THE CANADIAN YEARBOOK OF INTERNATIONAL LAW

2013

ANNUAIRE CANADIEN DE DROIT INTERNATIONAL

The Canadian Yearbook of International Law

VOLUME LI   2013   TOME LI

Annuaire canadien de droit international

Published under the auspices of
THE CANADIAN BRANCH, INTERNATIONAL LAW ASSOCIATION
AND
THE CANADIAN COUNCIL ON INTERNATIONAL LAW

Publié sous les auspices de
LA BRANCHE CANADIENNE DE L'ASSOCIATION DE DROIT INTERNATIONAL
ET
DU CONSEIL CANADIEN DE DROIT INTERNATIONAL

UBCPress
VANCOUVER, BC

Printed in Canada on acid-free paper

ISBN 978-0-7748-2877-2
ISSN 0069-0058

Canadian Cataloguing in Publication Data

The National Library of Canada has catalogued this publication as follows:

The Canadian yearbook of international law — Annuaire canadien de droit international

> Annual.
> Text in English and French.
> "Published under the auspices of the Canadian Branch, International Law Association and the Canadian Council on International Law."
> ISSN 0069-0058
>
> 1. International Law — Periodicals.
> I. International Law Association. Canadian Branch.
> II. Canadian Council on International Law.
> III. Title: The Canadian yearbook of international law.
> JC 21.C3   341'.05   C75-34558-6E

Données de catalogage avant publication (Canada)

Annuaire canadien de droit international — The Canadian yearbook of international law

> Annuel.
> Textes en anglais et en français.
> «Publié sous les auspices de la Branche canadienne de l'Association de droit international et du Conseil canadien de droit international.»
> ISSN 0069-0058
>
> 1. Droit international — Périodiques.
> I. Association de droit international. Branche canadienne.
> II. Conseil canadien de droit international.
> III. Titre: Annuaire canadien de droit international.
> JC 21.C3   341'.05   C75-34558-6E

UBC Press
University of British Columbia
2029 West Mall
Vancouver, BC V6T 1Z2
(604) 822-5959
www.ubcpress.ca

Communications to the *Yearbook* should be addressed to:
Les communications destinées à *l'Annuaire* doivent être adressées à:

THE EDITOR-IN-CHIEF/LE DIRECTEUR

THE CANADIAN YEARBOOK OF INTERNATIONAL LAW/
ANNUAIRE CANADIEN DE DROIT INTERNATIONAL

FACULTY OF LAW, COMMON LAW SECTION/
FACULTÉ DE DROIT, SECTION COMMON LAW

UNIVERSITY OF/UNIVERSITÉ D'OTTAWA
57 Louis Pasteur
Ottawa, Ontario K1N 6N5 Canada
john.currie@uottawa.ca

Contents / Matière

Book Reviews / Recensions de livres

THE CANADIAN YEARBOOK OF INTERNATIONAL LAW

2013

ANNUAIRE CANADIEN DE DROIT INTERNATIONAL

The *Canada–China FIPPA*:
Its Uniqueness and Non-Reciprocity

GUS VAN HARTEN

[O]ur China FIPPA stuck to the model, the model FIPPA ... This is a perfect example of ... a family of investment agreements that Canada has had in place since 1994 in terms of FIPPAs or ... investment chapters of free trade agreements. So there is no departure from our past practice in that regard.[1]

INTRODUCTION

The *Agreement between the Government of Canada and the Government of the People's Republic of China for the Promotion and Reciprocal Protection of Investments* (*Canada–China Foreign Investment Promotion and Protection Agreement* or *China FIPPA*) is one of three major trade or investment treaties now pursued by the government of Canada.[2] It is also the first treaty since the *North American Free Trade Agreement* (*NAFTA*) for which an official text is public that would subject all

Gus Van Harten is an Associate Professor at Osgoode Hall Law School at York University, Toronto, ON.

Editors' note: The *Agreement between the Government of Canada and the Government of the People's Republic of China for the Promotion and Reciprocal Protection of Investments* was ratified by Canada on 12 September 2014 and came into force on 1 October 2014, after this article went to press.

1 *Hupacasath First Nation v Minister of Foreign Affairs of Canada and Attorney General of Canada*, Federal Court Case No T-153-13 (Cross-Examination on Affidavit of Vernon John MacKay) (3 April 2013) at 9 [MacKay Cross-Examination].

2 *Agreement between the Government of Canada and the Government of the People's Republic of China for the Promotion and Reciprocal Protection of Investments* (9 September 2012), online: <http://www.international.gc.ca/trade-agreements-accords-commerciaux/agr-acc/fipa-apie/china-text-chine.aspx?lang=eng> [not yet in force] [*China FIPPA*]. On the reported delay in ratification by Canada, see Shawn McCarthy, "Pressure Mounts with Tories Ready to Ratify China Trade Deal by

legislatures, governments, and courts in Canada to investor-state arbitration (ISA) in relation to substantial foreign direct investment (FDI) stocks in Canada.[3] The ratification of the *China FIPPA* — along with two other proposed trade agreements[4] — would make Canada the most ISA-constrained country among Western developed states by far, based on the scope of ISA coverage of inward FDI in Canada.[5] Potential ratification of the *China FIPPA* is thus an important policy choice that will affect future decision makers for the long term.[6]

In this article, the *China FIPPA* is examined in the context of other trade and investment treaties that provide for ISA. Its text is compared especially to Canada's Model FIPPA, other FIPPAs, and trade agreements — including *NAFTA* — that provide for ISA.[7] The purpose is to highlight variations in the *China FIPPA* relative to Canada's other relevant treaties, which sets the stage for an evaluation of the *China FIPPA*'s novelty and non-reciprocity — in favour of China — in legal terms and, more tentatively, in its economic context. In summary, it is demonstrated that the *China FIPPA* is *de jure* non-reciprocal, and uniquely so,[8] because it:

• allows a general right of market access by Chinese investors to Canada but not by Canadian investors to China;

Thursday," *Globe and Mail* (30 October 2012), online: <http://www.theglobeand mail.com>; Susana Mas, "Delayed China Trade Deal Reflects Tory Dissent, NDP Says," *CBC News* (22 April 2013), online: CBC News <http://www.cbc.ca/news>.

3 *North American Free Trade Agreement between the Government of Canada, the Government of the United Mexican States, and the Government of the United States of America*, Can TS 1994 No 2, 32 ILM 296 and 605 (1993) (in force 1 January 1994) [*NAFTA*].

4 That is, the proposed *Canada—European Union Comprehensive Economic and Trade Agreement* (*CETA*) and the *Trans-Pacific Partnership* (*TPP*).

5 That is, a larger share of foreign direct investment (FDI) stocks in Canada than in the United States, Western Europe, and Australia would be covered by investor-state arbitration (ISA). See further discussion in note 177 in this article.

6 See text accompanying note 171 in this article.

7 Canada has concluded five trade agreements, including *NAFTA, supra* note 3, that provide for ISA and has concluded twenty-five foreign investment promotion and protection agreement (FIPPAs) (that is, bilateral investment treaties (BITs), all of which provide for ISA. The texts of the relevant treaties are available online at Department of Foreign Affairs, Trade and Development Canada (DFATD) <http://www.international.gc.ca/trade-agreements-accords-commerciaux/agr -acc/fipa-apie/index.aspx?lang=eng>. See also Annexes 1 and 2 in this article.

8 By its non-reciprocity in these respects, the *China FIPPA, supra* note 2, differs from all of Canada's FIPPAs and trade agreements that provide for ISA as well as Canada's Model FIPPA. Canada, "Agreement between Canada and [other

- excludes from the treaty's dispute settlement mechanisms, including ISA, decisions on investment screening by sub-national governments in China but not in Canada; and
- excludes from the treaty's dispute settlement mechanisms, including ISA, decisions on investment screening in China that, in Canada, would remain subject to thresholds and other limitations in the *Investment Canada Act.*[9]

It is explained further that the *China FIPPA* appears *de facto* non-reciprocal due to the relatively extensive liberalization of the Canadian economy as compared to that of the Chinese economy.[10] This is because the *China FIPPA* excludes from its national treatment obligation all existing measures that discriminate against foreign investors and because it locks in this unlevel feature of the existing playing field between Canada and China.

More broadly, it is highlighted that the *China FIPPA* departs from Canada's usual treaty practice in important ways. In particular, it:

- expressly allows a temporal "reach-back" on most-favoured-nation (MFN) treatment, such that the scope of MFN treatment is extended to post-1993 investment treaties, thus undermining Canada's post-2001 treaty language that aims to limit various FIPPA provisions in order to rebalance principles of investor protection and regulatory flexibility;[11]
- omits reservations to its obligations on performance requirements, including an Aboriginal rights reservation that is found in all of Canada's twenty-five FIPPAs and trade agreements that contain obligations on performance requirements;[12]

---

country] for the Promotion and Protection of Investments" (2004), online: <http://italaw.com/documents/Canadian2004-FIPA-model-en.pdf> [Canada's Model FIPPA].

[9] *Investment Canada Act*, RSC 1985, c 28 (1st Supp).

[10] See further text accompanying notes 106-8 in this article.

[11] This distinguishes the *China FIPPA* from Canada's Model FIPPA, *supra* note 8; *NAFTA, supra* note 3; Canada's other trade agreements that provide for ISA; and all but two of the twenty-five FIPPAs. These two FIPPAs also do not raise comparable issues for Canada concerning regulatory flexibility because they apply to little inward FDI. See Annex 2 in this article.

[12] This includes all of Canada's FIPPAs and trade agreements that provide for ISA and prohibit performance requirements. See further text accompanying notes 149-50 in this article.

- scales back Canada's well-established position on transparency in ISA by setting up a presumption that all documents, other than awards, filed or issued in ISA proceedings are confidential unless the respondent state decides to make them public;[13] and
- has a minimum lifespan of thirty-one years, including a sixteen-year effective minimum term and a fifteen-year survival clause, which goes beyond all but one other treaty concluded by Canada that provides for ISA.[14]

Finally, it is suggested that the *China FIPPA* is apparently *de facto* non-reciprocal because it provides for robust substantive investor protection and ISA, with corresponding fiscal risks and regulatory constraints for states in their role as capital importers, in a context where Chinese FDI stocks in Canada exceed Canadian FDI stocks in China by a factor of about three to one.[15]

The commentary in this article is specific to the *China FIPPA* and focuses on the FIPPA text in its legal and economic context. The analysis responds partly to claims by government of Canada officials, among others, that the *China FIPPA* is unremarkable because it continues Canada's past practice.[16] Other questions about the *China FIPPA* and its cost-benefit implications are raised in the conclusion of the article, along with a suggestion that the *China FIPPA*, due to its significance, uniqueness, and long-term irreversibility, should be subject to a comprehensive independent review before a decision is taken by the federal government to ratify it.

GENERAL CONTEXT

HISTORICAL ASPECTS

The *China FIPPA* is a bilateral investment treaty (BIT). BITs that provide for ISA date from the late 1960s.[17] At this time, major

---

[13] This distinguishes the *China FIPPA, supra* note 2; from Canada's Model FIPPA, *supra* note 8; NAFTA, *supra* note 3; and all ten of Canada's post-2001 FIPPAs and trade agreements that provide for ISA (that is, all relevant treaties since the federal government responded to issues arising from ISA confidentiality under *NAFTA*).

[14] See further text accompanying note 171 in this article.

[15] See further Table 2 in this article. This distinguishes the *China FIPPA* from all of Canada's relevant treaties except *NAFTA, supra* note 3.

[16] See, for example, MacKay Cross-Examination, *supra* note 1.

[17] Andrew Newcombe and Lluís Paradell, *Law and Practice of Investment Treaties* (Alphen aan den Rijn: Kluwer Law International, 2009) at 44-49.

Western European capital-exporting states began to develop model investment treaties in their relations with former colonies and developing states. The model was extended to relations with former East Bloc states and to relations among many transitioning and developing states. Around 1980, the United States developed its model investment treaty, and, from about 1990, the number of BITs providing for ISA expanded rapidly. ISA also began to be incorporated into trade agreements such as *NAFTA*. The *China FIPPA* is consistent with the general approach to BITs following this post-1990 expansion. Speaking generally, Canada adopted this overall approach, based especially on the US approach to BITs, after *NAFTA* entered into force in 1994, whereas China did so around 2000.[18] In particular, the *China FIPPA* is consistent with a muscular version of ISA based on the following elements:

- Investors can bring claims against states (but not vice versa) in relation to most or all aspects of the treaty rather than to a limited class of potential disputes, such as disputes over the amount of compensation to be paid in the event of an expropriation.
- Investors can bring claims in forums where voting power is concentrated in the hands of the major capital-exporting states,[19] pursuant to the International Centre for the Settlement of Investment Disputes's (ICSID) *Rules of Procedure for Arbitration Proceedings* (*ICSID Rules*), ICSID's *Rules Governing the Additional Facility for the Administration of Proceedings* (*ICISID Additional Facility Rules*), and the UN Commission on International Trade Law's (UNCITRAL) *Arbitration Rules of the United Nations Commission on International Trade Law* (*UNCITRAL Rules*), which locate significant powers over the arbitration process, including default arbitrator appointment powers, at the World Bank or the Permanent Court of Arbitration.[20]

---

18 Axel Berger, *China and the Global Governance of Foreign Direct Investment* (Bonn: German Development Institute, 2008) at 21-22; Monica CE Heymann, "International Law and the Settlement of Investment Disputes Relating to China" (2008) 11:3 J Int'l Econ L 507 at 515-16; Gordon Smith, "Chinese Bilateral Investment Treaties: Restrictions on International Arbitration" (2010) 76 Arbitration 58 at 58-59.

19 Gus Van Harten, "Investment Treaty Arbitration, Procedural Fairness, and the Rule of Law" in Stephan W Schill, ed, *International Investment Law and Comparative Public Law* (Oxford: Oxford University Press, 2010) 628 at 645-48.

20 International Centre for Settlement of Investment Disputes (ICSID), *Rules of Procedure for Arbitration Proceedings* (revised 26 September 1984 and 1 January

- Investors can bring claims without having to exhaust domestic remedies in the host state regardless of whether these remedies are capable of delivering justice.
- Investors are not precluded, according to most investment treaty awards,[21] from submitting contractual disputes with the host state or a related entity to the treaty's arbitration mechanism, even if the contract calls for the resolution of disputes exclusively in another forum.
- Arbitrators can discipline states based on broadly worded standards, including protection from treatment that is not fair and equitable, does not ensure full protection and security, is discriminatory in relation to domestic or third-state investors, or is an expropriation or tantamount to an expropriation.
- Arbitrators can review the conduct of virtually any branch or entity of the state, including at the sub-national level.
- Arbitrators can award monetary damages, as opposed to conventional public law remedies,[22] as a primary remedy where the state is found to have violated its treaty obligations.
- Foreign states can enforce an arbitration award against assets of the losing state, based on enforcement provisions of the *Convention on the Settlement of Investment Disputes between States and Nationals of Other States,* the *UN Convention on the Recognition and Enforcement of Foreign Arbitral Awards,* and/or the *Inter-American Convention on International Commercial Arbitration.*[23]

2003; original rules 1968), reprinted in ICSID, *Convention, Regulations and Rules* (Washington: ICSID, 2003) [*ICSID Rules*]; ICSID, *Rules Governing the Additional Facility for the Administration of Proceedings by the Secretariat of the International Centre for Settlement of Investment Disputes* (revised 1 January 2003; original rules 1978) (1992) 1 ICSID Rep 213 [*ICSID Additional Facility Rules*]; UN Commission on International Trade Law (UNCITRAL), *Arbitration Rules of the United Nations Commission on International Trade Law,* UN GA Res 31/98, UN GAOR, 31st Sess, Supp No 17, UN Doc A/31/17 (1976), c V, s C [*UNCITRAL Rules*].

21 Gus Van Harten, *Sovereign Choices and Sovereign Constraints: Judicial Restraint in Investment Treaty Arbitration* (Oxford: Oxford University Press, 2013) at 135-47.

22 Anne van Aaken, "Primary and Secondary Remedies in International Investment Law and National State Liability: A Functional and Comparative View" in Schill, *supra* note 19, 722 at 723, 725-30.

23 *Convention on the Settlement of Investment Disputes between States and Nationals of Other States,* 4 ILM 524 (1965) (in force 14 October 1966); *United Nations Convention on the Recognition and Enforcement of Foreign Arbitral Awards,* 330 UNTS 3 (in force 7 June 1959); *Inter-American Convention on International Commercial Arbitration,* 14 ILM 336 (1975).

On the one hand, these elements of the *China FIPPA* are common in BITs and trade agreements that provide for ISA. On the other hand, the *China FIPPA* does not reflect other elements of a muscular version of ISA in the following ways:

- Foreign investors can be blocked from forum-shopping in some circumstances — that is, from assuming the status of an investor covered by the agreement by establishing an intermediary company in the host state — due to the *China FIPPA*'s flexible denial-of-benefits clause.[24]
- Investors are not entitled to pre-establishment national treatment, although they are entitled to pre-establishment MFN treatment.
- Investors are precluded expressly from accessing, based on MFN treatment, more favourable dispute settlement provisions in other investment treaties, as otherwise permitted by about half of investment treaty tribunals that have opined on the issue.[25]

These aspects of the *China FIPPA* are significant even if they do not alter the FIPPA's position as a typical, muscular BIT. As such, the *China FIPPA*, like many treaties, gives a special status to foreign investors in the form of (1) substantive legal protections not enjoyed by other private parties, including domestic competitors, and (2) access to ISA, including relief from the customary duty to exhaust reasonably available domestic remedies before an international claim can be brought.

LEGAL ASPECTS

Among treaties that provide for ISA, the *China FIPPA* tracks most closely the structure of the *NAFTA* investment chapter, which was based originally on the US-prototype BIT and was adopted by Canada in many of its post-*NAFTA* FIPPAs and its Model FIPPA of 2004.[26] Thus, the *China FIPPA* may be said to fall within a North

---

[24] *China FIPPA*, *supra* note 2, art 16(2)-(3). Rachel Thorn and Jennifer Doucleff, "Disregarding the Corporate Veil and Denial of Benefits Clause: Testing Treaty Language and the Concept of 'Investor'" in Michael Waibel et al, eds, *The Backlash against Investment Arbitration* (Alphen aan den Rijn: Kluwer Law International, 2010) 3 at 25-26.

[25] Gus Van Harten, "Arbitrator Behaviour in Asymmetrical Adjudication: An Empirical Study of Investment Treaty Arbitration" (2012) 50 Osgoode Hall LJ 211 at 228, 237-38.

[26] Canada's Model FIPPA, *supra* note 8.

American species of BITs, albeit with important variations discussed in the next section of this article. In this section, a general overview of the *China FIPPA* is provided.

Broad Definition of Investment

The *China FIPPA* contains a typically broad definition of the concept of investment. The definition extends beyond physical assets such as land and buildings and beyond notions of FDI (based on ownership and control of assets) to include other concepts of asset ownership. For example, the *China FIPPA* includes in its definition of investment: resource concession rights, debt instruments (that is, portfolio investment), intellectual property rights, and "any other tangible or intangible ... property and related property rights acquired or used for business purposes."[27] Thus, like most treaties that provide for ISA, the *China FIPPA*'s coverage is wide-ranging in its application to the economic activities of foreign investors. The question of whether this breadth of application goes beyond comparable concepts in Canadian or other domestic law is beyond the scope of this article.[28]

Broad Definition of Investor, with an Important Qualification

The *China FIPPA* also has a broad definition of the concept of the investor. The definition includes any natural or corporate person that is a national of the other state party and that "seeks to make, is making or has made a covered investment."[29] Alternatively, the *China FIPPA* constrains forum shopping by foreign investors by allowing the host state to deny benefits of the *China FIPPA* to Canadian or Chinese investors (as applicable) that are controlled by investors from a third state or from the host state itself that have no substantial business activities in the host state's territory.[30] This denial-of-benefits clause is clearly more reliable for respondent states than are similar provisions in *NAFTA* and other FIPPAs

---

[27] *China FIPPA, supra* note 2, art 1(1).

[28] See, for example, Steven Shrybman, "Submissions to Standing Committee on International Trade Re: Abitibi Bowater NAFTA Claim Settlement," Submission to the House of Commons Standing Committee on International Trade (8 March 2011), online: <http://www.canadians.org/sites/default/files/Trade/Submissions_AbitibiBowater.pdf>.

[29] *China FIPPA, supra* note 2, art 1(2), (10)(a).

[30] *Ibid*, art 16(2)-(3).

because the clause allows a host state to deny benefits after ISA proceedings have been initiated without any express requirement of advance notice or consultation.[31]

Broad Application to State Measures

The *China FIPPA* applies broadly to any measures by Canada or China, including legislative, executive, or judicial measures of the federal government or of a provincial, territorial, or local government or First Nations authority.[32] This application reflects the principle of the state as a unified entity under international law and is typical of treaties providing for ISA.[33]

Inclusion of Core Substantive Standards

Much of the *China FIPPA*'s substantive content reflects many other treaties that provide for ISA.[34] Thus, the *China FIPPA* includes:

1. a minimum standard of treatment for investors, including "fair and equitable treatment" and "full protection and security";[35]
2. MFN treatment and national treatment at the post-establishment stage of an investment;[36]

---

[31] No other relevant treaties to which Canada is a party include the express clarification contained in the *China FIPPA* that access to ISA can be denied after the initiation of an ISA claim. *China FIPPA, supra* note 2, art 18(3). Compare *NAFTA, supra* note 3, art 1113(2); Canada's Model FIPPA, *supra* note 8, art 18(2). Thorn and Doucleff, *supra* note 24 at 25-26. Other treaties concluded by Canada that have more ambiguous denial-of-benefits provisions include Canada's FIPPAs with Costa Rica, the Czech Republic, Jordan, Latvia, Peru, Romania, the Slovak Republic, and Tanzania as well as Canada's trade agreements with Chile, Colombia, Panama, and Peru. In addition, seventeen of Canada's FIPPAs, the latest of which (with Croatia) entered into force in 2001, do not have any denial-of-benefits provisions. See further Annex 1 in this article.

[32] *China FIPPA, supra* note 2, art 2(1); see also art 2(2).

[33] See, for example, International Law Commission, "Draft Articles on the Responsibility of States for Internationally Wrongful Acts" in *Report of the International Law Commission,* UN GAOR, 56th Sess, Supp No 10 at c IV, para 76, UN Doc A/56/10 (2001), art 4(1).

[34] The *China FIPPA* also excludes, whether entirely or from ISA only, provisions on monopolies and regulatory transparency. That said, comparable provisions in other treaties have not figured prominently, if at all, in actual ISA cases and are apparently non-binding in important respects in Canada's Model FIPPA, *supra* note 8, arts 8, 19.

[35] *China FIPPA, supra* note 2, art 4(1).

[36] *Ibid,* arts 5(1)-(2), 6(1)-(2); see also art 11.

3. protection from direct or indirect expropriation, including a requirement for market-based compensation;[37]
4. provisions for the free transfer of capital;[38]
5. MFN treatment at the pre-establishment stage of an investment;[39]
6. a prohibition on performance requirements;[40] and
7. requirements on the make-up of senior management and boards of directors and on the entry of key personnel.[41]

Items (1) through (4) reflect the great majority of BITs, whereas items (5) to (7) mainly reflect the North American approach.

Limiting Language for Substantive Provisions

Consistent also with the North American approach, the *China FIPPA* contains limiting language in some of its substantive provisions. This limiting language applies to the *China FIPPA*'s provisions for a minimum standard of treatment and for MFN treatment (reflecting the approach in the *NAFTA* states' clarification in 2001 of the equivalent *NAFTA* provisions[42]) and to the *China FIPPA*'s expropriation clause (reflecting the post-2001 practice of the United States and Canada). In particular, on the minimum standard of treatment, the *China FIPPA* provides (1) that concepts of fair and equitable treatment and full protection and security do not require treatment beyond that required by the international law minimum standard of treatment as evidenced by general state practice accepted as law and (2) that a state's breach of another standard or treaty does not constitute a breach of the *China FIPPA*'s minimum standard.[43] In addition, the *China FIPPA*'s MFN treatment clause provides expressly that MFN treatment does not extend to aspects of dispute resolution mechanisms in other treaties.[44] Finally, the *China FIPPA* seeks to clarify and limit the concept of indirect expropriation in ways derived mainly from US takings law.[45]

---

[37] *Ibid*, art 10.
[38] *Ibid*, art 12.
[39] *Ibid*, art 5(1)-(2).
[40] *Ibid*, art 9.
[41] *Ibid*, art 7(1)-(3).
[42] NAFTA Free Trade Commission, *Notes of Interpretation of Certain Chapter 11 Provisions* (31 July 2001), (2001) 13(6) WTAM 139, art B(1).
[43] *China FIPPA, supra* note 2, art 4(2)-(3).
[44] *Ibid*, art 5(3).
[45] *Ibid*, Annex B.10; Andrea J Menaker, "Benefiting from Experience: Developments in the United States' Most Recent Investment Agreements" (2005) 12 UC Davis J Int'l L & Pol 121 at 124, n 8.

These limiting provisions reflect a post-2001 North American approach to the relevant substantive standards. That said, as for any treaty that provides for ISA, the limiting language is subject to interpretation by investment treaty arbitrators, and, in many cases, arbitrators under other treaties have adopted an expansive approach to ambiguous treaty language.[46] This interpretive trend appears especially important in the case of the *China FIPPA* due to its approach to MFN treatment, as discussed in the following section.

Other Limitations on Substantive Standards of Investor Protection

The *China FIPPA* includes other limiting aspects that reflect Canada's FIPPA practice. In particular, the *China FIPPA* has a clause — especially relevant to its allowance for free transfers of capital[47] — that may assist in protecting a host state's financial stability, although the version of this clause in the *China FIPPA* appears narrower than in most of Canada's other relevant treaties.[48] The *China FIPPA* also contains a partial carve-out for tax measures,[49] and its provisions on non-discrimination are subject to exceptions for existing discriminatory measures and for procurement, subsidies, and other matters.[50] These features — encompassing exceptions both from substantive standards and from dispute settlement provisions — are typical of Canada's treaties.

In addition, the *China FIPPA* contains general exceptions for health, environmental, and conservation measures, reflecting Canada's post-1993 treaty practice other than in *NAFTA* and one other trade agreement that provides for ISA.[51] The general exceptions state that the *China FIPPA* is not to be construed so as "to prevent a Contracting Party from adopting or maintaining measures,

---

[46] Van Harten, *supra* note 25 at 225-28, 237-40.

[47] *China FIPPA, supra* note 2, art 12(1).

[48] *Ibid,* art 12(4). Compare Canada's Model FIPPA, *supra* note 8, art 14(6). Only Canada's four pre-1994 FIPPAs do not contain the relevant clause.

[49] *China FIPPA, supra* note 2, art 14(1), (4), (5). The carve-out is partial because it does not apply to tax measures that lead to expropriation claims where the state parties do not agree, after the filing of the claim, that the relevant measure is not an expropriation.

[50] *Ibid,* art 8.

[51] Canada's four pre-1994 FIPPAs do not contain these general exceptions. *NAFTA* and Canada's trade agreement with Chile limit the exceptions to certain performance requirements. See, for example, *NAFTA, supra* note 3, art 1106(6). See further Annex 1 in this article.

including environmental measures" that are (1) necessary to ensure compliance with laws and regulations that are not themselves inconsistent with the *China FIPPA*, (2) necessary to protect human, animal, or plant life or health, or (3) relating to the conservation of living or non-living exhaustible natural resources, under certain conditions.[52]

These exceptions provide protection for various areas of government decision making, although the degree of protection is uncertain for several reasons. First, necessity requirements have been approached strictly by most of the investment treaty tribunals that have dealt with them in the comparable context of emergency economic measures.[53] Second, the exceptions are subject to other conditional language derived from the chapeau of Article XX of the *General Agreement on Tariffs and Trade (GATT)*, which provides additional discretion to arbitrators to limit the protection afforded by the exceptions.[54] Third, the exceptions may be diluted by the *China FIPPA*'s approach to MFN treatment, as discussed later in this article.[55] Fourth, and perhaps most importantly, arbitrators may conclude that a monetary award against a state in the context of ISA does not prevent the state from adopting a measure and, in turn, that none of the exceptions would excuse a state from any *China*

---

[52] *China FIPPA, supra* note 2, art 33(2). The agreement also has a general exception for cultural industries, which is similar to that found in Canada's other FIPPAs and trade agreements (art 33(1)).

[53] See, for example, *CMS v Argentina* (ICSID), 44 ILM 1205 (2005) at paras 316-17, 329, 331; *Enron v Argentina*, ICSID Case No ARB/01/3 (2007) at paras 303-9, 311-13; *Sempra v Argentina* (ICSID), 20 WTAM 117 (2007) at paras 347-55, 373-74; *National Grid v Argentina* (UNCITRAL) (3 November 2008) at paras 257-62, online: <http://italaw.com/sites/default/files/case-documents/ita0555.pdf>; *Suez and InterAgua v Argentina*, ICSID Case No ARB/03/17 (2010) at paras 235-43; *Total v Argentina*, ICSID Case No ARB/04/01 (2010) at paras 221-24, 345, 483-84; *EDF v Argentina*, ICSID Case No ARB/03/23 (2012) at paras 1171-73. Contrast *LG&E v Argentina* (ICSID), 46 ILM 40 (2006) at paras 228-61; *Continental Casualty v Argentina* (ICSID), 21 WTAM 181 (2008) at paras 173-81, 192-210, 227-36.

[54] *General Agreement on Tariffs and Trade*, 55 UNTS 194, Can TS 1948 No 31 (in force 1 January 1948), now incorporated by reference into the *General Agreement on Tariffs and Trade 1994*, 1867 UNTS 187, Annex 1A to the *Agreement Establishing the World Trade Organization*, 15 April 1994, 1867 UNTS 154, 33 ILM 1144 (1994) (in force 1 January 1995), art XX [*GATT*]; *China FIPPA, supra* note 2, art 33(2).

[55] This would depend, among other things, on whether the language defining the general exception in any post-1993 FIPPA was weaker than that in the *China FIPPA*. See Howard Mann, "The Canada-China Investment Treaty Sleight of Hand," *Embassy News* (8 January 2013).

FIPPA obligation to compensate investors who experience loss due to the state's actions in areas of health, environment, and conservation. Overall, while the exceptions may safeguard some state conduct from treaty liability, they remain untested in ISA and are subject to important qualifications.[56]

Institutional Structure

The *China FIPPA*'s institutional structure is consistent with the general approach taken in Canada's Model FIPPA, *NAFTA*, and other relevant treaties as well as in many other investment treaties. The *China FIPPA* provides for state-state arbitration;[57] investor-state arbitration;[58] the availability of the *ICSID Rules*, the *ICSID Additional Facility Rules*, and the *UNCITRAL Rules*;[59] the ICSID's secretary general as default appointing authority;[60] and binding interpretations by the state parties.[61] Its provisions on governing law,[62] public access,[63] finality and enforcement of awards,[64] and entry into force[65] also track the usual approach. However, there are some variations in the *China FIPPA*'s institutional structure. Perhaps the most important, as discussed in the following section, are the *China FIPPA*'s dilution of requirements for ISA transparency and its lengthy minimum lifespan.[66]

UNIQUENESS AND NON-RECIPROCITY

For Canada, the negotiation of the *China FIPPA* presumably called for more concessions than usual due to China's size and bargaining power relative to Canada's other treaty partners. It is therefore

---

56 See also Andrew Newcombe, "Canada's New Model Foreign Investment Protection Agreement" (August 2004) at 4-5, online: <http://italaw.com/documents/CanadianFIPA.pdf>.

57 *China FIPPA, supra* note 2, art 15.

58 *Ibid*, especially arts 20, 22.

59 *Ibid*, art 22(1).

60 *Ibid*, art 24(5).

61 *Ibid*, art 18(2).

62 *Ibid*, art 30.

63 *Ibid*, art 28.

64 *Ibid*, art 32.

65 *Ibid*, art 35.

66 See text accompanying notes 164 and 171 in this article.

noteworthy that the apparent starting point for negotiation of the *China FIPPA* was Canada's Model FIPPA. That said, it is also clear that important variations from its usual approach were accepted by Canada. The most important variations and corresponding non-reciprocal features[67] in the *China FIPPA* are evaluated in detail in this section. After this legal analysis, the *FIPPA* is also evaluated in its immediate economic context of China–Canada investment flows.

NON-RECIPROCITY ON MARKET ACCESS

Bilateral investment treaties, unlike trade agreements, do not provide for market access for goods or services. However, many BITs (and trade agreements) do provide for market access by investors and investments.[68] That is, they require the state parties to allow foreign investors to purchase domestic companies or other assets and, thus, to make "brownfield" or "greenfield" investments in the host state.[69] In this context, market access is often called pre-establishment national treatment because it involves an obligation by the host state not to discriminate between foreign and domestic investors even before a foreign investor has invested in the host state. Unlike many other BITs, the *China FIPPA* does not provide for this form of market access because its national treatment obligation does not extend to the pre-establishment stage of a foreign investment. In particular, the obligation does not include the terms "establishment" and "acquisition," alongside "expansion, management, conduct, operation and sale or other disposition," in its description of investment activities to which national treatment applies.[70] On the other hand, and extraordinarily in light of its more limited national treatment provision, the *China FIPPA*'s MFN treatment clause does extend to the pre-establishment stage of a foreign investment. It states: "Each Contracting Party shall accord to investors of the other Contracting Party treatment no less favourable than that it accords,

---

67 Some non-reciprocal aspects of the *China FIPPA*, *supra* note 2, such as its provision in Annex C.21(1) that Canadian (but not Chinese) investors must submit a dispute to domestic administrative procedures for four months before bringing a FIPPA claim, were not thought to be important enough to discuss in detail.

68 This element originates in US BITs and has been adopted in various forms in twenty-one of Canada's post-*NAFTA* FIPPAs or trade agreements that provide for ISA. See Annex 2 in this article.

69 Brownfield investment involves the acquisition of an existing company or business; greenfield investment involves the establishment of a new venture.

70 *China FIPPA*, *supra* note 2, art 6(1)-(2).

in like circumstances, to investors of a non-Contracting Party with respect to the *establishment, acquisition* ... or other disposition of investments in its territory."[71] Thus, while the *China FIPPA* does not require non-discrimination in market access between Chinese or Canadian investors (as applicable) and domestic investors, it does provide for non-discrimination in market access between Chinese or Canadian investors and third-state investors in each state.

This structure is unique among treaties concluded by Canada that provide for ISA (indeed, it may be unique among all treaties that provide for ISA). First, the great majority of Canada's treaties provide for pre-establishment national treatment.[72] Second, none of Canada's treaties that exclude pre-establishment national treatment obligations go on to extend MFN treatment to the pre-establishment stage. As discussed below, the upshot of this extraordinary feature of the *China FIPPA* is to obligate Canada, but not China, to open its economy to the other state's investors.

The absence of pre-establishment national treatment in the *China FIPPA* would be less noteworthy, in that it would be a reciprocal element of the treaty, if Canada and China currently permitted similar levels of market access. Yet clearly this is not the case as the Canadian economy is significantly more open to foreign investment than the Chinese economy. Put differently, Chinese investors are in general able to purchase assets in Canada that Canadian investors would not be able to purchase in China.[73] As a result, the *China FIPPA* preserves China's asymmetrical freedom to deny market access by

---

[71] *Ibid*, art 5(1)-(2) [emphasis added].

[72] All of Canada's five trade agreements that provide for ISA and all but four of Canada's twenty-one FIPPAs since *NAFTA* extend national treatment to the pre-establishment stage of a foreign investment. In contrast, Canada's four pre-1994 FIPPAs do not extend national treatment to the pre-establishment stage. See Annex 2 in this article.

[73] MacKay Cross-Examination, *supra* note 1 at 39: "[O]ver 90 percent of investment entering the Chinese market is subject to review under laws, regulations and rules." European Union Chamber of Commerce in China (EUCCC), *European Business in China Position Paper 2013/2014* (EUCCC, 2013) at 19-20: "China has used the vast size of its domestic marketplace to protect domestic companies and to place conditionalities on market access for foreign companies." Although the relevant rankings do not necessarily define good economic policy, China was listed as the most restrictive of fifty-five countries in the Organisation for Economic Co-operation and Development's (OECD) FDI Regulatory Restrictiveness Index as of September 2013, online: OECD <http://www.oecd.org/daf/inv/ColumnChart-FDI_RR_Index_2013.pdf>.

Canadian investors. Although reciprocal on its face, the *China FIPPA*'s implications are in this respect *de facto* unequal.[74]

Moreover, the *China FIPPA* establishes *de jure* non-reciprocity of market access because (1) Canada and China commit to provide market access to investors from the other state only where the other state already provides market access to investors from a third state[75] and (2) Canada, unlike China,[76] has concluded numerous FIPPAs since 1994 in which third-state investors are given expansive rights of market access to Canada.[77] For instance, the *Agreement between the Government of Canada and the Government of the Republic of Costa Rica for the Promotion and Protection of Investments* (*Costa Rica FIPPA*) states that

[e]ach Contracting State shall permit establishment of a new business enterprise or acquisition of an existing business enterprise or a share of such enterprise by investors or prospective investors of the other Contracting Party on a basis no less favourable than that which, in like circumstances, it permits such acquisition or establishment by: ... its own investors or prospective investors.[78]

Based on this provision in the *Costa Rica FIPPA*, Costa Rican investors obtain a general right to invest in Canada (and vice versa for Canadian investors in Costa Rica). Canada's commitment in this

---

[74] As an aside, the *China FIPPA*, *supra* note 2, preserves the state parties' ability to block takeovers of domestic firms, although the relevant provision is also non-reciprocal in important respects. See further text accompanying note 85 in this article.

[75] *China FIPPA*, *supra* note 2, arts 5, 8(1)(b).

[76] Stephan W Schill, "Tearing Down the Great Wall: The New Generation of Investment Treaties of the People's Republic of China" (2007) 15 Cardozo J Intl Comp L 73 at 86.

[77] The *China FIPPA* does not extend the requirement to provide market access based on most-favoured-nation (MFN) treatment to trade agreements or to pre-1994 FIPPAs. China FIPPA, *supra* note 2, art 8(1)(a)(i), (b).

[78] *Agreement Between the Government of Canada and the Government of the Republic of Costa Rica for the Promotion and Protection of Investments*, Can TS 1999 No 43, art III(1) (in force 29 September 1999) [*Costa Rica FIPPA*]. See also Canada's FIPPAs with Croatia (art III(1)(b)), Jordan (art 3(1)), Lebanon (art III(b)), Peru (art 3(1)), Tanzania (art 4(1)), and Uruguay (art III(b)), online: DFATD <http://www.international.gc.ca/trade-agreements-accords-commerciaux/agr-acc/fipa-apie/index.aspx?lang=eng>. See also Annex 2 in this article.

respect is subject to further exceptions in the *Costa Rica FIPPA*.[79]
Yet the general provision is for broad market access by the relevant
third-state investors (that is, Costa Rican). Under the *China FIPPA*,
the same right of market access would thus extend to Chinese
investors based on its provision for pre-establishment MFN treatment. This derivative right would be subject to the exceptions to
the original right in the *Costa Rica FIPPA*, although, as an illustration
of its scope, the *Costa Rica FIPPA* — unlike some other FIPPAs —
does not include exceptions for measures in various areas such as
atomic energy, air transportation, overseas and coastal shipping,
and ownership of real estate.[80] As a result, in the case of the *China
FIPPA*, Chinese investors would obtain a (non-reciprocal) right of
market access to Canada in any areas not exempted expressly in all
of Canada's post-1993 FIPPAs that provide for pre-establishment
national treatment for relevant third-state investors.[81] In contrast,
China has not committed in any of its BITs to pre-establishment
national treatment.[82] As a result, China would not be obliged under

---

[79] These include exceptions for existing non-conforming measures (so long as they
have been laid out by letter from Canada to Costa Rica within two years of the
Costa Rica FIPPA's entry into force) and for future measures in areas such as
social services, oceanfront land, and government securities. *Costa Rica FIPPA*,
supra note 78, Annex I, art II(1)(c), (2).

[80] Each of these areas is listed as exempted for the state party other than Canada,
but not for Canada, in at least one other post-1993 FIPPA that provides for pre-
establishment national treatment. See, for example, *Agreement between the
Government of Canada and the Government of the Republic of Croatia for the Promotion
and Protection of Investments*, Can TS 2001 No 4, Annex I, art II(1)(c) (in force 30
January 2001) [*Croatia FIPPA*]; *Agreement between the Government of Canada and
the Government of the Lebanese Republic for the Promotion and Protection of Investments*,
Can TS 1999 No 15, Annex I, art II(1)(d) (in force 19 June 1999).

[81] As an aside, it would make no difference that Costa Rica, Croatia, and Jordan
do not own substantial assets in Canada for the operation of MFN treatment and
market access, as discussed here, in the *China FIPPA*. What would entitle Chinese
investors to the same rights under the *China FIPPA* is that the relevant third-state
investors receive more favourable treatment at the pre-establishment stage.

[82] Schill, *supra* note 76. Chinese BITs that entered into force after 2006, the texts
of which were available via the UN Conference on Trade and Development's
(UNCTAD) database of Investment Instruments Online, were reviewed by the
author of the present article in order to confirm Schill's report on this aspect of
China's BIT policy. The author's review covered China's BITs with Colombia,
Cuba, France, India, Madagascar, Mexico, Portugal, Romania, Slovakia, South
Korea, and Switzerland, none of which were found to provide for pre-establishment
national treatment. China's BITs are available online: <http://www.unctadxi.
org/templates/DocSearch____779.aspx>.

the *China FIPPA* to allow a derivative right of market access by Canadian investors. Put differently, China has not made any sweetheart deal that must be extended to Canadian investors based on the FIPPA's provision for MFN treatment on market access. If China were to give market access in the future to third-state investors, Canadian investors would then be entitled to no less favourable treatment than these third-state investors. This is a big "if" in light of Canada's binding long-term concession on market access by Chinese investors.

By this roundabout path, the *China FIPPA* provides for market access by Chinese investors to Canada but excludes a right of market access by Canadian investors to China. This lack of reciprocity arises from the interaction between the *China FIPPA*'s unique structure — its provision for pre-establishment MFN treatment but not for pre-establishment national treatment — in combination with Canada's other FIPPAs that provide for pre-establishment national treatment. The resulting MFN-derived right of market access by Chinese investors would be subject only to exceptions that were present in all of Canada's post-1993 FIPPAs that provide for pre-establishment national treatment.[83] This non-reciprocal feature of the FIPPA is an extraordinary concession by Canada against the backdrop of other FIPPAs and BITs in general.

NON-RECIPROCITY ON INVESTMENT SCREENING

In the *China FIPPA*, Canada's federal government would retain the ability to screen Chinese investment in Canada under the *Investment Canada Act*.[84] According to the *China FIPPA*, investment screening by Canada and China is excluded from ISA and state-state arbitration:

1. A decision by Canada following a review *under the Investment Canada Act*, an Act respecting investment in Canada, with respect to whether or not to:

   (a) initially approve an investment that is subject to review; or
   (b) permit an investment that is subject to national security review;

   shall not be subject to the dispute settlement provisions under Article 15 and Part C of this Agreement.

---

[83] The right is also subject in the *China FIPPA, supra* note 2, to the federal government's ability to block foreign takeovers under the *Investment Canada Act, supra* note 9, as discussed later in this article.

[84] *Investment Canada Act, supra* note 9.

2. A decision by China following a review *under the Laws, Regulations and Rules relating to the regulation of foreign investment*, with respect to whether or not to:

(a) initially approve an investment that is subject to review; or

(b) permit an investment that is subject to national security review;

shall not be subject to the dispute settlement provisions under Article 15 and Part C of this Agreement.[85]

This carve-out preserves the ability of Canada and China to screen (and thus block) a particular foreign investment. However, the carve-out is non-reciprocal in two important respects. First, unlike Canada's other treaties that provide for ISA,[86] the carve-out applies to subnational governments in the case of Canada's treaty partner but not in the case of Canada. Canada has the right to screen Chinese investments under a federal statute, the *Investment Canada Act*, which is specified expressly in the *China FIPPA* and authorizes the federal government to screen foreign investment. As a result, if a provincial, local, or First Nations government took steps to block or frustrate a foreign takeover, or the federal government did so outside of the *Investment Canada Act*, the decision would not fall within the scope of the carve-out and would be subject to Canada's *China FIPPA* obligations on market access. To illustrate, when Quebec took steps to deter a proposed purchase of Rona by Lowe's in 2012, this conduct — understood as a restriction on pre-establishment national treatment — apparently would have violated the *China FIPPA* had the foreign purchaser been a Chinese company.[87]

In contrast, the *China FIPPA* provides China with the ability to screen Canadian investment under any of China's "Laws, Regulations and Rules relating to the regulation of foreign investment." None of these unspecified laws, regulations, or rules are limited to those enacted or enforced by China's national government, meaning that

---

85 *China FIPPA, supra* note 2, Annex D.34 [emphasis added].

86 See note 97 in this article.

87 Marina Strauss and Bertrand Marotte, "Quebec Eyes Buying Rona Shares to Block Lowe's," *Globe and Mail* (31 July 2012), online: Globe and Mail <http://wwwtheglobeandmail.com>. Incidentally, under *NAFTA, supra* note 3, art 1108(1)(a)(ii), subnational decisions are exempted from the *NAFTA* national treatment obligation.

Chinese subnational governments, including even local governments, would retain the ability to block Canadian investments.[88] As a result, even if China were to allow market access to third-state investors (and, by extension, to Canadian investors) in a future treaty, China would retain the ability to block market access by Canadian investors at any level of Chinese government.

Second, the carve-out for China is not limited to a specific legal instrument akin to the *Investment Canada Act*. Rather, the *China FIPPA* refers to "Laws, Regulations and Rules." This reference gives China the ability to screen Canadian investment on a much wider basis than Canada, whose flexibility in investment screening is limited to the *Investment Canada Act* (presumably as it stood at the time of the *China FIPPA*'s entry into force). This lack of reciprocity is important because, with the exception of review on national security grounds,[89] the *Investment Canada Act* has significant limitations as a vehicle for investment screening. For example, the *Investment Canada Act* authorizes the federal government to block an investment only if the investment involves the takeover of a Canadian company — the federal government cannot block greenfield investment.[90] Further, even if a Chinese investment involved the takeover of a Canadian firm, the *Investment Canada Act* permits review of the investment only if the value of the Canadian firm subject to the takeover exceeds a general threshold of $344 million (in 2013), a threshold that is expected to rise to $1 billion by 2018.[91] To illustrate, a series of large-scale land purchases by Chinese companies — which

---

[88] For an indication of the potential significance of this carve-out, see the comment by David Fung, vice chair of the Canada China Business Council (offered by him as a reason for Canada to conclude the *China FIPPA* but without reference to the FIPPA's carve-out for investment screening and existing discriminatory measures in China): "There are lots of horror stories about Canadian investments in China ... In Canada, our cities don't go and destroy somebody else's investment. But, in China, a mayor has a lot more power than our mayors in Canada." Quoted in Keith Norbury, "Canada-China FIPA: A Good Deal for Canadian Investors, or Not?" *Canadian Sailings* (14 April 2013), online: <http://www.canadiansailings.ca/?p=6437>.

[89] *Investment Canada Act, supra* note 9, s 25.1.

[90] *Ibid*, s 14(1).

[91] Industry Canada, "*Investment Canada Act:* Thresholds for Review," online: Industry Canada <http://www.ic.gc.ca/eic/site/ica-lic.nsf/eng/h_lk00050.html>. The thresholds are different for takeovers by state-owned enterprises (SOEs). See Industry Canada, "*Investment Canada Act:* Guidelines on Investment by State-Owned Enterprises: Net Benefit Assessment," online: Industry Canada <https://www.ic.gc.ca/eic/site/ica-lic.nsf/eng/lk00064.html#p2>.

is an issue that has attracted attention elsewhere[92] — could take place parcel by parcel below the *Investment Canada Act* threshold, with no ability under the *China FIPPA* for the Canadian federal government to screen the investment without exposure to viable ISA claims.

In addition, under the *Investment Canada Act*, there are ways in which foreign takeovers of Canadian firms may proceed without any review by the federal government.[93] For example, where a foreign-owned company is expanding, rather than acquiring, an existing business in Canada, the *Investment Canada Act* does not apply.[94] This aspect of the *Investment Canada Act* incidentally appeared to raise concern after the Canadian federal government approved the Chinese National Offshore Oil Company (CNOOC)'s takeover of Nexen in 2012.[95] The concern was that the approval, in combination with the *China FIPPA*, would allow further takeovers of Canadian assets by CNOOC without any additional review under the *Investment Canada Act*.[96]

Thus, in various respects, the *China FIPPA*'s carve-out of investment screening is non-reciprocal in favour of China. It limits Canada's ability to screen Chinese investments to review under the

---

92 Lorenzo Cotula et al, *Land Grab or Development Opportunity?* (London/Rome: International Institute for Environment and Development/Food and Agriculture Organization/International Fund for Agricultural Development, 2009) at 36, 55; Klaus Deininger and Derek Byerlee, *Rising Global Interest in Farmland* (Washington, DC: World Bank, 2011) at 53. For a discussion of how Chinese SOEs may purchase land directly to avoid investment screening under the Canadian federal government's 2012 restrictions on SOE takeovers in the resource sector, see Nathan Vanderklippe, "For China, An Oil Sands Investment That Can't Be Blocked," *Globe and Mail* (11 March 2014), online: Globe and Mail <http://www.theglobeandmail.com>.

93 *Investment Canada Act, supra* note 9, s 38; Industry Canada, "*Investment Canada Act:* Related-Business Guidelines," online: Industry Canada <https://www.ic.gc.ca/eic/site/ica-lic.nsf/eng/lk00064.html#p2> [Related-Business Guidelines].

94 *Ibid.*

95 Shawn McCarthy and Steven Chase, "Ottawa Approves Nexen, Progress Foreign Takeovers," *Globe and Mail* (7 December 2012), online: Globe and Mail <http://www.theglobeandmail.com>.

96 Kelly Cryderman, "Ottawa's Foreign Ownership Strategy Hurts Alberta, Mulcair Argues," *Globe and Mail* (19 February 2013), online: Globe and Mail <http://www.theglobeandmail.com>. The concern is credible assuming that the *China FIPPA*, if ratified, would implicitly preclude future changes to the *Investment Canada Act* (as conditioned by existing instruments such as the Related-Business Guidelines, *supra* note 93) that would expand the scope of Annex D.34 of the *China FIPPA*.

Investment Canada Act while preserving China's ability to screen Canadian investments at any level of government and without the thresholds or other limitations contained in the *Investment Canada Act*. This non-reciprocity is unique to the *China FIPPA* compared to Canada's other treaties that provide for market access subject to ISA.[97] It also highlights that the *Investment Canada Act* is not as watertight a means to regulate Chinese investment as some have claimed in relation to the *China FIPPA*.[98] For a watertight carve-out, Canada should have secured language equivalent to that obtained by China in the *China FIPPA* or by Canada in other FIPPAs.[99]

APPARENT NON-RECIPROCITY ON POST-ESTABLISHMENT
NATIONAL TREATMENT

The *China FIPPA* provides for post-establishment national treatment. However, it also includes broad exceptions to this general obligation of non-discrimination between domestic investors and established foreign investors.[100] Perhaps most importantly, the *China FIPPA*

---

[97] See Canada's FIPPAs with Costa Rica (Annex I(VI)(1)-(2)); Croatia (Annex I(VI) (1)-(2)); Ecuador (art II(4)(a)-(b)); Egypt (art II(4)(a)-(b)); Latvia (art II(4) (a)-(b)); Panama (art II(4)(a)-(b)); Philippines (art II(4)-(5)); Romania (art II(4)(a)-(b)); Trinidad and Tobago (art II(4)(a)-(b)); Ukraine (art II(4)(a)- (b)); Uruguay (Annex I(VI)(1)-(2)); and Venezuela (Annex II(3)(a)-(b)). See Annex 2 in this article; relevant treaty texts available online: DFATD <http:// www.international.gc.ca/trade-agreements-accords-commerciaux/agr-acc/ fipa-apie/index.aspx?lang=eng>.

[98] See, for example, Greg Kanargelidis, Aaron Libbey, and Tamara Nachmani, "Canada-China Investment Treaty: Ratification Process Begins," *Blakes Bulletin* (1 October 2012), online: Blakes <http://www.blakes.com/English/Resources/Bulletins/ Pages/Details.aspx?BulletinID=1702>: "[W]hile some critics have attacked the Canada-China FIPA, arguing it results in a forfeiture of Canadian sovereignty with respect to Chinese foreign investment in Canada, this exception [for the *Investment Canada Act*] ensures the Government of Canada retains the ability to exercise oversight in this area."

[99] For example, *Agreement between the Government of Canada and the Government of the Eastern Republic of Uruguay for the Promotion and Protection of Investments*, Can TS 1999 No 31, Annex I(VI)(1) (in force 2 June 1999): "Decisions of a Contracting Party as to whether or not to permit establishment of a new business enterprise, or acquisition of an existing business enterprise or a share of such enterprise, by investors or prospective investors of the other Contracting Party shall not be subject to dispute settlement [i.e. investor-state arbitration] under Article XII of this Agreement." See also agreements listed in note 97 in this article.

[100] *China FIPPA*, *supra* note 2, art 8(2)-(5). Less significantly, these exceptions also apply to the *China FIPPA*'s provisions on senior management requirements and on pre- and post-establishment MFN treatment.

exempts existing non-conforming measures in Canada and China from post-establishment national treatment (and from both pre- and post-establishment MFN treatment).[101] Thus, Canada and China, after an investment has been made, are permitted to continue to discriminate in favour of domestic investors to the detriment of investors of the other state so long as the discrimination is based on an existing, rather than a new, statute, regulation, policy, practice, and so on.[102] Further, Canada and China are required to lock in — that is, not increase — the existing levels of discrimination.[103]

With some important exceptions,[104] most of Canada's treaties that provide for ISA, such as the *China FIPPA*, exclude existing non- conforming measures from post-establishment national treat- ment.[105] Yet, for the *China FIPPA*, this feature seems especially noteworthy due to the *de facto* non-reciprocity it apparently creates. Indeed, it appears at present that there would be vastly more discriminatory measures in China than in Canada and that the measures in China may be more opaque and difficult for a Canadian investor to pinpoint as "existing" at a particular point in time than vice versa. In 2013, based on a survey of its members, the United States–China Business Council (USCBC) made the following report on the business environment in China:

Respondents most frequently claimed to have experienced protectionism in licensing and regulatory approvals, while also noting discriminatory enforcement and preferential policies favoring domestic Chinese compan- ies in many forms. Fundamentally, there continues to be a significant difference in how foreign companies are treated, both formally and in- formally, versus their domestic Chinese counterparts. As one respondent noted, "As long as the term 'foreign-invested company' exists [in Chinese

---

[101] *Ibid*, art 8(2)(a)(i).

[102] See the definition of "measure" in *ibid*, art 1(6).

[103] *Ibid*, art 8(2)(c).

[104] In Canada's Model FIPPA, three of Canada's trade agreements (including *NAFTA*), and two FIPPAs (with Jordan and Peru), the exception is limited to subnational measures and extends to national measures only where the exempted relevant measure is listed specifically. For example, Canada's Model FIPPA, *supra* note 8, art 9(1)(a)(i). Also, Canada's trade agreements with Chile and Colombia go further by requiring a negative-list approach for exempted state/provincial measures as well as national measures. See Annex 2 in this article.

[105] This is so for twenty-two of Canada's twenty-five FIPPAs. One other FIPPA (with Poland) appears not to provide for post-establishment national treatment at all. See Annex 2 in this article.

policies and regulations], the competition will not be very fair and the discrimination will exist in some way." In other words, there is an inherent element of bias in the system.

That bias shows up in numerous ways, many of them overlapping. While each of the top 10 challenges could stand on its own, these issues magnify each other and often make resolution of the problems more complicated.[106]

According to the USCBC report, among the top ten challenges faced by foreign companies in China, 61 percent of survey respondents have experienced challenges with administrative licensing, 49 percent have experienced tighter enforcement of rules for foreign companies, and 33 percent have reported that there were laws or regulations that specified differential treatment for domestic competitors.[107] Importantly, under the terms of the *China FIPPA*, these categories of reported discriminatory or protectionist treatment would be exempt from China's obligations of nondiscrimination due to the *China FIPPA*'s carve-out of existing discriminatory measures at all levels.

Assuming that the business environment reported by the USCBC affects Canadian as well as US investors in China and that its discriminatory and protectionist character goes well beyond the comparable experience of foreign investors in Canada, the *China FIPPA* would lock in a playing field that is not level in key respects. This conclusion was supported further by testimony of Canadian federal trade official Vernon MacKay with respect to the *China FIPPA*'s provisions on non-discrimination:

[Y]ou have to look at the two economies as they exist at the time that the treaty comes into force. And when you look at the Canadian economy, it's relatively open, in terms of protectionist measures and discriminatory measures. You look at the Chinese economy, and they are more protectionist and they do have rules in place that allow them to discriminate in favour

---

[106] US-China Business Council (USCBC), *USCBC 2013 China Business Environment Survey Results: Tempered Optimism Continues amid Moderating Growth, Rising Costs, and Persistent Market Barriers* (USCBC, 2013) at 5-6, online: USCBC <http://uschina.org/sites/default/files/USCBC%E2%80%942013Member%20Survey_0.pdf>. The USCBC reported that its survey was conducted by the USCBC with US- and China-based executives among USCBC members and that the survey included a cross-section of US companies that do business in China. Further information on methodology, such as the survey size, was not provided in the USCBC report.

[107] *Ibid* at 5-6, 11-12.

of Chinese investment ... So ... at the time that this comes into force, you will have a relatively open Canadian economy locked in place, in terms of its ability to discriminate, and a less open, more closed economy locked in place at the time it comes into force.[108]

A proper study of this apparent, *de facto* non-reciprocity arising from the *China FIPPA* would require a comprehensive analysis of China's approach to internal economic regulation compared to that of Canada's other treaty partners. To the author's knowledge, no such study has been carried out in relation to the *China FIPPA*. Based on available evidence, it is prudent to conclude that the *China FIPPA* is likely highly unequal in its effects due to the carve-out of existing discriminatory measures in Canada and China.

Incidentally, China's preservation of the right to maintain existing discriminatory measures would provide Chinese governments with a powerful tool to bargain with, or take punitive measures against, any Canadian investor in a situation of conflict over the investor's regulatory treatment. For example, if a decision maker in China wanted to "destroy" a Canadian investor,[109] it could pursue this goal without violating the *China FIPPA* by imposing discriminatory requirements pursuant to any law or regulation that existed at the time the *China FIPPA* entered into force. Thus, the non-reciprocity of post-establishment national treatment in the *China FIPPA* — and the greater flexibility that this preserves for Chinese discriminatory measures — undermines claims that the *China FIPPA* will provide strong protections for Canadian investors in China.

REACH-BACK IN THE SCOPE OF MFN TREATMENT

The *China FIPPA* contains provisions that appear to safeguard the regulatory interests of states in the face of its investor protections. In particular, language in the *China FIPPA* would likely constrain some of the far-reaching interpretations — common in investment treaty arbitration — of concepts of fair and equitable treatment, full protection and security, and indirect expropriation.[110] For Canada, this limiting language dates from 2001 when the *NAFTA* states issued a statement of interpretation to rein in *NAFTA* tribunals. Thereafter, Canada incorporated the language in its

---

108 MacKay Cross-Examination, *supra* note 1 at 40–41.

109 See Fung, *supra* note 88.

110 See text accompanying notes 43 and 45 in this article.

subsequent treaties.[111] The language in the *China FIPPA* has been highlighted by proponents of the agreement as cause for reassurance about its impacts on governments and legislatures.[112] Yet the applicability of the limiting language — assuming it has a meaningful effect on interpretations given to the relevant substantive standards[113] — is open to serious doubt due to the *China FIPPA*'s temporal "reach-back" on MFN treatment.[114]

Based on their obligations of MFN treatment, Canada and China must give no less favourable treatment to foreign investors from the other state party as compared to the treatment given in like circumstances to foreign investors from any third state. As such, the point of comparison for MFN treatment is the host state's treatment of third-state investors, while for national treatment it is the host state's treatment of domestic investors. In this respect, the *China FIPPA*'s MFN provision is unremarkable. More significantly, the *China FIPPA* extends expressly its MFN treatment obligation beyond any treatment given to third-state investors in *future* treaties to include any treatment given in *previous* treaties since 1994.[115] This approach differs from all but two FIPPAs concluded by Canada, in that it makes clear that MFN treatment extends to treatment afforded to third-state investors in past FIPPAs.[116] Other treaties concluded by

---

[111] Canada's Model FIPPA, *supra* note 8, art 38(1)-(4). See also Canada's post-2001 FIPPAs with the Czech Republic, Jordan, Latvia, Peru, Romania, the Slovak Republic, and Tanzania as well as Canada's trade agreements with Colombia, Panama, and Peru. See Annex 1 in this article.

[112] See, for example, MacKay Cross-Examination, *supra* note 1 at 43, 53, 66.

[113] For a contrary position, which was adopted by the Canadian federal government, that the limiting language makes no difference to the meaning of the substantive standard of fair and equitable treatment, see *Chemtura Corporation v Government of Canada* (UNCITRAL), Respondent Counter-Memorial (20 October 2008) at para 896. The tribunal in that case appeared not to resolve this particular issue. *Chemtura Corporation v Government of Canada* (UNCITRAL), Award (2 August 2010) at para 235.

[114] Mann, *supra* note 55.

[115] *China FIPPA*, *supra* note 2, art 8(1)(b) (MFN treatment does not apply to "treatment accorded under any bilateral or multilateral international agreement in force prior to 1 January 1994"). MFN treatment also does not extend to trade agreements (*China FIPPA*, *ibid*, art 8(1)(a)(i)) but this does not affect the present analysis because the express application of MFN treatment to post-1993 FIPPAs is sufficient to undermine Canada's post-2001 limiting language (assuming that the pre-2001 language provides more favourable treatment to foreign investors than the post-2001 language).

[116] That is, Canada's FIPPAs with Jordan (in 2009) and Tanzania (in 2013). See Annex 2 in this article.

Canada either preclude expressly,[117] or are silent on,[118] the application of MFN treatment to previous treaties. The *China FIPPA*'s express reach-back also differs from Canada's Model FIPPA, which says that MFN treatment "shall not apply to treatment under all bilateral or multilateral international agreements in force or signed prior to the date of entry into force of this Agreement."[119] Thus, while Canada's Model FIPPA states expressly that MFN treatment does not allow foreign investors to mix and match provisions from previous treaties as a creative legal strategy, the *China FIPPA* makes clear that they can.[120]

For present purposes, the significance of this complex reach-back on MFN treatment is that it puts the *China FIPPA*'s limiting language, highlighted earlier, at serious risk. Perhaps most significant is the risk to the *China FIPPA*'s limiting language on fair and equitable treatment and full protection and security, given the extent to which investment treaty tribunals have interpreted these concepts expansively in favour of claimant investors.[121] To elaborate, the *China FIPPA*'s limiting language appears to restrict such expansive interpretations by clarifying that the concepts in question "do not require treatment in addition to or beyond that which is required by the international law minimum standard of treatment of aliens as evidenced by State practice accepted as law."[122] In other words, the *China FIPPA* affirms that the concepts are limited to their

---

117 That is, Canada's FIPPA with Peru and the Canada-Chile trade agreement. See Annex 2 in this article.

118 This is the case for the remaining twenty-six of Canada's treaties that provide for ISA. See Annex 2 in this article.

119 Canada's Model FIPPA, *supra* note 8, Annex III(1).

120 Stephan W Schill, *The Multilateralization of International Investment Law* (Cambridge: Cambridge University Press, 2009) at 140-42. For a discussion of rationales for limiting this mix-and-match approach as well as limiting the implied application of MFN treatment to past treaties, see Tony Cole, *The Structure of Investment Arbitration* (Milton Park: Routledge, 2013) at 97-112.

121 Roland Kläger, *"Fair and Equitable Treatment" in International Investment Law* (Cambridge: Cambridge University Press, 2011) at 116-19; M Sornarajah, "Evolution or Revolution in International Investment Arbitration? The Descent into Normlessness" in Chester Brown and Kate Miles, eds, *Evolution in Investment Treaty Law and Arbitration* (Cambridge: Cambridge University Press, 2011) at 650-52; Stephan W Schill, "Fair and Equitable Treatment, the Rule of Law, and Comparative Public Law" in Schill, supra note 19, 152 at 159-70; Alexandra Diehl, *The Core Standard of International Investment Protection* (Alphen aan den Rijn: Kluwer Law International, 2012) ch 6.

122 *China FIPPA*, *supra* note 2, art 4(2).

customary meaning, based on the usual evidentiary requirements of customary international law, and thus guards against arbitrators introducing novel and intrusive state obligations as part of the obligations to guarantee fair and equitable treatment or full protection and security.[123] Similarly, on indirect expropriation, the *China FIPPA* provides, among other things:

> Except in rare circumstances, such as if a measure or series of measures is so severe in light of its purpose that it cannot be reasonably viewed as having been adopted and applied in good faith, a non-discriminatory measure or series of measures of a Contracting Party that is designed and applied to protect the legitimate public objectives for the well-being of citizens, such as health, safety and the environment, does not constitute indirect expropriation.[124]

This language likewise responds to expansive approaches by arbitrators in, for example, the early *NAFTA* award in *Metalclad v Mexico*, where the tribunal adopted a far-reaching approach to indirect expropriation.[125] It is unclear how ISA tribunals under the *China FIPPA* would respond to the limiting language on these concepts, given the prevalence of expansive approaches.[126] Yet the limiting language is at least an important factor weighing against expansive interpretations that may frustrate legitimate regulatory interests of Canada or China.[127]

---

[123] The language also makes clear the requirement that claimants, in order to establish a change in the content of customary international law, must supply evidence of state practice and *opinio juris* — a requirement to which few ISA tribunals have held claimants. See Matthew C Porterfield, "A Distinction without a Difference? The Interpretation of Fair and Equitable Treatment under Customary International Law by Investment Tribunals," *Investment Treaty News* (22 March 2013).

[124] *China FIPPA, supra* note 2, Annex B.10.

[125] *Metalclad v Mexico* (ICSID Additional Facility), 40 ILM 36 (2000) at para 103. See also *United Mexican States v Metalclad Corporation,* 2001 BCSC 664 at para 99. The *Metalclad* award is still widely cited by ISA tribunals. See, for example, *Occidental v Ecuador (No 2),* ICSID Case No ARB/06/11 (2012) at para 455.

[126] For example, ISA tribunals have incorporated new concepts into the customary international legal standard without requiring the claimant to provide evidence of corresponding state practice and *opinio juris*. See, for example, *Railroad Development Corporation v Guatemala,* ICSID Case No ARB/07/23 (2012) at paras 207-11, 216-19. See also Porterfield, *supra* note 123.

[127] Judging from the *NAFTA* experience, the limiting language has gone some way towards reining in arbitrators' approaches to relevant concepts even if

Critically, the *China FIPPA*'s reach-back on MFN treatment casts serious doubt on the effectiveness of all of the limiting language discussed earlier. This is because both Canada and China have concluded treaties since 1994 that do not incorporate the limiting language[128] and, as a result, have assumed a significant risk of being unable to rely on the *China FIPPA*'s limiting language due to their obligation to provide MFN treatment. In Canada's case, therefore, a Chinese investor would be able to argue that it is entitled to no less favourable treatment than that enjoyed by third-state investors under any of Canada's fourteen post-1994 FIPPAs in which fair and equitable treatment, full protection and security, and indirect expropriation are not subject to the limiting language.[129]

For various reasons, it is at least likely that an ISA tribunal would decide that the *China FIPPA*'s limiting language amounts to less favourable treatment relative to the treatment of third-state investors under Canada's other FIPPAs. First, MFN treatment has been interpreted broadly — in that it has been extended to treatment relating to dispute settlement provisions rather than simply to substantive provisions in other treaties — by about half of the twenty ISA tribunals that have faced and resolved this particular issue in publicly available awards up to May-June 2010.[130] Second, even if a tribunal under the *China FIPPA* adopted a more restrictive approach, by limiting MFN treatment to substantive provisions only, the *China FIPPA*'s limiting language would still be in jeopardy because it affects treatment relating to the agreement's substantive, rather than dispute settlement, provisions.

---

variation remains and even if, outside *NAFTA*, ISA tribunals typically take a more expansive approach. See Van Harten, *supra* note 25 at 225-28, 237-40, and the authorities cited in note 121 in this article. See also Luke Eric Peterson, "Evaluating Canada's 2004 Model Foreign Investment Protection Agreement in Light of Civil Society Concerns," Report for the Canadian Council for International Co-operation (June 2006).

128 For example, *Croatia FIPPA*, *supra* note 80; *Agreement on Encouragement and Reciprocal Protection of Investments between the Government of the People's Republic of China and the Government of the Kingdom of the Netherlands* (26 November 2001, in force 1 August 2004), online: UNCTAD <http://unctad.org/sections/dite/iia/docs/bits/china_netherlands.pdf>.

129 See Canada's FIPPAs with Armenia, Barbados, Costa Rica, Croatia, Ecuador, Egypt, Lebanon, Panama, the Philippines, Thailand, Trinidad and Tobago, Ukraine, Uruguay, and Venezuela. See Annex 1 in this article.

130 Van Harten, *supra* note 25 at 228, 238.

To illustrate, in *Paushok v Mongolia*, an ISA tribunal adopted a relatively restrictive (that is, respondent state-friendly) approach to MFN treatment by declining to extend the concept either to treatment in dispute settlement provisions or to treatment in any new substantive provision in other treaties.[131] According to the tribunal,

> [h]istorically, tribunals have tended to construe MFN clauses broadly and they have regularly accepted to import substantive rights into an investment treaty from treaties that the host State has signed with other countries. This broad interpretation has also led tribunals to allow the import of more favorable procedural rights. There are however other cases which have adopted a more restrictive interpretation concerning the import of procedural rights but this issue need not be addressed in the present case, the question relating simply to the import of substantive rights.
>
> .... The treaty is quite clear as to the interpretation to be given to the MFN clause ... the extension of substantive rights it allows only has to do with Article 3(1) which deals with fair and equitable treatment. If there exists any other BIT between Mongolia and another State which provides for a more generous provision relating to fair and equitable treatment, an investor under the Treaty is entitled to invoke it. But, such investor cannot use that MFN clause to introduce into the Treaty completely new substantive rights, such as those granted under an umbrella clause.[132]

Based on this approach and on the terms of the relevant BIT, the concept of MFN treatment was extended to substantive rights only in circumstances where a more generous version of the same substantive right had been included in the treaty with a third state. Yet, even on this restrictive approach, foreign investors under the *China FIPPA* would be relieved of its limiting language relating to fair and equitable treatment, full protection and security, and indirect expropriation on the basis that each concept forms part of a more generous version of the same substantive provisions in other FIPPAs that lack the limiting language.

Further, if an ISA tribunal under the *China FIPPA* adopted an approach going beyond *Paushok*, as is common in other ISA awards,[133] the tribunal could incorporate other provisions from other FIPPAs in order to expand investor protection. For example, the *China*

---

[131] *Paushok v Mongolia* (UNCITRAL), Award (28 April 2011), online: <http://italaw.com/sites/default/files/case-documents/ita0622.pdf>.

[132] *Ibid* at paras 565, 570.

[133] Van Harten, *supra* note 25 at 228, 238.

FIPPA's denial-of-benefits clause could be read down and rendered ineffective by reference to clauses in other FIPPAs that require Canada to give notice before invoking a denial-of-benefits clause in the face of an ISA claim. In this way, the reach-back on MFN treatment undermines a variety of limiting devices in the *China FIPPA*, with implications for the apparent balance struck in the agreement between investor protection and regulatory flexibility.

Incidentally, this analysis of the effect of the *China FIPPA*'s reach-back on MFN treatment has been rejected, or at least not adopted, by some commentators.[134] Yet it appears that the federal government itself determined, as part of its negotiating strategy for the *China FIPPA*, to jeopardize its post-2001 limiting language in order to obtain for Canadian investors a similar ability to avoid the *China FIPPA*'s limiting language in ISA claims against China. When questioned under oath about the *China FIPPA*'s reach-back on MFN treatment, Canadian federal trade official Vernon MacKay explained:

China has over a hundred of what we call bilateral investment treaties very similar to FIPPAs. Most of them we would not want access to because they're not high-ambition — what we would call a high-ambition treaty. But there were a few in the early 2000s with some European countries that are pretty high standard. They're not directly comparable, so it's hard to say, you know, just how much more advantageous they might be to an investor, but they were — they were ones that we were considering ...

The fair and equitable standards of some of these treaties are very broadly worded, certainly worded in ways that we would not word ours, which could lend themselves to an expansive interpretation which our Canadian investors may take advantage of in a Chinese market situation ...

[S]ome of these provisions were potentially more of a broader scope and could provide high — you know, more protection for a Canadian investor. So since — and just to clarify, the Canadian model, as we have included in here, does not include that reach-back to 1994, but it is — we have the policy flexibility, if I could say that, to modify that ... We use that 1994 reach-back as an incentive to get the other party to reach back as well.[135]

This testimony indicates that Canadian negotiators intended the reach-back on MFN treatment to expand the benefits of the *China*

---

134 For example, *Hupacasath First Nation v Canada (Foreign Affairs)*, 2013 FC 900 at para 103.

135 MacKay Cross-Examination, *supra* note 1 at 51-53.

FIPPA for foreign investors at the expense of the regulatory interests of both Canada and China and, by extension, at the expense of other actors who may benefit from state conduct otherwise safe-guarded by the limiting language. In turn, it is dubious, based on the existing record of investment treaty arbitration and McKay's testimony, for anyone to rely on the *China FIPPA*'s limiting language as a safeguard for regulatory decision making.[136]

INCORPORATION INTO THE *CHINA FIPPA* OF THE TRIMS PERFORMANCE REQUIREMENTS CLAUSE

Like many treaties that reflect the North American approach, the *China FIPPA* has a prohibition on performance requirements — essentially, measures that require foreign investors to export a cer-tain share of their production, to use domestic inputs, to employ domestic workers, and so on — that many states sometimes impose on foreign investors as a condition of operating in their territory and as part of a larger industrialization and development strategy.[137] The *China FIPPA*'s prohibition is not as far-reaching as the prohibi-tion in other treaties concluded by Canada, including *NAFTA*.[138] In particular, the *China FIPPA*'s prohibition is limited to the state parties' existing obligations under the World Trade Organization's (WTO) *Agreement on Trade-Related Investment Measures* (*TRIMS Agreement*), which essentially require that states not discriminate between foreign and domestic investors in the case of a trade-related performance requirement.[139]

Importantly, by transplanting the *TRIMS Agreement*'s obligations into an investment treaty, the *China FIPPA* subjects the relevant

---

[136] For example, DFATD, *Final Environmental Assessment of the Canada-China Foreign Investment Protection Agreement (FIPA)* (Ottawa: Government of Canada, undated), online: DFATD <http://www.international.gc.ca/trade-agreements-accords -commerciaux/agr-acc/china-chine/finalEA-china-chine-EEfinale.aspx?lang =eng> [*Environmental Assessment*]: "No new issues arose during the latter stages of the Canada-China FIPA negotiations with respect to potential environmental impacts in Canada ... [A]s is found in [Canada's Model FIPPA], Annex B.10 of the Canada–China FIPA provides that regulations designed and applied to advance legitimate public welfare objectives, such as those respecting health, safety and the environment, do not constitute an indirect expropriation."

[137] *China FIPPA, supra* note 2, art 9.

[138] Compare *NAFTA, supra* note 3, art 1106.

[139] In particular, the *China FIPPA* incorporates Article 2 and the Annex of the *Agreement on Trade-Related Investment Measures,* 1868 UNTS 186 (in force 1 January 1995) [*TRIMS Agreement*].

obligations to ISA instead of to WTO state-to-state adjudication.[140] In ISA, arbitrators typically award retrospective compensation directly to a private party; at the WTO, tribunals authorize only prospective trade remedies to compensate the successful WTO state.[141] Thus, in ISA, arbitrators award compensation that is calculated from the time of the state's conduct that was found to have violated the treaty. Unlike at the WTO, the state typically has no opportunity to correct the declared illegality before having to pay potentially vast amounts of compensation to the claimant investor. As a result, ISA introduces the prospect of uncertain, but irreversible and potentially very onerous, liability whenever a legislature, government, or court pursues a course of action that may cause loss to a foreign investor. This prospect raises wider issues about the use of monetary remedies as a remedy for unlawful sovereign conduct,[142] without any limit on the amounts that can be awarded.[143] More specifically, it highlights how the obligations of the *TRIMS Agreement* on performance requirements take a different form when transplanted into a FIPPA and subjected to ISA.[144]

Since the *TRIMS Agreement* obligations are rarely incorporated into FIPPAs or other BITs, it is unclear how they will be applied in an investment, as opposed to a trade, context, although it is clearly possible that the obligations will be given a broader meaning.[145] In any event, one may surmise the potential meaning of the *China FIPPA*'s prohibition on performance requirements by considering how the relevant *TRIMS* obligations have been

---

[140] Martin Molinuevo, *Protecting Investment in Services: Investor-State Arbitration Versus WTO Dispute Settlement* (Alphen aan den Rijn: Wolters Kluwer, 2012) at 72-74, 233-34.

[141] Also, in contrast to World Trade Organization (WTO) arbitration, the legal claims in ISA are formulated by private parties who are not subject to the treaty obligations and who do not have a corresponding interest to moderate their claims.

[142] van Aaken, *supra* note 22.

[143] Compare the monetary limits on penalties in person-to-government dispute resolution under Canada's *Agreement on Internal Trade — Consolidated Version, 2012*, Annex 1707.1(2), online: <http://www.ait-aci.ca/en/ait/ait_en.pdf> (providing for a maximum penalty of $5 million per case for the largest provinces).

[144] Two other FIPPAs refer to *TRIMS Agreement* obligations as prohibited performance requirements, but both of these FIPPAs include the aboriginal exception. See Canada's FIPPAs with Thailand and Costa Rica in Annex 1 in this article.

[145] Van Harten, *Investment Treaty Arbitration and Public Law* (Oxford: Oxford University Press, 2007) at 73-80.

interpreted at the WTO. In the recent WTO panel report on Ontario's *Green Energy Act*[146] and the feed-in-tariff (FIT) program, the WTO panel concluded:

> As to whether the measures are "trade-related", we note that the FIT Programme imposes a "Minimum Required Domestic Content Level" on electricity generators utilising solar PV and windpower technologies that, for the reasons we explain elsewhere in this section, compels them to purchase and use certain types of renewable energy generation equipment sourced in Ontario in the design and construction of their facilities. To this extent, we see the "Minimum Required Domestic Content Level" that is at issue in these disputes to be not unlike the domestic content requirements challenged in Indonesia — Autos, where the panel opined that "*by definition, [domestic content requirements] always favour the use of domestic products over imported products, and therefore affect trade.*"[147]

On this basis, it appears clear that a regulatory requirement for a foreign investor to use domestic suppliers or hire domestic workers — as forms of "domestic content" in the investor's activities — would not be consistent with the obligations of the *TRIMS Agreement* and, in turn, with the *China FIPPA*. This inconsistency is significant due to other aspects of the *China FIPPA*'s prohibition on performance requirements, which are discussed in the following section.

EXPANDED APPLICATION OF THE PERFORMANCE REQUIREMENTS CLAUSE

The *China FIPPA*'s incorporation of the obligations of the *TRIMS Agreement* on performance requirements is especially important because it does not incorporate all of the reservations and exceptions that usually apply to obligations on performance requirements in Canada's other treaties.[148] In particular, in many or all of Canada's

---

[146] *Green Energy Act*, SO 2009, c 12.

[147] *Canada – Certain Measures Affecting the Renewable Energy Generation Sector/ Canada — Measures Relating to the Feed-In Tariff Program*, WTO Docs WT/DS412/R, WT/DS426/R (2012) at para 7.111 (panel reports) [emphasis added]; *Canada – Certain Measures Affecting the Renewable Energy Generation Sector/ Canada — Measures Relating to the Feed-In Tariff Program*, WTO Docs WT/DS412/AB/R, WT/DS426/AB/R (2013) at para 5.6 (reports of the Appellate Body): "Domestic content requirements are one type of TRIM regulated under the TRIMS Agreement."

[148] For instance, of the twenty-four relevant treaties that contain an obligation on performance requirements, all have an exception for aboriginal rights and

other treaties that provide for ISA, obligations on performance requirements do not extend to various measures such as existing provincial and municipal measures[149] and measures that protect the rights and preferences of Aboriginal peoples.[150] On the latter measures, for example, *NAFTA* provides with respect to its prohibition on performance requirements that "Canada reserves the right to adopt or maintain any measure denying investors of another Party and their investments, or service providers of another Party, any rights or preferences provided to aboriginal peoples."[151]

It is noteworthy by contrast that the *China FIPPA* does not extend the same reservations to its obligations on performance requirements.[152] As a result, the *China FIPPA* would prohibit, and subject to ISA, a range of federal, provincial, and municipal measures in Canada as they affect Chinese investors. Further, US and other foreign investors in Canada would henceforth be entitled to the same insulation from performance requirements — on a non-reciprocal basis in comparison to Canadian investors in the United States or the other third state — due to the MFN treatment obligations in *NAFTA* and other treaties to which Canada is a party and that provide for ISA.

In this respect, the *China FIPPA* marks a significant departure from Canada's past practice on performance requirements and ISA,

---

preferences. Likewise, Canada's Model FIPPA, *supra* note 8, allows for similar reservations and exceptions. See further Annex 1 in this article.

[149] For example, *NAFTA*, *supra* note 3, art 1108(1)(a)(ii)-(iii) (the relevant obligations "do not apply to … any existing non-conforming measure that is maintained by … a state or province … or … a local government"). Note that this NAFTA clause provides that the reserved state and provincial measures must be listed within two years in a separate schedule. The schedule was never completed, leaving by implication a reservation for all existing non-conforming measures of states and provinces. The sole exceptions appear to be Canada's trade agreements with Chile and Colombia.

[150] See note 148 in this article.

[151] *NAFTA*, *supra* note 3, Annex II (Schedule of Canada). Similarly, other state measures in some areas, such as the protection of rights of disadvantaged minorities, are also exempted in *NAFTA* and some other FIPPAs. See further Annex 1 in this article.

[152] *China FIPPA*, *supra* note 2, art 8(2)(a)(i), Annex B.8, which incorporate into the *China FIPPA* a series of reservations contained in the *Free Trade Agreement between Canada and the Republic of Peru*, Can TS 2009 No 15, Annex II (in force 1 August 2009) and in the *Free Trade Agreement between China and the Republic of Peru* (28 April 2009, entered into force 1 March 2010), ch 10, online: <http://fta.mofcom.gov.cn/topic/enperu.shtml>.

which may have significant consequences for Canadian businesses and employees whose contracts or jobs are linked to a regulatory requirement in Canada that foreign investors use domestic suppliers or domestic workers. It appears especially relevant in the resource sector in light of government efforts to enhance value-added benefits of resource extraction in Canada for the Canadian economy. The potential conflict was highlighted in 2012 when Canada lost an ISA claim under *NAFTA* in *Mobil Investments Canada Inc and Murphy Oil Corp v Canada*.[153] In this case, a majority of the tribunal decided that Canada had violated *NAFTA*'s prohibition on performance requirements after changes were made to research-and-development (R & D) expenditure rules for domestic and foreign companies operating in Newfoundland and Labrador's offshore oil sector.[154] Surprisingly, the tribunal also concluded that the changes were not safeguarded by Canada's reservation under *NAFTA* relating to the law that authorized the R & D rules.[155] For present purposes, the decision indicates that prohibitions on performance requirements in the *China FIPPA* may clash with domestic social or economic policies.

The *China FIPPA*'s divergence from Canada's past practice on performance requirements appears particularly significant in relation to Aboriginal peoples. Besides the *China FIPPA*, all of Canada's treaties that prohibit performance requirements include a reservation from the prohibition for measures that protect Aboriginal rights and preferences. By implication, the *China FIPPA* would, however, prohibit any Canadian requirements that foreign investors use Aboriginal (that is, domestic) content as a condition of their operation in Canada. This change would appear to preclude aspects of so-called impact and benefit agreements that are sometimes required by law and that typically require that foreign investors use Aboriginal content, especially in the resource sector.[156] Thus, although

---

[153] *Mobil Investments Canada Inc and Murphy Oil Corp v Canada*, ICSID Case No ARB(AF)/07/4 (2012) (ICSID Additional Facility), online: <http://www.italaw.com/sites/default/files/case-documents/italaw1145.pdf>.

[154] *Ibid* at para 246.

[155] *Ibid* at paras 410-16. For a critical comment on the award, see Nigel Bankes, "From Regulatory Chill to Regulatory Concussion: NAFTA's Prohibition on Domestic Performance Requirements and an Absurdly Narrow Interpretation of Country Specific Reservations," Case Comment (6 May 2013), online: <http://ablawg.ca/wp-content/uploads/2013/05/Blog_NB_Mobil_Investments_May20131.pdf>.

[156] Sandra Gogal, Richard Riegert, and JoAnn Jamieson, "Aboriginal Impact and Benefit Agreements: Practical Considerations" (2005) 43 Alta L Rev 129;

such agreements are widespread as a means of accommodating Aboriginal rights and interests and of avoiding potential disputes,[157] it appears that they would be prohibited under the *China FIPPA* and subject to ISA.

In light of this change, one might have expected the federal government to consult with provincial and municipal governments and Aboriginal peoples to evaluate how existing measures may be affected specifically by the *China FIPPA*. One might also expect that governments would examine how the change could have an impact on domestic companies or workers that are connected to foreign companies. Yet in 2012, it was disclosed in litigation that the federal government did not consult with other policy actors after deciding that no consultation over the *China FIPPA* was required. According to testimony given by Canadian federal trade official Vernon MacKay,

the design of the treaty did not lead us to consult with aboriginal peoples, it did not lead us to consult with other policy communities such as municipalities, because our China FIPA stuck to the model, the model FIPA, which is an agreement that we have had in place since 1994, since the NAFTA. This is a perfect example of — it's a member of a family of investment agreements that Canada has had in place since 1994, in terms of FIPAs or also investment chapters of free trade agreements. So there is no departure from our past practice in that regard, and it did not lead us to a decision on whether we should be consulting more broadly than we already were.[158]

The testimony continues:

Question: [T]o your knowledge, was any consideration given to how the exercise of First Nations governance might be affected by the ratification of the Canada-China FIPA?

Courtney Fidler and Michael Hitch, "Impact and Benefit Agreements: A Contentious Issue for Environmental and Aboriginal Justice" (2007) 35:2 Environments Journal 49 at 61.

[157] A joint government taskforce reported in 2010 that aboriginal organizations and mining companies concluded ninety-one agreements during 1998-2008 that were "designed to secure both benefits for Aboriginal communities and certainty for exploration and mining companies" and that may include, for example, "preferential hiring practices for Aboriginal workers." Federal, Provincial and Territorial Social Licence Task Group, *Mining Sector Performance Report: 1998-2008* (Ottawa: Government of Canada, 2010) at 27.

[158] MacKay Cross-Examination, *supra* note 1 at 9.

Answer: There was no specific analysis done on that question, nor was there specific analysis done on how, for example, the FIPA might affect municipalities. And the reason for that is that it did not depart from our FIPA model, and we are very comfortable with the impacts of that FIPA model on the various policy communities that are covered by this treaty.[159]

This lack of consultation is problematic due to the *China FIPPA*'s uniqueness with respect to performance requirements and other issues and due to the potential impact of this uniqueness on Canadian companies, workers, Aboriginal peoples, and municipalities.

ALLOWANCE FOR CONFIDENTIALITY IN INVESTOR-STATE
ARBITRATION

When ISA first attracted attention in the late 1990s, it became apparent that ISA claims and proceedings could be kept secret at the discretion of the ISA tribunal. In response, the *NAFTA* governments issued an interpretive statement in 2001 that clarified that nothing in *NAFTA* precluded the *NAFTA* states from publishing ISA awards and other documents and that ISA hearings under *NAFTA* could be open to the public.[160] This clarification was an important and positive step in the wider context of ISA. Beginning in 2001, Canada incorporated requirements for ISA transparency in all of its treaties that provide for ISA.[161] Reflecting this shift, Canada's Model FIPPA of 2004 states:

1. Hearings held [in ISA] shall be open to the public. To the extent necessary to ensure the protection of confidential information, including business confidential information, the Tribunal may hold portions of hearings *in camera....*

---

159 *Ibid* at 11.

160 NAFTA Free Trade Commission, *supra* note 42, art B(1). Meg Kinnear and Robin Hansen, "The Influence of NAFTA Chapter 11 in the BIT Landscape" (2005) 12 UC Davis J Int'l L & Pol'y 101 at 111.

161 This includes Canada's Model FIPPA, *supra* note 8; all of Canada's post-2001 FIPPAs, including those with the Czech Republic (which entered into force in 2012 and adopts the presumption that all documents are public but like the *China FIPPA* provides that hearings are public if the respondent state so decides), Jordan, Latvia, Peru, Romania, the Slovak Republic, and Tanzania; and all of Canada's post-2001 trade agreements, including those with Colombia, Panama, and Peru. See Annex 1 in this article.

3. All documents submitted to, or issued by, the Tribunal shall be publicly available, unless the disputing parties otherwise agree, subject to the deletion of confidential information.

4. Notwithstanding paragraph 3, any Tribunal award under this Section shall be publicly available, subject to the deletion of confidential information.[162]

These provisions clarify that ISA hearings and awards are, as a general rule, public, subject to specific exemptions for confidential information. Further, as a general principle, all documents submitted or issued in ISA are public unless the investor and respondent states both agree to make them confidential. This degree of transparency did not reach the openness of a judicial proceeding, in which all documents before the court are public, subject to the court's discretion, but it did offer a relatively high level of public access in ISA and was clearly warranted due to the significance of ISA for public policy and public finance.[163]

The *China FIPPA* diverges considerably from this approach on ISA transparency:

1. Any Tribunal award ... shall be publicly available, subject to the redaction of confidential information. Where a disputing Contracting Party determines that it is in the public interest to do so and notifies the Tribunal of that determination, all other documents submitted to, or issued by, the Tribunal shall also be publicly available, subject to the redaction of confidential information.

2. Where, after consulting with a disputing investor, a disputing Contracting Party determines that it is in the public interest to do so and notifies the Tribunal of that determination, hearings held under this Part shall be open to the public. To the extent necessary to ensure the protection of confidential information, including business confidential information, the Tribunal may hold portions of hearings *in camera*.[164]

---

[162] Canada's Model FIPPA, *supra* note 8, art 38.

[163] Jeswald W Salacuse, *The Law of Investment Treaties* (Oxford: Oxford University Press, 2010) at 354-57; Andreas Kulick, *Global Public Interest in International Investment Law* (Cambridge: Cambridge University Press, 2012) at 1-2, 94-97; Valentina Vadi, *Public Health in International Investment Arbitration* (London: Routledge, 2013) at 20-21, 57-58; Van Harten, *supra* note 145 at 58-70.

[164] *China FIPPA*, *supra* note 2, art 28(1)-(2).

These provisions differ from Canada's established approach in two main ways. First, they create a general presumption that all ISA documents, other than awards, will not be public unless the respondent state decides to release them. Second, they establish a general presumption that ISA hearings will not be public unless the respondent state decides otherwise. In both respects, the *China FIPPA* shifts the default position from one of openness to one of confidentiality. The *China FIPPA* is the only treaty in which Canada has diluted ISA transparency in this way since 2001, when concerns about ISA confidentiality originally came to light.[165]

As a result, under the *China FIPPA*, information of relevance to the public — such as a government's submissions or reasons for an investor's claim — can be kept from public scrutiny. Faced with an embarrassing claim under the *China FIPPA*, it seems a government would have not only an incentive but also a right under the agreement to keep information about the claim, including the fact of its existence, confidential. In these circumstances, how would a member of the public or media seek further information about a claim if the claim itself were not public? On this basis, the *China FIPPA* appears to support a presumption that claims against Canada or China may be resolved behind the scenes by, for example, the payment of public funds, changes to government decisions, or pressure on the foreign investor.[166] Where a claim or settlement is controversial — such as in the case of Canada's *NAFTA* settlement in *Ethyl Corporation v Government of Canada*, where the federal government withdrew a legislative ban on a gasoline additive amidst heated public debate[167] — the public may be unable to know how ISA has

---

165 See note 160 in this article.

166 This extension of the period of presumed confidentiality, beyond the time at which an ISA claim is filed, exacerbates the existing concern that compensation may be paid or decisions altered due to ISA without public knowledge.

167 *Ethyl Corporation v Government of Canada* (UNCITRAL), 38 ILM 78 (1998). The settlement has been discussed as an apparent case of regulatory chill. See, for example, K Traynor, "How Canada Became a Shill for Ethyl Corporation" (1998) 23:3 Intervenor (Canadian Environmental Law Association), online: <http://www.cela.ca/print/954>. On this, it is suggested here that the *NAFTA* claim by Ethyl Corporation — the manufacturer of the gasoline additive in question — was a significant factor in the federal government's decision to withdraw its prohibition. Also, the fact that the case attracted controversy highlights the importance of public access to ISA documents and indicates the potential governmental interest in withholding embarrassing information about ISA claims and settlements.

affected government decisions. More broadly, the lack of openness also undermines the independence and fairness of ISA.[168]

Incidentally, since 2001, Canada had been a champion of ISA transparency in international forums. As recently as 2010, in submissions to an UNCITRAL working group on ISA transparency, Canada commented:

Canada's Foreign Investment Promotion and Protection Agreements (FIPAs) and Free Trade Agreements (FTAs) contain provisions protecting and promoting investment. *Over time, these treaties have included increasingly explicit provisions concerning the transparency* of treaty-based investor-State arbitration.

With respect to dispute settlement, the [FIPA] model was revised to promote transparency. Article 38 of the updated model *requires that all documents submitted to or issued by the Tribunal, including hearing transcripts, be made public* subject to redaction for confidential, privileged or third party business information. Further, *all hearings are to be open to the public,* subject only to closure when necessary to protect confidential business, privileged or third party information.[169]

The government of Canada clearly has retreated from this position in the *China FIPPA.*

DURATION

The *China FIPPA* has a relatively long minimum lifespan. Under *NAFTA,* Canada can withdraw from the treaty, including its investment chapter, with six months' notice.[170] Canada's Model FIPPA allows for termination after one year's notice, with a so-called survival clause that extends the treaty's obligations for another fifteen years in the case of investments existing at the time of termination; for a total effective minimum lifespan of sixteen years. The *China FIPPA,* in contrast, provides for a minimum term of fifteen years, after which either state party can withdraw on one year's notice, subject to a survival clause that extends the treaty for another fifteen years

---

[168] Theodor Meron, "Judicial Independence and Impartiality in International Criminal Tribunals" (2005) 99 AJIL 359 at 360-61; Van Harten, *supra* note 19.

[169] UNCITRAL Working Group II (Arbitration and Conciliation), 53d Sess, UN Doc A/CN.9/WG.II/WP.159/Add.1 (2010) [emphasis added].

[170] *NAFTA, supra* note 3, art 2205.

for existing investments.[171] Assuming substantial Chinese asset ownership in Canada at the time of termination, the *China FIPPA*, if ratified, would therefore endure for at least thirty-one years, unless both China and Canada agreed to the contrary. This provision puts the *China FIPPA*'s lifespan at the far upper end of Canada's treaties. As indicated in Table 1, only three FIPPAs currently in force — with Egypt, Hungary, and Poland — have a comparable minimum duration among the thirty relevant treaties to which Canada is a party. Only one FIPPA, similarly to the *China FIPPA*, has a formal minimum term of fifteen years. Only four FIPPAs have any formal minimum term at all.

TABLE 1
Minimum Duration of Canada's Treaties Providing
for Investor-State Arbitration

Treaty	Minimum term (in years)	Notice to terminate (in years)	Survival clause (in years)	Effective minimum duration (in years)
China FIPPA	15	1	15	31
Egypt FIPPA	15	1	15	31
Hungary FIPPA	10	1	20	31
Poland FIPPA	10	1	20	31
Tanzania FIPPA	10	1	15	26
Lebanon FIPPA	0	1	20	21
Russia FIPPA	0	1	20	21
Argentina FIPPA	0	1	15	16
Armenia FIPPA	0	1	15	16
Barbados FIPPA	0	1	15	16
Costa Rica FIPPA	0	1	15	16
Croatia FIPPA	0	1	15	16
Czech Republic FIPPA	0	1	15	16
Ecuador FIPPA	0	1	15	16
Jordan FIPPA	0	1	15	16
Latvia FIPPA	0	1	15	16
Panama FIPPA	0	1	15	16
Peru FIPPA	0	1	15	16
Philippines FIPPA	0	1	15	16

▶

[171] *China FIPPA, supra* note 2, art 35(1)-(3).

◄ TABLE 1

Treaty	Minimum term (in years)	Notice to terminate (in years)	Survival clause (in years)	Effective minimum duration (in years)
Philippines FIPPA	0	1	15	16
Romania FIPPA	0	1	15	16
Slovak Republic FIPPA	0	1	15	16
Thailand FIPPA	0	1	15	16
Trinidad and Tobago FIPPA	0	1	15	16
Uruguay FIPPA	0	1	15	16
Venezuela FIPPA	0	1	15	16
Ukraine FIPPA	0	1	10	11
NAFTA	0	0.5	0	0.5
Canada–Panama FTA	0	0.5	0	0.5
Canada–Peru FTA	0	0.5	0	0.5
Canada–Colombia FTA	0	0.5	0	0.5
Canada–Chile FTA	0	0.5	0	0.5
Averages per treaty:				
Mean	1.9	0.9	13	15.9
Median	7.5	0.75	10	15.25

Notes: Data compiled by author. All treaty texts are available online: DFATD <http://www.international.gc.ca/trade-agreements-accords-commerciaux/agr-acc/fipa-apie/force-vigeur.aspx?lang=eng>.

Further, the *China FIPPA* is obviously much more significant for Canada than Canada's FIPPAs with Egypt, Hungary, and Poland, due to the size of the investment relationship to which the *China FIPPA* would apply. Investors from Egypt, Hungary, and Poland, and, indeed, from all countries with which Canada has a FIPPA, do not own assets in Canada that are comparable in value to the assets of Chinese investors.[172] Among Canada's treaties that provide for ISA, only *NAFTA* compares in terms of the size of the investment relationships involved, and, unlike the *China FIPPA*, *NAFTA* can be terminated after six months' notice, with no survival clause.[173] The

---

[172] See note 176 in this article.

[173] That said, for Canada, the adjustment cost of terminating *NAFTA* may presumably be much greater than the cost of terminating the *China FIPPA* or any other of Canada's FIPPAs or trade agreements.

China FIPPA's thirty-one-year minimum lifespan is thus an important variation from Canada's usual practice, magnifying the significance of its other features.

BROADER CONTEXT OF THE CANADA–CHINA INVESTMENT RELATIONSHIP

This article has focused thus far on textual aspects of the *China FIPPA* that are novel or non-reciprocal. Evaluation of the *China FIPPA* in its wider context is beyond the scope of this article. However, tentative comments are offered in this section, using data on Canada–China FDI stocks as a commonplace measure of the relative significance of a BIT and, incidentally, as a further indicator of the *China FIPPA*'s *de facto* non-reciprocity in favour of China. To begin, the *China FIPPA* differs from *NAFTA* and other trade agreements that include investment obligations within a wider trade treaty. The *China FIPPA*, as a BIT, deals exclusively with investment and especially with the protection of foreign investors from various forms of state treatment. It is therefore much more feasible to evaluate the *China FIPPA* than *NAFTA* in its economic context of foreign ownership of assets, of costs and benefits arising from the additional legal protections for such assets, and of corresponding fiscal risks and legal constraints for the state.

This is important because, other than *NAFTA* (where Canada may be said to have exchanged commitments on investment for greater trade-based market access to the United States), no trade or investment treaty approaches the economic significance of the *China FIPPA* for Canada. That is, since *NAFTA*, the government of Canada has not agreed to any treaty providing for ISA in which the nationals of the other state party own substantial assets in Canada.[174] Instead, the government has followed the conventional approach of Western states by accepting treaty-based ISA only where the Western state occupies the capital-exporting position in the investing relationship with the other state party and, thus, where the Western state does not assume equivalent risks and constraints arising from ISA.[175] To illustrate, Table 2 outlines the amounts of inward and outward FDI — as a measure of foreign ownership — covered by Canada's relevant treaties.

174 By "substantial" assets, I mean $1 billion or more in inward FDI stocks.

175 Justin Carter, "The Protracted Bargain: Negotiating the Canada-China Foreign Investment Promotion and Protection Agreement" (2009) 47 Can YB Int'l L 197 at 205-6; Salacuse, *supra* note 163 at 91-97.

TABLE 2

Inward and Outward Foreign Direct Investment in Canada[1]

| Country | Inward FDI stocks (of foreign nationals in Canada, 2008-12, $ millions) | | Outward FDI stocks (of Canadian nationals in country, 2008-12, $ millions) | | Ratio of outward to inward FDI stocks |
	Annual average	Highest annual amount[2]	Annual average	Highest annual amount[2]	
USA	309,356	326,527	272,224	289,426	1:1.14
China	10,709	12,037	3,663	4,239	1:2.9
Barbados	697	842	53,689	59,305	77:1
Russia	653 (a)	1249 (h)	2267	4816	3.5:1
Panama	386 (f)	386 (f)	234 (b)	415 (g)	1:1.6
Mexico	192 (c)	121 (i)	5,021	5,569	26:1
Argentina	15 (a)	19 (h)	3,110	4,553	>100:1
Poland	15 (a)	40 (h)	420	299	28:1
Chile	7 (j)	7	12,249	13,726	>100:1
Thailand	4	4	721	380	>100:1
Colombia	1.5 (d)	1	1,147	1,762	>100:1
Armenia	NA	NA	x/NA	x/NA	–
Costa Rica	x	x	208 (a)	226 (h)	>100:1
Croatia	x	x	x/NA	x/NA	–
Czech Republic	x	x	271 (f)	271 (f)	>100:1
Ecuador	x	x	29 (a)	4 (h)	>29:1
Egypt	x	x	439 (a)	490 (h)	>100:1
Hungary	x	x	12,929	13,692	>100:1
Jordan	NA	NA	x/NA	x/NA	–
Latvia	NA	NA	x	x	–
Lebanon	x/NA	x/NA	x	x	–
Peru	x/NA	x/NA	5,895	6,908	>100:1
Philippines	x	x	454 (a)	761 (h)	>100:1
Romania	x	x	297	348	>100:1
Slovak Republic	x/NA	x/NA	x	x	–
Tanzania	x/NA	x/NA	x	x	–
Trinidad and Tobago	x	x	1,113	893	>100:1
Ukraine	x/NA	x/NA	x	x	–
Uruguay	x	x	692 (e)	999	>100:1
Venezuela	x	x	942	898	>100:1

[1] Compiled by author from Statistics Canada, Table 376-0051: Foreign Direct Investment (Stocks) in Canada and Canadian Direct Investment Abroad (Stocks) (May 2013). The symbol "x" denotes that confidential data is withheld; NA denotes data not available. Annual averages (medians) were calculated by the author and rounded to the nearest million. The notes indicate partial coverage where five-year data was unavailable for a particular country, as follows: (a) 2008–10 only; (b) 2008–09 only; (c) 2008–11 only; (d) 2008–10 and 2012 only; (e) 2008 and 2011–12 only; (f) 2008 only; (g) 2009 only; (h) 2010 only; (i) 2011 only; and (j) 2012 only.

[2] In 2012, unless indicated otherwise.

The data in Table 2 demonstrates that the *China FIPPA* would apply to far more FDI ($10.7 billion on average during 2008-12) than any of Canada's relevant treaties other than *NAFTA*. Thus, while other treaties concluded by Canada may create a significant risk of ISA claims by Canadian investors against another state, they do not raise a direct risk of ISA claims against Canada.[176] In this respect, the *China FIPPA* would entail a significant expansion of ISA coverage of foreign-owned assets in Canada. As an aside, if the federal government were to conclude the proposed Canada–European Union trade agreement and the US-led Trans-Pacific Partnership Agreement in addition to the *China FIPPA*, the great majority of inward FDI in Canada would be covered by ISA.[177]

The data in Table 2 also shows that the *China FIPPA* would apply to significant amounts of Canadian FDI in China ($3.7 billion on average during 2008–12). The additional legal protection of these assets based particularly on ISA is presumably a key rationale for the Canadian government's negotiation of the *China FIPPA*, even if it leaves gaps relative to other treaties in the extent of ISA protection it provides for Canadian investors by allowing China to continue to bar market access and to maintain an array of discriminatory measures. Yet, in principle, the availability of ISA for Canadian investors delivers a significant benefit to be weighed against costs to Canada.

One common approach to weighing relative costs and benefits of any BIT is to compare the relative amounts of foreign-owned assets between the state parties. By this measure, the overall costs of the *China FIPPA* for Canada exceed the overall benefits for Canadian investors on the basis that, during 2008–12, Chinese investment in Canada exceeded Canadian investment in China by a ratio of about three to one. Put differently, Canada occupies the capital-importing position under the *China FIPPA* and, as a result,

---

[176] There is also an indirect risk of claims based on forum shopping, although none appear to have materialized in Canada's case.

[177] That is, based on inward FDI stocks in 2013, Canada will have allowed approximately 83 percent of its foreign-owned economy to be covered by ISA. Other major countries, including the United States, western European states, Australia, and Japan, have not consented to ISA in treaties with one another. In contrast, Canada would have consented to ISA in treaties with all of the main capital exporters: the United States in *NAFTA* and the *TPP*; the UK, Germany, France, Netherlands, and Belgium-Luxembourg in the Canada-EU *CETA*; Japan in the *TPP*; and China in the *China FIPPA*.

has accepted more fiscal risk and regulatory constraint associated with ISA.[178]

In addition, going forward, there are tentative reasons to expect a greater increase in Chinese investment in Canada than vice versa. Chinese FDI stocks in Canada increased from an annual average of $334 million (during 2001–05) to $10.7 billion (during 2008–12). If one extrapolated from this rate of growth, Chinese FDI stocks would reach an annual average of $343 billion in 2015–19 and, a few years later, would exceed US FDI stocks in Canada extrapolated on the same basis. This timeframe would be approximately 25 percent of the minimum lifespan of the *China FIPPA*, assuming that it entered into force in 2014. By comparison, Canadian investment in China would have reached an average of $13 billion during 2015–19 and, in this same period, would be exceeded by Chinese FDI stocks in Canada by a ratio of about twenty-six to one.

This projection of disproportionate growth in Chinese investment in Canada is based on limited data. The projection is supported by public statements by Canadian officials seeking greater Chinese investment in Canada (especially the oil sands),[179] by the Canadian government's evident willingness not to insist on market access by Canadian investors in the *China FIPPA*, and by the Canadian government's statement in 2012 that China's total global FDI outflows are forecast by some experts to reach $1 trillion by 2020, compared to $64 billion in 2011.[180] On the other hand, the projection is contradicted by the government of Canada's statement in late 2012 that Chinese state-owned enterprises would in future face limits in acquiring control of Canadian companies in the oil sands and potentially elsewhere in the Canadian economy[181] and by media reports

---

[178] Andrew T Guzman, "Why LDCs Sign Treaties That Hurt Them: Explaining the Popularity of Bilateral Investment Treaties" (1998) 38 Va J Int'l L 639.

[179] See, for example, "Oil Sands Need China, Oliver Says on Visit," *National Post* (13 February 2012), online: National Post <http://www.nationalpost.com/index.html>.

[180] Department of Foreign Affairs and International Trade (DFAIT), *Responses to Questions submitted through the Chair of the House of Commons Standing Committee on International Trade on behalf of the Liberal Party* (Ottawa: undated) [received by author 9 November 2012; on file with author].

[181] Prime Minister of Canada, *Statement by the Prime Minister of Canada on Foreign Investment* (Ottawa: 7 December 2012), online: <http://www.pm.gc.ca/eng/news/2012/12/07/statement-prime-minister-canada-foreign-investment>: "In light of growing trends, and following the decisions made today, the Government of Canada has determined that foreign state control of oil sands development

of a drop-off in Chinese investment in Canada in 2013.[182] Overall, the projection should be approached with caution.

Another way of thinking about a treaty that provides for ISA is to liken it to a subsidy mechanism in which the host state insures the relevant foreign investors, via new substantive protections and access to ISA in addition to the domestic judicial system, against risks arising from the investors' activities in the host state.[183] The subsidy to foreign investors is financial because the host state assumes the potential cost of ISA litigation and awards. The subsidy also has administrative and political implications because the host state, in the face of the potential liability, presumably will vet or alter some decisions, with knock-on implications for other actors. To illustrate, in Canada, the *China FIPA* would appear to require expanded vetting of decisions through the federal government's Regulatory Impact Assessment program, which requires that regulatory proposals be assessed for compliance with Canada's investment obligations. For example,

[d]epartments and agencies are expected to demonstrate in regulatory impact analysis statements, when relevant, that their proposals do in fact meet Canada's international trade and other obligations ...

Is the proposed regulation a legitimate exercise of governmental regulatory power? Could it constitute expropriation?

[Footnote:] Canada's international trade and investment treaties typically contain a provision prohibiting the nationalization or expropriation of an investment of an investor from another party to that agreement, except where certain conditions have been met, including the payment of compensation ... [G]iven that expropriation can be very fact-specific, in situations where a proposed *regulation has the potential to substantially interfere with the operations of an investment in Canada, the regulatory body proposing*

---

has reached the point at which further such foreign control would not be of net benefit to Canada. Therefore, going forward, the Minister will find the acquisition of control of a Canadian oil-sands business by a foreign state-owned enterprise to be of net benefit only in an exceptional circumstance."

182 Nathan Vanderklippe, "Investment Deal with China Coming 'in Short Order': Baird," *Globe and Mail* (16 October 2013), online: Globe and Mail <http://theglobeandmail.com>.

183 Emma Aisbett, Larry Karp, and Carol McAusland, "Compensation for Indirect Expropriation in International Investment Agreements: Implications of National Treatment and Rights to Invest" (2010) 1:2 J Globalization & Development 5.

such a regulation should seek legal advice from the Trade Law Bureau to ensure compliance with Canada's international obligations.[184]

Although it is difficult to evaluate these governmental vetting processes from the outside, it is reasonable to expect that they involve expenditure of public resources and that they lead in some cases to changes in government decisions that will affect other actors beyond the relevant foreign investor.

Of course, other factors besides FDI flows — as a rough measure of the quasi-subsidy offered by the state parties to each other's investors — may affect the relative costs and benefits of a FIPPA. For instance, it might be said that Canada is more or less likely than China to avoid fiscal risks associated with ISA or that Canada is more or less likely to change government decisions due to fiscal or symbolic incentives created by ISA. Along these lines, it has been argued that, because Canada provides a more predictable and rules-based economic environment, Chinese investors are less likely than Canadian investors to benefit from the *China FIPPA*.[185] Yet, based on publicly available information, Canada has faced over thirty ISA claims under *NAFTA* — of which about half have progressed to a fully constituted arbitration or a known settlement — whereas China has faced one minor ISA claim despite having concluded more than 100 BITs, including about twelve muscular BITs with significant capital exporters.[186] Further, it appears relevant that aspects of the *China FIPPA* — including China's ability to discriminate against and potentially punish Canadian investors via its right to continue with existing discriminatory measures — may reduce the

---

[184] Treasury Board of Canada Secretariat, *Guidelines on International Regulatory Obligations and Cooperation* (Ottawa: Queen's Printer, 2007), online: Treasury Board Secretariat <http://www.tbs-sct.gc.ca/rtrap-parfa/iroc-cori/iroc-cori01-eng.asp#Toc175098395> [emphasis added].

[185] Milos Barutciski and Matthew Kronby, "Investment Agreement with China Will Benefit Canada," *Globe and Mail* (2 November 2012), online: Globe and Mail <http://theglobeandmail.com>.

[186] These include BITs with Belgium-Luxembourg, Finland, France, Germany, India, the Netherlands, Norway, Russia, South Korea, Spain, Sweden, and Switzerland: UNCTAD, "Full List of Bilateral Investment Agreements Concluded [by China], 1 June 2013," online: UNCTAD <http://unctad.org/Sections/dite_pcbb/docs/bits_china.pdf>. Other BITs concluded by China with major economies, especially Austria, Australia, Denmark, Italy, Japan, New Zealand, and the United Kingdom, date from the 1980s and would not reflect China's shift towards a more muscular regime of ISA since the early 2000s.

China FIPPA's value for Canadian investors that experience conflict with the Chinese government.[187]

For these reasons, relative FDI stocks between Canada and China offer a useful, albeit approximate, gauge of the *China FIPPA*'s relative costs and benefits, especially because other potential factors are difficult to quantify and do not appear obviously to favour either state party. On this measure, the *China FIPPA* favours China by a substantial margin. Most importantly, other than *NAFTA*, Canada's capital-importing position under the *China FIPPA* would distinguish it from other treaties concluded by Canada. If ratified, the *China FIPPA* would mark an important change from Canada's approach to ISA in that it would be the first occasion, since the ISA boom began in the late 1990s, on which the Canadian government will have consented to a treaty that carries a significant and unequal risk of ISA claims against Canada.

CONCLUSION

The analysis in this article has focused on the *China FIPPA*'s novelty and non-reciprocity. The *China FIPPA* was evaluated in these respects with reference to its provisions on market access and investment screening; post-establishment national treatment; MFN treatment; performance requirements; ISA transparency; and duration. This text-based examination was followed by a discussion of the *China FIPPA*'s wider significance, given Canada's capital-importing position in relation to China. Criticisms of the *China FIPPA* have been specific to the treaty and have not aimed to address wider concerns about ISA or the international investment regime.[188]

This article has also not examined a range of broader questions about the *China FIPPA*. For example, how might the Canada–China investment relationship evolve over the next sixteen or thirty-one years? Is there evidence that the *China FIPPA* will contribute to new investment in Canada or China and that the benefits of new investment will outweigh the *China FIPPA*'s costs? How would new investment affect each country's economic, environmental, or social priorities? What may have motivated the Canadian government to accept the significant elements of non-reciprocity in the *China*

---

[187] See text accompanying note 109 in this article.

[188] See, for example, David Gaukrodger and Kathryn Gordon, "Investor-State Dispute Settlement: A Scoping Paper for the Investment Policy Community," OECD Working Paper on International Investment no 2012/3 (OECD Investment Division, 2012).

FIPPA?[189] Does the ongoing volatility of ISA call for closer attention of the role of ISA in Canada's FIPPA program? Is the *China FIPPA*'s reliance on ISA unacceptable due to its encroachment on democratic choice and judicial independence? Does the experience of ISA under *NAFTA* and BITs give cause for reassurance or heightened concern?

These questions have also not been addressed in any public study of the *China FIPPA*. They would become more pressing, albeit in hindsight, if the *China FIPPA* were ratified and Canada faced a major ISA claim by a Chinese investor. Alternatively, despite assumptions to the contrary in the Canadian government's flawed environmental assessment of the *China FIPPA*,[190] Canada might benefit from concluding a non-reciprocal *China FIPPA* if doing so were essential to attracting substantial quality investment from China or, incidentally, to opening markets for Canadian exports. Due to the many outstanding questions it raises, as well as its novelty, significance, and

---

[189] Carter, *supra* note 175 at 216.

[190] The *Environmental Assessment, supra* note 136, is of little use as an evaluation of environmental impact and seems more a public relations document. It discounts any environmental impact of the *China FIPPA* on the assumption that there would be no direct causative relationship between the *China FIPPA* and increased investment flows: "As new flows of investment from China into Canada (or Canada into China) cannot be directly attributed to the presence of a FIPA, there can be no causal relationship found between the implementation of such a treaty and environmental impacts in Canada. It is for this reason that the claim made in the initial environmental assessment, that no significant environmental impacts are expected based on the introduction of a Canada-China FIPA, is upheld." The absence of a causative relationship in this respect was assumed in the environmental assessment based partly on the assertion that "this type of government-to-government treaty cannot directly facilitate new investments or directly create new opportunities for investment." This assertion is inaccurate in that many BITs, including FIPPAs provide for a right of market access by foreign investors. The assertion was also contradicted by the Prime Minister's Office's in a statement on the *China FIPPA* that was cited but not addressed in this respect in the environmental assessment: "Once implemented, the Canada-China FIPA will facilitate investment flows, contributing to job creation and economic growth in Canada": Prime Minister of Canada, *Canada-China Foreign Investment Promotion and Protection Agreement (FIPA)* (Ottawa, 8 February 2012), online: <http://www.pm.gc.ca/eng/news/2012/02/08/canada-china-foreign-investment-promotion-and-protection-agreement-fipa>. Finally, the environmental assessment's discounting of environmental impacts of the *China FIPPA* is undermined seriously by the assessment's failure to consider how a BIT may have environmental impacts due to new legal rights it bestows on foreign investors — whether or not their investment decisions are linked to the *China FIPPA* — and the corresponding fiscal risks and regulatory constraints for host states.

long-term irreversibility, it is suggested that the *China FIPPA* calls for a thorough, independent, and public review prior to ratification by Canada.

Sommaire

L'Accord sur la promotion et la protection des investissements étrangers Canada-Chine (APPIE Chine) est un accord novateur et, à plusieurs niveaux, non réciproque — au profit de la Chine. À titre d'exemples, l'*APPIE Chine* donnerait un droit général d'accès au marché canadien par les investisseurs chinois, mais pas au marché chinois par les investisseurs canadiens; accorderait une plus grande marge de manœuvre pour le dépistage des investissements à la Chine qu'au Canada; omettrait une réserve canadienne de longue date applicable aux exigences de performance qui favorisent les peuples autochtones; et diluerait la position établie du Canada en matière de transparence dans l'arbitrage entre investisseurs et États. L'auteur discute de ces questions, ainsi que d'autres enjeux qui ressortent du texte de l'*APPIE Chine*, tout en comparant ce texte à celui d'autres traités sur le commerce et les investissements étrangers qui prévoient l'arbitrage entre investisseurs et États, plus particulièrement ceux auxquels le Canada est partie. De surcroît, l'auteur place l'*APPIE Chine* dans son contexte économique immédiat, soit celui des taux d'investissements actuels entre le Canada et la Chine. L'article se veut une riposte partielle aux prétentions de représentants canadiens en matière de commerce international que l'*APPIE Chine* n'est pas du tout remarquable mais est plutôt conforme à la pratique bien-établie du Canada en matière de la promotion et la protection des investissements étrangers.

Summary

The *Canada–China Foreign Investment Promotion and Protection Agreement (China FIPPA)* is novel and, in key respects, non-reciprocal in favour of China. For example, it would provide a general right of market access by Chinese investors to Canada but not by Canadian investors to China; allow wider scope for investment screening by China than by Canada; omit a long-standing Canadian reservation for performance requirements that favour Aboriginal peoples; and dilute Canada's established position on transparency in investor-state arbitration. These and other textual aspects of the *China FIPPA* are highlighted in comparison to other trade and investment treaties, especially those to which Canada is a party, that provide for investor-state arbitration. The *China FIPPA* is also examined in the current economic context of investment flows between Canada and China. The article responds partly to claims by Canadian trade officials that the *China FIPPA* is unremarkable because it simply continues Canada's past foreign investment promotion and protection practice.

Data on Limiting Language, Exceptions, Reservations, and Disclosure Provisions in Canada's Treaties Providing for ISA

Treaty	Year of entry into force	Limiting language on fair and equitable treatment	Limiting language on expropriation	General exception for health/ environmental/ conservation measures	Financial stability exception	Prohibition on performance requirements?	Aboriginal reservation for prohibition on performance requirements?	Reservation for disadvantaged minorities for prohibition on performance requirements?	Presumptive disclosure of ISA documents?
Model FIPPA	NA	Yes	Yes	Yes	Yes	Yes	Yes (c)	Yes (c)	Yes
Argentina FIPPA	1993	No	No	No	No	No	NA	NA	No
Armenia FIPPA	1999	No	No	Yes	Yes	Yes	Yes	No	No
Barbados FIPPA	1997	No	No	Yes	Yes	Yes	Yes	No	No
Chile FTA	1997	No	No	Yes (a)	No (b)	Yes	Yes	Yes	No
Colombia FTA	2011	Yes	Yes.	Yes	Yes	Yes	Yes	Yes	Yes
Panama FTA	2013	Yes	Yes	Yes	Yes	Yes	Yes	Yes	Yes
Peru FTA	2009	Yes	Yes	Yes	Yes	Yes	Yes	Yes	Yes
China FIPPA	NA	Yes	Yes	Yes	No	Yes	No	No	Yes
Costa Rica FIPPA	1999	No	No	Yes	Yes	Yes	Yes	No	No
Croatia FIPPA	2001	No	No	Yes	Yes	Yes	Yes	No	No
Czech Republic FIPPA	2012	Yes	Yes	Yes	Yes	No	NA	NA	Yes
Ecuador FIPPA	1997	No	No	Yes	Yes	Yes	Yes	No	No
Egypt FIPPA	1997	No	No	Yes	Yes	Yes	Yes	No	No
Hungary FIPPA	1993	No	No	No	No	No	NA	NA	No
Jordan FIPPA	2009	Yes	Yes	Yes	Yes	Yes	Yes	Yes	Yes

Treaty	Year							
Latvia FIPPA	2011	Yes	Yes	Yes	Yes	Yes	No	Yes
Lebanon FIPPA	1999	No	No	Yes	Yes	Yes	No	No
NAFTA	1994	Yes	No	Yes (a)	Yes	Yes	Yes	Yes
Panama FIPPA	1998	No	No	Yes	Yes	Yes	No	No
Peru FIPPA	2007	Yes	Yes	Yes	Yes	Yes	Yes	Yes
Philippines FIPPA	1996	No	No	Yes	Yes	Yes	No	No
Poland FIPPA	1990	No	No	No	No	NA	NA	No
Romania FIPPA	2011	Yes	Yes	Yes	Yes	Yes	No	Yes
Russia FIPPA	1991	No	No	No	No	NA	NA	No
Slovak Republic FIPPA	2012	Yes	Yes	Yes	No	NA	NA	Yes
Tanzania FIPPA	2013	Yes	Yes	Yes	Yes	Yes	Yes	Yes
Thailand FIPPA	1998	No	No	Yes	Yes	Yes	No	No
Trinidad and Tobago FIPPA	1996	No	No	Yes	Yes	Yes	No	No
Ukraine FIPPA	1995	No	No	Yes	Yes	Yes	No	No
Uruguay FIPPA	1999	No	No	Yes	Yes	Yes	No	No
Venezuela FIPPA	1998	No	No	Yes	Yes	Yes	No	No

Notes: Data collected from texts of all of Canada's foreign investment promotion and protection agreements (FIPPAs) and free trade agreements (FTAs) that provide for investor-state arbitration (ISA) and that were in force as of 27 January 2013. The relevant treaty texts are available online: DFATD <http://www.international.gc.ca/trade-agreements-accords-commerciaux/agr-acc/fipa-apie/index.aspx?lang=eng>. "NA" means not applicable; (a) denotes that general exceptions are limited to certain performance requirements only; (b) denotes that the treaty excludes related investments such as in financial institutions, loans, etc; (c) denotes that the treaty allows for annexes that in other FIPPAs include the relevant reservation; (d) denotes negative-list requirement for exempted national measures; (e) denotes negative-list requirement for exempted national and state/provincial measures; (f) denotes that the treaty does not provide for post-establishment national treatment; (g) denotes express application of MFN treatment to future treaties only.

ANNEX 2

Data on Denial of Benefits and Market Access Provisions in Canada's Treaties that Provide for ISA

Treaty	Year of entry into force	Denial of benefits clause	Denial of benefits clause with express allowance to deny after claim	Market access based on pre-establishment national treatment (pre-E NT)	Exemption of pre-E NT obligation from ISA or exemption of Investment Canada Act from ISA/ pre-E NT	Exemption of existing non-conforming measures from post-establishment NT	Market access based on pre-establishment MFN treatment (pre-E MFN)	Exemption of pre-E MFN from ISA or exemption of Investment Canada Act from ISA/ pre-E MFN	Express application of MFN treatment to past treaties
Model FIPPA	NA	Yes	No	Yes	Yes	Yes (d)	Yes	Yes	No (g)
Argentina FIPPA	1993	No	NA	No	NA	Yes	No	NA	No
Armenia FIPPA	1999	No	NA	No	NA	Yes	No	NA	No
Barbados FIPPA	1997	No	NA	No	NA	Yes	No	NA	No
Chile FTA	1997	Yes	No	Yes	No	Yes (e)	Yes	Yes	No (g)
Colombia FTA	2011	Yes	No	Yes	Yes	Yes (e)	Yes	Yes	No
Panama FTA	2013	Yes	No	Yes	Yes	Yes (d)	Yes	Yes	No
Peru FTA	2009	Yes	No	Yes	Yes	Yes (d)	Yes	Yes	No
China FIPPA	NA	Yes	Yes	No	NA	Yes	No	Yes	Yes
Costa Rica FIPPA	1999	Yes	No	Yes	Yes	Yes	Yes	Yes	No
Croatia FIPPA	2001	No	NA	Yes	Yes	Yes	Yes	Yes	No
Czech Republic FIPPA	2012	Yes	No	No	NA	Yes	No	NA	No
Ecuador FIPPA	1997	No	NA	Yes	Yes	Yes	Yes	Yes	No

Egypt FIPPA	1997	No	NA	Yes	Yes	Yes	Yes	Yes	No
Hungary FIPPA	1993	No	NA	No	NA	Yes	No	NA	No
Jordan FIPPA	2009	Yes	No	Yes	Yes	Yes (d)	Yes	Yes	Yes
Latvia FIPPA	2011	Yes	No	Yes	Yes	Yes	Yes	Yes	No
Lebanon FIPPA	1999	No	NA	Yes	Yes	Yes	Yes	Yes	No
NAFTA	1994	Yes	No	Yes	Yes	Yes (d)	Yes	Yes	No
Panama FIPPA	1998	No	NA	Yes	Yes	Yes	Yes	Yes	No
Peru FIPPA	2007	Yes	No	Yes	Yes	Yes (d)	Yes	Yes	Yes
Philippines FIPPA	1996	No	NA	Yes	Yes	Yes	Yes	Yes	No
Poland FIPPA	1990	No	NA	No	NA	No (f)	No	NA	No
Romania FIPPA	2011	Yes	No	Yes	Yes	Yes	Yes	Yes	No
Russia FIPPA	1991	No	NA	No	NA	Yes	No	NA	No
Slovak Republic FIPPA	2012	Yes	No	No	NA	Yes	No	NA	No
Tanzania FIPPA	2013	Yes	No	Yes	Yes	Yes	Yes	Yes	Yes
Thailand FIPPA	1998	No	NA	Yes	Yes	Yes	Yes	Yes	No
Trinidad and Tobago FIPPA	1996	No	NA	Yes	Yes	Yes	Yes	Yes	No
Ukraine FIPPA	1995	No	NA	Yes	Yes	Yes	Yes	Yes	No
Uruguay FIPPA	1999	No	NA	Yes	Yes	Yes	Yes	Yes	No
Venezuela FIPPA	1998	No	NA	Yes	Yes	Yes	Yes	Yes	No

Annex 2 ... *continued*

Notes: Data collected from texts of all of Canada's foreign investment promotion and protection agreements (FIPPAs) and free trade agreements (FTAs) that provide for investor-state arbitration (ISA) and that were in force as of 27 January 2013. The relevant treaty texts are available online: DFATD <http://www.international.gc.ca/trade-agreements-accords-commerciaux/agr-acc/fipa-apie/index.aspx?lang=eng>. "NA" means not applicable; (a) denotes that general exceptions are limited to certain performance requirements only; (b) denotes that the treaty excludes related investments such as in financial institutions, loans, etc; (c) denotes that the treaty allows for annexes that in other FIPPAs include the relevant reservation; (d) denotes negative-list requirement for exempted national measures; (e) denotes negative-list requirement for exempted national and state/provincial measures; (f) denotes that the treaty does not provide for post-establishment national treatment; (g) denotes express application of MFN treatment to future treaties only.

More Honey Than Vinegar:
Peer Review As a Middle Ground between
Universalism and National Sovereignty

ELVIRA DOMÍNGUEZ-REDONDO AND

EDWARD R. McMAHON

INTRODUCTION

D r. Martin Luther King famously suggested that the arc of the moral universe is long and that it bends towards justice.[1] This vision is reflected in growing and evolving global acceptance of the universality of human rights values. The positive correlation between justice, especially as evidenced by respect for human rights, and the prevention of conflict has been well articulated.[2] It has been argued that a generalized understanding is now developing regarding the conceptualization and implementation of human rights that diverges from the first, second, and third world doctrines, which dominated the global human rights agenda until the end of the Cold War.[3] Although elements of the philosophies underpinning Western,

---

Elvira Domínguez-Redondo is asssociate professor of international law at Middlesex University in London, United Kingdom. Edward R McMahon is research associate professor in the Department of Community Development and Applied Politics and the Department of Political Science at the University of Vermont in Burlington, United States. The authors want to thank Alice Donald for her valuable comments on earlier drafts.

[1] On the origin of the expression and its use by Martin Luther King, see Joshua Cohen, *The Arc of the Moral Universe and Other Essays* (Cambridge, MA: Harvard University Press, 2010) at 17, n 4. A modern and interesting reformulation of the idea can be found in David Keane, "Survival of the Fairest: Evolution and Geneticization of Human Rights" (2010) 30:3 Oxford J Legal Stud 467.

[2] See, for example, UN General Assembly, *In Larger Freedom: Towards Development, Security and Human Rights for All: Report of the Secretary-General*, UN Doc A/59/2005 (21 March 2005).

[3] Elvira Domínguez-Redondo, "Role of the UN in the Promotion and Protection of Human Rights" in Azizur Rahman Chowdhury and Jahid Hossain Bhuiyan, eds, *An Introduction to International Human Rights Law* (Boston: Brill, 2010) 119 at 121-25.

socialist, and developing countries' doctrines on human rights continue to permeate inter-governmental human rights debates, albeit with many nuances no longer captured in traditional East-West or North-South divides, the current period is marked by a "broad consensus on the need to consider respect for human rights a *sine qua non* for full international legitimization."[4] An interesting proposition is that the existence of a "global consensus" in international law is the result of the overlapping views of a few powerful countries.[5] Still, the voices contesting the universality of global values as foundations of international law, and particularly as foundations of the international human rights regime, are far from silenced.

This article explores the potential of strategies, rather than philosophies, for the implementation of human rights as a means of reconciling the universalist and relativist conceptual approaches. In doing so, it engages with the eternal issue of "sovereignty" as an impediment to strengthening the international human rights regime. The founders of the United Nations were unable to overcome their concerns regarding limitations to their sovereignty, including transferring various governance competencies to international organizations. As a result, Article 2(7) of the *Charter of the United Nations* (*UN Charter*) maintains the principle of state sovereignty, constraining the organization's powers to intervene in the domestic affairs of member states, with the sole exception of collective action under Chapter VII in response to the breach of, or threats to, international peace and security.[6] Despite this strong assertion, articulated among the principles of the organization, references to human rights included elsewhere in the *UN Charter* have been used as a foundation for an increasingly active UN human rights regime, permeating (at least nominally) all of the spheres of activity and structures of the United Nations.[7]

---

[4] Antonio Cassese, *International Law* (Oxford: Oxford University Press, 2001) at 354.

[5] Using the examples of the United States, the European Union, and China, see Anu Bradford and Eric A Posner, "Universal Exceptionalism in International Law" (2011) 52:1 Harv Int'l LJ 3.

[6] *Charter of the United Nations*, Can TS 1945 No 7 (in force 24 October 1945) [*UN Charter*].

[7] On the 1997 UN reforms, aimed at mainstreaming human rights, see Elvira Domínguez-Redondo, "The Millennium Development Goals and the Human Rights Based Approach: Reflecting on Structural Chasms with the United Nations System" (2009) 13:1 Int'l JHR 29 at 31. In her 2011 annual report, the UN high commissioner for human rights highlighted the approval of the following policy

The evolution of the UN human rights regime has been signifi-cantly influenced by the changing cast of dominant state actors. The more developed Organisation for Economic Co-operation and Development (OECD) countries have generally been more open to accepting and promoting some evolving international norms, even though these may result in diminished sovereignty. They have been frequently prepared to specifically criticize and "call out" states deemed to be violating commonly accepted human rights principles. By contrast, the Non-Aligned Movement, then the G-77, and, more recently, the emerging powers known as BRICS (Brazil, Russia, India, China and South Africa) have had a different approach.[8] The change in the relative participation and influence of emerging powers, many of which did not participate actively in the develop-ment of earlier conceptions of the international human rights machinery, has led to a significant debate. As the human rights machinery has grown, these states have aligned themselves, at least in theory, with a conception of human rights that is more consonant with the notion of state sovereignty, in which cultural differences often significantly contribute to the formulation of normative stan-dards (for example, the discussion on the defamation of religions).[9]

---

documents as key components of the efforts to mainstream human rights: (1) *Human Rights Due Diligence Policy* (approved by the UN Secretary General in 2011); (2) the *Joint Policies on Human Rights for Peace Missions* (endorsed in September 2011 by the UN Department of Peacekeeping Operations, the Depart-ment of Political Affairs, and the Department of Field Support); and (3) the *Human Rights Mainstreaming Mechanism under the United Nations Development Group*, United Nations Development Group, "UNDG Human Rights Mainstreaming Mechanism Operational Plan 2011-2013" (2011), online: <http://undg.org/docs/12173/UNDG-HRM%20OperationalPlan%20Nov%202011.pdf>. See Office of the High Commissioner for Human Rights, *OHCHR Report 2011* (2012) at 190. See also Domínguez-Redondo at 11-12, 42-43, 59-60, 70-72, 79-81, 92-94.

8 One example of this is demonstrated in Edward R McMahon, *The First Cycle of the Universal Periodic Review Mechanism of the United Nations Human Rights Council: A Work in Progress* (Berlin: Friedrich Ebert Stiftung, 2012) at 24-26, online: <http://www.fes-globalization.org/geneva/documents/08_2012_UPR%20McMahon.pdf>. See also Miko Lempinen, *The United Nations Commission on Human Rights and the Different Treatment of Governments* (Turku: Åbo Akademi University, 2005) at 167-92.

9 Between 1999 and 2011, the Commission on Human Rights and the Human Rights Council (HRC) adopted resolutions, sponsored by the Organisation of Islamic Countries, on "defamation of religions," which implied some endorse-ment of controversial limitations to the right of freedom of expression. HRC Resolution 16/18 (2011) has changed this trend, replacing the focus on "combating defamation" with "combating religious intolerance." See HRC,

The biggest impact, however, lies in their insistence that apolitical technical co-operation, rather than value-laden "naming and shaming," is the appropriate approach by which to advance human rights. As a result, these states continue to resist measures deemed to monitor their compliance with human rights obligations without their express consent and, therefore, remain proponents of a restrictive conception of sovereignty.[10] At the same time, however, a range of methodological approaches, such as the responsibility-to-protect concept (R2P) and peer-review mechanisms, both developed with the explicit support of G-77 states, reflect moves in this era of globalization towards more flexible interpretations of national sovereignty.

Two of the major initiatives focusing on governance and human rights are the UN Human Rights Council's Universal Periodic Review (UPR) and the African Peer Review Mechanism (APRM). Both approaches are relatively new. The APRM was implemented in 2003 and the UPR in 2008. They represent, at least in theory, a fresh approach as they do not involve conditionality and have the potential to minimize North-South and other cleavages between regions.[11]

This article begins by explaining the context in which peer review mechanisms were conceived as a means of addressing the long-standing denunciation of the political selectivity of investigation and/or condemnation of situations in particular territories.[12] It

---

Combating Intolerance, Negative Stereotyping and Stigmatization of, and Discrimination, Incitement to Violence and Violence against, Persons Based on Religion or Belief, HRC Res 16/18 (2011), UNGAOR, 16th Sess, UN Doc A/HRC/Res/16/18 (2011). However, proposals to introduce a ban on defamation of religion are still an incendiary topic in human rights fora. See, for example, Daniel Osabu-Kle, *Compatible Cultural Democracy: The Key to Development in Africa* (Peterborough, ON: Broadview Press, 2000). See also Brett G Scharffs, "International Law and the Defamation of Religion Conundrum" (2013) 11:1 Rev Faith & International Affairs 66.

[10] See Elvira Domínguez-Redondo, "The Universal Periodic Review: Is There Life beyond Naming and Shaming in Human Rights Implementation?" (2012) 4 NZL Rev 673.

[11] "Conditionality" refers to a specific set of conditions attached to the disbursement of policy-based lending or budget support. See Stefan Koeberle et al, eds, *Conditionality Revisited: Concepts, Experiences, and Lessons* (Washington, DC: World Bank, 2005) at 6.

[12] On the motivations and political background surrounding the creation of the UPR, see Elvira Domínguez-Redondo, "The Universal Periodic Review of the UN Human Rights Council: An Assessment of the First Session" (2010) 7:3 Chinese J Int'l L 721 at 722-24.

explores the gap between the universalist and cultural relativist human rights perspectives and highlights the role of human rights in what is claimed to be a progressive erosion of the sovereignty of states. This exploration sets the scene to consider the nascent role of one international organization's peer review process — the UPR — at the UN Human Rights Council in contrast to other, more traditional (and coercive) methods of influencing state behaviour regarding human rights. Through the prism of the UPR, this article will challenge common perceptions regarding regional blocs and the pursuit of national and regional policies on human rights issues and explain the potential of such a mechanism to showcase existing or emerging customary law. Furthermore, it will explore the role and potential of inter-governmental mechanisms based on peer review assessment in the prevention of human rights violations and conflict mitigation. In examining the last point, it will focus on the outcomes of the UPR but will also refer to the APRM.

Overall, this article aims to demonstrate that peer review mechanisms may, if used wisely, "thread the needle" by addressing national sovereignty concerns while concomitantly promoting adherence to universal human rights standards. It also posits the idea that the establishment of peer review mechanisms with which states are voluntarily engaging for the promotion and protection of human rights may be a reflection of a level of "maturity" of human rights law as a subject of international law.

UNIVERSAL PERIODIC REVIEW: A CONTEMPORARY
INTER-GOVERNMENTAL APPROACH TO IMPLEMENTING
HUMAN RIGHTS

While no general norm of international law obliges states to choose any particular means of monitoring their compliance with agreed standards or in resolving disputes, the vast majority of international disputes involving states and/or international organizations follow a pattern. Diplomatic means of dispute settlement are attempted first and other, more adversarial, means are used when diplomatic means do not bear fruit.[13] In extreme cases where there is a threat to peace and security, the UN Security Council may decide a course of action that also follows the logic of gradually increasing severity of measures, from less to more aggressive, as exemplified in Articles 41 and 42 of the *UN Charter*.

---

[13] On means used to resolve international disputes, see Ian Brownlie, "The Peaceful Settlement of International Disputes" (2009) 8:2 Chinese J Int'l L 267.

Contrary to other areas regulated by international law, human rights implementation mechanisms have rarely been left in the hands of states alone. Politicization is understood as being synonymous with inefficiency and injustice when it comes to assessing the work of human rights bodies. The actions of inter-governmental bodies such as the UN General Assembly, the Human Rights Council, or the Security Council are, by definition, political. Therefore, ever since the United Nations decided it had competence to address human rights violations, reversing its original position based on Article 2(7) of the *UN Charter*, these organs have used numerous expert bodies to assist in this work.[14] This practice has provided legitimacy to their human rights work since initial reliance on governmental representatives alone met with fierce criticism.[15] In addition, the non-reciprocal nature of human rights, the inequality between parties (individual versus state), and the configuration of human rights as legal claims protecting individuals from abuses of (state) power have all led to a very particular legal conception of human rights. As a result, the measures and mechanisms considered suitable for the implementation of human rights have frequently been based on legal principles articulated by independent experts, reflected in the myriad of *UN Charter-* and treaty-based human rights bodies that have been created under the auspices of the United Nations.

[14] On the declaration of non-competence with respect to allegations of human rights violations, see ECOSOC Resolution 75(V) of 5 August 1947, UN Doc E/573, ESCOR, 5th Sess, Suppl No 1 at 20, endorsing the decision of the UN Commission on Human Rights during its second session (UN Doc E/259 (1946) at para 22). The only entry point for petitions to UN organs, until 1967, was restricted to those addressed to the now inoperative Trusteeship Council and the "24 Committee" that monitored implementation of the 1960 *Declaration on the Granting of Independence to Colonial Countries and Peoples*, GA Res 1654 (XVI), UN Doc A/RES/1654 (XVI) (27 November 1961). See, for example, Nigel Rodley, "Monitoring Human Rights by the UN System and Nongovernmental Organizations" in Donald P Kommers and Gilburt D Loescher, eds, *Human Rights and American Foreign Policy* (Notre Dame, IN: University of Notre Dame Press, 1979) 157 at 161-62. On the change of position of the organization, reflected in ECOSOC Resolution 1235 (XLII), ESCOR 42nd Sess, UN Doc E/4393 (6 June 1967) Suppl No 1 at 17, see Elvira Domínguez-Redondo, "Rethinking the Legal Foundations of Control in International Human Rights Law: The Case of Special Procedures" (2011) 29:3 Nethl Q HR 261.

[15] On the criticisms and legal questions raised regarding the decision of the former UN Commission on Human Rights to use its own members (governmental representatives) as mandate holders of the first "special procedures," see Theo van Boven, "Fact-Finding in the Field of Human Rights" (1973) 3 Israel YB Human

This development does not mean that extra-legal, non-adjudicatory methods of work, where the aim is other than to discern whether or not a state has failed to honour its human rights obligations, are alien to UN human rights monitoring bodies. Mandate holders of special procedures of the UN Human Rights Council and experts on treaty bodies offer technical co-operation to states and use tools aimed at protecting potential victims of human rights violations, often without entering into an assessment of the legality of the situation.[16] Treaty bodies have demonstrated the potential for achieving positive results through engaging in constructive dialogue with the state concerned.[17] In addition, "confidential enquiries" to investigate widespread or systematic violations are foreseen in the *Convention against Torture and Other Cruel, Inhuman or Degrading Treatment or Punishment* (Article 20), the *Optional Protocol to the Convention on the Rights of Persons with Disabilities* (Article 6), and the *Optional Protocol to the Convention on the Elimination of Discrimination against Women* (Article 8).[18]

Until recently, inter-governmental mechanisms of human rights implementation under UN auspices attained modest results, reinforcing the view that human rights monitoring was at an advantage in the hands of third parties, such as independent experts. The first example illustrating this point consisted of the establishment, in

Rights 93 at 97-101; Robert Miller, "United Nations Fact-Finding Missions in the Field of Human Rights" (1970–73) 5 Australian YB Int'l L 40 at 44, 54. See also "Membership of the Working Group on Enforced and Involuntary Disappearances: Opinion of the Office of Legal Affairs (dated 15 September 1989)," in Bretram G Ramcharan, ed, *The Principle of Legality in International Human Rights Institutions: Selected Legal Opinions* (The Hague: Martinus Nijhoff, 1997) 135.

16 On the emphasis placed on dialogue and co-operation in the mandates of special procedures and the humanitarian element of their work, see Bertram Ramcharan, *The Protection Role of UN Human Rights Special Procedures* (The Hague: Brill, 2009).

17 Michael K Addo, "Practice of the Human Rights Treaty Bodies in the Reconciliation of Cultural Diversity with Universal Respect for Human Rights" (2010) 32:3 Hum Rts Q 601.

18 *Convention against Torture and Other Cruel, Inhuman or Degrading Treatment or Punishment*, 1465 UNTS 85, Can TS 1987 No 36 (in force 26 June 1987) [*Convention against Torture*]; *Optional Protocol to the Convention on the Rights of Persons with Disabilities*, UN Doc A/61/611 (2006) (in force 3 May 2008); *Optional Protocol to the Convention on the Elimination of Discrimination against Women*, 2131 UNTS 83 (in force 22 December 2000). The Committee on Economic Social and Cultural Rights now also has this power under Article 11 of the *Optional Protocol to the International Covenant on Economic Social and Cultural Rights*, UN Doc A/63/435 (2008) (in force 5 May 2013).

1956, of a system of periodic reports to be submitted by states to the then UN Commission on Human Rights[19] on progress achieved within their territories in advancing the rights enshrined in the *Universal Declaration of Human Rights*,[20] the *Declaration on the Granting of Independence to Colonial Countries and Peoples*,[21] and the *Declaration on the Elimination of All Forms of Racial Discrimination*.[22] The purpose of periodic reports was not to criticize or evaluate the situation of human rights in a given country but, rather, to gather information and serve as a "valuable incentive to Governments' efforts to protect human rights" and promote their implementation.[23] The consensus among commentators at the time, still shared today, is that this mechanism did not result in any meaningful outcome[24] in its twenty-

[19] See ECOSOC Resolution 624B (XXII), ESCOR 22nd Sess, UN Doc E/2929 (1 August 1956) Suppl No 1 at 12; UN Commission on Human Rights, *Annual Reports on Human Rights*, Res I, UN Doc E/2844-3/CN/4/731 (1956). The most important reform to the reporting system was introduced by ECOSOC Resolution 1074C (XXXIX), ESCOR 39th Sess, UN Doc E/4117 (28 July 1965) Suppl No 1 at 23. See also ECOSOC Resolution 728B (XXVIII), ESCOR 28th Sess, UN Doc E/3290 (30 July 1959) Suppl No 1 at 18; ECOSOC Declaration 1596 (L), ESCOR 50th Sess, UN Doc E/5044 (21 May 1971) Suppl No 1 at 20; and ECOSOC Res 1978/20, ESCOR 1978, UN Doc E/1978/78 (5 May 1978) Suppl No 1 at 27. See further Philip Alston, "Reconceiving the UN Human Rights Regime: Challenges Confronting the New UN Human Rights Council" (2006) 7:1 Melbourne J Int'l L 185 at 207-15.

[20] *Universal Declaration of Human Rights*, GA Res 217A(III), UNGAOR, 3d Sess, Supp No 13, UN Doc A/810 (1948).

[21] *Declaration on the Granting of Independence to Colonial Countries and Peoples*, GA Res 1514(XV), UN Doc A/RES/1514(XV) (14 December 1960).

[22] *Declaration on the Elimination of All Forms of Racial Discrimination*, GA Res 1904(XVIII), UN Doc A/RES/1904(XVIII) (20 November 1963).

[23] ECOSOC Resolution 1074C (XXXIX), *supra* note 19 at para 3. See also Antônio Cançado Trindade, "Co-Existence and Co-Ordination of Mechanisms of International Protection of Human Rights (at Global and Regional Levels)" (1987) 202:II Rec des Cours 302.

[24] See Ineke Boerefijn, *The Reporting Procedure under the Covenant on Civil and Political Rights: Practice and Procedures of the Human Rights Committee* (Antwerp: Intersentia-Hart, 1999) at 9-13; Tom J Farer, "The UN and Human Rights: More Than a Whimper, Less Than a Roar" in Adam Roberts and Benedict Kingsbury, eds, *United Nations, Divided World* (Oxford: Clarendon Press, 1988) 95 at 123-24; Peter Haver, "The United Nations Sub-Commission on Prevention of Discrimination and Protection of Minorities" (1982) 21:1 Colum J Transnat'l L 103 at 117-19; Samuel Hoare, "The UN Commission on Human Rights" in Evan Luard, ed, *The International Protection of Human Rights* (London: Thames and Hudson) 59 at 79-87; Marc Schreiber, "La pratique récente des Nations Unies dans le

five-year existence.[25] Nevertheless, periodic reporting has been incorporated into all of the core international human rights treaties since then. Other equally flawed processes have included: (1) the much criticized "complaint procedures" (formerly 1503 procedure) whose impact is limited due to its confidentiality;[26] (2) the still unused inter-state complaint mechanisms under some treaty-based bodies;[27] and (3) the limited number of cases brought to the International Court of Justice (ICJ) based on human rights violations.[28] In brief, past experience of human rights mechanisms dependent on inter-governmental bodies for their implementation suggests that states have not been particularly committed to the enforcement of human rights in other jurisdictions.

It is therefore unsurprising that when the idea of the UPR was first mooted as an inter-governmental mechanism for the promotion of human rights relying on inter-active dialogues *inter pares,*

---

domaine de la protection des droits de l'homme" (1975) 145:II Rec des Cours 297 at 325-32; Louis B Sohn, "Human Rights: Their Implementation and Supervision by the United Nations" in Theodor Meron, ed, *Human Rights in International Law: Legal and Policy Issues,* volume 2 (Oxford: Clarendon Press, 1984) 369 at 373.

[25] For decisions terminating the mechanism, see GA Resolution 35/209, UN Doc A/RES/35/209 (17 December 1980), followed by UN Commission on Human Rights Declaration 10 (XXXVII) (13 March 1981) and ECOSOC Declaration 1981/151 , ESCOR 1981, UN Doc E/1981/81 (8 May 1981) Suppl No 1 at 46. See also Miko Lempinen and Martin Scheinin, *The New Human Rights Council: The First Two Years* (Turku: Åbo Akademi University Institute for Human Rights, 2007) at 14-15.

[26] See HRC Resolution 5/1, UN Doc A/HRC/RES/5/1 (18 June 2007). See also Elvira Domínguez-Redondo, "La Comisión de Derechos Humanos a Debate: el procedimiento 1503 ["Future of the UN Commission on Human Rights: 1503 procedure"] (2006) 2 Revista Iberoamericana de Derechos Humanos 34.

[27] The possibility of inter-state complaints is foreseen in the *Convention against Torture, supra* note 18, art 21; the *International Convention on the Rights of Migrant Workers and Members of Their Families,* 2220 UNTS 3 (in force 1 July 2003), art 74; the *International Convention on the Elimination of Racial Discrimination,* 660 UNTS 195 (in force 4 January 1969), arts 11-13; the *International Covenant on Civil and Political Rights,* 999 UNTS 171 (in force 23 March 1976), arts 41-43; the *International Convention for the Protection of All Persons from Enforced Disappearance,* UN Doc A/61/488 (2006) (in force 23 December 2010), art 32; and the *Optional Protocol to the International Covenant on Economic, Social and Cultural Rights, supra* note 18, art 10.

[28] See Domínguez-Redondo, *supra* note 10 at 684-85. See also Rosalyn Higgins, "Human Rights in the International Court of Justice" (2007) 20:4 Leiden J Int'l L 745.

many were sceptical, if not openly against it.[29] Experience has challenged this reflexive attitude, however, and the initial scepticism has given way to grounds for belief that many governments are engaging seriously with the mechanism.[30] Assessments regarding state compliance with recommendations must await the end of the second cycle, at which time judgments on whether recommendations agreed to in the first cycle have been implemented. Research, however, shows high levels of acceptance of recommendations made during the process,[31] and there is significant data indicating positive on-the-ground impact of the UPR in the short term.[32] Its capacity to provide unprecedented data highlights the rather mediocre human rights performance of the permanent members of the UN Security Council, five countries enjoying *de facto* immunity from strong action by the UN Commission and Human Rights Council until now.[33] In addition, topics consistently overlooked under the international human rights mechanisms, such as minority rights[34] and sexual orientation rights,[35] are finding accommodation under the UPR.[36]

There are other positive outcomes. Peer review mechanisms for the implementation of human rights such as the UPR and the lesser

[29] On the criticisms expressed, see Domínguez-Redondo, *supra* note 10 at 679-80.

[30] By April 2013, the only country not to have participated as a state under review was Israel (in the fifteenth session in January 2013).

[31] McMahon, *supra* note 8 at 13.

[32] "Universal Periodic Review: On the Road to Implementation" (2013) at 5, online: <http://www.upr-info.org/IMG/pdf/2012_on_the_road_to_implementation. pdf> ["UPR"].

[33] Rhona Smith, "To See Themselves As Others See Them": The Five Permanent Members of the Security Council and the Human Rights Council's Universal Periodic Review" (2013) 35:1 Hum Rts Q 1.

[34] Joshua Castellino, "No Room at the International Table: The Importance of Designing Effective Litmus Tests for Minority Protection at Home" (2013) 35:1 Hum Rts Q 201.

[35] The first ever UN resolution addressing human rights violations based on sexual orientation was adopted in June 2011. HRC, *Human Rights, Sexual Orientation and Gender Identity*, UN HRC Res 17/19, UNGAOR, 17th Sess, UN Doc A/HRC/ Res/17/19 (2011).

[36] For an analysis of the treatment of lesbians, gays, bisexuals, and transsexuals during the first eight sessions of the UPR, see UPR, "Issue Analysis: Lesbians, Gays, Bisexuals, Transsexuals" (2011), online: <http://www.upr-info.org/IMG/ pdf/issue_analysis_lgbts.pdf>. Minority rights are among the top ten issues raised during the UPR process. See McMahon, *supra* note 8 at 20.

known APRM are, perhaps ironically, relying on traditional sovereign state diplomacy to further human rights implementation.[37] We argue that this trend is positive at three levels: (1) at a theoretical level, it reveals an evolving maturity of the human rights regime with a capacity to detach from exclusively legalistic approaches to human rights implementation; (2) at a policy level, it has generated evidence of measured positive outcomes of peer review mechanisms, suggesting a preference for more co-operative approaches to human rights implementation as a first and complementary step to other more legalistic/adversarial means of implementation; and (3) peer review mechanisms offer both a theoretical and pragmatic framework under which to reconcile universalist and relativist approaches to human rights, accommodating international legal obligations while also formally accommodating the concept of sovereignty.

INTEGRATING UNIVERSALISM AND CULTURAL RELATIVISM

Proponents of universal values argue that all human beings have certain basic human rights such as the freedoms of religion, speech, association, and thought. The *Universal Declaration of Human Rights* is the most seminal document legitimizing this perspective, profoundly and positively affecting human rights globally.[38] In 1948, the UN General Assembly proclaimed the declaration to be a "common standard of achievement for all peoples and all nations."[39] This sense of universalism is rooted in other jurisprudential theories such as natural law theory — that is, belief in a higher, divinely ordained law and its secular counterpart, the theory of rationalism.

---

[37] On the meaning of peer review in academia and within different inter-governmental bodies, among others, see Tamara Lewis Arredondo, "The Universal Periodic Review Mechanism of the United Nations Human Rights Council: Transforming the Human Rights Discourse" (PhD thesis, Maastricht University, 2013) at 85-108 [unpublished]. On the meaning attached to the expression "peer review" or the finally adopted "periodic review" for the UPR, see Felice D Gaer, "A Voice Not an Echo: Universal Periodic Review and the UN Treaty Body System" (2007) 7:1 Human Rights LR109 at 112-21. On the position of regional groups regarding this issue, see Claire Doole and Juan Gasparini, "Enhancing Council Credibility," *Infosud Human Rights Tribune*, (2006) online <http://www.infosud.org/Enhancing-Council-credibility,862>.

[38] William Schabas, "Introductory Essay: The Drafting and Significance of the Universal Declaration of Human Rights" in William Schabas, ed, *The Universal Declaration of Human Rights: Travaux Préparatoires*, volume 1 (Cambridge: Cambridge University Press, 2013) xxi. *Universal Declaration of Human Rights, supra* note 20.

[39] *Universal Declaration of Human Rights, supra* note 20.

Some proponents have sought to justify an emerging consensus on the right to democratic forms of government.[40] Another strand holds that since human rights are universal, their global observance leads to improvements in living standards throughout the world. One of the most influential proponents of this perspective is Nobel Prize winner Amartya Sen who has argued not only that personal freedom and individual rights are global in nature but also that they are inextricably linked to economic development.[41] The internationalization of human rights — that is, the treatment of human rights as a subject of international law and politics,[42] reinforces its foundational claim of universality. This claim is closely linked to liberal and constitutional conceptions of international law, based on shared global values.

The purported universality of some of these foundational values of international law has been the cause of unease and contestation among international lawyers.[43] Third World approaches to international law have also pointed out that the universality of international law is a sub-product of colonialism.[44] Similarly, the universality of human rights is an issue that has been hotly contested for decades by cultural relativists. They argue either that (1) such rights do not exist or (2) to the extent that such rights exist, they must be fully mediated and interpreted through the particular social, cultural, and historical prisms of the societies in which people live. The *Universal Declaration of Human Rights* was challenged at its birth by the American Anthropological Association, which queried how the declaration could "be applicable to all human beings, and not be a statement of rights conceived only in terms of the values prevalent in countries of Western Europe and America."[45]

---

40 Thomas Franck, "The Emerging Right to Democratic Governance" (1992) 86:1 AJIL 46.

41 Amartya Sen, *Development As Freedom* (New York: Anchor Books, 1999).

42 See Louis Henkin, *The Age of Rights* (New York: Columbia University Press, 1996) at 13-29.

43 See Jean d'Aspremont, "The Foundations of the International Legal Order" (2007) 18 Finnish YB Int'l L 219 at 219. See also Jean d'Aspremont, "Re-inforcing the (Neo-) Hobbesian Representations of International Law" (2010) 13 J Int'l Relations & Development 85.

44 Antony Anghie and BS Chimni, "Third World Approaches to International Law and Individual Responsibility in Internal Conflicts" (2003) 2:1 Chinese J Int'l L 77.

45 Johannes Morsink, *The Universal Declaration of Human Rights: Origins, Drafting and Intent* (Philadelphia: University of Pennsylvania Press, 1999) at ix.

Proponents of these views have spoken against a broad-based interpretation of human rights — for example, through the "Asian
values" argument.[46] Some leading developing world figures, such
as Singapore's former Chief Minister Lee Kuan Yew, have strongly
contested universal interpretations of human rights and suggested
instead that there are "Asian values" based on regional, rather than
on universal, norms.[47]

Rhonda Calloway suggests that this critique provides an alternative to Western states' perspectives, emphasizing state sovereignty,
respect for hierarchy and authority, and socio-economic rights. This
view holds that Western political culture is too individualistic, suffers
from a crumbling civil society, and has sought to impose its values
inappropriately in non-Western contexts. Counter-arguments suggest that Asia is not homogenous and that there cannot be one
over-arching set of values and that the Asian values argument has
tended to be advanced by Asian governments or their supporters
who benefit politically from doing so.[48] This issue has also arisen in
the clash of Middle Eastern or, more precisely, Islamic values and
those of Western states. Ali Mazrui has focused on various aspects
of this question, arguing that compatibility exists between the two
cultures and that the West (his term) has much to learn from Islamic
values.[49] Other authors have noted that discrepancies in approach
may have less to do with Islam than with the economic, social, and
political distortions inherent in the Middle Eastern oil-based *rentier*
contexts.[50]

A similar debate has taken place regarding African approaches
to human rights and democracy. African intellectuals in the post-
independence period argued that single-party democracy was

---

[46] Adamantia Pollis and Peter Schwab, "Human Rights: A Western Construct with
Limited Applicability" in Adamantia Pollis and Peter Schwab, eds, *Human Rights:
Cultural and Ideological Perspectives* (New York: Praeger, 1979) 1.

[47] Fareed Zakaria, "Culture Is Destiny: Conversation with Lee Kuan Yew" (1994)
83 Foreign Affairs 109.

[48] See, for example, RL Callaway, "The Rhetoric of Asian Values" in RL Callaway
and J Harrelson-Stephens, eds, *Exploring International Human Rights: Essential
Readings* (Boulder, CO: Lynne Reinner Publishers, 2007); Fareed Zakaria, "The
Dustbin of History: Asian Values" (2012) Foreign Policy 1.

[49] See, for example, Ali Mazrui, "*Islamic and Western Values*" (1997) Foreign Affairs
76; Ali Mazrui, *Islam Between Globalization and Counterterrorism* (Trenton, NJ: Africa
World Press, 2004).

[50] Larry Diamond, Marc F Plattner, and Daniel Brumberg, eds, *Islam and Democracy
in the Middle East* (Baltimore, MD: John Hopkins University Press, 2003) at xii.

possible and feasible in Africa. Presidents Julius Nyerere of Tanzania and Kenneth Kaunda of Zambia were ardent proponents of this theory, and President Yoweri Museveni of Uganda developed a "no-party" variation on this theme. While this perspective has been discredited due to the abuses of human rights and economic decline that accompanied the suppression of political pluralism, a germ of truth lies in the fact that political institutions cannot be grafted wholesale from one context into another, as they were from Europe to Africa with disastrous results after colonial rule. This argument has been adapted and developed by Daniel Osabu-Kle, although his approach is stronger in critiquing the impact of Western models than in proposing realistic and workable models of governance that reflect regional realities and universal values.[51]

In recent years, an increasing number of commentators have sought common ground between the complete adherence to immutable universal values, including human rights, and full cultural relativism in which rights can only be defined in the context of the particular society in question. These perspectives include the further articulation of the concept of a "right to culture," in which the relativist regard for difference is made the subject of a universal right to express this different identity and examples by which universalist legal frameworks accommodate difference to reflect different traditions. Such thinking has been spurred on by the work of the United Nations itself. The landmark 1993 *Vienna Declaration and Program of Action* states that

[a]ll human rights are universal, indivisible and interdependent and inter-related. The international community must treat human rights globally in a fair and equal manner, on the same footing, and with the same emphasis. While the significance of national and regional particularities and various historical, cultural and religious backgrounds must be borne in mind, it is the duty of States, regardless of their political, economic and cultural systems, to promote and protect all human rights and fundamental freedoms.[52]

Similarly, Jack Donnelly seeks to articulate what he views as the reality of both universal and contextual elements in human existence

---

51 Daniel T Osabu-Kle, *Compatible Cultural Democracy: The Key of Development in Africa* (Toronto: University of Toronto Press, 2000).

52 *Vienna Declaration and Program of Action*, 12 July 1993, UN Doc A/CONF.154/23 at para 5.

by developing the concept of "relative universality," although he recognizes that the devil can be in the detail when one determines how much weight to assign to the "relative" or the "universal" aspects of this concept.[53] Michael Goodhart argues that one way to move beyond the divide is for analysts to avoid conceptualizing rights as either universal or relative.[54] Michael Brown struggles with this dichotomy, stating that

[c]lassical cultural relativism ... has been debated by scholars for more than a half-century. Today's consensus is that, as originally conceived, cultural relativism has significant flaws ... Yet there is much to be said for the clarity and conciseness of classical cultural relativism's claim that cultures constitute different life-worlds, as long as they are not taken too literally.[55]

Adamantia Pollis and Peter Schwab, whose previous work has fallen squarely into the cultural relativist camp, have also evolved in their thinking, largely because of the reality of the phenomenon of globalization. They take the approach of integrating cultural elements into a universal concept of human rights, as opposed to fundamentally questioning the universality concept itself.[56]

A related cleavage occurs in discussions concerning the nature and definition of human rights. One school of thought has focused on human rights as primarily civil and political in nature, as reflected in the work of non-governmental organizations (NGOs) such as Freedom House and Human Rights Watch. Hugo Bedau, for example, has argued that, at their core, human rights are "negative" in nature, in the sense that they are focused on protecting the individual from abuses by the government.[57] Others, such as Henry

---

[53] Jack Donnelly, "The Relative Universality of Human Rights" (2007) 29:2 Hum Rts Q 281.

[54] Michael Goodhart, "Human Rights and Global Democracy" (2008) 22:4 Ethics & Int'l Affairs 395.

[55] Michael F Brown, "Cultural Relativism 2.0" (2008) 49:3 Current Anthropology 363 at 371.

[56] Adamantia Pollis, "A New Universalism" in Adamantia Pollis and Peter Schwab, eds, *Human Rights: New Perspectives, New Realities* (Boulder, CO: Lynne Rienner Publishers, 2000) 9.

[57] Hugo A Bedau, "Human Rights and Foreign Assistance Programs" in Peter G Brown and Douglas Maclean, eds, *Human Rights and US Foreign Policy* (Lexington, MA: Lexington Books, 1979) 29.

Shue, have argued that human rights should be seen as "positive," expanding the role of government in addressing basic human economic, social, and cultural needs.[58] This discussion has been coloured by regional and geopolitical considerations, as Western states have tended to define human rights in the former terms, while communist bloc countries before the fall of the Iron Curtain and those in the developing world (especially governments) have argued for the broader interpretation. Richard Claude and Burns Weston, among others, have built on the concept introduced by Karel Vasak of "first-generation" civil and political rights, "second-generation" economic, social, and cultural rights, and "third-generation" "solidarity" rights,[59] which represent a further extension of the rights concept into the areas of global redistribution of wealth, the sharing of global resources, and the right to peace.[60]

As with the universalist and cultural relativity themes, some more recent observers have sought to identify bridges between "negative" and "positive" definitions of human rights. In a move that received considerable attention in the press and academia, the highly respected and influential American Anthropological Association altered its stance on the *Universal Declaration on Human Rights* in 1999, stating that its

working definition [of human rights] builds on the Universal Declaration of Human Rights (UDHR), the International Covenants on Civil and Political Rights, and on Social, Economic, and Cultural Rights, the Conventions on Torture, Genocide, and Elimination of All Forms of Discrimination Against Women, and other treaties which bring basic human rights within the parameters of international written and customary law and practice.[61]

---

58 Henry Shue, *Basic Rights: Subsistence, Affluence and US Foreign Policy* (Princeton, NJ: Princeton University Press, 1996) at 52.

59 Karel Vasak, "Human Rights: A Thirty Year Struggle — The Sustained Efforts to Give Force of Law to the Universal Declaration of Human Rights" (1977) UNESCO Courier 29.

60 See Richard P Claude and Burns H Weston, eds, *Human Rights in the World Community*, 3rd edition (Philadelphia: University of Pennsylvania Press, 2006) at 19-20.

61 American Anthropological Association, "Declaration on Anthropology and Human Rights" (June 1999), online: <http://www.aaanet.org/about/Policies/statements/Declaration-on-Anthropology-and-Human-Rights.cfm>. See further Karen Engle, "From Skepticism to Embrace: Human Rights and the American Anthropological Association from 1947-1999" (2001) 23:3 Hum Rts Q 536.

Leonard Rubenstein has suggested that human rights groups have an important role to play in promoting economic, social, and cultural rights by (1) collaborating with partner organizations in the developing world in lobbying for systems and services that meet needs in a manner consistent with human rights requirements; (2) advocating for resources to fulfil economic, social, and cultural rights, especially by lobbying for funds from wealthy countries; and (3) monitoring compliance by states with the increasingly explicit obligations to protect, respect, and fulfil these rights.[62] Bonny Ibhawoh has noted some movement on the part of Western state-oriented human rights NGOs to include economic, social, and cultural rights in their agendas. He has also emphasized the role that indigenous human rights organizations in the developing world can play to help further this debate.[63]

These themes represent, in varying ways, attempts to find "middle ground," to attenuate some of the highly polarized, partisan, and ideological thinking that was a feature of the Cold War, shifted onto a North/South axis, and that has subsequently evolved as a result of the "global war on terror" that followed the 11 September 2001 attacks. Proposals to achieve a paradigm shift reconciling the tension between universalists and relativists have also included: (1) proposals to move from a "representation of culture as abstract and static to one based on the reality of culture as practice";[64] (2) the cross-cultural approach advocated by Abdullahi An-Na'im;[65] (3) the "inclusive universality" promoted by Eva Brems;[66] and (4) the

[62] Leonard S Rubenstein, "How International Human Rights Organizations Can Advance Economic, Social and Cultural Rights: A Response to Kenneth Roth" (2004) 26:4 Hum Rts Q 845.

[63] Bonny Ibhawoh, "Beyond Naming and Shaming: Methodological Imperatives of Economic, Social and Cultural Rights Advocacy" (2008) African YB Int'l L 49.

[64] Addo, *supra note* 17 at 608-10, focusing in particular on the work of Ann-Belinda S Preis, "Human Rights As Cultural Practice: An Anthropological Critique" (1996) 18 Hum Rts Q 286.

[65] Addo, *supra* note 17 at 610-12, relying on the following works to sustain his arguments: Abdullahi An-Na'im, *Human Rights in Cross-Cultural Perspectives: A Quest for Consensus* (Pennsylvania: University of Pennsylvania Press, 1995); Abdullahi An-Na'im, "Religious Minorities under Islamic Law and the Limits of Cultural Relativism" (1987) 9 Hum Rts Q 1; Abdullahi An-Na'im, "Human Rights in the Muslim World: Socio-Political Conditions and Scriptural Imperatives" (1990) 3 Harv Hum Rts J 13.

[66] Addo, *supra* note 17 at 612-13, based on arguments developed in Eva Brems, "Reconciling Universality and Diversity in International Human Rights: A

approach based on "legal practice" articulated by Douglas Donoho.[67] After summarizing the shortcomings of these approaches, Michael Addo has suggested that the working methods of UN human rights treaty bodies could offer a model of good practice for managing the tensions between universalist and cultural relativist schools of thought.[68] We suggest that the creation of the UPR (and other international organization, peer review processes) also reflects this ambitious, albeit imperfect, compromise, which promotes a global conception of human rights while acknowledging the realities of regional and/or cultural differentiation.

Recent research suggests that there is robust evidence supporting the proposition that states ratify treaties because they intend to comply with them.[69] It is therefore fair to deduce that the engagement of states with international mechanisms reflects a level of commitment to them, at least at the time of engagement. In the case of the UPR, for example, all states have engaged with the system (with the exception of Israel for a few months during the second cycle in 2013).[70] This record suggests, assuming these conclusions can be applied to other human rights commitments and mechanisms, at least some commitment on the part of participating states towards human rights implementation.[71]

It is not the objective of this article to refute the widespread, but uncorroborated, belief about the limited impact of *UN Charter*-based bodies, such as the Human Rights Council and its subsidiary bodies, due to their characterization as political organs.[72] Contrary to Addo's assertion that a legal approach is a necessary condition to achieving reconciliation between cultural diversity and universal respect for human rights,[73] this article argues that it is the more

---

Theoretical and Methodological Framework and its Application in the Context of Islam" in Adrás Sajó, ed, *Human Rights with Modesty: the Problem of Universalism* (The Hague: Martinus Nijhoff, 2004) 213.

[67] Addo, *supra* note 17 at 613-14. This approach is articulated by Douglas L Donoho in "Relativism Versus Universalism in Human Rights: The Search for Meaningful Standards" (1990-91) 27 Stanford Journal of International Law 345.

[68] Addo, *supra* note 17 at 613-14..

[69] Beth A Simmons, *Mobilizing for Human Rights: International Law in Domestic Politics* (Cambridge: Cambridge University Press, 2009) at 80-111.

[70] Israel returned to the UPR a few months later, in November 2013.

[71] Simmons, *supra* note 69.

[72] Conversely, increasing evidence seems to point in a totally different direction. See Domínguez-Redondo, *supra* note 10; McMahon, *supra* note 8.

[73] Addo, *supra* note 17 at 602, 614-15.

co-operative techniques used by human rights bodies in recent years, rather than the nature (that is, legal or political) of such bodies, that seems to be adding value to existing human rights implementation mechanisms. Preliminary research provides reason for optimism regarding the beneficial effects of peer review mechanisms on the enjoyment of human rights on the ground.[74]

Whatever the reasons behind it, the scale of engagement of states with the UPR is unprecedented, as is the data it is generating on levels of respect for global human rights as well as the evidence of *opinio juris* in relation to human rights and international humanitarian law. The preparation of state reports for the UPR and the interactive dialogue is particularly useful as a tool to identify and blend different sets of social values at the universal level since it allows "the identification of the positions which the responsible organs of governments have officially adopted."[75] In addition, the existence of this data has facilitated innovative research measuring the impact of the UPR. The efficiency of other UN human rights bodies has only been tested in recent times, after decades of existence,[76] while quantitative and qualitative analyses of the UPR's impact were available less than five years after its implementation.[77] This phenomenon is related to the quantity and quality of data generated by the UPR itself, which is relatively standard and comparable for all states.[78] It is also not dependent on restricted sources for certain countries or rights, a bane often undermining the reliability of conclusions reached by researchers engaged in empirical analyses of the effectiveness of human rights mechanisms prior to the UPR.[79]

---

[74] See "UPR," *supra* note 32; Domínguez-Redondo, *supra* note 10; McMahon, *supra* note 8. These include some specific examples of changes that have occurred in state promotion of human rights as a result of the UPR.

[75] Christian Tomuschat, *Human Rights: Between Idealism and Realism*, 2nd edition (New York: Oxford University Press, 2008) at 71.

[76] While similar works with different conclusions have proliferated since, the first relevant attempt to test empirically the effectiveness of the UN human rights machinery was undertaken by Oona Hathaway, "Do Human Rights Treaties Make a Difference?" (2002) 112 Yale LJ 1935.

[77] See "UPR," *supra* note 32; McMahon, *supra* note 8.

[78] On the impact of the UPR on equal treatment of states, see Rhona Smith, "Equality of 'Nations Large and Small': Testing the Theory of the Universal Periodic Review in the Asia-Pacific" (2011) 2 Asia Pac J HR & L 36.

[79] See, for example, Eric A Posner, "Some Skeptical Comments on Beth Simmon's 'Mobilizing for Human Rights'" (2010) 44:3 NYUJ Int'l L & Pol 819; Ryan Goodman and Derek Jinks, "Measuring the Effects of Human Rights Treaties" (2003) 14:1 EJIL 171.

This is the first comprehensive source of information allowing an analysis of the standards used in practice when states examine human rights performance in a peer context. For instance, by analyzing the types of action verbs utilized in recommendations and ranking them on a scale from one (minimal action) to five (specific action), it is possible to develop a picture of the extent to which recommendations are "softer" — that is, easier for states to accept — or "harder" — requiring more critical human rights reforms (and posing greater costs for states in rational choice terms).[80]

Evolving Perspectives on National Sovereignty and Human Rights

States have not only committed themselves to protecting the rights of all within their jurisdiction, but they have also accepted that human rights no longer fall within their exclusive domestic jurisdiction. When obligations *erga omnes* are violated,[81] including gross human rights violations, states other than directly injured states may invoke international responsibility.[82] In extreme scenarios, there is discussion of the "right" (of humanitarian intervention)[83] or even the responsibility to intervene (that is, R2P), if necessary, using armed force.[84] The discourse over the R2P principle, its endorsement as a concept by states in 2005,[85] and the United Nations-sanctioned interventions in Libya and Côte d'Ivoire in 2011[86] have been interpreted as a confirmation that "human rights concerns have effectively become internationalized and the rights of non-interference

---

[80] See McMahon, *supra* note 8.

[81] On the concept and its consequences in terms of responsibility, see Eric A Posner, "Erga Omnes Norms, Institutionalization and Constitutionalism in International Law" (2009) 165 J Institutional & Theoretical Economics 5.

[82] See *Report of the International Law Commission on the Work of Its Fifty-third Session*, UNGAOR, 53d Sess, UN Doc A/56/10 (2001) at 318.

[83] Anne Orford, *Reading Humanitarian Intervention: Human Rights and the Use of Force in International Law* (Cambridge: Cambridge University Press, 2003).

[84] Gareth Evans, *The Responsibility to Protect: Ending Mass Atrocity Crimes Once and For All* (Washington, DC: Brookings Institution Press, 2009); Anne Orford, *International Authority and the Responsibility to Protect* (Cambridge: Cambridge University Press, 2011).

[85] *2005 World Summit Outcome*, GA Res 60/1, UNGAOR, 60th Sess, UN Doc A/Res/60/1 (2005) at paras 139-45.

[86] See UNSC Resolution 1973, 6498th Mtg, UN Doc S/Res/1973 (2011) and UNSC Resolution 1975, 6508th Mtg, UN Doc S/Res/1975 (2011).

and non-use of force have been qualified as a result ... [T]hose states advocating an absolute right to non-interference clearly represent a minority."[87]

Louis Henkin was one of the most enthusiastic proponents of the argument that state sovereignty becomes subsidiary when this foundational principle of international law clashes with the promotion and protection of human rights. He viewed human rights law as a real "revolution" of international law, changing its content, sources, and means of implementation.[88] The erosion of the principle of sovereignty has been welcomed as a positive effect of the human rights regime at the international level. Sovereignty and human rights have traditionally been seen as being in an antagonistic relationship — Article 2(7) of the *UN Charter* has often been used by states as a shelter from scrutiny in relation to human rights.[89]

Others suggest that human rights have re-conceptualized sovereignty rather than eroded it. Anne Peters, for instance, argues that the impact of human rights in international law may culminate in a wholesale redefinition of the legal status of state sovereignty through which the antinomy between human rights and sovereignty will be eliminated.[90] Human rights would be more than limitations on state sovereignty. Rather, sovereignty would find its source and purpose (*telos*) "in humanity understood as the principle that the state must protect human rights, interests, needs and security."[91] As a result, Peters claims that "sovereignty has already been relegated to the status of a second-order norm which is derived and geared

---

[87] Theresa Reinold, *Sovereignty and the Responsibility to Protect* (New York: Routledge, 2013) at 153.

[88] Louis Henkin, "Human Rights and State 'Sovereignty'" (1995-96) 25 Ga J Int & Comp L 31; see also Louis Henkin, "That 'S' Word: Sovereignty, and Globalization, and Human Rights, et cetera" (1999-2000) 68:1 Fordham L Rev 1. Other commentators arguing in a similar direction include Michael W Reisman, "Sovereignty and Human Rights in Contemporary International Law" (1999) 84:4 AJIL 866; Felix Ermacora, "Human Rights and Domestic Jurisdiction (Article 2, Paragraph 7 of the Charter)" (1968) 124:II Rec des Cours 371; Rosalyn Higgins, *The Development of International Law through the Political Organs of the United Nations* (London: Oxford University Press, 1963) at 118-30.

[89] On the use of Article 2(7) by states before the UN General Assembly and the former Commission on Human Rights between 1975 and 1991, see Menno T Kamminga, *Inter-State Accountability for Violations of Human Rights* (Philadelphia: University of Pennsylvania Press, 1992) at 88-111.

[90] Anne Peters, "Humanity as the A and Ω of Sovereignty" (2009) 20:3 EJIL 513 at 543.

[91] *Ibid.*

towards the protection of basic human rights, needs, interest, and security."[92]

Similarly, Karel Wellens sees a demonstration of the "irreversible humanisation of international law" in the growing recognition of the responsibility to protect concept.[93] The R2P principle did constitute an attempt at redefining sovereignty. Francis Deng and others argued in 1996 that responsibility, understood as the obligation of the state "to preserve life-sustaining standards for its citizens," is the essence of, and a necessary condition for, sovereignty.[94] In Anne Orford's words, "[i]n its various formulations, the responsibility to protect concept can be seen as an attempt to redefine and delimit domestic and international jurisdiction, and to reassert the primacy of the UN in the face of proliferating functionalist claimants to international authority."[95]

The acceptance of monitoring mechanisms and peer-to-peer accountability — understood as mandating, reporting, surveillance, monitoring, and dispute settlement — has intensified significantly in the last century in many areas regulated by international law.[96] The real innovation brought by human rights was not that states should be accountable for their legal commitments towards other states. Rather it was that the human rights regime, preoccupied with the rights of individuals within a state's jurisdiction, "could be brought under this broader accountability trend in public international law."[97] Through their own consent, states have gradually allowed and increased the role and standing of individuals in international law and generated space for legal challenges of human rights violations before domestic and international bodies.

Nonetheless, a new concept of sovereignty dependent on human rights compliance remains at odds with the legal and political realities of contemporary international law.[98] The fact that human rights

---

92 *Ibid* at 544.

93 Karel Wellens, "Revisiting Solidarity as a (Re-)Emerging Constitutional Principle: Some Further Reflections" in Rüdiger Wolfrum and Chie Kojima, eds, *Solidarity: A Structural Principle of International Law* (Heidelberg: Springer, 2010) 3 at 10.

94 Francis M Deng et al, *Sovereignty as Responsibility: Conflict Management in Africa* (Washington DC: Brookings Institution, 1996) at xvii; on the gradual erosion of sovereignty, see also 6-10.

95 Orford, *supra* note 84 at 178.

96 Simmons, *supra* note 69 at 27-31.

97 *Ibid* at 27.

98 For commentary on the conceptual flaws and political limits of Anne Peters' proposal, see Emily Kidd White et al, "Humanity as the A (Alpha) and (Omega)

— and humanitarian — arguments are increasingly used to justify governmental action beyond borders is often mistaken for a real shift away from the centrality of sovereignty in international law and relations. This can be illustrated through the universal acceptance of the principle of R2P and the UN's commitment to its "implementation."[99] In its final version, the concept is firmly located within the powers of the UN Security Council, the structure of which is, of course, rooted in sovereign authority. It therefore falls to a collection of nation-states to authorize (collective) humanitarian interventions, including through the use of force. This power, as is well known, does not find its legal foundations in the *UN Charter* but, rather, in customary law or a functional approach to the competence of organs of international organizations.[100] In addition, the modern endorsement of R2P does not create new legal obligations on the part of states to prevent or to respond to genocide, war crimes, ethnic cleansing, and crimes against humanity.[101] Rather, the power of the concept relies on the fact that "it develops an ambitious conceptual framework aimed at systematising and giving formal expression to the protective authority exercised by international actors in the decolonised world since 1960."[102]

The R2P concept remains hotly contested, as evidenced by the allegations of misuse of UN Security Council Resolution 1973 in 2011, which authorized the establishment of a "no-fly zone" over Libya, provoking an ongoing controversy.[103] It is also critiqued for

---

of Sovereignty: Four Replies to Anne Peters' *Special Anniversary Article*" (2009) 20:3 EJIL 545.

[99] See UN General Assembly Resolution 63/308, UN Doc A/RES/63/308 (2009); UN Secretary-General, "Implementing the Responsibility to Protect: Report of the Secretary-General," UN Doc A/63/677 (2009). On the institutionalization of the concept, see Orford, *supra* note 84 at 17-22.

[100] Orford, *supra* note 84 at 167-72.

[101] UN Secretary-General, *supra* note 99 at para 11. A very interesting critique to the responsibility-to-protect (R2P) concept as redefining sovereignty and distinguishing sovereignty *de facto* and *de jure*, can be found in Jeremy Moses, "Sovereignty as Irresponsibility? A Realist Critique of the Responsibility to Protect" (2013) 39:1 Rev Int'l Studies 113.

[102] Orford, *supra* note 84 at 3; see also at 103-39, explaining the role of R2P as a tool for recognizing lawful authority.

[103] See, for example, Ambassador Vitaly Churkin, President of the Security Council, Press Conference, News and Media: United Nations Webcast, online: <http://www.unmultimedia.org/tv/webcast/2011/12/press-conference-ambassador-vitaly-churkin-president-of-the-security-council.html>. See also John Murphy,

being only selectively applied, as in the failure of the Security Council to invoke it in the case of the Syrian civil war.[104] The ICJ may have repeatedly recognized, in principle, the existence of obligations owed to the international community as a whole (that is, *erga omnes* obligations). However, its reasoning in the *Legal Consequences for States of the Continued Presence of South Africa in Namibia (South West Africa)*,[105] *Barcelona Traction, Light and Power Company, Limited (Belgium v Spain)*,[106] *Case Concerning East Timor (Portugal v Australia)*,[107] and *Military and Paramilitary Activities in and against Nicaragua (Nicaragua v United States of America)*[108] reveals that it has not enforced the legal consequences of such a recognition. Instead, the ICJ has refused claims by parties that have a specific legal interest in a dispute but are not directly affected.[109] Likewise, an empirical assessment of the real influence of human rights litigation concludes that claims about the impact of human rights on sovereignty are exaggerated.[110] After engaging in a thorough analysis to test whether facts support the narrative about the transformation of sovereignty, focusing on the extreme scenarios of military intervention, Theresa Reinold concludes: "Overall, the case studies dictate the sobering conclusion that we have not (yet) moved beyond Westphalia, and that sovereignty as responsibility continues to be a moral aspiration more than anything else."[111]

Alongside those who disagree that sovereignty has been "eroded,"[112] those who acknowledge that sovereignty does wield less power than

---

"Responsibility to Protect (R2P) Comes of Age? A Sceptic's View" (2012) 18 ILSA J Int'l & Comp L 413.

[104] Aidan Hehir, "The Permanence of Inconsistency: Libya, the Security Council, and the Responsibility to Protect" (2013) 38:1 Int'l Security 137.

[105] *Legal Consequences for States of the Continued Presence of South Africa in Namibia*, Second Phase, Judgment, [1966] ICJ Rep 6.

[106] *Barcelona Traction, Light and Power Company, Limited (Belgium v Spain)*, [1970] ICJ Rep 3.

[107] *Case Concerning East Timor (Portugal v Australia)*, [1995] ICJ Rep 90.

[108] *Military and Paramilitary Activities in and against Nicaragua (Nicaragua v United States of America)*, Merits, Judgment, [1986] ICJ Rep 4.

[109] See Karl Zemanek, "New Trends in the Enforcement of Erga Omnes Obligations" (2000) 4 Max Planck YB UN L 1 at 11.

[110] Chandra Lekha Sriram, "Human Rights Claims vs the State: Is Sovereignty Really Eroding?" (2006) 1:1 Interdisciplinary J HR L 107.

[111] Reinold, *supra* note 87 at 155.

[112] See Richard H Steinberg, "Who Is Sovereign?" (2004) 40:2 Stan J Int'l L 329.

in the past do not always view this development as being positive. Attenuating sovereignty does not *ipso facto* lead to greater capacity for the international community to modify states' behaviour towards compliance with internationally accepted human rights standards. The activities of international financial institutions and non-state actors that led to the post-2007 global economic crisis, for example, have negatively affected the enjoyment of human rights. These developments, alongside unregulated globalization, have reified the need to reclaim, rather than cede, sovereignty for better rights protection.[113] Citizens expect to be protected by their politicians, but "States have been shedding power to globalisation."[114] In the words of Martti Koskenniemi,

[w]hen questions of economic distribution, environmental protection, security, or human rights are conceived of as essentially global, best dealt with by the best forms of functional expertise available globally, then no room is left for communities to decide on their preferences.[115]

This notion invokes "the paradox of national power and international solidarity," whereby in order to project and implement a sense of international solidarity, national power is needed.[116] In reference to international investment regimes, which are "arguably the most effective and sovereignty-intrusive of our international regimes at the global level," José Alvarez concludes that we have not moved too far from the Westphalian system of nation-states.[117] Evidence suggests that states are on a "path to sovereign

---

[113] Matthew S Weinert, "Bridging the Human Rights-Sovereignty Divide: Theoretical Foundations of a Democratic Sovereignty" (2007) 8:2 HR Rev 5.

[114] Philip Stephens, "Leaders Who Generate Diminishing Returns," *Financial Times* (19 January 2012) at 7, online: Financial Times <http://www.ft.com>.

[115] Martti Koskenniemi, "What Use for Sovereignty Today" (2011) 1:1 Asian J Int'l L 61 at 68.

[116] Jean-Marc Coicaud, "Making Sense of National Interest and International Solidarity" in Jean-Marc Coicaud and Nicholas J Wheeler, eds, *National Interest and International Solidarity: Particular and Universal Ethics in International Life* (Tokyo: United Nations University Press, 2008) 288 at 289. See also Simon Chesterman, Michael Ignatieff, and Ramesh Thakur, eds, *Making States Work: State Failure and the Crisis of Governance* (Tokyo: United Nations University Press, 2005) at 1, 359.

[117] José A Alvarez, "State Sovereignty Is Not Withering Away: A Few Lessons for the Future" in Antonio Cassese, ed, *Realizing Utopia: The Future of International Law* (Oxford: Oxford University Press, 2012) 26 at 31.

re-empowerment"[118] and that even "Grotians" are sceptical about the virtues of diminished sovereignty when faced with the backlash against the international investment regime, International Monetary Fund (IMF) conditionality, or the role of the UN Security Council as legislator.[119]

This tension concerning state sovereignty *vis-à-vis* the promotion and protection of human rights lies at the core of the divide between states favouring "co-operative" or, conversely, "confrontational" strategies to prompt respect for human rights.[120] Beyond doctrinal debates and academic constructions of sovereignty that are difficult to translate into legal and political realities, there is a reluctance to accept human rights implementation mechanisms that use confrontational approaches towards states and that are perceived as violating the principle of non-intervention. This is the official position of the so-called Like-Minded Group of states, whose members have publicly acknowledged that they have been co-operating on a concerted strategy since 1996 in order to avoid tools aimed at "forcing states to co-operate" with human rights mechanisms.[121]

It is nonetheless difficult to accurately locate states' positions as either opponents or advocates of confrontational approaches to human rights implementation since political motivations often lead to changes of position depending on national and regional interests.[122] The portrayal of such differences as characteristic of a North-South divide leads to an artificial polarization, with potentially long-term damaging effects for the human rights agenda.[123] In fact, developing countries as a group no longer hold a unified, sovereignty-trumps-all approach to human rights. Some developing countries currently align themselves with positions analogous to those normally associated with Western states. A record of political alliances within the UN Human Rights Council during 2008–09 reveals that

[t]he Asian Group, the Eastern European Group, and GRULAC [the Group of Latin American and Caribbean States] never spoke or voted as a group

---

[118] *Ibid* at 32.

[119] *Ibid* at 34.

[120] See Domínguez-Redondo, *supra* note 10 at 679-80.

[121] Domínguez-Redondo, *supra* note 14 at 274-75. See also Alston, *supra* note 19 at 204-7.

[122] See Lempinen, *supra* note 8.

[123] International Service for Human Rights, "Human Rights Monitor, no 64/2008" (2008) at 11.

and continued to serve as "swing regions" on a range of thematic and country issues. Russia, China, and Cuba almost always joined the African Group and OIC [Organization of Islamic States] positions while Japan, Republic of Korea, Ukraine, Chile and Argentina generally took similar positions as the EU.[124]

The antagonism towards mechanisms that intrude on state sovereignty is visible even among states who led the creation of international human rights standards and monitoring mechanisms. Two contemporary examples of Western countries asserting sovereignty at variance with universal human rights values demonstrate this antagonism clearly. The first concerns the United States in its reluctance to ratify the *Convention on the Rights of the Child*[125] or the *Convention on the Rights of Persons with Disabilities*[126] as well as its unwillingness to allow unfettered access to human rights experts seeking to investigate the situation in Guantanamo Bay.[127] The second concerns British posturing towards human rights treaties and their implementation, especially its resistance to implementing the European Court of Human Rights' decisions regarding prisoners' rights to vote.[128] Others with a history of colonialism, including

---

[124] Democracy Coalition Project, "Human Rights Council Report Card: Government Positions on Key Issues 2008-2009" (2009), online: <http://www.demcoalition.org/site09-2008/2005_html/unhrc-related-documents.html>. See also Sibylle SS Scheipers, "Civilization vs Toleration: The New UN Human Rights Council and the Normative Foundations of the International Order" (2007) 10:3 J Int'l Relations & Development 219 at 234-36.

[125] *Convention on the Rights of the Child*, 1577 UNTS 3, Can TS 1992 No 3, 28 ILM 1457 (in force 2 September 1990). On the concerns about US sovereignty in relation to every human rights convention and this one in particular, see Lainie Rutkow and Joshua T Lozman, "Suffer the Children? A Call for the United States Ratification of the United Nations Convention on the Rights of the Child" (2006) 19 Harv Hum Rts J 161.

[126] *Convention on the Rights of Persons with Disabilities*, 2515 UNTS 3, Can TS 2010 No 8, 46 ILM 443 (in force 3 May 2008). Senator Mike Lee led the opposition to ratification of the convention in the US Senate on 4 December 2012 using the argument that ratification would pose a threat to American sovereignty. Jim Abrams, "Disability Treaty Downed by Republican Opposition," *Huffington Post* (4 December 2012), online: Huffington Post <http://www.huffingtonpost.com>. See also Sally Chaffin, "Challenging the United States Position on a United Nations Convention on Disability" (2006) 15 Temp Pol & Civ Rts L Rev 121.

[127] See *Report of the Chairperson of the Working Group on Arbitrary Detention*, UN Doc E/CN.4/2006/120 (26 February 2006).

[128] Alice Donald, Jane Gordon, and Philip Leach, "The UK and the European Court of Human Rights," Research Report 83 (2012) Equality and Human Rights Commission 126.

the 'Asian bloc,' continue to contest a conception of human rights that places limits on state sovereignty through the use of confrontational approaches.[129] Asian governments have tended to assert the sovereignty argument from a different perspective — one based on the "Asian values" debate summarized earlier. Respect for sovereignty is claimed, not on the grounds of Article 2(7) of the *UN Charter*, nor on the grounds of consent as the basis of international law, but, rather, on the grounds of culture.[130]

A significant number of countries tend to view the human rights discourse as neo-colonialist, with the potential to destroy cultural diversity while moving societies towards Western homogenization. China, Colombia, Cuba, Indonesia, Iran, Iraq, Malaysia, Mexico, Myanmar, Pakistan, Singapore, Syria, Vietnam, and Yemen have all been labelled as "culturally relativist" in relation to human rights, especially within the context of the UPR mechanism, despite their non-contestation of the principle of universality of human rights as such.[131] A high degree of correlation exists between states identified as culturally relativist and those Like-Minded Group states advocating non-confrontational approaches to human rights implementation — eight of the fourteen "culturally relativist" states are members of the Like-Minded Group.[132]

---

[129] See, for instance, the portrayal of the post-Cold War era as a "Westphalian order" versus an emerging "Eastphalian" order based on what it is described as a "Western-inspired effort to limit sovereignty and qualify the principle of non-interference" using international law standards such as human rights, humanitarian intervention, or the responsibility to protect. Sung Won Kim, *Human Security with an Asian Face?* (2010) 17:1 Ind J Global Legal Stud 83 at 85.

[130] Karen Engle, "Culture and Human Rights: The Asian Values Debate in Context" (2000) 32:2 NYUJ Int'l L & Pol 291; see also Joshua Castellino and Elvira Domínguez-Redondo, *Minority Rights in Asia: A Comparative Legal Analysis* (Oxford: Oxford University Press, 2006) at 11-26.

[131] See Christina M Cerna, "Universality of Human Rights and Cultural Diversity: Implementation of Human Rights in Different Socio-Cultural Contexts" (1994) 16:3 Hum Rts Q 740 at 740; Diane Otto, "Rethinking the Universality of Human Rights Law" (1997) 29:1 Colum HRL Rev 1 at 10, n 46. Confirming the list based on the UPR review, see Roger Lloret Blackburn, *Cultural Relativism in the Universal Periodic Review of the Human Rights Council,* ICIP Working Papers 2011/ 03 (Barcelona: Institut Català por la Pau, 2011) at 9, 14, online: <http://www. icpt.cat>.

[132] The divisive HRC *Resolution on Promoting Human Rights and Fundamental Freedoms through a Better Understanding of Traditional Values of Humankind,*" HRC Resolution 12/21, UNGAOR, 12th Sess, UN Doc A/HRC/RES/12/21 (2009), was sponsored by Russia and co-sponsored by Bolivia, Cuba, Algeria, Bangladesh, Belarus, Burundi, Cameroon, Chad, China, Djibouti, Egypt, Ethiopia, Gabon, Iran,

The United States has led the trend towards the reassertion of sovereignty in relation to investment treaties, confirming that a more nuanced analysis of the North-South narrative is necessary:

Critics of "hegemonic" international law, and particularly of economic legal regimes such as the IMF or that governing investment, would have not predicted that the world's leading capital exporter, the state that has the most to gain from enhancing international protections for foreign investors, that has done the most to dismantle the Calvo doctrine that once barred investors from resorting to any forum other than local courts, and that produced the most investor-protective BIT in existence, would be leading the drive in the opposite direction.[133]

One positive outcome of the UPR mechanism is that it provides evidence that while there are some significant differences in how the OECD and G-77 states approach the UPR (OECD states tend to use "harder" recommendations), more democratic states tend to use the UPR more actively, irrespective of region.[134] This is consistent with other research regarding the engagement of states with UN treaty bodies.[135]

Given the problems and uncertainties surrounding more interventionist approaches to implementing universal human rights norms, a voluntary and non-coercive approach such as peer review takes on added appeal. The UPR mechanism is, by its global approach and particular methodology, a forum and a tool that provides space for a more empirically based approach that attenuates North-South differences regarding human rights. Being public and transparent, it meets the desirable criteria not fulfilled by other diplomatic means of implementing international rules, thus conferring some legitimacy on the mechanism. At the same time, the UPR

Kazakhstan, Kyrgyzstan, Lebanon, Madagascar, Malaysia, Morocco, Myanmar, Nigeria, Pakistan, Singapore, Sri Lanka, Syrian Arab Republic, Tunisia, Vietnam, and Zambia.

[133] Alvarez, *supra* note 117 at 36.

[134] Edward R McMahon, "Herding Cats and Sheep: Assessing State and Regional Behavior in the Universal Periodic Review of the United Nations Human Rights Council" (2010) at 1, 15, Table 5, online: UPR <http://www.upr-info.org/IMG/pdf/McMahon_Herding_Cats_and_Sheeps_July_2010.pdf>.

[135] See, for example, Eric Neumayer, "Do International Human Rights Treaties Improve Respect for Human Rights" (2005) 49 J Confl Resolution 925; Simmons, *supra* note 69.

mechanism is also consonant with arguments reaffirming the importance of sovereignty as a means of human rights protection.

PEER REVIEWS AND CONFLICT MITIGATION

The tentative, but ongoing, bridging of the universalism versus national sovereignty divide has important implications for multilateral actions promoting universal norms of human rights protection and peaceful conduct. Beginning with the 1948 adoption by states of the *Universal Declaration of Human Rights*, and especially after the dissolution of the Soviet bloc, the international community has developed a range of tools to promote human rights. In ascending interventionist order, these include: (1) international organization norm setting; (2) co-operative approaches to human rights monitoring and implementation, including peer review; (3) "naming and shaming" — that is, value-driven, country-specific critiques, typically not only by human rights NGOs and expert human rights bodies but also sometimes by governments; (4) targeted sanctions; and (5) R2P's third pillar, relating to the use of armed force for (collective) humanitarian intervention.

The latter two approaches represent, in essence, tough love, while peer review occupies the opposing bookend, reflecting a less confrontational and critical approach to nurturing respect for human rights. The more interventionist mechanisms entail greater immediate costs both for implementing states and those that are the objects of these interventions, while peer review entails lower costs for both recommending states and states being reviewed. The more intrusive forms of intervention are typically aimed at situations involving massive human rights violations, while peer review, designed to be a regular part of state-to-state interactions, deals more with the "lesser" sins of autocratic rule and lower-level human rights violations. Given the costs entailed by the more interventionist approaches, they are best left sheathed to the maximum extent possible. By contrast, peer review represents a more user-friendly methodology with a focus on institutions and policies supporting human rights on a day-to-day basis, which, if properly used, can have a prophylactic effect, promoting human rights to reduce the number of instances requiring more interventionist actions.

Expanding the scope and impact of peer review creates the potential to extend international human rights and democratic norms by mainstreaming them. As such, they can become accepted as normal and regular parts of international discourse. The international organization peer review mechanisms are, by definition, creations of the member states of the organization undertaking them. They have in common a tendency to be the products of a consensus decision-making process based on the states' own willingness to engage. This reality, in turn, means that they almost invariably rely more on the carrot of positive reinforcement and inducements rather than on the stick of punitive measures. They are not designed to be quick response mechanisms for crisis situations, but, instead, their utility lies in their preventive function in establishing conditions so crises do not arise.

The UPR and APRM both emphasize follow-up actions to be taken as a result of the review. By their consensual and largely voluntary nature, peer review mechanisms are evolutionary rather than revolutionary in nature, and it is true that limited follow-up enforcement mechanisms and deficits in political will, resources, and discipline can all be impediments. There can be a tendency to make overly rosy assessments of particular human rights or governance situations or to fail fully to address key issues. The "you scratch my back and I'll scratch yours" syndrome can act as a disincentive for states to engage energetically in peer review.

Peer review does, however, demonstrate a willingness of states to submit themselves to the examination, judgment, and recommendations of other states on how to improve human rights and/or governance performance, if the perceived costs of doing so are manageable. And the costs of not doing so are now rising, except for the small minority of incorrigible states that care little about international attitudes and actions. There is evidence that even states that are more resistant to external criticism may respond better to implementation mechanisms relying on co-operative, rather than confrontational, approaches.[136] Should the UPR and other peer review mechanisms succeed in fulfilling their promise, they could reduce the need for more interventionist approaches by deterring future human rights abuses, which, in turn, would reduce the pressure and expectations of robust R2P third-pillar interventions.

Few analysts have yet made a systematic and comprehensive connection between how peer review does, or can, contribute to preventing conflict. Preliminary evidence exists, however, suggesting possible grounds for linking peer review and conflict prevention. Indeed, the latter issue is addressed in some peer reviews. For example, a UPR recommendation from Australia to Equatorial Guinea

---

[136] Anna Spain, "Integration Matters: Rethinking the Architecture of International Dispute Resolution" (2010) 32:1 U Pennsylvania J Int'l L 1.

has called for this country to "[c]ease all forms of forced displace-ment, in accordance with the Guiding Principles on Internal Displacement of 1998."[137] Similarly, a Canadian recommendation to Sudan, which was accepted by Khartoum, stated that it should "end attacks against civilians and ... ensure unimpeded humanitar-ian access to the camps of internally displaced persons in Darfur."[138] A relevant APRM example is a recommendation to Kenya to "[d]evelop and implement coherent land policy to address land ownership, use, tenure and administration."[139] Similarly, an objective in Burkina Faso's APRM national plan of action is the "Early Warning Program: Conflict Prevention."[140] In addition, the APRM's democ-racy and good political governance theme, for example, specifically includes the mandate to "[p]revent and reduce intra- and inter-country conflicts." And the UPR human rights focus implicitly embraces conflict prevention, while many recommendations relate to causes or results of conflict.[141]

These mechanisms reflect a formal commitment of states to par-ticipate in this process. Although some participating governments may be more motivated by the appearance of participation than by its reality, states increasingly find themselves bound to com-mitments and precedents simply by engaging in the process. Such participation represents in effect a tool for enmeshing states in a heightened acceptance of international human rights norms.

Considerable thought has been given to the ways in which the international community, including international organizations, can prevent conflict.[142] There is also a modest amount of literature

[137] Office of the High Commissioner for Human Rights, *Report of the Working Group on the Universal Periodic Review: Equatorial Guinea*, 6th Sess, UN Doc A/HRC/16/13 (2010) at 20.

[138] Office of the High Commissioner for Human Rights, *Report of the Working Group on the Universal Periodic Review: Sudan*, 11th Sess, UN Doc A/HRC/18/16 (2011) at 16.

[139] Africa Peer Review Mechanism, *Country Review Report of the Republic of Kenya* (2006) at 325.

[140] Africa Peer Review Mechanism, *Country Review Report of Burkina Faso* (2008) at 400.

[141] Some related issues in UPR recommendations include asylum seekers, corrup-tion, counter-terrorism, detention conditions, enforced disappearances, extra-judicial executions, freedom of association and of the press, extra-judicial human rights violations by state agents, and internally displaced people.

[142] For a seminal report on this subject, see Carnegie Commission on Preventing Deadly Conflict, *Preventing Deadly Conflict: Final Report* (Washington DC: Carnegie Corporation, 1997).

on how peer reviews may do so.[143] The Zimbabwean scholar-activist Webster Zambara argues that one of the greatest shifts in the international humanitarian order heralded by the end of the Cold War in 1990 has been the concept of holding state sovereignty accountable to international human rights standards. He suggests that while the concept of R2P has generally focused on humanitarian intervention at a macro level, "the period since the 1990s has also witnessed an increase of micro-level institutions, in the form of National Human Rights Institutions (NHRIs) that can advance R2P."[144] NHRIs also figure prominently in the UPR process.

In discussing the "enabling environment" surrounding the R2P concept, Dorota Gierycz has cited the existence of

[v]arious protection tools available within the UN human rights machinery, in particular the Human Rights Council with its new Universal Periodic Review (UPR) system and the special procedures, and the OHCHR, with its extensive field presence tasked with public reporting and support to national protection systems and public defenders. It concludes that those tools could play a much stronger role in preventing and addressing atrocities — through timely provision of information, early warning or thorough analysis of protection conditions in various countries.[145]

Mark Malan has drawn a link between the APRM and conflict prevention, suggesting that in the African context, "in terms of long-term conflict prevention and early warning, it is the political and governance component of the New Partnership for Africa Development (NEPAD) peer review that holds most promise."[146]

---

143 See, for example, Fabrizio Pagani, "Peer Review: A Tool for Cooperation and Change—An Analysis of the OECD Working Method" (2002) OECD Secretary General, online: <http://www.oecd.org/dataoecd/33/16/1955285.pdf>; Ross Herbert and Steven Gruzd, *The African Peer Review Mechanism: Lessons from the Pioneers* (Johannesburg, South Africa: South African Institute for International Affairs, 2008); Marie Chene and Gillian Dell, "Comparative Assessment of Anti-Corruption Conventions' Review Mechanisms: U4 Expert Answer," *Transparency International* (2008), online: <http://www.u4.no/publications/comparative-assessment-of-anti-corruption-conventions-review-mechanisms/downloadasset/369>.

144 Jeremy Sarkin and Mark Paterson, "Africa's Responsibility to Protect: Introduction" (2010) 2:4 Global Responsibility to Protect 339 at 352.

145 Dorota Gierycz, *NUPI Report: The Responsibility to Protect: A Legal and Rights-Based Perspective* (Oslo, Norway: Norwegian Institute of International Affairs, 2008).

146 Mark Malan, "Conflict Prevention in Africa: Theoretical Construct or Plan of Action? KAIPTC Paper 3 (2005) at 6. at 14, online: <http://www.kaiptc.org/Publications/Occasional-Papers/Documents/no_3.aspx>.

CONCLUSION: PEER REVIEW AS A MIDDLE GROUND BETWEEN
UNIVERSALISM AND NATIONAL SOVEREIGNTY

This article has presented the traditional universalist versus cultural relativist human rights divide and suggests that a middle path may be emerging. Against this backdrop, we have outlined the toolbox of international efforts designed to actualize universal norms. Viewing this array of mechanisms as a continuum from voluntary to coercive measures, we argue that the more collaborative approaches that minimize confrontation may have, over the long term, the salutary effect of attenuating arguments that national sovereignty shields countries from implementing universal norms.

A key mechanism for navigating these challenges is that of peer review, whereby states agree to have their conduct scrutinized by their peers. This emphasis carries practical policy implications for international organizations and national governments alike — namely that support for peer review should be enhanced and that priority should be given to increasing its effectiveness. This preventative approach has the potential to reduce the need for more interventionist and coercive measures. It can also help to further minimize the civil and political versus economic, social, and cultural rights divide by including both sets of rights within its purview. This more collaborative and less confrontational approach to improving human rights observance calls to mind the adage that it is easier to catch bees with honey than vinegar, although some circumstances will undoubtedly continue to warrant the stronger dosage.

The preparation of state reports for the UPR and the interactive dialogue can be particularly useful as a tool to identify and blend different sets of social values at the universal level.[147] The UPR has the potential to showcase existing or emerging customary law, shedding light on state practice and the validity of arguments normally sustained by those taking either side of the universalist/relativist debate.[148] The UPR and the APRM can be seen as manifestations of the internationalization of human rights and evidence that human rights compliance and domestic implementation have permeated the agendas of all of the governments of the world, particularly when engaging in institutionalized fora as the UN Human Rights Council. From early international efforts to create a regime that would ban slavery, plant the seed of minority protection, and develop modern international humanitarian law to initiatives to establish a

[147] Tomuschat, *supra* note 75 at 71.

[148] Domínguez-Redondo, *supra* note 10 at 703-5.

means of prosecuting individuals for atrocities against humanity,[149] the introduction of peer review mechanisms reveals a maturity achieved by the human rights machinery within international law and politics. Being on the agenda of every foreign affairs ministry, states have started to treat human rights compliance as they would other topics in their international portfolio — that is, by using diplomatic mechanisms in addition to legal, expert-led mechanisms. The results so far suggest that states are more willing to engage with a more "political" means of dealing with international human rights matters. At the same time, a key characteristic of the UPR is that it is a public process, where the influence of civil society and other human rights bodies has considerable weight.

There is evidence that states are not particularly committed to the enforcement of human rights in other jurisdictions. This has been attributed to the particularities of human rights enforcement, which is reliant on collective action, and could be a feature held in common with other fields where reciprocity plays a limited role. Conversely, other international rules governed by the regime of reciprocity have been more successful in terms of compliance.[150] Karl Zemanek concludes that institutional mechanisms of implementation (namely reporting, inspection, verification, and investigation systems, complaint procedures, and non-violent sanctions) in the fields of human rights law, environmental law, arms control, and disarmament law, "although they may indirectly encourage compliance, are not effective means for enforcing the *erga omnes* obligations deriving from these regimes."[151]

If nothing else, the UPR has proven successful in engaging all states in its process, participating not only to defend their own human rights record but also to understand and interrogate (or support) that of every other state. This article does not suggest that peer review mechanisms should, by definition, replace other, more confrontational, legal-based approaches. Different strategies can be mutually supportive, and treaties play an important role in the promotion of human rights. Without the kind of principled guidance offered in international treaties, efforts could become dissipated, actors could work at cross-purposes, and the coherent

[149] Paul Gordon Lauren, *The Evolution of International Human Rights* (Philadelphia, PA: University of Pennsylvania Press, 2003).

[150] Eric A Posner, "Human Rights, the Laws of War and Reciprocity" (2013) 6:2 Law & Ethics of Human Rights 147.

[151] Zemanek, *supra* note 109 at 16.

message of the priority of rights observance could become garbled. Treaties do not guarantee clarity, and there is much room to disagree on the proper interpretation of their content. However, in their absence, it would be much harder for all actors concerned to target the promotion of human rights, condition trade agreements in a coherent way, or have any yardstick to engage in a meaningful review of states under peer review mechanisms.[152]

Peer review processes are works in progress, but they possess the potential to enmesh states within a web of heightened respect for universal human rights norms, thus preventing conflict. A longer-term perspective suggests that peer review represents a potentially inexorable dynamic. The slow-grinding operation of national and international bureaucracies has a good chance, over time, of shifting the debate and creating a "new normal" in terms of international standards of domestic political behaviour. Peer review scrutinizes the domestic affairs of states, blunting the traditional concept of sovereign independence — governments that have agreed to join cannot avoid review by claiming that matters in their countries are not open to scrutiny. And governments increasingly are coming under pressure from international financial institutions, other international organizations, fellow governments, and domestic public opinion to participate. Standing aloof now carries a stigma that governments have something to hide or are otherwise seeking to shield authoritarian tendencies from public view. This perception, in turn, can have deleterious effects on aid, trade, and other aspects of bilateral and multilateral relations. No longer are only serious international crimes to be made open to review. Peer review also serves to empower domestic voices in favour of human rights promotion and protection by providing tangible evidence of the interest of the international community in these issues and by spotlighting these human rights defenders, providing to some extent a protective shield for their activities.[153]

---

[152] Simmons, *supra* note 69 at 375.

[153] See, for example, the remarks of Laura Laserre, president of the Human Rights Council, "Closing Comments, UPR Report of Bahrain, 13th Universal Periodic Review," Webcast (News and Media, United Nations Webcast, 25 May 2012), online: <http://www.unmultimedia.org/tv/webcast/2012/05/closing-comments-upr-report-of-bahrain-13th-universal-periodic-review.html>.

Sommaire

Les mécanismes d'évaluation par les pairs, tels l'Examen Périodique Universel, s'appuient sur la diplomatie traditionnelle entre États souverains comme moyen contemporain d'assurer la mise en œuvre des droits de la personne. Cet article soutient qu'il s'agit d'un développement positif pour plusieurs raisons. Tout d'abord, sur le plan théorique, il révèle une maturation du régime des droits de la personne par sa capacité de se détacher des approches exclusivement juridiques pour la mise en œuvre de ces droits. Deuxièmement, au niveau politique, il y a suffisamment de preuves de résultats positifs attribuables aux mécanismes d'examen par les pairs pour soutenir une préférence pour cette approche plus coopérative comme mesure préalable et complémentaire à d'autres moyens plus controversés, telles des approches juridiques ou interventionnistes (par exemple, le troisième pilier du concept de la responsabilité de protéger). Enfin, les mécanismes d'examen par les pairs offrent un cadre théorique et pragmatique pour concilier les approches conceptuelles universalistes et relativistes aux droits de la personne, servant à satisfaire à la fois ceux qui préconisent le respect du droit international des droits de la personne et ceux mettant l'accent sur le respect de la souveraineté étatique.

Summary

Peer review mechanisms, such as the Universal Periodic Review, rely upon traditional sovereign state diplomacy for contemporary human rights implementation. This article argues that this is a positive development for several reasons. First, at a theoretical level, it reveals an evolving maturity of the human rights regime through its capacity to detach from exclusively legalistic approaches to human rights implementation. Second, at a policy level, there is enough evidence of measured positive outcomes of peer review mechanisms to suggest a preference for more co-operative approaches to ensuring human rights compliance as a first and complementary step to other more controversial legal/adversarial means of implementation (such as the third pillar of the R2P concept). Finally, peer review mechanisms offer a theoretical and pragmatic framework conciliating between universalist and relativist conceptual approaches to human rights, accommodating and integrating views that call for compliance with international human rights law as well as those emphasizing respect for sovereignty.

La révision de 2012 de l'Accord de l'OMC sur les marchés publics: son contexte et les dimensions de son champ d'application

PHILIPPE PELLETIER

INTRODUCTION

Les marchés publics représentent généralement une proportion très importante de l'économie des États, de 15 pour cent à 20 pour cent du PIB national.[1] Ils permettent aux gouvernements de fournir au public des infrastructures primordiales pour le développement d'un pays, comme les réseaux routiers, les ports, les aéroports, les hôpitaux et les systèmes d'égouts, ainsi que des services publics essentiels sur le plan social, comme l'éducation et les soins

Philippe Pelletier, avocat, Canada (Québec), et juriste, division de la propriété intellectuelle (DPI), Secrétariat de l'OMC. Le présent document a été produit par son auteur et les opinions qui y sont exposées revêtent un caractère exclusivement personnel. Elles ne sauraient être considérées comme reflétant la position de l'OMC, ou celle de ses membres ou de son secrétariat. L'auteur tient aussi à remercier pour leurs conseils et encouragements Robert D Anderson, conseiller et chef d'équipe chargé des marchés publics et de la politique de la concurrence, DPI, Secrétariat de l'OMC, et Charles-Emmanuel Côté, docteur en droit et professeur agrégé à la faculté de droit de l'Université Laval. L'auteur est également reconnaissant envers Kodjo Osei-Lah, conseiller, DPI, Secrétariat de l'OMC, pour des discussions utiles sur des questions sous-jacentes.

[1] Les marchés publics se réfèrent généralement à l'achat de marchandises, de services généraux et de services de construction par ou pour le compte d'organismes gouvernementaux. OCDE, "La taille des marchés publics" (12 mars 2002), en ligne: OCDE <http://www.oecd.org/dataoecd/34/19/1845948.pdf>. Voir également Robert D Anderson et al, "Assessing the Value of Future Accessions to the WTO Agreement on Government Procurement (GPA): Some New Data Sources, Provisional Estimates, and an Evaluative Framework for Individual WTO Members Considering Accession" (2012) 21 PPLR 4. Une version antérieure de cet article a été publiée en tant que document de travail de l'OMC, ERSD-2011-15, (2011): <http://www.wto.org/french/res_f/reser_f/ersd201115_f.htm>.

de santé.[2] Ces marchés étant exclus du champ d'application des principales règles commerciales multilatérales de l'OMC, ils sont essentiellement régulés ou réglementés au niveau mondial par l'*Accord sur les marchés publics* de l'OMC (*AMP*).[3]

Au cours des dernières années, l'importance de cet Accord s'est accrue à la fois pour libéraliser les marchés publics et pour assurer une bonne gouvernance.[4] Dans le contexte de la crise économique et de l'augmentation des dépenses publiques consacrées aux infrastructures, son envergure et son efficacité ont été réaffirmées par certains pays désireux de relancer leur économie nationale. L'Accord a joué un rôle décisif durant cette période en protégeant les marchés publics couverts de certaines politiques protectionnistes qui auraient pu se transformer en guerre commerciale.[5]

Aujourd'hui, l'Accord est sur le point de prendre un nouvel envol, puisque les négociations dont il faisait l'objet ont abouti à la fin de l'année 2011. De fait, une entente de principe mettant fin à plus de dix ans de négociations a été entérinée à Genève le 15 décembre 2011, lors de la huitième Conférence ministérielle de l'OMC.[6] Les résultats corrigés des négociations ont été formellement adoptés

---

[2] Voir, pour une analyse de l'importance de politiques saines en matière de marchés publics et de la concurrence afin de favoriser l'innovation et l'accès aux technologies médicales: Anna Caroline Müller et Philippe Pelletier, "Competition Policy and Government Procurement: Two Missing Links in the Debate on Public Health" (à venir) document de travail de l'OMC.

[3] *Accord sur les marchés publics*, annexe 4B de l'*Accord de Marrakech instituant l'Organisation mondiale du commerce* (15 avril 1994), 1915 RTNU 104 (entrée en vigueur: 1er janvier 1996) [*AMP* 1994]. L'*AMP* est un accord plurilatéral, ce qui signifie que seuls les membres qui y ont souscrit y sont liés. Actuellement, 43 membres sont visés par l'Accord. L'*AMP* ne s'applique *pas* automatiquement à tous les marchés publics des Parties à l'Accord. Au contraire, son champ d'application est déterminé, pour chaque Partie, dans les annexes de l'Appendice I de l'*AMP*. Les principes fondamentaux de l'Accord sont la non-discrimination, la transparence et l'équité procédurale. Les principaux éléments contenus dans l'*AMP* servent à garantir l'application effective de ces trois principes.

[4] Voir, pour une analyse des récents développements et défis futurs entourant l'*AMP*, Sue Arrowsmith et Robert D Anderson, dir, *The WTO Regime on Government Procurement: Challenge and Reform*, Cambridge, University Press, 2011.

[5] Le directeur général de l'OMC Pascal Lamy, allocution d'ouverture, Symposium de l'OMC sur l'AMP, présentée à Genève, 11 février 2010, en ligne: OMC <http://www.wto.org/french/news_f/sppl_f/sppl147_f.htm>.

[6] OMC, Réunion au niveau ministériel du Comité des marchés publics (tenue le 15 décembre 2011), *Décision sur les résultats des négociations au titre de l'article XXIV:7 de l'Accord sur les marchés publics*, GPA/112 (2011), en ligne: OMC <http://docsonline.wto.org> [Réunion ministérielle].

par les Parties le 30 mars 2012.[7] Plus récemment, le 6 avril 2014, l'*AMP* révisé est officiellement entré en vigueur.[8]

La conclusion de ces négociations, qui ne faisaient pas partie du Cycle de Doha, est importante pour plusieurs raisons.[9] D'abord et avant tout, elle apporte des avantages substantiels à toutes les Parties en ce qui concerne l'accès aux marchés. L'élargissement de la portée de l'*AMP* résultant de la conclusion des négociations a été estimé par le Secrétariat de l'OMC à la hauteur de 80 à 100 milliards de dollars US, propulsant ainsi la portée globale de l'*AMP* révisé à des sommets historiques (évaluée à environ 1 700 milliards de dollars US).[10] Ces gains d'accès aux marchés publics des Parties résultent essentiellement du fait que de nouvelles entités contractantes ont

---

[7] OMC, Réunion formelle des Parties à l'Accord de l'OMC sur les marchés publics tenue à Genève pour les chefs de délégation (tenue le 30 mars 2011), *Adoption des résultats des négociations au titre de l'article XXIV:7 de l'Accord sur les marchés publics, après leur vérification et examen, comme il est prescrit au paragraphe 5 de la Décision ministérielle du 15 décembre 2011 (GPA/112)*, GPA/113 (2012), en ligne: OMC <http://docsonline.wto.org> [*Décision du Comité adoptant les résultats des négociations au titre de l'AMP 1994*].

[8] *Protocole portant amendement de l'Accord sur les marchés publics*, 30 mars 2012 (entrée en vigueur: 6 avril 2014) [*AMP révisé*]. L'*AMP révisé* est entré en vigueur le 6 avril 2014 pour les dix Parties suivantes: (1) Canada; (2) Union européenne; (3) Hong Kong, Chine; (4) Islande; (5) Israël; (6) Liechtenstein; (7) Norvège; (8) Singapour; (9) Taipei chinois et (10) les États-Unis. Il est entré en vigueur pour le Japon le 16 avril 2014 et pour les Pays-Bas pour le compte d'Aruba le 4 juin 2014. Par la suite, l'*AMP* révisé entrera en vigueur pour les trois Parties restantes (l'Arménie, la Corée et la Suisse) le trentième jour suivant la date de dépôt de leur instrument d'acceptation. *Ibid*, voir paragraphe 2 de la Décision et paragraphe 3 du Protocole.

[9] Voir, pour une discussion sur la conclusion des négociations, Robert D Anderson, "The Conclusion of the Renegotiation of the WTO Agreement on Government Procurement: What It Means for the Agreement and for the World Economy" (2012) 21 PPLR 83.

[10] Il convient de noter que chacune des Parties à l'AMP ne bénéficiera pas nécessairement de la totalité de cette extension du champ d'application de l'Accord, car des dérogations propres à chaque Partie peuvent s'appliquer dans certains cas. Voir OMC, *Rapport annuel 2012 de l'OMC* (2012), à la p 25, en ligne: OMC <http://www.wto.org/french/res_f/booksp_f/anrep_f/anrep12_f.pdf>; voir également OMC, Comité sur les marchés publics, *Rapport (2012) du Comité des marchés publics*, GPA/116, en ligne: OMC <http://docsonline.wto.org> [*Rapport (2012) du Comité*]. La portée de l'*AMP 1994* a été évaluée à environ 1 600 milliards de dollars US pour 2008. Le bureau du Représentant américain au commerce, communiqué, "The WTO Government Procurement Agreement: A Tremendous Opportunity for China" (non daté), en ligne: <http://shenyang.usembassy-china.org.cn/wto-gpa.html>.

été adjointes aux engagements des Parties, ainsi que de nouveaux services et marchandises, et qu'on y a inclus de nouvelles formes de passation de marchés publics, comme les arrangements construction-exploitation-transfert (CET).[11]

De plus, bien que la conclusion de l'*AMP* révisé insuffle un élan vigoureux à l'ouverture des marchés, elle ne constitue pas la fin du processus visant à libéraliser les marchés publics. Au contraire, la conclusion des négociations permettra aux Parties d'engager un nouveau cycle de négociations ayant comme point de départ un ensemble de nouveaux programmes de travail du Comité sur les marchés publics qui traiteront de questions n'ayant pu être résolues lors des négociations précédentes, comme la participation des petites et moyennes entreprises aux marchés publics visés par l'Accord, et les considérations en matière d'approvisionnement public durable. Ces questions ont fait l'objet de décisions spécifiques du Comité et elles seront abordées lors de ces travaux.[12]

Ensuite, la conclusion des négociations permet de faire entrer en vigueur le texte révisé et amélioré de l'Accord. Cette version modernise effectivement le texte de l'*AMP*, notamment en instaurant des normes relatives à l'utilisation des moyens électroniques de passation de marchés publics. De plus, avec ses flexibilités supplémentaires pour les pays en développement, le texte révisé devrait faciliter l'adhésion à l'*AMP* de membres de l'OMC qui ne sont pas déjà signataires. À cet égard, la liste des Parties à l'Accord s'allonge et un large éventail de membres de l'OMC, dont la Chine, envisage actuellement d'accéder à l'*AMP* (*voir Encadré 1 pour la liste des Parties à l'AMP*). La valeur de nouvelles adhésions est loin d'être négligeable et pourrait représenter plusieurs milliards de dollars en gains d'accès aux marchés. À titre d'exemple, un document de travail de l'OMC a estimé que l'adhésion à l'*AMP* par un certain nombre de membres de l'OMC pourrait résulter en gains d'accès aux marchés représentant chaque année entre 440 et 1 227 milliards de dollars US.[13]

---

[11] L'augmentation du champ d'application est aussi le résultat des ajouts suivants: (1) l'abaissement des valeurs de seuil par certaines Parties; (2) l'élimination progressive complète par une Partie (Israël) de son régime d'opérations de compensation et (3) l'élimination de plusieurs mesures et pratiques discriminatoires qui étaient incluses dans les engagements des Parties sous l'*AMP*. Rapport (2012) du Comité, *ibid*, au para 7. Pour une discussion plus détaillée sur les améliorations du champ d'application, voir section 2 ci-dessous.

[12] *Décision du Comité adoptant les résultats des négociations au titre de l'AMP 1994*, *supra* note 7. Voir section 1.

[13] Voir Anderson et al, *supra* note 1.

ENCADRÉ 1: LES PARTIES À L'AMP ET LES DIFFÉRENTS
PROCESSUS D'ADHÉSION À L'ACCORD

L'*AMP* est un accord plurilatéral, ce qui signifie que seuls les membres qui y ont souscrit y sont liés. Actuellement, les quarante-trois membres de l'OMC visés par l'Accord sont les suivants: l'Arménie; le Canada; la Corée; les États-Unis; Hong Kong, Chine; l'Islande; Israël; le Japon; le Liechtenstein; le Royaume des Pays-Bas pour le compte d'Aruba; la Norvège; Singapour; la Suisse; le Taipei chinois et l'Union européenne, y compris ses 28 États membres. Parmi les adhésions récentes à l'Accord, celle de la Croatie a pris effet le 1er juillet 2013 (par son adhésion à l'Union européenne), celle de l'Arménie le 15 septembre 2011 et celle du Taipei chinois en juillet 2009. De plus, le Monténégro et la Nouvelle-Zélande deviendront les prochaines parties à l'AMP, car leurs demandes d'adhésion ont abouti le 29 octobre 2014.

En dehors des Parties actuelles à l'Accord, 15 autres membres de l'OMC ont (i) déjà entamé leur processus d'accession à l'*AMP* (par exemple, la Chine, la Nouvelle-Zélande, le Monténégro, la Moldavie et l'Ukraine);[14] ou (ii) pris des engagements pour accéder à l'*AMP* par leur protocole d'accession respectif à l'OMC.[15] Les derniers pays à avoir pris de tels engagements sont la Fédération de Russie, le Monténégro et le Tadjikistan, qui se sont engagés à accéder à l'*AMP* au cours des trois dernières années. Ces membres sont à différentes étapes de leur processus d'accession.[16] Ceux de la Chine, de la Moldavie et de l'Ukraine font actuellement

---

[14] Les autres membres de l'OMC ayant déjà entamé leur processus d'accession à l'AMP sont les suivants: l'Albanie, la Géorgie, la Jordanie, le Sultanat d'Oman et la République kirghize.

[15] Les cinq membres s'étant engagés à accéder à l'AMP sont les suivants: (1) l'ancienne République yougoslave de Macédoine; (2) la Mongolie; (3) le Royaume d'Arabie saoudite; (4) la Fédération de Russie et (5) le Tadjikistan.

[16] Voir, pour une discussion plus détaillée sur l'état d'avancement des différents processus d'adhésion, OMC, *Comité sur les marchés publics, Rapport (2013) du Comité des marchés publics*, GPA/121, en ligne: OMC <http://docsonline.wto.org> [*Rapport (2013) du Comité*].

l'objet d'une attention toute particulière. En ce qui concerne la Chine, son processus d'accession s'est intensifié et elle a soumis, à la fin 2013, une nouvelle offre révisée pour accéder à l'*AMP*. De plus, elle s'est engagée à soumettre une nouvelle offre révisée en 2014 et à rendre sa législation nationale conforme aux prescriptions de l'*AMP* (surtout concernant son initiative quant à l'innovation autochtone).

Cette conclusion constitue un bel exemple d'une négociation qui apporte des avantages considérables non seulement à ses Parties, mais aussi au système commercial multilatéral en général. La crédibilité de ce système est désormais renforcée, surtout par rapport aux difficultés entourant la conclusion du Cycle de Doha,[17] car la conclusion des négociations de l'*AMP* a démontré que l'OMC peut produire des résultats significatifs et mener à terme des négociations. Plusieurs ministres des Parties à l'*AMP* ont mis l'accent sur ce point. Par exemple, l'ancien représentant américain au commerce, Ron Kirk, a dit que

la décision du Comité d'approuver les résultats des négociations sur l'*AMP* était aussi très importante pour l'OMC en tant qu'institution. Elle démontrait la capacité de l'Organisation – à force de persévérance et de travail acharné accompli dans un esprit de collaboration – à conclure des accords qui renforçaient et clarifiaient les règles et à multiplier les débouchés par le biais de l'accès aux marchés. Les États-Unis espéraient vivement que cette avancée aurait un effet accélérateur sur d'autres dossiers en négociation à l'OMC.[18]

---

[17] Le Cycle de Doha de négociations commerciales entre les membres de l'OMC a été lancé officiellement à la quatrième conférence ministérielle de l'OMC, tenue à Doha (Qatar), en novembre 2001. Il vise à réformer en profondeur le système commercial international en réduisant les obstacles au commerce et certaines règles commerciales révisées. Le programme de travail comprend environ 20 domaines. Voir OMC, *Programme de travail de Doha*, OMC Conseil général, OMC Doc WT/L/579 (2004); OMC, *Déclaration ministérielle*, OMC Doc WT/MIN(01)/DEC/1 (2001), 4ᵉ sess.

[18] OMC, Comité des marchés publics, *Compte rendu de la réunion formelle au niveau ministériel* (tenue le 15 décembre 2011), GPA/M/45 (2012), aux para 20 et 25, en ligne: OMC <http://docsonline.wto.org>.

Un autre événement a contribué de manière considérable à accroître l'importance de l'*AMP* au niveau mondial (outre la conclusion des négociations): l'augmentation des accords commerciaux bilatéraux et régionaux (ACR) libéralisant les marchés publics. En particulier, un nombre élevé et croissant d'ACR a utilisé l'*AMP* comme modèle pour libéraliser les marchés publics (*voir Encadré 2*).[19] En pratique, cette tendance a pour effet d'étendre la portée des principes de l'*AMP* bien au-delà des Parties actuelles à l'Accord. Cette convergence des normes dans le secteur des marchés publics au niveau international rend également possible une expansion importante des membres de l'*AMP* (dans l'éventualité où les pays appliquant des règles similaires à l'*AMP* décideraient d'y accéder).

Encadré 2: Traitement des marchés publics dans les accords commerciaux régionaux

Des études récentes ont permis de fournir des informations pertinentes sur le traitement des marchés publics dans les accords commerciaux régionaux.[20] Les découvertes principales de ces analyses sont les suivantes: premièrement, dans le cas des ACR contenant des dispositions détaillées sur les marchés publics, le texte de l'*AMP* 1994 (et, plus récemment, le texte révisé de l'*AMP*) a manifestement servi de modèle pour les chapitres pertinents, avec des exceptions occasionnelles et sporadiques. Cette tendance se révèle tant pour les accords impliquant les Parties à l'*AMP* que pour ceux engageant des non-Parties. Cela veut dire que plusieurs pays se sont déjà engagés dans les faits, tout en étant actuellement à l'extérieur de l'*AMP* (par exemple, les principaux pays en développement d'Amérique latine), à mettre en œuvre au

---

[19] Voir, par exemple, Anderson et al, "Government procurement provisions in regional trade agreements: a stepping stone to GPA accession?" dans Arrowsmith et Anderson, *supra* note 4 au ch 20 aux pp 561-656; Robert D Anderson, Anna Caroline Müller, et Philippe Pelletier, "Government Procurement Provisions in Recent regional Trade Agreements: Characterization, Analysis and Implications vis-à-vis the WTO Agreement on Government Procurement" (à venir) document de travail de l'OMC.

[20] *Ibid.*

niveau national des disciplines manifestement influencées par l'*AMP*.

Deuxièmement, en comparant les engagements d'accès au marché dans les ACR avec ceux de l'*AMP*, on constate que ce dernier sert aussi de modèle. C'est particulièrement vrai pour les ACR conclus entre Parties à l'*AMP*, et entre Parties et non-Parties à l'*AMP*. Certains ACR conclus entre non-Parties à l'*AMP* ont même utilisé l'*AMP* comme modèle pour définir et structurer leurs engagements.

Dans l'ensemble, les auteurs de ces études concluent que la coexistence de l'*AMP* avec les dispositions concernant les marchés publics dans les ACR entraîne relativement peu d'effets négatifs (ou d'effets "bol de spaghetti"), auxquels on fait souvent référence par exemple dans le contexte des consolidations tarifaires relatives au commerce des marchandises qui divergent entre les accords, sur le plan bilatéral/régional et sur le plan multilatéral.

L'un des objectifs principaux du présent document consiste à clarifier et à rendre plus accessible le champ d'application de l'*AMP* révisé. En effet, malgré une certaine simplification résultant de la conclusion des négociations, cette partie de l'*AMP* demeure particulièrement technique et complexe. Une telle démarche pourrait s'avérer utile pour déterminer les possibilités d'accès aux marchés découlant de l'*AMP* révisé. Les débouchés à l'exportation sont aussi susceptibles d'intéresser les fournisseurs des autres membres de l'OMC ayant pour objectif d'accéder à l'Accord.

Ce document est divisé en deux sections. La première débute en décrivant les principaux éléments de l'Accord révisé, ainsi que les événements marquants de l'histoire des négociations internationales visant à libéraliser les marchés publics, pour ensuite présenter — d'une façon générale — les principaux éléments du texte de l'*AMP* révisé. La seconde section aborde la portée de l'Accord révisé sur les marchés publics en traitant des éléments du texte ayant des conséquences pour l'accès aux marchés, ainsi que des principes fondamentaux liés au champ d'application de l'Accord. Elle présente ensuite une analyse approfondie de l'Appendice I de l'*AMP*, incluant les listes d'engagements des Parties.

Afin d'expliquer certains aspects de l'*AMP* révisé, sur lesquels pratiquement aucun écrit scientifique n'a encore été publié, nous avons privilégié dans le présent document une approche à caractère essentiellement descriptif.

L'ABOUTISSEMENT DE PLUS DE 65 ANS DE NÉGOCIATIONS

L'HISTOIRE SANS FIN DES NÉGOCIATIONS INTERNATIONALES VISANT À LIBÉRALISER LES MARCHÉS PUBLICS

Il y a plus de 65 ans commençait une longue série de négociations visant à établir un cadre multilatéral efficace en matière de marchés publics et à parvenir à un accroissement de leur libéralisation. En décembre 2011, le dernier cycle de ces négociations, dont l'*AMP* faisait l'objet, s'est conclu au niveau international. Bien que cette conclusion constitue une avancée importante et que la liste des Parties à l'*AMP* n'ait jamais été aussi longue, elle ne constitue pas la fin des négociations visant à libéraliser les marchés publics. Au contraire, cette conclusion permet aussi d'entamer un nouveau cycle de négociations en vue de libéraliser encore davantage les marchés publics et d'améliorer l'Accord.

La nécessité pour les Parties à l'*AMP* de négocier de façon quasi permanente une plus grande libéralisation découle de l'histoire des négociations précédentes sur les marchés publics, et en particulier des lacunes laissées dans la portée de l'Accord par les cycles antérieurs des négociations. Afin de bien comprendre cette nécessité de négocier de façon quasi permanente une libéralisation accrue des marchés publics, ainsi que la structure et la complexité du champ d'application de l'*AMP*, il convient d'examiner succinctement les principaux cycles de négociations internationaux sur les marchés publics.

Les principaux cycles de négociations qui seront abordés dans cette section sont les suivants: (i) les balbutiements à l'OIC et le *GATT* de 1947; (ii) la nouvelle tentative au sein de l'OCDE; (iii) la conclusion de l'*AMP* du Cycle de Tokyo; (iv) l'*AMP* de 1994 et les négociations lors du Cycle de l'Uruguay; et (v) la révision de l'*AMP* 1994 et l'adoption de l'*AMP* révisé en 2012.

Les balbutiements: l'OIC et le GATT 1947

La première vraie tentative pour inclure les marchés publics dans les négociations commerciales multilatérales a eu lieu autour de

1945, dans le cadre des négociations entourant l'Organisation internationale du commerce (OIC).[21] Les États-Unis avaient alors proposé, dans leur projet initial de Charte de l'OIC, de soumettre les marchés publics aux obligations de traitement national et de la nation la plus favorisée (NPF).[22] L'idée générale de cette proposition consistait à éliminer la discrimination entre les marchandises des États signataires, dans l'attribution des marchés publics. Finalement, quoique cette idée ait fait l'objet de négociations intensives, les marchés publics ont été très largement exclus de l'accord final.[23] Néanmoins, bien que l'OIC n'ait jamais vu le jour, une partie des résultats des négociations de la Charte de l'OIC apparaîtra sous la forme de l'*Accord général sur les tarifs douaniers et le commerce* de 1947 (*GATT*), mais les marchés publics resteront largement exclus de cet accord.[24]

En particulier, alors que le *GATT* 1947 contient des obligations générales relatives au traitement national et de la nation la plus favorisée, les marchés publics sont exclus de ces obligations. Tout d'abord, l'article III (8) du *GATT* 1947 exclut de façon explicite les marchés publics de la clause du traitement national.[25] La

---

[21] Annet Blank et Gabrielle Marceau, "The History of the Government Procurement Negotiations Since 1945" (1996) 5 PPLR 77; Sue Arrowsmith, *Government Procurement in the WTO*, The Hague, Kluwer Law International, 2003 aux pp 31-32.

[22] Blank et Marceau, *supra* note 21 aux pp 79-88.

[23] Arrowsmith, *supra* note 21 à la p 32; *Charte de La Havane instituant une organisation internationale du commerce*, dans Acte final de la Conférence des Nations Unies sur le commerce et l'emploi, 24 mars 1948, RT Can 1948 n°32 à la p 3 (jamais entrée en vigueur).

[24] *Accord général sur les tarifs douaniers et le commerce*, 30 octobre 1947, 55 RTNU 187 (entrée en vigueur: 1er janvier 1948) [*GATT* 1947]. La seule disposition traitant des marchés publics insérée dans le *GATT* de 1947 est l'article XVII (2) traitant des entreprises commerciales d'État qui impose, d'une façon très modeste, un effort nécessitant un traitement équitable du commerce des autres parties contractantes.

[25] Voir, pour une interprétation de l'article III (8) du *GATT* 1947, *Canada — Certaines mesures affectant le secteur de la production d'énergie renouvelable (plainte du Japon)* (2012), et *Canada — Mesures relatives au programme de tarif de rachat garantis (plainte de l'Union européenne)* (2012) OMC Doc WT/DS412/R et WT/DS426/R (Rapports des groupes spéciaux). Les groupes spéciaux ont remis les rapports sous la forme d'un document unique constituant deux rapports. *Canada — Certaines mesures affectant le secteur de la production d'énergie renouvelable (plainte du Japon)* (2013), et *Canada — Mesures relatives au programme de tarif de rachat garantis (plainte de l'Union européenne)* (2013) OMC Doc WT/DS412/AB/R et WT/DS426/AB/R (Rapports de l'Organe d'appel) aux para. 5.74-5.79. L'Organe d'appel a remis les rapports

non-application de la clause NPF du *GATT* 1947 (article I) aux marchés publics est légèrement plus controversée, car elle n'exclut pas explicitement les marchés publics. Néanmoins, il est générale-ment avancé que la clause NPF du *GATT* 1947 ne s'applique pas aux marchés publics.[26]

Nouvelle tentative au sein de l'OCDE

Il faudra attendre les années 1960 pour que reprennent les travaux sur les marchés publics au niveau international[27] et ils auront lieu dans l'enceinte de l'Organisation de coopération et de développe-ment économiques (OCDE). Même s'ils n'ont pas donné un accord définitif, ils ont joué un rôle crucial dans le développement des disciplines sur les marchés publics. En particulier, c'est dans le forum de l'OCDE qu'ont été élaborés les principes généraux et certaines règles procédurales qui formèrent la base des textes régissant les disciplines internationales sur les marchés publics.[28]

En ce qui concerne la portée d'un éventuel accord, certaines questions-clés ont été résolues à ce stade. Par exemple, il a été convenu que le champ d'application d'un accord futur serait ini-tialement limité aux entités du gouvernement central.[29] Il a égale-ment été établi que le champ d'application d'un accord futur ne serait pas fondé sur une définition commune d'entités visées par l'*AMP*, mais sur des listes spécifiques d'entités couvertes par l'Ac-cord, listes que les Parties auraient préalablement négociées et acceptées, car elles leur auraient offert des niveaux de libéralisation réciproques. En 1975, le résultat des travaux de l'OCDE a donné un projet d'instrument sur les politiques gouvernementales en

---

sous la forme d'un document unique constituant deux rapports de l'Organe d'appel distincts.

[26] L'*AMP* semble aussi basé sur les mêmes prémisses, car si la clause NPF du *GATT* 1947 devait s'appliquer aux marchés publics, les avantages d'adhérer à l'*AMP* seraient grandement réduits du fait que les membres de l'OMC, qui ne sont pas parties à l'*AMP*, pourraient bénéficier des engagements de libéralisation des Parties sous l'*AMP*, sans avoir à prendre d'engagements réciproques. Voir, pour une discussion plus détaillée sur le sujet, Arrowsmith, *supra* note 21 aux pp 61 à 63; Robert D Anderson et Sue Arrowsmith, "The WTO Regime on Government Procurement: Past, Present and Future," dans Arrowsmith et Anderson, *supra* note 4 au ch 1 à la p 6.

[27] Blank et Marceau, *supra* note 21 aux pp 31-32.

[28] *Ibid* aux pp 79-88.

[29] Arrowsmith, *supra* note 21 aux pp 31-32.

matière de marchés publics.[30] Par contre, aucun accord définitif n'a pu être conclu à cette époque, surtout à cause des désaccords entre les Parties sur les listes d'entités couvertes et les seuils d'application.

Le premier accord plurilatéral sur les marchés publics: l'AMP du Cycle de Tokyo

Ensuite, une étape marquante est survenue dans le cadre général du cycle de négociations commerciales du Cycle de Tokyo.[31] En 1976, dans le cadre de ces négociations, un sous-groupe a été créé pour travailler sur les marchés publics; on y a transféré les résultats des travaux qui avaient déjà eu lieu au sein de l'OCDE.[32] Le fait d'importer ces travaux dans ce forum de négociations commerciales — y compris le projet d'instrument sur les politiques gouvernementales en matière de marchés publics[33] — a grandement facilité les négociations, car de nombreuses questions avaient déjà été résolues entre les principaux acteurs des négociations. Le résultat final donna naissance, en 1979, au premier accord plurilatéral sur les marchés publics, appelé *l'Accord sur les marchés publics du Cycle de Tokyo* (*AMP du Cycle de Tokyo*).[34]

Bien que l'*AMP du Cycle de Tokyo* constitue une étape cruciale, il demeure extrêmement limité à bien des égards. D'une part, seulement 23 membres y ont adhéré,[35] et d'autre part, sa portée était loin

---

[30] OCDE, *Projet d'instrument relatif aux politiques, procédures et pratiques d'achats gouvernementaux* (1975).

[31] Voir, Mark L Jones, "The GATT-MTN System and the European Community as International Frameworks for the Regulation of Economic Activity: the removal of barriers to trade in Government Procurement" (1984) 8 Md J Contemp Legal Issues 53; Richard A Horsh, "Eliminating Nontariff Barriers to International Trade: the MTN Agreement on Government Procurement" (1979) 12 NYUJ Int'l L & Pol 315; Jacques HJ Bourgeois, "The Tokyo Round Agreements on Technical Barriers and on Government Procurement in International and EEC Perspective" (1982) 19 CML Rev 5.

[32] *GATT*, Note communiquée par le Secrétariat de l'OCDE, *Projet d'instrument relatif aux politiques, procédures et pratiques d'achats gouvernementaux*, MTN/NTM/W/81 (1977), en ligne: OMC <http://docsonline.wto.org>.

[33] OCDE, *supra* note 30.

[34] *Accord sur les marchés publics*, (12 avril 1979), 1235 RTNU 259 (entrée en vigueur: 1er janvier 1981) [*AMP du Cycle de Tokyo*].

[35] Les Parties de l'*AMP du Cycle de Tokyo* étaient les suivantes: Autriche; Canada; Espagne (1982); États-Unis; Finlande; Grèce (1982); Hong Kong, Chine; Japon;

d'être exhaustive. L'*AMP du Cycle de Tokyo* ne couvrait que les marchés publics de marchandises, effectués par un certain nombre d'entités du gouvernement central, comme l'indiquent les listes spécifiques d'entités préalablement négociées par les Parties.[36] Les marchés publics de services étaient exclus, tout comme les marchés publics effectués par les entités de gouvernements sous-centraux, et tout autre type d'entités. L'*AMP du Cycle de Tokyo* s'appliquait aux marchés publics d'une valeur égale ou supérieure à 150 000 droits de tirage spéciaux (DTS).

Afin de remédier aux lacunes de l'*AMP du Cycle de Tokyo*, un engagement a été pris de poursuivre les négociations, tant sur le texte de l'Accord que sur sa portée. Ainsi, l'article IX (6) (b) de l'*AMP du Cycle de Tokyo* indiquait qu'au plus tard à l'expiration d'un délai de trois ans, à compter de la date d'entrée en vigueur de l'Accord, les Parties devaient engager de nouvelles négociations en vue d'atteindre deux objectifs principaux: (i) élargir la portée de l'Accord sur une base de réciprocité mutuelle et étendre le champ d'application aux marchés publics de services; et (ii) améliorer le texte de l'Accord.[37] Les négociations visaient également à faciliter l'adhésion à l'Accord, notamment pour les pays en développement.

Ce nouveau cycle de négociations a été officiellement conclu en 1988, sans toutefois avoir totalement atteint ses objectifs. Durant ces négociations, les Parties ont mis surtout l'accent sur l'amélioration du texte de l'Accord. Il fallut attendre la conclusion du cycle de négociations suivant pour voir la portée de l'Accord s'élargir de façon considérable. Malgré tout, une amélioration a été introduite à la portée de l'AMP du Cycle de Tokyo en réduisant les seuils d'application de 150 000 DTS à 130 000 DTS. Les résultats de ces négociations ont été inclus dans le Protocole d'amendement de 1987, entré en vigueur en janvier 1988.[38]

Norvège; Singapour; Suède; Suisse; Portugal (1983) et Union européenne et ses États membres à cette époque (Allemagne, Belgique, Danemark, France, Irlande, Italie, Luxembourg, Pays-Bas et Royaume-Uni).

[36] *AMP du Cycle de Tokyo, supra* note 34, art 1.

[37] Les termes "élargir", "étendre" et "améliorer" ont pris des sens bien définis. "Élargir" visait à élargir les listes d'entités gouvernementales; "étendre" visait l'inclusion des marchés publics de service et "améliorer" visait l'amélioration du texte de l'Accord. Blank et Marceau, *supra* note 21 à la p 43.

[38] *Protocole portant modification de l'Accord sur les marchés publics* (2 février 1987), BISD 14e suppl à la p 12 (entrée en vigueur: 14 février 1988).

*L'Accord de l'OMC sur les marchés publics: les négociations
lors du Cycle d'Uruguay*

Les négociations

À partir de 1988, parallèlement aux négociations commerciales du Cycle de l'Uruguay,[39] les Parties à l'Accord ont continué à négocier.[40] Comme la majeure partie des négociations visant à améliorer le texte de l'Accord avait alors déjà été complétée, elles ont mis l'accent sur l'élargissement de la portée de l'Accord. En particulier, elles visaient à élargir les listes d'entités gouvernementales et à étendre le champ d'application aux marchés publics de services, incluant les services de construction. Ces négociations aboutirent en 1994 à l'Accord de l'OMC sur les marchés publics (l'*AMP* 1994).[41]

Un événement marquant de ces négociations fut la signature, en 1993, d'un protocole d'entente entre les États-Unis et l'Union européenne, afin de mettre fin à un différend lié à la portée de l'Accord.[42] La conclusion de ce protocole d'entente, jumelée à l'objectif général visant à conclure le cycle de négociations de l'Uruguay avant la fin de l'année 1993, eut un effet catalyseur sur les négociations. En effet, au moment où les négociations de l'*AMP* entraient dans leur phase finale, plusieurs questions en suspens ont été réglées. Par exemple, les Parties se sont mises d'accord sur le fait que les résultats des négociations prendraient la forme d'un nouvel Accord, plutôt qu'un deuxième amendement à l'AMP du Cycle de Tokyo. Il a également été convenu que le nouvel Accord serait

---

[39] Pour une discussion plus détaillée sur le cycle de négociations commerciales de l'Uruguay, voir Dominique Carreau et Patrick Juillard, *Droit international économique*, 4ᵉ éd, Paris, Dalloz, 1998 aux pp 113-33; Michael J. Trebilock et Robert Howse, *Regulation of International Trade*, 3ᵉ éd, Londres, 2005 aux pp 24-25.

[40] Gerard de Graaf et Matthew King, "Towards a More Global Government Procurement Market: The Expansion of the GATT Government Procurement Agreement in the Context of the Uruguay Round" (1995) 29 Int'l Law 435; Arrowsmith, *supra* note 21 aux pp 44-50; Blank et Marceau, *supra* note 21 à la p 43.

[41] *AMP 1994*, *supra* note 3.

[42] *Accord sous forme de mémorandum d'entente entre la Communauté économique européenne et les États-Unis d'Amérique concernant la passation de marchés publics*, (10 mai 1993), OJ (L 125) ou OJEC, L 125 [*Protocole d'entente ÉU-UE*]. Le protocole d'entente ÉU-UE contenait trois éléments principaux: (1) il ouvrait les marchés publics dans le secteur de l'électricité; (2) il prévoyait la négociation d'un accord bilatéral sur les marchés publics couverts et (3) il prévoyait le lancement d'une étude conjointe sur les valeurs des marchés publics des offres respectives des deux Parties.

plurilatéral, de sorte que l'adhésion à l'OMC n'entraînerait pas automatiquement l'adhésion à l'*AMP*.[43]

Les négociations pour le nouvel *AMP* se sont officiellement achevées le 15 décembre 1993, pour concorder avec la date définitive de l'accord général de l'ensemble du Cycle d'Uruguay de l'OMC.[44] Par contre, en pratique, il s'est avéré impossible de conclure tous les aspects des négociations liés à la portée de l'Accord avant la date butoir du 15 décembre 1993. En particulier, il restait un certain nombre de questions à régler entre les États-Unis et l'Union européenne pour ce qui est des marchés publics couverts. Les Parties ont donc décidé d'utiliser le temps disponible avant la date de signature de l'Acte final du Cycle d'Uruguay et de l'*AMP*, prévue le 15 avril 1994 à Marrakech, pour finaliser les négociations sur la portée de l'Accord.

Afin de remédier à l'impossibilité de conclure avant la date butoir du 15 décembre 1993 les négociations sur la portée de l'Accord, les Parties y ont introduit la possibilité de déroger à l'obligation de non-discrimination.[45] Cette possibilité visait à assurer un équilibre entre les droits et les obligations des Parties quant à la portée de l'Accord. Ainsi, des clauses de réciprocité, à la fois sectorielles et propres à chaque pays, et des clauses de non-application de certaines dispositions de l'Accord (par exemple, les procédures de recours internes [article XX]) ont fait leur apparition dans l'Accord. Initialement, il s'agissait d'introduire ces clauses de façon temporaire et de les éliminer avant l'entrée en vigueur de l'Accord, mais plusieurs clauses sont restées dans l'*AMP* 1994 après son entrée en vigueur.[46]

La portée de l'*AMP* 1994 a été considérablement améliorée au cours des mois précédant la signature effective de l'Accord. En particulier, une étude parue en mars 1994 sur la valeur des marchés publics des États-Unis et de l'Union européenne a joué un rôle décisif en facilitant la conclusion d'un accord bilatéral sur l'accès à leurs marchés publics respectifs.[47] Cet accord entre les États-Unis et

---

43 Blank et Marceau, *supra* note 21 à la p 48.

44 *GATT*, Comité des marchés publics, *Compte rendu de la réunion* (tenue le 15 décembre 1993), GPR/M/50, (1994), en ligne: OMC <http://docsonline.wto.org>.

45 *AMP* 1994, *supra* note 3, art III.

46 Blank et Marceau, *supra* note 21 à la p 50.

47 Les deux Parties s'étaient mises d'accord pour commander cette étude dans le cadre du Protocole d'entente entre les ÉU et l'UE de 1993. Voir *Protocole d'entente*

l'Union européenne a subséquemment été incorporé à l'*AMP* 1994. De la même manière, les résultats des négociations sur la portée de l'Accord entre d'autres Parties y ont aussi été incorporés. L'ensemble de ces ajouts a considérablement accru les marchés publics couverts par l'*AMP* 1994. Enfin, l'Accord a été signé comme convenu en avril 1994 à Marrakech, dans le cadre de l'Acte final contenant les accords conclus lors du Cycle d'Uruguay. Il est entré en vigueur le 1er janvier 1996.

Dans le contexte plus large des négociations au titre des règles multilatérales de l'OMC, il a été convenu de conserver l'exclusion des marchés publics de l'obligation de non-discrimination du *GATT* de 1947 dans le *GATT* de 1994,[48] et de permettre des exclusions similaires dans l'*Accord général sur le commerce des services* (*AGCS*).[49] Ainsi, l'article XIII (1) de l'*AGCS* exclut de façon explicite les marchés publics des principales règles de cet Accord (par exemple, des clauses du traitement national [article XVII], de la nation la plus favorisée [article II] et de l'accès aux marchés [article XVII]). Néanmoins, afin d'éviter que les marchés publics de services restent indéfiniment exclus des règles commerciales multilatérales, l'article XIII (2) de l'*AGCS* a établi un mandat de négociations multilatérales sur les marchés publics de services. Toutefois, ces négociations sont toujours en cours et il semble actuellement difficile d'imaginer une conclusion dans un futur rapproché.[50]

Résultats

L'*AMP* de 1994 améliore à plus d'un titre l'*AMP du Cycle de Tokyo*. L'amélioration-clé de l'*AMP* 1994 concerne l'élargissement considérable de la portée de l'Accord, qui a été estimé à environ 450

ÉU-UE, supra note 42; Deloitte et Touche, "Study *of Public Procurement Opportunities: European Union and Government of the United States*" (1994).

48 *Accord général sur les tarifs douaniers et le commerce de 1994*, annexe 1A de l'*Accord de Marrakech instituant l'Organisation mondiale du commerce*, 15 avril 1994, 1867 RTNU 125 (entrée en vigueur: 1er janvier 1995) [*GATT* 1994]. Voir note 24 et texte correspondant.

49 *Accord général sur le commerce des services*, annexe 1B de l'*Accord de Marrakech instituant l'Organisation mondiale du commerce* (15 avril 1994), 1869 RTNU 141 (entrée en vigueur: 1er janvier 1995) [*AGCS*].

50 Il est important de souligner que ces négociations ne sont pas directement liées aux négociations plurilatérales en vertu de l'*AMP* et qu'ainsi, elles peuvent progresser à leur propre rythme.

milliards d'ECU par an, soit environ dix fois la valeur des marchés publics qui étaient soumis à l'*AMP du Cycle de Tokyo*.[51] Ces gains d'accès aux marchés résultent principalement de l'adjonction de nouveaux types d'entités et de nouveaux secteurs aux engagements des Parties, sous l'*AMP du Cycle de Tokyo*.

En particulier, l'*AMP* 1994 ajoute deux nouvelles catégories aux entités gouvernementales centrales déjà couvertes par l'*AMP du Cycle de Tokyo*. La première catégorie couvre les entités gouvernementales sous-centrales. Cela inclut des États, des provinces, des cantons et des municipalités. La deuxième catégorie englobe toutes les autres entités gouvernementales soumises à l'*AMP* 1994, par exemple les entités des services d'utilité publique qui sont soumises au contrôle du gouvernement ou majoritairement financées par celui-ci. Par ailleurs, une autre grande amélioration concerne l'extension du champ d'application de l'*AMP* 1994 aux marchés publics de services, incluant les services de construction.[52] Ces nouveaux secteurs s'ajoutent aux marchés publics de marchandises déjà couverts sous l'*AMP du Cycle de Tokyo*.

En ce qui concerne le texte de l'Accord, il introduit plusieurs améliorations tout en restant généralement basé sur les principes et les éléments essentiels de l'*AMP du Cycle de Tokyo*. Par exemple, il intègre des règles plus souples pour la passation des marchés publics, afin de permettre aux nouvelles entités sous-centrales soumises à l'*AMP* 1994 de s'adapter plus facilement. Il améliore aussi significativement la mise en œuvre de l'Accord en incluant une obligation pour les Parties d'établir des procédures internes permettant à un fournisseur de déposer un recours pour violation de

---

[51] Union européenne, *Livre vert de la Commission européenne, Les marchés publics dans l'Union européenne: pistes de réflexion pour l'avenir*, COM 583 (1997), en ligne: EC <http://www.europarl.europa.eu/sides/getDoc.do?pubRef=-//EP//TEXT+REPORT+A4-1997-0309+0+DOC+XML+V0//FR#Contentd1392847e350>.

[52] Il est opportun de rappeler que l'*AGCS* exclut les marchés publics de services du champ d'application des principales règles commerciales multilatérales de l'OMC concernant le commerce des services. L'*AMP* comble ainsi une lacune du système commercial multilatéral en libéralisant et en réglementant une partie des marchés publics de services. De plus, l'exemption des marchés publics des principales règles de l'AGCS, incluant la clause NPF, permet aux Parties à l'*AMP* de ne pas accorder les avantages du traitement national et de leurs engagements dans le secteur des marchés publics de services sous l'*AMP*, sur une base NPF, aux autres membres de l'OMC, n'ayant pas accepté des disciplines similaires. *AGCS*, *supra* note 49, art XIII(1) et le texte correspondant; voir également, pour une discussion plus détaillée, Arrowsmith, *supra* note 21 aux pp 60-68.

l'Accord.[53] De plus, en cas de différend, il permet aux Parties de recourir aux dispositions du Mémorandum d'accord sur les règles et procédures régissant le règlement des différends de l'OMC, qui contient de grandes améliorations par rapport au mécanisme de résolution des différends de l'*AMP du Cycle de Tokyo.*[54]

Par contre, bien que cet accord constitue une avancée très importante, il contient toujours quelques lacunes. D'une part, le nombre d'adhésions demeure limité, et d'autre part, même si la portée de l'*AMP* 1994 — considérée collectivement — est dix fois supérieure à celle de l'*AMP du Cycle de Tokyo,* il manque toujours une grande part des marchés publics des Parties pouvant être libéralisée au niveau international. Finalement, la complexité des règles qui délimitent le champ d'application de l'*AMP* 1994, avec ses mesures discriminatoires et ses clauses de non-application à la fois sectorielles et propres à chaque pays, laisse place à de multiples améliorations.

La révision de l'Accord de l'OMC sur les marchés publics

Les négociations

Une fois de plus, reconnaissant que la conclusion de l'*AMP* 1994 ne constituait pas la fin des négociations visant à libéraliser les

---

[53] *AMP* 1994, *supra* note 3, art XX.

[54] Les intervenants n'ont pas toujours été satisfaits de l'expérience vécue avec le mécanisme de résolution des différends de l'*AMP du Cycle de Tokyo.* Par exemple, une des critiques majeures est liée au fait que le Comité sur les marchés publics devait adopter par consensus les recommandations du Groupe spécial. Rappelons que toute Partie, incluant les Parties aux différends, pouvait bloquer ou retarder significativement l'adoption d'un rapport du Groupe spécial. Pour remédier à cette situation, le Mémorandum d'accord sur le règlement des différends de l'OMC a introduit plusieurs améliorations. Ainsi, un rapport du Groupe spécial ne nécessite plus l'adoption par consensus, mais plutôt le contraire — c'est-à-dire qu'un rapport sera automatiquement adopté à moins que les Parties décident, par consensus, de ne *pas* l'adopter, ou qu'une Partie au litige interjette appel du rapport. Cette possibilité d'interjeter appel constitue une autre innovation majeure du Mémorandum d'accord sur le règlement des différends. *Ibid*, art XXII; *Mémorandum d'accord sur les règles et procédures régissant le règlement des différends,* annexe 2 de l'*Accord de Marrakech instituant l'Organisation mondiale du commerce* (15 avril 1994), 1869 RTNU 426 [*Mémorandum d'accord sur le règlement des différends*]. Voir, pour une discussion générale sur le mécanisme de règlement des différends de l'OMC, Carreau et Juillard, *supra* note 39 aux pp 68-89; Trebilock et Howse, *supra* note 39 au ch 4; Charles-Emmanuel Côté, *La participation des personnes privées au règlement des différends internationaux économiques: l'élargissement du droit de porter plainte à l'OMC,* Bruxelles, Bruylant, 2007; et Arrowsmith, *supra* note 21 aux pp 358-79.

marchés publics et à améliorer l'Accord, un autre engagement à poursuivre les négociations y a été intégré. L'article XXIV (7) (b) et (c) de l'*AMP* 1994 indique qu'au plus tard à l'expiration d'un délai de trois ans à compter de la date d'entrée en vigueur de l'*AMP* 1994, les Parties engageront de nouvelles négociations en vue d'atteindre trois objectifs principaux, à savoir: (1) améliorer le texte de l'Accord; (2) réduire et éliminer progressivement les mesures discriminatoires qui subsistent; et (3) étendre le plus possible le champ d'application de l'Accord entre toutes les Parties sur une base de réciprocité mutuelle, en prenant en considération les besoins des pays en développement. Les négociations visaient également à faciliter l'adhésion à l'Accord par d'autres membres de l'OMC, notamment les pays en développement. Notons que les négociations en vertu de l'*AMP* ne faisaient pas partie du Cycle de Doha et qu'elles pouvaient ainsi progresser à leur rythme.

Les négociations ont commencé en 1997 et se sont déroulées à la fois sous la forme de consultations bilatérales entre les Parties et sous la forme de discussions plurilatérales informelles. Tout d'abord, afin d'améliorer le texte de l'*AMP*, les négociateurs se sont mis provisoirement d'accord en décembre 2006 sur un texte révisé de l'Accord, sous réserve d'une vérification juridique — qui a été achevée pour l'essentiel en 2007 — et d'un résultat des négociations mutuellement satisfaisant concernant la portée de l'Accord — qui a été atteint en décembre 2011 (sous réserve de rectifications de nature purement formelle).[55]

En ce qui concerne l'aspect des négociations liées à la portée de l'Accord, les modalités ont été adoptées en 2004[56] et les négociations ont subséquemment commencé avec des échanges d'offres et de demandes entre les Parties. Ces négociations se sont poursuivies pendant plusieurs années sans résultat concluant. Selon les rapports publics, jusqu'en 2009 il semblait impossible de conclure les négociations liées à la portée de l'Accord parce que toutes les Parties n'avaient pas les mêmes ambitions. Toutefois, vers la moitié de l'année 2009, un regain de dynamisme et de détermination a

---

55 Voir OMC, Comité sur les marchés publics, *Rapport (2006) du Comité des marchés publics*, GPA/89 (2006), en ligne: OMC <http://docsonline.wto.org>; *Décision du Comité adoptant les résultats des négociations au titre de l'AMP 1994*, *supra* note 7.

56 OMC, Comité sur les marchés publics, *Modalités des négociations sur l'extension de la portée de l'Accord et l'élimination des mesures et pratiques discriminatoires*, GPA/79, (2004), en ligne: OMC <http://docsonline.wto.org>.

émergé dans les négociations et il est apparu possible de conclure ces négociations dans un futur rapproché.[57]

Sur la base des progrès réalisés en 2010, les négociations ont continué en 2011, avec l'objectif de conclure les négociations, sous tous leurs aspects, et de présenter l'*AMP* révisé à la huitième Conférence ministérielle de l'OMC. Comme l'année avançait, les attentes augmentaient et la pression sur certaines Parties est devenue particulièrement intense, surtout pour que les trois plus grandes Parties à l'*AMP* — Union européenne, Japon, États-Unis — s'accordent et règlent les différends qui subsistaient.[58] Les détails ultimes concernant la portée de l'Accord se sont négociés jusqu'à la toute dernière minute précédant l'adoption de la décision qui entérinait la conclusion des négociations.

Cette intensité a porté ses fruits et toutes les Parties ont fait les compromis nécessaires pour parvenir à un accord de principe qui, le 15 décembre 2011, mettait fin à la renégociation de l'*AMP* 1994.[59] Les résultats corrigés des négociations ont été formellement adoptés par les Parties le 30 mars 2012. La décision formalisant la conclusion comprenait trois éléments principaux: (1) un élargissement considérable de la portée de l'Accord (voir section 2); (2) une entente permettant de faire entrer en vigueur la version révisée et améliorée du texte de l'Accord (voir section 1) et (3) un ensemble de nouveaux programmes de travail du Comité (voir section 1). L'*AMP* révisé est officiellement entré en vigueur le 6 avril 2014, soit environ deux ans après l'adoption des résultats des négociations.[60]

Selon les rapports publics, les progrès dans les négociations ont été facilités grâce à cinq éléments majeurs.[61] Le premier de ceux-ci a été la présentation de nouvelles offres d'accès aux marchés par certaines Parties à l'*AMP*, comme l'offre historique du Canada de

---

[57] Philippe Pelletier, "Vers un nouvel Accord de l'OMC sur les marchés publics" (2011) 1:4 Bulletin des avocats hors Québec, en ligne: <http://www.avocatshorsquebec.org>.

[58] *Ibid.*

[59] Réunion ministérielle, *supra* note 6.

[60] *Décision du Comité adoptant les résultats des négociations au titre de l'AMP 1994*, *supra* note 7.

[61] OMC, Comité sur les marchés publics, *Rapport (2010) du Comité des marchés publics*, GPA/106 au para. 33, en ligne: OMC <http://docsonline.wto.org>; OMC, Comité sur les marchés publics, *Rapport (2011) du Comité des marchés publics*, GPA/110 aux para 32-36, en ligne: OMC <http://docsonline.wto.org>.

soumettre à l'*AMP* une partie de ses marchés publics régionaux, soit l'ensemble de ses provinces et territoires, conformément à un accord bilatéral entre le Canada et les États-Unis.[62] Cette offre a eu un réel effet catalyseur sur les négociations (voir Encadré 3).

ENCADRÉ 3: L'OFFRE DU CANADA CONSISTANT À SOUMETTRE SES MARCHÉS PUBLICS RÉGIONAUX À L'AMP[63]

Dès l'entrée en vigueur de l'*AMP*, le 1er janvier 1996, le gouvernement du Canada y a soumis ses entités fédérales. Par contre, il en a exclu ses entités provinciales et territoriales, et ce, jusqu'en 2011. En réponse à cette exclusion, le Canada fut lui-même exclu d'une part des concessions de plusieurs Parties à l'*AMP*, comme l'Union européenne, l'Islande, le Japon, la Corée, le Liechtenstein, la Norvège, la Suisse et les États-Unis, ce qui priva les entreprises canadiennes de précieux marchés publics régionaux un peu partout dans le monde.

En février 2010, le Canada accepta pour la première fois d'ouvrir une part de ses marchés publics régionaux aux États-Unis, en échange d'engagements similaires et de la levée par les États-Unis des obstacles empêchant les entreprises canadiennes de participer aux projets d'infrastructure américaine financés en vertu du plan de relance américaine.[64] En février 2010, les résultats de cette entente connexe ont parallèlement été offerts aux autres Parties à l'*AMP*, sous conditions d'une négociation de concessions "mutuellement acceptables". En échange de cette offre historique, par le Canada, de soumettre ses provinces et territoires à

---

62   *Accord entre le gouvernement du Canada et le gouvernement des États-Unis d'Amérique en matière de marchés publics*, (12 février 2010), RT Can 2010 n°5 (entrée en vigueur: 16 février 2010) [*Accord sur les marchés publics Canada-États-Unis*].

63   Voir, pour une analyse plus détaillée, David Collins, "Canada's Sub-central Government Entities and the Agreement on Government Procurement: past and Present," dans Arrowsmith et Anderson, *supra* note 4 au ch 7 aux pp 175-96.

64   *Accord sur les marchés publics Canada-États-Unis*, *supra* note 62; *American Recovery and Reinvestment Act of 2009*, Pub L N°111.5, HR1.

l'*AMP*, les fournisseurs canadiens ont obtenu un meilleur accès aux entités régionales des autres Parties à l'OMC, dont ils étaient exclus jusqu'alors. Par exemple, avec l'entrée en vigueur de l'*AMP*, les fournisseurs canadiens ont eu accès, en plus des marchés publics régionaux des États-Unis, aux marchés publics régionaux de l'Union européenne, du Japon, de la Corée, de la Norvège et de la Suisse. Il est à noter que l'accès à ces marchés publics régionaux s'ajoute aux autres élargissements de la portée de l'*AMP* découlant de la conclusion des négociations (voir section 2).[65]

Le deuxième élément majeur à avoir fait progresser les négociations a été la possibilité d'intégrer dans les futurs programmes de travail du Comité, depuis la fin de 2010, des questions ne pouvant être résolues dans le cadre des négociations en cours. Des discussions ont alors eu lieu sur un certain nombre de sujets susceptibles d'être inclus dans les futurs programmes de travail, dont la participation des petites et moyennes entreprises (PME) aux marchés publics visés par l'Accord, et les considérations en matière d'approvisionnement public durable (voir section 1). Cette possibilité s'est avérée essentielle pour que les Parties trouvent l'équilibre entre les éléments pouvant encore être raisonnablement abordés dans le cadre des négociations précédentes et ceux devant être abordés dans le cadre des futurs travaux du Comité.[66]

Le troisième élément décisif a été le soutien inconditionnel que toutes les Parties ont manifesté à l'égard d'une "feuille de route" présentée par le président du Comité pour conclure les négociations à temps pour la huitième Conférence ministérielle de l'OMC. Cette feuille de route visait en priorité à faire en sorte que toutes les questions dont le Comité était saisi, dans le cadre des négociations, reçoivent en permanence toute l'attention voulue.

Un quatrième élément majeur a été la perception généralisée des Parties à l'*AMP*, que la conclusion des négociations faciliterait également l'adhésion de nouveaux membres, grâce aux flexibilités supplémentaires ainsi qu'aux meilleures dispositions de traitement

[65] Voir *AMP révisé, supra* note 8.
[66] Pelletier, *supra* note 57.

spécial et différencié pour les pays en développement, qui étaient comprises dans le texte révisé de l'*AMP*1994. À cet égard, les progrès dans les négociations semblent aussi être liés à la présentation d'un document de travail de l'OMC estimant que les futures accessions à l'Accord apporteraient aux Parties des gains considérables en matière d'accès aux marchés publics.[67]

Un cinquième élément a été déterminant vers la fin des négociations, lorsqu'il est devenu évident pour les Parties qu'en plus d'être bénéfique pour elles, la conclusion des négociations apporterait des avantages significatifs à l'ensemble du système commercial multilatéral. Étant donné les sérieuses difficultés entourant la conclusion du Cycle de Doha, la perception généralisée indiquant que la conclusion des négociations de l'*AMP* renforcerait la crédibilité du système commercial multilatéral a joué un rôle-clé dans les derniers moments des négociations, incitant les Parties à faire les compromis nécessaires pour parvenir à un accord.

L'*AMP* révisé: négociations futures et nouveaux programmes de travail du Comité

Tout en reconnaissant l'importance de la conclusion de cette étape des négociations, les Parties ont concédé que certaines questions restaient irrésolues et que l'Accord contenait toujours des imperfections. D'une part, le nombre d'adhésions demeure encore limité, et ce, même si la liste des Parties à l'Accord s'allonge et qu'un nombre considérable de membres de l'OMC envisage d'accéder à l'*AMP* révisé, comme la Chine, la Moldavie et l'Ukraine. D'autre part, même si la portée de l'*AMP* révisé atteint maintenant des sommets historiques, il y manque encore une part considérable des marchés publics des Parties pouvant être libéralisée au niveau international.

Ainsi, afin de répondre aux questions en suspens et d'améliorer l'Accord, le texte révisé de l'*AMP* intègre un autre engagement à poursuivre les négociations. L'article XXII (7) indique qu'au plus tard à l'expiration d'un délai de trois ans, à compter de la date d'entrée en vigueur du Protocole d'amendement, les Parties engageront de nouvelles négociations en vue d'atteindre trois objectifs principaux:[68] (1) améliorer le texte de l'Accord; (2) réduire et

---

67 Anderson et al, *supra* note 1.

68 Il est important de rappeler que les négociations en vertu de l'*AMP* ne font pas partie du Cycle de Doha (ou autres cycles futurs) des négociations à l'OMC, et peuvent ainsi progresser à leur propre rythme.

éliminer progressivement les mesures discriminatoires qui subsistent; et (3) étendre le plus possible le champ d'application de l'Accord entre toutes les Parties, sur une base de réciprocité mutuelle et en prenant en considération les besoins des pays en développement. Les négociations visent également à faciliter l'adhésion à l'Accord par d'autres membres de l'OMC, notamment les pays en développement.

En plus de cet engagement à poursuivre les négociations en vertu de l'article XXII (7), le texte révisé contient à l'article XXII (8) un nouvel élément indiquant que le Comité adoptera des programmes de travail sur une multitude de sujets pour faciliter la mise en œuvre de l'Accord et des négociations prévues à l'article XXII (7). Le Comité a déjà pris des décisions spécifiques sur un certain nombre de ces programmes traitant de questions qui n'ont pu être résolues:[69] (1) un programme de travail visant à faciliter la participation aux marchés publics des petites et moyennes entreprises (PME); (2) un programme de travail visant à améliorer l'établissement et la communication de données statistiques; (3) un programme de travail sur les marchés publics durables; (4) un programme de travail sur les exclusions et restrictions énoncées dans les annexes concernant les Parties; et (5) un programme de travail sur les normes de sécurité dans les marchés publics internationaux.

Outre ces programmes, qui ont été officiellement lancés le 25 juin 2014, le Comité sur les marchés publics a dressé une liste de travaux à faire et dont il prévoit la date de commencement à une date ultérieure.[70] Cette liste, qui pourra être périodiquement révisée, comprend (1) l'examen de l'utilisation, de la transparence et des cadres juridiques des partenariats public-privé et de leur relation avec les marchés publics couverts; (2) les avantages et inconvénients de l'élaboration d'une nomenclature commune pour les marchandises et les services; et (3) les avantages et les inconvénients d'élaborer des avis normalisés.

À l'évidence, les programmes de travail susmentionnés sont de nature exploratoire; néanmoins, ils peuvent contribuer à l'évolution de l'Accord et à son administration. Plusieurs aspects des nouveaux

---

[69] Voir *Décision du Comité adoptant les résultats des négociations au titre de l'AMP 1994*, *supra* note 7, Appendice 2.

[70] *Ibid*, Décision du Comité des marchés publics sur l'adoption de programmes de travail, Appendice 2; *AMP révisé*, *supra* note 8, art XXII (8) (b) (i). Voir, pour une discussion sur les futurs programmes de travail du Comité, Anderson, *supra* note 9.

programmes de travail concernent des questions de portée.[71] Par exemple, le programme de travail sur les exclusions et restrictions énoncées dans les annexes abordera certainement des préoccupations des Parties pour ce qui est de l'accès aux marchés. Ce programme de travail visera à accroître la transparence, pour ce qui est de la portée et de l'effet des exclusions et restrictions spécifiées dans les annexes, ainsi que pour donner des renseignements sur celles-ci et faciliter les négociations, afin d'accroître la portée prévue par l'article XXII (7) de l'Accord.

Un autre exemple est le programme de travail visant la participation des PME aux marchés publics. Bien que toutes les Parties reconnaissent qu'il est important de faciliter la participation des PME aux marchés publics, toutes n'adoptent pas les mêmes approches pour y arriver et cela peut devenir une préoccupation d'un point de vue d'accès aux marchés. Ce programme de travail examinera donc les mesures et les politiques concernant les PME auxquelles les Parties ont recours pour aider, promouvoir, encourager ou faciliter la participation des PME aux marchés publics et il établira un rapport sur les résultats de cet examen, où seront identifiées les meilleures pratiques pour promouvoir et faciliter la participation des PME des Parties aux marchés publics visés par l'Accord. Les Parties encourageront alors l'adoption de ces pratiques. Les Parties se sont aussi engagées d'une part à éviter d'adopter des mesures discriminatoires qui favoriseraient uniquement les PME nationales, et d'autre part à dissuader les Parties accédant à l'*AMP* d'adopter de telles mesures et politiques.

Un exemple supplémentaire concerne le programme de travail visant à promouvoir le recours à des pratiques de développement durable en matière de passation de marchés, en conformité avec l'Accord. Le Comité identifiera les mesures et les politiques qu'il considère comme une pratique de passation de marchés publics durable, compatible avec le principe de l'optimisation des ressources et avec les obligations commerciales internationales des Parties, et il établira un rapport indiquant les mesures et les politiques constituant les meilleures pratiques. La question de la durabilité des pratiques en matière de marchés publics est particulièrement intéressante parce que dans certaines juridictions, on considère qu'elle

---

[71] À l'évidence, les programmes de travail susmentionnés répondent à la fois à des préoccupations sociopolitiques partagées par l'ensemble des Parties et aux intérêts qu'au moins certaines d'entre elles continuent d'avoir dans les négociations.

concerne principalement les mesures visant à promouvoir la passation de marchés écologiques, alors que dans d'autres, elle englobe
également des considérations de politique sociale.[72]

Finalement, il existe un intérêt de longue date pour les normes
de sécurité dans les marchés publics internationaux, en particulier
de la part de l'Union européenne, en ce qui concerne l'accès aux
marchés. Le programme de travail sur le sujet examinera les meilleures pratiques s'y rapportant et pouvant être adoptées pour protéger la sécurité publique à la lumière des dispositions de l'article
X, concernant les spécifications techniques et la documentation
relative à l'appel d'offres.

Somme toute, bien que l'entrée en vigueur de l'*AMP* révisé constitue une avancée importante, elle ne marque pas la fin des négociations internationales visant à libéraliser les marchés publics, car un
nouveau cycle de négociations commencera d'ici peu. Dans l'inter-
valle, l'entrée en vigueur de l'*AMP* révisé est très importante, car
en plus d'élargir considérablement la portée de l'Accord (voir
section 2), elle permet au texte révisé et amélioré de l'*AMP* d'entrer
en vigueur (voir section 1).

LE TEXTE RÉVISÉ DE L'*AMP* DE L'OMC: INTRODUCTION GÉNÉRALE

Le texte révisé de l'*AMP* améliore significativement le texte de l'*AMP*
1994, tout en demeurant basé sur les mêmes principes,
c'est-à-dire la non-discrimination, la transparence et l'équité procédurale.[73] La version révisée de l'Accord réorganise complètement
le texte, introduit des flexibilités supplémentaires et reformule intégralement ses différentes dispositions afin de le rendre plus facile
à comprendre. Elle a aussi été mise à jour afin de prendre en
compte l'évolution de la pratique des marchés publics, notamment
en ce qui concerne l'utilisation des moyens électroniques.

L'*AMP* a également renforcé son rôle en tant qu'instrument assurant la bonne gouvernance et la gestion efficace des ressources
publiques en mettant l'accent sur la transparence, l'obligation red-
ditionnelle et les conditions de concurrence non discriminatoire.[74]

---

[72] Voir Anderson, *supra* note 9.

[73] Sur ce sujet, Sue Arrowsmith, "The Revised Agreement on Government
Procurement: Changes to the procedural rules and other transparency provisions," dans Arrowsmith et Anderson, *supra* note 4 au ch 10 aux pp 285-336.

[74] OMC, Comité des marchés publics, *Compte rendu de la réunion formelle au niveau
ministériel* (tenue le 3 décembre 2013), GPA/M/54 (2014) au para 1.7, en ligne:
OMC <http://docsonline.wto.org>.

En plus d'avoir adopté ces principes généraux, l'*AMP* révisé promeut de façon explicite la bonne gouvernance et décourage la corruption. Pour être plus précis, l'Accord exige que les entités contractantes procèdent à la passation de marchés publics couverts d'une manière transparente et impartiale, qui évite les conflits d'intérêts et empêche les pratiques frauduleuses.[75] Une telle obligation envoie un signal clair: les Parties à l'Accord considèrent que l'*AMP*, en plus d'être un Accord commercial international, est aussi un Accord servant la lutte mondiale contre la corruption et pour la bonne gouvernance. Cet aspect de l'*AMP* est unique en son genre à l'OMC et dans le contexte plus large des obligations découlant de son système commercial multilatéral.

De plus, les obligations contenues dans le texte de l'*AMP* révisé codifient les bonnes pratiques reconnues internationalement dans le domaine des marchés publics.[76] Ainsi, l'*AMP* est grandement compatible avec la *Loi type de la Commission des Nations unies pour le droit commercial international* (*CNUDCI*) sur la passation des marchés, incluant la révision de 2011 qui a inspiré la législation nationale de nombreux pays.[77] Il renforce aussi d'autres instruments internationaux, comme les directives de la Banque mondiale et les travaux de l'OCDE sur la prévention de la corruption. De plus, et comme mentionné ci-dessus, l'*AMP* a servi de modèle à plusieurs accords commerciaux bilatéraux et régionaux libéralisant les marchés publics (voir Encadré 2). Ces éléments contribuent à favoriser une certaine convergence des normes dans le secteur des marchés publics au niveau international et ils montrent que les disciplines de base de l'*AMP* ont une grande influence, au-delà de la composition actuelle de ses membres.

---

[75] *AMP révisé*, *supra* note 8, art IV (2) (b) et (c) et sixième considérant du préambule.

[76] Voir Müller et Pelletier, *supra* note 2; Anderson et al, *supra* note 1.

[77] Loi type de la *CNUDCI* de 2011, qui remplace la loi type de 1994, a été élaborée de manière à favoriser l'harmonisation des normes internationales en matière de passation des marchés publics et tient notamment compte des dispositions de l'*AMP révisé*. *Loi type de la Commission des Nations unies pour le droit commercial international sur la passation des marchés*, Rés AG 66/95, Doc off AG NU, 66ᵉ sess, supp n°17, Doc NU A/66/17 (2011), en ligne: CNUDCI <http://www.uncitral.org/uncitral/fr/uncitral_texts/procurement_infrastructure/2011Model.html> [*Loi type de la CNUDCI de 2011*]; Caroline Nicholas, "Work of UNCITRAL on Government Procurement: Purpose, Objectives and Complementarity with the Work of the WTO," dans Arrowsmith et Anderson, *supra* note 4 au ch 24 aux pp 746-72.

Afin de bien comprendre et de saisir la portée du texte révisé de l'*AMP*, il convient d'examiner succinctement ses principales caractéristiques: (1) les principes fondamentaux de l'*AMP*: la non-discrimination et la transparence; (2) l'équité procédurale: normes minimales en matière de procédures de passation des marchés publics; (3) les dispositions relatives aux moyens de faire respecter l'Accord; et (4) les dispositions spéciales pour les pays en développement.

Les principes fondamentaux: la non-discrimination et la transparence

L'*AMP* établit un cadre de droits et d'obligations entre ses Parties en ce qui concerne les mesures[78] dans le domaine des marchés publics *couverts* par l'*AMP*, qu'ils soient ou non passés exclusivement ou partiellement par des moyens électroniques.[79] La pierre angulaire des règles de l'Accord est la non-discrimination. Pour s'assurer que cette règle est respectée, l'*AMP* porte aussi une attention particulière à la transparence des mesures ayant trait aux marchés publics.

En ce qui concerne toute mesure ayant trait aux marchés publics couverts, l'*AMP* prévoit que chaque Partie, y compris ses entités contractantes, accordera un traitement non discriminatoire aux marchandises et aux services de toute autre Partie et aux fournisseurs de toute autre Partie. Pour être plus précis, ce traitement non discriminatoire doit ne pas être moins favorable que celui accordé par la Partie, y compris par ses entités contractantes aux marchandises, aux services et aux fournisseurs nationaux (traitement national), et aux marchandises, aux services et aux fournisseurs de toute autre Partie (obligation de la nation la plus favorisée).[80] En outre, chaque Partie est tenue de veiller à ce que ses entités n'établissent pas de discrimination entre les fournisseurs établis sur le territoire national, en raison du degré de contrôle ou de participation étrangers[81] ou pour le motif que les marchandises ou les services offerts par ce fournisseur pour un marché donné seraient les marchandises ou les services d'une autre Partie.[82]

---

[78] *AMP révisé, supra* note 8, art I(i). Le terme "mesure" s'entend de toute loi, réglementation, procédure, directive ou pratique administratives ou de toute action d'une entité contractante concernant un marché public couvert.

[79] *Ibid*, art II(1).

[80] *Ibid*, art IV(1).

[81] *Ibid*, art IV(2)(a).

[82] *Ibid*, art IV(2)(b).

L'Accord accorde une grande importance aux procédures assurant la transparence des mesures ayant trait aux marchés publics couverts, pour s'assurer que le principe fondamental de non-discrimination est respecté et que l'accès aux marchés publics couverts est donné aux marchandises, aux services et aux fournisseurs des autres Parties. Ainsi, il contient une obligation générale de publier des renseignements sur le système de passation des marchés publics.[83] Chaque Partie a l'obligation de publier le plus rapidement possible toutes lois, réglementations, décisions judiciaires et décisions administratives d'application générale. De la même façon, chaque Partie doit publier dans des médias officiellement désignés toute procédure concernant les marchés publics couverts et toute modification afférente.[84] De plus, elle doit recueillir des statistiques sur ses marchés publics couverts par l'Accord et les communiquer au Comité sur les marchés publics.[85]

L'équité procédurale: normes minimales en matière de procédures de passation des marchés publics

L'Accord contient aussi un certain nombre de normes minimales détaillées que les entités contractantes doivent respecter, d'une part pour garantir l'application effective des principes de non-discrimination et d'autre part pour assurer l'équité procédurale et l'optimisation des ressources financières. Dans le cadre de l'*AMP*, ces normes en matière de procédures de passation servent aussi à garantir l'accès aux marchés publics couverts et à s'assurer que les marchandises, les services et les fournisseurs nationaux et étrangers peuvent se concurrencer équitablement, de façon transparente et non discriminatoire.

Le texte révisé a été mis à jour afin de prendre en compte l'évolution de la pratique des marchés publics, notamment en ce qui concerne l'utilisation des moyens électroniques.[86] Il intègre également une flexibilité supplémentaire pour les autorités contractantes des Parties, par exemple sous la forme de délais de préavis plus courts lorsque des outils électroniques sont utilisés.[87]

---

[83] *Ibid*, art VI.

[84] *Ibid*, art VI(2).

[85] *Ibid*, art XVI(4).

[86] Voir notamment *ibid*, art IV(3).

[87] Voir notamment *ibid*, art XI(5).

Dispositions relatives aux moyens de faire respecter l'Accord

L'*AMP* est un accord international juridiquement contraignant. Il contient deux mécanismes pour faire respecter l'Accord (ou la législation nationale qui le met en œuvre). Tout d'abord, l'établissement d'un mécanisme d'examen national. Un tel mécanisme, permettant aux fournisseurs de déposer un recours pour violation des règles pertinentes, est largement reconnu comme étant un moyen efficace d'assurer la transparence, l'équité et la prévisibilité des systèmes de passation des marchés nationaux.[88] Pour cette raison, l'article XVIII requiert que toutes les Parties établissent un système indépendant de contestation des adjudications au niveau national, pour les fournisseurs estimant qu'un marché public couvert a été traité de manière incompatible avec les prescriptions de l'Accord. Ce système de contestation doit accorder une procédure de recours administratif ou judiciaire qui soit efficace, transparente, non discriminatoire, et qui s'applique en temps opportun. Il est prévu que les organes nationaux de recours doivent avoir le pouvoir d'ordonner des mesures correctives ou une compensation pour la perte ou les dommages subis. De plus, en attendant l'issue des procédures de contestation, il faut prévoir rapidement des mesures transitoires pour préserver la possibilité qu'a le fournisseur de participer au marché public.[89]

Par ailleurs, bien qu'on l'invoque assez rarement, le Mémorandum d'accord sur les règles et procédures régissant le règlement des différends de l'OMC s'applique aussi aux différends survenant entre les Parties dans le cadre de l'Accord.[90] Afin de traiter avec le caractère plurilatéral de l'Accord, l'article XX contient certaines règles particulières. Par exemple, il prohibe les mesures dites de "rétorsion croisée."[91]

Dispositions spéciales pour les pays en développement

Une autre amélioration-clé du nouveau texte concerne la clarification des mesures transitoires de traitement spécial et différencié qui sont offertes aux pays en développement, incluant les pays les

---

[88] Daniel I Gordon, "Constructing a Bid Protest Process: The Choices That Every Procurement Challenge System Must Make" (2006) 35:3 PCLJ.

[89] *AMP révisé, supra* note 8, art XVIII(7).

[90] *Ibid*, art XX.

[91] Voir *ibid.*, art XX (3); *Mémorandum d'accord sur le règlement des différends, supra* note 54.

moins avancés qui adhèrent à l'Accord.[92] Ces mesures ont l'avantage d'assurer une transition en douceur en évitant de perturber trop fortement l'économie nationale. Celle-ci peut également s'adapter progressivement à une intensification de la concurrence. Espérons que cette version de l'Accord, avec ses flexibilités supplémentaires, facilitera les futures adhésions à l'*AMP*.

En vertu de l'article V de l'*AMP* révisé, les mesures transitoires qui peuvent être offertes, sous réserve de négociations, comprennent notamment (1) un programme de préférences en matière de prix; (2) une opération de compensation;[93] (3) l'inclusion progressive d'entités ou de secteurs spécifiques; et (4) une valeur de seuil plus élevée que sa valeur de seuil permanente. De plus, il a été convenu que pendant une période de trois à cinq ans il serait possible de différer l'application de toute obligation spécifique figurant dans l'Accord, à l'exception du principe de non-discrimination aux produits, services et fournisseurs des autres Parties (Article VI (1) (b)). À la demande du pays concerné, ces délais peuvent être prolongés par décision du Comité sur les marchés publics.[94]

CONCLUSION DE LA PREMIÈRE PARTIE

La première section du présent document a mis en lumière l'importance d'avoir conclu, en décembre 2011, le dernier cycle de négociations dont l'*AMP* faisait l'objet, ce qui a permis de faire aboutir une longue série de négociations internationales s'étant poursuivies

---

[92] Voir, pour une analyse plus détaillée, Anna Caroline Müller, "Special and Differential Treatment and other Special Measures for Developing Countries under the Agreement on Government Procurement: the Current Text and New Provisions," dans Arrowsmith et Anderson, *supra* note 4 au ch 11 aux pp 339-76; et pour une analyse approfondie avec une référence particulière à l'Afrique, voir Nicholas Niggli et Kodjo Osei-Lah, "Infrastructure provision and Africa's Trade and Growth Prospects: Potential Role and Relevance of the WTO Agreement on Government Procurement (GPA)," (à venir) document de travail de l'OMC. Voir, pour une discussion générale sur le traitement spécial et différencié à l'OMC, Charles-Emmanuel Côté, "De Genève à Doha: genèse et évolution du traitement spécial et différencié des pays en développement dans le droit de l'OMC" (2010) 56:1 RD McGill 115.

[93] L'expression "opérations de compensation" s'entend de toute condition ou de tout engagement qui encourage le développement local ou améliore le compte de la balance des paiements d'une Partie, telle que l'utilisation d'éléments d'origine nationale, l'octroi de licences pour des technologies, l'investissement, les échanges compensés et les actions ou prescriptions similaires. *AMP révisé*, *supra* note 8, art II(1).

[94] *Ibid*, art V(6).

sur plus de 65 ans. À cet égard, nous avons relaté les événements marquants de l'histoire de ces négociations, tout en notant que malgré l'incontestable avancée qu'elle représente, leur conclusion ne constitue pas la fin des négociations visant à libéraliser les marchés publics. Au contraire, elle permet d'entamer un nouveau cycle de négociations en vue de libéraliser davantage les marchés publics et d'améliorer l'Accord. Nous avons aussi introduit le texte de l'*AMP* révisé, nous avons décrit ses principaux éléments et noté que le texte révisé améliore significativement le texte de l'*AMP* 1994, tout en demeurant basé sur les mêmes principes et les mêmes éléments fondamentaux. Afin de bien comprendre l'*AMP* révisé et la nécessité de négocier de façon quasi permanente une libéralisation accrue des marchés publics, il convient aussi d'examiner la portée de l'Accord révisé, incluant les quelques lacunes laissées par la conclusion du dernier cycle de négociations de l'*AMP*.

L'ÉLARGISSEMENT DU CHAMP D'APPLICATION DE L'*AMP* RÉVISÉ

L'*AMP* révisé est d'abord et avant tout un accord commercial. Dans ce contexte, il est essentiel d'avoir une bonne compréhension de sa portée, afin d'apprécier pleinement son importance pour l'économie mondiale et de déterminer les débouchés à l'exportation, qui pourraient s'avérer très lucratifs pour les fournisseurs des Parties à l'*AMP*.[95] Évidemment, ces débouchés sont aussi susceptibles d'intéresser les fournisseurs des autres membres de l'OMC désirant accéder à l'Accord. Sur deux plans distincts, la conclusion des négociations a eu des effets favorables pour la portée de l'*AMP*. D'une part, la nouvelle version du texte de l'Accord clarifie certains éléments ayant des effets sur sa portée, et d'autre part, la conclusion des négociations a donné lieu à une augmentation substantielle des marchés publics couverts.

Dans la prochaine section, nous chercherons à clarifier et à rendre plus accessible la portée de l'*AMP* révisé et ses améliorations. Cet objectif est particulièrement pertinent, car malgré une certaine simplification, les règles qui définissent le champ d'application de l'*AMP* demeurent techniques et complexes. D'une façon plus précise, nous aborderons, dans un premier temps, la portée de l'Accord

---

95 Voir, pour une discussion sur la portée de l'AMP, Robert D Anderson et Kodjo Osei-Lah, "The Coverage Negotiations under the Agreement on Government Procurement: Context, Mandate and Present," dans Arrowsmith et Anderson, *supra* note 4 au ch 6 aux pp 149-74.

révisé sur les marchés publics en traitant des éléments du texte de l'Accord ayant des conséquences pour l'accès aux marchés. Dans un second temps, nous mettrons en lumière les principes fondamentaux liés au champ d'application de l'*AMP* révisé. Enfin, dans un troisième temps, nous présenterons une analyse approfondie de l'Appendice I de l'*AMP*, incluant des listes d'engagements des Parties (les annexes de l'Appendice I).

L'INCIDENCE DU TEXTE DE L'*AMP* RÉVISÉ SUR SA PORTÉE ET SON CHAMP D'APPLICATION

Le texte révisé de l'*AMP* touche à sa portée, soit directement soit indirectement, en clarifiant et en simplifiant certains éléments. La présente section abordera succinctement les deux éléments suivants qui ont des conséquences pour l'accès aux marchés: (1) la définition des marchés publics couverts par l'*AMP* révisé et (2) les exclusions prévues dans le texte de l'Accord.

La définition des marchés publics couverts par l'AMP révisé

L'*AMP* ne s'applique *pas* automatiquement à tous les marchés publics des Parties. Il s'applique seulement aux marchés publics passés, pour les besoins des pouvoirs publics de marchandises, de services ou d'une combinaison des deux, comme il est spécifié dans les annexes de l'Appendice I de l'*AMP* concernant chaque Partie (voir Encadré 4 pour une description de la structure de base de l'Appendice I). En particulier, tel qu'énoncé à l'article II, l'Accord s'applique (1) aux marchés publics des entités contractantes que chaque Partie a énumérées dans les annexes 1 à 3 de l'Appendice I, concernant respectivement les entités du gouvernement central, les entités des gouvernements sous-centraux et toutes les autres entités dont l'Accord couvre les marchés publics (voir section 2); (2) aux marchés publics de marchandises, telles qu'énumérées à l'annexe 4 de l'Appendice I (voir section 2); et (3) aux marchés publics de services (incluant les services de construction) figurant dans les listes contenues aux annexes 5 et 6 (voir section 2).

L'*AMP* s'applique seulement lorsque la valeur des marchés publics est égale ou supérieure à la valeur de seuil spécifiée dans les annexes de l'Appendice I. Il s'agit d'un élément important, car les marchés publics qui ne répondent pas aux seuils ne sont pas soumis aux exigences prévues par l'*AMP*. L'*AMP* indique aussi que les marchés publics couverts ne se réfèrent pas uniquement aux achats simples, mais aussi à tous les autres types d'arrangement d'acquisition, comme le crédit-bail et la location.[96]

De plus, désormais l'*AMP* indique clairement que les marchés publics visés par l'Accord ne doivent pas être acquis pour être vendus ou revendus dans le commerce ni pour servir à la production ou à la fourniture de marchandises ou de services destinés à la vente ou à la revente dans le commerce.[97] Le fait d'inclure cette clause clarifie et harmonise le texte de l'*AMP* avec le texte utilisé dans le *GATT* et l'*AGCS*.[98] Il s'agit d'une amélioration importante qui pourrait

---

ENCADRÉ 4: LA STRUCTURE DE L'APPENDICE I DE L'AMP

L'Appendice I comprend les sept annexes suivantes (voir l'article II [4]):

- L'ANNEXE 1, les *entités du gouvernement central* dont les marchés sont couverts par l'Accord;
- L'ANNEXE 2, les *entités des gouvernements sous-centraux* dont les marchés sont couverts par l'Accord;
- L'ANNEXE 3, toutes les *autres entités* dont les marchés sont couverts par l'Accord;
- L'ANNEXE 4, les *marchandises* couvertes par l'Accord;
- L'ANNEXE 5, les *services*, autres que les services de construction, couverts par l'Accord;
- L'ANNEXE 6, les *services de construction* couverts par l'Accord et
- L'ANNEXE 7, toutes *notes générales*.

Les annexes spécifient également les valeurs de seuil à partir desquelles les marchés publics sont soumis aux disciplines de l'Accord. En outre, les annexes de la plupart des Parties contiennent aussi des notes qui qualifient et précisent l'application de l'Accord. Les marchandises sont couvertes si elles ne sont pas spécifiquement exclues.

---

[96] *AMP révisé, supra* note 8, art II(2)(b).

[97] *Ibid,* art II(2)(a)(ii).

[98] Il a été expliqué ci-dessus que, tandis que les marchés publics sont généralement exclus du traitement national et de la clause NPF en vertu du *GATT* et de l'*AGCS*,

finir par jouer un rôle significatif dans la résolution des questions relatives à l'inclusion des entreprises publiques fonctionnant entièrement sur une base commerciale dans les engagements des Parties. Cette question compte particulièrement pour les pays qui sont en voie d'adhérer à l'Accord et qui ont un large secteur public comprenant un grand nombre d'entreprises publiques, comme la Chine et l'Ukraine.[99]

Les exclusions communes aux Parties

Afin de s'assurer qu'un marché public donné est couvert par l'*AMP*, il convient de vérifier qu'il n'est pas autrement exclu du champ d'application de l'Accord par un des trois moyens suivants: (1) les différentes exceptions prévues à l'article II(3) de l'*AMP*, qui codifient un certain nombre de dérogations communes aux Parties; (2) les exceptions concernant la sécurité nationale et l'exception générale prévue à l'article III, qui autorisent des dérogations aux obligations de l'Accord; et (3) les notes de chaque annexe et les notes générales spécifiées à l'annexe 7 de l'Appendice I, qui contiennent des exceptions (voir section 2). La présente sous-section concerne les deux premiers types d'exclusions.

L'article II(3) de l'*AMP* codifie des dérogations communes qui étaient préalablement incluses dans les listes d'engagements des Parties et qui ont été transformées en dérogations générales dans le texte de l'Accord. Il s'agit d'une nette amélioration, car cela simplifie la compréhension de la portée de l'Accord révisé et harmonise l'application d'un nombre de dérogations communes. Ainsi, cet article indique qu'à moins que les engagements spécifiques des Parties n'en disposent autrement, l'Accord ne s'applique pas: (1) à l'acquisition ou à la location de terrains ou de biens immobiliers; (2) aux accords non contractuels ou à toute forme d'aide qu'une Partie fournit; (3) aux marchés ou à l'acquisition de services de

---

les achats destinés à la vente ou à la revente dans le commerce ou pour servir à la production ou à la fourniture de marchandises ou de services destinés à la vente ou à la revente dans le commerce sont, dans une certaine mesure, exclus de cette dérogation et sont donc réglementés par le *GATT* et l'*AGCS*. Voir *GATT* 1947, *supra* note 24; *GATT* 1994, *supra* note 48; *AGCS*, *supra* note 49 et le texte correspondant.

[99] Voir, par exemple, Ping Wang, "Coverage of the WTO's Agreement on Government Procurement: Challenges of Integrating China and Other Countries with a Large State Sector into the Global Trading System" (2007) 10 J Int'l Econ L 887.

dépositaire et autres types de services financiers, et au placement de la dette publique; et (4) aux contrats d'emploi public. En outre, l'article II(3) indique que l'*AMP* ne s'applique pas aux marchés publics passés: (1) dans le but de fournir une assistance internationale, y compris une aide au développement;[100] (2) conformément à un accord international relatif au stationnement de troupes ou à l'exécution conjointe d'un projet par les pays signataires; ou (3) conformément aux règles particulières d'une organisation internationale, ou financée par des dons, des prêts ou une autre aide au niveau international.

L'article III de l'*AMP* prévoit deux autres types d'exclusions, certaines concernant la sécurité nationale et d'autres, plus générales, pour protéger par exemple la moralité publique, l'ordre public, la santé et la vie humaine et animale. Le premier paragraphe de cet article autorise des dérogations aux obligations de l'Accord pour protéger par exemple les intérêts essentiels de la sécurité nationale des États se rapportant aux marchés d'armes, de munitions ou de matériel de guerre. Par ailleurs, plusieurs Parties ont déjà exclu d'une façon explicite dans leurs listes d'engagements les marchés publics de matériel militaire effectués par leurs entités dans le secteur de la défense nationale (voir section 2).[101] Cette exception s'applique aussi aux marchés publics indispensables à la sécurité nationale ou aux fins de la défense nationale, comme les réserves stratégiques de pétrole, le transport aérien de sécurité et la sûreté nucléaire.[102]

Le deuxième paragraphe de cet article autorise aussi, sous certaines conditions, des exceptions générales afin de protéger la

---

[100] Cette exception dans le texte de l'Accord a pour effet d'exclure l'aide liée apportée aux pays en développement. Voir, pour une analyse plus détaillée, Annamaria La Chimia, "Untying Aid through the Agreement on Government Procurement: A Means to Encourage Developing Countries' Accession to the Agreement and to Improve Aid Effectiveness ?" dans Arrowsmith et Anderson, *supra* note 4 au ch 13 aux pp 390-425.

[101] Dans la pratique, les exclusions explicites dans les annexes signifient que les Parties n'ont pas besoin de fournir une justification pour ne pas appliquer l'Accord à ces achats. À titre d'exemple, les contrats pour le matériel militaire et les marchandises expressément exclus peuvent, en vertu de l'*AMP*, être conclus en toute légalité avec l'industrie nationale et cela, pour plusieurs raisons, y compris pour des raisons économiques telles que la préservation de l'emploi. Voir Arrowsmith, *supra* note 21 aux pp 129-30.

[102] Voir, par exemple, *AMP révisé*, *supra* note 8, la note générale 9 du Taipei Chinois et la note 5 à l'annexe 1 des États-Unis.

moralité publique, l'ordre public ou la sécurité publique, la santé et la vie humaine et animale, la préservation des végétaux ou la propriété intellectuelle. Enfin, il permet aux Parties d'appliquer des mesures se rapportant à des marchandises fabriquées ou des services fournis par des personnes handicapées, des institutions philanthropiques ou des détenus.

En résumé, le texte de l'*AMP* met en place les règles de base définissant le champ d'application de l'Accord et spécifie un certain nombre d'exclusions communes à tous. En ce qui concerne les détails des engagements d'accès au marché, il faut se référer aux annexes à l'Appendice I de l'*AMP*.

DÉFINIR LES ENGAGEMENTS D'ACCÈS AU MARCHÉ DANS LES ANNEXES À L'APPENDICE I DE L'*AMP* RÉVISÉ: LES PRINCIPES FONDAMENTAUX

Dans la présente section, nous abordons les principes fondamentaux liés au champ d'application de l'*AMP* révisé. D'une part, nous soulignons l'importance des négociations afin d'établir les listes d'engagements des Parties, ainsi que le rôle-clé joué par le principe de la réciprocité mutuelle dans ces négociations. D'autre part, nous traitons des différentes approches adoptées par les Parties pour définir la portée de l'*AMP*.

L'importance des négociations et l'application du principe
de la réciprocité mutuelle

Tout d'abord, il est important de souligner qu'aucun niveau prédéterminé ou uniforme n'est prévu par l'Accord pour la libéralisation et qu'il n'y a pas de règles communes encadrant la façon de définir les engagements d'accès au marché dans les annexes à l'Appendice I de l'*AMP* révisé (à l'exception de la structure de base de l'Appendice I, définie à l'article II(4)). À cet égard, les Parties jouissent d'un certain degré de flexibilité et les engagements de libéralisation de chaque Partie sont négociés individuellement, sur une base de réciprocité mutuelle, en prenant en considération les besoins des pays en développement.[103]

Dans la conduite des négociations, les Parties ont adopté différentes variantes du principe de la réciprocité mutuelle. Dans certaines situations, les Parties ont utilisé la réciprocité "formelle", où sont échangées des concessions dans un secteur contre d'autres

---

[103] Voir, par exemple, l'*AMP révisé, supra* note 8, art XXII(7).

concessions dans le même secteur (par exemple, dans les marchés publics de services).[104] Dans d'autres situations, les Parties ont adopté un format plus souple du principe de réciprocité mutuelle, avec l'objectif de parvenir à un équilibre des concessions d'accès aux marchés, qui reconnaît les circonstances particulières de chaque Partie. Par exemple, les Parties ont effectué des échanges entre différents secteurs afin de parvenir à un équilibre global de concessions.[105] Cette souplesse dans les négociations est également appliquée dans les négociations avec les membres de l'OMC qui sont candidats à l'adhésion à l'*AMP*.

Historiquement, la réciprocité mutuelle a joué et continue de jouer un rôle très important pour étendre la portée de l'*AMP*. On peut illustrer le rôle de la réciprocité mutuelle en prenant l'exemple des entités des gouvernements sous-centraux et des services d'utilité publique. Comme mentionné précédemment, les entités des gouvernements sous-centraux et les services d'utilité publique n'étaient pas couverts par l'*AMP du Cycle de Tokyo* et leur inclusion initiale a été négociée au cours du Cycle de l'Uruguay, qui a abouti à l'*AMP* 1994. En raison de contraintes politiques et pratiques, il existait de grandes variations dans les niveaux de libéralisation que les Parties étaient disposées à offrir sous l'*AMP*. Il est finalement devenu impossible d'établir un niveau global et uniforme de libéralisation dans l'*AMP*. Afin de prendre en considération les circonstances spécifiques de chaque Partie et les différents niveaux de libéralisation offerts par celles-ci, les Parties ont accepté, sur la base de la réciprocité mutuelle, d'adopter une application plus flexible de la clause NPF dans certaines situations spécifiques. Par exemple, plusieurs Parties ont accepté de soumettre leurs entités sous-centrales ou des secteurs de services d'utilité publique, mais elles n'offrent ces

---

[104] Une critique concernant la réciprocité "formelle" est qu'elle réduit les possibilités d'échanges mutuellement bénéfiques — des concessions dans un secteur ne peuvent pas être échangées contre d'autres concessions — et, donc, en général, la portée globale de l'Accord est réduite. Voir Arrowsmith, *supra* note 21 à la p 110.

[105] À titre d'exemple, une forme flexible de la réciprocité mutuelle a été utilisée dans des négociations importantes entre les États-Unis et l'Union européenne ayant mené à l'*AMP* 1994, au cours desquelles l'équivalence économique des concessions était devenue une question centrale. L'étude de la firme Deloitte et Touche a été utilisée pour négocier les engagements dans certains domaines-clés — notamment au niveau sous-central et pour l'accès des marchés publics dans le secteur de l'électricité. Ces négociations étaient fondées sur la valeur monétaire des opportunités offertes. *Ibid*, aux pp 109-10; *Protocole d'entente ÉU-UE*, *supra* note 42 et note.

concessions qu'aux Parties ayant fait des concessions équivalentes.[106] Cela a été fait par l'application de clauses de dérogations propres à chaque Partie (voir section 2). La récente conclusion des négociations a permis de réduire le nombre de dérogations propres à chaque pays.[107]

Les principales approches adoptées par les Parties

Afin de définir les marchés publics couverts par l'Accord dans l'Appendice I de l'*AMP*, les Parties ont utilisé différentes approches. En général, étant donné qu'il n'y a pas d'approche obligatoire ni de règle commune en la matière, les Parties sont libres d'adopter l'approche de leur choix pour définir leurs engagements de libéralisation. Néanmoins, en examinant les nombreuses annexes de l'Appendice I de l'*AMP*, il est possible d'identifier deux grandes tendances, à savoir (1) une approche par liste d'entités ou de secteurs et (2) une approche de type générique (*voir Encadré 5 pour une description des différentes approches*).

ENCADRÉ 5: DESCRIPTION DES PRINCIPALES APPROCHES ADOPTÉES PAR LES PARTIES POUR DÉFINIR LES MARCHÉS PUBLICS COUVERTS PAR L'*AMP*

Les deux grandes approches adoptées par les Parties pour définir leurs marchés publics couverts par l'*AMP* sont les suivantes: (1) l'approche par liste d'entités ou de secteurs et (2) l'approche de type générique.[108]

---

[106] À titre d'illustration, au cours des récentes négociations, la réciprocité mutuelle a aussi joué un rôle important afin de permettre d'étendre la portée de l'*AMP révisé* aux transports par chemins de fer, et ce, même si cet élément n'est offert qu'aux Parties ayant également offert des engagements équivalents dans le même secteur (voir section 2).

[107] Voir section 2.

[108] Il convient de noter que les listes d'engagements des Parties peuvent combiner les différentes approches et qu'il n'est pas toujours possible de distinguer clairement entre une approche générique descriptive et une approche générique de définition ou d'établir avec précision si une liste positive est exhaustive ou indicative.

Approche par liste d'entités ou de secteurs: Les listes d'entités ou de secteurs peuvent être soit *positives* soit *négatives*. Une liste est positive lorsque les éléments qui sont couverts par l'*AMP* sont individuellement énumérés dans la liste. Une liste est négative lorsque les éléments qui sont couverts par l'*AMP* sont ceux qui ne sont pas individuellement énumérés dans la liste.

En plus de ce qui précède, une liste peut aussi être qualifiée *d'exhaustive* ou *d'indicative*. Par exemple, une *liste est exhaustive* lorsque les éléments énumérés représentent toute l'étendue des engagements de cette Partie. Sur la base de la formulation utilisée, aucun engagement — autre que ceux énumérés dans la liste — ne semble avoir été pris par cette Partie. Or, si un élément n'est pas mentionné dans la liste, il ne fait pas partie des engagements de cette Partie.[109]

Une liste est indicative lorsqu'elle désigne une gamme plus large d'éléments qui partagent des caractéristiques identiques ou similaires et qui sont aussi destinés à être couverts par les engagements d'une Partie, mais qui ne sont pas expressément énumérés.[110] Lorsque la liste indicative est utilisée, elle est toujours combinée à une approche générique. La présence d'une telle liste a pour effet d'accroître la prévisibilité et la transparence des engagements d'accès au marché, définis par une approche générique.

Approche générique: En ce qui concerne l'approche générique, les éléments couverts par l'*AMP* sont précisés par

---

[109] À cet égard, il est important de noter qu'une *liste exhaustive* n'est exhaustive qu'en ce qui a trait aux engagements spécifiés à l'Appendice I. En d'autres termes, la liste exhaustive ne contient pas nécessairement tous les éléments (par exemple, les entités) d'une Partie à un niveau donné. Par exemple, selon cette terminologie, si une Partie a 25 entités au niveau du gouvernement central et n'en a désignées que 20 à l'annexe 1 selon la formulation suivante: "Les entités suivantes sont couvertes: [la liste des 20 entités]," alors cette liste peut être caractérisée comme étant exhaustive, indépendamment du fait qu'il y a cinq autres entités qui pourraient être couvertes par la Partie.

[110] À cet égard, par définition, une liste indicative ne constitue pas une liste exhaustive.

référence à une caractéristique commune distinctive ou à un ensemble de caractéristiques. Cela peut être fait par une *description générale* (par exemple "agences de l'exécutif," "universités d'État," "organismes publics au niveau local ne présentant pas un caractère industriel ou commercial"), ou d'une *définition*, qui peut être basée sur une notion juridique et qui, en outre, peut être qualifiée par référence à une législation nationale, à un secteur donné, avec ou sans l'application d'une clause, soi-disant "attrape-tout."[111]

ANALYSE DES ANNEXES À L'APPENDICE I DE L'*AMP* RÉVISÉ

La présente section met en lumière un aspect fondamental de la portée de l'*AMP* révisé, à savoir son Appendice I. Plus précisément, elle contient une analyse approfondie des listes d'engagements des Parties (les annexes de l'Appendice I) et identifie également, dans de multiples dimensions, les améliorations substantielles de la portée de l'*AMP* révisé. Afin d'avoir une vue d'ensemble de l'Appendice I de l'*AMP* révisé, il convient d'analyser les quatre éléments suivants: (1) les entités gouvernementales couvertes par l'*AMP* et énumérées dans les annexes 1 à 3; (2) les types de contrats couverts, qui sont inventoriés dans les annexes 4 à 6; (3) les seuils applicables; et (4) les dérogations diverses spécifiées dans les engagements des Parties.

Le caractère particulièrement descriptif de cette section se justifie par le fait que nous visons à expliquer le contenu hautement technique des annexes de l'Appendice I de l'*AMP* révisé, sur lequel pratiquement aucun écrit scientifique n'a encore été publié. Les renseignements exposés dans la présente section ne représentent qu'un premier effort pour extraire des informations concernant les engagements des Parties sous l'*AMP* révisé et pour les synthétiser.

Les entités gouvernementales couvertes par l'AMP

L'identification du type d'entités couvertes par l'*AMP* est une question cruciale pour fixer les limites de la portée de l'Accord. Au fil du temps, avec la diversification de l'activité étatique, cette question est devenue de plus en plus complexe. Outre les formes classiques

---

[111] Par exemple, "toute autorité ou unité administrative centralisée et décentralisée." Dans ce cas, la cause "attrape-tout" est caractérisée par le mot "toute."

des ministères et des autorités municipales, les organismes qui exercent des pouvoirs publics peuvent aussi inclure des organismes gouvernementaux commerciaux indépendants appartenant à l'État, ou des entreprises ou coentreprises établies en partenariat avec le secteur privé. En outre, il est particulièrement difficile de fixer les limites de passation des marchés publics dans les économies en transition, où l'activité du secteur public peut être omniprésente et en constante évolution (comme en Chine, en Géorgie, en Moldavie et en Ukraine).[112]

Dans son ensemble, les entités couvertes par l'*AMP* révisé sont très diversifiées. Ainsi, les Parties à l'Accord, considérées conjointement, désignent un minimum de 5200 entités et sans doute beaucoup plus.[113] Les entités visées par l'Accord se répartissent en trois grands groupes, que chaque Partie a énumérés dans les annexes 1 à 3 de l'Appendice I et qui couvrent, respectivement, les entités du gouvernement central, les entités des gouvernements sous-centraux et toutes les autres entités dont les marchés sont couverts par l'Accord. D'un point de vue général, la désignation des entités couvertes par l'*AMP* a fait l'objet de négociations détaillées et varie selon les Parties. Nous considérerons donc chaque groupe d'entités à son tour.

Les entités du gouvernement central (annexe 1)

L'annexe 1 couvre les *entités du gouvernement central* dont les marchés sont libéralisés par l'Accord. Les engagements des Parties à cet égard comprennent, par exemple, les services et les ministères gouvernementaux centraux. Pour les Parties ayant un système fédéral, cela concerne les organismes du niveau fédéral. Pour certaines

---

[112] Il est intéressant de noter qu'en pratique l'accent est généralement mis sur l'identification des entités qui sont les plus susceptibles de discriminer en faveur de l'industrie nationale. Les entités non susceptibles de s'engager dans un comportement discriminatoire — par exemple, parce que la pression commerciale sur leurs marchés les force à se procurer des marchandises et des services commercialement — ne sont généralement pas couvertes par l'AMP, même lorsqu'elles sont de propriété publique. Voir Arrowsmith, *supra* note 21 aux pp 114-15.

[113] Le nombre exact d'entités couvertes par l'*AMP révisé* n'est pas déterminé, car un certain nombre de Parties utilise des approches génériques, sans leur liste indicative, pour désigner les entités dont les marchés publics sont libéralisés par l'Accord. Lorsque de telles approches sont utilisées, les annexes de l'*AMP révisé* ne permettent pas, à elles seules, d'identifier avec précision la gamme complète des entités visées par l'Accord.

Parties, cette annexe contient aussi des entités qui fonctionnent au niveau national, en totalité ou en grande partie, et qui sont indépendantes de la structure classique des services et des ministères, mais qui sont publiques dans le sens où elles sont contrôlées ou financées dans une large mesure par un gouvernement.[114]

En général, les Parties désignent la quasi-totalité de leurs entités à ce niveau de gouvernement.[115] Considérées conjointement, les Parties à l'Accord désignent au moins 1700 entités, et sans doute beaucoup plus.[116] Ces entités comprennent, dans une large mesure, celles précédemment régies par l'*AMP* 1994 (ainsi que par l'*AMP du Cycle de Tokyo*) et plus de 400 nouvelles entités résultant de la conclusion des négociations en mars 2012.[117] Généralement, les engagements de libéralisation concernant les entités de l'annexe 1 sont accessibles à toutes les Parties.[118]

Deux observations générales se dégagent des engagements des Parties au niveau du gouvernement central: la principale approche adoptée par les Parties pour définir leurs engagements de libéralisation à l'annexe 1 est la liste positive et exhaustive

---

[114] Lorsque de telles entités indépendantes centrales ne sont pas énumérées dans l'annexe 1, elles le sont souvent à l'annexe 2. Le choix de l'annexe revêt une importance pratique et stratégique, puisque les règles de procédure applicables aux entités de l'annexe 1 sont plus strictes que celles applicables aux entités mentionnées aux annexes 2 et 3 et les seuils applicables sont plus élevés aux annexes 2 et 3 qu'à l'annexe 1.

[115] De façon très significative, cela comprend aussi les entités dans le secteur de la défense nationale (par exemple, les ministères de la défense, les corps policiers ou autres entités avec des activités liées à la défense ou la sécurité), mais l'achat de certaines marchandises sensibles pour la sécurité nationale est expressément exclu de l'Accord (voir section 2).

[116] Voir note 113.

[117] À la suite de la conclusion des négociations en mars 2012, les neuf Parties suivantes ont désigné de nouvelles entités au niveau du gouvernement central: (1) l'Union européenne; (2) Hong Kong, Chine; (3) Israël; (4) la Corée; (5) le Liechtenstein; (6) les Pays-Bas pour le compte d'Aruba; (7) la Norvège; (8) la Suisse et (9) les États-Unis. Voir, l'*AMP révisé, supra* note 8.

[118] Une exception à ce principe concerne les nouveaux engagements de l'Union européenne à l'annexe 1, qui ne sont pas offerts de façon uniforme à toutes les Parties. Trois niveaux de libéralisation sont offerts aux Parties. Premièrement, l'ouverture complète à: (1) l'Islande; (2) le Liechtenstein; (3) aux Pays-Bas pour le compte d'Aruba; (4) la Norvège et (5) la Suisse. Deuxièmement, certaines entités nouvelles pour: (1) Israël; (2) le Japon; (3) le Taipei chinois et (iv) les États-Unis. Troisièmement, aucune nouvelle ouverture pour: (1) l'Arménie; (2) le Canada; (3) Hong Kong, Chine; (4) la Corée et (5) Singapour. *Ibid*, annexe 1 de l'Union européenne.

d'entités.[119] Certaines Parties ont aussi adopté une approche fondée sur des clauses génériques avec des clauses "attrape-tout" et des listes positives d'entités;[120] et neuf Parties ont pris explicitement des engagements de libéralisation ayant trait aux entités adjudicatrices qui sont subordonnées à leurs entités énumérées à l'annexe 1.[121]

Les entités gouvernementales sous-centrales (annexe 2)

L'annexe 2 de l'Appendice I de l'*AMP* vise les *entités des gouvernements sous-centraux* dont les marchés publics sont couverts par l'*AMP*. Ainsi, pour les Parties avec un gouvernement au niveau sous-central (États, provinces ou cantons), cette annexe dresse la liste des ministères visés, ainsi que des administrations municipales et des organismes associés.

Considérées conjointement, les Parties à l'Accord désignent au moins 2000 entités des gouvernements sous-centraux, et sans doute beaucoup plus.[122] La conclusion des négociations a permis d'en ajouter environ 200.[123] En particulier, le Canada a convenu d'étendre la portée de l'Accord à l'ensemble de ses provinces et territoires (ajoutant plus de 100 entités supplémentaires).

Quatre observations générales se dégagent des engagements de libéralisation des Parties au niveau du gouvernement sous-central: dans l'ensemble, et malgré certaines lacunes individuelles, toutes

---

[119] Les dix Parties suivantes ont adopté l'approche de la liste positive: (1) l'Arménie; (2) le Canada; (3) Hong Kong, Chine; (4) Israël; (5) la Corée; (6) le Liechtenstein; (7) les Pays-Bas pour le compte d'Aruba; (8) Singapour; (9) le Taipei chinois et (10) les États-Unis. *Ibid.*

[120] Les cinq Parties suivantes ont adopté une approche généralement fondée sur des clauses génériques: (1) l'Union européenne; (2) l'Islande; (3) le Japon; (4) la Norvège et (5) la Suisse. *Ibid.*

[121] Les neuf Parties suivantes font expressément référence à l'inclusion d'entités subordonnées à leurs entités énumérées à l'annexe 1: (1) l'Arménie; (2) l'Union européenne; (3) l'Islande; (4) le Japon; (5) la Corée; (6) le Liechtenstein; (7) la Norvège; (8) le Taipei chinois et (9) les États-Unis. À titre d'exemple, l'Union européenne a pris des engagements de libéralisation concernant toute entité subordonnée aux pouvoirs adjudicateurs énumérés à l'annexe 1, à condition qu'elle ne soit pas dotée d'une personnalité juridique distincte (note 3 à l'annexe 1 de l'Union européenne), et les engagements des États-Unis incluent les marchés publics par les entités subordonnées aux entités énumérées à l'annexe 1 des États-Unis (note 1 à l'annexe 1 des États-Unis). *Ibid.*

[122] Voir note 113.

[123] Celles-ci comprennent des entités dans les quatre Parties suivantes: (1) le Canada; (2) le Japon; (3) la Corée et (4) le Taipei chinois. *Ibid.*

les Parties ayant un niveau de gouvernement sous-central y ont pris des engagements;[124] les principales approches adoptées pour prendre des engagements ont été la liste positive d'entités et la clause générique. Cinq Parties ont adopté l'approche de la liste positive[125] et sept Parties ont adopté une approche fondée sur des clauses génériques.[126] Un certain nombre de Parties ont combiné les différentes approches pour définir certains éléments de leurs engagements de libéralisation; trois Parties ont pris explicitement des engagements de libéralisation ayant trait aux entités adjudicatrices qui sont subordonnées à leurs entités énumérées à l'annexe 2;[127] et neuf Parties font référence à la législation nationale pertinente pour définir certains aspects de leurs engagements de libéralisation.[128]

---

[124] Les trois Parties suivantes n'ont pas de niveau de gouvernement sous-central: (1) Hong Kong, Chine; (2) les Pays-Bas pour le compte d'Aruba et (3) Singapour. Voir l'*AMP révisé, supra* note 8.

[125] Les cinq Parties sont les suivantes: (1) le Canada; (2) Israël; (3) la Corée; (4) le Taipei chinois et (5) les États-Unis. *Ibid.*

[126] Les sept Parties sont les suivantes: (1) l'Arménie; (2) l'Union européenne; (3) l'Islande; (4) le Japon; (5) le Liechtenstein; (6) la Norvège et (7) la Suisse. *Ibid.*

[127] Les trois Parties sont les suivantes: (1) le Japon; (2) la Corée et (3) le Taipei chinois. *Ibid.* À titre d'exemple, le Japon a pris des engagements de libéralisation concernant les entités subordonnées aux entités visés à l'annexe 2, tels que les subdivisions internes, et certaines organisations et succursales (note 1 à l'annexe 2 du Japon); et les engagements de la Corée incluent les marchés publics par les entités subordonnées sous le contrôle direct des entités énumérées à l'annexe 2, ainsi que certains bureaux et succursales, à condition qu'elles ne soient pas dotées d'une personnalité juridique distincte (note 1 à l'annexe 2 de la Corée). *Ibid.*

[128] Les neuf Parties sont les suivantes: (1) le Canada; (2) l'Union européenne; (3) le Japon; (4) la Corée; (5) le Liechtenstein; (6) la Norvège; (7) la Suisse; (8) le Taipei chinois et (9) les États-Unis. *Ibid.* À titre d'exemple, l'Union européenne a pris des engagements de libéralisation concernant "*Tous les* "*pouvoirs adjudicateurs*" *des unités administratives telles que définies par le règlement 1059/2003 — règlement NUTS*"; et les engagements du Japon couvrent tous les gouvernements préfectoraux intitulés "*To*," "*Do*," "*Fu*" *et* "*Ken*" et toutes les villes désignées intitulées "*Shitei toshi*," couvertes par la "*Local Autonomy Law*" du Japon. Voir CE, *Règlement (CE) 1059/2003 du Parlement européen et du Conseil du 26 mai 2003 relatif à l'établissement d'une nomenclature commune des unités territoriales statistiques (NUTS)*, (2003), JO L154, tel que modifié en dernier lieu par le *Règlement (CE) 1137/2008 du Parlement européen et du Conseil du 22 octobre 2008 portant adaptation à la décision 1999/468/CE du Conseil de certains actes soumis à la procédure visée à l'article 251 du traité, en ce qui concerne la procédure de réglementation avec contrôle* (2008), JO L311 à la p 26; Japon, *Local Autonomy Law*, Law N°67 (1947).

Historiquement, les engagements à l'égard des entités couvertes par l'annexe 2 étaient particulièrement soumis à des dérogations propres à chaque Partie, mais la conclusion des négociations en a significativement réduit le nombre. En particulier, le fait que le Canada ait intégré l'ensemble de ses provinces et territoires a permis d'éliminer de nombreuses dérogations. Néanmoins, il subsiste un certain nombre de dérogations propres à chaque Partie à l'égard des entités couvertes par l'annexe 2.[129]

De plus, quatre Parties ont des clauses de non-application des procédures de recours internes (article XVIII), en ce qui concerne les recours intentés contre l'adjudication de certains marchés publics effectués par les entités visées par l'annexe 2.[130] Ces clauses de non-application s'appliquent seulement aux fournisseurs de produits et de services de quelques Parties. Ainsi, sans exclure littéralement le droit des Parties concernées d'exploiter certains marchés publics, ce type de clauses nie le droit de leurs fournisseurs de contester une violation de l'Accord pour les marchés publics spécifiés. De ce fait, ces clauses réduisent la sécurité juridique des Parties ainsi affectées. L'objectif principal de ce type de clause semble être de parvenir à un équilibre temporaire des engagements, avec l'objectif ultime d'obtenir des concessions supplémentaires. En effet, la formulation de ces clauses suggère qu'elles seront éliminées lorsque la Partie sujette à la clause aura offert un niveau d'engagements acceptable par la Partie qui l'applique.

---

129   Par exemple, afin de calibrer et de balancer les marchés publics offerts par le Canada, certaines Parties ont exclu les marchandises, services et fournisseurs en provenance du Canada en ce qui concerne les marchés publics passés par leurs entités des gouvernements sous-centraux opérant au niveau local (par exemple, les municipalités). Un autre exemple est l'exclusion, par l'Union européenne, de l'Islande, du Liechtenstein et de la Norvège des services et fournisseurs de services en provenance des États-Unis des marchés publics passés par les entités visées à l'annexe 2. En d'autres termes, seules les marchandises en provenance des États-Unis sont couvertes.

130   Une telle clause peut prendre la forme suivante: "Les dispositions de l'article XVIII ne sont pas applicables aux fournisseurs de produits et de services des Parties suivantes: [Parties A, B et C] en ce qui concerne les recours intentés contre l'adjudication de marchés par les organismes mentionnés à l'annexe 2, tant qu'il n'aura pas été constaté que ces Parties ont complété leurs listes respectives d'entités des gouvernements sous-centraux." Les quatre Parties ayant adoptées de telles clauses sont les suivantes: (1) l'Union européenne (note 3 à l'annexe 2); (2) l'Islande (note 4 à l'annexe 2); (3) le Liechtenstein (note 2 à l'annexe 2) et (4) la Suisse (note générale 2 à l'annexe 7). Voir l'*AMP révisé*, *supra* note 8 et section 2.

Les autres entités, y compris les fournisseurs de services d'utilité publique dont les marchés sont couverts par l'Accord (annexe 3)

L'annexe 3 de l'Appendice I de l'*AMP* couvre toutes les *autres entités* dont les marchés publics sont couverts par l'Accord. Cette annexe désigne principalement, mais pas uniquement, des organismes publics et des entreprises publiques qui fournissent des services d'utilité publique, comme la production et la fourniture de gaz et d'électricité, la distribution d'eau, l'exploitation de réseaux de transports urbains (tramways, métros, chemins de fer, etc.) et la fourniture d'installations portuaires et aéroportuaires.[131] Certaines Parties ont également inclus dans l'annexe 3 d'autres types d'entités, comme des instituts de recherche, des établissements d'enseignement, des universités et des laboratoires.

Considérées conjointement, les Parties à l'Accord désignent au moins 1500 entités, et sans doute beaucoup plus.[132] Suite à la conclusion des négociations, il y a eu des ajouts importants au niveau des autres entités gouvernementales (y compris des entreprises publiques),[133] comprenant par exemple de nouvelles entités dans les secteurs des transports ferroviaires ou urbains,[134] des entités dans le secteur des services postaux[135] et d'autres types d'entités.[136]

Quatre observations générales se dégagent des engagements de libéralisation des Parties au niveau des *autres entités*, y compris les fournisseurs de services d'utilité publique: (1) les principaux secteurs de services d'utilité publique libéralisés par les Parties sont la production, le transport ou la distribution d'eau potable; la production, le transport ou la distribution d'électricité; les aéroports,

---

[131] Voir, pour une discussion sur les engagements de libéralisation concernant les entreprises publiques sous l'*AMP*, Ping Wang, "The Procurement of State Trading Enterprises under the WTO Agreements: A Proposal for a Way Forward," dans Arrowsmith et Anderson, *supra* note 4 au ch 8 aux pp 197-251; Wang, *supra* note 99.

[132] Voir note 113.

[133] Des améliorations ont aussi été apportées dans la portée des engagements des Parties par l'élimination d'un certain nombre de dérogations qui étaient précédemment incluses dans l'*AMP* 1994.

[134] Voir, notamment, les quatre Parties suivantes: (1) l'Union européenne; (2) Islande; (3) Israël et (4) la Corée. Voir l'*AMP révisé*, *supra* note 8.

[135] Voir, notamment, les deux Parties suivantes: (1) le Liechtenstein et (2) la Suisse. *Ibid.*

[136] Voir, notamment, les quatre Parties suivantes: (1) le Canada; (2) Israël; (3) la Corée et (iv) le Taipei chinois. *Ibid.*

les ports maritimes ou intérieurs; les transports urbains, les transports par chemins de fer y compris les trains à grande vitesse; et les services postaux; (2) dans l'ensemble, malgré des lacunes individuelles, toutes les Parties sauf une ont pris des engagements à l'annexe 3;[137] (3) les principales approches adoptées pour définir les engagements ont été la liste positive d'entités et la clause générique; et (4) huit Parties ont adopté l'approche de la liste positive;[138] et six Parties ont adopté une approche généralement fondée sur des clauses génériques, en se basant sur une définition par référence à la législation nationale et aux secteurs d'utilité publique, avec une clause "attrape-tout" et avec des listes positives et indicatives d'entités;[139] six Parties font référence à la législation nationale pertinente pour définir certains aspects de leurs engagements à l'annexe 3.[140]

Les Parties n'offrent pas une libéralisation uniforme des marchés publics dans le secteur des services d'utilité publique. Par exemple, tandis que pratiquement tous ces marchés publics sont libéralisés par l'Union européenne et par les pays de l'Association européenne de libre-échange (AELE), ce n'est pas le cas de toutes les autres Parties. Pour contrer ce manque d'uniformité dans la libéralisation des services d'utilité publique, les Parties ont généralement appliqué le principe de la réciprocité sectorielle. Ainsi, l'accès aux marchés publics dans ce secteur est généralement conditionnel à l'ouverture réciproque des marchés par d'autres Parties dans le même secteur. Cette situation s'est traduite par l'application de certaines clauses de dérogations sectorielles et propres à chaque Partie basées sur la réciprocité.[141] Néanmoins, la conclusion des négociations a permis de réduire le nombre de dérogations dans

---

[137] La seule Partie sans engagements à ce niveau est la suivante: les Pays-Bas pour le compte d'Aruba. *Ibid.*

[138] Les huit Parties sont les suivantes: (1) le Canada; (2) Hong Kong, Chine; (3) Israël; (4) le Japon; (5) la Corée; (6) Singapour; (7) le Taipei chinois et (8) les États-Unis. *Ibid.*

[139] Les six Parties sont les suivantes: (1) l'Arménie; (2) l'Union européenne; (3) l'Islande; (4) le Liechtenstein; (5) la Norvège et (6) la Suisse. *Ibid.*

[140] Les six Parties sont les suivantes: (1) l'Arménie; (2) l'Union européenne; (3) l'Islande; (4) le Liechtenstein; (5) la Norvège et (6) la Suisse. *Ibid.*

[141] Par exemple, l'Union européenne et les pays de l'AELE ont entièrement ou majoritairement exclu le Canada de l'ensemble de leurs engagements de libéralisation des services d'utilité publique, et ce, tant qu'elles n'auront pas constaté que le Canada assure à leurs entreprises un accès comparable et effectif au marché de ses services d'utilité publique. Le Japon, la Corée et les États-Unis

certains secteurs de services d'utilité publique, comme les transports urbains et l'électricité.

Les marchandises et services (incluant les services de construction) couverts par l'AMP

L'identification des types de contrats couverts par l'*AMP* est aussi une question primordiale pour fixer les limites de la portée de l'Accord. Afin de désigner les différents types de contrats couverts, l'*AMP* distingue trois catégories, comprenant les marchandises, les services et les services de construction, qui sont respectivement énumérées dans les annexes 4 à 6 de l'Appendice I. D'un point de vue général, la désignation des types de contrats couverts par l'*AMP* a fait l'objet de négociations détaillées et elle varie entre les Parties. Cela est particulièrement vrai en ce qui concerne les services. Chaque type de contrat sera considéré à tour de rôle au sein de la section suivante.

Les marchandises (annexe 4)

L'annexe 4 de l'Appendice I de l'*AMP* vise les marchandises couvertes par l'Accord. Sous l'*AMP* révisé, tous les marchés publics de marchandises sont couverts (par les entités visées et d'une valeur supérieure au seuil d'application), sauf s'ils sont expressément exclus. Toutes les Parties désignent les marchandises couvertes dans leur annexe 4 à l'aide d'une note indiquant, dans des termes plus ou moins similaires, que l'Accord vise tous les marchés publics de marchandises par les entités figurant dans les annexes 1 à 3, à moins que l'Accord en dispose autrement. Il s'agit d'une approche par liste négative.

Bien que la présence d'une annexe consacrée aux marchandises constitue une nouveauté de l'*AMP* révisé, en pratique il s'agit uniquement d'un changement de présentation. En effet, les marchés publics de marchandises étaient déjà couverts sous l'*AMP du Cycle de Tokyo* et sous l'*AMP* 1994. Néanmoins, l'ajout de cette annexe constitue une nette amélioration pour la clarté et la prévisibilité de la portée de l'Accord. La conclusion des négociations a également permis d'étendre le champ d'application de l'*AMP* à certains aspects des marchandises, qui étaient jusqu'alors non couverts. Cette libéralisation supplémentaire a essentiellement été réalisée par la

---

sont aussi exclus d'une partie des services d'utilité publique libéralisés par l'Union européenne et les pays de l'AELE.

suppression ou la réduction de l'étendue de dérogations pré-existantes sous l'*AMP* 1994.[142]

Comme dans le cadre de l'*AMP* 1994, la principale exception — pour ce qui est des marchandises — concerne les marchés publics dans le secteur de la défense nationale. Généralement, les entités dans ce secteur sont couvertes par l'Accord (par exemple, les ministères ou départements de la défense, les corps policiers ou autres entités avec des activités liées à la défense ou la sécurité), mais l'Accord exclut expressément l'achat par celles-ci de certaines marchandises. Cette exception prend la forme d'une exclusion générale des marchés publics par les entités liées à la défense nationale, et dans la majorité des cas elle est jumelée à une liste de produits et de matériel militaire non sensibles et couverts par les entités liées à la défense nationale.

Ces listes ne couvrent généralement pas les produits de nature exclusivement militaire: armes, munitions, missiles, véhicules de combat, blindés ou appareils spatiaux, avions de chasse, etc. En revanche, elles couvrent des produits comme le matériel ferroviaire, le matériel de construction, les cordages, câbles, chaînes, produits chimiques, produits pharmaceutiques et matériel médical, matériel d'informatique générale, meubles, etc. Deux observations se dégagent des listes de produits et de matériel militaire non sensibles et couverts par l'Accord: d'abord, toutes les Parties qui se sont engagées à libéraliser leurs entités dans le secteur de la défense nationale excluent les marchés publics passés par ces entités.[143] Ces exclusions sont jumelées à des listes de produits et de matériel militaire non sensibles et couverts par ces entités. Neuf de ces Parties ont inclus à l'annexe 4 leur liste de produits non sensible pour la défense.[144] Ensuite, les produits non sensibles pour la défense sont définis par référence à deux systèmes principaux de codification et de classification des marchandises: (1) la Classification fédérale des approvi-

---

[142] Des améliorations dans le champ d'application des marchandises ont été fournies par des suppressions ou des réductions de l'étendue de dérogations pré-existantes (notamment par le Canada et Israël). En outre, la Suisse fournit une expansion des marchés publics visés par l'ajout, à son annexe 4, de marchandises supplémentaires dans la liste de marchandises non sensibles pour les marchés publics liés à la défense. Voir l'*AMP révisé*, *supra* note 8.

[143] Les onze Parties sont les suivantes: (1) l'Arménie; (2) le Canada; (3) l'Union européenne; (4) l'Islande; (5) le Japon; (6) la Corée; (7) la Norvège; (8) Singapour; (9) la Suisse; (10) le Taipei chinois et (11) les États-Unis. *Ibid.*

[144] Les trois Parties suivantes ont inclus leur liste à l'annexe 1: (1) l'Arménie; (2) Singapour et (3) les États-Unis. *Ibid.*

sionnements (FSC);[145] et (2) le Système harmonisé (SH) ou systèmes connexes.[146]

Cette dérogation vise à assurer la sécurité et la défense nationale des Parties, et en théorie le paragraphe 1 de l'article III de l'*AMP* révisé (concernant la sécurité) pourrait aussi s'appliquer à de nombreux achats de matériel militaire, si cet équipement était couvert par les annexes. Toutefois, les exclusions explicites dans les annexes évitent aux Parties de fournir une justification pour ne pas appliquer l'Accord à ces achats.

Les services (annexe 5)

L'annexe 5 de l'Appendice I de l'*AMP* désigne les *services* couverts par l'Accord, autres que les services de construction. Dans son ensemble, les services couverts comprennent ceux précédemment régis par l'*AMP* 1994 et plus de 50 nouveaux secteurs résultant de la conclusion des négociations. À titre d'exemple, presque toutes les Parties ont étendu, à divers degrés, la portée de l'Accord à des secteurs de services supplémentaires,[147] incluant une libéralisation accrue des services de télécommunications par huit Parties.[148]

Les engagements varient entre les Parties, et dans l'ensemble, la libéralisation ne va pas aussi loin que celle des marchés publics de marchandises. Ainsi, les engagements des Parties comprennent, entre autres, des services fournis aux entreprises (comme les services

---

[145] Les sept Parties suivantes ont utilisé les positions tarifaires désignées dans les chapitres de la classification fédérale des approvisionnements (FSC): (1) l'Arménie; (2) le Canada; (3) le Japon; (4) la Corée; (5) Singapour; (6) le Taipei chinois et (7) les États-Unis. *Ibid.* De plus amples renseignements sur le FSC sont disponibles dans le "Federal Procurement Data System Product and Service Code Manual" à l'adresse suivante: US <http://www.acquisition.gov/>.

[146] La Suisse a utilisé le Système harmonisé (SH), l'Union européenne et l'Islande ont utilisé la nomenclature combinée (NC) et la Norvège a utilisé la nomenclature de Bruxelles du Conseil de coopération douanière (CCD). De plus amples renseignements sur: (1) le SH et la CCD sont disponibles à l'adresse suivante: OMD <http://www.wcoomd.org/fr.aspx> et (2) sur la NC à l'adresse suivante: CE <http://ec.europa.eu/taxation_customs/customs/customs_duties/tariff_aspects/combined_nomenclature/index_fr.htm>.

[147] Les douze Parties suivantes ont offert des services supplémentaires: (1) l'Union européenne; (2) Hong Kong, Chine; (3) Islande; (4) Israël; (5) Japon; (6) Corée; (7) Liechtenstein; (8) les Pays-Bas pour le compte d'Aruba; (9) Norvège; (10) Singapour; (11) Suisse et (12) les États-Unis. Voir l'AMP révisé, *supra* note 8.

[148] Les huit Parties sont les suivantes: (1) l'Union européenne; (2) Hong Kong, Chine; (3) Islande; (4) Liechtenstein; (5) les Pays-Bas pour le compte d'Aruba; (6) Norvège; (7) Suisse et (8) les États-Unis. Voir l'*AMP révisé*, *supra* note 8.

informatiques), des services de télécommunications, des services concernant l'environnement, des services financiers, des services relatifs au tourisme et aux voyages, et des services de transports aériens et routiers.

Des observations générales se dégagent des engagements des Parties pour ce qui est des services: le champ d'application des catégories de services mentionnées à l'annexe 5 est généralement défini en référence à la Classification centrale de produits provisoire des Nations unies (CPC Prov.), tel que défini dans une note informelle du Secrétariat de l'OMC;[149] les services couverts sont désignés dans une liste positive par toutes les Parties, sauf l'Arménie et les États-Unis. De leur côté, les États-Unis ont adopté une liste négative de services et couvrent tous les services, sauf ceux énumérés; l'Arménie, elle, couvre tous les services définis dans la note informelle du Secrétariat, sans exception;[150] les huit secteurs suivants sont couverts en totalité ou en grande partie par les Parties: (1) services de télécommunications (CPC Prov. 752); (2) services d'informatique et services connexes (CPC Prov. 84); (3) certains services de transport (aériens [CPC Prov. 731] et routiers [CPC Prov. 712]); (4) services concernant l'environnement (CPC Prov. 940); (5) services de courrier (CPC Prov. 7512); (6) certains services professionnels (services comptable, services d'architecture, services d'ingénierie, etc.) (CPC Prov. 862, 863, 867); (7) les services d'assurance et services connexes (CPC Prov. 812, 814); et (8) certains services fournis aux entreprises;[151] seule une ou quelques Parties (pas plus de trois) s'engagent dans les secteurs et sous-secteurs suivants: (1) services de recherche-développement (CPC Prov. 85); (2) services postaux (CPC Prov. 7511); (3) certains services de transport (ferroviaires [CPC Prov. 711], maritimes [CPC Prov. 721], par voies navigables intérieures [CPC Prov. 722] et par conduites [CPC Prov. 713]);[152] (4) services

---

[149] *GATT*, Cycle de l'Uruguay, Groupe de négociation sur les services, Note du Secrétariat, *Classification sectorielle des services*, (1991), MTN.GNS/W/120, en ligne: OMC <http://docsonline.wto.org>. Ces services sont désignés conformément à la Classification centrale de produits provisoire des Nations Unies (CPC Prov.), en ligne: UNSD <http://unstats.un.org/unsd/cr/registry/regcst. asp?Cl=9&Top=2&Lg=2>.

[150] *Ibid.*

[151] Voir les codes CPC Prov. suivants: 871, 864, 865, 866, 8676, 881,883, 5115, 8675, 633, 8861-8866, 874 et 88 442.

[152] Voir les codes CPC Prov. suivants: 7211, 7214, 745, 711, 722, 713, 741, 742, 749, 95, 97, 98 et 99.

de distribution;[153] (5) services de radio et télévision (CPC Prov. 9613); (6) services récréatifs, culturels et sportifs;[154] et (7) certains services de santé[155] et d'éducation,[156] ainsi que des services fournis aux entreprises.[157]

Comme mentionné, les Parties ne libéralisent pas de manière uniforme les marchés publics de services. Pour faire face à ce manque d'uniformité, les Parties ont généralement insisté sur la libéralisation réciproque des marchés publics d'un service donné comme condition d'accès à leurs marchés publics pour le même type de service. L'application de la réciprocité dans le secteur des services signifie que, dans les faits, des Parties n'ont pas accès à certains services parce qu'ils ne libéralisent pas eux-mêmes ces services. Ainsi, neuf Parties ont fondé leurs engagements sur la base de la réciprocité mutuelle.[158] Ces Parties ont spécifié, à l'aide d'une note, que l'*AMP* vise les services précisés dans leurs engagements, en ce qui concerne une Partie donnée, seulement dans la mesure où cette Partie a accordé un accès réciproque aux services en question.

Enfin, l'*AMP* fixe les règles sur la façon dont sont conduits les marchés publics, mais les questions relatives à l'accès ou au commerce des services en général sont régies par l'*AGCS*.[159] En d'autres termes, les concessions sur les marchés publics de services dans

---

153 Voir les codes CPC Prov. suivants: 621, 622, 631, 632, 6111, 6113, 6121 et 8929.

154 Voir les codes CPC Prov. suivants: 9619, 962, 963 et 964.

155 Voir les codes CPC Prov. suivants: 9311, 9319 et 933.

156 Voir les codes CPC Prov. suivants: 921, 922 et 923.

157 Voir les codes CPC Prov. suivants: 884, 885, 887 et 872.

158 Ces neuf Parties sont les suivantes: (1) le Canada; (2) l'Union européenne; (3) l'Islande; (4) la Corée; (5) le Liechtenstein; (6) la Norvège; (7) la Suisse; (8) le Taipei chinois et (9) les États-Unis. Voir l'*AMP révisé, supra* note 8.

159 L'article IV(7) de l'*AMP* prévoit explicitement que les principes de non-discrimination de l'*AMP* (art IV(1) et (2)) ne s'appliqueront pas aux mesures non spécifiques à la passation des marchés publics, telles que les mesures touchant le commerce des services autres que celles qui régissent les marchés couverts par l'*AMP*. Cette disposition indique clairement que l'*AMP* fixe les règles sur la façon dont les marchés publics sont conduits, mais qu'il ne traite pas des questions relatives à l'accès aux marchés publics des services ou au commerce des services en général. Ces mesures restent soumises aux règles de l'*AGCS*. *Ibid*, art IV(7). Voir aussi Robert D Anderson et al, "The Relationship between Services Trade and Government Procurement Commitments: Insights from Relevant WTO Agreements and Recent RTAs" (à venir) document de travail de l'OMC; Arrowsmith, *supra* note 21 aux pp 104-5; Patrick Low, Aaditya Mattoo et Arvind Subramanian, "Government Procurement in Services" (1995) 20 World Competition 5.

l'*AMP* sont soumises à toutes les conditions d'accès aux marchés qui s'appliquent pour chaque Partie en vertu de l'*AGCS*.[160]

Les services de construction (annexe 6)

L'annexe 6 de l'*AMP* fournit les détails sur les services de construction et les formes de partenariats public-privé (PPP) qui sont couverts par les Parties. Sous l'*AMP* révisé, toutes les Parties s'engagent maintenant d'une façon complète à l'égard des marchés publics de services de construction (CPC Prov. 51).[161] Il s'agit d'une nette amélioration de l'*AMP* révisé, par rapport à l'*AMP* 1994. De plus, le texte révisé de l'*AMP* innove et fournit maintenant une définition commune des services de construction, indiquant que l'expression "service de construction" s'entend d'un service ayant pour objectif la réalisation, par quelque moyen que ce soit, de travaux de génie civil ou de construction, au sens de la division 51 de la CPC Prov.[162]

De plus, à la suite de la conclusion des négociations en mars 2012, trois Parties (Union européenne,[163] Japon,[164] Corée[165]) ont expli-

[160] À cet égard, six Parties ont explicitement spécifié, à l'aide d'une note, dans des termes plus ou moins similaires, que leurs engagements dans le domaine des services sont sous réserve des limitations et conditions concernant l'accès aux marchés et le traitement national spécifiés dans leurs listes d'engagements respectifs au titre de l'*AGCS*. Les six Parties sont les suivantes: (1) le Canada; (2) Israël; (3) Liechtenstein; (4) Singapour; (5) le Taipei chinois et (6) la Suisse. *Ibid.* Du point de vue de l'auteur, ces spécifications ne semblent pas nécessaires compte tenu des observations qui précèdent.

[161] Néanmoins, il convient de noter qu'il existe toujours certaines variations dans les seuils d'application pour la libéralisation des marchés publics des services de construction, en particulier au niveau des annexes 2 et 3 (voir section 2).

[162] *AMP révisé, supra* note 8, art 1(c).

[163] Les engagements de l'Union européenne à cet égard sont offerts uniquement aux six Parties suivantes: (1) l'Islande; (2) le Liechtenstein; (3) la Norvège; (4) les Pays-Bas pour le compte d'Aruba; (5) la Suisse et (6) la Corée (pour cette dernière Partie, un seuil d'application différent de 15 000 000 DTS est applicable).

[164] Les engagements du Japon à cet égard proviennent de la précision voulant que les marchés publics de projets de construction assujettis à la loi japonaise sur la promotion de l'initiative de financement privé soient couverts par l'*AMP*. Voir *AMP révisé, supra* note 8, note à l'annexe 6 du Japon; Japon, *Act on Promotion of Private Finance Initiative*, Law N°117, 1999, tel que modifié en dernier lieu au 30 novembre 2011; OMC, Comité des marchés publics, *Notification des législations nationales, Communication du Japon*, GPA/111 (2011), en ligne: OMC <http://docsonline.wto.org>.

[165] La Corée vise les contrats de CET pour les entités visées à l'annexe 1 avec un seuil d'application de 5 000 000 DTS et à l'annexe 2 avec un seuil d'application de 15 000 000 DTS.

tement étendu la portée de l'*AMP* aux contrats de "construction-exploitation-transfert de propriété" (CET), concessions de travaux publics ou autres formes de partenariats public-privé. Cela est en soi un ajout très important au champ d'application de l'*AMP*.

Les seuils applicables

L'article II (2) (c) de l'*AMP* stipule que l'Accord s'applique lorsque la valeur des marchés publics est égale ou supérieure à la valeur de seuil spécifiée dans les annexes de l'Appendice I. Les contrats qui ne répondent pas aux seuils ne sont pas soumis aux exigences prévues par l'*AMP*. D'un point de vue général, l'*AMP* vise à libéraliser les marchés publics à l'international, et en pratique l'*AMP* est destiné à s'appliquer aux marchés publics d'une certaine envergure. C'est la principale raison pour laquelle les seuils de l'*AMP* sont généralement assez élevés. Cela a aussi pour effet de protéger les plus petits contrats contre les forces de la concurrence internationale et de donner une protection *de facto* aux entreprises nationales, notamment les PME.

Dans son ensemble, et nonobstant certaines réductions des seuils d'application par cinq Parties,[166] les valeurs de seuil applicable sont les mêmes sous l'*AMP* révisé que celles précédemment applicables sous l'*AMP* 1994. Dans l'*AMP*, les valeurs de seuil doivent être négociées individuellement, mais de façon générale, les Parties appliquent presque toutes les mêmes seuils, qui constituent les "valeurs de seuil généralement applicables" sous l'*AMP* (voir Encadré 6 ci-dessous). Certaines Parties ont néanmoins adopté des seuils différents.

Habituellement, les Parties spécifient séparément les seuils applicables pour les marchés publics de marchandises, services et services de construction, selon le type d'entité concerné. Les seuils dans les annexes sont exprimés en Droit de tirage spécial (DTS). Conformément à une Décision du Comité, ces valeurs sont ensuite converties par chaque Partie en monnaie nationale et notifiées au Secrétariat de l'OMC.[167]

---

[166] Voir notamment Israël, le Japon, la Corée, les Pays-Bas pour le compte d'Aruba et les États-Unis. Voir l'*AMP révisé, supra* note 8.

[167] OMC, Comité sur les marchés publics, *Décision sur les questions de procédure relevant de l'Accord sur les marchés publics*, GPA/1 (1996), annexe 3, en ligne: OMC <http://docsonline.wto.org>.

ENCADRÉ 6: VALEURS DE SEUIL GÉNÉRALEMENT APPLICABLES
(EXPRIMÉES EN DTS)

Niveau des entités	Marchandises	Services	Services de construction
Annexe 1 (gouvernement central)	130 000	130 000	5 000 000
Annexe 2 (gouvernements sous-centraux)	200 000	200 000	5 000 000
Annexe 3 (autres entités)	400 000	400 000	5 000 000

Les cinq observations suivantes se dégagent des valeurs de seuil appliquées par les Parties: (1) dans chaque annexe, neuf Parties appliquent le même ensemble uniforme de seuils pour les marchés publics de marchandises, de services et de services de construction (voir Encadré 6);[168] (2) toutes les Parties, sauf deux,[169] appliquent des valeurs de seuil de 130 000 DTS en matière de marchés publics de marchandises et de services effectués par les entités visées à l'annexe 1; (3) toutes les Parties ayant un niveau de gouvernement sous-central, sauf trois,[170] appliquent des valeurs de seuil de 200 000 DTS en matière de marchés publics de marchandises et de services effectués par les entités visées à l'annexe 2;[171] (4) toutes les Parties, sauf quatre,[172] appliquent des valeurs de seuil de 400 000 DTS en

---

168 Ces neuf Parties sont les suivantes: (1) l'Arménie; (2) l'Union européenne; (3) Hong Kong, Chine; (4) Islande; (5) Liechtenstein; (6) Norvège; (7) Singapour; (8) Suisse et (9) le Taipei chinois. Voir l'*AMP révisé, supra* note 8.

169 Le Japon et les Pays-Bas pour le compte d'Aruba appliquent des valeurs de seuil de 100 000 DTS pour les mêmes types de marchés publics. Il est aussi intéressant de noter que le Japon a en outre spécifié, à l'égard des services en matière d'architecture, ingénierie et autres techniques (CPC Prov 867) des valeurs de seuil spécifiques de 450 000 DTS pour les entités visées aux annexes 1 et 3 et de 1 500 000 DTS pour les entités visées à l'annexe 2. *Ibid.*

170 Les trois Parties suivantes ont des seuils différents: le Canada et les États-Unis (355 000 DTS) et Israël (250 000 DTS). *Ibid.*

171 Les trois Parties suivantes n'ont pas de niveau de gouvernement sous-central: (1) Hong Kong, Chine; (2) les Pays-Bas pour le compte d'Aruba et (3) Singapour. *Ibid.*

172 Les quatre Parties suivantes ont des seuils différents: le Canada et Israël (355 000 DTS); le Japon (130 000 DTS) et les États-Unis (l'équivalent en DTS de

matière de marchés publics de marchandises et de services effectués par les entités visées à l'annexe 3;[173] et (5) toutes les Parties, sauf quatre,[174] appliquent des valeurs de seuil de 5 000 000 DTS en matière de marchés publics de services de construction effectués par toutes les entités.[175]

Historiquement, les seuils étaient particulièrement soumis à la réciprocité entre les Parties, mais la conclusion des négociations a atténué le phénomène. Néanmoins, il subsiste un certain nombre de dérogations propres à chaque Partie et fondées sur la réciprocité quant aux seuils applicables pour faire face aux variations des valeurs de seuil entre les Parties.[176] De plus, cinq Parties ont des clauses de non-application des procédures de recours internes (article XVIII) s'appliquant à certains fournisseurs en ce qui concerne les recours intentés contre l'adjudication de marchés publics dont la valeur est

---

250 000 de dollars US pour la liste A des entités et 400 000 DTS pour la liste B des entités). *Ibid.*

[173] Les onze Parties qui appliquent des valeurs de seuil de 400 000 DTS sont les suivantes: (1) l'Arménie; (2) l'Union européenne; (3) Hong Kong, Chine; (4) Islande; (5) Corée; (6) Liechtenstein; (7) les Pays-Bas pour le compte d'Aruba; (8) Norvège; (9) Singapour; (10) Suisse et (11) le Taipei chinois. *Ibid.*

[174] Les quatre Parties suivantes ont des seuils différents: les Pays-Bas pour le compte d'Aruba (4 000 000 DTS); Israël (8 500 000 DTS); la Corée (15 000 000 DTS) et le Japon (4 500 000 DTS pour les entités visées à l'annexe 1 et pour la liste B des entités à l'annexe 3 et 15 000 000 DTS pour les entités visées à l'annexe 2 et pour la liste A des entités à l'annexe 3). *Ibid.*

[175] Les onze Parties sont les suivantes: (1) l'Arménie; (2) l'Union européenne; (3) Hong Kong, Chine; (4) Islande; (5) Corée; (6) Liechtenstein; (7) les Pays-Bas pour le compte d'Aruba; (8) Norvège; (9) Singapour; (10) Suisse et (11) le Taipei chinois. *Ibid.*

[176] Des exemples de dérogations spécifiques à chaque Partie fondées sur la réciprocité pour faire face aux variations des valeurs de seuil entre les Parties comprennent les suivantes: l'Union européenne applique des seuils plus élevés pour les arrangements de construction-exploitation-transfert (CET) en provenance de la Corée (15 000 000 DTS) aux annexes 2 et 3, ainsi que pour les marchandises et les services du Canada (355 000 DTS). Les États-Unis appliquent des seuils plus élevés pour les services de construction de la Corée et les fournisseurs de ces services (15 000 000 DTS). De plus, les marchés publics visés par le Taipei chinois sont seulement couverts par l'AMP à l'égard de chaque Partie, lorsque la valeur des seuils est la même ou supérieur à celle appliquée par l'autre Partie pour la même catégorie de marchés publics (note générale 1). Cette note générale du Taipei chinois ne s'applique pas à Israël et aux États-Unis au niveau de l'annexe 2.

inférieure au seuil appliqué à la même catégorie de marchés publics par certaines Parties.[177]

Dérogations diverses

Après avoir précisé la portée des engagements des Parties en termes d'entités, de types de contrats et de seuils d'application, il importe de se pencher sur un autre aspect important du champ d'application de l'*AMP*, à savoir les dérogations. Il convient de noter que des dérogations ou des conditions afférentes aux engagements peuvent être spécifiées par une Partie, soit dans l'annexe 7 de l'*AMP* qui contient toutes les notes générales, soit directement dans les notes afférentes à chaque annexe.[178]

Ce qui suit contient quelques détails supplémentaires concernant la nature et la portée des dérogations suivantes: (1) des dérogations ou des notes visant à assurer la précision et la clarté des engagements des Parties; (2) des dérogations relatives à une entité particulière, un produit, un secteur de services ou un autre élément; (3) des dérogations relatives à certaines considérations de politique intérieure, qui utilisent les marchés publics comme outil de politique sociale ou environnementale; et (4) des dérogations propres à chaque pays.

Premièrement, certaines Parties utilisent leurs notes ou les notes générales pour fournir plus de précision, de clarté et de transparence en ce qui concerne leurs engagements. Ainsi, quatre Parties ont exclu — à l'aide d'une note — les marchés publics passés par les entités mentionnées aux annexes 1 et 2 dans les secteurs de l'eau potable, de l'énergie, du transport ou des télécommunications, sauf s'ils sont couverts à l'annexe 3;[179] quatre Parties ont exclu les marchés publics passés par une entité visée pour le compte d'une entité non visée;[180] et trois Parties ont indiqué que si une entité adjuge un

---

[177] Les cinq Parties ayant adoptées de telles clauses sont les suivantes: (1) l'Union européenne; (2) l'Islande; (3) le Liechtenstein; (4) la Norvège et (5) la Suisse. *Ibid* et section 2. Voir note 130 et le texte correspondant.

[178] Il convient aussi de noter qu'à certaines occasions, des dérogations ou des conditions afférentes au champ d'application ont été spécifiées directement dans les listes d'engagements des Parties (par exemple, directement après une entité ou un service). Voir aussi pour une discussion sur le sujet, Anderson et Osei-Lah, *supra* note 95.

[179] Ces Parties sont les suivantes: (1) l'Union européenne; (2) l'Islande; (3) le Liechtenstein et (4) la Norvège. Voir l'*AMP révisé*, *supra* note 8.

[180] Ces Parties sont les suivantes: (1) le Canada; (2) Singapour; (3) le Taipei chinois et (4) les États-Unis. *Ibid.*

contrat non visé par l'*AMP*, aucun produit ou service constituant un élément de ce contrat ne doit être interprété comme étant couvert par l'Accord.[181]

Deuxièmement, les exemples abondent en ce qui concerne les dérogations relatives à une entité particulière, un produit, un secteur de services ou un autre élément des engagements des Parties. Ainsi, neuf Parties ont une note indiquant que l'*AMP* ne s'applique pas aux marchés publics portant sur des produits agricoles passés en application de programmes de soutien à l'agriculture ou de programmes d'aide alimentaire;[182] certaines Parties ont aussi des dispositions explicites dans leurs annexes restreignant l'application de l'*AMP* aux marchés publics de marchandises et de services entre des entités publiques;[183] six Parties ont une note excluant les marchés publics visant l'achat, le développement, la production ou la coproduction d'éléments de programmes par des organismes de radiodiffusion et aux marchés concernant les temps de diffusion.[184]

Troisièmement, comme nous l'avons vu, le champ d'application de l'*AMP* est très flexible. Certaines Parties ont utilisé cette flexibilité pour inclure des dérogations afin d'appliquer et de maintenir des politiques relatives à des considérations de politique intérieure, en utilisant les marchés publics comme outil de politique sociale ou environnementale. Par exemple, l'*AMP* ne s'applique pas: au Canada pour les marchés réservés aux petites entreprises et aux entreprises détenues par des minorités,[185] et pour les provinces et les territoires, l'Accord ne s'applique pas aux préférences ni aux restrictions liées à des programmes de promotion du développement des régions défavorisées;[186] en Corée, aux marchés publics réservés aux petites et moyennes entreprises en vertu de

---

[181] Ces Parties sont les suivantes: (1) le Canada; (2) le Taipei chinois et (3) les États-Unis. *Ibid.*

[182] Ces Parties sont les suivantes: (1) l'Arménie; (2) le Canada; (3) l'Union européenne; (4) l'Islande; (5) la Corée; (6) le Liechtenstein; (7) la Norvège; (8) le Taipei chinois et (9) les États-Unis. *Ibid.*

[183] Par exemple, le Canada exclut totalement les marchés publics passés entre une entité ou entreprise publique et une autre entité ou entreprise publique. *Ibid*, note générale 4 du Canada.

[184] Ces Parties sont les suivantes: (1) l'Union européenne; (2) l'Islande; (3) le Liechtenstein; (4) la Norvège; (5) le Taipei chinois et (6) la Suisse. *Ibid.*

[185] *Ibid*, note générale 2 du Canada.

[186] *Ibid*, note 2 à l'annexe 2 du Canada.

la législation coréenne spécifiée;[187] au Japon, aux marchés publics attribués à des coopératives ou à des associations en vertu de la législation japonaise spécifiée;[188] aux États-Unis, aux marchés réservés aux petites entreprises et aux entreprises détenues par des minorités.[189] De plus, les États peuvent appliquer des préférences ou des restrictions liées à des programmes favorisant le développement des régions défavorisées ou à des entreprises détenues par des minorités, d'anciens combattants handicapés ou des femmes.[190] De plus, en Israël, compte tenu de ses besoins en termes de développement, un régime d'opération de compensation[191] peut être appliqué pendant une période de transition prédéfinie.[192] Dans certains cas, des Parties ont limité l'application de l'*AMP* à l'égard des Parties appliquant des politiques secondaires afin de maintenir la réciprocité. Par exemple, cinq Parties ont des clauses de non-application des procédures de recours internes (article XVIII) s'appliquant aux fournisseurs de produits et de services de trois Parties (Japon, Corée, États-Unis), en ce qui concerne les recours intentés contre l'adjudication de marchés publics aux fournisseurs des autres Parties qui sont des PME.[193]

Quatrièmement, pour contrer le manque d'uniformité dans les engagements (par exemple, dans les services d'utilité publique et les municipalités), des Parties ont adopté des clauses de non-application propres à chaque Partie. Ainsi, une Partie peut exclure de ses engagements certains produits, services ou entités. En réponse, une autre Partie, couvrant par ailleurs le même type de produits, services ou entités, peut restreindre dans la même mesure

---

[187] *Ibid*, note 2 à l'annexe 1; note 2 à l'annexe 2; note 1 à l'annexe 3 et la note à l'annexe 5 de la Corée.

[188] *Ibid*, note 2 à l'annexe 1; note 2 à l'annexe 2 et note 1 à l'annexe 3 du Japon.

[189] *Ibid*, note générale 1 des États-Unis.

[190] *Ibid*, note 2 à l'annexe 2 des États-Unis. Les États-Unis ont aussi inclus une note indiquant qu'une réserve peut inclure toute forme de préférence, comme le droit exclusif de fournir un bien ou un service, ou de toute préférence de prix.

[191] Voir note 93.

[192] Voir la note sur le régime d'opération de compensation à l'annexe 7 d'Israël, *AMP révisé, supra* note 8.

[193] Ces cinq Parties sont les suivantes: (1) l'Union européenne; (2) l'Islande; (3) le Liechtenstein; (4) la Norvège et (5) la Suisse. *Ibid*. Voir aussi note 130 et le texte correspondant.

l'accès à ses marchés publics à l'égard des fournisseurs de la première Partie. Ainsi, dans les faits, des secteurs sont offerts seulement aux Parties ayant ouvert leurs marchés publics au même niveau. Ces exclusions ont pris la forme de clauses de non-application propres à chaque Partie. Souvent, ces dérogations reflètent un effort pour parvenir à la réciprocité des engagements. Par exemple, un certain nombre de Parties ont convenu qu'en principe, l'*AMP* révisé allait s'appliquer à leurs secteurs d'utilité publique ou à leurs municipalités, mais ont refusé d'offrir ces concessions aux Parties n'offrant pas des engagements semblables.

Enfin, la conclusion des négociations a permis de supprimer de nombreuses exclusions ou restrictions sectorielles ou propres à certains pays, et qui étaient incluses dans les annexes de l'*AMP* 1994. Ainsi, au moins dix Parties ont supprimé des exclusions ou restrictions dans des secteurs d'utilité publique, comme les transports urbains et l'électricité, et dans des entités mentionnées à l'annexe 2.[194] Le fait que le Canada ait intégré l'ensemble de ses provinces et territoires a permis d'éliminer de nombreuses dérogations, et Israël s'est engagé à éliminer totalement son régime d'opérations de compensation.

CONCLUSION DE LA SECONDE PARTIE

Dans la seconde partie du présent document, nous avons examiné la portée de l'Accord révisé sur les marchés publics. D'une part, nous avons abordé les éléments du texte ayant des conséquences pour l'accès aux marchés. À cet égard, nous avons analysé la définition des marchés publics couverts par l'*AMP*, ainsi qu'un certain nombre d'exclusions prévues dans le texte. Nous avons aussi vu les principes fondamentaux entourant la définition des engagements d'accès au marché dans les annexes à l'Appendice I de l'Accord, incluant le rôle-clé de la réciprocité mutuelle dans la conduite des négociations et les différentes approches adoptées par les Parties.

D'autre part, dans cette partie du document nous avons mis en lumière un aspect fondamental de la portée de l'*AMP* révisé, à savoir son Appendice I, incluant les listes d'engagements des Parties. La portée de l'Accord atteint maintenant des sommets historiques à

---

[194] Cela inclus, par exemple, les dix Parties suivantes: (1) le Canada; (2) l'Union européenne; (3) l'Islande; (4) Israël; (5) la Corée; (6) le Japon; (7) le Liechtenstein; (8) la Norvège; (9) la Suisse et (10) le Taipei chinois. *Ibid.*

la suite des améliorations substantielles apportées au champ d'application de l'*AMP* révisé. Ainsi, considérées conjointement, les Parties à l'Accord désignent au moins 5200 entités, et sans doute beaucoup plus.[195] Ce nombre inclut 1700 entités du gouvernement central, 2000 entités des gouvernements sous-centraux, et 1500 entités pour ce qui est des autres entités gouvernementales (y compris les entreprises publiques).

Quant à la portée des services (incluant les services de construction) et des marchandises visés, elle n'a jamais été aussi large. Ainsi, sous l'*AMP* révisé, presque toutes les Parties ont, à divers degrés, étendu la portée de l'Accord à des secteurs de services supplémentaires, comme les services de télécommunications. Considérés conjointement, plus de 50 secteurs de services supplémentaires ont été ajoutés. De plus, toutes les Parties offrent maintenant des engagements d'accès au marché complet pour les marchés publics de services de construction (CPC Prov. 51) et trois Parties ont explicitement étendu la portée de leurs engagements aux accords de "construction-exploitation-transfert de propriété" (CET), de concessions de travaux publics ou autres formes de partenariats public-privé. Certaines Parties ont aussi apporté des améliorations dans le champ d'application des marchandises.

Ensuite, en ce qui concerne les autres types d'ajouts, quatre Parties ont offert de réduire leurs seuils d'application, Israël s'est engagé à éliminer totalement son régime d'opérations de compensation et au moins dix Parties ont supprimé des exclusions ou restrictions sectorielles ou propres à certains pays, qui étaient antérieurement inclus dans leurs annexes.

Enfin, il convient de rappeler que les renseignements exposés ici ne représentent qu'un premier effort pour extraire des informations concernant les engagements des Parties et pour les synthétiser. Nous pensons néanmoins que ces données peuvent, d'une part, apporter une aide considérable aux décideurs confrontés à des choix dans ce domaine, et d'autre part, contribuer à identifier les débouchés à l'exportation susceptibles d'intéresser les fournisseurs des Parties à l'*AMP* et d'autres membres de l'OMC désirant accéder à l'Accord. Nous espérons aussi que les renseignements, sources et observations connexes présentés ici stimuleront la réflexion et susciteront de nouvelles analyses sur le sujet.

---

[195] Voir note 113.

CONCLUSION

En somme, les marchés publics sont essentiellement régulés ou réglementés, au niveau mondial, par l'*AMP* et l'importance de cet Accord s'est consolidée au cours des dernières années. L'*AMP* est aujourd'hui sur le point de prendre un nouvel envol, car les négociations dont il faisait l'objet ont abouti à la fin de l'année 2011. La conclusion de ces négociations, qui ne faisaient pas partie du Cycle de Doha, est importante pour plusieurs raisons et les résultats des négociations comprenaient trois éléments principaux: (1) un engagement à poursuivre les négociations; (2) une version révisée et améliorée du texte de l'Accord et (3) un élargissement considérable de la portée de l'Accord.

Tout d'abord, il a été mis en évidence que la conclusion du dernier cycle de négociations — dont l'*AMP* faisait l'objet — a constitué l'aboutissement d'une longue série de négociations internationales échelonnées sur plus de 65 ans. Nous avons donc passé en revue les grands événements de l'histoire des négociations internationales visant à libéraliser les marchés publics. Nous avons aussi mis en évidence le fait que la conclusion des négociations permettra d'entamer un nouveau cycle de négociations en vue de libéraliser davantage les marchés publics et d'améliorer l'Accord. Ce nouveau cycle de négociations aura comme point de départ un ensemble de nouveaux programmes de travail du Comité traitant de questions n'ayant pas été résolues lors des négociations précédentes.

De plus, nous avons souligné que la conclusion des négociations permettra de faire entrer en vigueur le texte révisé et amélioré de l'Accord. À cet égard, nous avons décrit ses principaux éléments et mentionné que ce texte améliore grandement la version de l'*AMP* 1994, tout en demeurant basé sur les mêmes principes et les mêmes éléments principaux. Il a été mis à jour afin de prendre en compte l'utilisation des moyens électroniques, de promouvoir de façon explicite la bonne gouvernance et de décourager la corruption. De plus, cette version de l'*AMP*, avec ses flexibilités supplémentaires pour les pays en développement, devrait faciliter les futures adhésions à l'*AMP* par les membres de l'OMC qui ne sont pas encore signataires. La valeur des adhésions futures pourrait représenter plusieurs milliards de dollars en gains d'accès aux marchés (estimée entre 440 et 1 227 milliards de dollars US chaque année) et accroître significativement la portée de l'Accord.

Ensuite, en ce qui concerne la portée des engagements de libéralisation des Parties, il ressort de l'analyse que l'*AMP* révisé constitue incontestablement une avancée importante et que la portée de l'Accord atteint maintenant des sommets historiques (évaluée à environ 1 700 milliards de dollars US). À elle seule, la conclusion des négociations apporte de considérables avantages additionnels à toutes les Parties dans le domaine de l'accès aux marchés (estimés entre 80 et 100 milliards de dollars US). Dans un autre ordre d'idées, le présent document visait spécialement à clarifier et à rendre plus accessible la portée de l'*AMP* révisé. Cet aspect est particulièrement important, car malgré une certaine simplification, les règles qui définissent le champ d'application de l'*AMP* demeurent techniques et parfois complexes.

Enfin, on sait que l'*AMP* révisé est officiellement entré en vigueur le 6 avril 2014. L'entrée en vigueur de l'*AMP* fait suite à l'engagement pris par les ministres à la Conférence ministérielle de Bali de décembre 2013 de tout faire pour atteindre ce but dans les deux ans suivant l'adoption de l'Accord révisé.[196] En félicitant les Parties, le directeur général de l'OMC, Roberto Azevêdo, a déclaré:

> Ce résultat est très positif. L'Accord sur les marchés publics révisé aura pour effet d'ouvrir des marchés et de promouvoir la bonne gouvernance dans l'économie des membres participants. La rapidité avec laquelle ce résultat a été obtenu montre l'importance que les Parties accordent à l'*AMP* et prouve une fois encore que, après le succès du paquet de Bali, l'OMC s'est remise au travail. Le texte modernisé de l'*AMP* révisé et les engagements en matière d'accès aux marchés élargis devraient inciter d'autres membres de l'OMC à prendre en considération les avantages qui pourraient découler de l'accession à l'Accord.[197]

Dans cette optique, et compte tenu des difficultés entourant la conclusion du Cycle de Doha, la conclusion des négociations de l'*AMP* (ainsi que la rapide entrée en vigueur de l'Accord révisé) renforce la crédibilité du système commercial multilatéral en démontrant que l'OMC peut produire des résultats significatifs et mener à terme des négociations. Dans ce contexte, certains observateurs ont suggéré que la réussite de l'*AMP*, dans son format

---

[196] Voir OMC, Réunion au niveau ministériel du Comité des marchés publics (tenue le 3 décembre 2013), Déclaration, GPA/122 (2013), en ligne: <OMC http://docsonline.wto.org>.

[197] OMC, communiqué, "Entrée en vigueur de l'Accord sur les marchés publics révisé" (7 avril 2014), en ligne: <http://www.wto.org/french/news_f/news14_f/gpro_07apr14_f.htm>.

plurilatéral, pourrait servir d'ores et déjà de modèle de négociations dans d'autres contextes.[198]

Summary

Government procurement is mainly regulated at the international level by the plurilateral WTO *Agreement on Government Procurement* (*GPA*). Following conclusion of a renegotiation of the agreement in 2011 and the entry into force of the revised *GPA* on 6 April 2014, this WTO instrument is about to take on enhanced significance. While the entry into force of the revised *GPA* brings new momentum to the opening of markets, it does not mark the end of the process of liberalization of public procurement. To assist in understanding the ongoing need to negotiate ever greater liberalization of public procurement markets and to fully appreciate the importance of the revised *GPA* for the global economy, this article begins by briefly describing significant milestones in the historical process of public procurement liberalization and then presents an overview of the main features of the revised *GPA*. This article then sets out a thorough analysis of the parties' market access commitments under the revised *GPA* (contained in the Appendix I annexes) because, despite some simplification resulting from the *GPA* renegotiation, this part of the agreement remains highly technical and complex. This analysis and related observations may provide assistance to decision makers confronted with choices in this area and help identify export opportunities that are likely to be of interest to suppliers of the parties to the *GPA* and of other WTO members considering accession to the agreement.

---

[198] Voir, par exemple, Inside US Trade, "Services Plurilateral Talks Remain at Technical Level on Scope, Coverage" (30 mars 2012), en ligne: Inside US Trade <http://insidetrade.com/Inside-US-Trade/Inside-U.S.-Trade-03/30/2012/ services-plurilateral-talks-remain-at-technical-level-on-scope-coverage/menu -id-710.html> (date d'accès: 18 mai 2014); Le bureau du Représentant américain au commerce, communiqué, "U.S. Trade Representative Ron Kirk Notifies Congress of Intent to Negotiate New International Trade Agreement on Services" (15 janvier 2013), en ligne: US Trade Representative <http://www.ustr. gov/about-us/press-office/press-releases/2013/january/ustr-kirk-notifies -congress-new-itas-negotiations> (date d'accès: 18 mai 2014); Inside US Trade, "USTR Notifies Congress On Green Goods Talks, Kicking Off 90-Day Period," (24 mars 2014), en ligne: Inside US Trade <http://insidetrade.com/2014 03242465292/WTO-Daily-News/Daily-News/ustr-notifies-congress-on-green -goods-talks-kicking-off-90-day-period/menu-id-948.html> (date d'accès: 18 mai 2014).

Sommaire

Les marchés publics sont essentiellement régulés ou réglementés, au niveau mondial, par l'*Accord plurilatéral sur les marchés publics* de l'OMC (*AMP*). Cet Accord est aujourd'hui sur le point de prendre un nouvel envol, car les négociations dont il faisait l'objet ont abouti à la fin de l'année 2011 et l'*AMP* révisé est entré en vigueur le 6 avril 2014. Bien que l'entrée en vigueur de l'*AMP* révisé insuffle un élan vigoureux à l'ouverture des marchés, elle ne constitue toutefois pas la fin du processus visant à libéraliser les marchés publics. Afin de comprendre la nécessité de négocier de façon quasi permanente une libéralisation accrue des marchés publics et d'apprécier pleinement l'importance de l'*AMP* révisé pour l'économie mondiale, cet article décrit succinctement les événements marquants de l'histoire des négociations internationales visant à libéraliser les marchés publics et présente ensuite, d'une façon générale, les principaux éléments du texte de l'*AMP* révisé. De plus, cet article contient une analyse approfondie des listes d'engagements des Parties à l'*AMP* révisé (les annexes à l'Appendice I) car, malgré une certaine simplification résultant de la conclusion des négociations, cette partie de l'*AMP* révisé demeure particulièrement technique et complexe. Ces renseignements et observations connexes pourraient, d'une part, apporter une aide aux décideurs confrontés à des choix dans ce domaine et, d'autre part, aider à identifier les débouchés à l'exportation qui sont susceptibles d'intéresser les fournisseurs des Parties à l'*AMP* et des autres Membres de l'OMC désirant accéder à l'Accord.

Nuclear Non-Proliferation and "Preventive Self-Defence": Why Attacking Iran Would Be Illegal

PATRICK C.R. TERRY AND KAREN S. OPENSHAW

Make no mistake: a nuclear-armed Iran is not a challenge that can be contained ... And that is why the United States will do what we must to prevent Iran from obtaining a nuclear weapon.[1]

There is a legal discussion that has been missing here ... They only say, is it sensible to attack Iran or not? And most people say it is not. But for us lawyers, it is significant that actually this would be a terrible setback for the interpretation of the UN Charter and the growing legal inhibitions against the use of armed force.[2]

Patrick CR Terry is a professor of law at the University of Public Administration in Kehl, Germany. He holds a PhD in public international law (University of Kent, United Kingdom (UK)), an LLM in international law and international relations (Kent), and two German law degrees (Ministry of Justice Stuttgart and University of Tübingen). He also worked as a judge in Germany for a number of years. Karen S Openshaw holds a PhD in public international law (Kent). Her doctoral research focused on state succession to sovereign debt. She holds post-graduate diplomas in English law and international law and relations and practised for a number of years as a solicitor in the UK. The authors would like to thank the editorial team of the *Canadian Yearbook of International Law* for their helpful suggestions. Any errors are, of course, the authors' responsibility (all URLs were last accessed on 1 August 2014).

[1] Barack Obama, "Remarks by the President to the UN General Assembly" (speech delivered at the United Nations General Assembly, 25 September 2012), online: White House <http://www.whitehouse.gov/the-press-office/2012/09/25/remarks-president-un-general-assembly>.

[2] Interview of Hans Blix, former head of the International Atomic Energy Agency (IAEA) and former UN weapons inspector in Iraq, by Rebecca Lowe (17 April 2012) in *Blix Condemns "Shocking" Lack of Legal Debate over Iran Nuclear Threat*, online: International Bar Association <http://www.ibanet.org/Article/Detail.aspx?ArticleUid=42842918-96dc-4682-900c-ef86bddcb5dc>. See also Shiv Malik, "Hans Blix Urges Britain to Relinquish Trident Nuclear Programme," *The Guardian* (26 May 2013), online: The Guardian <http://www.theguardian.com/world/2013/may/26/hans-blix-trident-abandon-britain-nuclear>.

INTRODUCTION

In the early 1990s, American and Israeli concerns began to mount that Iran was actively seeking to develop nuclear weapons. Intelligence estimates were regularly produced claiming that Iran was a couple of years, or a decade, or more than a decade, away from obtaining nuclear weapons and suitable delivery systems.[3] Preventing Iran from becoming a nuclear-weapons state became an overriding goal of US foreign policy in the Middle East. In this goal, the United States was energetically supported, and indeed encouraged, by Israel. However, the European Union (EU), Russia, and China — to varying degrees — came to be supportive of this objective as well.

Iran has always denied that its intention is to acquire nuclear weapons, insisting instead that it wishes only to exercise its right to make use of nuclear technology for civilian purposes.[4] The crisis surrounding Iran's nuclear program escalated in 2002, however, when it emerged that Iran had built uranium enrichment sites of which it had not informed the International Atomic Energy Agency (IAEA), in apparent contravention of its obligations under the *Treaty on the Non-Proliferation of Nuclear Weapons* (*Nuclear Non-Proliferation Treaty* or *NPT*).[5] For many in the international community, this information confirmed their worst suspicions. Despite Iran's protestations to the contrary, its behaviour seemed to suggest that it was not merely conducting research into the — perfectly legal — civilian uses of nuclear technology.

Although there is still no definite proof that Iran is trying to acquire the "bomb," it is widely assumed that Iran's objective is indeed to achieve at least nuclear weapons capability. Nevertheless, there

---

[3] David Hastings Dunn, "'Real Men Want to Go to Tehran': Bush, Pre-emption and the Iranian Nuclear Challenge" (2007) 83:1 Int'l Affairs 19 at 26. See also Peter Oborne and David Morrison, *A Dangerous Delusion: Why the West Is Wrong about Nuclear Iran* (London: Elliott and Thompson, 2013) at 95-96.

[4] Jeffrey T Richelson, *Spying on the Bomb: American Nuclear Intelligence from Nazi Germany to Iran and North Korea* (New York: WW Norton and Company 2006) at 505-6.

[5] *Treaty on the Non-Proliferation of Nuclear Weapons*, 1 July 1968, 749 UNTS 1 (in force 5 March 1970), online: IAEA <http://www.iaea.org/Publications/Documents/Treaties/npt.html> [*NPT*]. There are currently 190 states parties to the *NPT*, including the five (recognized) nuclear weapons states. On 11 May 1995, the Review and Extension Conference of the Parties to the *NPT* decided that the treaty should continue in force indefinitely, in accordance with Article X(2) of the *NPT*.

are doubts within the West's intelligence community. In particular, US intelligence agencies have repeatedly pointed out that they believe Iran halted its nuclear weapons program in 2003 and that, although Iran may currently be pursuing nuclear weapons capability, it has yet to decide whether to actually build nuclear weapons.[6]

This doubt has not deterred the United States and Israel from repeatedly warning that "all options [are] on the table" in order to prevent Iran from obtaining nuclear weapons.[7] Israel, which disagrees with US intelligence reports on Iran, has been more forthright than the United States in its warnings that it will not accept a nuclear-armed Iran.[8] The United States has in the past asserted an ostensible right of "preventive" self-defence, which would allow it to destroy Iranian weapons of mass destruction (WMD) capabilities in order to avert any possible threat they may pose (the so-called "Bush doctrine"). Whether and how this doctrine can be reconciled with international law is contentious.

Hopes that the election and subsequent re-election of US President Barack Obama would lessen the tensions between the United States and Iran remain unfulfilled, despite the initial conciliatory tone adopted by the Obama administration.[9] Instead, under

---

[6] See, for example, United States, National Intelligence Council, *National Intelligence Estimate — Iran: Nuclear Intentions and Capabilities* (Washington, DC: National Intelligence Council, November 2007), online: <http://www.dni.gov/files/documents/Newsroom/Reports%20and%20Pubs/20071203_release.pdf> [2007 US National Intelligence Estimate]; Mark Mazzetti, "US Says Iran Ended Atomic Arms Work," *New York Times* (3 December 2007), online: New York Times <http://www.nytimes.com/2007/12/03/world/middleeast/03cnd-iran.html?_r=2&hp&oref=slogin&>; David Albright and Paul Brannan, "US Intelligence Estimates and the Iranian Nuclear Program" (9 April 2012), online: Institute for Science and International Security <http://isis-online.org/uploads/isis-reports/documents/US_Intelligence_Estimates_and_the_Iranian_Nuclear_Program_9April2012.pdf>; Tabassum Zakaria and Mark Hosenball, "Special Report: Intel Shows Iran Nuclear Threat Not Imminent," *Reuters* (23 March 2012), online: Reuters <http://www.reuters.com/article/2012/03/23/us-iran-usa-nuclear-idUSBRE82M0G020120323>.

[7] Obama, *supra* note 1.

[8] See, for example, Benjamin Netanyahu, "Address to the UN General Assembly" (speech delivered to the United Nations General Assembly, 27 September 2012), online: Jewish Press <http://www.jewishpress.com/news/un/pm-netanyahus-speech-to-the-united-nations-general-assembly-in-new-york/2012/09/27/5/>; David Patrikarakos, *Nuclear Iran, The Birth of an Atomic State* (London: IB Tauris, 2012) at 271-72.

[9] Patrikarakos, *supra* note 8 at 243-46.

Obama, the United States has imposed extremely tough sanctions on Iran.[10] Nor will the interim deal on Iran's nuclear program reached between Iran and the permanent five members of the UN Security Council plus Germany (P5+1)[11] — prompted by the election of the moderate cleric Hassan Rouhani to the Iranian presidency — necessarily translate into a full and final agreement that will avert the threat of a military strike.[12] Furthermore, a series of US–Israeli covert operations appears to have been undertaken in the last few years, involving the assassination of nuclear scientists within Iran[13] and acts of cyber-warfare, such as the introduction of computer viruses (for example, Stuxnet and Flame).[14] Such acts are hardly conducive to creating an atmosphere of mutual trust. The Iranian government, on the other hand, has sometimes given the impression of playing for time, thereby arousing even more suspicions as to its intentions.[15]

---

[10] Oborne and Morrison, *supra* note 3 at 62-65.

[11] That is, the negotiations between Iran and the five permanent members of the Security Council, being the United States, Russia, China, France, and the UK. They are joined by Germany, as well as the High Representative for Foreign Affairs and Security Policy for the European Union (EU). See *Joint Plan of Action* (24 November 2013), online: EU <http://eeas.europa.eu/statements/docs/2013/131124_03_en.pdf>.

[12] Under the *Joint Plan of Action, supra* note 11, Iran has agreed to curtail certain of its uranium enrichment activities, not to commission the Arak heavy water reactor and to allow greater access to IAEA inspectors. In return, it has been granted limited sanctions relief, including access to around US $4 billion in hitherto frozen overseas bank accounts. The deadline for reaching a comprehensive agreement on Iran's nuclear program — originally set to expire on 20 July 2014 — has been extended by a further four months, to 24 November 2014.

[13] Adrian Blomfield, "Assassination of Iranian Nuclear Scientist Is a Familiar Story," *Daily Telegraph* (11 January 2012), online: The Telegraph <http://www.telegraph.co.uk/news/worldnews/middleeast/iran/9007055/Assassination-of-Iranian-nuclear-scientist-is-a-familiar-story.html>; Karl Vick and Aaron J Klein, "Who Assassinated an Iranian Nuclear Scientist? Israel Isn't Telling," *Time* (13 January 2012) online: Time <http://content.time.com/time/world/article/0,8599,2104372,00.html>; Patrikarakos, *supra* note 8 at 269-70.

[14] David E Sanger, "Obama Order Sped Up Wave of Cyberattacks against Iran," *New York Times* (1 June 2012), online: New York Times <http://www.nytimes.com/2012/06/01/world/middleeast/obama-ordered-wave-of-cyberattacks-against-iran.html?ref=stuxnet&_r=0>; Jim Finkle, "Researchers Say Stuxnet Was Deployed against Iran in 2007," *Reuters* (26 February 2013), online: Reuters <http://www.reuters.com/article/2013/02/26/us-cyberwar-stuxnet-idUSBRE91P0PP20130226>; Patrikarakos, *supra* note 8 at 264-66.

[15] Patrikarakos, *supra* note 8 at 257-63, 272-79. On the missteps and squandering of opportunities on the part of both the Obama administration and the Iranian

On 3 June 2013, Yukiya Amano, director-general of the IAEA, voiced his impatience with the progress achieved so far: "Despite the intensified dialogue between the agency and Iran ... no agreement has been reached on the structured approach document. To be frank, for some time now we have been going round in circles."[16] Meanwhile, the prospect of a US–Iran rapprochement, while lauded in Europe,[17] has met with scepticism, if not outright hostility, in Israel and Saudi Arabia.[18] Many US lawmakers are also suspicious of Iran's intentions, seeking to exert pressure on the Obama administration to adopt a strict stance towards Iran in the current negotiations.[19] Consequently, the possibility that the United States will eventually take military action to curtail Iran's alleged nuclear weapons program cannot be ruled out.

With these developments in mind, this article examines the lawfulness of such a potential military venture. After outlining the political background to the nuclear crisis, the obligations imposed by the *NPT* will be scrutinized, since Iran's violations of this treaty are often cited as potential justification for responsive measures. While this examination will confirm that there are good reasons for accusing Iran of violating the *NPT*, it will also reveal the United

---

regime in their dealings with each other, see Trita Parsi, *A Single Roll of the Dice: Obama's Diplomacy with Iran* (New Haven, CT: Yale University Press, 2012).

16 Yukiya Amano, director-general of the IAEA, "Iran Nuclear Talks Going Round in Circles — IAEA Chief," *BBC News* (3 June 2013), online: BBC <http://www.bbc.co.uk/news/world-middle-east-22756844>.

17 Laurence Norman and Jay Solomon, "Iran, U.S. Talks Seen As 'Good Start'," *Wall Street Journal* (26 September 2013), online: Wall Street Journal <http://online.wsj.com/news/articles/SB10001424052702304526204579099969288 1998588>.

18 Jeffrey Heller, "Israel, Saudis Speaking Same Language on Iran: Livni," *Reuters* (24 October 2013), online: Reuters <http://www.reuters.com/article/2013/10/24/us-israel-saudi-diplomacy-idUSBRE99N0NO20131024>; Atul Aneja, "Israel, Saudi Arabia Unhappy with U.S. on Iran Outreach," *The Hindu* (25 October 2013), online: The Hindu <http://www.thehindu.com/todays-paper/tp-international/israel-saudi-arabia-unhappy-with-us-on-iran-outreach/article5270385.ece>.

19 See Paul Lewis, "Hopes Raised for US–Iran Talks but Hawks in Congress Threaten Any Deal," *Guardian* (3 October 2013), online: Guardian <http://www.theguardian.com/world/2013/oct/03/us-iran-talks-threatened-congress-sanctions>; Julian Pecquet, "Iran Debate Shifts to the House," *Al-Monitor* (21 May 2014), online: Al-Monitor <http://www.al-monitor.com/pulse/originals/2014/05/iran-debate-house-franks-nuclear-deal.html?utm_source=dlvr.it&utm_medium=twitter>.

States' own non-adherence to some of the treaty's provisions as well as its tolerance for, if not encouragement of, nuclear proliferation among certain of its allies. Calling for responsive action against Iran under the guise of upholding the international legal order therefore leaves the United States and its allies open to charges of hypocrisy. The concept of "preventive" self-defence will then be analyzed, and it will be shown that such a use of force is clearly unlawful and should remain so. The article will conclude by pointing out that, in their attempts to extend their influence over the Middle East, both Iran and the United States pay scant attention to international law.

BACKGROUND

Iran's interest in nuclear technology pre-dates the current regime. Under Shah Mohammad Reza Pahlavi, during whose reign Iran was allied to the United States, the country initiated nuclear research, albeit officially only for civilian use.[20] In 1970, Iran ratified the *NPT*. It is, however, often assumed that the Shah's real aim was to acquire nuclear weapons.[21] While some describe the Shah's nuclear weapons program as "rather restrained,"[22] others quote the Shah as having declared, in 1974, "sooner than you think, we will have nuclear arms."[23]

It is widely believed that Iran's nuclear weapons program was terminated after the Islamic revolution in 1979 because Ayatollah

---

[20] Ervand Abrahamian, "Empire Strikes Back: Iran in US Sights" in André Schiffrin, ed, *Inventing the Axis of Evil: The Truth about North Korea, Iran, and Syria* (New York: New Press, 2004) 98. See also Oborne and Morrison, *supra* note 3 at 38-41; Dafna Linzer, "Past Arguments Don't Square with Current Iran Policy," *Washington Post* (27 March 2005) online: Washington Post <http://www.washingtonpost.com/wp-dyn/articles/A3983-2005Mar26.html>; Patrikarakos, *supra* note 8 at 14-47.

[21] Harald Müller, "Nukleare Krisen und transatlantischer Dissens, Amerikanische und europäische Antworten auf aktuelle Probleme der Weiterverbreitung von Kernwaffen". (2003) HSFK-Report 9/2003 1 at 5; Benjamin M Greenblum, "The Iranian Nuclear Threat: Israel's Options under International Law" (2006-07) 29 Hous J Int'l L, 55 at 61. Ali M Ansari, *Confronting Iran, The Failure of American Foreign Policy and the Roots of Mistrust* (London: Hurst and Company, 2006) at 199-200, points out that this was well-known in the United States. See also Shahram Chubin, *Iran's Nuclear Ambitions* (Washington DC: Carnegie Endowment for International Peace, 2006) at 7; Patrikarakos, *supra* note 8 at 58-70.

[22] Kenneth M Pollack, *The Persian Puzzle: The Conflict between Iran and America* (New York: Random House Trade, 2005) at 258.

[23] Abrahamian, *supra* note 20 at 137, n 93, quoting from a report in the *Christian Science Monitor*. See also Patrikarakos, *supra* note 8 at 59-60.

Khomeini was said to view nuclear weapons as "un-Islamic."[24] However, the exposure of Iran to Iraq's WMD (chemical weapons) during the Iran–Iraq War of 1980–88 — to the indifference of the international community — supposedly prompted a reassessment within the Iranian regime regarding the usefulness of nuclear weapons.[25] It is assumed that Iran's nuclear weapons program was relaunched in the mid- or late 1980s.[26]

Exactly what progress Iran has made to date, however, remains uncertain. Contradictory intelligence analyses are published regularly, ranging from the alarmist to much more conservative estimates.[27] Nevertheless, there is little doubt within the international community that Iran is actively pursuing nuclear weapons capability.[28] This certainty is mainly attributable to Iran's concealment of two nuclear research plants at Natanz and Arak, the existence of which came to light via a dissident Iranian organization.[29] Subsequent inspections carried out by the IAEA revealed "traces of uranium" concentrated at high levels — a necessary ingredient for producing nuclear weapons.[30] While claiming that this concentration was owing to the contamination of instruments by the supplier, Iran was unable or unwilling to name the state concerned.[31] Furthermore, Iran has frequently demonstrated its research into ballistic missiles — which can serve as delivery systems for nuclear weapons.[32] Other

---

[24] Pollack, *supra* note 22 at 259; Müller, *supra* note 21 at 6.

[25] John Simpson, "Iran's Nuclear Capability and Potential to Develop Atomic Weapons" in The Emirates Center for Strategic Studies and Research, ed, *Iran's Nuclear Program, Realities and Repercussions* (Abu Dhabi: Emirates Center for Strategic Studies and Research, 2006) 11 at 11; Müller, *supra* note 21 at 6; Chubin, *supra* note 21 at 7, 19.

[26] Pollack, *supra* note 22 at 259; Chubin *supra* note 21 at 7. See also Abrahamian, *supra* note 20 at 137, suggesting the program was relaunched in the early 1990s.

[27] Simpson, *supra* note 25 at 30-32; Greenblum, *supra* note 21 at 69; Oborne and Morrison, *supra* note 3 at 95-96.

[28] Dunn, *supra* note 3 at 25-26; Richelson, *supra* note 4 at 503-5; Simpson *supra* note 25 at 11; Greenblum, *supra* note 21 at 62-63.

[29] That is, the National Council of Resistance of Iran, a coalition comprising various Iranian opposition groups, the most prominent of which, Mojahideen-e-Khalq, was previously viewed as a terrorist organization by the United States and numerous European countries. See Pollack, *supra* note 22 at 361; Ansari, *supra* note 21 at 198; Müller, *supra* note 21 at 7.

[30] Greenblum, *supra* note 21 at 62.

[31] Müller, *supra* note 21 at 8.

[32] James Noyes, "Iran's Nuclear Program: Impact on the Security of the GCC" in Emirates Center for Strategic Studies and Research, ed, *Iran's Nuclear Program,*

states have thus concluded that Iran is attempting to deceive the world so far as its nuclear ambitions are concerned.[33]

From a strategic viewpoint, Iran has every reason to pursue a nuclear weapons program.[34] With the exception of the embattled Assad government in Syria, Iran has no "reliable allies," but it does have a number of powerful enemies.[35] It is bordered by Afghanistan, where many US troops are still stationed,[36] while Gulf states, especially Saudi Arabia, see Iran as a rival and a potential danger. Former US President George W. Bush named Iran as one of the states belonging to the "axis of evil,"[37] and regime change in Iran has — certainly in the past — been quasi-official US government policy.[38] In addition, Iran has been confronted with three nuclear weapons states in the region: India, Pakistan, and Israel,[39] the latter, of course, being the state with which Iran regards itself as being in "acute religious and ideological conflict."[40] Iran's government has also

---

Realities and Repercussions (Abu Dhabi: Emirates Center for Strategic Studies and Research, 2006) 63 at 70-71.

[33] Dunn, *supra* note 3 at 25-26; Simpson, *supra* note 25 at 11; George Perkovich, "Iran's Nuclear Program after the 2005 Elections" in Emirates Center for Strategic Studies and Research, *supra* note 32, 37 at 38-39.

[34] Simpson, *supra* note 25 at 11; Abrahamian, *supra* note 20 at 139.

[35] Noyes, *supra* note 32 at 68; Chubin, *supra* note 21 at 11, 15.

[36] Dunn, *supra* note 3 at 24; Chubin, *supra* note 21 at 14.

[37] George W Bush, "2002 State of the Union Address" (speech delivered to the US Congress, 29 January 2002), online: Washington Post <http://www.washington post.com/wp-srv/onpolitics/transcripts/sou012902.htm>.

[38] White House, *National Security Strategy of the United States of America* (March 2006), online: White House <http://georgewbush-whitehouse.archives.gov/nsc/nss/ 2006/> [*NSS* 2006]; Seymour M Hersh, "Preparing the Battlefield," *New Yorker* (7 July 2008) online: New Yorker <http://www.newyorker.com/reporting/ 2008/07/07/080707fa_fact_hersh?currentPage=all>; Dunn, *supra* note 3 at 19, 34; Perkovich, *supra* note 33 at 53-54; Noyes, *supra* note 32 at 65, Abrahamian, *supra* note 20 at 96; Ansari, *supra* note 21 at 204; Müller, *supra* note 21 at 33; Chubin, *supra* note 21 at 21.

[39] Noyes, *supra* note 32 at 66; Abrahamian, *supra* note 20 at 139; Patrikarakos, *supra* note 8 at 60.

[40] Simpson, *supra* note 25 at 11; Dunn, *supra* note 3 at 36. Winston P Nagan and Craig Hammer, "The New Bush National Security Strategy and the Rule of Law" (2004) 22:3 Berkeley J Int'l L 375 at 433-34, make the same point in regard to Iraq's interest in acquiring nuclear weapons. Although, as Parsi points out, Iran and Israel have in the past been prepared to co-operate to further mutual interests. Parsi, *supra* note 15 at 20-23.

observed North Korea's development of a nuclear weapons capability, with an American military intervention there now seeming a very remote possibility.[41] India and Pakistan have not suffered any severe consequences as a result of obtaining nuclear weapons,[42] and the United States' treatment of Israel's stockpile of nuclear weapons has left American accusations against Iran smacking of double standards.[43]

The invasion of Iraq in 2003, which demonstrated the overwhelming superiority of American conventional weaponry, very likely further enhanced the desirability of obtaining nuclear weapons from Iran's point of view.[44] As former Indian Army Chief of Staff Sundarji stated in the aftermath of the 1991 Gulf War: "[D]on't fight the United States unless you have nuclear weapons."[45] Iran's strategic position is therefore such that a nuclear weapons program would make sense. This is reinforced by Iran's wish — also based on Persian history — to become the dominant power in the Middle East and to challenge the traditional post-Second World War American role there.[46]

The United States, on the other hand, has many reasons to prevent the emergence of a nuclear-armed Iran.[47] Iran's government has

---

[41] Christian Henderson, "The Bush Doctrine: From Theory to Practice" (2004) 9 J Confl & Sec L 3 at 19; Abrahamian, *supra* note 20 at 139; Chubin, *supra* note 21 at 8.

[42] Dunn, *supra* note 3 at 25; Richard Falk, "The Illegitimacy of the Non-Proliferation Regime" (1997) 4 Brown J World Affairs 73 at 78; Ansari, *supra* note 21 at 201.

[43] Chamundeeswari Kuppuswamy, "Is the Nuclear Non-Proliferation Treaty Shaking at Its Foundations? Stock Taking after the 2005 NPT Review Conference" (2006) 11 J Confl & Sec L 141 at 149; Dunn, *supra* note 3 at 36; Abdel Monem Said Aly, "In the Shadow of the Israeli Nuclear Bombs: Egyptian Threat Perceptions" (1996) 3 Brown J World Affairs 151 at 152-53; Falk, *supra* note 42 at 77; Noyes, *supra* note 32 at 74-75; Sverre Lodgaard, "Bombing Iran: Is It Avoidable?" in Emirates Center for Strategic Studies and Research, *supra* note 32, 113 at 113; Ansari, *supra* note 21 at 201; Chubin, *supra* note 21 at 126; Oborne and Morrison, *supra* note 3 at 32-34.

[44] Dunn, *supra* note 3 at 23; Noyes, *supra* note 32 at 69; Henderson, *supra* note 41 at 19.

[45] Quoted in Guy B Roberts, "The Counterproliferation Self-Help Paradigm: A Legal Regime for Enforcing the Norm Prohibiting the Proliferation of Weapons of Mass Destruction" (1998-99) 27 Denver J Int'l L & Pol'y 483 at 498. Thomas Graham, Jr, "National Self-Defense, International Law, and Weapons of Mass Destruction" (2003) 4 Chicago J Int'l L 1 at 12, attributes this statement to Indian Defence Secretary Fernandez.

[46] Kuppuswamy, *supra* note 43 at 150; Simpson, *supra* note 25 at 11; Perkovich, *supra* note 33 at 37, 40; Noyes, *supra* note 32 at 65, 67; Chubin, *supra* note 21 at 16, 113.

[47] Lodgaard, *supra* note 43 at 115.

often proclaimed its undying animosity towards the United States, and its former president, Mahmoud Ahmadinijad, was renowned for making outrageous statements and threats.[48] Some have therefore claimed that Iran might even provide anti-American or anti-Israeli terrorists with "a dirty bomb" in the hope of not being found out.[49] Many also fear that Iran may be tempted to use nuclear weapons to blackmail other states in the region, especially Saudi Arabia and other Persian Gulf states, which remain vitally important because of their central role in supplying the world with oil.[50] Such a situation might also lead to further nuclear weapons proliferation in the area, with states such as Saudi Arabia and Egypt being potential candidates for embarking on such a project.[51]

Israel is another obvious concern for the United States. Not only might Israel be in danger were Iran to acquire nuclear weapons[52] — irrational statements by Iranian government officials have led some to doubt whether Israel's own nuclear weapons would serve as an effective deterrent[53] — but Israel itself might react in an irrational way to an Iranian threat, sparking a major confrontation in the region.[54] Last but not least, even the best possible scenario would leave a nuclear-armed Iran posing a serious challenge to American dominance in the strategically important Middle East.[55] While India and Pakistan have so far refrained from questioning

---

[48] Such as denying the Holocaust or stating that Israel must be "wiped off" the map — although some claim the latter threat was never made and can be traced back to an incorrect translation. See, for example, Oborne and Morrison, *supra* note 3 at 79-80; Pollack, *supra* note 22 at 376.

[49] Dunn, note *supra* 3 at 33; Perkovich, *supra* note 33 at 58-59; Greenblum, *supra* note 21 at 81-82.

[50] Perkovich, *supra* note 33 at 58.

[51] Kuppuswamy, *supra* note 43 at 149; Dunn, *supra* note 3 at 32; Noyes, *supra* note 32 at 75-77; Pollack, *supra* note 22 at 377; Müller, *supra* note 21 at 31; Chubin, *supra* note 21 at 129.

[52] Louis René Beres, "Israel, Iran and Preemption: Choosing the Least Unattractive Option under International Law" (1995-96) 14 Dick J Int'l L 187 at 189-91; Chubin, *supra* note 21 at 119.

[53] Beres, *supra* note 52 at 197-98; Greenblum, *supra* note 21 at 79-80.

[54] Müller, *supra* note 21 at 10; Chubin, *supra* note 21 at 130-33; Aly, *supra* note 43 at 157. See also Seymour M Hersh, *The Samson Option, Israel, America and the Bomb* (London: Faber and Faber, 1993) at 225-40, stating that during the 1973 Arab-Israeli War, Israel seriously contemplated using nuclear weapons.

[55] Lodgaard, *supra* note 43 at 115-16; Chubin, *supra* note 21 at 115-17, 125; Oborne and Morrison, *supra* note 3 at 20, 90.

US hegemony in the wider region, this would almost certainly not be the case if Iran became a nuclear weapons state.[56] As Ali Ansari has pointed out, both the Unites States and Iran are basically "imperial powers," whose interests are bound to clash.[57]

THE *NPT*

The United States and its allies, and even the UN Security Council, have invoked Iran's conduct contrary to the *NPT* as justification for imposing sanctions.[58] Only very recently, some have argued that military intervention in Syria's civil war would be justified by the Syrian government's alleged use of chemical weapons, contending that the ban on the use of chemical weapons is of such importance that military enforcement is necessary to uphold international law.[59] That Iran's alleged violations of the *NPT* could be employed to similar ends does not seem unlikely, making it relevant to examine Iran's conduct in this respect. Whether such an argument could convincingly be sustained, however, also depends on the attitude of the United States and its allies to nuclear proliferation in general.

Both Iran and the United States are parties to the *NPT*. As required by Article III(4) of the treaty, Iran concluded a *Safeguards Agreement* with the IAEA in 1974 — the IAEA being responsible for verifying that states are fulfilling their treaty obligations.[60] Owing to the ease

---

[56] See Chubin, *supra* note 21 at 115-17 (quoting former US Secretary of State Condoleezza Rice: "No one wants to see a Middle East that is dominated by an Iranian hegemony ... Iran is pursuing policies in the Middle East that are, if not 180, 170 degrees counter to the kind of Middle East that we would build"); Kuppuswamy, *supra* note 43 at 150. See also Dunn, *supra* note 3 at 25, 32.

[57] Ansari, *supra* note 21 at 234. See also Chubin, *supra* note 21 at 115.

[58] See, for example, The White House, *National Security Strategy of the United States of America* (May 2010), online: <http://www.whitehouse.gov/sites/default/files/rss_viewer/national_security_strategy.pdf> at 24 [*NSS* 2010].

[59] Frederik Pleitgen and Tom Cohen, "'War-Weary' Obama Says Syria Chemical Attack Requires Response," *CNN* (30 August 2013), online: CNN <http://edition.cnn.com/2013/08/30/world/europe/syria-civil-war/>; "U.S. Secretary of State Kerry Makes Statement on Syria," *Reuters* (30 August 2013), online: Reuters <http://www.reuters.com/article/2013/08/30/us-syria-crisis-kerry-transcript-idUSBRE97T0RR20130830>; "Obama Says US Has 'Obligation' to Act on Syria, Cites Intel Findings," *Fox News* (30 August 2013), online: Fox News <http://www.foxnews.com/politics/2013/08/30/kerry-says-clear-evidence-chemical-weapons-used-in-syria-as-intelligence/>.

[60] IAEA, *Information Circular: Text of the Agreement between Iran and the IAEA for the Application of Safeguards in Connection with the Treaty on the Non-Proliferation of*

with which certain states, such as Iraq, had circumvented IAEA inspections in the past, it was seen as being necessary to strengthen the IAEA's ability to monitor state parties' activities more effectively. This was to be achieved by ratification, by state parties, of an optional additional protocol adopted by the IAEA in 1997.[61] Iran signed the additional protocol in December 2003 but has yet to ratify it.

IRAN'S CONDUCT

As a result of the 2002 disclosure that Iran had uranium enrichment plants that it had failed to report to the IAEA as required under its *Safeguards Agreement,* Iran came under close scrutiny by the agency, which in turn was being placed under considerable pressure by the United States. Iran's overall co-operation with the IAEA has been found to be wanting in every IAEA report on the implementation of the *Safeguards Agreement* since 2002.[62] This ultimately led to the resolution of 4 February 2006, adopted by the IAEA Board of Governors, in which Iran's non-co-operation with the IAEA was referred to the UN Security Council in accordance with Article 12(c) of the *Statute of the International Atomic Energy Agency.*[63]

Since the Security Council has been seized of the matter, the relationship between Iran and the IAEA has not improved. In September 2012, the IAEA Board of Governors adopted a resolution

---

Nuclear Weapons, Doc INFCIRC/214 (15 May 1974), online: IAEA <http://www. iaea.org/Publications/Documents/Infcircs/Others/infcirc214.pdf> [*Safeguards Agreement*].

[61] *Model Protocol Additional to the Agreement(s) between State(s) and the International Atomic Energy Agency for the Application of Safeguards,* Doc INFCIRC540 (Corr) (May 1997), online: IAEA <http://www.iaea.org/Publications/Documents/ Infcircs/1997/infcirc540c.pdf>. To date, 124 states have concluded additional protocols with the IAEA that are now in force. See IAEA, *Safeguards and Verifications: Status of Additional Protocols (as of 6 August 2014),* online: IAEA <http:// www.iaea.org/safeguards/protocol.html>.

[62] See, for example, IAEA, *Implementation of the NPT Safeguards Agreement in the Islamic Republic of Iran, Report of 28 April 2006,* Doc GOV/2006/27 (2006) at 7, online: IAEA <http://www.iaea.org/Publications/Documents/Board/2006/ gov2006-27.pdf>.

[63] *Statute of the International Atomic Energy Agency,* 276 UNTS 3 (in force 29 July 1957), online: IAEA <http://www.iaea.org/About/statute.html>. This step was possible under Article 19 of the *Safeguards Agreement, supra* note 60; IAEA, *Implementation of the NPT Safeguards Agreement in the Islamic Republic of Iran, Resolution of 4 February 2006,* Doc GOV/2006/14 (2006) at 2, paras 2, 4, online: IAEA <http://www.iaea. org/Publications/Documents/Board/2006/gov2006-14.pdf>.

in which it lamented Iran's lack of co-operation.[64] In its report of February 2013, the IAEA reiterated that Iran had not undertaken the necessary steps to fulfil its obligations under the *Safeguards Agreement*.[65] The Security Council itself has meanwhile adopted six resolutions on Iran's nuclear program.[66] Despite the Security Council's repeated demands that Iran suspend its uranium enrichment and reprocessing activities, Iran has refused to do so. For its part, the Security Council initially reacted to Iran's non-compliance by imposing limited sanctions under Article 41 of the *Charter of the United Nations* (*UN Charter*).[67] These have subsequently been tightened. Russian and Chinese opposition to further sanctions led the EU[68] and the United States[69] to implement measures unilaterally.

[64] IAEA, *Implementation of the NPT Safeguards Agreement and Relevant Provisions of United Nations Security Council Resolutions in the Islamic Republic of Iran, Resolution of 13 September 2012*, Doc GOV/2012/50 (2012) at paras 1-3, online: IAEA <http://www.iaea.org/Publications/Documents/Board/2012/gov2012-50.pdf>.

[65] IAEA, *Implementation of the NPT Safeguards Agreement and Relevant Provisions of Security Council Resolutions in the Islamic Republic of Iran, Report of 21 February 2013*, Doc GOV/2013/6 (2013) at paras 62, 65, online: IAEA <http://www.iaea.org/Publications/Documents/Board/2013/gov2013-6.pdf>.

[66] UN Security Council (SC) Resolution 1696, UNSCOR, 2006, UN Doc S/RES/1696 (2006); SC Resolution 1737, UNSCOR, 2007, UN Doc S/RES/1737 (2007); SC Resolution 1747, UNSCOR, 2007, UN Doc S/RES/1747 (2007); SC Resolution 1803, UNSCOR, 2008, UN Doc S/RES/1803 (2008); SC Resolution 1835, UNSCOR, 2009, UN Doc S/RES/1835 (2009); SC Resolution 1929, UNSCOR, 2010, UN Doc S/RES/1929 (2010). At the time of writing, there have been four further UNSC resolutions renewing the mandate of the Iran Sanctions Committee: SC Resolution 1984, UNSCOR, 2011, UN Doc S/RES/1984 (2011); SC Resolution 2049, UNSCOR, 2012, UN Doc S/RES/2049 (2012); SC Resolution 2105, UNSCOR, 2013, UN Doc S/RES/2105 (2013); and SC Resolution 2159, UNSCOR, 2014, UN Doc S/RES/2159 (2014).

[67] *Charter of the United Nations*, 26 June 1945, Can TS 1945 No 7 (in force 24 October 1945), art 41 [*UN Charter*].

[68] EC, *Council Regulation (EU) 264/2012 of 23 March 2012 amending Regulation (EU) No 359/2011 Concerning Restrictive Measures Directed against Certain Persons, Entities and Bodies in View of the Situation in Iran*, [2012] OJ, L87/26; EC, *Council Regulation (EU) No 267/2012 of 23 March 2012 Concerning Restrictive Measures against Iran and Repealing Regulation (EU) No 961/2010*, [2012] OJ L88/1.

[69] The *Iran Freedom and Counter-Proliferation Act* (Subtitle D of Title XII of *National Defence Authorization Act for Fiscal Year 2013*, Pub L No 112-239, 112th Cong, 2 January 2013) imposes, in combination with Executive Order 13645 of 3 June 2013 (78 FR 33945, 5 June 2013), a wide range of sanctions even on non-US companies and financial institutions, including those deemed to be providing support to key Iranian industries. The measures took effect on 1 July 2013. For reporting on enforcement of the sanctions notwithstanding an interim deal

The IAEA has accused Iran of not complying with Article III(1) of the *NPT*,[70] which has led many states to allege that Iran is violating its obligation not to seek nuclear weapons under Article II of the *NPT*. By disregarding the Security Council's resolutions, Iran has also contravened Article 25 of the *UN Charter*.

THE UNITED STATES' CONDUCT

There is little doubt that the United States has violated, and is violating, its obligations under Article VI of the *NPT*.[71] No significant steps have been taken by any of the nuclear weapons states towards eliminating nuclear weapons.[72] The United States has not even ratified the *Comprehensive Nuclear-Test-Ban Treaty*.[73] On taking office, President Obama proclaimed his vision of a "world without nuclear weapons," and he announced that the United States would be working towards this goal.[74] Six years later, the picture is decidedly mixed.

---

between Iran and the P5+1 on Iran's nuclear program, see Rick Gladstone, "U.S Issues Penalties over Violations of Iran Sanctions," *New York Times* (6 February 2014), online: New York Times <http://www.nytimes.com/2014/02/07/world/middleeast/us-issues-penalties-over-violations-of-iran-sanctions.html?_r=0>. President Obama has also chosen to maintain, for a further year from 15 March 2014, the national emergency with respect to Iran declared by President Clinton in Executive Order 12957 of 15 March 1995 (60 FR 14616, 17 March 1995): see *Notice to the Congress: Continuation of the National Emergency with Respect to Iran*, White House Press Release, Washington, DC (12 March 2014), online: White House <http://www.whitehouse.gov/the-press-office/2014/03/12/notice-congress-continuation-national-emergency-respect-iran>.

[70] Maurice Andem, "The Treaty on the Non-Proliferation of Nuclear Weapons (NPT)" (1995) 64 Nordic J Int'l L 575 at 585.

[71] The International Court of Justice (ICJ) has reaffirmed that Article VI of the *NPT* imposes an international obligation. *Legality of the Threat or Use of Nuclear Weapons*, Advisory Opinion, [1996] ICJ Rep 226 at paras 102-3, 105 (F). See also Mike Moore, "Can the Nuclear Powers Continue to Have It Both Ways?" (1997) 4 Brown J World Affairs 83 at 86-87.

[72] Kelly J Malone, "Preemptive Strikes and the Korean Nuclear Crisis: Legal and Political Limitations on the Use of Force" (2003) 12 Pac Rim L & Pol'y J 807 at 828; Andem, *supra* note 70 at 583; Falk, *supra* note 42 at 76, 79-80; Moore, *supra* note 71 at 85; Graham, *supra* note 45 at 14-15.

[73] *Comprehensive Nuclear-Test-Ban Treaty*, UN Doc A/50/1027 (1996) (not yet in force). The US Senate rejected ratification in 1999. See Graham, *supra* note 45 at 14; Nagan and Hammer, *supra* note 40 at 400, 402.

[74] "Remarks by President Barack Obama" (speech delivered at Hradcany Square, Prague, Czech Republic, 5 April 2009), online: White House: <http://www.whitehouse.gov/the_press_office/Remarks-By-President-Barack-Obama-In-Prague-As-Delivered>.

Reductions in the number of nuclear weapons have been made up for by improvements in quality.[75]

Recent US foreign policy has also severely undermined the non-proliferation regime.[76] The *United States–India Nuclear Cooperation Approval and Non-Proliferation Enhancement Act (123 Agreement)* proposed in 2006,[77] and ratified in 2008,[78] exposes the *NPT* regime to renewed charges of discrimination,[79] as it allows India to acquire nuclear technology from the United States for civilian use despite developing nuclear weapons and not being a party to the *NPT*. Although requiring India to reach a *Safeguards Agreement* with the IAEA — which it subsequently did[80] — the *123 Agreement* does not oblige India to give up its nuclear weapons.[81]

---

[75] Stockholm International Peace Research Institute, "Nuclear Force Reductions and Modernizations Continue; Drop in Peacekeeping Troops; No Progress in Cluster Munitions Control—New SIPRI Yearbook out Now," Press Release (3 June 2013); "Nuclear Forces Reduced While Modernizations Continue, says SIPRI," Press Release (16 June 2014) online: Stockholm International Peace Research Institute <http://www.sipri.org/media/pressreleases/2013/YBlaunch _2013>; <http://www.sipri.org/media/pressreleases/2014/nuclear_May_2014>.

[76] Falk, *supra* note 42 at 73-74, 76-77; Lodgaard, *supra* note 43 at 113.

[77] *Joint Statement by President George W Bush and Prime Minister Manmohan Singh,* White House Press Release, Washington, DC (18 July 2005), online: US Dept of State Archive <http://2001-2009.state.gov/p/sca/rls/pr/2005/49763.htm>. The name for such agreements derives from section 123 of the US *Atomic Energy Act of 1954,* Pub L 83-703, which governs co-operation between the United States and other states on nuclear matters.

[78] *United States–India Nuclear Cooperation Approval and Non-proliferation Enhancement Act,* Pub L 110-369, 110th Cong (8 October 2008).

[79] It should be noted that France almost immediately followed suit, concluding an agreement on nuclear co-operation with India in 2008. See "Text of Indo-France Nuclear Deal," *Times of India* (30 September 2008), online: Times of India <http://timesofindia.indiatimes.com/india/Text-of-Indo-France-nuclear -deal/articleshow/3545557.cms>; "India and France in Nuclear Deal," *BBC News* (30 September 2008), online: BBC <http://news.bbc.co.uk/1/hi/7644377.stm>.

[80] *Agreement between the Government of India and the International Atomic Energy Agency for the Application of Safeguards to Civilian Nuclear Facilities,* Doc INFCIRC754 (29 May 2009) (in force 11 May 2009), online: IAEA <http://www.iaea.org/Pub-lications/Documents/Infcircs/2009/infcirc754.pdf>.

[81] Kuppuswamy, *supra* note 43 at 145; Oborne and Morrison, *supra* note 3 at 36-37. See also "India Joins World Nuclear Club amid Warnings over Spread of Weapons," *The Times* (8 September, 2008) 33, reporting on the decision of the Nuclear Suppliers' Group (founded to combat proliferation, and made up of forty-five states that supply nuclear technology) to allow nuclear technology exports to India despite India not being a state party to the *NPT*.

The United States' treatment of Israel has aroused similar concerns. Although Israel is not a party to the *NPT*, has not allowed any inspections of its nuclear facilities (in clear contravention of UN Security Council Resolution 487[82]), and has acquired nuclear weapons, these facts have not deterred the United States from supporting Israel in virtually every respect.[83] The United States' reaction to Pakistan's acquisition of nuclear weapons also hardly served as a deterrent, notwithstanding Pakistani scientist Abdul Khan's notorious proliferation network. Sanctions initially imposed by the United States were quickly lifted.[84] The behaviour of the United States and its allies in relation to the *NPT*, as well as their acceptance of nuclear proliferation among allied states, severely undermines the argument that responsive measures — *in extremis*, the use of force — against Iran are necessary to uphold the *NPT*. The accusation that Iran has violated the *NPT*'s provisions may even fall foul of the "clean hands doctrine."[85]

PREVENTIVE SELF-DEFENCE

The United States has nevertheless claimed the right to intervene militarily in "rogue states" when such action is deemed necessary in order to prevent those states from acquiring WMD. As explained in the Bush administration's 2002 *National Security Strategy* (*NSS*),[86] this right is justified on the basis of the grave danger that such

---

[82] See SC Resolution 487, UNSCOR, 1981, UN Doc S/RES/487 (1981) at operative para 5.

[83] See Hersh, *supra* note 54 at 225-40, 262-83 (describing US support notwithstanding its awareness of Israeli nuclear efforts from the 1950s onwards). See also Nagan and Hammer, *supra* note 40 at 434 (arguing that a "single nuclear power in the Middle East" is a "major security threat for all states and peoples in the region"); Falk, *supra* note 42 at 77; Kuppuswamy, *supra* note 43 at 150; Aly, *supra* note 43 at 153-54; Noyes, *supra* note 32 at 74-75; Lodgaard, *supra* note 43 at 113, 138-39; Oborne and Morrison, *supra* note 3 at 32-34; Patrikarakos, *supra* note 8 at 152-53.

[84] See Centre for Arms Control and Non-Proliferation, *India–Pakistan Sanctions Legislation Factsheet*, online: <http://armscontrolcenter.org/issues/nonproliferation/articles/india_pakistan_sanctions/#>.

[85] Whereby claimants alleging treaty violations by another party must themselves not be at fault. See *Diversion of Water from the River Meuse (Netherlands v Belgium)* (1937), PCIJ (Ser A/B) No 70 at 24-25.

[86] White House, *National Security Strategy of the United States of America* (September 2002), online: <http://www.state.gov/documents/organization/63562.pdf> at 14 [*NSS* 2002].

weapons pose, which requires "anticipatory action ... even if uncertainty remains as to the time and place of the enemy's attack."[87] Iran is clearly viewed as such a "rogue state" by many in the United States.[88] Although the Obama administration's *NSS* of 2010 no longer mentions preventive self-defence, it does not explicitly repudiate it either.[89] Furthermore, there is widespread agreement that President Obama's and others' repeated declarations that "all options remain on the table" in order to prevent Iran from acquiring nuclear weapons includes the option of using force.[90] Only the concept of preventive self-defence could possibly provide a legal justification for such action. Whether such an understanding of self-defence is consistent with international law is, however, extremely contentious.

Various attempts have been made to reconcile the concept of preventive self-defence with the law on the use of force. The main argument involves the claim that anticipatory self-defence is permitted under the *UN Charter* and/or is supported by state practice and *opinio juris* and that this "traditional" concept merely has to be adjusted to accommodate the new dangers posed by WMD. Others, however, acknowledge that the concept of preventive self-defence cannot be reconciled with the current state of the law, while contending that new rules need to be developed by the international community in order to cope with the latest threats posed by the proliferation of WMD. Some have gone so far as to argue that destroying WMD sites would not amount to a violation of Article 2(4) of the *UN Charter* in the first place. The most far-reaching argument is made by Michael Glennon, who, as will be seen, disputes the validity of the current rules on the use of force in general. A detailed analysis of these arguments will show that the concept of

---

[87] *Ibid* at 15.

[88] *NSS* 2006, *supra* note 38 at 2, 20. President Obama refers to "outliers" rather than "rogue states." "'Outliers Like Iran and North Korea' Are Exceptions to New Policy on Nukes, Obama Says," *NY Daily News* (6 April 2010), online: NY Daily News <http://www.nydailynews.com/news/politics/outliers-iran-north -korea-exceptions-new-policy-nukes-obama-article-1.163742>.

[89] *NSS* 2010, *supra* note 58.

[90] "President Obama's Speech to the General Assembly," *supra* note 1; "Obama Says Iran Nuclear Row 'Larger' Than Syria Crisis," *BBC News* (15 September 2013), online: BBC News <http://www.bbc.co.uk/news/world-middle-east-24102723>; Maya Shwayder, "Panetta: US May Have to Use Force against Iran," *Jerusalem Post* (1 November 2013), online: Jerusalem Post <http://www.jpost.com/Iranian -Threat/News/Panetta-US-may-have-to-use-military-force-against-Iran-330373>.

preventive self-defence is clearly contrary to international law and should remain so.

TERMINOLOGY

Before embarking on such a discussion, however, it is worthwhile trying to clarify what is meant by terms such as "anticipatory," "preventive," and "pre-emptive" self-defence, especially as the 2002 *NSS* undoubtedly muddied the terminological waters and the term "pre-emptive," in particular, is not used consistently in the literature.[91] "Anticipatory self-defence" normally refers to the use of force in order to repel an attack that is imminent — that is, one that is just about to occur. As famously encapsulated by US Secretary of State Daniel Webster in 1841, in relation to the *Caroline* incident of a few years earlier,[92] a state is permitted to use force in order to counter an attack that has not yet commenced provided there exists "a necessity of self-defence, instant, overwhelming, leaving no choice of means, and no moment for deliberation."[93] In addition to the imminence requirement, the use of force must be necessary (in that it is not possible to avert the attack by other, peaceful means) and proportionate to the threat (or not "unreasonable or excessive," as Webster put it).[94]

Some question the relevance of the *Caroline* incident regarding anticipatory self-defence, claiming that the destruction of the *Caroline* was not anticipatory but, rather, an action in self-defence in the course of an ongoing armed conflict.[95] It must be acknowledged, however, that there is widespread agreement that anticipatory

[91] On the problem of inconsistent usage of terms in this area, see Whitley RP Kaufman, "What's Wrong with Pre-emptive War?" (paper delivered at the Joint Services Conference on Professional Ethics, 27-28 January 2005), online: <http://isme.tamu.edu/JSCOPE05/Kaufman05.html>.

[92] An 1837 incident in which the American ship *Caroline* was attacked by British troops because of its supposed use in aiding rebels seeking to overthrow British rule in Canada.

[93] Letter from Daniel Webster to Lord Ashburton (27 July 1842), online: Yale Law School, the Avalon Project <http://avalon.law.yale.edu/19th_century/br-1842d.asp#web1>.

[94] *Ibid.*

[95] Yoram Dinstein, *War, Aggression and Self-Defence*, 4th edition (Cambridge: Cambridge University Press, 2005) at 184-85; Joel R Paul, "The Bush Doctrine: Making or Breaking Customary International Law?" (2003–04) 27 Hastings Int'l & Comp L Rev 457 at 463.

self-defence was viewed as lawful under customary international law before the *UN Charter* came into force in 1945, no matter how the *Caroline* incident is categorized.[96] Whether it survived the adoption of the *Charter* is a much more contentious point, as will be discussed later in this article.

In contrast to "anticipatory self-defence," "preventive self-defence" usually describes the use of force to counter a threatened attack that cannot be classified as imminent — that is, a threat that is more distant in time and, hence, lacking the "imminence" criterion of the *Caroline* formulation. As defined by Allen Buchanan and Robert Keohane, it is "the initiation of military action in anticipation of harmful actions that are neither presently occurring nor immediately impending."[97] "Pre-emptive self-defence" has become something of a problematic phrase. Following its use in the 2002 *NSS* and its consequent association with the Bush doctrine, "pre-emptive" has frequently been interpreted as meaning the same as "preventive" — that is, a defensive use of force to neutralize a threat that is not yet imminent. Many authors have used the term in this sense or have employed the terms "pre-emptive" and "preventive" interchangeably.

However, a more purist approach maintains that the term "pre-emptive" is in fact synonymous with "anticipatory" (in the *Caroline* sense of denoting a response to an imminent or immediate threat

---

96 Malone, *supra* note 72 at 809-10; Erin L Guruli, "The Terrorism Era: Should the International Community Redefine Its Legal Standards on Use of Force in Self-Defense?" (2004) 12 Willamette J Int'l L & Disp Resol 100 at 105, 119; David Sloss, "Forcible Arms Control: Preemptive Attacks on Nuclear Facilities" (2003) 4 Chicago J Int'l L 39 at 53; Gregory A Raymond and Charles W Kegley, "Preemption and Preventive War" in Howard M Hensel, ed, *The Legitimate Use of Military Force: The Just War Tradition and the Customary Law of Armed Conflict* (Aldershot, UK: Ashgate Publishing, 2008) 99 at 100-1; Terry D Gill, "The Temporal Dimension of Self-Defense: Anticipation, Pre-emption, Prevention and Immediacy" in Michael N Schmitt and Jelena Pejic, eds, *International Law and Armed Conflict: Exploring the Faultlines: Essays in Honour of Yoram Dinstein* (Leiden: Martinus Nijhoff, 2007) 113 at 121; W Thomas Mallison and Sally V Mallison, "The Israeli Aerial Attack of June 7, 1981, Upon the Iraqi Nuclear Reactor: Aggression or Self-Defense?" (1982) 15 Vand J Transnat'l L 417 at 422-23; Istvan Pogany, "Nuclear Weapons and Self-Defence in International Law" in Istvan Pogany, ed, *Nuclear Weapons and International Law* (Aldershot, UK: Avebury, 1987) 63 at 75; Roberts, *supra* note 45 at 505; Donald R Rothwell, "Anticipatory Self-Defence in the Age of International Terrorism" (2005) 24 UQLJ 337 at 339-40.

97 Cited in Jack S Levy, "Preventive War and Democratic Politics" (2008) 52 Int'l Studies Q 1 at n 19. See also James Mulcahy and Charles O Mahony, "Anticipatory Self-Defence: A Discussion of the International Law" (2006) 2 Hanse LR 231 at 236.

of attack) and that the 2002 *NSS* was therefore describing the *preventive* use of force.[98] This confusion stems from the slippery use of language in the 2002 *NSS*, which, while using the concept of "pre-emption" and asserting that such a defensive use of force is permissible under existing international law,[99] nevertheless confers on it an altogether more expansive meaning — one that would allow force to counter a much more remote attack than customary law would allow.[100]

Adding to this confusion, "anticipatory self-defence" has also been used as an umbrella term for any use of force undertaken to avert an attack that has not yet begun, encompassing both "pre-emptive self-defence" and "preventive self-defence."[101] In an attempt to avoid confusion, this article will refrain from using the term "pre-emptive" where possible and will instead use the terms "anticipatory" to refer to the use of force in self-defence against an imminent attack, in keeping with the *Caroline* formula, and "preventive" to describe the use of force to forestall a future attack that cannot be categorized as imminent in this sense.

PREVENTIVE SELF-DEFENCE IS NOT ILLEGAL AS THERE ARE NO RULES ON THE USE OF FORCE?

According to Michael Glennon, the *UN Charter*-based rules on the use of force have become inoperative owing to desuetude — since

---

[98] See Miriam Sapiro, "Iraq: The Shifting Sands of Preemptive Self-Defense" (2003) 97 AJIL 599 at 599; Levy, *supra* note 97 at 2. See also Nicholas Rengger, "The Greatest Treason? On the Subtle Temptations of Preventive War" (2008) 84 Int'l Affairs 949 at 950.

[99] "Legal scholars and international jurists often conditioned the legitimacy of *preemption* on the existence of an *imminent* threat." *NSS* 2002, *supra* note 86 at 15 [emphasis added].

[100] "The United States has long maintained the option of preemptive actions to counter a sufficient threat to our national security. The greater the threat, the greater is the risk of inaction — and the more compelling the case for taking anticipatory action to defend ourselves, *even if uncertainty remains as to the time and place of the enemy's attack*." *Ibid* [emphasis added].

[101] See, for example, Jeff Collins, "The Case for Pre-emption (Not Prevention) in Public International Law," *Globalized World Post* (23 January 2012), online: Globalized World Post <http://thegwpost.com/2012/01/23/the-case-for-pre-emption-not-prevention-in-public-international-law/>. Mulcahy and Mahony, *supra* note 97 at 237, also seem to use "anticipatory" as an all-encompassing term that can include the preventive use of force: "[I]t should not be forgotten that the use of anticipatory self-defence where there is an emerging threat is permissible under the Charter regime where the Security Council gives its consent."

they have been violated so often, they no longer reflect the law.[102] The failure of the UN system, it is argued, is attributable to ignoring realities: namely, the failure to recognize the power and exceptionalism of the hegemon, currently the United States. The desire of the United States to retain its "towering pre-eminence" within the international community means it will "use," "avoid," or "ignore" the Security Council as necessary in order to "maintain a unipolar system."[103] Glennon has more recently reiterated his stance on the *UN Charter*'s rules on the use of force and has tentatively suggested using traditional "policy analysis" as a basis for deciding whether to enforce non-proliferation militarily.[104]

However, state practice actually evidences the contrary, since governments unfailingly offer legal justifications for even the most indefensible of actions and routinely seek advice on international legal issues, especially concerning the use of force.[105] In response, Glennon claims that states' actions speak louder than words, but he fails to acknowledge that, in attempting to justify their actions on the basis of *UN Charter* rules, states implicitly confirm their validity. Consequently, Glennon's conclusion that non-compliance is to be seen as a withdrawal of consent does not follow. There are formal ways of withdrawing consent, and the fact that states, following their own violations, nevertheless continue to apply the same

---

[102] Michael J Glennon, "The UN Security Council in a Unipolar World" (2003–04) 44 Va J Int'l L 91 at 98-100. A more nuanced version of this argument can be found in Michael J Glennon, "The Rise and Fall of the UN Charter's Use of Force Rules" (2003–04) 27 Hastings Int'l & Comp L Rev 497.

[103] Glennon, "The UN Security Council," *supra* note 102 at 94, 102.

[104] Michael J Glennon, "Pre-empting Proliferation: International Law, Morality, and Nuclear Weapons" (2013) 24 EJIL 109 at 109-17, 123-27.

[105] Thomas M Franck, "The Power of Legitimacy and the Legitimacy of Power: International Law in an Age of Disequilibrium" (2006) 100 AJIL 88 at 96; Mary Ellen O'Connell, *The Power and Purpose of International Law: Insights from the Theory and Practice of Enforcement* (Oxford: Oxford University Press, 2008) at 1, see also at 114, 169; Nico Krisch, "International Law in Times of Hegemony: Unequal Power and the Shaping of the International Legal Order" (2005) 16 EJIL 369 at 374; Yasuaki Onuma, "International Law in and with International Politics: The Functions of International Law in International Society" (2003) 14 EJIL105 at 112-13, 125-26, 128; Oscar Schachter, *International Law in Theory and Practice* (Dordrecht: Martinus Nijhoff, 1991) at 6-7; Arthur Watts, "The Importance of International Law" in Michael Byers, ed, *The Role of Law in International Politics* (Oxford: Oxford University Press, 2009) 5 at 7; Louis Henkin, *How Nations Behave: Law and Foreign Policy*, 2nd edition (New York: Council on Foreign Relations, 1979) at 65; Rüdiger Wolfrum, "American-European Dialogue: Different Perceptions of International Law" (2004) 64 ZaöRV 255 at 256.

rules to other states strongly implies that there has been no such withdrawal.

Glennon's reasoning that the rules on the use of force have become invalid owing to a lack of enforcement is similarly unconvincing. As Anthony D'Amato has observed, this is also true of many areas of domestic constitutional law. Ultimately, domestic constitutional courts can only hope and expect that the government will comply with their decisions, since they have, in truth, no practical means of enforcing compliance.[106] Moreover, many areas of criminal law, such as the rules on theft or tax evasion, suffer from a severe lack of enforcement in most states, but nobody would seriously question the legal status of these rules or suggest that the activities they prohibit are in fact permitted.[107] Even the rules on speeding limits, which are routinely flouted by the majority of motorists in many states, do not forfeit their "legal" quality as a consequence of such repeated violation, and no motorist charged with a speeding-related offence ever attempts to argue that the rule they have allegedly broken is no longer a rule simply because many drivers have chosen to ignore it or have been lucky enough to escape prosecution.

Lastly, using "policy analysis" in order to decide whether to use force could in no way provide a substitute for international legal rules. Even the most positivist international lawyer will acknowledge that states weigh the benefits and disadvantages of going to war before reaching a decision and that international law will be only one of many factors considered. Of course, the same applies in the domestic context. The pickpocket, knowing that theft is illegal, will nevertheless weigh his or her chances of stealing a purse and gaining a worthwhile amount of money against the chances of being caught and punished. No one would seriously suggest that this weighing of chances should supplant the prohibition on theft.

NO VIOLATION OF ARTICLE 2(4) OF THE *UN CHARTER?*

In relation to Israel's attack on Iraq's Osiraq nuclear reactor in 1981, D'Amato questioned whether this action violated Article 2(4) of the *UN Charter*, as Iraq had neither lost any territory nor had "its

---

[106] Anthony D'Amato, "Is International Law Really 'Law'?" (1984–85) 79 Northwestern UL Rev 1293 at 1293-301, reprinted in Martti Koskenniemi, ed, *International Law* (Aldershot, UK: Dartmouth Publishing, 1992).

[107] O'Connell, *supra* note 105 at 8; Franck, *supra* note 105 at 92-93; Wade Mansell and Emily Haslam, "John Bolton and the United States' Retreat from International Law" (2005) 14 Social & Legal Studies 459 at 470.

governmental authority vis-à-vis other sovereign governments [been] diminished."[108] D'Amato's assessment was based on the very narrow view that the use of force is prohibited under Article 2(4) only when it is directed against another state's "territorial integrity or political independence" or is "inconsistent with the Purposes of the United Nations."[109] Given more recent, similar arguments by certain US commentators concerning the potential use of force in response to breaches of international law in Syria, it is worthwhile considering the strength of this line of reasoning.[110]

In fact, the *travaux préparatoires* contradict any assertion that the authors of Article 2(4) intended to limit the scope of its prohibition by including the closing references to territorial integrity, political independence, and UN purposes.[111] Phrases such as "territorial integrity" and "political independence" were included as illustrative examples, mainly at the behest of smaller states that felt their independence required an iron-clad guarantee within the *UN Charter*. The scope of the ban on the use of force in Article 2(4) was not to be limited in any way.[112]

---

108 Anthony D'Amato, "Israel's Air Strike upon the Iraqi Nuclear Reactor" (1983) 77 AJIL 584 at 585.

109 *UN Charter, supra* note 67, art 2(4).

110 See, for example, Jordan Paust, "US Use of Limited Force in Syria Can be Lawful under the UN Charter," *JURIST-Forum* (10 September 2013), online: JURIST <http://www.jurist.org/forum/2013/09/jordan-paust-force-syria.php>; Anthony D'Amato, "The Meaning of Article 2(4) in the U.N. Charter," Northwestern Public Law Research Paper no 13-30 (6 September 2013), online: SSRN <http://ssrn.com/abstract=2321806>.

111 D'Amato himself acknowledged that the contrary view "commands some support in the *travaux préparatoires*." D'Amato, *supra* note 108 at 585.

112 Ian Brownlie, "The Use of Force in Self-Defence" (1961) 37 Brit YB Int'l L 183 at 232-37, especially 233-36. See also Ian Brownlie, *International Law and the Use of Force by States* (Oxford: Oxford University Press, 1963) at 265-68; Rex J Zedalis, "Protection of Nationals Abroad: Is Consent the Basis of Obligation?" (1990) 25 Tex Int'l LJ 209 at 223-24; Edward Gordon, "Article 2(4) in Historical Context" (1984–85) 10 Yale J Int'l L 271 at 276; CHM Waldock, "The Regulation of the Use of Force by Individual States in International Law" (1952) 81 Rec des Cours 451 at 493; Thomas R Krift, "Self-Defense and Self-Help: The Israeli Raid on Entebbe" (1977–78) IV Brook J Int'l L 43 at 52; John R D'Angelo, "Resort to Force by States to Protect Nationals: The US Mission to Iran and Its Legality under International Law" (1980–81) 21 Va J Int'l L 485 at 499; Oscar Schachter, "International Law in the Hostage Crisis: Implications for Future Cases" in Paul H Kreisberg, ed, *American Hostages in Iran: The Conduct of a Crisis* (New Haven, CT: Yale University Press, 1985) 325 at 330.

D'Amato's interpretation can also hardly be reconciled with the *UN Charter*'s overriding purpose, reflected in its preamble and in Article 1(1), of outlawing the use of force as far as possible.[113] Those who drafted the *UN Charter*, having just experienced the devastation of the Second World War, were well aware of the dangers posed by a return to pre-war gunboat diplomacy.[114] Not surprisingly, the International Court of Justice (ICJ) and the UN General Assembly have rejected a restrictive interpretation of Article 2(4).[115] State practice also fails to support a narrow view of the scope of the Article 2(4) prohibition. In the case of the Israeli attack on the Osiraq reactor — which is the only case to date in which a state has claimed a right of anticipatory self-defence, as will be shown later in this article — Israel sought to justify its actions on the basis of Article 51, clearly implying a *prima facie* violation of Article 2(4).[116] There is therefore no basis for concluding that the scope of the ban on the use of force in Article 2(4) is limited by this provision's closing language. It therefore follows that any US strike against Iranian nuclear facilities would constitute a *prima facie* infringement of Article 2(4).[117]

---

[113] Jeffrey A Sheehan, "A Response to Paust" (1978) 2 Fletcher Forum 92. See also Zedalis, *supra* note 112 at 222.

[114] Ulrich Beyerlin, "Die israelische Befreiungsaktion von Entebbe in völkerrechtlicher Sicht" (1977) ZaöRV 213 at 216-19; Michael Hakenberg, *Die Iran-Sanktionen der USA während der Teheraner Geiselaffäre aus völkerrechtlicher Sicht* (Frankfurt: Peter Lang, 1988) at 240; Zedalis, *supra* note 112 at 222; Schachter, *supra* note 112 at 330.

[115] *Corfu Channel Case (United Kingdom v Albania)*, Merits, [1949] ICJ Rep 4 at 34-35 [*Corfu Channel*] (although the ICJ did not specifically mention Article 2(4), it seems UK activities in Albanian waters would not have contravened Article 2(4) if the restrictive interpretation were correct); *Military and Paramilitary Activities in and against Nicaragua (Nicaragua v United States of America)*, [1986] ICJ Rep 14 at paras 187-201 [*Nicaragua*]; James P Rowles, "Military Responses to Terrorism: Substantive and Procedural Constraints in International Law" (1987) 81 Am Soc Int'l L Rev 307 at 309; *Declaration on Inadmissibility of Intervention in Domestic Affairs of States and Protection of Their Independence and Sovereignty*, GA Res 2131 (XX), UNGAOR, 20th Sess, UN Doc A/RES/20/2131 (1965); *Declaration on Principles of International Law Concerning Friendly Relations and Cooperation among States in Accordance with the Charter of the United Nations*, GA Res 2625(XXV), UNGAOR, 25th Sess, UN Doc A/RES/25/2625 (1970); *Definition of Aggression*, GA Res 3314 (XXIX), UNGAOR, 29th Sess, UN Doc A/RES/3314 (XXIX) (1974).

[116] See text accompanying note 175 in this article.

[117] Sloss, *supra* note 96 at 50-53.

PREVENTIVE SELF-DEFENCE DOES NOT CONTRAVENE ARTICLE 51?

Proponents of the legality of preventive self-defence usually contend that it is no more than an aspect of anticipatory self-defence (and, hence, does not contravene the *Caroline* imminence standard). This argument in turn is premised on the contention that the legality of anticipatory self-defence, as part of pre-*Charter* customary international law, has remained unaffected by the *UN Charter*. Before testing the validity of the second limb of this argument — that is, whether a right of anticipatory self-defence in fact survived the adoption of the *UN Charter* — it is worth examining in detail the first claim — that preventive self-defence does not flout the imminence criterion. Doing so illuminates some of the difficulties intrinsic to the concept of preventive self-defence, including the problem of distinguishing between defensive force and acts of aggression.

The conflation of preventive and pre-emptive/anticipatory self-defence in the 2002 *NSS* serves as a useful means of portraying the preventive use of force as being permissible under existing customary law. This depiction was in turn dependent upon a reconceptualization of the imminence criterion, which, the document suggested, needed to be reinterpreted to deal effectively with a species of threat very different from that which confronted the world of the mid-nineteenth century: "We must adapt the concept of imminent threat to the capabilities and objectives of today's adversaries."[118] Governments cannot be expected to wait until an irrational regime or terrorist group is on the point of launching a nuclear, chemical, or biological weapon threatening large-scale death and destruction, but they are permitted, indeed required, to take action "against such emerging threats before they are fully formed."[119]

The notion that the *Caroline* criterion of imminence is no longer fit for purpose and needs to be modified in order to deal with inchoate, but potentially lethal, terrorist- and WMD-related threats has received a cautious welcome among some members of the United Kingdom's (UK) political class. This recognition suggests doubt as to whether it is possible to accommodate the Bush doctrine of preventive/pre-emptive use of force within the current bounds of what counts as an imminent attack. In a 2002–03 report on the war against terrorism, the UK House of Commons Foreign Affairs Committee was of the opinion:

[118] *NSS* 2002, *supra* note 86 at 15.

[119] *Ibid*, preamble.

that the notion of "imminence" should be reconsidered in the light of new threats to international peace and security — regardless of whether the doctrine of pre-emptive self-defence is a distinctively new legal development. We recommend that the Government work to establish a clear international consensus on the circumstances in which military action may be taken by states on a pre-emptive basis.[120]

Similarly, in its 2003–04 report on the same issue, the committee concluded that "the concept of 'imminence' in anticipatory self-defence may require reassessment," but it advised that the UK government, "in the event of the legitimisation of the doctrine of anticipatory self-defence ... persuade its allies to limit the use of the doctrine to a 'threat of catastrophic attack'" so as to guard against possible misuse by unscrupulous states.[121] Meanwhile, in a 2004 debate in the House of Lords, Lord Goldsmith, then UK attorney-general in the administration of Tony Blair, stated his belief that "what constitutes an 'imminent' armed attack will develop to meet new circumstances and new threats" and that "[i]t must be right that states are able to act in self-defence in circumstances where there is evidence of further imminent attacks by terrorist groups, even if there is no specific evidence of where such an attack will take place or of the precise nature of the attack."[122] Many academics and commentators, and even some international lawyers, have also called for the concept of imminence to be extended to encompass more remote threats — principally from terrorist actors — than the strict customary law standard envisages.[123]

---

[120] Cited in Daniel Bethlehem, "Self-Defense against an Imminent or Actual Armed Attack by Nonstate Actors" (2012) 106 AJIL 770 at 771.

[121] Cited in *ibid* at 772.

[122] Cited in *ibid.*

[123] See, for example, *ibid* at 774; Guruli, *supra* note 96 at 119; Jane E Stromseth, "Law and Force after Iraq: A Transitional Moment" (2003) 97 AJIL 628 at 638 (pleading, however, for a more moderate adjustment than envisaged by the Bush doctrine); Ruth Wedgwood, "The Fall of Saddam Hussein: Security Council Mandates and Preemptive Self-Defense" (2003) 97 AJIL 576 at 582; John Yoo, "International Law and the War in Iraq" (2003) 97 AJIL 563 at 573; Matt S Nydell, "Tensions between International Law and Strategic Security: Implications of Israel's Preemptive Raid on Iraq's Nuclear Reactor" (1983–84) 24 Va J Int'l L 459 at 488 (merely stating, however, that nuclear weapons pose a "new challenge" to the concept of necessity and imminence); Marshall Silverberg, "International Law and the Use of Force: May the United States Attack the Chemical Plant at Rabta?" (1990) 13 BC Int'l & Comp L Rev 53 at 58; Mark E Newcomb, "Non-Proliferation, Self-Defense, and the Korean Crisis" (1994) 27 Vand J Transnat'l L 603 at 620.

Following this logic, however, is to arrive at the somewhat paradoxical outcome that an imminent threat need no longer be imminent — at least in the ordinary sense of being immediately impending or just about to take place. Conceptual clarity alone would seem to dictate that, rather than stretching the imminence requirement to the breaking point, proponents of the preventive use of force would be better served by dispensing with it altogether. This could be achieved either by arguing that imminence is not a necessary condition of the customary right of anticipatory self-defence[124] or, if conceding that the preventive use of force is currently unlawful, adopting the normative position that it should be lawful and that it is necessary to persuade the international community accordingly.

It is also important to note that what distinguishes preventive from anticipatory/pre-emptive self-defence is not merely a matter of timing (how far in advance of a threatened attack is it permissible to use force to deflect that attack) but something more fundamental. Differences in the objectives sought, the type of calculations made, and the level of force to be employed are altogether more consequential. In contrast to anticipatory self-defence, which necessarily targets a specific and clearly identifiable threat, the focus of preventive self-defence tends not to be a particular hazard but, rather, a source of future hazards, whether this be a terrorist organization, a state believed to be harbouring such an organization, or a state or regime constituting a potential threat in and of itself.

Consequently, as David Luban points out, it is possible to differentiate between a one-off preventive attack aimed at removing a suspected future threat — such as Israel's attack on the Iraqi Osiraq nuclear reactor in 1981, which otherwise left Iraq's territory intact and its incumbent regime untouched — and preventive war aimed at regime change, such as the war that was waged on Iraq in 2003.[125] As the Council on Foreign Relations observed in response to the Bush doctrine,

[t]raditionally, preemption constitutes a "war of necessity" based on credible evidence of imminent attack ... But the Bush administration has

---

124 See Maria Benvenuta Occelli, "'Sinking' the *Caroline*: Why the Caroline Doctrine's Restrictions on Self-Defense Should Not Be Regarded as Customary International Law" (2003) 4 San Diego Int'l LJ 467.

125 David Luban, "Preventive War" (2004) 32 Philosophy & Public Affairs 207 at 214.

expanded the definition to include actions that more clearly resemble preventive war. Preventive wars are essentially "wars of choice" that derive mostly from a calculus of power, rather than the precedent of international law, convention and practice. In choosing preventive wars, policymakers project that waging a war, even if unprovoked, against a rising adversary sooner is preferable to an inevitable war later when the balance of power no longer rests in their favour.[126]

Pursuing preventive war as a means of gaining geostrategic advantage is well summarized by Jack Levy:

Preventive war is a strategy designed to forestall an adverse shift in the balance of power and driven by better-now-than-later logic. Faced with a rising and potentially hostile adversary, it is better to fight now rather than risk the likely consequences of inaction — a decline in relative power, diminishing bargaining leverage, and the risk of war under less favourable circumstances later.[127]

Were the United States to launch a preventive strike against Iran's territory in response to Iran's growing nuclear capability, this could amount to either a "preventive attack" or a "preventive war" depending on the outcome sought and the degree of force employed. If the goal was to remove the current Islamic regime and replace it with one more amenable to US interests,[128] then this goal would clearly fall under the rubric of a "preventive war," as with the overthrow of Saddam Hussein in 2003. Alternatively, if the objective was to destroy or disable a number of Iranian nuclear facilities, without seeking to unseat the incumbent regime, such a use of force might more accurately be described as a "preventive attack," although this could well depend on the number and type of sites attacked and the level of death and destruction caused.[129]

---

[126] Council on Foreign Relations, *The Bush Administration's Doctrine of Preemption (and Prevention): When How, Where?* (1 February 2004), online: Council of Foreign Relations <http://www.cfr.org/world/bush-administrations-doctrine-preemption-prevention-/p6799>.

[127] Levy, *supra* note 97 at 1.

[128] On the possibility of US-engineered "regime change" in Iran, whether by military or non-military means, see Elliott Abrams, "Regime Change" in Robert D Blackwill, ed, *Iran: The Nuclear Challenge* (New York: Council on Foreign Relations, 2012) 43.

[129] On the feasibility of various military actions (by Israel) aimed at disrupting Iran's nuclear program, see Whitney Raas and Austin Long, "Osirak Redux?

The notion of "preventive war" — in which the use of force is aimed not at eliminating an obvious and defined threat but, rather, at removing a regime regarded as posing a future threat — points to a wider philosophical problem with the concept of "preventive self-defence." Can such a use of force correctly be described as defensive at all? For Whitley Kaufman, the concept of preventive self-defence is inherently contradictory, and relaxing the imminence requirement would have the effect of transforming the use of force from the defensive into its opposite:

> [T]he very purpose of defensive force is to ward off an attack: that is what renders it "defensive." In contrast, the use of force to prevent possible future threats is no longer defensive in the strict sense, but offensive. That is to say, it is no longer "defensive" in nature. For the very idea of self-defense intrinsically involves action aimed at removing or pre-empting an immediate threat.[130]

Once the link between an act of force and the threat to which it is supposedly a response is substantially weakened, the opportunities for error, manipulation, and outright abuse multiply considerably, inviting recourse to the very wars of aggression that the *UN Charter* sought to stamp out.

There is also the more fundamental issue of whether anticipatory self-defence itself still forms part of customary international law. Those who maintain that it does tend to argue either that Article 51 does not regulate customary international law on self-defence or, more commonly, that Article 51 explicitly confirms the validity of pre-*Charter* customary rules.

Self-Defence Is Not Regulated by the UN Charter?

This approach is based on the argument that Article 2(4) does not trench on the customary international law right of self-defence as it stood in 1945:

> We must presuppose that rights formerly belonging to member states continue except in so far as obligations inconsistent with those existing rights are assumed under the Charter ... [I]t is, therefore, fallacious to

---

Assessing Israeli Capabilities to Destroy Iranian Nuclear Facilities" (2007) 31 Int'l Security 7.

[130] Kaufman, *supra* note 91 at 3.

assume that members have only those rights which general international law accords them except and in so far as they have surrendered them under the Charter.[131]

This theory assumes that the ban on the use of force in Article 2(4) did not apply to self-defence. When the *UN Charter* was drafted, the delegates were united in their belief that the use of force in self-defence was justified and, hence, not subject to the ban.[132] Therefore, the customary international law rules on self-defence were not curtailed by Article 2(4). Article 51 was not really necessary and was included only at the behest of members of various regional security pacts.[133] Furthermore, Article 51 applied only "if an armed attack occurs." Other cases of rightful self-defence under customary international law were not regulated under the *UN Charter* and therefore remained intact.[134]

This approach is to be rejected. It is true that rights not surrendered under a treaty, such as the *UN Charter*, generally remain intact. This does not, however, apply when a treaty purports to regulate an area of the law generally. There can be no doubt that the *UN Charter* was intended to regulate the use of force in international relations. Article 2(4) stipulated a ban on the use of force; Article 51 set out one of the few exceptions to this prohibition.[135] By agreeing to the ban on the use of force in Article 2(4), and by allowing for only two exceptions,[136] UN member states have renounced all other customary rights to use force against other member states they may have had before the *UN Charter* came into force. Between the *Charter*'s ban and its narrow exceptions relating to the use of force, there

---

[131] Derek William Bowett, *Self-Defence in International Law* (Manchester: Manchester University Press, 1958) at 184-85.

[132] *Ibid* at 185-86.

[133] *Ibid* at 182-84, 187-93.

[134] See, for example, the argument to this effect by the then Lord Chancellor, Viscount Kilmuir, speaking in the House of Lords at the time of the Suez crisis in 1956. House of Lords, UK, *Parliamentary Debates*, vol 199, col 1243-1365 at 1351-52 (1 November 1956), online: <http://hansard.millbanksystems.com/lords/1956/nov/01/egypt>.

[135] Brownlie, "The Use of Force in Self-Defence," *supra* note 112 at 239-41; Brownlie, *International Law, supra* note 112 at 269-75.

[136] That is, use of force in individual or collective self-defence under the *UN Charter*, *supra* note 67, art 51, or as authorized by the Security Council acting under its Chapter VII powers.

is simply no room for generous customary international legal entitlements.

Logic also militates against the contrary approach. Should pre-*Charter* customary international law on self-defence have remained undisturbed by the *UN Charter*, this would lead to the paradoxical situation that self-defence against an "armed attack" — arguably the most severe form of aggression — would be subject to more stringent rules than would the use of force in response to other, lesser forms of aggression that traditionally sufficed in order to give rise to a right of self-defence.[137] This illogical result can be avoided only if Derek Bowett's approach is followed, whereby the phrase "if an armed attack occurs" is given no meaning.[138] However, such an approach to treaty interpretation cannot be accepted.[139]

It should also be noted that, while the ICJ has so far avoided ruling on the legality of anticipatory self-defence as such,[140] it nevertheless concluded, in *Military and Paramilitary Activities in and against Nicaragua (Nicaragua v United States of America)*, that, by 1986 (the date of the judgment), customary international law also stipulated that forceful self-defence could be exercised only by a state that had been "the victim of an armed attack."[141] This approach makes the foregoing discussion obsolete, as any "non-regulated" customary international law on self-defence would by now be closely aligned with *UN Charter* law, at least as far as the requirement of an actual "armed attack" is concerned. It must therefore be concluded that pre-*Charter* customary international law on the use of force in self-defence cannot provide UN member states with additional grounds for resorting to the use of force.

Article 51 Confirms Pre-UN Charter Custom on Self-Defence?

Most who argue that anticipatory self-defence is permitted under the *UN Charter*, however, do not claim that this is because of the

---

137 Dinstein, *supra* note 95 at 185.

138 Bowett, *supra* note 131 at 184.

139 Oscar Schachter, "The Right of States to Use Armed Force" (1983-84) 82 Mich L Rev 1620 at 1633-34.

140 *Nicaragua, supra* note 115 at paras 187-201, esp at para 194; *Case Concerning Armed Activities on the Territory of the Congo (Democratic Republic of the Congo v Uganda)*, [2005] ICJ Rep 168 at para 143 [*DRC v Uganda*]. See also Guruli, *supra* note 96 at 106.

141 *Nicaragua, supra* note 115 at para 195. See also *DRC v Uganda, supra* note 140 at paras 142-47; *Oil Platforms (Islamic Republic of Iran v United States of America)*, [2003] ICJ Rep 161 at para 51 [*Iran v US*].

direct applicability of pre-*Charter* customary international law but, instead, argue that such a right is in accordance with, and confirmed by, Article 51.[142] This view's popularity is almost certainly due to the fact that the right of self-defence in Article 51 is the one clear exception to the ban on the use of force, as far as individual states are concerned. The argument originates in the phrase "nothing ... shall impair the inherent right of individual ... self-defence" in Article 51. By preserving the "inherent" right of self-defence, Article 51, it is concluded, reaffirms and thereby incorporates existing, pre-*Charter* rules on self-defence.[143] This argument differs from the one outlined earlier in that, according to this view, Article 51 explicitly confirms (rather than fails to regulate) pre-*Charter* customary international law on self-defence. As anticipatory self-defence was lawful prior to the *UN Charter* coming into force, the argument continues, it has remained so under Article 51. This interpretation is said to be confirmed by state practice and *opinio juris* since 1945.[144]

Adopting such a broad interpretation of Article 51 would severely undermine the *UN Charter*'s main goal of preserving the peace and could hardly be reconciled with the ICJ's view of the *Charter*'s effect on permissible conduct between member states.[145] Moreover, if pre-Second World War customary international law on the right of self-defence had been incorporated into the *Charter*, it would in effect render the prohibition of the use of force meaningless, with all of the appalling consequences that the drafters of the *UN Charter* wished to avoid.[146] Many of the same arguments made in response

---

[142] Kristen Eichensehr, "Defending Nationals Abroad: Assessing the Lawfulness of Forcible Hostage Rescues" (2008) 48 Va J Int'l L 451 at 461; Richard B Lillich, "Forcible Protection of Nationals Abroad: The Liberian 'Incident' of 1990" (1992) 35 German Yearbook of International Law 205 at 216-17; D'Angelo, *supra* note 112 at 498; Christine Gray, *International Law and the Use of Force*, 3rd edition (Oxford: Oxford University Press, 2008) at 156-57.

[143] Geoffrey Marston, "Armed Intervention in the 1956 Suez Canal Crisis: The Legal Advice Tendered to the British Government" (1988) 37 ICLQ 773 at 795-96, 800. See also JR Gainsborough, *The Arab-Israeli Conflict, A Politico-Legal Analysis* (Aldershot: Gower Publishing, 1986) 83 at 85; Steven F Day, "Legal Considerations in Noncombatant Evacuation Operations" (1992) XL Nav L Rev 45 at 50; Mitchell Knisbacher, "The Entebbe Operation: A Legal Analysis of Israel's Rescue Action" (1977-1978) 12 J Int'l Econ L 57 at 64-65; Eichensehr, *supra* note 142 at 465.

[144] Raymond and Kegley, *supra* note 96 at 101-2; Roberts, *supra* note 45 at 513-14.

[145] See *Corfu Channel, supra* note 115 at 34-35, rejecting the notion that "self-help" justified British mine-sweeping operations in Albanian waters.

[146] Beyerlin, *supra* note 114 at 219-21, 240.

to the contention that Article 51 does not regulate self-defence at all can also be made here, in particular, those underscoring the illogicality of constraining self-defence in cases of "armed attack" while leaving other "inherent" rights of self-defence untouched.[147] There were many instances prior to 1945 when the use of force in self-defence was seen as justified, notwithstanding the fact that an "armed attack" had not occurred. The *UN Charter*'s aim — as confirmed by the preamble and Article 1(1) — was, however, to limit the use of force as far as practically possible. Ignoring the threshold requirement of an "armed attack" would achieve exactly the opposite and would raise the question of why the phrase was included in Article 51 in the first place.[148] Had its authors wanted to include anticipatory self-defence — as defined in 1841 or at any other time before 1945 — as a legitimate use of force under Article 51, there is no reason why they should not have said so explicitly.[149]

It has been suggested that the phrase "where an armed attack occurs" was included only at the request of some Latin American states that wanted to preserve the legality of their regional security treaties, without any other meaning being attached to the phrase.[150] This rationale would imply, however, that the drafters of the *UN Charter* were bad jurists who failed to realize what the consequences of such a wording might be — an implication that should be treated with caution, considering that it is proponents of this argument who are attempting to interpret the *Charter* provisions *contra legem*.[151]

---

[147] See text accompanying notes 137-40 above.

[148] Brownlie, "The Use of Force in Self-Defence," *supra* note 112 at 239-41, pointing out that the right of self-defence had, between 1920 and 1945, become "vague" and that it therefore seemed highly unlikely that the *UN Charter*'s framers would have attempted to preserve such an indeterminate customary right. See also Brownlie, *International Law, supra* note 112 at 269-75; Beyerlin, *supra* note 114 at 221-23, 230-31; Krift, *supra* note 112 at 52.

[149] W Michael Reisman and Andrea Armstrong, "The Past and Future of the Claim of Preemptive Self-Defense" (2006) 100 AJIL 525 at 532-33; Elizabeth Wilmshurst, "The Chatham House Principles of International law on the Use of Force in Self-Defence" (2006) 55 ICLQ 963 at 964; D'Amato, "Israel's Air Strike," *supra* note 108 at 587-88.

[150] Pogany, *supra* note 96 at 72; Niaz A Shah, "Self-Defence, Anticipatory Self-Defence and Pre-emption: International Law's Response to Terrorism" (2007) 12 J Confl & Sec L 95 at 99-100.

[151] See Graham, *supra* note 45 at 3-4, quoting the Deputy US negotiator at the San Francisco conference in 1945, H Stassen, as saying that the language of Article 51 was "intentional and sound. We did not want exercised the right of self-defense before an armed attack had occurred."

Lastly, the argument that interpretation of Article 51 must accommodate a right of self-defence as recognized in the *Caroline* correspondence is also not convincing. As the Anglo-American exchange of notes in the *Caroline* incident demonstrates, the phrase "armed attack" was neither discussed nor even mentioned (likely due to the fact that an "armed attack" was not a prerequisite of the right to use force in self-defence in the mid-nineteenth century, in contrast to the situation under the *UN Charter*). The views on self-defence expressed by the British and American representatives in 1841–42 can therefore have no bearing on the interpretation of the phrase "if an armed attack occurs." As Jörg Kammerhofer has argued in another context, the emphasis put on the *Caroline* incident in the context of self-defence is in truth an attempt to make us "believe that a statement on the law on the use of force made in 1842 is still correct despite the developments over the last 165 years" — a view he correctly describes as "not corroborated in any way."[152] Thus, the notion that anticipatory self-defence as an element of the right of self-defence has "survived," or been confirmed by the *UN Charter*, falls to be rejected.[153] Therefore, *a fortiori*, preventive self-defence, which would not even require an "imminent" attack but would permit the use of force to combat emerging, potential future threats, cannot be reconciled with Article 51.[154]

"NEW" CUSTOMARY INTERNATIONAL LAW?

Proponents of the legality of anticipatory self-defence often argue that their view is supported by state practice and *opinio juris* since 1945. Some argue that, even if the *UN Charter* outlawed anticipatory self-defence, post-Second World War developments have resulted in the creation of a new customary international legal right of

---

152 Jörg Kammerhofer, "The *Armed Activities* Case and Non-State Actors in Self-Defence Law" (2007) 20 Leiden J Int'l L 89 at 99.

153 It is worth noting, however, that there is no great difference in the practical application of the law between those who claim a right of anticipatory self-defence in the case of a truly imminent attack and the view supported here. As some have argued, if an aggressor state takes "irrevocable" steps towards launching an attack, that attack must be seen as "occurring." "Interceptive" self-defence against an attack that has obviously already begun is lawful under Article 51 of the *Charter*. See, for example, Dinstein, *supra* note 95 at 185, 187-92; Tarcisio Gazzini, *The Changing Rules on the Use of Force in International Law* (Manchester, UK: Manchester University Press, 2005) at 152-53.

154 Dinstein, *supra* note 95 at 186-87; Malone, *supra* note 72 at 826; Graham, *supra* note 45 at 17; Sapiro, *supra* note 98 at 606.

anticipatory self-defence. It should be noted that such new rules would not necessarily contravene the generally accepted *jus cogens* status of the ban on the use of force, as it can be argued that such a status applies to the core of the ban on the use of force but not automatically to the detailed circumstances in which force is exceptionally permitted.[155]

When examining state practice and *opinio juris*, it is, however, striking how rarely states have actually justified their use of force on the basis of anticipatory self-defence.[156] While the United States and Israel have quite frequently stated that they were using force with the additional aim of "preventing future attacks," this has nearly always been in circumstances where attacks against American or Israeli interests have already taken place.[157] The legal question that has tended to arise in such instances, therefore, is whether the use of force was a lawful exercise of the right of *responsive* (as distinct from *anticipatory*) self-defence or, rather, an (unlawful) armed reprisal.[158]

There have been only three well-known instances in which the state using force could be seen as having acted in "anticipatory" self-defence because no prior attack had occurred:[159] the US blockade of Cuba during the Cuban Missile Crisis in 1962,[160] the Israeli

---

[155] Antonio Cassese, "Terrorism Is Also Disrupting Some Crucial Legal Categories of International Law" (2001) 12 EJIL 993 at 1000; Rein Müllerson, "Jus ad Bellum: Plus Ça Change (Le Monde) Plus C'est la Même Chose (Le Droit)?" (2002) 7 J Conflict & Sec L 149 at 169.

[156] Guruli, *supra* note 96 at 119; Gray, *supra* note 142 at 130; Pogany, *supra* note 96 at 73. However, see Secretary-General, *Report of the Secretary-General, In Larger Freedom: Towards Development, Security and Human Rights for All*, UNGAOR, 59th Sess, UN Doc A/59/2005 (21 March 2005) at para 124.

[157] Reisman and Armstrong, *supra* note 149 at 527; Gray, *supra* note 142 at 131-32. However, see Rothwell, *supra* note 96 at 343-45, arguing that the US raid on Libya in 1986 was a case of anticipatory self-defence, although acknowledging that this characterization is "clouded due to the ongoing tensions" between the two countries. In fact, Libyan involvement in the terrorist attack on a Berlin discotheque is generally seen as the main reason for the subsequent US attack, so that the raid cannot serve as a classic example of anticipatory self-defence.

[158] See, for example, W Michael Reisman, "The Raid on Baghdad: Some Reflections on Its Lawfulness and Implications" (1994) 5 EJIL 120 at 126.

[159] Gray, *supra* note 142 at 131, mentioning a fourth case, the Iraqi attack on Iran in 1980, which Iraq originally characterized as "preventive" self-defence. However, as Gray points out, Iraq quickly changed its position and justified its actions on the basis of a prior attack by Iran.

[160] Stephen G Rademaker, "Use of Force after 9/11" (2004–05) 5 Chicago J Int'l L 461at 465; Wedgwood, *supra* note 123 at 584; Newcomb, *supra* note 123 at 623-25; Mallison and Mallison, *supra* note 96 at 423-24.

attack on Egypt at the outset of the Six-Day War in 1967,[161] and the 1981 Israeli attack on the Iraqi nuclear reactor at Osiraq. However, the US naval blockade of Cuba in 1962[162] and the 1967 Israeli attack on Egypt[163] must be discounted, because in both instances the states concerned did not justify their actions on the basis of a right of anticipatory self-defence. The United States justified its blockade of Cuba, which was designed to prevent Russia from delivering military equipment (missiles) to Cuba, not on the grounds of self-defence but, rather, by invoking regional security arrangements under Chapter VIII of the *UN Charter*,[164] a point emphasized by the US legal adviser to the US State Department in a contemporary legal analysis.[165] Israel, in 1967, claimed it was acting in self-defence because Egypt's prior actions amounted to an armed attack on Israel, allowing the latter to respond.[166] International

---

[161] Raymond and Kegley, *supra* note 96 at 102; Gill, *supra* note 96 at 134-39; Charles Pierson, "Preemptive Self-Defense in an Age of Weapons of Mass Destruction: Operation Iraqi Freedom" (2004–05) 33 Denv J Int'l L & Pol'y 150 at 166-67; Newcomb, *supra* note 123 at 621-22.

[162] D'Amato, "Israel's Air Strike," *supra* note 108 at 588, n 19; John Quigley, "Israel's Destruction of Iraq's Nuclear Reactor: A Reply" (1995) 9 Temp Int'l & Comp LJ 441 at 441; Gray, *supra* note 142 at 131; Pierson, *supra* note 161 at 163; Gazzini, *supra* note 153 at 149-50.

[163] Sapiro, *supra* note 98 at 601; Gray, *supra* note 142 at 130-31; Gazzini, *supra* note 153 at 150.

[164] See *Resolution of the Council of the Organization of American States* (22 October 1962), (1962) 47 Dep't St Bull 722, invoking Article 6 of the *Inter-American Treaty of Reciprocal Assistance*, 21 UNTS 77 (in force 3 December 1948), which does not require an "armed attack." See further Wedgwood, *supra* note 123 at 584; Sapiro, *supra* note 98 at 601; Gray, *supra* note 142 at 131; Nydell, *supra* note 123 at 484-85, (pointing out that the US government explicitly rejected the idea of justifying its actions on the basis of self-defence because no "armed attack" had occurred and it did not want to set a precedent); Pierson, *supra* note 161 at 164; Roberts, *supra* note 45 at 528; Gazzini, *supra* note 153 at 149-50.

[165] Abram Chase, "The Legal Case for U.S. Action on Cuba" (1962) 47 Dep't St Bull 763 at 764.

[166] *Yearbook of the United Nations 1967* (New York: United Nations Office of Public Information, 1967) at 176; Knesset Lexicon, *Six Days War*, online: The Knesset <http://www.knesset.gov.il/lexicon/eng/six_days_eng.htm>; Gray, *supra* note 142 at 130-31; Pogany, *supra* note 96 at 73; Sapiro, *supra* note 98 at 601; Gazzini, *supra* note 153 at 150. See also Paul, *supra* note 95 at 466 (describing the Israeli position as "arguable" given that Egypt had occupied the buffer zone between Egypt and Israel prior to the Israeli attack and had blockaded Israeli shipping). But see Quigley, *supra* note 162 at 442-43 (calling Israel's accusations against Egypt "false").

reaction to Israel's attack can also be described as being, at best, inconclusive.[167]

Only when Israel attacked the Iraqi nuclear reactor in 1981 did it rely on anticipatory self-defence (see the discussion later in this article).[168] However, the Israeli actions were condemned unanimously by the UN Security Council.[169] Much has been made of the fact that not every state supporting this Security Council resolution explicitly denounced the alleged right of anticipatory self-defence during the debates (for example, the United States), which some have interpreted as implicit acceptance of the concept.[170] However, no state explicitly embraced the concept either, and many plainly rejected it.[171] In any event, as explained later in this article, Israel's action is better categorized as an example of preventive self-defence. It can be concluded, therefore, that state practice and *opinio juris* since 1945 do not support the concept of anticipatory self-defence.[172] Consequently, no "new" customary international law to that effect has developed since the Second World War.

---

[167] Arab and Soviet bloc states condemned the Israeli attack as "aggression." See Paul, *supra* note 95 at 466. But see Gill, *supra* note 96 at 136 (claiming an "overwhelming majority of states" supported the Israeli actions — a rather surprising assessment given that a Yugoslav draft resolution calling for Israel's immediate and unconditional withdrawal garnered a deeply divided vote of 53: 46: 20 in the UN General Assembly). See also Gazzini, *supra* note 153 at 150 (describing international reaction as "consistently negative").

[168] D'Amato, "Israel's Air Strike," *supra* note 108 at 587-88; Sapiro, *supra* note 98 at 601; Gray, *supra* note 142 at 133; Pogany, *supra* note 96 at 73; Silverberg, *supra* note 123 at 60.

[169] SC Resolution 487, *supra* note 82.

[170] Paul, *supra* note 95 at 467-68; Gill, *supra* note 96 at 140-41; Pogany, *supra* note 96 at 73-74 (interpreting the statements of the United States, the UK, Sierra Leone, and Niger as — at least — implicitly accepting the legality of anticipatory self-defence); Henderson, *supra* note 41 at n 41. See also Pierson, *supra* note 161 at 167-68 (while acknowledging there was no consensus within the UN Security Council on the legality of anticipatory self-defence, somewhat paradoxically concluding that this demonstrated worldwide support).

[171] Quigley, *supra* note 162 at 441; Gray, *supra* note 142 at 133; Pogany, *supra* note 96 at 74 (naming Uganda, Algeria, Brazil, Spain, Ireland, Syria, Guyana, Mexico, and the Soviet Union as explicitly rejecting the notion of anticipatory self-defence during the UN Security Council debate).

[172] See Gray, *supra* note 142 at 130 (stating that the "vast majority of states" rejects the concept of anticipatory self-defence).

PREVENTIVE SELF-DEFENCE AS EMERGING LAW?

If there is no right in international law at present to engage in anticipatory, much less preventive, self-defence, can it be argued that such a right is in the process of developing? Moreover, in any event, is it desirable, given the potential devastation that can be wreaked by WMD, that the law on the use of force should be amended to recognize such a right? Some supporters of preventive self-defence argue that state practice and, especially, *opinio juris* are beginning to evidence the emergence of a new norm allowing "forcible counter-proliferation" or preventive self-defence measures.[173] Others observe that there is a tendency among American proponents of preventive self-defence to assume that American actions and positions can create new international law without any analysis of the practice or views of other states.[174] It is, however, unlikely that this US-centric view will be accepted by others, particularly powerful states such as China, Russia, or India. Turning to state practice, there have so far been three possible cases of preventive self-defence concerning WMD since the Second World War, each of which is examined briefly in the following sections.

Israel's Attack on Iraq in 1981

On 7 June 1981, Israeli fighter jets attacked and destroyed an Iraqi nuclear reactor near Baghdad. Four people were killed. Israel subsequently justified its actions on the basis of anticipatory self-defence. According to the Israelis, intelligence reports had shown that Iraq was trying to develop nuclear weapons at the site, contrary to its assertions that it was engaged only in research into the civilian use of nuclear technology. As Iraq had repeatedly expressed its hostile intent towards Israel, it was necessary for Israel to prevent Iraq from acquiring nuclear weapons: "Israel said that, in destroying the 'Osirak' nuclear reactor, it had performed an act of self-preservation and exercised its inherent right of self-defence. A threat of nuclear obliteration was being developed by Iraq against Israel."[175]

---

173 Guruli, *supra* note 96 at 120-22; Paul, *supra* note 95 at 469 (describing these views); Pierson, *supra* note 161 at 177.

174 Gray, *supra* note 142 at 134; Thomas M Franck, "What Happens Now? The United Nations after Iraq" (2003) 97 AJIL 607 at 620. See, for example, Guruli, *supra* note 96 at 120-22 (claiming that the invasion of Iraq in 2003 led to new norms "emerging," despite acknowledging that the invasion was extremely controversial).

175 *Yearbook of the United Nations 1981* (New York: United Nations Office of Public Information, 1981) at 277.

International reaction was "overwhelmingly negative."[176] The UN Security Council unanimously condemned Israel's actions and ordered it to pay Iraq reparations for the damage caused.[177] While the United States limited its criticism to the fact that Israel had not first explored peaceful remedies,[178] no state explicitly endorsed Israel's interpretation of its right of self-defence.[179] The *Yearbook of the United Nations* for 1981 summarizes the debate before the Security Council, in which many non-Council members also participated, as follows:

> Most speakers in the debate condemned Israel's attack as a violation of the United Nations Charter and international law and as a threat to international peace and security. They could not accept Israel's argument that it had acted in self-defence to prevent a nuclear strike against it; they said Article 51 of the Charter limited the right of self-defence to a case of armed attack and did not allow for preventive action. They considered Israel's attack a dangerous precedent, rejected Israel's allegation that the Iraqi reactor was intended to produce nuclear weapons and underlined the right of States to develop nuclear energy for peaceful purposes.[180]

Invasion of Iraq in 2003

One of the reasons given for the invasion of Iraq by the "coalition of the willing" in March 2003 was Saddam Hussein's continued research into and stockpiling of WMD.[181] Not only was this allegation

---

[176] See *Armed Israeli Aggression against the Iraqi Nuclear Installations and Its Grave Consequences for the Established International System Concerning the Peaceful Uses of Nuclear Energy, the Non-Proliferation of Nuclear Weapons and International Peace and Security*, GA Res 36/27, UNGAOR, 36th Sess, UN Doc A/RES/36/27, (1981), condemning the Israeli actions (only the United States and Israel opposed the resolution). See also Paul, *supra* note 95 at 468; Louis René Beres and Yoash Tsidddon-Chatto, "Reconsidering Israel's Destruction of Iraq's Osiraq Nuclear Reactor" (1995) 9 Temp Int'l & Comp LJ 437 at 437 (who, however, go on to demand a re-evaluation); Beres, *supra* note 52 at 203; Gill, *supra* note 96 at 140; Silverberg, *supra* note 123 at 60; Mallison and Mallison, *supra* note 96 at 441; Roberts, *supra* note 45 at 530; Michael Byers, *War Law: International Law and Armed Conflict* (London: Atlantic Books, 2005) at 73.

[177] SC Resolution 487, *supra* note 82.

[178] *Yearbook of the United Nations 1981*, *supra* note 175 at 276.

[179] Paul, *supra* note 95 at 467-68; Graham, *supra* note 45 at 11 (quoting former British Prime Minister Margaret Thatcher as saying: "Armed attack in such circumstances cannot be justified. It represents a grave breach of international law.")

[180] *Yearbook of the United Nations 1981*, *supra* note 175 at 277.

[181] Rademaker, *supra* note 160 at 462-63.

later proved to be untrue, but the United States was the only state within the coalition that officially based its legal justification for the invasion on, *inter alia,* preventive self-defence.[182] The other coalition members officially justified their intervention solely on the ground of the (controversial) theory of "implied authorization" by the UN Security Council and past Security Council resolutions.[183] Even the United States mainly focused on this argument.[184]

International reaction to the invasion was negative.[185] The United States itself was able to list only forty-nine states that supported the

---

[182] Malone, *supra* note 72 at 816; Rademaker, *supra* note 160 at 462-65; Paul, *supra* note 95 at 474; Graham, *supra* note 45 at 13; Franck, *supra* note 174 at 611; Gray, *supra* note 142 at 182; David P Fidler, "International Law and Weapons of Mass Destruction: End of the Arms Control Approach?" (2004) 14 Duke J Comp & Int'l L 39 at 73; Rothwell, *supra* note 96 at 349; Henderson, *supra* note 41 at 14; Byers, *supra* note 176 at 79.

[183] *Letter dated 20 March 2003 from the Permanent Representative of the United Kingdom of Great Britain and Northern Ireland to the United Nations Addressed to the President of the Security Council,* UN Doc S/2003/350 (2003); Gerry Simpson, "The War in Iraq and International Law" (2005) 6 Melbourne J Int'l L 167 at 173-75; Fidler, *supra* note 182 at 73; Stromseth, *supra* note 123 at 629, n 4. For accounts questioning such a justification, see Paul, *supra* note 95 at 459-61; Franck, *supra* note 174 at 611-14; Rothwell, *supra* note 96 at 349; Henderson, *supra* note 41 at 10; Gazzini, *supra* note 153 at 221; Byers, *supra* note 176 at 79.

[184] *Letter dated 20 March 2003 from the Permanent Representative of the United States of America to the United Nations Addressed to the President of the Security Council,* UN Doc S/2003/351 (2003) (relying almost exclusively on SC Resolutions 1441 and 678 as providing legal justification for the attack on Iraq, although the necessity to "defend" the United States and the "international community" is also mentioned in one sentence). See also Rademaker, *supra* note 160 at 464-65; Stromseth, *supra* note 123 at 629, n 4 (pointing out that the United States did not base its justification on "pre-emptive" self-defence before the Security Council); Gill, *supra* note 96 at 142; Gazzini, *supra* note 153 at 221, 232.

[185] The then UN secretary-general, Kofi Annan, declared in 2004 that "[f]rom our point of view and the U.N. Charter point of view, it was illegal" (quoted in John R Crook, "Contemporary Practice of the United States Relating to International Law" (2005) 99 AJIL 269 at 269). See also *Dutch Military Mission to Iraq, Conclusions of the Committee of Inquiry on Iraq* (21 April 2010) online <http://vorige. nrc.nl/multimedia/archive/00267/rapport_commissie_i_267285a.pdf> at paras 18, 20 of the English summary at 530-31. In a case before the German Federal Administrative Court (the *Bundesverwaltungsgericht)* in 2005, the court declared that there were grave doubts as to the legality, under international law, of the attack on Iraq by the United States and the UK, as both governments could not rely on authorization by the UN Security Council nor on Article 51. *Bundesverwaltungsgericht,* Urteil/Judgment (21 June 2005), *BVerwG 2WD 12.04,* online: <http://www.bverwg.de/entscheidungen/pdf/210605U2WD12.04.0.pdf>. See further "War Would Be Illegal" (letter from 16 leading legal academics in

invasion[186] (including states, such as Palau, which are completely dependent on the United States) — obviously a minority of the more than 190 states worldwide.[187] Major states such as Russia, China, France, and Germany openly opposed the invasion, and it is well known that the United Kingdom tried nearly everything possible to obtain a UN Security Council resolution backing the invasion. In the end, it failed to secure the nine votes necessary (disregarding probable French, Russian, and Chinese vetoes),[188] and it subsequently abandoned its efforts.[189] Even within the British and US governments, grave doubts as to the legality of the attack on Iraq were expressed.[190]

Britain), *The Guardian* (7 March 2003) 29, online: The Guardian <http://www.theguardian.com/politics/2003/mar/07/highereducation.iraq>); Tom Bingham, *The Rule of Law* (London: Allen Lane, 2010) at 122-24; Phillipe Sands, *Lawless World* (London: Penguin Books, 2006) at 174-204, 258-75; Franck, *supra* note 105 at 95, 97, 103; Hanspeter Neuhold, "Law and Force in International Relations: European and American Positions" (2004) 64 ZaöRV 263 at 276-78; Simpson, *supra* note 183 at 172-78; Gray, *supra* note 142 at 135; Gazzini, *supra* note 153 at 221.

186 Wedgwood, *supra* note 123 at 577 (quoting from a "White House Information Sheet"). See also Gray, *supra* note 142 at 183 (referring to "about forty-five states [that] were willing to offer military or political support to the USA," of which none justified its support on the basis of preventive self-defence).

187 Paul, *supra* note 95 at 472-73; Gray, *supra* note 142 at 181-83.

188 *UN Charter, supra* note 67, art 27(3). This attempt was based on UK Prime Minister Tony Blair's rather novel and questionable theory of the "unreasonable veto," whereby a veto cast in contravention of UN principles — presumably as understood by the UK — would be deemed invalid.

189 Reisman and Armstrong, *supra* note 149 at 537; Henderson, *supra* note 41 at 13.

190 See the evidence provided to the Chilcot Inquiry by Sir Michael Wood, legal adviser to the UK Foreign and Commonwealth Office from 1999-2006: Iraq Inquiry, Statement by Sir Michael Wood, 26 January 2010, at para 15, online: <http://www.iraqinquiry.org.uk/media/43477/wood-statement.pdf>. The deputy legal adviser to the UK Foreign and Commonwealth Office, Elizabeth Wilmshurst, resigned from her post because she believed the Iraq War to be a "crime of aggression," as she explained in her evidence to the Chilcot Inquiry. See Iraq Inquiry, transcript of Elizabeth Wilmshurst (26 January 2010), online: Iraq Inquiry <http://www.iraqinquiry.org.uk/media/44211/20100126pm-wilmshurst-final.pdf>. In his draft advice of 14 January 2003, the UK attorney general (who, of course, later changed his mind), concluded "that resolution 1441 does not revive the authorisation to use of force [sic] contained in resolution 678 in the absence of a further decision by the Security Council." *Iraq Inquiry: Attorney General's Draft Advice to Prime Minister* at 5, online: <http://www.iraqinquiry.org.uk/media/46493/Goldsmith-draft-advice-14January2003.pdf>.

Israel's Attack on Syria in 2007

On 6 September 2007, Israel carried out an attack on what is believed to have been a Syrian nuclear reactor ("Operation Orchard"). Syria acknowledged that the attack had taken place and, of course, denounced Israel for its actions, but it denied that a nuclear reactor had been hit, instead claiming that an unused military building had been destroyed.[191] In his memoirs, former President George W. Bush confirms the attack took place and adds that there had been prior discussions between Israel and the United States in which the two states had failed to reach agreement on whether action was necessary.[192] Israel never provided an official justification for its use of force against Syria and, for some time, even refused to acknowledge that any sort of military action had taken place. Even the Israeli media were not permitted to report on the matter until a couple of weeks later.[193]

Owing to Israel's silence and Syria's denials as to the nature of the site destroyed, there was almost no official international reaction to the incident. Apart from Syria, only North Korea condemned Israel's actions.[194] The head of the IAEA at the time, Mohamed

---

See further Helen Pidd and Hélène Mulholland, "Lord Goldsmith Changed Legal View of Iraq War in Two Months, Says Adviser," *The Guardian* (26 January 2010), online: The Guardian <http://www.guardian.co.uk/uk/2010/jan/26/iraq-war-illegal-chilcot-inquiry>. Similarly, in the United States, Richard Perle, chairman of the Defense Policy Board Advisory Committee in the Bush administration, declared, during a visit to the UK, that "in this case international law stood in the way of doing the right thing" as "international law ... would have required us to leave Saddam Hussein alone." See Oliver Burkeman and Julian Borger, "War Critics Astonished as US Hawk Admits Invasion Was Illegal," *The Guardian* (20 November 2003) 4, online: The Guardian <http://www.theguardian.com/uk/2003/nov/20/usa.iraq1>.

[191] David E Sanger and Mark Mazzetti, "Israel Struck Syrian Nuclear Project, Analysts Say," *New York Times* (14 October 2007) online: New York Times <http://www.nytimes.com/2007/10/14/washington/14weapons.html?pagewanted=all&_r=0>; see also Erich Follath and Holger Stark, "The Story of 'Operation Orchard': How Israel Destroyed Syria's Al Kibar Nuclear Reactor," *Der Spiegel* (2 November 2009) online: Spiegel Online International <http://www.spiegel.de/international/world/the-story-of-operation-orchard-how-israel-destroyed-syria-s-al-kibar-nuclear-reactor-a-658663.html>.

[192] George W Bush, *Decision Points* (London: Virgin Books, 2010) at 420-22.

[193] Amir Oren, "IDF Lifts Censorship of Sept. 6 IAF Strike on Target inside Syria," *Haaretz* (2 October 2007) online: Haaretz <http://www.haaretz.com/news/idf-lifts-censorship-of-sept-6-iaf-strike-on-target-inside-syria-1.230392>.

[194] "Israel Condemned for Intrusion into Syria's Territorial Air" (11 September 2007), online: KCNA <http://www.kcna.co.jp/item/2007/200709/news09/12.htm>.

ElBaradei, criticized Israel's actions, accusing it of "bomb[ing] first and ask[ing] questions later."[195] Against this backdrop of international silence, it is impossible to draw any conclusions. Israel never publicly justified its use of force, Syria denied the target had been a nuclear facility, and the international community refrained from comment. The incident cannot therefore serve to support the notion that the right to preventive self-defence is an "emerging norm."

Furthermore, despite claims by some authors of (sometimes very tenuous) implicit support in various national security strategies,[196] Israel and Australia[197] are actually the only states that have officially backed the American concept of preventive self-defence directed against other states.[198] State practice and *opinio juris* do not, therefore, support the notion that a right of preventive self-defence is currently emerging. If anything, the attitude of the international community towards the concept, and towards military intervention in general, seems to have hardened since the Iraq War, as has recently been demonstrated by the generally negative response, both within and outside of the United States, to the Obama administration's threat to bomb Syrian chemical sites following the use — allegedly by government forces — of nerve gas against civilians.[199]

---

[195] "IAEA Chief Criticizes Israel over Syria Raid," *Reuters* (28 October 2007), online: Reuters <http://www.reuters.com/article/2007/10/28/idUSN28442767>.

[196] See Reisman and Armstrong, *supra* note 149 at 540-46 (claiming implicit acceptance of "pre-emptive self-defence" in the national security strategies and/or statements made by officials of Japan, the UK, China (only regarding Taiwan), France, India, Israel, North Korea, Russia, Taiwan (only regarding China), and Iran). However, most of the material quoted deals only with terrorist threats, casting doubt on the degree of support for "pre-emptive" self-defence directed against other states (a point conceded by the authors at 547). See also Raymond and Kegley, *supra* note 96 at 107 (presenting a similar list, albeit limited to statements made by individual politicians).

[197] Guruli, *supra* note 96 at 119; Reisman and Armstrong, *supra* note 149 at 538-40 (also quoting former Australian Prime Minister John Howard as saying, in 2002, that "preemptive action is a self-evidently defensible and valid principle"). Gray, *supra* note 142 at 177; Henderson, *supra* note 41 at 10.

[198] Christian M Henderson, "The 2006 National Security Strategy of the United States: The Pre-emptive Use of Force and the Persistent Advocate" (2007) 15 Tulsa J Comp & IL 1 at 3, 16; Gray, *supra* note 142 at 177-78 (pointing out that the United States failed to gain the explicit approval of the North Atlantic Treaty Organization and of the UK regarding its doctrine); Shah, *supra* note 150 at 115.

[199] Ronald Brownstein, "America's Sharp Turn Inward," *National Journal* (5 September 2013), online: National Journal <http://www.nationaljournal.com/political-connections/america-s-sharp-turn-inward-20130905>; Tom Mludzinski,

Some supporters of preventive self-defence, while acknowledging that the concept cannot be reconciled with international law as it now stands,[200] nevertheless argue that the rules on the use of force should be amended in light of the ineffectiveness of the *NPT*'s non-proliferation regime and the substantial danger posed by the acquisition by "rogue states" of nuclear weapons or other WMD.[201] "Forcible counter-proliferation"[202] or preventive self-defence must be legalized as a last resort if states refuse to forsake WMD. Not only can the use of force in these instances make the world safer, it can also serve to enforce the rule of law by compelling states to adhere to the non-proliferation regime.[203] When vital national security issues are at stake (such as when "rogue" regimes acquire WMD), states cannot be expected to refrain from the use of force.[204]

Although expressing some valid concerns, these arguments are nevertheless not convincing. It is certainly true that there are states whose past behaviour makes their acquisition of WMD worrisome. Iran's former president, for example, with his inflammatory statements, seemed intent on reinforcing perceptions that Iranian WMD capability should be prevented.[205] The main weakness of the "forcible counter-proliferation" theory is, however, its ability to destroy any semblance of stability in international relations and the rule

"The British Aren't Coming: Syria and the Legacy of Iraq," *Daily Telegraph* (5 September 2013), online: The Telegraph <http://www.telegraph.co.uk/news/worldnews/middleeast/syria/10289553/The-British-arent-coming-Syria-and-the-legacy-of-Iraq.html>; Marc Young, "Syria Crisis Exposes Rifts in U.S.-German Ties," *Yahoo News* (12 September 2013), online: Yahoo News <http://news.yahoo.com/syria-crisis-exposes-rifts-in-us-german-ties–222905636.html>.

[200] Paul, *supra* note 95 at 469; Greenblum, *supra* note 21 at 56-57, 103.

[201] Roberts, *supra* note 45 at 484; Beres, *supra* note 52 at 201-03; Silverberg, *supra* note 123 at 86-87; Pierson, *supra* note 161 at 174-75; Newcomb, *supra* note 123 at 631-33; Greenblum, *supra* note 21 at 57.

[202] Roberts, *supra* note 45 at 483, 517-18, 518-27.

[203] Pierson, *supra* note 161 at 171; Beres and Tsiddon-Chatto, *supra* note 176 at 439; Beres, *supra* note 52 at 205-06; Roberts, *supra* note 45 at 497.

[204] Newcomb, note *supra* 123 at 618; Beres and Tsiddon-Chatto, *supra* note 176 at 438 ("international law is not a suicide pact!"); Beres, *supra* note 52 at 188 (claiming that pre-emption is necessary to avoid "genocide"); Greenblum, *supra* note 21 at 111-12.

[205] It should be noted that Ahmadinejad's egregious pronouncements are by no means indicative of the thinking of all members of Iran's political class. See Parsi, *supra* note 15 at 82; Trita Parsi, *Treacherous Alliance: The Secret Dealings of Israel, Iran, and the US* (New Haven, CT: Yale University Press, 2007) at 9.

of law.[206] Its supporters seem to believe that it would be possible to restrict the legality of recourse to military intervention to cases where the United States or, possibly, Israel deems such action necessary. This perception, however, overlooks the basic principle in international law of sovereign equality.[207] Once preventive self-defence is legalized, there is no reason why India should not decide that Pakistan is a "rogue state" that might threaten India in the future with nuclear weapons, entitling India to strike preventively (or vice versa). Extended to other WMD, there are many more situations in the world that could be argued to justify the preventive use of force between states.[208] It should also not be forgotten that today's ally is often tomorrow's "rogue state" (Iran being a prime example) and vice versa.[209]

It should therefore come as no surprise that the UN secretary-general's High-Level Panel on Threats, Challenges and Change concluded with respect to preventive self-defence:

For those impatient with such a response [necessity of collective action in cases of acquisition of WMD with hostile intent], the answer must be that, in a world full of perceived potential threats, the risk to the global order and the norm of non-intervention on which it continues to be based is simply too great for the legality of unilateral preventive action, as distinct

---

[206] It has been suggested that the breakdown of the rule of law in international affairs may in fact be the intention of some of the concept's proponents. See, for example, Gill, *supra* note 96 at 149; Quigley, *supra* note 162 at 444; Graham, *supra* note 45 at 11-12; Stromseth, *supra* note 123 at 636; Sapiro, *supra* note 98 at 603; Sloss, *supra* note 96 at 54; Reisman and Armstrong, *supra* note 149 at 548-50; Raymond and Kegley, *supra* note 96 at 106 (describing US President Eisenhower's reaction to the suggestion of pre-empting the emerging Chinese nuclear capability as follows: "He wouldn't even listen to anyone seriously that came in and talked about such a thing"); Mallison and Mallison, *supra* note 96 at 429, 444-46; Shah, *supra* note 150 at 112 (also pointing out the similarities of the theory to German arguments preceding the First World War); Henderson, *supra* note 41 at 22; Gazzini, *supra* note 153 at 221-22; Byers, *supra* note 176 at 76.

[207] Paul, *supra* note 95 at 458, correctly describes such an argument as "not a doctrine of law" but "simply a unilateral assertion of power."

[208] *Ibid* at 458; Sapiro, *supra* note 98 at 599, 605; Gray, *supra* note 142 at 186 (adding the example of China/Taiwan); Shah, *supra* note 150 at 103-4; Henderson, *supra* note 198 at 28; Henderson, *supra* note 41 at 5; Byers, *supra* note 176 at 76.

[209] A similar point is made by Nagan and Hammer, *supra* note 40 at 429 (observing that the United States may no longer be able to "pick and choose which rogue state to coddle and which to destroy" if the Bush doctrine were to be accepted universally).

from collectively endorsed action, to be accepted. Allowing one to so act is to allow all.[210]

The Non-Aligned Movement (NAM), which comprises 118 states, explicitly endorsed the panel's rejection of "preventive" self-defence:

NAM emphasizes that Article 51 of the UN Charter is restrictive and recognizes "the inherent right of individual or collective self-defence if an armed attack occurs against a Member of the United Nations". This Article should not be re-written or re-interpreted. This is supported by the practice of the UN and in accordance with international law pronounced by the International Court of Justice, the principal judicial organ of the UN, concerning this question.

NAM stresses its deep concern over the intention of a group of States to unilaterally re-interpret or re-draft the existing legal instruments, in accordance with their own views and interests. NAM reemphasises that the integrity of international legal instruments must be maintained by Member States.[211]

The practical limitations of the doctrine are also considerable. It is virtually impossible to eliminate all aspects of WMD capability by way of preventive military strikes.[212] Indeed, a military attack might itself lead the targeted state (and others) to redouble efforts to gain WMD capability.[213] Many argue that this is exactly what happened after the Israeli attack on the Iraqi nuclear reactor.[214] Consequently, not only is there no sign that a new norm authorizing preventive

---

[210] *Report by the Secretary-General's High-level Panel on Threats, Challenges and Change: A More Secure World: Our Shared Responsibility*, UNGAOR, 59th Sess, UN Doc A/59/565 (December 2004) at para 191, online: <http://www.unrol.org/files/gaA.59.565_En.pdf>.

[211] *Comments of the Non-Aligned Movement on the Observations and Recommendations Contained in the Report of the High-level Panel on Threats, Challenges and Change*, Non-Aligned Movement Position Paper (28 February 2005), online: <http://www.un.int/malaysia/NAM/Positionpaper280205.doc> at 43.

[212] Dunn, *supra* note 3 at 30; Perkovich, *supra* note 33 at 57.

[213] Graham, *supra* note 45 at 10; Lodgaard, *supra* note 43 at 121; Raymond and Kegley, *supra* note 96 at 103; Newcomb, *supra* note 123 at 631 (who nevertheless supports "pre-emptive" self-defence); Henderson, *supra* note 41 at 19; Byers, *supra* note 176 at 76.

[214] Lodgaard, *supra* note 43 at 117; Raymond and Kegley, *supra* note 96 at 103; Mallison and Mallison, *supra* note 96 at 443.

self-defence is in the process of forming, but also there remain strong grounds for resisting such a development.

It must therefore be concluded that an "armed attack" as specified in Article 51 of the *UN Charter* remains a prerequisite for the lawful use of force in self-defence, even in situations involving WMD. This, of course, does not mean that military action cannot be taken to counter a threat that falls short of an armed attack — even a relatively remote threat; only that such action must comply with the other exception to the general prohibition on the use of force — that is, it must be sanctioned by a resolution of the UN Security Council acting under its Chapter VII powers. To those who object that a lack of agreement within the Security Council — and especially the use of the veto power by one or more of the five permanent members — may prevent effective measures being taken, it can only be reiterated that there is no credible alternative. Allowing states to determine individually at what point preventive force should be employed to neutralize a perceived future threat by another state encourages dangerously subjective assessments and is ultimately likely to increase, rather than lessen, the risk of wide-scale threats to international peace and security.

Conclusion

Although the latest negotiations between Iran and the P5+1 have rekindled hopes of a diplomatic resolution to the crisis surrounding Iran's nuclear program, Iran and the United States have yet to divert conclusively from the collision course on which both, unfortunately, appear set. It seems likely that Iran is pursuing nuclear weapons capability in violation of its treaty obligations under the *NPT*, while the United States has repeatedly stressed that it will not accept a nuclear-armed Iran and, hence, has refused to forgo the "military option." The anger expressed by the United States' major Middle Eastern allies (Israel and Saudi Arabia) at the possibility of a deal being struck between Iran and the P5+1, coupled with the Obama administration's decision (so far) to refrain from taking military action to help remove Syria's President Bashar al-Assad, may require that the United States be seen to adopt a firm stance in regard to Iran's nuclear program — one that could very well extend to the use of force should the latest talks fail to produce the desired outcome and Iran be deemed to have edged uncomfortably close to the nuclear capability threshold.

Some argue that the United States cannot attack Iran because of its involvement in Afghanistan and its dependence on Iran's goodwill there, not to mention the dire consequences that such an attack would have on world oil markets. Both the United States and Iran also share a common objective in helping Iraq rid itself of the militant jihadist group ISIS (Islamic State of Iraq and Syria) currently occupying large swaths of Iraqi territory in the north of the country. In addition, any conflict with Iran could spark a region-wide conflagration, perhaps provoking attacks on American troops stationed in the Gulf and prompting Iran to attack the Gulf Emirates or even Saudi Arabia — all states that are already trying to cope with internal dissent and the Sunni–Shia conflict. Moreover, Israel may very well become involved if Hezbollah or others decide to retaliate by attacking Israel.

These are certainly grave considerations, but they must be balanced against other American concerns regarding the Middle East. The United States is unlikely to accept a dominant Iran in this oil-rich and, therefore, strategically important area as long as its current regime is in power. Nuclear weapons would certainly greatly increase Iran's influence. Israel's role should not be overlooked either. The United States might feel compelled to act in order to prevent Israel from acting, with even more unpredictable results. Lastly, some US politicians may be more worried about a perceived loss of credibility if a nuclear-armed Iran were to emerge than about preserving peace in the area.

Iran shows no signs of backing down either. It realizes that nuclear weapons would greatly enhance its power and standing, especially in the Middle East, bringing it nearer to realizing its goal of regional dominance. Iran has, of course, also noticed that the "united front" against it is not very united, and it will therefore be tempted to exploit divisions in order to buy time.[215] Furthermore, its nuclear program is one of the few government agendas that enjoy widespread support among Iran's population. Giving way would amount to losing face.

Meanwhile, both governments have in the past continued to stoke the conflict. US government officials have regularly threatened Iran, some American politicians still favour an aggressive policy of regime change, and Israel has rarely paused in its relentless campaign against Iran. All of this contributes to making nuclear weapons an even more attractive option for Iran's rulers.[216] The former Iranian president, on the other hand, was infamous for making outrageous

---

[215] Dunn, *supra* note 3 at 29.

[216] *Ibid*; Oborne and Morrison, *supra* note 3 at 22.

statements and threats, thereby reinforcing fears of a nuclear-armed Iran[217] and strengthening the hand of those in Washington who would prefer to intervene militarily sooner rather than later. The election of a more moderate Iranian president and the recommencement of diplomatic talks have revived hopes that a negotiated settlement may be achieved. Or, perhaps, as Kenneth Waltz has suggested, the world will come to accept a nuclear-armed Iran — an outcome he argues is "the best possible result: the one most likely to restore stability to the Middle East."[218] However, given the unfulfilled hopes that followed Obama's first election, Israel's evident refusal to accept such a state of affairs, and the fact that major decisions in Iran ultimately rest with its more hard-line supreme leader, Ayatollah Ali Khamenei, there is no reason to be overly optimistic.[219]

International law certainly cannot be said to figure prominently in American or Iranian calculations regarding the nuclear crisis. While both states will always attempt to justify their actions on the basis of international law, they are currently mainly influenced by strategic concerns. Consequently, although developing nuclear weapons and engaging in preventive self-defence are both unlawful, this is unlikely to exert much influence over decision makers in either state. Nevertheless, international law has an important role to play. It still offers the only opportunity for states to escape an anarchic world order and conduct their relations in a civilized manner. The sooner the United States and Iran realize that it is in their own interests to adhere to international law, the better. They might otherwise live to regret the precedents they set.[220]

---

[217] Perkovich, *supra* note 33 at 48.

[218] Kenneth N Waltz, "Why Iran Should Get the Bomb" (July/August 2012) 91:4 Foreign Affairs 2, online: Council on Foreign Relations <http://sistemas.mre.gov.br/kitweb/datafiles/IRBr/pt-br/file/CAD/LXII%20CAD/Pol%C3%ADtica/Why%20Iran%20Should%20Get%20the%20Bomb.pdf>.

[219] Although it should be noted that Khamenei, in 2005, issued a *fatwa* outlawing the possession of nuclear weapons. See Oborne and Morrison, *supra* note 3 at 76-79.

[220] See, for example, Reisman and Armstrong, *supra* note 149 at 545 (quoting former Iranian Defence Secretary Shamkhani as claiming a right of "pre-emptive" self-defence against US troops in the Middle East in 2004); Nagan and Hammer, *supra* note 40 at 408, n 129 (quoting Henry Kissinger as remarking: "It is not in the American national interest to establish pre-emption as a universal principle available to every nation.")

Sommaire

La poursuite par l'Iran de la technologie nucléaire continue d'engendrer des tensions dans les relations américano-iraniennes. Plusieurs dirigeants américains doutent les prétentions de l'Iran que son programme d'enrichissement d'uranium vise à fournir du combustible à des fins civiles et non pas à développer des armes nucléaires. En dépit de progrès diplomatiques réalisés à ce jour, une résolution de l'impasse demeure insaisissable, avec des éléments puissants dans les deux États résistant à tout compromis et les alliés régionaux clés des États-Unis, soit l'Israël et l'Arabie Saoudite, s'opposant fermement aux négociations entre l'administration Obama et le gouvernement d'Hassan Rouhani. Il en découle qu'une attaque américaine sur l'Iran, afin de retarder sérieusement le programme nucléaire de ce dernier, demeure une possibilité distincte. Rappelant les origines de la situation actuelle, y-inclus le non-respect par l'Iran et les États-Unis de leurs obligations en vertu du *Traité sur la non-prolifération des armes nucléaires*, les auteurs évaluent la prétendue légalité d'une éventuelle attaque militaire américaine contre l'Iran selon le droit international régissant le recours à la force armée entre les États. La conclusion tirée est qu'une utilisation préventive de la force armée serait — et doit demeurer — illicite, et que le respect par les deux pays de leurs obligations juridiques respectives offre toujours la meilleure voie à suivre pour la résolution de leur différend.

Summary

Iran's pursuit of nuclear technology continues to place a major strain on US–Iranian relations, with many US decision makers still sceptical of Iran's claims that its uranium-enrichment program is aimed only at providing fuel for civilian purposes, not at developing nuclear weapons capability. In spite of the diplomatic progress made to date, the conclusion of a comprehensive agreement resolving the issue remains elusive, with powerful elements in both states resistant to any compromise, and the United States' key regional allies, Israel and Saudi Arabia, strongly opposed to the Obama administration's decision to negotiate with the government of Hassan Rouhani. Consequently, a US attack on Iran in order to (at least) severely delay Iran's nuclear program remains a distinct possibility. After outlining the causes of the current situation, and noting the extent to which both Iran and the United States have disregarded their obligations under the *Treaty on the Non-Proliferation of Nuclear Weapons*, this article considers the lawfulness of a potential US military strike against Iran, examining in detail relevant international legal rules governing the use of force. The conclusion reached is that such a preventive use of force would be — and should remain — illegal and that adherence to their respective legal obligations still offers the best way forward for both countries.

Renewable Energy and Trade: Interpreting against Fragmentation

MAUREEN IRISH

INTRODUCTION

Several disputes have been notified to the World Trade Organization (WTO) over measures relating to renewable energy.[1] These disputes raise issues concerning the interpretation of specific WTO obligations as well as questions over the relationship between the trade and climate change treaty regimes. This

---

Maureen Irish is a professor in the Faculty of Law at the University of Windsor. The author is grateful for comments from Marcia Valiante in the Faculty of Law at the University of Windsor; from the *Canadian Yearbook of International Law*'s anonymous reviewer; and from students in her International Economic Law classes as well as the participants in the Dean's Lunch-and-Learn meeting held in the Faculty of Law at the University of Windsor in October 2013. Zlatina Georgieva, Laura Sardella, and André Rivard provided helpful research support, funded by the Law Foundation of Ontario. The author appreciates the ongoing assistance of Annette Demers, acting law librarian at the Paul Martin Law Library at the University of Windsor.

[1] At the time of writing, the following matters had been notified: DS412 *Canada – Certain Measures Affecting the Renewable Energy Generation Sector* (complainant Japan); DS419 *China – Measures Concerning Wind Power Equipment* (complainant United States); DS426 *Canada – Measures Relating to the Feed-In Tariff Program* (complainant European Union); DS443 *European Union and a Member State – Certain Measures Concerning the Importation of Biodiesels* (complainant Argentina); DS452 *European Union and Certain Member States – Certain Measures Affecting the Renewable Energy Generation Sector* (complainant China); DS456 *India – Certain Measures Relating to Solar Cells and Solar Modules* (complainant United States); DS459 *European Union – Certain Measures on the Importation and Marketing of Biodiesel and Measures Supporting the Biodiesel Industry* (complainant Argentina); DS473 *European Union – Antidumping Measures on Biodiesel from Argentina* (complainant Argentina); DS476 *European Union and its Member States – Certain Measures Relating to the Energy Sector* (complainant Russia). As well, several applications for antidumping and countervailing duties are underway in domestic procedures. See Timothy Meyer, "Energy Subsidies and the World Trade Organization" (2013) 17(22) Am Soc Int'l L Insights 1.

article is divided into two main parts. The first surveys potential claims under the WTO agreements and outlines exemptions and defences available in these agreements. The second discusses approaches to interpretation, addressing the objective of sustainable development and the position of the WTO legal regime within public international law more generally.

The argument presented is that WTO jurisprudence can support important non-trade public policy goals, especially when WTO provisions are interpreted in light of the promotion of sustainable development, an objective recognized in the preamble to the *Agreement Establishing the World Trade Organization (WTO Agreement)*.[2] An analysis of the position of the WTO agreements within public international law also favours the integration of trade law with other international treaties. This article endorses the view that WTO law should not be interpreted in isolation, unconnected to other areas of global public policy and international law.

It is no surprise that measures relating to renewable energy appear in dispute settlement proceedings before the WTO. The last few decades have witnessed the development of new treaties and tribunals in several areas of international law. This enhanced activity is a positive response to the increased intensity of human exchange around the globe and to identified needs for new rules. The growth of tribunals has led to concerns over fragmentation, as differing legal regimes add their own views and understandings. In response, numerous suggestions have been made to encourage the harmonious interaction of tribunals or even to accept some competition among them. The greater complexity of the legal system is not solely or even mainly a question of choice of forum, however. Overlaps and tensions among substantive norms are now a common feature of many international disputes, including those within the jurisdiction of a single forum. As the coverage of international law expands, there is an increased role for methods of interpreting various treaties and other obligations harmoniously, as the disputes over measures relating to renewable energy demonstrate.

RENEWABLE ENERGY AND WTO LAW

This part of the article examines potential claims and defences in WTO law, with particular attention to the WTO Appellate Body decision in *Canada – Certain Measures Affecting the Renewable Energy*

---

[2] *Agreement Establishing the World Trade Organization*, 1867 UNTS 154 (1994), 33 ILM 1144 (in force 1 January 1995) [*WTO Agreement*].

Generation Sector[3] and three other recent Appellate Body decisions: *United States – Measures Affecting the Production and Sale of Clove Cigarettes*,[4] *United States – Measures Concerning the Importation, Marketing and Sale of Tuna and Tuna Products*,[5] and *United States – Certain Country of Origin Labelling (COOL) Requirements*.[6] The comments should not be taken as arguing that any particular domestic laws breach WTO obligations since much depends on a detailed analysis of each case in its own context. The analysis proceeds with reference to the following three hypothetical measures.

COUNTRY A

To enhance energy security, Country A has decided to support the development of a domestic green energy industry for the production of electricity. Suppliers who generate electricity from solar or wind power get a premium price when they sell this electricity to . the public distribution grid. The suppliers must be locally established to qualify. As well, any suppliers of solar or wind energy earn an additional premium if they use equipment that was manufactured in Country A. A further premium is added to the price for any solar or wind energy suppliers located in the northeast region of the country, which has higher unemployment rates and lower income per capita than the rest of Country A.

COUNTRY B

To encourage the use of green energy in transportation, Country B requires, by regulation, that all gasoline sold in the country contain a certain level of ethanol or some other bio-fuel. To qualify, the bio-fuel must be responsible for no more than 35 percent of the

---

[3] The dispute over the feed-in tariff program in Ontario is the first one to make its way through the dispute settlement system. *Canada – Certain Measures Affecting the Renewable Energy Generation Sector*, Doc WT/DS412/AB/R, Appellate Body Report (24 May 2013); *Canada – Measures Relating to the Feed-In Tariff Program*, Doc WT/DS426/AB/R, Appellate Body Report (24 May 2013) [*Canada – Renewable Energy*].

[4] *United States – Measures Affecting the Production and Sale of Clove Cigarettes*, Doc WT/DS406/AB/R, Appellate Body Report (24 April 2012) [*US – Clove Cigarettes*].

[5] *United States – Measures Concerning the Importation, Marketing and Sale of Tuna and Tuna Products*, Doc WT/DS381/AB/R, Appellate Body Report (13 June 2012) [*US – Tuna II*].

[6] *United States – Certain Country of Origin Labelling (COOL) Requirements*, Doc WT/DS384/AB/R, Appellate Body Report (23 July 2012) [*US – COOL*].

volume of the greenhouse gases (GHGs) that the same amount of fossil fuel would produce. The comparison between bio-fuels and fossil fuels takes account of GHGs produced during the entire life cycle of the fuel, including cultivation, extraction, refining, transportation to market, and emissions on consumption. In the regulation, the level of ethanol or other bio-fuel required gradually increases over a period of years. Grants are available from the government for 20 percent of the cost of adapting motor vehicles to the new requirements as the bio-fuel levels increase.

COUNTRY C

To meet its commitment to reduce GHGs, country C has adopted a system of carbon taxes. The taxes apply to certain industrial sectors that emit high levels of GHGs. In order to secure legislative approval for the carbon tax, the government of Country C has agreed that the taxes will only apply once a manufacturer has surpassed a certain annual volume of production. As well, the government has agreed to apply border tax adjustments on imports that compete with the goods produced by the target industries. The imports are charged a tax equivalent to the domestic carbon tax. Exporters and importers are not granted a free allowance before the tax applies.

CLAIMS IN WTO LAW: DISCRIMINATION, BORDER TAXES, AND SUBSIDIES

This section addresses potential claims in WTO law relating to non-discriminatory treatment, border adjustments, and subsidies.

Non-Discriminatory Treatment

A central WTO requirement in support of trade is the obligation of national treatment. Imported goods are not to face discrimination in comparison to the treatment of like goods produced domestically. As expressed in Article III:4 of the *General Agreement on Tariffs and Trade* (*GATT*), imported products must receive "treatment no less favourable than that accorded to like products of national origin in respect of all laws, regulations and requirements affecting their internal sale, offering for sale, purchase, transportation, distribution or use."[7] A government measure is examined under this provision

---

[7] *General Agreement on Tariffs and Trade*, 55 UNTS 194, Can TS 1948 No 31 (in force 1 January 1948), now incorporated by reference into *General Agreement on Tariffs*

for both *de jure* and *de facto* treatment of imports. The premium for the use of locally manufactured equipment in the Country A measure described earlier is an example of an explicit *de jure* preference. Such content requirements are usually fairly straightforward examples of breaches of Article III:4, since imports are not eligible for the beneficial treatment given to goods of national origin. The requirement that all solar and wind energy be from local suppliers in order to qualify for the measure in Country A would also be a domestic content requirement in the same category, assuming electricity is considered a product rather than a service.[8]

In *Canada – Renewable Energy*, the measure at issue involved purchases of electricity by the government of the province of Ontario.[9] The feed-in tariff program allowed Ontario-based producers of electricity generated from renewable sources such as wind and solar power to feed into the provincial grid. Much like the hypothetical measure in country A, the program paid premium prices in comparison to the prices for electricity produced from other sources. In order to qualify for the feed-in tariff, the generating companies had to meet a domestic content requirement involving the use of locally manufactured equipment. The panel found that the domestic content requirement for equipment was in breach of Article III:4, and this finding was not disturbed on appeal.[10]

The main defence on this point was that Article III:4 did not apply to the feed-in tariff, since it was "procurement by governmental agencies of products purchased for governmental purposes and not with a view to commercial resale" within the terms of *GATT* Article III:8(a). A government procurement measure is not subject to the

---

and Trade 1994, 1867 UNTS 187 (in force 1 January 1995, art III:4), Annex 1A to the *WTO Agreement, supra* note 2 [*GATT*].

8   In *Canada – Renewable Energy, supra* note 3, electricity was treated as a good or product rather than a service, although Japan did not explicitly agree to this characterization. Panel Reports, *Canada–Certain Measures Affecting the Renewable Energy Generation Sector*, WT/DS412/R and *Canada–Measures Relating to the Feed-In Tariff Program*, WT/DS426/R at para 7.11, n 46 [*Canada–Renewable Energy*, Panel Report].

9   *Canada – Renewable Energy, supra* note 3.

10 *Ibid* at para 6.1(b)(iv); *Canada – Renewable Energy*, Panel Report, *supra* note 8 at para 7.166. The measure thereby also breached Article 2.1 of the *Agreement on Trade-Related Investment Measures*, as it was a trade-related investment measure "that is inconsistent with the provisions of Article III … of GATT." *Agreement on Trade-Related Investment Measures*, 1868 UNTS 186 (in force 1 January 1995) at art 2.1.

national treatment obligation. The Appellate Body rejected the government procurement defence, reasoning that Article III:8(a) applies only in relation to the obligations in Article III and, thus, only to products in a competitive relationship with the potential imports in question. Procurement of desks for government offices, for example, can favour local manufacturers and discriminate against imported desks. Ontario's feed-in tariff provided beneficial treatment to locally manufactured generating equipment, but the procurement in question was for electricity. Since generating equipment and electricity are not products that compete with each other, the Appellate Body ruled that the government procurement exclusion in Article III:8(a) did not apply.[11]

The Appellate Body's analysis is puzzling since it appears to reverse course on the treatment of production and processing methods (PPMs) and reopens the controversy over the identification of like goods. In 1991, the unadopted *GATT* panel report in the first dispute of *US – Tuna I* had ruled against distinguishing between imported and domestic tuna in accordance with the acceptability of fishing methods. It stated that such a PPM distinction would threaten the multilateral framework for trade since "each contracting party could unilaterally determine the life or health protection policies from which other contracting parties could not deviate without jeopardizing their rights under the General Agreement."[12] The Appellate Body took a very different view in the more recent *US – Tuna II* dispute involving the same main parties. This 2012 decision was rendered under provisions of the *Agreement on Technical Barriers to Trade (TBT Agreement)*, which require national treatment and prohibit technical regulations that are more trade restrictive than necessary to fulfil a legitimate objective.[13] The US measure at issue in this more recent dispute made dolphin-friendly labelling available only if certain fishing methods had been followed. The panel held that one of the legitimate objectives of the measure was to ensure that the US market not be used to encourage fishing methods

---

[11] *Canada – Renewable Energy, supra* note 3 at para 5.79.

[12] *United States – Restrictions on Imports of Tuna*, Doc DS21/R, GATT Panel Report (3 September 1991), BISD 39S/155, 30 ILM 1594 (1991) at para 5.27 [unadopted] [*US Tuna I*]. See further *United States – Restrictions on Imports of Tuna*, Doc DS29/R, GATT Panel Report (16 June 1994), 33 ILM 839 (1994) [unadopted].

[13] *Agreement on Technical Barriers to Trade*, 1868 UNTS 120 (in force 1 January 1995) [*TBT Agreement*].

harmful to dolphins.[14] The Appellate Body found a breach of the national treatment obligation in Article 2.1 of the *TBT Agreement* because the less favourable treatment of Mexican tuna was not due exclusively to a legitimate regulatory distinction.[15] When Mexico argued that the US measure was unilateral and coercive, the Appellate Body simply noted that Article 2.2 of the *TBT Agreement* permits some trade restrictiveness and that the question was whether this level of restrictiveness was necessary to fulfil the objectives.[16]

The decision in *US – Tuna II* seemed to signal a new approach to PPMs, one that would involve examining them as part of the regulatory treatment of goods, rather than the identification of like products.[17] It appeared that their trade restrictiveness could be considered along with the restrictive effects of other aspects of the measure at issue, for both the *TBT Agreement* and the *GATT*, given the strong connections between these two agreements. Now the reasoning in *Canada – Renewable Energy* returns the focus, under the *GATT*, to the like products question. The Appellate Body stated in *Canada – Renewable Energy* that it was not deciding whether inputs and processes of production are part of procurement, and thus excluded from the national treatment obligation,[18] but its interpretation of *GATT* Article III:8(a) leaves no room to consider the measure at issue as a PPM.

---

14 *US – Tuna II, supra* note 5 at paras 242, 302. The other legitimate objective was to ensure that consumers were not misled by deceptive labelling about fishing methods.

15 *Ibid* at para 297. See also *ibid* at para 407(d). The use of regulatory distinctions in the interpretation of Article 2.1 of the *TBT Agreement, supra* note 13, is discussed more fully later in this article.

16 *US – Tuna II, supra* note 5 at paras 335, 338. The Appellate Body reversed a Panel finding of breach of Article 2.2 of the *TBT Agreement* because the Panel had incorrectly assessed Mexico's argument over a less restrictive alternative measure. Due to a lack of evidence, the Appellate Body did not rule on whether there was a breach of Article 2.2. In 2001, the Appellate Body found that a distinction based on production and processing methods was justified pursuant to *GATT* Article XX. *United States – Import Prohibition of Certain Shrimp and Shrimp Products, Recourse to Article 21.5 of the DSU by Malaysia,* Doc WT/DS58/AB/RW, Appellate Body Report (21 November 2001).

17 This possibility has been hinted at by Andrew Green, "Climate Change, Regulatory Policy and the WTO: How Constraining Are Trade Rules?" (2005) 8(1) J Int'l Econ L 143 at 160.

18 *Canada – Renewable Energy, supra* note 3 at para 5.63, n 523.

The Appellate Body's interpretation of *GATT* Article III:8(a) is also potentially at variance with its choice of comparative market prices in the subsidy analysis in *Canada – Renewable Energy*. In order to decide whether prices provide a benefit within the definition of a subsidy in Article 1.1(b) of the *Agreement on Subsidies and Countervailing Measures* (*SCM Agreement*), the Appellate Body held that a comparison should be made to market prices for electricity produced from renewable sources, not to prices for electricity in general.[19] Even if final consumers of electricity may not distinguish between renewable and non-renewable sources, governments at the wholesale level do make this distinction, according to the Appellate Body, and benchmark prices should be chosen from the separate market for renewable sources.[20] It seems odd that the process of production (that is, a PPM) can be acknowledged in this manner for the definition of the market, but not for other aspects of the analysis.

The treatment of PPMs will be an ongoing challenge in WTO jurisprudence for government procurement and also for general regulatory measures. Increasing attention is being paid to international supply chains for health, human rights, and security matters, and renewable energy disputes will commonly involve PPMs. The concerns expressed in the first *US – Tuna* decision over extraterritoriality will need to be recognized and considered.[21] It cannot be just any difference in policies between countries that will permit differences in the treatment of imports. Guidance is needed as to how close the link to goods must be in order to qualify as a PPM. The domestic content requirement for the generating equipment in *Canada – Renewable Energy* could easily have been seen as too distant from the final electricity produced. Instead of entering into this discussion, the Appellate Body took a step backwards by focusing on a narrow view of like products.

In addition, the competitiveness test for *GATT* Article III:8 is only a partial answer to the like products question. The complainants in *Canada – Renewable Energy* challenged the domestic content requirement for generating equipment, but not the fact that generating facilities had to be located in Ontario.[22] In the decision,

---

[19] *Agreement on Subsidies and Countervailing Measures*, 1869 UNTS 14 (in force 1 January 1995), art 1.1(b) [*SCM Agreement*].

[20] *Canada – Renewable Energy, supra* note 3 at paras 5.175–5.178.

[21] *US – Tuna I, supra* note 12.

[22] See *Canada – Renewable Energy*, Panel Report, *supra* note 8 at para 7.66. Hypothetically, there might have been a possibility of generating facilities in

there was no analysis of whether renewable and non-renewable energy are in competition with each other for the purposes of the application of *GATT* Article III:8. In the result, there is no decision from the Appellate Body on whether electricity from renewable sources and electricity from non-renewable sources are like products. The issue of how the national treatment standard will be applied to renewable energy remains open, to be determined in future disputes.

For measures that pass the initial competitiveness test of *Canada – Renewable Energy*, the rest of *GATT* Article III:8(a) will apply—in particular, the requirement that the procurement be "for governmental purposes and not with a view to commercial resale." Although the analysis was not necessary for its decision, the Appellate Body addressed the meaning of this language. Referring to the French and Spanish versions, the Appellate Body determined that "purposes" should relate to the needs ("*besoins*," "*necesidades*") of governments in the discharge of their functions.[23] This interpretation covers goods consumed by governments and also goods provided to recipients as part of government functions, such as pharmaceuticals purchased by a public hospital for use in the treatment of patients.[24] A commercial resale, according to the Appellate Body, would be one at arm's length and with a general profit orientation, at least over the long term.[25] This view of commercial resale

---

some contiguous area of the United States wishing to connect to the Ontario transmission grid, but it appears that this argument was not raised by the United States in its third party submissions. *Ibid*, Annex B-11 (Integrated Executive Summary of the United States). Canada has reported that the Ontario government issued a ministerial directive that removed large-capacity projects from the content requirement for equipment and lowered the requirement for smaller projects. As well, the province is proceeding with a statutory change that will permit procurement of electricity under the feed-in tariff free from the requirement. *Canada – Certain Measures Affecting the Renewable Energy Generation Sector*, Doc WT/DS412/17/Add.1, Status Report by Canada (14 March 2014); *Canada – Measures Relating to the Feed-In Tariff Program*, Doc WT/DS426/17/Add.1, Status Report by Canada (14 March 2014).

[23] *Canada – Renewable Energy, supra* note 3 at para 5.67. For Canada's arguments, see Alan H Kessel, "Canadian Practice in International Law at the Department of Foreign Affairs and International Trade in 2010-11" (2011) 49 Can YB Int'l L 381 at 413-17. The arguments of the United States are summarized in *Canada–Renewable Energy*, Panel Report, *supra* note 8, Annex B-11 (Integrated Executive Summary of the United States).

[24] *Canada – Renewable Energy, supra* note 3 at para 5.68, n 514.

[25] *Ibid* at para 5.71.

raises the possibility that if an electricity distribution system is entirely public and charges user fees designed only to recover costs, a government procurement defence will shield explicit local preferences from *GATT* Article III.[26] A privatized utility operating for profit could not be made subject to the same local preferences without a contravention of *GATT* Article III. Some further clarification of the interpretation of commercial resale will likely be needed to resolve future disputes.

The *Canada – Renewable Energy* decision is mainly concerned with government procurement and a subsidy issue that is discussed in more detail later in this article. Perhaps the Appellate Body's view of PPMs will be restricted to these contexts. The interpretation could have consequences, however, for PPMs relating to many areas of regulation, both for explicit *de jure* discrimination as in Ontario's feed-in tariff and for complaints of breaches of *GATT* Article III:4 through *de facto* discrimination.

Claims of *de facto* discrimination require comparing the treatment of imports and the treatment of like domestic products. In the hypothetical case involving the bio-fuel measure of Country B, if an importer argues that the methodology used to calculate GHG production favoured domestic bio-fuel over imported bio-fuel, this argument would be a claim of a *de facto* breach of *GATT* Article III:4. In addition to the identification of like products, analysis of a *de facto* discrimination claim requires assessment of the treatment accorded to the two groups of products. Then, if it is determined that there is a breach of *GATT* Article III:4, the breach could be justified under *GATT* Article XX, which provides exemptions from the *GATT* obligations for certain measures, such as those protecting health or relating to the conservation of natural resources.[27] Disputes over national treatment thus involve the interaction of three elements: like products, their treatment, and, finally, possible exemptions should a measure be found to be non-compliant.

---

[26] Ontario's electricity system operated as a hybrid system, in which public and private entities were involved in generation, transmission, distribution, and retailing. Electricity was sold to retail consumers by a provincial government agency, by local distribution companies (including public municipal utilities), and by some licensed private sector retailers. *Canada – Renewable Energy*, Panel Report, *supra* note 8 at paras 7.22, 7.25, 7.35, 7.57. For a survey of Canadian provincial electricity policies, see Marcia Valiante, "A Greener Grid? Canadian Policies for Renewable Power and Prospects for a National Sustainable Electricity Strategy" (2013) 25 J Envtl L Prac 41.

[27] *GATT*, *supra* note 7, art XX(b), (g).

Interpretation of the national treatment obligation was central to the Appellate Body decisions in *US – Clove Cigarettes* and *US – Tuna II*, examined in this section and also in *US – COOL*, which is discussed in less detail. All three were decided under the *TBT Agreement*, concerning regulations applying to goods. The *TBT Agreement* requires that imports receive national treatment (Article 2.1) and also that any technical regulation not be more trade restrictive than necessary to achieve a legitimate objective (Article 2.2). In the three decisions, some progress was made on PPMs, on the definition of like products, and on coordinating the analysis between the *GATT* and the *TBT Agreement*. *Canada – Renewable Energy* may have obscured some of this progress, however, at least on PPMs.

In past *GATT* disputes over like products, a major question has been whether the purpose of the measure at issue should influence the selection of the products for comparison. Called the "aim-and-effects" test, this approach would say that if distinctions are made between goods for legitimate, non-protectionist purposes, then the distinctions are not discriminatory and deference should be granted to the choices made by the regulating government.[28] The traditional test for determining like products has been to look to physical characteristics, end use, consumer tastes and habits, and tariff classification.[29] In *US – Clove Cigarettes*, the Appellate Body reaffirmed that the determination is judged on these traditional factors.[30] While it declined to apply an aim-and-effects test,[31] the Appellate Body did not completely reject consideration of the purpose of a measure. It noted the difficulties of specifying the purpose of a measure and of trying to identify like products based on factors

---

[28] For thorough analysis of arguments supporting an aim-and-effects test in the determination of like products, see Julia Ya Qin, "Defining Nondiscrimination under the Law of the World Trade Organization" (2005) 23 Boston U Int'l LJ 215. Qin would also use the reference to "discrimination between countries where the same conditions prevail" in the introductory paragraph of *GATT* Article XX to support extended consideration of regulatory purpose for analysis of exemptions under this article. I am grateful to Chios Carmody for remarks on this issue.

[29] GATT Working Party, *Border Tax Adjustments*, Doc L/3464 (2 December 1970), BISD 18S/97 at para 18.

[30] *US – Clove Cigarettes*, *supra* note 4 at paras 112-13.

[31] An aim-and-effects test had been rejected earlier in *Japan – Taxes on Alcoholic Beverages*, Docs WT/DS8/AB/R, WT/DS10/AB/R, WT/DS/11/AB/R, Appellate Body Report (1 November 1996).

relevant to such a purpose. Although the Appellate Body agreed with the Panel that the imported clove cigarettes were like domestically produced menthol cigarettes, the Appellate Body found that the Panel had concentrated its examination of consumer tastes and habits too narrowly on the views of current and potential young smokers, guided by the purpose of the measure. which was to reduce smoking among this group.[32] Regulatory goals may play a role, according to the Appellate Body, but only "to the extent that they have an impact on the competitive relationship between and among the products concerned."[33] Future WTO jurisprudence will undoubtedly elaborate on the meaning of the need for an impact on the competitive relationship. The reasoning in *US – Clove Cigarettes* now presents an opportunity for the purpose of a regulatory measure to have some relevance in the identification of like products, albeit subject to the traditional factors and to a demonstration of some influence on competition.

For renewable energy, regulatory purpose could be relevant in the choice of like products for comparison. Some forms of renewable energy may have distinct characteristics that could be considered under the traditional factors. Solar energy from panels on a building, for example, differs from conventional electricity in that it is intermittent and not vulnerable to grid failure.[34] Electricity from the public grid will not present those distinctions, however. A measure that does not conform to *GATT* Article III might, of course, be justified by one of the exemptions under *GATT* Article XX. A strong argument against using purpose in the *GATT* Article III analysis is that such an interpretation fails to acknowledge the presence of *GATT* Article XX, which lists certain legitimate exempted purposes. Since there is an exemption clause in the *GATT*, the argument is that the clause should be given effect and examination of regulatory purpose should take place in accordance with the terms of *GATT* Article XX.[35]

---

[32] *US – Clove Cigarettes, supra* note 4 at para 137.

[33] *Ibid* at para 119. For detailed analysis, see Weihuan Zhou, "*US–Clove Cigarettes* and *US–Tuna II (Mexico)*: Implications for the Role of Regulatory Purpose under Article III:4 of the GATT" (2012) 15(4) J Int'l Econ L 1075.

[34] Robert Howse and the Renewable Energy and International Law (REIL) Project, "World Trade Law and Renewable Energy: The Case of Non-tariff Measures" (2006) 6 J Eur Envtl Planning L 500 at 504.

[35] James Flett has argued in favour of an "aim-and-effects" test for the review of the treatment standard required in trade agreements and also in investment

If the regulatory purpose has a subordinate role in identifying like products, then consumer views as to the purpose might be in the same category. The issue of how consumer perceptions affect the like products test has been debated since the Appellate Body decision in *European Communities – Measures Affecting Asbestos and Asbestos-Containing Products* reversed a panel ruling that a health risk would be considered only under the *GATT* Article XX exemptions· and not in the determination of like products. In the view of the Appellate Body, the dangerous nature of asbestos meant that the health risks would be bound to influence consumers' behaviour and thus had to be part of the analysis of consumer tastes and habits.[36] For electricity from the grid, the issue would likely be whether to reflect the views of certain consumers who choose to pay more for power that they know has been produced from renewable sources. The Appellate Body in *Canada – Renewable Energy* did consider that consumers were increasingly prepared to make this distinction.[37] The consumer perceptions factor is a controversial one, as it is difficult to control for consumer views that are mercantilist or anti-trade,[38] and the analysis could end too early with a conclusion that there are no domestic like products for comparison purposes. If the reasoning in *US – Clove Cigarettes* applies, it seems to deal only with

---

agreements, which often lack an exemption clause. See James Flett, "WTO Space for National Regulation: Requiem for a Diagonal Vector Test" (2013) 16(1) J Int'l Econ L 37. A major hurdle for the analysis is the one identified of respect for differing treaty texts. As investment agreements are updated, more may be modified to include specific exemption clauses.

[36] *European Communities – Measures Affecting Asbestos and Asbestos-Containing Products*, Doc WT/DS135/AB/R, Appellate Body Report (5 April 2001) at para 122. The decision can also be explained by the physical differences between asbestos fibres and the polychloryl vinyl fibres suggested as domestic like products. Zhou, *supra* note 33 at 1084; Maureen Irish, "Global Public Policy and the World Trade Organization after Shrimp/Turtle and Asbestos" (2004) 42 Can YB Int'l L 253 at 307-9.

[37] *Canada – Renewable Energy, supra* note 3 at para 5.177.

[38] In *US – COOL, supra* note 6, Canada argued unsuccessfully that the purpose of the US requirement for detailed records on where cattle were born, raised, and slaughtered was trade protectionism rather than the provision of information to consumers (at para 354). The panel had relied on evidence of a social norm that consumers want information on the origin of products (at para 441). While the Appellate Body was unsupportive of the panel's reference to social norms to identify legitimate objectives (at para 448), it upheld the panel determination that the objective of the US measure to provide consumer information was legitimate (at para 453).

market impact. Unless their impact on competition is significant, thus, consumer perceptions about the purpose of a measure are not likely to have much influence on the choice of like products.

In the recent *US – Tuna II* decision, the Appellate Body also dealt with another contentious issue that could affect both the identification of like products and the assessment of the treatment of imports. In the decision, the Appellate Body found that the panel had incorrectly ruled that there was no breach of national treatment under Article 2.1 of the *TBT Agreement* because any discrimination against Mexican tuna was due to factors unrelated to the foreign origin of the tuna. This argument, that distinctions among products are only prohibited if they are related to origin, was not precisely an aim-and-effects test but had been presented in the past as a way of increasing the space for domestic regulation.[39] In *US – Tuna II*, the Appellate Body ruled quite conclusively that the argument is "difficult to reconcile with the fact that a measure may be *de facto* inconsistent with Article 2.1 [of the *TBT Agreement*] even when it is origin-neutral on its face."[40] Although the Appellate Body was analyzing treatment rather than the identification of like products, the rejection of the origin-specific argument was decisive and can be expected to be influential in future disputes on the determination of like products, as well as less favourable treatment, in both the *GATT* and the *TBT Agreement*.

In *US – Clove Cigarettes*, the Appellate Body took the welcome step of establishing coherence between the *GATT* and the *TBT Agreement*. The decision reads the two agreements together, in a manner that relieves the concern over the lack of a general exemption clause in the *TBT Agreement*. The worry had been that the national treatment standard in Article 2.1 of the *TBT Agreement* did not seem to be subject to exemptions, even though the corresponding national treatment obligation in *GATT* Article III is subject to the general exemptions of *GATT* Article XX. The Appellate Body resolved the mismatch by interpreting the sixth recital in the preamble of the *TBT Agreement* so as to provide legitimate objectives that can justify what would otherwise be less favourable treatment of imports in

---

[39] See Michael Ming Du, "The Rise of National Regulatory Autonomy in the GATT/ WTO Regime" (2011) 14(3) J Int'l Econ L 639 at 656-64; Richard G Tarasofsky, "Heating Up International Trade Law: Challenges and Opportunities Posed by Efforts to Combat Climate Change" (2008) 1 Carbon & Climate L Rev 7 at 9; Green, *supra* note 17 at 164-66.

[40] *US – Tuna II*, *supra* note 5 at para 225.

breach of Article 2.1. The sixth recital serves as context for interpretation and an expression of the object and purpose of the *TBT
Agreement*. In the result, Article 2.1 does not prohibit detrimental
impact on imports "where such detrimental impact stems exclusively from legitimate regulatory distinctions."[41] This interpretation
will remove most of the risk that a measure might be justified pursuant to an exemption in *GATT* Article XX but, nevertheless, be in
breach of Article 2.1 of the *TBT Agreement*. The approach of the Appellate Body to reading the *GATT* and the *TBT Agreement* together
should promote predictability.[42] It is argued later in this article that
climate change treaties and public international law are relevant to
the interpretation of the exemptions under *GATT* Article XX. The
same approach should also apply to the use of legitimate objectives
in the *TBT Agreement*.

In Article 2.1 of the *TBT Agreement*, the new thinking from *US –
Clove Cigarettes* and *US – Tuna II* will apply to comparisons to
domestic like products and also to comparisons to like products
from any other country. In the *GATT*, non-discrimination regarding trade from other countries is governed by the most-favoured-
nation (MFN) obligation of *GATT* Article I:1:

---

[41] *US – Clove Cigarettes, supra* note 4 at para 174. The idea that a detrimental impact
must be due exclusively to a legitimate regulatory distinction might be considered
as establishing a test that differs from the requirement in the introductory paragraph of *GATT* Article XX that measures not constitute arbitrary or unjustifiable
discrimination between countries where the same conditions prevail. Zhou
argues that the two tests are not that far apart, since they would both depend on
the reasonable availability of alternate less discriminatory means. Zhou, *supra*
note 33 at 1120.

[42] It is not clear what effect the interpretation of "treatment no less favourable" in
US – Clove Cigarettes, supra note 4, will have on interpretation of the same phrase
in *GATT* Article III:4. Since the *GATT* context is different and includes the
specific exemptions of *GATT* Article XX, there may be no need to consider
legitimate objectives directly at the stage of a *GATT* Article III analysis. There
could be a possible linkage to a consideration of purpose in the identification
of like products, as outlined earlier. Another issue that will undoubtedly be explored in future WTO jurisprudence is how the *US – Clove Cigarettes* interpretation
of Article 2.1 will relate to the legitimate objectives listed in Article 2.2 of the *TBT
Agreement*. In *US – COOL, supra* note 6, for example, if the Appellate Body had
completed the Article 2.2 analysis and determined that the obstacle to trade was
justified by the objective of providing consumer information, would it still have
been able to find that the same measure breached Article 2.1 because the information demanded was disproportionate to the same objective? Will a proportionality analysis be used for both Articles 2.1 and 2.2 ?

With respect to customs duties and charges of any kind imposed on or in connection with importation or exportation ... and with respect to all rules and formalities in connection with importation and exportation, and with respect to all matters referred to in paragraphs 2 and 4 of Article III, any advantage, favour, privilege or immunity granted by any Member to any product originating in or destined for any other country shall be accorded immediately and unconditionally to the like product originating in or destined for the territories of all other Members.

There may be some question as to whether providing imports with treatment that is no less favourable than the treatment of the comparison products under Article 2.1 of the *TBT Agreement* and *GATT* Article III:4 will carry the same meaning as granting imports an advantage, favour, privilege, or immunity immediately and unconditionally under *GATT* Article I:1. In principle, the interpretation should be the same and the new thinking should also apply to *GATT* Article I:1. There has been discussion in the literature and in some WTO decisions over what is meant by granting an advantage unconditionally and whether conditions are permissible so long as they are not origin specific.[43] This debate has now likely been superseded by the rejection of the origin-specific argument in *US – Tuna II*, as outlined earlier. If a distinction based on sustainable production of a bio-fuel, for example, meets the test of no less favourable treatment in Article 2.1 of the *TBT Agreement* and *GATT* Article III:4, it should not constitute a failure to provide imports with an advantage, favour, privilege, or immunity that is available to like products from other countries. Future WTO disputes may address this issue of coordination between the MFN standard and the national treatment standard.

In summary, the Appellate Body decision in *Canada – Renewable Energy* addressed the scope of the government procurement defence and the analysis of subsidies, examined later in this article. The decision leaves the important question of the treatment of PPMs unresolved. On *de facto* discrimination, the recent Appellate Body decisions in *US – Clove Cigarettes*, *US – Tuna II*, and *US – COOL* have modified the approach to like products and non-discrimination. The like products test will continue to use the traditional approach based on competition, but with some possible influence relating to

---

[43] Charles Benoit, "Picking Tariff Winners: Non-Product Related PPMs and DSB Interpretations of 'Unconditionally' within Article I:1" (2010–11) 42 Geo J Int'l L 583.

regulatory purpose. The problem of a potentially absolute non-discrimination obligation in Article 2.1 of the *TBT Agreement* has been resolved. *GATT* provisions will be read as part of the context of the *TBT Agreement* in light of the acknowledgment of legitimate objectives, including environmental protection, in the preamble of the *TBT Agreement*. This new thinking will very likely apply as well to interpretation of the MFN obligation in *GATT* Article I:1.

Border Adjustments

Some of the current measures on climate change and renewable energy use carbon taxes that vary with the amount of GHG production associated with particular sectors. Trade concerns over carbon taxes can relate to the position of domestic producers in competition with foreign producers who are not subject to such a tax and also to the risk of "carbon leakage," which would undermine the effectiveness of the measure if domestic production moved to a tax-free jurisdiction, resulting in no overall reduction of GHG emissions. Border taxes on imports are often suggested as a way of alleviating these concerns.

GATT Article III:2 requires that imported goods "not be subject, directly or indirectly, to internal taxes ... in excess of those applied, directly or indirectly, to like domestic products." Article II:2(a) allows countries to impose on imports "a charge equivalent to an internal tax imposed consistently with the provisions of paragraph 2 of Article III in respect of the like domestic product or in respect of an article from which the imported product has been manufactured or produced in whole or in part."

If the internal tax is a simple charge on a particular product, such as a block of cement, then the *GATT* provisions permit a border tax in the same amount on imported blocks of cement. Interpretation is more complicated if the tax varies with the amount of GHGs emitted during the production process. If what is taxed domestically are the emissions themselves, then there is some question as to whether a border tax would be an adjustment "in respect of an article from which the imported product has been manufactured or produced." The GHGs have not become part of the product and neither has the energy that was expended when the GHGs were emitted during production. In a sense, the question posed is one that necessarily follows general acceptance of PPMs as outlined earlier — how close must the connection to the goods be in order for a measure to be considered to affect the determination of like products, the treatment of goods, or, in this case, product taxes? As

Joost Pauwelyn points out, we would not expect to impose an adjustment to try to balance out differences in levels of income tax imposed on manufacturers in countries of export and import. It is only for product taxes that *GATT* Article II permits an adjustment.[44]

A tax on GHG emissions during production is probably a "hidden tax," on which existing *GATT* authority does not provide a clear answer.[45] Some debate in the literature mentions footnote 61 to Annex II of the *SCM Agreement*, which lists "energy" as a production input for which a tax remission can be granted on exports without having the remission considered a prohibited export subsidy.[46] The argument is that for border adjustments tax levies on imports were intended to match tax remissions on exports.[47] Others find this argument unpersuasive[48] and conclude that the *GATT* consistency of a border tax adjustment is uncertain, such that justification under *GATT* Article XX may be needed.[49]

---

[44] Joost Pauwelyn, "U.S. Federal Climate Policy and Competitiveness Concerns: The Limits and Options of International Trade Law," Working Paper, Nicholas Institute for Environmental Policy Solutions, Duke University, April 2007, online: <http://www.nicholas.duke.edu/institute> at 18.

[45] GATT Working Party, *Border Tax Adjustments*, Doc L/3464 (2 December 1970), BISD 18S/97 at para 15: "taxes occultes." The French version of *GATT* Article II:2(a) refers to "*une marchandise qui a été incorporée dans l'article importé*," seeming to require that the product tax be on components that have been incorporated into the imported goods, which does not describe greenhouse gases (GHGs) emitted during production. See Patrick Low, Gabrielle Marceau, and Julia Reinaud, "The Interface between the Trade and Climate Change Regimes: Scoping the Issue," Centre for Trade and Economic Integration (paper prepared for the conference on Climate Change, Trade and Competitiveness: Issues for the WTO held on 16-18 June 2010), Doc ERSD-2011-1, online: <http://www.wto.org/english/res_e/reser_e/ersd201101_e.pdf> at 8-10; Pauwelyn, *supra* note 44 at 20.

[46] *SCM Agreement*, *supra* note 19, Annex II, n 61.

[47] Warren H Maruyama, "Climate Change and the WTO: Cap and Trade versus Carbon Tax?" (2011) 45(4) J World Trade 679; Christine McIsaac, "Opening a GATE to Reduced Global Emissions: Getting over and into the WTO" (2010) 44(5) J World Trade 1053.

[48] Charles E McLure, Jr, "The GATT Legality of Border Adjustments for Carbon Taxes and the Cost of Emission Permits: A Riddle, Wrapped in a Mystery, Inside an Enigma" (2011) 11 Florida Tax Rev 221.

[49] Pauwelyn, *supra* note 44; Paul-Erik Veel, "Carbon Tariffs and the WTO: An Evaluation of Feasible Policies" (2009) 12(3) J Int'l Econ L 749 at 771-75; Ryan Vanden Brink, "Competitiveness Border Adjustments in US Climate Change Proposals Violate GATT: Suggestions to Utilize GATT's Environmental Exceptions" (2010) 21 Colo J Int'l Envtl L Pol'y 85.

If a country chooses a cap-and-trade system instead of a carbon tax, it might impose an obligation at the border to purchase emission certificates covering the imports. The debate over border tax adjustments would apply if this obligation were considered a tax. If it were not, national treatment and MFN treatment would still be required in accordance with the WTO provisions on non-discrimination discussed earlier.[50]

In summary, countries that adopt carbon taxes could decide, like Country C in the hypothetical example provided earlier, that they should apply border tax adjustments. The intent may be to protect competing domestic producers, and it may also be to discourage producers from relocating to another jurisdiction that does not apply carbon taxes. *GATT* Article II on border tax adjustments might not cover carbon tax adjustments.

Subsidies

Current measures to encourage the use of renewable energy could be subject to WTO rules on subsidies. *GATT* Articles VI and XVI set out basic provisions on subsidies and countervailing duties, which are levied by importing members on subsidized imported products. These provisions are elaborated upon and expanded in the *SCM Agreement*. In addition to countervailing duties, subsidies may lead to complaints by members in WTO dispute settlement proceedings.[51]

[50] A counter-argument is that trade in the emission certificates can be detached from goods and classified as a service subject to the *General Agreement on Trade in Services*, 1869 UNTS 183 (in force 1 January 1995) [*GATS*], but not to provisions that relate to products. Classification will depend on the details of any particular measure and, probably, on the availability of secondary markets in emission certificates. A measure could also be subject to rules under the *GATT,* the *TBT Agreement,* and the *GATS*. If the *GATS* applies exclusively, then any national treatment requirement would depend on whether a commitment had been made under Article XVI of the *GATS*. The exemption clauses would be *GATS* Articles XIV and XIV*bis*; and subsidies would be governed by *GATS* Article XV rather than the *SCM Agreement, supra* note 19. See generally Howse and REIL Project, *supra* note 34, for the argument that the *GATS* has wide application to energy trade; Erich Vranes, "Climate Change and the WTO: EU Emission Trading and the WTO Disciplines on Trade in Goods, Services and Investment Protection" (2009) 43(4) J World Trade 707. Note that *GATS* Article XIV does not include an exemption for measures relating to conservation of exhaustible natural resources. Joshua Meltzer, "Climate Change and Trade: The EU Aviation Directive and the WTO" (2012) 15(1) J Int'l Econ L 111 at 150.

[51] Subsidies for bio-fuels such as ethanol may be subject to obligations in the WTO *Agreement on Agriculture,* 1867 UNTS 410 (in force 1 January 1995), a topic not

The *SCM Agreement* defines a subsidy as having some form of government financial contribution, or price, or income support and as conferring a benefit. A remedy may be available if the subsidy is directed not to the general public but, rather, specifically to particular enterprises or industries.[52] The *SCM Agreement* contains requirements for the imposition of countervailing duties or the use of WTO dispute settlement procedures, including injury to competing producers or other adverse effects.[53] In addition, the *SCM Agreement* prohibits export subsidies and subsidies that are contingent on the use of domestic over imported goods.[54]

There are quite a few hurdles to overcome before a renewable energy measure would be subject to a remedy. First, the measure must be a subsidy. If there is no benefit, or no government support or financial contribution of the sort described in Article 1 of the *SCM Agreement*, then the measure is not a subsidy.[55] Even if it is a subsidy, it must be a prohibited subsidy[56] or it must meet further requirements, including specificity[57] and adverse effects.

The subsidies issue was analyzed extensively by the Appellate Body in *Canada – Renewable Energy*. It was argued that payments under the Ontario feed-in tariff program constituted prohibited subsidies contingent on the use of domestic over imported goods, contrary to Article 3.1(b) of the *SCM Agreement*. The crucial question was whether the complainants had demonstrated that the feed-in tariff program provided a benefit to domestic producers of wind and solar energy, within the definition of a subsidy. Although the

---

addressed in this article. See Paolo D Farah and Elena Cima, "Energy Trade and the WTO: Implications for Renewable Energy and the OPEC Cartel" (2013) 16(3) J Int'l Econ L 707 at 716.

[52] *SCM Agreement, supra* note 19, arts 1-2, 8.1.

[53] *Ibid*, arts 5-7, 15.

[54] *Ibid*, art 3.

[55] For analysis, see Robert Howse, "Climate Mitigation Subsidies and the WTO Legal Framework: A Policy Analysis" (May 2010), International Institute for Sustainable Development, online: <http://www.iisd.org> at 8-16; Howse and REIL Project, *supra* note 34 at 510-14.

[56] Prohibited subsidies are presumed to be specific. *SCM Agreement, supra* note 19, art 2.3.

[57] For a discussion of whether climate change subsidies could be specific, see Craig Forcese, "The Kyoto Rift: Trade Law Implications of Canada's Kyoto Implementation Strategy in an Era of Canadian-US Environmental Divergence" in Kevin Kennedy, ed, *The First Decade of NAFTA: The Future of Free Trade in North America* (Ardsley, NY: Transnational, 2004) 393 at 402-8.

Appellate Body determined that the complainants had presented adequate information, the panel had improperly defined the market for comparison, and there were insufficient factual findings to permit the Appellate Body to complete the analysis. In the result, there was no determination of a breach of Article 3.1(b) of the *SCM Agreement.* Contrary to the panel, the Appellate Body decided that the appropriate market for comparison was limited to solar and wind energy.[58] The Appellate Body acknowledged that the definition of a subsidy does not leave room for "legitimate policy considerations"[59] — that is, legitimate objectives — but still treated renewable energy sources separately, as this was crucial for the long-term "viability and sustainability" of the electricity market.[60] Government intervention in electricity markets ensures that consumers have reliable, uninterrupted electricity service. According to the Appellate Body, government goals are not just immediate and short term, but can also include a long-term goal of "stable access ... increasingly from renewable sources."[61]

It was argued earlier in the discussion of *GATT* Article III that the definition of the comparator market in *Canada – Renewable Energy* uses a PPM and is at odds with the Appellate Body's competitiveness approach to the government procurement issue in the same dispute. The definition of the comparator market seems to be pushing towards a consideration of regulatory purpose similar to the "aim-and-effects" test that has been advocated in the past for the determination of like products. As renewable energy disputes make their way through the WTO dispute settlement system, a very significant question will be whether the ordinary subsidies rules apply against climate change measures[62] or whether some exemptions can be found. There is no general exemption clause in the *SCM Agreement.* Members might try to use *GATT* Article XX exemptions in defence of a claim, since the *SCM Agreement* is an elaboration of *GATT* Articles XVI and VI.[63] It is true, however, that

---

[58] *Canada – Renewable Energy, supra* note 3 at para 5.178.

[59] *Ibid* at para 5.185.

[60] *Ibid* at para 5.186.

[61] *Ibid* at para 5.187.

[62] See generally Tracey Epps and Andrew Green, *Reconciling Trade and Climate: How the WTO Can Help Address Climate Change* (Cheltenham, UK: Edward Elgar, 2010) at 103-21.

[63] For discussion, see Howse, *supra* note 55 at 17-19; Bradly J Condon, "Climate Change and Unresolved Issues in WTO Law" (2009) 12(4) J Int'l Econ L 895 at

the provisions of the *SCM Agreement* are much more detailed than the related *GATT* articles, and, unfortunately, the *SCM Agreement* does not have a helpful preamble like the preamble to the *TBT Agreement*. Any defence would likely refer to the objective of sustainable development in the preamble to the *WTO Agreement* and the general background of the *UN Framework Convention on Climate Change (UNFCCC)*, approaches that are addressed later in this article.[64]

The *SCM Agreement* originally contained a list of non-actionable subsidies that would not be subject to a remedy. These subsidies were for research, regional development, and adaptation to new environmental requirements.[65] The regional development subsidy in Country A's electricity measure and the adaptation grant in Country B's bio-fuel measure, outlined earlier, might both have qualified as non-actionable based on this list. However, the *SCM Agreement*'s list of non-actionable subsidies was temporary and has been allowed to lapse. Not all countries have removed the list from their domestic legislation. In Canadian legislation, for example, these subsidies have remained non-actionable and will not be subject to countervailing duties.[66] Countries do not have to impose counter-vailing duties whenever permitted in the *SCM Agreement*. Individual countries are free to decide that they wish to exempt climate change subsidies from such duties and could also consider doing this pursu-ant to their obligations under the *UNFCCC*.[67] In summary, there is

---

903-4; Luca Rubini, "Ain't Wastin' Time No More: Subsidies for Renewable Energy, the SCM Agreement, Policy Space and Law Reform" (2012) 15(2) J Int'l Econ L 525 at 559-70; Aaron Cosbey and Petros C Mavroidis, "A Turquoise Mess: Green Subsidies, Blue Industrial Policy and Renewable Energy: The Case for Redrafting the Subsidies Agreement of the WTO" (2014) 17(1) J Int'l Econ L 11; Rajib Pal, "Has the Appellate Body's Decision in *Canada – Renewable Energy / Canada – Feed-In Tariff Program* Opened the Door for Production Subsidies?" (2014) 17(1) J Int'l Econ L 125; Sherzod Shadikhodjaev, "First WTO Judicial Review of Climate Change Subsidy Issues" (2013) 107(4) Am J Int'l L 864. Farah and Cima, *supra* note 51 at 727, argue that the *SCM Agreement* is *lex specialis* and that the *GATT* provisions continue to apply as *lex generalis*.

[64] *WTO Agreement, supra* note 2; *United Nations Framework Convention on Climate Change*, 1771 UNTS 107 (in force 21 March 1994) [*UNFCCC*].

[65] *SCM Agreement, supra* note 19, art 8.

[66] *Special Import Measures Act*, RSC 1985, c S-15, s 30.4(3).

[67] Remedies within the *SCM Agreement, supra* note 19, arts 4, 7, 9, would theoreti-cally remain open.

some confusion over the application of the *SCM Agreement* to renewable energy, an area in which governments make significant use of subsidies. In particular, there is a need to resolve the question of whether exemptions for legitimate objectives are available.

DEFENCES IN WTO LAW, *GATT* ARTICLE XX

Much of WTO law includes environmental protection as an integral part of the trade analysis. For issues relating to renewable energy and trade, there has been some progress in recent WTO disputes, although the treatment of PPMs remains unresolved. The threat of a national treatment obligation under Article 2.1 of the *TBT Agreement* that would be immune from exemptions has been removed. As seen earlier, the *TBT Agreement* will be read subject to the sixth recital of its preamble, which mentions environmental protection. Although interpretation of *GATT* provisions will benefit from this new thinking, its MFN and national treatment obligations will still be judged in the context of particular measures. There could be a finding of breach of *GATT* Articles I or III or also of *GATT* Article II on border adjustments. For such *GATT* violations, analysis would then turn to the exemption clause — Article XX.

The most relevant parts of *GATT* Article XX are as follows:

Subject to the requirement that such measures are not applied in a manner which would constitute a means of arbitrary or unjustifiable discrimination between countries where the same conditions prevail, or a disguised restriction on international trade, nothing in this Agreement shall be construed to prevent the adoption or enforcement by any Member of measures: ...

   (b) necessary to protect human, animal or plant life or health; ...

   (g) relating to the conservation of exhaustible natural resources if such measures are made effective in conjunction with restrictions on domestic production or consumption;

The exemptions of Article XX protect measures that would otherwise breach another GATT provision. Even if a measure fails to provide MFN or national treatment, it can still be justified so long as the discrimination is not arbitrary or unjustifiable and so long as the measure is not a disguised restriction on international trade.

Arguments in defence of climate change and renewable energy measures are likely to invoke Article XX(g). In *Brazil – Measures Affecting Imports of Retreaded Tyres*, the Appellate Body mentioned that Article XX(b) on the protection of health could also be used to justify climate change measures.[68]

The defence of a renewable energy measure under Article XX could also invoke the objective of sustainable development in the preamble to the *WTO Agreement.*[69] As well, on a more basic level, a climate change measure cannot be understood properly as simply the isolated expression of domestic public policy. It is, rather, a topic of major global concern on which there are significant ongoing negotiations pursuant to the *UNFCCC,* a treaty regime that has more member countries than the WTO.[70] Article 3 of the *UNFCCC* lists certain fundamental principles, including:

1. The Parties should protect the climate system for the benefit of present and future generations of humankind, on the basis of equity and in accordance with their common but differentiated responsibilities and respective capabilities. Accordingly, the developed country Parties should take the lead in combating climate change and the adverse effects thereof ...

5. The Parties should cooperate to promote a supportive and open international economic system that would lead to sustainable economic growth and development in all Parties, particularly developing country parties, thus enabling them better to address the problems of climate change. Measures taken to combat climate change, including unilateral ones, should not constitute a means of arbitrary or unjustifiable discrimination or a disguised restriction on international trade.

The initial GHG reduction commitments of certain developed countries for the period 2008–12 were set out in the *Kyoto Protocol*

---

68 *Brazil – Measures Affecting Imports of Retreaded Tyres,* Doc WT/DS332/AB/R, Appellate Body Report (17 December 2007) at para 151. See Condon, *supra* note 63 at 914.

69 "*Recognizing* that their relations in the field of trade and economic endeavour should be conducted with a view to ... expanding the production of and trade in goods and services, while allowing for the optimal use of the world's resources in accordance with the objective of sustainable development, seeking both to protect and preserve the environment and to enhance the means for doing so in a manner consistent their respective needs and concerns at different levels of economic development." *WTO Agreement, supra* note 2, preamble, para 1.

70 The *UNFCCC, supra* note 64, currently has 196 parties. For more information, see <http://unfccc.int>.

to the *UNFCCC*.[71] Developing countries were not subject to these reduction commitments, in light of the principle of common but differentiated responsibilities and respective capabilities (CBDR) acknowledged in Article 3(1) of the *UNFCCC*. At a meeting of the Conference of the Parties in Cancun in 2010, developing countries agreed to take nationally appropriate mitigation actions, with the support of enhanced financial, technological, and capacity-building resources provided by developed countries.[72] A WTO member defending a climate change measure under *GATT* Article XX is quite likely to argue that the measure is part of its commitment to mitigate GHG emissions under the *UNFCCC* and (as applicable) the *Kyoto Protocol*. An interpretation that failed to take these global developments into account could hardly be said to reflect the objective of sustainable development.

GATT Article XX is available should justification be needed for any measures found in breach of other provisions of *GATT*. Under the introductory paragraph of Article XX, measures that appear to lack even-handedness, or that discriminate in favour of domestic producers or among various countries of export, will be subject to particular scrutiny. It will be noted that Article 3.5 of the *UNFCCC* adopts the language of *GATT* Article XX, prohibiting arbitrary or unjustifiable discrimination and disguised restrictions on international trade. For any measures that reach this stage of analysis, there is some question as to how the *UNFCCC* would affect the interpretation of *GATT* Article XX. May — or must — the measure

---

[71] *Kyoto Protocol to the United Nations Framework Convention on Climate Change*, 37 ILM 22 (1998) (in force 16 February 2005) [*Kyoto Protocol*]. The second commitment period runs from 2013 to 2020. *Report of the Conference of the Parties Serving as the Meeting of the Parties to the Kyoto Protocol on Its Eighth Session, held in Doha from 26 November to 8 December 2012*, Doc FCCC/KP/CMP/2012/13/Add.1, Decision 1/CMP.8 (2012).

[72] *Report of the Conference of the Parties on Its Sixteenth Session Held in Cancun from 29 November to 10 December 2010*, Doc FCCC/CP/2010/7/Add.1, Decision 1/CP.16 (2010) at paras 48-52 (affirming on this point the earlier Copenhagen Agreement that was noted but not adopted by the Conference of the Parties in 2009). *Report of the Conference of the Parties on Its Fifteenth Session, Held in Copenhagen from 7 to 19 December 2009*, Doc FCCC/CP/2009/11/Add.1, Decision 2/CP.15 (2009). At the meeting in Durban in 2011, the Conference of the Parties decided to negotiate a new "protocol, another legal instrument or an agreed outcome with legal force under the Convention" by 2015, to take effect in 2020. *Report of the Conference of the Parties on Its Seventeenth Session Held in Durban from 28 November to 11 December 2011*, Doc FCCC/CP/2011/9/Add.1, Decision 1/CP.17 (2011) at para 2.

be graduated so as to reflect the GHG mitigation commitments of various countries?[73] If the imports are from a country that has met all of its *UNFCCC* commitments, is there a legitimate basis for imposing an additional burden? May — or must — the measure discriminate in favour of imports from developing countries?[74] Fabio Morosini argues that the reference to discrimination "between countries where the same conditions prevail" in the introductory paragraph of *GATT* Article XX operates like CBDR within the WTO, requiring that the circumstances of developing countries be taken into account in the assessment of conditions.[75]

The question is presented directly for any border adjustments that do not comply with *GATT* Article II. It is clear that in any *GATT* Article XX analysis of such border adjustments a desire by domestic producers to avoid international competition will not be a good defence. If the reason for the adjustment is economic protectionism, it will not qualify as a measure about conservation or health.[76] Aspects of a domestic carbon tax that shield producers from international competition, such as free allowances in an emission-trading system as in Country C's hypothetical carbon tax example provided earlier, would have to be discounted in the calculation of any adjustment.[77] For border adjustments, a goal of controlling carbon leakage

---

[73] There would likely be a strong argument that any tax or other burden would have to involve a calibrated measure. See *US – Tuna II, supra* note 5 at para 297.

[74] See Michael Hertel, "Climate-Change-Related Trade Measures and Article XX: Defining Discrimination in Light of the Principle of Common but Differentiated Responsibilities" (2011) 45(3) J World Trade 653 at 677: "The crux of CBDR is that discrimination results where countries in which different conditions prevail are treated the same ... This approach would require unilateral trade measures to be 'graded' in accordance with countries' mitigation responsibilities ... to be a permissible use of coercion and compliant with the *chapeau*."

[75] Fabio Morosini, "Trade and Climate Change: Unveiling the Principle of Common but Differentiated Responsibilities from the WTO Agreements" (2010) 42 Geo Wash Int'l L Rev 713.

[76] Julia O'Brien, "The Equity of Levelling the Playing Field in the Climate Change Context" (2009) 43(5) J World Trade 1093 at 1110. As O'Brien argues, the same issue can affect the interpretation of GATT Article III as applied to the border adjustment: "Unless an exporting country could be expected to reduce its carbon emissions to an equal degree as the importing country, a carbon tax that charged imported goods the equivalent of what they would have had to pay if they had been produced domestically would amount to placing an inequitable tax burden on producers in the exporting country and may thus be inconsistent with the second sentence of Article III(2)." *Ibid* at 1108-9.

[77] It has been argued that such discounting would also be required for adjustments to be acceptable under Article II. See Pauwelyn, *supra* note 44 at 21-22; McLure,

in order to make a climate change measure effective stands a some-what better chance of success, but it may not be persuasive.[78]

In summary, *GATT* Article XX will protect some renewable energy measures if needed. A link to sustainable development and the international climate change negotiations will bolster the *bona fides* of a defence. The link will similarly be relevant for interpretation of legitimate objectives under the *TBT Agreement*, which mention the environment specifically, in language that is close to but differs somewhat from that of *GATT* Article XX. It is hard to see how these provisions could be interpreted in isolation from climate change negotiations and commitments. For border tax adjustments to be exempted under *GATT* Article XX, they would need to be based on something other than competitiveness. The principle of CBDR in the *UNFCCC* could be problematic for such adjustments. Whatever conclusions are reached on the mandates of the WTO panels and the Appellate Body (a question to be addressed later in this article), integration of substantive climate law is required for a full analysis of a *GATT* Article XX defence.

Interpreting against Fragmentation

Sustainable Development

The first recital of the preamble of the *WTO Agreement* states that the parties aim to increase standards of living and production of goods and services while

allowing for the optimal use of the world's resources in accordance with the objective of sustainable development, seeking both to protect and preserve the environment and to enhance the means for doing so in a manner consistent with their respective needs and concerns at different levels of economic development.[79]

Géraud de Lassus Saint-Geniès has identified two paradigms of sustainable development.[80] The first, which would cover the *WTO*

---

supra note 48 at 285-87. In addition, free allowances for exporters could be seen as illegal export subsidies. Maruyama, *supra* note 47.

[78] Vanden Brink, *supra* note 49.

[79] *WTO Agreement, supra* note 2, preamble.

[80] Géraud de Lassus Saint-Geniès, "Les piliers économique et environnemental du développement durable: conciliation ou soutien mutuel? L'éclairage apporté

Agreement recital, sees trade and environmental protection as distinct from one another and requiring conciliation or balancing. The second is the paradigm of integration, in which elements are not in conflict but, rather, are mutually supportive, so that promotion of one is inherently promotion of the other. According to de Lassus Saint-Geniès, this second paradigm has gained increasing prominence since the mid-1990s. Paragraph 31 of the Doha Declaration of 2001, for example, establishes negotiations on the relationship between WTO rules and multilateral environmental agreements "with a view to enhancing the mutual supportiveness of trade and environment."[81]

While the paradigm of mutual supportiveness appears frequently in recent treaties and negotiated texts, de Lassus Saint-Geniès argues that the International Court of Justice (ICJ) returned to the conciliation paradigm in *Pulp Mills on the River Uruguay (Argentina v Uruguay)*, with an emphasis on procedural duties such as consultation and negotiation.[82] Both paradigms coexist within the fluid, broad concept of sustainable development, which includes CBDR,[83] also reflected in the *WTO Agreement*'s preambular recognition of the parties' "respective needs and concerns at different levels of development."[84] Sustainable development therefore provides an interpretive link between WTO law and the *UNFCCC*.

As the title of his article indicates, de Lassus Saint-Geniès addresses the economic and environmental pillars of sustainable development, but not social development, which is often considered a third pillar.[85]

---

par la Cour internationale de Justice dans l'*Affaire des Usines de pâte à papier sur le fleuve Uruguay (Argentine c Uruguay)*" (2010) 48 Can YB Int'l L 151.

81 *WTO Ministerial Declaration*, Doc WT/MIN(01)/DEC/1 (20 November 2001) at para 31.

82 *Pulp Mills on the River Uruguay (Argentina v Uruguay)*, Judgment, [2010] ICJ Rep 14, reflecting the decision in *Case Concerning the Gabčíkovo-Nagymaros Project (Hungary v Slovakia)*, [1997] ICJ Rep 78.

83 See Philippe Sands, *Principles of International Environmental Law*, 2nd edition (Cambridge: Cambridge University Press, 2003) at 148.

84 *WTO Agreement*, *supra* note 2, preamble.

85 *Johannesburg Declaration on Sustainable Development*, Annex to Resolution 1, *Report of the World Summit on Sustainable Development*, UN Doc A/CONF.199/20 (26 August–4 September 2002) at para 5. A possible fourth pillar is cultural protection. See Véronique Guèvremont, "La reconnaissance du pilier culturel du développement durable: vers un nouveau mode de diffusion des valeurs culturelles au sein de l'ordre juridique mondial" (2012) 50 Can YB Int'l L 163.

The first recital of the preamble to the *WTO Agreement* also emphasizes only the first two pillars. There may be an argument that a wider view of sustainable development could be found in general public international law. The extra premium for regional development in Country A's hypothetical electricity measure, for example, could raise this issue.

The recognition of sustainable development as an objective of the WTO should guide teleological interpretation pursuant to Article 31(1) of the *Vienna Convention on the Law of Treaties* (*VCLT*).[86] This approach requires that treaties be interpreted in light of their object and purpose. Teleological interpretation supports the suggestions made earlier that less favourable treatment, border adjustments,[87] and the *GATT* Article XX exemption clause[88] should be interpreted in a way that takes account of the *UNFCCC*.

Interpretation that follows the ordinary meaning of terms pursuant to the same Article 31(1) of the *VCLT* would serve as an additional basis for use of the principle of mutual supportiveness in the second paradigm of sustainable development identified by de Lassus Saint-Geniès. This approach could apply widely, as more and more legal instruments adopt the language of mutual supportiveness. The principle of mutual supportiveness requires a harmonious reading of texts, assuming complementarity and absence of conflict. Ordinary meaning, thus, calls for wide, non-hierarchical interpretation of any texts that are linked by mutual supportiveness.

Article 31(3)(c) of the *VCLT* provides a further mechanism for an interpretive link. Article 3(2) of the WTO's *Understanding on Rules and Procedures Governing the Settlement of Disputes* (*DSU*) confirms that the customary rules of interpretation in public international law apply in the WTO system.[89] There is general agreement that those rules are expressed in the *VCLT*.[90] Article 31(3)(c) of the *VCLT* provides that interpretation is to take account of "any relevant

---

86 *Vienna Convention on the Law of Treaties*, 1155 UNTS 331, Can TS 1980 No 37 (in force 27 January 1980) [*VCLT*].

87 O'Brien, *supra* note 76.

88 Hertel, *supra* note 74.

89 *Understanding on Rules and Procedures Governing the Settlement of Disputes*, 1869 UNTS 401, 33 ILM 1226 (1994) (in force 1 January 1995) [*DSU*].

90 See *United States – Standards for Reformulated and Conventional Gasoline*, Doc WT/DS2/AB/R, Appellate Body Report (20 May 1996) at 16; *Japan – Taxes on Alcoholic Beverages*, Docs WT/DS8/AB/R, WT/DS10/AB/R, WT/DS11/AB/R, Appellate Body Report (1 November 1996) at 9-12.

rules of international law applicable in the relations between the parties." There has been strong criticism of the WTO Panel's view in *European Communities – Measures Affecting the Approval and Marketing of Biotech Products* that Article 31(3)(c) applies to external treaty rules only when there is completely common membership in the WTO agreement being interpreted and the external treaty.[91] An interpretive use of customary international law or general principles of law would not present this problem, but it has arisen concerning the use of an external treaty.

The 2006 report to the International Law Commission (ILC) on the fragmentation of international law rejects the interpretation in the *EC – Biotech* decision.[92] The ILC study group noted that a requirement of identical membership would tend to isolate major multilateral agreements from each other, given that their wider membership would create greater chances of slight differences in

---

[91] *European Communities – Measures Affecting the Approval and Marketing of Biotech Products*, Doc WT/DS291-293/R, Report of the Panel (21 November 2006) at para 7.68 [*EC – Biotech*]. Note that not all parties in the case were members of the treaties in question. See Epps and Green, *supra* note 62 at 226; Panagiotis Delimatsis, "The Fragmentation of International Trade Law" (2011) 45(1) J World Trade 87, discussing (at 114) the Appellate Body's view in *European Communities – Customs Classification of Frozen Boneless Chicken Cuts* that the Harmonized System (HS) constitutes context for interpretation of the WTO agreements under Article 31(2)(a) of the *VCLT* due to a consensus among *GATT* contracting parties to use the HS as a basis for their WTO tariff schedules, despite the fact that not all members are parties to the HS. *European Communities – Customs Classification of Frozen Boneless Chicken Cuts*, Docs WT/DS269/AB/R and WT/DS286/AB/R, Appellate Body Report (27 September 2005) at para 199; *International Convention on the Harmonized Commodity Description and Coding System*, with Protocol of Amendment,1503 UNTS 167, Can TS 1988 No 38 (in force 1 January 1988) [*HS*]. Prior to the *EC – Biotech* decision, Joost Pauwelyn canvassed arguments both for and against a requirement of common membership for purposes of application of Article 31(3)(c) of the *VCLT*. Joost Pauwelyn, *Conflict of Norms in Public International Law: How WTO Law Relates to Other Rules of International Law* (Cambridge, MA: Cambridge University Press, 2003) at 253-63. The opposing positions were argued by the European Union and the United States in *European Communities and Certain Member States – Measures Affecting Trade in Large Civil Aircraft*. The Appellate Body rejected the view of *EC–Biotech*, but did not completely resolve the issue. *European Communities and Certain Member States – Measures Affecting Trade in Large Civil Aircraft*, Doc WT/DS316/AB/R (1 June 2011) at paras 80-82, 310-13, 839-55.

[92] International Law Commission (ILC), *Fragmentation of International Law: Difficulties Arising from the Diversification and Expansion of International Law*, Report of the Study Group of the International Law Commission (finalized by Martti Koskenniemi), UN Doc A/CN.4/L.682 (13 April 2006) at para 450 [*ILC Study Group Report*].

their respective membership.[93] The study group urged the application of Article 31(3)(c) of the *VCLT* whenever all parties to a given dispute are also parties to relevant treaties, in furtherance of a principle of systemic integration that would ensure that treaty interpretation takes account of the broader international legal framework.[94]

The strength of this developing principle of systemic integration remains to be seen. Some commentators have noted that the original discussion over Article 31(3)(c) of the *VCLT* related mainly to making the reference to external law dynamic, rather than frozen, as of the time of the conclusion of the treaty.[95] However, the ILC study group views Article 31(3)(c) as supporting the general public interest in a coherent international legal system for the "common good of human kind."[96] It seems clear at least that the principle of systemic integration would apply only if treaties can be read together. It does not presume that all conflicts would disappear or that other rules of treaty interpretation would be displaced.[97]

In this sense, the principle of systemic integration appears less ambitious than the principle of mutual supportiveness within sustainable development. If treaties are clearly intended to be mutually supportive and non-hierarchical, there may be additional reluctance to move to rules of priority, although the ILC study group considers that priority rules would nevertheless be present in the background.[98] De Lassus Saint-Geniès suggests that the principle of mutual supportiveness facilitates the development of consensus in treaty negotiations, but it is difficult to apply in dispute settlement.[99]

---

[93] *Ibid* at para 470.

[94] *Ibid* at para 472.

[95] Campbell McLachlan, "The Principle of Systemic Integration and Article 31(3)(c) of the Vienna Convention" (2005) 54 ICLQ 279 at 291-93; Vassilis P Tzevelekos, "The Use of Article 31(3)(c) of the *VCLT* in the Case Law of the ECtHR: An Effective Anti-Fragmentation Tool or a Selective Loophole for the Reinforcement of Human Rights Teleology? Between Evolution and Systemic Integration" (2009-10) 31 Mich J Int'l L 621 at 634. See further Benn McGrady, "Fragmentation of International Law or 'Systemic Integration' of Treaty Regimes: *EC – Biotech Products* and the Proper Interpretation of Article 31(3)(c) of the Vienna Convention on the Law of Treaties" (2008) 42(4) J World Trade 589 at 597.

[96] *ILC Study Group Report, supra* note 92 at paras 479-80.

[97] McGrady, *supra* note 95 at 607-8.

[98] *ILC Study Group Report, supra* note 92 at paras 277, 412.

[99] de Lassus Saint-Geniès, *supra* note 80 at 173-75.

In a contested matter, a less onerous principle of systemic integration may be more suitable.

Article 31(3)(c) of the *VCLT* directs interpreters to "take account of" other relevant rules that apply in the relations between parties. The direction does not dictate what particular effect the other rules must have. In past decisions, the Appellate Body has occasionally referred to non-WTO treaties without checking for common membership,[100] using them as evidence of ordinary meaning or as a sort of law dictionary.[101] These external references will have some effect on the decision because they become part of the reasoning, but the force of the reference to external rules of law is not set out in Article 31(3)(c).

In summary, sustainable development is an objective of the WTO and should be part of the teleological interpretation of WTO law. In addition, to the extent that aspects of sustainable development reflect customary international law or general principles of law, they can be taken into account in the interpretive process pursuant to Article 31(3)(c) of the VCLT. The same article will also support an interpretive link to treaties under the *UNFCCC*, reflecting interpretation that promotes coherence and systemic integration.

THE WTO WITHIN PUBLIC INTERNATIONAL LAW

In the preceding section, it was noted that non-WTO treaties applicable among the parties to a WTO dispute can be used to guide interpretation of WTO instruments pursuant to Article 31(3)(c) of the VCLT. The general availability of public international law in the WTO dispute settlement system is addressed in this section, along with the possibility that an *UNFCCC* treaty might have additional force if it applies independently, instead of simply being used as an aid to interpretation. Should there be something more detailed that could come from such a treaty, either now or in the future — for example, a range of permissible or even compulsory remedies or some specific defence to a trade claim — there would be an

---

[100] Benn McGrady, "Necessity Exceptions in WTO Law: Retreaded Tyres, Regulatory Purpose and Cumulative Regulatory Measures" (2009) 12(1) J Int'l Econ L 153 at 170-71, referring to *United States – Tax Treatment for "Foreign Sales Corporations" – Recourse to Article 21.5 of the DSU by the EC*, Doc WT/DS108/AB/RW, Appellate Body Report (20 January 2002), and *United States – Import Prohibition of Certain Shrimp and Shrimp Products*, Doc WT/DS58/AB/R, Appellate Body Report (6 November 1998).

[101] See McLachlan, *supra* note 95 at 315; Pauwelyn, *supra* note 91 at 262.

argument for giving such provisions independent application in WTO disputes. For example, what if a future climate agreement allowed for adaptation subsidies that cover the 20 percent grants in Country B's hypothetical bio-fuel measure?[102] Or what if future climate negotiators decided to promote the use of carbon taxes and negotiated an agreement specifically permitting border tax adjustments that take no account of domestic-free allowances, as in the hypothetical carbon tax measure in Country C?

A leading contribution to the debate on the law applicable in WTO dispute settlement procedures was Joost Pauwelyn's groundbreaking 2003 book *Conflict of Norms in Public International: How WTO Law Relates to Other Rules of International Law.*[103] Pauwelyn's thorough scholarship marked a turning point in thinking about the relationship between trade and other areas of international law. In *Conflict of Norms,* Pauwelyn starts from the observation that WTO law exists within the general system of public international law. While standing to bring a claim before the dispute settlement mechanism must be based in one of the WTO agreements,[104] nothing prevents respondent countries from defending themselves on the basis of non-trade law, in his view. Under Articles 7.1 and 11 of the *DSU*, the mandate of the panels is to examine the dispute, assessing the applicability of, and conformity with, the covered WTO agreements and to "make such other findings as will assist the Dispute Settlement Body" to make recommendations and rulings. Unless parties have contracted out of the rest of public international law, Pauwelyn maintains, these "other findings" could relate to defences based on non-WTO international law.[105]

In the academic commentary on this issue, one potential limit on this wide view of the applicability of general international law relates

---

[102] For the suggestion that the non-actionable category of subsidies in the *SCM Agreement, supra* note 19, should be revived for climate change measures, see Debra P Steger, "The Subsidies and Countervailing Measures Agreement: Ahead of Its Time or Time for Reform?" (2010) 44(4) J World Trade 779 at 795.

[103] Pauwelyn, *supra* note 91. A preview of the thesis was published in 2001. Joost Pauwelyn, "The Role of Public International Law in the WTO: How Far Can We Go?" (2001) 95 Am J Int'l L 535.

[104] Pauwelyn, *supra* note 91 at 81-86. Article 1.1 of the *DSU, supra* note 89, confirms that the dispute settlement mechanism applies to disputes brought pursuant to the WTO agreements.

[105] Pauwelyn, *supra* note 103 at 559-65. The ILC study group agrees with this distinction between jurisdiction and applicable law. *ILC Study Group Report, supra* note 92 at para 45.

to Articles 3.2 and 19.2 of the *DSU*, which stipulate that rulings under the dispute settlement mechanism "cannot add to or diminish the rights and obligations provided in the covered agreements." Lorand Bartels, who is prepared to take a wide approach to applicable law, nevertheless concludes from these provisions that non-WTO law can never have priority over the WTO-covered agreements.[106] In a different view, others, relying in part on Article 31(3)(c) of the *VCLT* argue that the meaning of WTO rights and obligations cannot be established until they are properly interpreted and if that interpretation requires taking account of non-WTO law, then such interpretation neither adds to nor diminishes WTO rights and obligations.[107]

In a book review of *Conflict of Norms,* Joel Trachtman takes issue with the applicability of non-WTO law in the dispute settlement mechanism. He argues that international tribunals are not like courts of general jurisdiction and that "states are not held under international law to have accepted mandatory jurisdiction of international tribunals to apply law without their consent."[108] He also disagrees with a further argument by Pauwelyn that WTO members are able to modify their WTO obligations bilaterally by entering into a subsequent conflicting treaty covering some but not all WTO members. Trachtman maintains that waivers and amendments pursuant to Articles IX and X of the *WTO Agreement* provide the only means of modifying WTO obligations with effect before WTO panels and the Appellate Body.[109]

A possible response to the first of Trachtman's arguments relates back to the original position that WTO law exists within general public international law.[110] When states submit matters for decision by an international tribunal under public international law, they

---

[106] Lorand Bartels, "Applicable Law in WTO Dispute Settlement Proceedings" (2001) 35(3) J World Trade 499.

[107] Delimatsis, *supra* note 91; O'Brien, *supra* note 76; Hertel, *supra* note 74; Andrew D Mitchell, *Legal Principles in WTO Disputes* (Cambridge: Cambridge University Press, 2008) at 96. The Appellate Body in *Chile – Taxes on Alcoholic Beverages* considered Articles 3.2 and 19.2 of the *DSU*, holding that proper interpretation of WTO provisions would neither add to nor diminish rights and obligations. *Chile – Taxes on Alcoholic Beverages,* Docs WT/DS87/AB/R and WT/DS110/AB/R, Appellate Body Report (12 January 2000) at para 79.

[108] Joel Trachtman, 'Book Review of *Conflict of Norms in Public International Law* by Joost Pauwelyn' (2004) 98 Am J Int'l L 855 at 858.

[109] *Ibid* at 858-59.

[110] Pauwelyn, *supra* note 91 at 73.

cannot be expected to delineate all of the areas of law that might be relevant, at the risk of having a claim fail because they forgot to mention some fundamental doctrine such as territorial sovereignty or state recognition. A WTO dispute is submitted pursuant to the *DSU* as it is interpreted. The response would thus maintain that general public international law applies unless the parties have effectively contracted out of it.

The issue concerning modification is more complex. Pauwelyn's thesis on modification starts with the distinction between reciprocal treaties and integral treaties. Reciprocal treaties are bilateral or involve a grouping of bilateral relations, while integral treaties establish collective rights and obligations among their members.[111] The distinction is reflected in Article 41 of the *VCLT*, which deals with modification of multilateral treaties among some but not all of the parties. Such modification is possible if it "does not affect the enjoyment by the other parties of their rights under the treaty or the performance of their obligations" and "does not relate to a provision, derogation from which is incompatible with the effective execution of the object and purpose of the treaty as a whole."[112] If either of these circumstances applies, then the treaty is integral and cannot be partially modified in this manner. According to Pauwelyn, the WTO agreements are in the reciprocal category and thus can be modified by a subset of WTO members. Not all academic commentators agree with this classification. Chios Carmody notes the expectation interests created through WTO rules and the interaction between producers and consumers worldwide and concludes that WTO obligations are collective rather than bilateral.[113] Trachtman's view is that Articles IX and X of the *WTO Agreement* set out an exclusive system for modification of WTO rights and obligations and that WTO members have contracted out of Article 41 of the *VCLT*.[114]

111 *Ibid* at 52-56.

112 *VCLT, supra* note 86, art 41(1)(b)(i)-(ii). Suspension of a multilateral treaty by a subset of the parties is subject to the same conditions, pursuant to Article 58 of the *VCLT*.

113 Chios Carmody, "WTO Obligations As Collective" (2006) 17(2) Eur J Int'l L 419.

114 See further Gabrielle Marceau, "Conflicts of Norms and Conflicts of Jurisdictions: The Relationship between the WTO Agreement and MEAs and Other Treaties" (2001) 35(6) J World Trade 1081 at 1104-5. If all parties to the subsequent agreement are content with its application, there will be no disputes filed among

The issue is significant for any practical consequences that flow from the distinction between using an external treaty to assist with interpretation of WTO agreements and applying this external treaty independently. The external treaty may be quite detailed. It may be wider than WTO law.[115] It may be in irresolvable conflict with the WTO provision. Generous interpretation of the rules applying to an adaptation subsidy, as in Country B's hypothetical bio-fuel measure, might be possible, for example, in light of the provisions of an external treaty. It would be much more difficult to take a similarly generous view of a border adjustment that gives trade protectionism to domestic producers, such as in Country C's hypothetical carbon tax measure.

If a subsequent climate treaty were to expressly permit border adjustments that conflict with WTO obligations, it might operate as a modification of these obligations. Even if it is concluded that official modification is not possible (because WTO obligations are collective) or not effective (unless it is done under Articles IX and X of the *WTO Agreement*), the legal arguments would be similar, if we accept that the WTO agreements are not outside the realm of public international law altogether. The external treaty would still be there and could be part of the applicable law. The real challenge is whether the panels and Appellate Body can make a decision based on an external treaty rather than on a WTO provision. This is a difficult proposition to defend, as the WTO dispute settlement mechanism was not put in place in order to enforce non-WTO treaties. The panels and the Appellate Body might decline jurisdiction or decide that the complainant has not proved its case.[116] They might conclude that the WTO provisions do not set out the relevant obligation when properly interpreted. In these circumstances, the ICJ would be a more effective forum for dispute resolution.

It could be that at the end of the analysis we circle back to a position not far from that of the ILC study group, emphasizing the

---

them, of course. Problems would arise if differing interpretations develop or if outside parties decide to bring complaints.

[115] Custom may, of course, be wider as well. In the context of the security exception under *GATT* Article XXI, see Maureen Irish, "Trade, Border Security, and Development" in Yong-Shik Lee et al, eds, *Law and Development Perspective on International Trade Law* (Cambridge, MA: Cambridge University Press, 2011) 81.

[116] See further Joost Pauwelyn, "How to Win a World Trade Organization Dispute Based on Non-World Trade Organization Law: Questions of Jurisdiction and Merits" (2003) 37(6) J World Trade 997.

importance of Article 31(3)(c) of the *VCLT*, the principle of systemic integration, and the need to read international obligations in a harmonious way. In this exercise, it seems to be agreed that law "applicable in the relations between the parties" for the purposes of the *VCLT* refers to public international law in general, not to whatever part of public international law is dealt with by a specialized tribunal. There might be an argument that the identification of applicable law before a particular tribunal affects the availability of an external provision as an aid to interpretation, but no one appears to be taking this position. Even those who argue that non-WTO law is not applicable in the WTO dispute settlement mechanism do not object to external law being used as an aid to interpretation pursuant to Article 31(3)(c).[117] The focus remains on interconnection, coherence, and the need for satisfactory approaches to treaty interpretation.

A further major contribution of Pauwelyn's *Conflict of Norms* is his analysis of what constitutes a conflict in interpreting public international law. International lawyers accept that in case of a conflict, some legal obligations have peremptory status over others.[118] Absent such priority of one treaty provision over the other, there will be an attempt to resolve any conflict through interpretation. As part of the methodology, certain priority rules, such as *lex specialis* or *lex posterior*, may help to resolve the problem. Pauwelyn's analysis in *Conflict of Norms* expands what is meant by a conflict. The classic definition of a conflict, as expressed by Wilfred Jenks, is fairly narrow: "A conflict in the strict sense of direct incompatibility arises only where a party to the two treaties cannot simultaneously comply with its obligations under both treaties."[119] Pauwelyn expands this definition to include what Jenks refers to as a divergence, which occurs when a party taking advantage of the provisions of one treaty is thereby placed in breach of a second treaty.[120] Pauwelyn refers to this idea as one treaty permitting what the other prohibits. He agrees with Jenks that the right to do something could be as central to the object of one treaty as the prohibition in another.[121] The right to

---

117 Trachtman, *supra* note 108 at 857.

118 *VCLT, supra* note 86, arts 53, 64 (on peremptory norms); *ILC Study Group Report, supra* note 92 at paras 324-409.

119 C Wilfred Jenks, "The Conflict of Law-Making Treaties" (1953) 30 Brit YB Int'l L 401 at 426.

120 *Ibid.*

121 Pauwelyn, *supra* note 91 at 166-74.

take certain action in an environmental treaty, for example, could be equally central to that treaty as is a prohibition of that same action to a WTO agreement.[122] The narrow sense of conflict resolves the problem too easily and always in favour of the prohibition, which complies with both treaties. The relationship between the WTO agreements and non-WTO treaties is, of course, not always this simple. Pauwelyn's wide view of treaty conflict as inconsistency or incompatibility relating to the same subject matter[123] means that interpretive techniques of harmonious reading will have wide application.

Whether interpretation involves two treaties that are both considered applicable or simply the use of an external treaty as an interpretive aid under Article 31(3)(c) of the *VCLT*, a key step will be to find a meaning that reflects the two sources without giving priority to one over the other. It was argued earlier that the views advanced in this article regarding WTO obligations and exceptions are supported by teleological interpretation reflecting sustainable development. They should also be supported through integrated interpretation before any consideration of the priorities among treaties.

Should the integrated approach not resolve the problem and a conflict remain, the next step is to look to rules of priority. If no particular hierarchical priority attaches to one of the provisions, then the *lex specialis* principle applies. Under this principle, which is also used in domestic statutory interpretation, a particular or specific provision takes priority over a more general one.[124] Jenks

[122] *Ibid* at 187-88.

[123] *Ibid* at 168. The wide view of a conflict is now part of WTO jurisprudence. The Panel in *United States – Certain Measures Affecting Imports of Poultry from China* refers to both the strict view of conflict arising "where ... obligations are mutually exclusive in the sense that a Member cannot comply with both obligations at the same time" and the wider view "where a rule in one agreement prohibits what a rule in another agreement explicitly permits." *United States – Certain Measures Affecting Imports of Poultry from China*, Doc WT/DS392/R, Panel Report (25 October 2010) at para 7.63, n 240, citing for the first view *Turkey – Restrictions on Imports of Textile and Clothing Products*, Doc WT/DS34/R, Panel Report (adopted with the Appellate Body Report, 19 November 1999) at para 9.92, and for the second view *European Communities – Regime for the Importation, Sale and Distribution of Bananas*, Doc WT/DS27/R, Panel Report (adopted with Appellate Body Report25 September 1997) at para. 7.159. The Panel in *US – Poultry from China* decided that it was not dealing with a conflict but, rather, a question of the order in which it should address claims.

[124] *ILC Study Group Report, supra* note 92 at paras 36, 56-122.

quotes Hugo Grotius in explaining this preference for that "which is most specific and approaches most nearly to the subject in hand."[125] The ILC study group examines several applications of the principle in international decisions and notes the difficulty of determining what is specific and what is general, considering, in particular, specificity as to parties and as to subject matter. As the study group comments, specificity as to subject matter depends on context and regulatory purpose.[126] This description of *lex specialis* is very close to the "pith and substance" principle suggested by Jenks as a way of determining "which of two conflicting norms really deals with the essentials of the matter and must therefore be regarded as of primary authority."[127] If it were necessary to decide, a treaty interpreter would have to determine whether a particular measure at issue was essentially about trade or about climate change. In effect, use of the *lex specialis* principle is part of a full teleological interpretation of object and purpose pursuant to Article 31 of the *VCLT*.[128]

If the conflict cannot be otherwise resolved, then Article 30(3) of the *VCLT* adopts the *lex posterior* principle, giving priority to the later treaty. This principle is awkward when applied to major multilateral treaty systems such as the WTO and the *UNFCCC*. When parties have not given a clear indication of their intentions, it could be unsettling if interpretation of their obligations were to change depending on which treaty system had most recently convened a major negotiating conference. For the imaginary climate treaty suggested earlier, specifically permitting Country C's hypothetical

---

125 Jenks, *supra* note 119 at 446, quoting Hugo Grotius, *De Jure Belli et Pacis*, Book II, Cap VXI, s XXIX(1), translated by Francis W Kelsey and reprinted in James Brown Scott, ed, *The Classics of International Law,* volume 2 (Oxford: Clarendon Press, 1925) at 428. See also *ILC Study Group Report, supra* note 92 at para 59.

126 *Ibid* at para 118: "The example ... was that of maritime carriage of hazardous substances. Depending on what the interpreter sees as the relevant consideration, the case comes under one or another set of rules as *lex specialis*: is the point of the law to advance trade, flag or coastal State jurisdiction, or environmental protection? None [of] these perspectives enjoys intrinsic priority over the others. This is why, in a hard case, a justifiable decision would have to take all of these into account."

127 Jenks, *supra* note 119 at 450.

128 *Lex specialis* is not solely a priority rule, replacing one norm with another. It can operate to indicate the appropriate intensity of one norm in relation to another or to create partial carve-outs that leave more general provisions in place across a range of meanings. Legislative measures, after all, may have more than one purpose. As an interpretive technique, *lex specialis* can function as part of a general teleological approach. See further Marceau, *supra* note 114 at 1093.

border tax adjustments, *lex specialis* would be a more reliable reflection of the parties' intentions than *lex posterior*. Remedies would remain an issue, of course, should a panel or the Appellate Body conclude that the external treaty has priority over WTO agreements. In its report, the ILC study group recommended further study of multilateral treaties and specialized treaty regimes.[129]

As between the WTO and the *UNFCCC*, instances of irresolvable conflict will be uncommon. The more likely situation is that of opportunities for harmonious interpretation. Environmental policy is integrated into the WTO, not inconsistent with it. Treaty negotiators will attempt to avoid direct conflict situations. If problems arise, however, interpretive methodology must be adequate to the task. In summary, there is debate as to whether non-WTO treaties are part of the law applicable before WTO panels and the Appellate Body. This is the major issue posed by the ground-breaking scholarship of Pauwelyn. In addition, he proposes a wide notion of conflict that will require integrated interpretation in a range of instances. On this view, the identification of conflict is not done in a formal way that looks only to whether it is impossible to conform to both treaties. Pauwelyn's more substantive view reflects the object and purpose of the treaties in question. The argument made in this article is supported by this approach as well as by teleological interpretation. Multilateral treaty regimes should be interpreted in an integrated way, whether through identification of the applicable law or under Article 31(3)(c) of the *VCLT*.

CONCLUSIONS

There is much within existing WTO jurisprudence that can support environmental protection and help to resolve disputes over measures relating to renewable energy, especially if obligations and exemptions are interpreted in light of the objective of sustainable development. To ensure coherence, WTO provisions must be addressed within the broader international legal context, which includes the *UNFCCC* and treaties negotiated thereunder. It is impossible to ignore the modern proliferation of international treaties, regimes, and tribunals as governments grapple with the problems posed in our interconnected world. The growth of international tribunals raises important questions about decision making

---

[129] *ILC Study Group Report, supra* note 92 at para 493.

and doctrinal isolation.[130] Procedural and jurisdictional rules may resolve some frictions between tribunals,[131] but potential conflicts are likely to arise more and more frequently in circumstances involving only single tribunals, where there is no question of involvement by another forum.

Approaches to the interpretation of public international law should presume and support coherence, rather than accepting fragmentation that would leave significant questions unresolved. Governments negotiate multiple treaties with the expectation that all will be applicable at the same time and the objectives of all will be simultaneously advanced. Disputes over renewable energy are likely to highlight the importance of reflecting these expectations in the interpretation of WTO provisions.

Sommaire

Plusieurs litiges relatifs à l'énergie renouvelable sont en cours à l'Organisation mondiale du commerce (OMC). L'Organe d'appel a rendu sa première décision dans ce domaine, sur le tarif de rachat de l'électricité de la province de l'Ontario. Ces litiges soulèvent à nouveau la question de la relation entre le droit commercial international et la protection de l'environnement. Plusieurs tendances dans la jurisprudence récente de l'OMC devraient permettre de résoudre la plupart des difficultés qui se posent, bien que le problème crucial du traitement des méthodes de production et de transformation demeure obscur suite à la décision *Canada – Énergie renouvelable*. Des questions théoriques fondamentales sous-tendent ces débats. L'expansion récente du nombre de régimes et de tribunaux internationaux met en évidence l'importance des approches à l'interprétation du droit international public. Au fur et à mesure

---

[130] Tomer Broude, "Principles of Normative Integration and the Allocation of International Authority: The WTO, the Vienna Convention on the Law of Treaties, and the Rio Declaration" (2008-09) 6(1) Loy U Chicago Int'l L Rev 173; Harlan Grant Cohen, "Finding International Law, Part II: Our Fragmenting Legal Community" (2012) 44 NYUJ Int'l L & Pol 1049.

[131] Chester Brown argues that international tribunals have inherent powers to deal with instances of parallel procedures, including powers to dismiss or suspend proceedings and power to enjoin parties from pursuing a parallel claim. Chester Brown, *A Common Law of International Adjudication* (Oxford: Oxford University Press, 2007) at 242-55.

que les pays négocient d'avantage de traités pour répondre aux besoins de la société internationale, des conflits et des chevauchements entre dispositions sont susceptibles d'apparaître. Les opinions divergentes concernant le recours aux traités non-OMC dans le cadre du règlement des différends à l'OMC illustrent, par ailleurs, les problèmes qui pourraient surgir dans d'autres foires. Pour parvenir à des résolutions viables des différends concernant l'énergie renouvelable — et bien d'autres — une approche à l'interprétation qui vise l'intégration harmonieuse de diverses obligations internationales, conformément à l'intention des négociateurs, est à désirer.

Summary

Several disputes relating to renewable energy are underway at the World Trade Organization (WTO). The Appellate Body has released its first decision on this subject on the feed-in tariff for electricity in the province of Ontario. The disputes raise once again the issue of the relationship between international trade law and environmental protection. Evolving WTO jurisprudence should be able to resolve many of the difficulties, although the crucial problem of the treatment of production and processing methods remains obscure after the *Canada – Renewable Energy* decision. Questions of fundamental theory lie close to the surface of these debates. The recent expansion in the number of international regimes and tribunals highlights the importance of approaches to interpretation in public international law. As countries negotiate new treaties to address the needs of global society, potential conflicts and overlapping provisions are likely to appear. Differences of opinion about reliance on non-WTO treaties in the WTO dispute settlement system illustrate problems that can be anticipated in several fora. To achieve workable solutions for renewable energy disputes and many others, interpretation should promote the harmonious integration of obligations, in accordance with the intent of the negotiators.

Notes and Comments / Notes et commentaires

The Scottish Independence Referendum in an International Context

JURE VIDMAR

INTRODUCTION

On 18 September 2014, Scotland will hold a referendum on independence.[1] Under international law, such referenda generally do not create a "right to independence," and, even if successful, they only rarely result in the emergence of a new state.[2] Independence is not an entitlement under international law, and states usually oppose any such aspirations of their sub-units.[3] Scotland seems to be one of the few exceptions to this general pattern, as the referendum is formalized by an agreement between the governments of the United Kingdom (UK) and Scotland.[4]

Jure Vidmar is Professor of Public International Law in the Faculty of Law at Maastricht University; Research Fellow at St John's College at the University of Oxford; and Extraordinary Lecturer in the Centre for Human Rights in the Faculty of Law at the University of Pretoria.

Editors' note: This article went to press before the Scottish independence referendum took place.

1 See *Scottish Independence Referendum Act 2013*, ASP 2013, c 14, online: <http://www.legislation.gov.uk/asp/2013/14/pdfs/asp_20130014_en.pdf> [*Referendum Act*].

2 For an overview of a number of unsuccessful attempts at secession, see James Crawford, *The Creation of States in International Law*, 2nd edition (Oxford: Oxford University Press, 2006) at 403-14.

3 See *Reference re Secession of Quebec*, [1998] 2 SCR 217 at para 132 [*Quebec* case].

4 See *Agreement between the United Kingdom Government and the Scottish Government on a Referendum on Independence for Scotland* (15 October 2012), online: <http://

The UK government has thus committed itself to accepting the outcome of the referendum, whatever it may be. Although the *Scottish Independence Referendum Act 2013* does not specify the winning majority, it is taken for granted that the future legal status of Scotland would be determined by a simple majority of all votes cast.[5] An independent Scotland could thus result from a vote favouring independence falling (significantly) below 50 percent of all those eligible to vote.[6] What would this mean for the legitimacy of the outcome, in light of comparative international practice?

The Scottish referendum also cannot be detached from the announcement by UK Prime Minister Cameron that the UK may hold a referendum on whether to remain in, or leave, the European Union (EU).[7] A Scottish vote for independence would effectively also mean a vote for the exit of Scotland from the EU.[8] It is unclear, however, whether a vote against independence would mean a vote to remain within the UK as part of the EU or a vote to remain within the UK regardless of its EU membership. Could this circumstance compromise the legitimacy of the Scottish referendum?

This article begins from the premise established in James Crawford and Alan Boyle's report, *Referendum on the Independence of Scotland: International Law Aspects* (*Referendum* report), that, in the case of independence, Scotland would become a new state without automatic EU membership, while the "rump" UK would continue the UK's present international personality, including EU membership.[9] The article then extends the debate to issues not considered in the

---

www.scotland.gov.uk/About/Government/concordats/Referendum-on-independence> [*UK–Scotland Agreement*]. See also S Tierney, "Legal Issues Surrounding the Referendum on Independence for Scotland" (2013) 9 Eur Constitutional L Rev 359 at 362, affirming that the *UK–Scotland Agreement* "contrasts sharply with so many States where the issue of secessionist or sovereignist referendums has been the source of such deep and protracted disagreement."

5 See A Lecours and S Kerr, "Towards the Scottish Referendum" (2012) 3 Federal News 3, online: <http://ideefederale.ca/documents/Dec_2012_ang.pdf>, arguing that the UK government was willing to accept this relatively low threshold because opinion polls consistently show that even it would not be met. *Referendum Act, supra* note 1.

6 See "Panel Base Survey," *Sunday Times* (29 July 2013), online: Sunday Times <http://www.panelbase.com/news/TheSundayTimesScottishPollTables290713.pdf>.

7 See "David Cameron Promises in/out Referendum on EU," *BBC News* (23 January 2013), online: BBC News <http://www.bbc.co.uk/news/uk-politics-21148282>.

8 See text accompanying notes 109-13 later in this article.

9 See James Crawford and Alan Boyle, *Opinion: Referendum on the Independence of Scotland – International Law Aspects* (2013), part V, online: <https://www.gov.uk/

Referendum report. In particular, it places the Scottish independence referendum in comparative context by examining international practice and legislation relating to independence referenda. In doing so, the article elucidates some potential problems and ambiguities that could follow from the Scottish vote.

While international law does not prescribe exactly how an independence question must be phrased or a winning majority qualified, the article demonstrates that there nevertheless exists an international standard of clarity, albeit a loose one.[10] In terms of a winning majority, Scotland could become independent with the lowest support, in absolute terms, in post-Cold War international practice, but this would not necessarily delegitimize the outcome. However, it is more problematic that the effect of holding two referenda (one on Scottish independence, the other on the UK's membership in the EU) could bring an element of internationally impermissible ambiguity to the outcome of the former. The EU is a complex supranational legal structure with crucial implications for the parameters of the future status of Scotland as well as the rights and duties of its citizens.[11] Scots, therefore, have a right to know whether the alternative to independence is the UK within or outside of the EU.

In this context, the article rejects an expansive reading of the EU citizenship doctrine[12] and develops the argument that, in the case of Scottish independence, certain categories of people would nevertheless retain some limited rights stemming from current EU citizenship. This is an effect of the *Convention for the Protection of Human Rights and Fundamental Freedoms* (*European Convention on Human Rights* or *ECHR*).[13] The same would apply for certain categories of people should the UK opt for exiting the EU.

THE LEGAL EFFECTS OF INDEPENDENCE REFERENDA INTERNATIONALLY

In its advisory opinion in *Western Sahara*, the International Court of Justice (ICJ) pronounced that "the application of the right of

---

government/uploads/system/uploads/attachment_data/file/79408/Annex_A.pdf>.

[10] Compare *Clarity Act*, SC 2000, c 26, s 1(3), online: <http://laws-lois.justice.gc.ca/eng/acts/C-31.8/FullText.html>.

[11] See text accompanying notes 112-13 later in this article.

[12] Crawford and Boyle, *supra* note 9 at paras 176-80.

[13] *Convention for the Protection of Human Rights and Fundamental Freedoms*, 213 UNTS 221, ETS No 5 (in force 3 September 1953) [*ECHR*].

self-determination requires a free and genuine expression of the will of the peoples concerned."[14] Such an expression is usually formalized through a referendum on the future legal status of a territory. In the aftermath of the First World War, several referenda on the legal status of European territories took place under the auspices of the League of Nations.[15] Referenda were also held in the process of decolonization after the Second World War.[16] The post-Cold War period saw the emergence of a number of new states, and independence referenda were held in several of the territories of the Soviet Union, the Socialist Federal Republic of Yugoslavia (SFRY), Eritrea, East Timor, Montenegro, and South Sudan.

There were notable absences of independence referenda in the Czechoslovakia[17] and Kosovo contexts.[18] However, as the ICJ remarked in *Western Sahara*, the requirement for consultation may be dispensed with where the will of the people is obvious and unambiguous.[19] This was the case·in some instances of decolonization, where referenda were not held but the will of the people was nevertheless clear.[20] The same cannot be said for the dissolution of Czechoslovakia. No referendum was held, and it was unclear whether separation really was the will of the people,[21] yet the Czech Republic and Slovakia nevertheless emerged as new states.[22]

Outside the colonial context, independence is not an entitlement under international law.[23] As a consequence, a referendum is (subject to the caveat noted in the preceding paragraph) a necessary but not a sufficient requirement for independence. Recent practice has indeed witnessed a number of referenda in favour of independence,

---

[14] *Western Sahara*, Advisory Opinion, [1975] ICJ Rep 12 at para 55 [*Western Sahara*].

[15] H Brady and C Kaplan, "Eastern Europe and the Former Soviet Union" in D Butler and A Ranney, eds, *Referendums around the World: The Growing Use of Direct Democracy* (Washington, DC: AEI Press, 1994) 174 at 175.

[16] R Miller, "Self-Determination in International Law and the Demise of Democracy" (2003) 41 Colum J Transnat'l L 601 at 612. See also Y Beigbeder, *International Monitoring of Plebiscites, Referenda and National Elections: Self-Determination and Transition to Democracy* (Dordrecht: Martinus Nijhoff, 1994) at 91.

[17] Crawford, *supra* note 2 at 402.

[18] See Jure Vidmar, *Democratic Statehood in International Law: The Emergence of New States in Post-Cold War Practice* (Oxford: Hart, 2013) at 190, 196.

[19] *Western Sahara*, *supra* note 14 at para 55.

[20] *Ibid.*

[21] Vidmar, *supra* note 18 at 190.

[22] *Ibid.*

[23] *Quebec case*, *supra* note 3 at para 132.

which, however, did not result in the creation of new states.[24] Under international law, independence referenda are, therefore, not binding on the central government. This conclusion, however, must be qualified in light of one of the pronouncements of the Supreme Court of Canada in *Reference re Secession of Quebec*. Referring to the principle of democracy entrenched in Canadian constitutional law, the Court held that in a democratic state an expression of the will of the people in favour of independence cannot be ignored.[25] An obligation would arise for both sides to negotiate the future legal status of the independence-seeking territory.[26] The Supreme Court of Canada made it clear, however, that such negotiations need not necessarily lead to independence.[27]

It follows that independence referenda generally do not have direct or self-executing legal effects. At best, they can trigger an obligation to negotiate, but they do not create a right to independence. The central government can nevertheless commit itself in advance to respecting the outcome of the vote, as in the referenda in East Timor,[28] Montenegro,[29] and South Sudan.[30] It seems that binding referenda are more of an exceptional feature used in an internationalized peace process rather than a standard applicable in constitutional democracies. Scotland is an exception in this regard. Unlike the situation of Quebec, the central government is committed to entering into negotiations with a predetermined outcome — that is, independence — should the majority of Scottish voters support it. However, what is considered to be a majority?

In the *Quebec* case, the Supreme Court of Canada expressed the general threshold for validity of an independence referendum: "The referendum result, if it is to be taken as an expression of the democratic will, must be free of ambiguity both in terms of the question asked and in terms of the support it achieves."[31] The definition of the phrase "free of ambiguity" was further specified by the *Clarity*

[24] Crawford, *supra* note 2 at 403-14.

[25] *Quebec* case, *supra* note 3 at para 87.

[26] *Ibid* at para 91.

[27] *Ibid.*

[28] Crawford, *supra* note 2 at 561.

[29] See Assembly of the Republic of Montenegro, *Skupstina Republike Crne Gore* (24 May 2006), online: <http://www.skupstina.me/index.php?strana=fiksna&id=401>.

[30] See South Sudan Referendum Commission, *Results for the Referendum of Southern Sudan* (2011), online: <http://southernsudan2011.com>.

[31] *Quebec* case, *supra* note 3 at para 87.

Act, passed in 2000 by the Parliament of Canada.[32] With regard to the winning majority, the Act specifies that clarity of the decision may be determined by: "(a) the size of the majority of valid votes cast in favour of the secessionist option; (b) the percentage of eligible voters voting in the referendum; and (c) any other matters or circumstances ... consider[ed] to be relevant."[33] While the *Clarity Act* refers to, *inter alia*, the percentage of participating eligible voters, the threshold for success of a referendum is not quantified.

The next section will consider recent international practice with regard to setting the winning majority for independence referenda. It will be argued that the "Quebec clarity formula" captures a general international standard applicable to independence referenda according to which the exact threshold for the success of a referendum depends on specific social factors in each situation.

Determining an Unambiguous Winning Majority

Winning Majorities in International Practice

Since 1991, a number of independence referenda have taken place in the contexts of (1) the dissolution of the Soviet Union and the SFRY; (2) "belated decolonization," and (3) negotiated secessions. Most of these situations were characterized by armed conflict and/or a breakdown of the constitutional order. Independence referenda were sometimes held under international auspices in the context of peace settlements. The Scottish circumstance is different, and this difference should be kept in mind when the Scottish referendum is compared to other independence referenda in contemporary practice. Nevertheless, the relatively extensive international practice of recent decades provides some guidelines as to how the requirement for an "unambiguous majority" should be defined.

The referendum situation in the Soviet Union was confusing. In the complicated internal political situation, Mikhail Gorbachev called for an all-Union referendum on "the preservation of the Union of Soviet Socialist Republics as a renewed federation of equal sovereign republics, in which the rights and freedoms of an individual of any nationality will be fully guaranteed."[34] The required majority for the preservation of the Soviet Union was 50 percent of all votes cast, while other referendum rules were very unclear and the results open to different interpretations "so that success could

---

[32] *Clarity Act, supra* note 10 at ss 1-2.

[33] *Ibid* at s 2(2).

[34] Cited in Brady and Kaplan, *supra* note 15 at 187.

be claimed for a variety of different outcomes."[35] The consequences of a negative answer, either by the entire population of the Soviet Union or by a single republic, were not specified. Furthermore, the question did not specify the exact status of the republics in a new federation. The referendum was thus rife with ambiguities.

The referendum was boycotted by six out of fifteen republics: Armenia, Estonia, Georgia, Latvia, Lithuania, and Moldova.[36] Estonia, Latvia, and Lithuania had already held referenda on independence prior to the all-Union referendum. In the Baltic States, a majority of all votes cast was required, but in all instances a majority of all those eligible to vote was achieved.[37] Armenia organized a separate independence referendum after the all-Union referendum. Independence was supported by 99.3 percent of those who voted, with a turnout of 95.1 percent.[38]

Of those Soviet republics that did not boycott the all-Union referendum, special referenda on independence were held prior to dissolution of the Soviet Union on 8 December 1991 in Turkmenistan[39] and Ukraine,[40] where independence was also supported by overwhelming majorities of all those eligible to vote. After the Soviet Union had already been officially dissolved,[41] popular consultations were also held in Azerbaijan[42] and Uzbekistan.[43] In the effective

[35] *Ibid* at 188.

[36] *Ibid.*

[37] See further I Ziemele, *State Continuity and Nationality: The Baltic States and Russia: Past Present and Future as Defined by International Law* (Leiden: Martinus Nijhoff, 2005) at 27-29 (Estonia), 32-34 (Latvia), 38-40 (Lithuania).

[38] Brady and Kaplan, *supra* note 15 at 193.

[39] Independence, along with the question on foreign and domestic policies, was supported by 97.4 percent of those who voted, with a turnout of 94.1 percent. *Ibid.*

[40] With a participation rate of 84.18 percent, 90.32 of votes cast were in favour of independence. This means that 76.03 percent of all those eligible to vote supported an independent Ukraine. See *Electoral Geography: Ukraine*, online: <http://www.electoralgeography.com/new/en/countries/u/ukraine/ukraine -independence-referendum1991.html>.

[41] See *Agreement on the Establishment of the Commonwealth of Independent States*, 31 ILM 138 (1992). See also *Protocol to the Agreement Establishing the Commonwealth of Independent States signed at Minsk on 8 December 1991 by the Republic of Belarus, the Russian Federation and Ukraine*, 31 ILM 147 (1992).

[42] The independence of Azerbaijan was confirmed by 99.6 percent of those who voted, with a turnout of 95.3 percent of all those eligible to vote. Brady and Kaplan, *supra* note 15 at 193. The independence of Uzbekistan was confirmed by 98.2 percent of those who voted, with a turnout of 94 percent of all those eligible to vote (*ibid*).

[43] The independence of Uzbekistan was confirmed by 98.2 percent of those who voted, with a turnout of 94 percent of all those eligible to vote. *Ibid.*

absence of any alternative, independence was confirmed virtually unanimously. In three Soviet republics (Kazakhstan, Kirghizia, and Uzbekistan), no specific referenda on independence were held, but the question of the all-Union referendum was modified to imply the potential creation of a sovereign state. Support for independence in all of these situations was once again overwhelming.[44] Conversely, Russia remained loyal to the all-Union referendum question, and preservation of a renewed Soviet Union was a majority preference.[45] However, this popular decision could not change the political reality of the time — the Soviet Union was collapsing, regardless of what Russians preferred. Finally, neither the all-Union referendum (in any of its variations) nor any specific independence referendum was ever held in Moldova.[46] Independence referenda in the Soviet Union were held in the complicated political circumstances of a virtually non-functioning federation.

Due to the peculiarity of the Soviet situation, comparisons with Scotland should be made carefully. It is worth noting that the referenda rules generally required a majority of all votes cast with a turnout of at least 50 percent. However, the majorities that were actually achieved in practice were overwhelming, comfortably above 50 percent of all those eligible to vote. In the absence of an alternative to independence, referenda in the republics other than Russia and Moldova merely confirmed the collapse of the federation.

The dissolution of the SFRY had a different dynamic. The process was internationalized through the work of the Badinter Commission,[47]

---

[44] In Kazakhstan, the turnout was 88.2 percent, while 94.1 percent of valid votes responded affirmatively to the question asked (which implied independence). *Ibid* at 190-91. In Kirghizia, the turnout was 92.9 percent and the question was answered affirmatively by 94.6 percent of those who cast their votes (*ibid*). In Uzbekistan, the turnout was 95.4 percent and the question was answered affirmatively by 93.7 percent of those who cast their votes (*ibid* at 193). Unlike Kazakhstan and Kirghizia, Uzbekistan also held a special referendum on independence, which took place after the Soviet Union had already been transformed into the Commonwealth of Independent States.

[45] The answer to the original question of the all- European Union (EU) referendum was affirmative by 71.3 percent of those who cast their votes, with a turnout of 75.4 percent of registered voters. *Ibid.* The question on popular election of the Russian president was supported by 69.9 percent of those who cast their votes (*ibid* at 194).

[46] *Ibid* at 193.

[47] See further S Terrett, *The Dissolution of Yugoslavia and the Badinter Arbitration Commission: A Contextual Study of Peace-Making Efforts in the Post-Cold War World* (Aldershot, UK: Ashgate, 2000) at 31.

but three out of four referenda were held before the commission started its work. Conversely, the referendum in Bosnia-Herzegovina was held at the explicit request of the Badinter Commission.[48] The Croatian referendum prescribed, as a winning threshold, "the majority of those who cast votes, under the condition that a majority of those eligible to vote cast their votes in the referendum."[49] With a turnout of 83.56 percent of all those eligible to vote, 94.17 percent of votes were cast in favour of independence.[50] In absolute terms, these numbers mean that the independence of Croatia was supported by 78.69 percent of all those eligible to vote. Bosnia-Herzegovina used its general *Referenda Act,* which required decision making by a majority of all votes cast.[51] The legitimacy of the vote may be questioned because of the boycott by the ethnic Serbian population (31.3 percent of the entire population of Bosnia-Herzegovina). The result was nevertheless 63 percent of all those eligible to vote choosing independence.[52] In Macedonia, a majority of all votes cast was also prescribed, but independence was comfortably supported by an absolute majority of 72.16 percent of all those eligible to vote.

The referenda rules employed in these Yugoslav republics are generally in line with those applied in the Soviet republics. A majority of all votes cast is usually supplemented by a 50 percent turnout requirement. However, an absolute majority of all those eligible to vote was nevertheless easily achieved in all situations. An exception was in Slovenia, which explicitly prescribed a threshold of the majority of all those eligible to vote.[53] Since the Slovenian referendum was not legally binding on the central authorities of the

48 Arbitration Commission of the Conference on Yugoslavia (Badinter Commission), *Opinion 4,* (1992) 31 ILM 501 (11 January 1992) at para 3.

49 *Constitution of the Republic of Croatia* (1990), art 87(2), online: <http://narodne-novine.nn.hr/clanci/sluzbeni/232289.html> [author's own translation].

50 See Andrija Hebrang, *A Short Summary of Croatian History,* online: <http://www.andrija-hebrang.com/povijest.htm#nastanak> [in Croatian].

51 *Act on Referenda of the Socialist Republic of Bosnia-Herzegovina,* Official Gazette of the Socialist Republic of Bosnia and Herzegovina, No 29/77 (1977) [on file with author].

52 See National Congress of the Republic of Bosnia-Herzegovina, *Referendum o nezavisnosti Bosne i Hercegovine* [*Referendum on Independence of Bosnia-Herzegovina*] (1992), online: <http://republic-bosnia-herzegovina.com/?p=306>.

53 *Plebiscite on the Sovereignty and Independence of the Republic of Slovenia,* Official Gazette of the Republic of Slovenia, No 44-2102/1990 (2 December 1990), art 3 [on file with author] [*Slovenian Plebiscite*].

SFRY, the high threshold aimed at achieving a higher degree of legitimacy for Slovenia's claim to independence, in the sense later spelled out in the Canadian *Clarity Act*.[54] The prescribed threshold was comfortably achieved.[55] Notably, no other independence referendum in contemporary practice has prescribed such a demanding threshold.

Outside of the 1991–92 "Yugoslav independence package," Montenegro opted for independence in 2006. Unlike the referenda held in the context of the dissolution of the SFRY, the referendum in Montenegro was legally binding and triggered a constitutional formula for secession.[56] It was also an exception with regard to the prescribed majority. The opinion polls were suggesting a fifty-fifty split between the "unionists" and the "secessionists."[57] Given the recent history of armed conflict in the area as well as the proximity of Kosovo, which had not declared independence at the time, the EU feared a potential outburst of violence and a spill-over effect if Montenegro declared independence with virtually half of its population opposing this move.[58] The "unionists" were also threatening a boycott of the referendum.[59] This move would further delegitimize the vote.

In response, the EU imposed the *Act on Referendum on State-Legal Status of the Republic of Montenegro* (*Independence Referendum Act*), which prescribed a minimum turnout and a higher burden on the "secessionists."[60] Under this formula, the constitutionally entrenched mechanism for secession would be triggered by 55 percent of all votes being cast for secession, with a turnout of at least 50 percent plus one of eligible voters.[61] Such a majority was designed

---

[54] *Clarity Act, supra* note 10, s 2(2).

[55] See Government of the Republic of Slovenia, *Od plebiscita do samostojnosti* [*From the Plebiscite to Independence*], online: <http://www.ukom.gov.si/10let/pot/kronologija>.

[56] See *Constitution of the State Union of Serbia and Montenegro* (2003), online: <http://www.arhiva.srbija.gov.rs/vesti/2003-02/05/333116.html>, art 60.

[57] See Dragoljub Vukovic, *Crnogorsko javno mnjenje uoči referenduma* (23 December 2000), online: <http://www.aimpress.ch/dyn/pubs/archive/data/200012/01223-005-pubs-pod.htm>.

[58] International Crisis Group, *Briefing No 169: Montenegro's Independence Drive* (7 December 2006), online: <http://www.crisisgroup.org/en/regions/europe/balkans/montenegro/169-montenegros-independence-drive.aspx> at 1.

[59] *Ibid.*

[60] *Act on Referendum on State-Legal Status of the Republic of Montenegro*, Official Gazette of the Republic of Montenegro, No 12/06 (2 March 2006).

[61] *Ibid*, art 6.

to give the "unionists" a reasonable hope of winning the referendum and thus averted their boycott.[62] Greater legitimacy was also achieved by avoiding the prospect of Montenegro becoming independent by a close 50 percent vote. Independence was in the end supported by a narrow margin of 55.53 percent of all votes cast with a turnout of 86.49 percent of all those eligible to vote.[63]

The barely achieved threshold has been described as a political gamble, as it was quite possible that the result could have fallen in the "grey zone" between 50 and 55 percent.[64] In such a circumstance,

Montenegro's government would have been legally unable to declare independence. At the same time it would have viewed the referendum result as a mandate to further weaken the State Union. The unionists would have viewed the result as a victory and demanded immediate parliamentary elections and closer ties with Belgrade.[65]

The referendum rules in Montenegro demonstrate that an "unambiguous majority" is not a concept that can be universally quantified. It depends crucially on social and political factors specific to the society that is consulted on the future legal status of its territory. It should be noted, however, that in absolute terms, the independence of Montenegro was supported by 48 percent of all those eligible to vote. If the Slovenian standard of an absolute majority had been applied,[66] Montenegro would have been unable to declare independence. This experience suggests that in those rare circumstances where independence referenda are binding and neither option is widely favoured over the other, the future legal status of the territory can, ultimately, depend on the choice of the winning majority threshold.

Another legally binding referendum was held in South Sudan, where the preference for independence was virtually unanimous.[67] The rules for this referendum, in the context of a peace process,

---

[62] International Crisis Group, *supra* note 58 at 2.

[63] Assembly of the Republic of Montenegro, *supra* note 29.

[64] International Crisis Group, *Briefing No 42: Montenegro's Referendum* (30 May 2006), online: <http://www.crisisgroup.org/en/regions/europe/balkans/montenegro/b042-montenegros-referendum.aspx> at 6.

[65] *Ibid.*

[66] Compare *Slovenian Plebiscite, supra* note 53.

[67] South Sudan Referendum Commission, *supra* note 30.

are also instructive.[68] The prescribed winning majority was 50 percent plus one of all votes cast, with a required turnout of at least 60 percent.[69] South Sudan thus also raised the threshold but did so with respect to the required participation rate. Both criteria were easily satisfied, as independence was supported by an overwhelming 98.83 percent of those who voted, with a turnout of 97.58 percent.[70]

There was, however, an element of ambiguity in the rules governing the UN-sponsored binding referendum on independence in East Timor. The referendum was grounded in the *Agreement between the Republic of Indonesia and the Portuguese Republic on the Question of East Timor (1999 Agreement)*, which was concluded on 5 May 1999.[71] The popular consultation was also endorsed in Security Council Resolution 1246.[72] Neither instrument specified the required winning majority. The *1999 Agreement* left interpretation of the referendum results to the UN secretary-general.[73] Some guidelines may have been implicit in the pre-referendum report of the secretary-general, in which he stated: "[S]hould the popular consultation result in a majority of the East Timorese people rejecting the proposed special autonomy, the Government of Indonesia would take the constitutional steps necessary to terminate Indonesia's links with East Timor."[74] The reference to the "majority of the East Timorese people,"[75] rather than the "majority of all votes cast," could be interpreted as a requirement that the decision be made by the more demanding majority of all those eligible to vote. This conclusion is not straightforward, however, as voters were deciding on two competing questions: either independence or autonomy within Indonesia. If neither option won an absolute majority, the

---

[68] See *Comprehensive Peace Agreement* (2005), online: United Nations <http://unmis. unmissions.org/Portals/UNMIS/Documents/General/cpa-en.pdf>. See also *Southern Sudan Referendum Act 2009*, online: United Nations <http://unmis. unmissions.org/Portals/UNMIS/Referendum/SS%20Referendum%20MOJ -Englis.pdf>.

[69] *Ibid*, art 41.

[70] South Sudan Referendum Commission, *supra* note 30.

[71] *Agreement between the Republic of Indonesia and the Portuguese Republic on the Question of East Timor*, UN Doc S/1999/513 (5 May 1999), arts 1–6 [*1999 Agreement*].

[72] Security Council Resolution 1246, UN Doc S/RES/1246 (11 June 1999) at para 1.

[73] *1999 Agreement*, *supra* note 71, arts 1-6.

[74] *Report of the Secretary General: The Question of East Timor*, UN Doc A/53/951 (5 May 1999) at para 2.

[75] *Ibid*.

UN secretary-general would probably have had no other choice but to declare the winning option to be the one that received more votes.

The ambiguity did not prove to be a difficulty in practice. Independence was supported by 78.5 percent of all votes cast, with a turnout of 98.6 percent.[76] The expression of the will of the people was thus clear and unambiguous. It should also be mentioned that after a lengthy armed conflict in Ethiopia, the central government accepted the independence of Eritrea.[77] The UN-observed referendum was a mere formality. With a participation of 93.9 percent, 99.8 percent of votes cast were in favour of independence.[78]

THE WINNING MAJORITY IN SCOTLAND IN LIGHT OF
INTERNATIONAL PRACTICE

The earlier analysis of international practice shows that there is no universally prescribed threshold for independence referenda. There is a general requirement that the majority be clear and unambiguous. In different social and political situations, differently qualified majorities lead to such clarity. Do the rules governing the Scottish referendum ensure the required clarity? The Scottish *Referendum Act* does not specify a winning majority. However, given the controversy over the 1979 Scottish devolution referendum, which imposed a threshold participation rate of 40 percent,[79] the UK government is willing this time to accept the lower threshold of a majority of all votes cast.[80] This is indeed the most common majority prescribed for independence referenda. At the same time, it is true that in international practice a participation threshold is generally also prescribed, which will not be the case in Scotland in 2014. Furthermore, even where only a simple majority of all votes cast is required, a majority of all those eligible to vote is almost always achieved in practice. Independence is indeed often supported virtually unanimously. According to the opinion polls, this is not going to

---

[76] Crawford, *supra* note 2 at 561.

[77] *Ibid* at 402.

[78] *Ibid*.

[79] See, for example, "The 1979 Referendums," *BBC News* (30 September 1979), online: BBC News <http://www.bbc.co.uk/news/special/politics97/devolution/scotland/briefing/79referendums.shtml>. See further, for example, D Balsom, "The Scottish and Welsh Devolution Referenda of 1979: Constitutional Change and Popular Choice" (1972) 32 Parliamentary Affairs 394.

[80] Lecours and Kerr, *supra* note 5 at 4.

happen in Scotland.[81] The independence advocates can hope for a majority of all votes cast, while higher expectations would be illusory.

Disregarding the rather peculiar dissolution of Czechoslovakia, which took place probably against the will of its people(s),[82] Montenegro is the only contemporary instance of state creation with popular support below 50 percent of all those eligible to vote.[83] If the outcome of Montenegro's referendum had not been legally binding, doubts would have lingered over its potential to trigger the "Quebec formula" — that is, negotiations on the future legal status without a predetermined outcome.[84] Indeed, where a referendum is not binding on the central government, either by law or by political pledge, the rule seems simply to be: the higher the support for independence, the stronger the claim for independence. However, there is no automaticity. Below 50 percent of all those eligible to vote, a claim to independence may be seen as weak and the will of the people not sufficiently clear.[85] Politically, the central government could oppose independence on the basis that it is supported by less than half of the electorate.

Binding referenda are different, as the mechanism for secession is triggered by a pre-determined majority. Such referenda are rare in practice but when they happen, the negotiations on future legal status are no longer open-ended — there is a commitment to independence on both sides. Scotland falls within this camp. And if Scotland became independent with less than 50 percent of all those eligible to vote, it would not be unprecedented in international practice. It is notable, however, that in Montenegro the threshold was set higher than in Scotland. It thus seems that the Scottish referendum rules are, in fact, most favourable for the independence camp in comparative international practice. First, they demand a simple majority of all votes cast but no turnout threshold. Second, achieving this comparatively low threshold would suffice for the central government to accept Scottish independence. Scotland could thus become independent with the lowest popular support in comparative contemporary practice (again disregarding the Czech Republic and Slovakia, where no referenda were held).

[81] "Panel Base Survey," *supra* note 6.

[82] Crawford, *supra* note 2 at 402.

[83] Assembly of the Republic of Montenegro, *supra* note 29.

[84] Compare *Quebec* case, *supra* note 3 at para 87.

[85] *Ibid.*

However, this circumstance does not necessarily de-legitimize the potential path to Scotland's independence.

One should take into account that Scotland is being compared here to situations where independence was determined predominantly in circumstances of armed conflict and ethnic tensions. In such situations, achieving statehood is often seen as a means of collective self-preservation.[86] This circumstance is absent in Scotland, as it is in Quebec.[87] And unlike many other examples in international practice, the UK is not on the brink of constitutional collapse. Continuing its current status within the UK is a viable option for Scotland, and there exists no strong "remedial element" that would virtually harmonize the will of the people. For these reasons, it would be unfair to impose on Scotland a requirement for a majority akin to those achieved in, for example, Armenia, Slovenia, Eritrea, or East Timor.

In light of domestic dissatisfaction with the 40 percent turnout requirement imposed in the 1979 devolution referendum,[88] it thus seems reasonable to conclude that a majority of all votes cast would represent a legitimate and clear expression of the will of the Scottish people in favour of independence. After all, those who expressly oppose independence have a chance to lift the bar by participating and voting against independence. It should also be noted that the Venice Commission adopted, in Resolution 235, a Code on Good Practice at Referendums, which expressly recommends that "no provision be made for rules on quorums."[89] In the commission's reasoning, a turnout threshold "means that it is in the interests of a proposal's opponents to abstain rather than to vote against it,"[90] while an approval requirement higher than a simple majority should

---

[86] See *ibid* at para 126 for an analogy with the so-called "remedial secession" doctrine. The court reasoned: "The recognized sources of international law establish that the right to self-determination of a people is normally fulfilled through internal self-determination — a people's pursuit of its political, economic, social and cultural development within a framework of an existing state. A right to external self-determination (which in this case potentially takes the form of the assertion of a right to unilateral secession) arises in only the most extreme of cases and, even then, under carefully defined circumstances."

[87] *Ibid.*

[88] "The 1979 Referendums," *supra* note 79.

[89] European Commission for Democracy through Law (Venice Commission), Resolution 235 (30 May 2007), online: <https://wcd.coe.int/ViewDoc.jsp?id=1133019> at para 50.

[90] *Ibid* at para 51.

not be imposed as it "may be so high as to make change excessively difficult."[91] It follows from this reasoning that a simple majority of all votes cast should decide. The Scottish referendum thus also falls within the parameters of the Venice Commission's recommendation.[92] In terms of the winning majority, the Scottish referendum rules therefore also meet the clarity standard. However, do Scots know for what kind of an arrangement they are voting if they vote to remain within the UK?

ASKING AN UNAMBIGUOUS REFERENDUM QUESTION

As noted by the Supreme Court of Canada, an impermissible ambiguity could stem not only from the degree of voter support for independence but also from the phrasing of the referendum question.[93] This section shows that, textually, the Scottish question meets the clarity standard in an exemplary manner. However, a problem arises because of the potential effects of holding two referenda: one on Scotland's independence and one on the UK's place in the EU (should the latter take place). The argument is developed that the EU is a complex legal structure with crucial implications for the nature and structure of the UK as well as the rights and duties of its citizens. It is thus problematic if Scots do not know whether a vote to remain part of the UK means a vote to remain part of the UK within the EU.

INTERNATIONAL PRACTICE ON REFERENDA QUESTIONS

With regard to phrasing the referendum question, some guidance again follows from Canadian responses to independence referenda

---

91 *Ibid* at para 52.

92 The view of the Venice Commission needs to be taken with some caution. The recommendation refers to referenda as an instrument of direct democracy in general, not to independence referenda in particular. It is questionable whether general referenda rules can readily be transplanted to consultations on the legal status of territory. Most independence referenda do impose a minimum threshold, albeit usually in terms of the required turnout. Independence referenda often take place in circumstances of conflict and ethnic tensions and a path to independence with a very narrow relative majority may indeed be problematic. As argued earlier, in the case of Montenegro, imposing a minimum turnout threshold and raising the required majority in fact added to the legitimacy of the vote rather than undermined it. The Venice Commission's recommendation, therefore, should not be applied across the board to all referenda. The standard may be reasonable in Scotland but is not automatically applicable worldwide.

in Quebec. The Supreme Court of Canada's requirement that the phrasing of the question be "free of ambiguity"[94] was further developed by the *Clarity Act*. In this context, the Act provides:

[A] clear expression of the will of the population of a province that the province cease to be part of Canada could not result from

(*a*) a referendum question that merely focuses on a mandate to negotiate without soliciting a direct expression of the will of the population of that province on whether the province should cease to be part of Canada; or

(*b*) a referendum question that envisages other possibilities in addition to the secession of the province from Canada, such as economic or political arrangements with Canada, that obscure a direct expression of the will of the population of that province on whether the province should cease to be part of Canada.[95]

Drafters of the *Clarity Act* evidently had in mind the two previous referenda questions in Quebec, both of which implied a future economic association with Canada.[96] The referendum question in 1980 did not ask directly about independence but, rather, about a mandate for the government of Quebec to negotiate a new arrangement with the rest of Canada, possibly leading to independence.

---

[93] *Quebec* case, *supra* note 3 at para 87.

[94] *Ibid.*

[95] *Clarity Act, supra* note 10, s 1(4).

[96] In 1980, the referendum question read: "The Government of Québec has made public its proposal to negotiate a new agreement with the rest of Canada, based on the equality of nations; this agreement would enable Québec to acquire the exclusive power to make its laws, administer its taxes and establish relations abroad in other words sovereignty and at the same time, to maintain with Canada an economic association including a common currency; any change in political status resulting from these negotiations will be submitted to the people through a referendum; on these terms, do you agree to give the Government of Québec the mandate to negotiate the proposed agreement between Québec and Canada?" And in 1995: "Do you agree that Québec should become sovereign, after having made a formal offer to Canada for a new economic and political partnership, within the scope of the Bill respecting the future of Québec and of the agreement signed on 12 June 1995?" reprinted in P Dumberry, "Lessons Learned from the Quebec Secession Reference before the Supreme Court of Canada" in M Kohen, ed, *Secession: International Law Perspectives* (Cambridge: Cambridge University Press, 2006) 416 at 418, 420.

While reflecting the Quebec experience, the minimum standard set by the *Clarity Act* is relevant beyond the specific Canadian context and has universal validity. Indeed, a misleading question could not yield a "free and genuine expression of the will of the people," as required by the ICJ in *Western Sahara*.[97] In post-1990 practice on independence referenda, some questions put forward have attracted doubt as to whether they really were unambiguous. For example, the referenda questions in Croatia and Macedonia implied a possibility of a future arrangement within Yugoslavia,[98] while referenda in Bosnia-Herzegovina,[99] Estonia, Latvia, and Lithuania[100] implied that these entities might already be states, such that the questions did not clearly ask about the alteration of legal status.

---

[97] *Western Sahara, supra* note 14 at para 55.

[98] The Croatian referendum questions read: "1. Do you agree that the Republic of Croatia, as a sovereign and independent state which guarantees the cultural autonomy and all civil liberties of Serbs and members of other nationalities in Croatia, shall enter into an association of sovereign states together with other republics (according to the suggestion of the Republic of Croatia and the Republic of Slovenia for solving the state crisis in the SFRY)? 2. Do you agree that the Republic of Croatia shall remain in Yugoslavia as a unitary federal state (according to the suggestion of the Republic of Serbia and the Socialist Republic of Montenegro for solving the state crisis in the SFRY)?" *Decree on the Call for A Referendum on Independence of the Republic of Croatia,* Official Gazette of the Republic of Croatia, No 21 (2 May 1991) [author's own translation, on file with author]. And the Macedonian referenum questions: "Are you in favour of an independent Macedonia with a right to enter into a future association of sovereign states of Yugoslavia?": "Ден што веднаш стана историја [*Den shto vednash stana istorija*]" online: <http://star.dnevnik.com.mk/default.aspx?pbroj=1349 &stID=2147477716> [author's own translation].

[99] The Bosnian referendum question read: "Do you support sovereign and independent Bosnia-Herzegovina, a state of equal citizens, peoples of Bosnia-Herzegovina – Muslims, Serbs, Croats and people of other nationalities who live in Bosnia-Herzegovina?" *Act on Referenda of the Socialist Republic of Bosnia-Herzegovina,* Official Gazette of the Socialist Republic of Bosnia and Herzegovina, No 29/77 (1977) [author's own translation, on file with author].

[100] The Lithuanian question read: "Are you for the independent and democratic state of Lithuania?" See Francis X Clines, "Lithuania Votes Overwhelmingly for Independence from Moscow," *New York Times* (10 February 1991), online: <http://query.nytimes.com/gst/fullpage.html?res=9D0CE1D61E3DF933A257 51C0A967958260>. The Estonian question read: "Do you want restoration of the Independence of the Republic of Estonia?" See R Taagepera, *Estonia: Return to Independence* (Boulder, CO: Westview, 1993) at 193. And the Latvian question read: "Do you support the democratic and independent statehood of the Republic of Latvia?" See Ziemele, *supra* note 37 at 34.

These situations involved difficult political circumstances, in some cases even of emerging armed conflict. In Croatia, the question on independence had to be somewhat "disguised," as the federal authorities fiercely opposed any independence aspirations. The less specific wording used gave the Croatian authorities the ability to claim that the vote would not necessarily lead to independence but, instead, only to a possible restructuring of the federation. However, there was no doubt among the population that this was a vote on independence.[101] The Baltic referenda questions must be understood in the context of claims to continuity of the international legal personality enjoyed by the Baltic states in the inter-war period. The referenda questions were therefore carefully phrased so as not to imply that these states would be created anew, as this would undermine the continuity claim. However, there was no doubt that the people were being asked about independence from the Soviet Union. Similarly, Bosnia-Herzegovina held a referendum under international pressure, several months after declaring independence.[102] In the view of its government, Bosnia-Herzegovina was thus already a state at the time of the referendum, and the question was thus phrased in such a way as not to imply that it had yet to become one.

The referendum questions in these difficult political circumstances cannot be closely scrutinized against the Canadian standards of clarity, which were drafted with a peaceful situation in mind. While their phrasing may evoke some ambiguity, it was nevertheless clear in all of these situations that these were referenda on independence. As a matter of general principle, however, the referendum question must consult on independence directly (not merely implicitly) and should not obscure the issue of independence within a broader question. Applying this standard to Scotland, the question would be impermissible if it obscured the issue of independence by, for example, proposing a monetary union with the UK or EU membership for Scotland. The question does not do that. Textually, the Scottish referendum question is exemplary in its clarity: "Should Scotland be an independent country? Yes/No."[103] The problem lies elsewhere.

---

101 D Rai, *Statehood and the Law of Self-Determination* (The Hague: Kluwer Law International, 2002) at 349.

102 Badinter Commission, *supra* note 48 at para 3.

103 UK Electoral Commission, *Referendum on Independence for Scotland: Advice of the Electoral Commission on the Proposed Referendum Question* (January 2013) at 33,

THE SCOTTISH AMBIGUITY

In January 2013, Prime Minister David Cameron announced the possibility of a referendum on the UK's continued EU membership. According to Prime Minister Cameron, the referendum would take place should the Conservatives win at the next general election.[104] Opinion polls show that 53 percent of Scots would vote for the UK to remain in the EU, "only" 34 percent would vote for the UK to exit, and 61 percent think that an independent Scotland should seek to join the EU.[105] This is quite different from England, where 50 percent would prefer that the UK exit the EU and "only" 42 percent are in favour of staying.[106] Consequently, not only may EU membership be an important consideration in a potential EU referendum, but it will also be in the background of decision making in Scottish voting booths in 2014.

Imagine a Scottish voter who would vote for independence but only if it did not effectively mean an exit by that voter from the EU.[107] How should she or he vote? If she or he votes against independence from the UK, it might indeed end up being a vote against remaining within the EU — depending on the outcome of the potential, subsequent EU referendum. What is more, if the UK eventually leaves the EU, it is quite likely that a vote for Scottish independence would turn out to have been a vote for remaining within the EU. Such a result would follow because it is more likely that an independent Scotland would join the EU in due course than that the UK, if it left, would re-join the EU any time soon. A potential EU referendum thus brings an element of ambiguity to the Scottish independence referendum. A formalistic objection could be made that, in 2014, Scots will be voting on secession from the UK, not from the EU, as the latter is not a state. However, it will now be argued that the complexity and the "special nature" of the EU legal system have important implications for the rights and duties

---

online: <http://www.electoralcommission.org.uk/__data/assets/pdf_file/0007/153691/Referendum-on-independence-for-Scotland-our-advice-on-referendum-question.pdf>.

[104] "David Cameron Promises in/out Referendum on EU," *supra* note 7.

[105] See "Scotland and the EU: The Polling Evidence," *Newsnet Scotland* (16 February 2013), online: <http://newsnetscotland.com/index.php/scottish-opinion/6761-scotland-and-the-eu-the-polling-evidence>.

[106] *Ibid.*

[107] *Treaty on the Functioning of the European Union*, [2010] OJ C83/47, art 20 [*TFEU*].

of UK citizens, including those eligible to vote in the Scottish referendum.[108]

THE IMPORTANCE OF THE EU ELEMENT

Boyle and Crawford demonstrate that by exiting the UK, Scotland would effectively also exit the EU.[109] While international law supports automatic succession to certain treaties — in particular, those of human rights and humanitarian character[110] — there is no automatic succession to closed treaties that establish international organizations or other institutionalized supra-state arrangements.[111] As established by the Court of Justice of the European Union (CJEU) in *Van Gend en Loos v Nederlandse Administratie der Belastingen*, the EU is not only an international treaty regime but also "constitutes a new legal order of international law for the benefit of which the states have limited their sovereign rights, albeit within limited fields, and the subjects of which comprise not only Member States but also their nationals."[112] The EU question thus critically affects the future status of Scotland and the rights and duties of its people. Through independence, Scots would exit not only the UK but also a supranational arrangement to which member states have transferred some of their sovereign powers and which grants to the citizens of its member states Union citizenship and rights stemming from it.[113]

Since there is no precedent of a territory exiting the EU in which the facts and circumstances would be Scotland-like,[114] there has been speculation on how EU citizenship doctrine could influence the

---

[108] Compare *Van Gend en Loos v Nederlandse Administratie der Belastingen*, C-26/62 [1963] ECR 1 at 12 [*Van Gend en Loos*].

[109] Crawford and Boyle, *supra* note 9 at paras 142-67.

[110] A Rasulov, "Revisiting State Succession to Humanitarian Treaties: Is There a Case for Automaticity?" (2003) 14 Eur J Int'l L 141. See also Crawford and Boyle, *supra* note 9 at paras 134-42.

[111] *Ibid* at paras 119-33.

[112] *Van Gend en Loos, supra* note 108 at 12.

[113] *TFEU, supra* note 107, art 20.

[114] See Tierney, *supra* note 4 at 21, giving the examples of Algeria and Greenland but concluding that these situations were different because Algeria was effectively a French colony — and thus an instance of decolonization — while Greenland did not become independent and actually held a referendum on withdrawal from the European Economic Community. According to Tierney, the novel situation in the Scottish case is that Scotland would not be seeking to leave the EU but, in fact, to join it.

EU status of an independent Scotland. Boyle and Crawford caution that the CJEU could potentially decide that Scots simply may not be deprived of their EU citizenship rights.[115] This is more speculation than argument and is based on the CJEU's case law affirming the importance of the rights stemming from EU citizenship.[116] However, this issue has been explored further, and there appear to be two ways in which EU citizenship doctrine may be relevant in the context of Scottish independence. The first pertains to the question of whether Scottish citizens could remain EU citizens without retaining UK nationality. The second, expanded argument uses EU citizenship doctrine as a premise for establishing Scotland's automatic accession to the EU.

The CJEU's citizenship doctrine should not be understood too broadly, in the sense of "once an EU citizen always an EU citizen." Most citizenship cases referred to in this context deal with the extent of the rights of a person who is undoubtedly a national of an EU member state.[117] This is not analogous to the issues pertaining to Scotland's potential independence. The facts were, however, different in *Rottmann v Freistaat Bayern*, where EU citizenship was indeed lost when the person involved became stateless.[118] Yet it is also quite different from what is at stake in the case of Scotland.

Article 20(1) of the *Treaty on the Functioning of the European Union* (*TFEU*) provides: "Citizenship of the Union is hereby established. Every person holding the nationality of a Member State shall be a citizen of the Union. Citizenship of the Union shall be additional to and not replace national citizenship."[119] Union citizenship thus depends on citizenship of a member state. If an independent Scotland were not a member of the EU, Scottish citizenship alone would not carry EU citizenship with it. Otherwise it would need to be accepted that one can be an EU citizen directly — that is, without being a citizen of an EU member state. This would be in clear conflict with Article 20(1) of the *TFEU*. Even in *Rottmann*, the CJEU did

---

[115] Crawford and Boyle, *supra* note 9 at para 171.

[116] *Ibid* at paras 176-78.

[117] See, for example, *Rudy Grzelczyk v CPAS*, C-184/99, [2001] ECR I-6193; *Zhu and Chen v Secretary of State for the Home Department*, C-200/02, [2004] ECR I-9925; *Ruiz Zambrano v ONEM*, C-34/09, [2011] ECR I-1177.

[118] *Rottmann v Freistaat Bayern*, C-135/08, [2010] ECR I-1449 [*Rottmann*].

[119] *TFEU*, *supra* note 107, art 20(1).

not rule that EU citizenship can never be lost. Rather, it continued to subordinate EU citizenship to citizenship of a member state.[120]

If EU citizenship in the "exit situation" were not lost, not only would citizens of an independent Scotland retain EU citizenship, but so would UK citizens in all circumstances, even if they decide that the UK should leave the EU. This would create an asymmetric situation in which UK citizens would enjoy Union citizenship rights in EU member states, while non-UK EU citizens would no longer enjoy these rights in the UK. The more expansive reading of EU citizenship doctrine suggests that in order to preserve the EU citizenship of Scots, Scotland itself would be entitled to automatic succession to EU treaties.[121] Stephen Tierney describes this interpretation as "simply not plausible," as it overstretches the CJEU's citizenship doctrine to have implications for treaty succession.[122]

A more plausible argument is, however, presented by David Edward, who not only accepts the premise that there would be no automatic accession to the EU for Scotland but also sees the independence of Scotland as a matter coming within the purview of Article 50 of the *Treaty on European Union (TEU)*, which regulates the circumstances in which a member state wishes to leave the EU.[123] Pursuant to Article 50, the future relationship of Scotland with the EU would be subject to negotiations[124] and to a two-year withdrawal period, unless negotiated otherwise.[125] Negotiations would have to be conducted in good faith and result in the amendment of EU treaties to acknowledge an independent Scotland and a diminished

---

[120] The court decided, rather, that when a national court decides on withdrawal of a fraudulently obtained citizenship, it needs to consider whether this is proportionate, in light of EU law. *Rottmann, supra* note 118 at para 55.

[121] A O'Neill, "A Quarrel in a Faraway Country?: Scotland, Independence and the EU," *Eutopia Law* (14 November 2011), online: <http://eutopialaw.com/2011/11/14/685>.

[122] Tierney, *supra* note 4 at 22.

[123] *Treaty on European Union*, [2010] OJ C83/13, art 50 [*TEU*]. See D Edward, "Scotland and the European Union," *Scottish Constitutional Futures* (17 December 2012) at paras 3-4, online: <http://www.scottishconstitutionalfutures.org/OpinionandAnalysis/ViewBlogPost/tabid/1767/articleType/ArticleView/articleId/852/David-Edward-Scotland-and-the-European-Union.aspx>.

[124] *TEU, supra* note 123, art 50(2).

[125] *Ibid*, art 50(3).

UK.[126] Scots would thus never lose EU citizenship, and Scotland would not accede to the EU as a new member state. Rather, Scotland would emerge as a new state under international law, but under EU law the territory would never leave the Union.

A negotiated entry into the EU at the moment of independence may seem to be an elegant solution and it may even be politically likely, but doubts linger over the claim that this would result from Article 50 of the *TEU*, which is concerned with the withdrawal of EU member states rather than territories seceding from member states and wishing to be EU members.[127] What is more, even if Edward's Article 50 argument were correct in principle, it rightly acknowledges that there would be no automatic accession. Rather, the outcome would still be determined by negotiations. As soon as the applicable law does not predetermine a certain outcome, such an outcome cannot be presumed. One can certainly accept the obligation to negotiate in good faith, but the outcome is nevertheless pushed to the realm of political negotiation rather than legal automaticity. The negotiations could become complicated and uncertain for reasons having little to do with Scotland but, instead, having to do with matters internal to EU member states. It must therefore be concluded that a vote for independence would lead to (at least) uncertainty with regard to EU membership.

FREEZING SOME EXISTING EU CITIZENSHIP RIGHTS

Thus far, it has been established that Scotland's EU membership would not be automatic and EU citizenship could be lost for those Scottish citizens who would not also retain UK citizenship. However, it is arguable that some aspects of citizenship rights extant at the moment of independence would be retained by some categories of people, even if Scotland found itself outside the EU. This effect would not follow directly from EU law but, rather, from the *ECHR*,[128] to which Scotland would succeed automatically,[129] due to a doctrine developed by the European Court of Human Rights (ECtHR) in *Kuric and Others v Slovenia*.[130]

Upon achieving independence, Slovenia denied the continued right of residency to a number of citizens of other states emerging

---

[126] Edward, *supra* note 123 at para 19.

[127] See further Tierney, *supra* note 4 at 24.

[128] *ECHR, supra* note 13.

[129] Crawford and Boyle, *supra* note 9 at paras 134-41.

[130] *Kuric and Others v Slovenia*, No 26828/06, [2013] 56 EHRR 20 [*Kuric*].

from the former SFRY who had, while the SFRY still existed, established their permanent residency in Slovenia.[131] According to the ECtHR in *Kurić,* withdrawing the right to permanent residency from these foreign citizens upon Slovenia's independence was a violation of the ECHR's right to private and family life.[132] The court recalled that the *ECHR* does not give a citizen of a party to the convention a right of residence in another state party.[133] However, in some circumstances, restrictions on the right of residency can interfere with the ECHR's right to private and family life.[134] As the Court put it in the case of Slovenia: "[P]rior to Slovenia's declaration of independence, [the applicants] had been lawfully residing in Slovenia for several years, [and] had, as former SFRY citizens, enjoyed a wide range of social and political rights."[135] The court continued:

[A]n alien lawfully residing in a country may wish to continue living in that country without necessarily acquiring its citizenship. As shown by the difficulties faced by the applicants, for many years, in obtaining a valid residence permit, the Slovenian legislature failed to enact provisions aimed at permitting former SFRY citizens holding the citizenship of one of the other republics to regularise their residence status if they had chosen not to become Slovenian citizens or had failed to do so. Such provisions would not have undermined the legitimate aims of controlling the residence of aliens or creating a corpus of Slovenian citizens, or both.[136]

Following this logic, once you have legally established permanent residency, you retain the right of residence even if the legal status of either your home or your host state changes, and, as a result of this change, your new citizenship status alone would no longer give you a right to residence. What matters is that you had the right at the moment of the change of territorial status. It is notable that the court established that non-citizen residents enjoy this guarantee under the *ECHR*'s right to private and family life in their own right. It does not depend on, for example, a family relationship with a citizen of the host state.

---

131 *Ibid* at paras 21-39.

132 *Ibid* at para 337.

133 *Ibid* at para 355.

134 *Ibid.*

135 *Ibid* at para 356.

136 *Ibid* at para 357.

In the context of two UK referenda, this doctrine has implications for several categories of people: (1) potential future Scottish citizens residing in a rump UK; (2) potential future Scottish citizens residing in other EU member states; (3) UK citizens residing in other EU member states; (4) non-UK EU citizens residing in the UK; and (5) non-UK EU citizens residing in Scotland. Following the *Kuric* doctrine, it appears that regardless of what happens in either referendum, in all circumstances the identified categories of people would retain their present residence rights. This would be so regardless of whether Scotland became independent without joining the EU and regardless of whether the UK exited the EU.

In other terms, even if EU citizenship is lost due to a change in the legal status of a territory, the *ECHR* protects the right of residence of those lawfully residing in territories covered by EU law at the moment of independence. Importantly, this effect would "cement" existing residence rights but would not extend the applicability of EU law to the territories exiting the EU (whether an independent Scotland, a rump UK, or the UK as it currently exists). The *ECHR* effect would also diminish the negative impact of Scotland's exit from the UK on those people with EU citizenship rights at the moment of independence.

This effect further undermines the strength of the EU citizenship argument with regard to Scotland's continued EU membership due to the fact that this argument is underpinned by the premise that an independent Scotland must be an EU member in order to protect extant EU citizenship and free movement rights, which would otherwise be lost "at the midnight hour."[137] However, rights stemming from EU citizenship would not simply be terminated "at the midnight hour." The *ECHR* will continue to protect those prospective Scottish citizens who, at the moment of independence, reside in EU member states as well as those EU citizens who, at the critical moment, reside in Scotland. EU citizenship is thus not necessary to "freeze" these existing rights. Hence, the effects of the EU citizenship doctrine for the future status of Scotland in the EU should not be exaggerated.

In the end, it has to be presumed that, following independence, Scotland's EU membership would be neither automatic nor guaranteed. It would rather depend on the outcome of political negotiations. And neither would UK citizens continue to enjoy EU

---

[137] Compare Edward, *supra* note 123 at para 12.

citizenship rights should they opt for exiting the EU. The *ECHR* would, however, prevent revocation of the right of residence in respect of the categories of people identified earlier.

CONCLUSION

The UK government is committed to respecting the will of the people of Scotland. International law does not require it to do so. Such an acceptance is indeed rare in comparative practice. In most circumstances, successful referenda merely contribute to the legitimacy of a claim for independence but are not sufficient for the emergence of a new state. International standards do not specify precise winning majorities or referendum questions, yet both need to satisfy the threshold requirement of clarity. Clarity is a society-and situation-specific concept. In terms of winning majorities, the most commonly prescribed threshold is that of a majority of all votes cast. A minimum turnout is usually also prescribed, most commonly 50 percent of all those eligible to vote. A majority of all those eligible to vote has only been prescribed on one occasion, but it is nevertheless achieved in practice in most situations. Exceptions exist, however, and Montenegro has become independent with less than half of the electorate endorsing that outcome. In Scotland, the opinion polls currently suggest that independence would not win a relative majority. Even if this turns around, one cannot reasonably expect a majority of all those eligible to vote. Scotland could thus become only the second state in contemporary practice to be created by a minority vote in absolute terms.

However, the Scottish referendum is not easily compared with most other independence referenda in recent international practice. Where independence results from years of oppression and a long struggle for independence, near universal support for independence can be expected. Scotland is also the only example in contemporary practice (outside an internationalized peace settlement context) where the central government has committed itself, in advance, to respecting the outcome. In addition, given domestic criticism of the 40 percent turnout requirement in the 1979 devolution referendum, it is plausible that, in the Scottish circumstances, the clarity threshold can be met by a less qualified majority, potentially even significantly below 50 percent of all those eligible to vote.

No automatic accession of Scotland to the EU can be presumed, and EU citizenship for Scottish citizens is not guaranteed. A vote for an independent Scotland is, at least *prima facie,* also a vote for Scotland outside of the EU. Moreover, with the possibility of an EU referendum also in the equation, it is now unclear whether or not a vote for the UK in the Scottish referendum would also mean a vote for remaining in the EU. This article has argued that the EU is a legal order with critical implications for the legal status of Scotland, the extent of Scottish sovereignty, its economic development, and the daily lives of its citizens, within Scotland itself and also when they travel abroad. The complexity of the EU legal order makes EU membership a factor that needs to be clarified before Scots decide on independence. Otherwise, the vote will be flawed with impermissible ambiguity.

However, holding an EU referendum before the Scottish independence referendum is not a solution. Opinion polls suggest that EU support in Scotland is significantly higher than the UK average. This could result in the UK remaining within the EU due to Scottish votes. In the next step, Scotland could opt for independence, having effectively forced the rump UK to remain in the EU against the wishes of a majority of its people. Yet the opposite could also happen if Scots voted to remain within the UK, motivated, *inter alia,* by the fact that independence would also mean Scotland's *prima facie* exit from the EU. In the next step in this alternative scenario, predominantly English votes could take Scotland, together with the rest of the UK, out of the EU anyway.

In order to avoid ambiguity and ensure fairness, the UK should first settle Scotland's status by allowing the Scottish independence vote to proceed and its outcome to sink in. A reasonable time frame should then be allowed before holding an EU referendum in order to avoid its potential influences on the Scottish independence vote. The required reasonable time frame cannot be defined in terms of an exact number of years. However, in order to avoid the mutual influence of the two referenda, it may be too early to hold the EU referendum in the next parliamentary term. The EU dimension is such an important determinant of the future legal status of Scotland that Scots have a right to know whether, at least in the near future, the alternative to independence is the UK within or outside the EU. If the two referenda were to fall too close to each other, the clarity of the outcome of the independence referendum would be unduly compromised.

Sommaire

Il n'existe pas, en droit international, de normes procédurales universellement applicables aux référendums sur l'indépendance. Cependant, la pratique comparative contemporaine révèle une exigence minimale de clarté quant à la majorité gagnante requise ainsi que sur la question référendaire elle-même. L'auteur démontre que l'Écosse pourrait devenir un état indépendant avec le plus faible soutien populaire dans la pratique internationale récente, mais que ceci ne remettrait pas en cause la légitimité du vote. Même le texte de la question référendaire écossaise est un modèle de clarté. Cependant, la possibilité d'un référendum sur le retrait éventuel du Royaume-Uni de l'Union européenne (UE) complique la situation. L'auteur prétend qu'advenant son indépendance du Royaume-Uni (R-U), l'Écosse quitterait également l'UE s'il n'en est pas convenu autrement. Mais avec un éventuel référendum sur le retrait du R-U de l'UE à l'horizon, les Écossais ne peuvent savoir si un vote pour demeurer partie du R-U est également un vote pour demeurer partie de l'UE. Étant donné la complexité et l'importance de l'ordre juridique de l'UE, les Écossais ont le droit de savoir si l'alternative à l'indépendance est de demeurer partie du R-U à l'intérieur, ou à l'extérieur, de l'UE. Si les deux référendums sont trop rapprochés l'un de l'autre, la clarté du référendum sur l'indépendance écossaise pourrait être indûment compromise.

Summary

There are no universally applicable procedural standards under international law for independence referenda. However, in contemporary comparative practice, a minimum requirement has emerged for clarity of both the winning majority and the referendum question. This article demonstrates that Scotland could become an independent state with the lowest popular support in recent international practice, yet this outcome would not compromise the legitimacy of the vote. Even the referendum question is an exemplar of textual clarity. However, the possibility of a referendum on the United Kingdom's (UK) exit from the European Union (EU) complicates the matter. The author argues that, with independence, Scotland would, *prima facie,* also exit the EU, unless negotiated otherwise. However, with a potential referendum on the UK's EU membership on the horizon, Scots do not know whether a vote to remain within the UK is also a vote to remain within the EU. Given the complexity and significance of the EU legal order, Scots have a right to know whether, at least in the near future, the alternative to independence is the UK within or outside the EU. If the two referenda fall too close to each other, the clarity of the Scottish independence referendum could be unduly compromised.

Does International Criminal Law Create Humanitarian Law Obligations? The Case of Exclusively Non-State Armed Conflict under the *Rome Statute*

ALAIN-GUY TACHOU-SIPOWO

INTRODUCTION

Defining the concept of armed conflict has been a continual challenge for international humanitarian law (IHL) since 1949, particularly with respect to non-international armed conflict (NIAC).[1] A definition is important because it can clarify whether IHL, or some other body of law, applies to a given situation.[2] While the 1949 *Geneva Conventions*[3] have taken a more effective approach to this issue by shifting the focus from the subjective concept of "declared war" to the more objective notion of "armed conflict,"[4] most writers have remained consistently critical with respect to the

---

Alain-Guy Tachou-Sipowo, LL.D. (Laval, 2014) is Lecturer in International Law and former Supervisor of the International Criminal Court's Legal Tools Project — Canadian Partnership at the International Criminal and Humanitarian Law Clinic in the Faculty of Law at Laval University, Quebec.

[1] For a comprehensive overview of the concept of non-international armed conflict, see Anthony Cullen, *The Concept of Non-International Armed Conflict in International Humanitarian Law* (Cambridge: Cambridge University Press, 2010).

[2] Sylvain Vité, "Typology of Armed Conflicts in International Humanitarian Law: Legal Concepts and Actual Situations" (2009) 91:873 Int'l Rev Red Cross 69 at 70 (arguing that, "depending on how the situations are legally defined, the rules that apply vary from one case to the next").

[3] *Geneva Convention (I) for the Amelioration of the Condition of the Wounded and Sick in Armed Forces in the Field*, 75 UNTS 31 (12 August 1949); *Geneva Convention (II) for the Amelioration of the Condition of Wounded, Sick and Shipwrecked Members of Armed Forces at Sea*, 75 UNTS 85 (12 August 1949); *Geneva Convention (III) Relative to the Treatment of Prisoners of War*, 75 UNTS 135 (12 August 1949); *Geneva Convention IV Relative to the Protection of Civilian Persons in Time of War*, 75 UNTS 287 (12 August 1949) [*Geneva Conventions*].

[4] According to the concept of "armed conflict," IHL may apply once some "specific factual conditions are met." See Vité, *supra* note 2 at 72, referring to Jean Pictet et al, eds, *Geneva Convention I for the Amelioration of the Condition of the Wounded and*

negative definition of NIAC and, in particular, its high threshold.[5] As a result of IHL's relative institutional vacuum, the search for a more suitable definition of NIAC had to await the creation, in the early 1990s, of the ad hoc United Nations (UN) criminal tribunals.[6] Among their inestimable contributions has been the clarification of the concept of armed conflict, particularly in the non-international context.

This article takes a critical look at the contributions of the International Criminal Tribunal for the Former Yugoslavia (ICTY) to the definition of NIAC, more particularly in the context of conflicts exclusively between non-state organized armed groups — that is, non-state armed conflicts (NSAC).[7] Endorsed by the *Rome Statute of the International Criminal Court* (ICC)[8] and applauded by many scholars as well as the International Committee of the Red Cross (ICRC),[9]

Sick in Armed Forces in the Field: Commentary (Geneva: International Committee of the Red Cross, 1952) at 32; Robert Kolb, *Jus in bello: Le droit international des conflits armés* (Basel and Brussels: Helbing and Lichtenhahn/Bruylant, 2003) at 72.

[5] Unlike international armed conflict, which exists even with a low level of violence, the existence of internal armed conflict is appraised through the lens of "protracted violence," meaning in essence that the conflict must reach a certain degree of intensity and that the parties must be organized. See *Prosecutor v Tadić*, International Criminal Tribunal for the Former Yugoslavia (ICTY) Case no IT—94-1-AR72, Decision on the Defense Motion for Interlocutory Appeal on Jurisdiction (2 October 2005) at para 70 (Appeals Chamber) [*Tadić*]; *Prosecutor v Boskoski*, ICTY Case no IT-04-82, Judgment (10 July 2008) at para 175 (Trial Chamber); *Prosecutor v Rutaganda*, International Criminal Tribunal for Rwanda (ICTR) Case no ICTR-96-3, Judgment (6 December 1999) at para 93 (Trial Chamber I).

[6] *Security Council Resolution 808 (1993)*, UNSCOR, 3175th Mtg, UN Doc S/RES/808 (1993) at para 1, establishing an international tribunal for the prosecution of persons responsible for serious violations of international humanitarian law committed in the territory of the former Yugoslavia since 1991; *Security Council Resolution 955 (1994)*, UNSCOR, 3453rd Mtg, UN Doc S/RES/955 (1994) at para 1, establishing "an international tribunal for the sole purpose of prosecuting persons responsible for genocide and other serious violations of international humanitarian law committed in the territory of Rwanda and Rwandan citizens responsible for genocide and other such violations committed in the territory of neighbouring States, between 1 January 1994 and 31 December 1994."

[7] *Tadić*, *supra* note 5.

[8] *Rome Statute of the International Criminal Court*, 2187 UNTS 3, arts 8(2)(e)-(f) (entered into force 1 July 2002) [*Rome Statute*].

[9] ICRC, *How Is the Term "Armed Conflict" Defined in International Humanitarian Law?* Opinion Paper (March 2008) at 4, online: ICRC <http://www.icrc.org/web/eng/siteengo.nsf/html/armed-conflict-article-170308>.

this newly defined category of conflict poses daunting challenges with regard to the nature of the legal regime applicable to it.

In the following section, it is argued that the international legal foundations upon which this innovation has been built are weak, considering the reasoning of the ICTY in *Prosecutor v Tadić* and the legislative history of common Article 3 of the *Geneva Conventions*.[10] The next section will look at the implications for the IHL regime of offences committed in NSAC. It asserts that war crimes arising out of such conflicts form the basis of an IHL regime, the implementation of which is likely to be catalyzed by the *Rome Statute*'s complementarity principle. In addition, the scope of IHL rules ensuing from the provisions of the *Rome Statute* regarding NSAC will be discussed. The analysis will show that the elements of these provisions are incomplete for IHL purposes. Indeed, setting aside the principle of distinction, they are insufficient and vague with respect to the principle of proportionality and limitations on the means and methods of warfare.

The final section recognizes the need to bring NSAC within the scope of IHL, particularly in the political context of failed states. However, it will argue that IHL cannot be the sole applicable regime, as the conflicts it would seek to regulate lie at the intersection of various legal relations. Therefore, it will be necessary to distinguish between the law-enforcement paradigm, governed by international human rights law (IHRL) and which may find application in regard to the taking up of arms by non-state groups against the state or a UN force, and the armed-conflict paradigm, in which conflict between non-state entities and a law enforcement mechanism as well as conflict exclusively between non-state entities are governed by IHL.

Exclusively NSAC as a Category of NIAC

The *Tadić* Decision on Jurisdiction

While common Article 3 of the *Geneva Conventions* does not define the concept of NIAC, *Protocol II Additional to the Geneva Conventions and Relating to the Protection of Victims of Non-International Armed Conflicts (Additional Protocol II)*, which was adopted to develop the protections set out in this provision, states explicitly that it applies to armed conflicts that

---

[10] *Geneva Conventions, supra* note 3, art 3.

take place in the territory of a High Contracting Party between its armed forces and dissident armed forces or other organized armed groups which, under responsible command, exercise such control over a part of its territory as to enable them to carry out sustained and concerted military operations and to implement this Protocol.[11]

This provision, however, as is the case with the *Geneva Conventions* in general, provides no guidance in regard to the meaning of "armed conflict" itself,[12] not to mention the notion of "military operations," which are the material manifestations of armed conflict.

Therefore, the approach of the ad hoc tribunals to this issue was highly anticipated. The ICTY's *Tadić* decision on 2 October 1995 is authoritative in this regard.[13] In this case, the defence objected, unsuccessfully, that the ICTY lacked jurisdiction *ratione materiae*.[14] It argued that the material jurisdiction of the tribunal, as set forth in Articles 2, 3, and 5 of the *Statute of the International Criminal Tribunal for the Former Yugoslavia*,[15] was limited to crimes committed in the context of international armed conflict and that, even if proven,

---

[11] *Protocol Additional (II) to the Geneva Conventions of 12 August 1949, and Relating to the Protection of Victims of Non-International Armed Conflicts*, 1125 UNTS 609, art 1(1) (entered into force 7 December 1978) [*Additional Protocol II*].

[12] In the commentary by the International Committee of the Red Cross (ICRC) on the third *Geneva Convention*, Pictet attempts a definition of "armed conflict": "[A]ny difference arising between States and leading to the intervention of members of armed forces is an armed conflict." Jean Pictet, *Commentary on the Geneva Convention of 12 August 1949 Relative to the Treatment of Prisoners of War* (Geneva: ICRC, 1958) at 23. It therefore seems that resort to armed forces in the context of a dispute between states may suffice for an international armed conflict to exist, while for a NIAC, "protracted armed violence" between the parties must be shown. *Tadić, supra* note 5; Rogier Bartels, "Timelines, Borderlines and Conflicts: The Historical Evolution of the Legal Divide between International and Non-International Armed Conflicts" (2009) 91:893 Int'l Rev Red Cross 35 at 38.

[13] Andrew J Carswell, "Classifying the Conflict: A Soldier's Dilemma" (2009) 91:893 Int'l Rev Red Cross 143 at 150.

[14] Tadić was charged with wilful killing, torture or inhuman treatment, wilfully causing great suffering or serious injury to body or health, as war crimes and crimes against humanity. *Prosecutor v Tadić*, ICTY Case no IT-94-1-T, Opinion and Judgement (7 May 1997) at para 9 (Trial Chamber).

[15] Article 2 of the *ICTY Statute* provides for the prosecution of grave breaches of the *Geneva Conventions* of 1949, Article 3 for violations of the law or customs of war, and Article 5 for crimes against humanity. see *Statute of the International Criminal Tribunal for the Former Yugoslavia*, approved by (and annexed to) *Security Council Resolution 827 (1993)*, UN Doc S/RES/827 (1993) at para 2 [*ICTY Statute*].

the crimes charged against the accused had been committed in the context of an internal armed conflict.[16] On appeal, the defence also argued that no armed conflict existed in the region at the time the alleged crimes were said to have occurred.

The Appeals Chamber decided that "an armed conflict exists whenever there is a resort to armed force between States or protracted armed violence between governmental authorities and organized armed groups or between such groups within a State."[17] This passage was received within the legal community with some enthusiasm, as it filled the void left by the absence of an authoritative definition of the notion of armed conflict. Yet, from a legal standpoint, the basis for appending the words "between such groups within a State" to the definition were questionable.

First, Tadić's defence did not question the existence of an armed conflict on the grounds of participation but, rather, on the grounds of geographical and temporal scope. In other words, the issues were whether IHL was applicable, in the case of armed conflict, on the whole or only in part of the territory in which the conflict was occurring and at what point in time the conflict ends.[18] Therefore, it can be argued that the statement of the Appeals Chamber was nothing but an *obiter dictum*.[19]

Second, encapsulating conflict exclusively between non-state armed groups in the definition of armed conflict appeared not to be grounded in the drafting history of the *Geneva Conventions*. The only provision of the *Geneva Conventions* and their additional protocols from which the subjection of NSAC to IHL could be inferred is common Article 3.[20] This article provides for respect of some minimum guarantees by each party to the conflict "[i]n the case of

---

[16] *Tadić, supra* note 5 at para 65.

[17] *Ibid* at para 70.

[18] *Ibid* at para 67.

[19] The answer addressing the defence's concern was as follows: "International humanitarian law applies from the initiation of ... armed conflict and extends beyond the cessation of hostilities until a general conclusion of the peace is reached, yet, in the case of internal conflicts, a peaceful settlement is achieved. Until that moment, international humanitarian law continues to apply in the whole territory of the warring states or, in the case of internal conflicts, the whole territory under the control of a party, whether or not actual combat takes place there." *Tadić, supra* note 5 at para 70.

[20] Robin Geiß, "Armed Violence in Fragile States: Low-Intensity Conflicts, Spillover Conflicts, and Sporadic Law Enforcement Operations by Third Parties" (2009) 91:873 Int'l Rev Red Cross 127 at 133.

armed conflict not of an international character occurring in the territory of one of the High Contracting Parties."[21] As has been argued by Robert Ash, "[t]he final records of the 1949 Conference provide no indication that article 3 dealt with ... anything other than civil wars and their close relations, such as rebellions, insurgencies, or colonial wars."[22] Moreover, most of the delegations, including those of Canada and the United States, defined the expression "conflict not of an international character" as "covering only a limited type of civil war."[23]

In fact, an overwhelming majority of delegations, while accepting that internal conflicts should be regulated by IHL, construed the notion of "conflict not of an international character" as necessarily involving a state as a party to the conflict.[24] The principal divergences between the delegates was, rather, twofold: first, the determination of the threshold according to which recourse of a state to armed force against a segment of its population would amount to a conflict not of an international character subject to IHL and, second, whether the *Geneva Conventions* had to be applied to such a conflict in part or in full.[25]

Far from its etymological meaning of "any internal armed conflict between persons of [the] same country"[26] or "war between the citizens of one country,"[27] civil war is now commonly understood as

[21] *Geneva Conventions, supra* note 3, art 3.

[22] Robert Weston Ash, "Square Pegs and Round Holes: Al-Qaeda Detainees and Common Article 3" (2007) 17:2 Ind Int'l & Comp L Rev 269 at 290.

[23] Switzerland Federal Political Department, *Final Record of the Diplomatic Conference of Geneva of 1949*, volume 2(B) (Buffalo, NY: William S Hein and Company, 2004) at 13.

[24] Indeed, the United Kingdom understood the notion of "conflict not of an international character" as meaning "situations in which one of the combatants was the lawful government (e.g. in the case of civil war)." For Norway, "[i]t was not a conflict between ... individuals." For Spain, "[t]he conventions should only be applied in cases where the legal government was obliged to have recourse to the regular military forces against insurgents militarily organised and in possession of a part of the national territory." For Mexico, non-international armed conflict referred to "civil wars, wars of resistance or wars of liberation." See *ibid* at 10 (UK), 11 (Norway and Spain), 333 (Mexico).

[25] David A Elder, "The Historical Background of Common Article 3 of the Geneva Convention of 1949" (1979) 11:1 Case W Res J Int'l L 37 at 46.

[26] *Black's Law Dictionary*, 10th edition (St Paul, MN: Thomson Reuters, 2014), *sub verbo* "civil war."

[27] *New Lexicon Webster's Encyclopedic Dictionary of the English Language*, deluxe edition (New York: Lexicon Publications, 1989) *sub verbo* "civil war."

an armed conflict in which one side is necessarily a state.[28] It therefore refers to an "armed conflict between some segment of a State's
population and the ruling government of that State."[29] While this
approach, reaffirmed by *Additional Protocol II*, may have been under-
standable in 1949, it is now seen as failing to reflect the current reality of the "privatization" of war. New thinking has therefore emerged
as to the place of NSAC under IHL.

ENDORSEMENT BY THE ICC

The first proposal for regulating NSAC under IHL came from the
ICRC during the conference for the adoption of *Additional Protocol II*.[30] The proposal would have applied IHL to situations where
"the established government had disappeared or was too weak to
intervene."[31] Governments, who considered this to be "merely a
theoretical textbook example," bluntly rejected this proposal.[32]
Yet, the ICRC commentary contradictorily considers that while
NSAC is not covered by *Additional Protocol II*, "only common article
3 will apply."[33] This view is based on the assumption that common
Article 3 has remained an autonomous text unaffected by the protocol. This seems at odds with the supplementary character of the
protocol. Since *Additional Protocol II* stipulates that it does not alter
the conditions of application of common Article 3, it should consequently be admitted that the definition of NIAC as a conflict involving a state is not altered either.[34] This position is reinforced by
the language of Article 1, paragraph 1, of the protocol.

---

[28] Ann Hironaka, *Never-Ending Wars: The International Community, Weak States, and the Perpetuation of Civil War* (Cambridge, MA: Harvard University Press, 2005) at 3.

[29] Ash, *supra* note 22 at 279.

[30] Claude Pilloud et al, *Commentary on the Additional Protocols of 8 June 1977 to the Geneva Conventions of 1949* (Dordrecht: ICRC/Martinus Nijhoff, 1987) at 1351. However, the Institute of International Law, at its Wiesbaden session on 14 August 1975, defined the concept of civil war as clashes between "two or more groups which in the absence of any established government contend with one another for the control of the State." Institute of International Law, *The Principle of Non-Intervention in Civil Wars*, Wiesbaden Session, 8th Commission (Institute of International Law, 14 August 1975), art 1(1)(b).

[31] Pilloud et al, *supra* note 30 at 1351.

[32] *Ibid.*

[33] *Ibid.*

[34] *Additional Protocol II, supra* note 11, art 1(1).

Indeed, *Additional Protocol II*'s stipulation that the conditions of application of common Article 3 remain unchanged refers mainly to determining the threshold at which an internal uprising against a state becomes a NIAC, triggering the application of common Article 3. In 1949, states had not set such a minimum threshold, in contrast to *Additional Protocol II*, which expressly does not apply to situations of internal disturbances and tensions such as riots, isolated and sporadic acts of violence, and other acts of a similar nature.[35] It follows that the conditions of application that remain unchanged include those pertaining to the nature of the parties to the conflict, which necessarily comprise a state. Common Article 3 will continue to apply to conflicts of low intensity and organization, while the more rigorous criteria of *Additional Protocol II* will have to be met for the protocol to be invoked.[36] Common Article 3 remains autonomous in this regard, and the conflicts to which it applies should have the same structure as originally conceived in 1949 — that is, uprisings within a state in defiance of the government.[37] Consequently, taking into account both their drafting history and their express wording, common Article 3 and *Additional Protocol II* regulate conflicts in which at least one party is a state, whatever their differences with respect to requirements regarding the degree of organization of the parties and the intensity of hostilities.

Yet, a teleological approach to interpreting these two legal frameworks — one advanced by the ICRC, supported by the *Tadić* jurisdiction judgment, and now widely endorsed,[38] would submit NSAC to

---

[35] *Ibid*, art 1(2).

[36] Alexander Zahar and Göran Sluiter, *International Criminal Law* (Oxford: Oxford University Press, 2008) at 118.

[37] Charles Lysaght, "The Scope of Protocol II and Its Relation to Common Article 3 of the Geneva Conventions of 1949 and Other Human Rights Instruments" (1983) 33 Am UL Rev 9 at 14.

[38] James G Stewart, "Towards a Single Definition of Armed Conflict in International Humanitarian Law: A Critique of Internationalized Armed Conflict" (2003) 85:850 Int'l Rev Red Cross 313 at 319; Dieter Fleck, *The Handbook of International Humanitarian Law*, 2nd edition (Oxford: Oxford University Press, 2008) at 609; Geiß, *supra* note 20 at 133. For the modern approach to the notion of non-international armed conflict, see International Law Association (Committee on the Use of Force), "Initial Report on the Meaning of Armed Conflict in International Law" (paper prepared for the Rio De Janeiro Conference, 2008) at 6, online: <http://www.ila-hq.org/en/committees/index.cfm/cid/1022>. See also Mary Ellen O'Connell, "Defining Armed Conflict" (2009) 13:2 J Confl & Sec L 393 at 393-400.

the regulation of IHL. However, in accordance with the minority *Tadić* opinion rejecting this progressive interpretation,[39] the ICTR has chosen not to depart from the plain wording of the two instruments.[40] Ruling on the applicability of common Article 3 and *Additional Protocol II*, the ICTR Trial Chamber found, in 1999, that an international armed conflict is distinct from a NIAC in that the latter is "conducted *by a State* and another armed force which does not qualify as a State."[41]

Subsequently, in *Prosecutor v Musema*, the ICTR Trial Chamber held that "a non-international conflict is distinct from an international armed conflict because of the legal status of the entities opposing each other: the parties to the conflict are not sovereign States, but the *government of a single State* in conflict with one or more armed factions within its territory."[42] This stance appears to be more in line with the intentions of states,[43] while the approach in *Tadić* significantly departs from it. In any event, the ICC is now positioned in favour of the teleological approach, both in its statute and in the case law.

[39] Christopher Greenwood, "Scope of Application of Humanitarian Law" in Fleck, *supra* note 38, 54.

[40] See also International Institute of Humanitarian Law, *The Manual on the Law of Non-International Armed Conflict* (San Remo, Italy: International Institute of Humanitarian Law, 2006) at 2, online: <http://www.dur.ac.uk/resources/law/ NIACManualIYBHR15th.pdf>: "Non-international armed conflicts are armed confrontations occurring within the territory of a single State and in which the armed forces of no other State are engaged against the central government."

[41] *Prosecutor v Kayishema & Ruzindana*, ICTR Case no ICTR-95-1-T, Judgment and Sentence (21 May 1999) at para 170 [emphasis added]. It is noteworthy that one year before, in *Prosecutor v Jean-Paul Akayesu*, ICTR Case no ICTR-96-4-T, Judgment (2 September 1998) at paras 619-21 [*Akayesu*], the Trial Chamber, in ruling on the applicability of common Article 3, referred to the 1995 *Tadić* decision.

[42] *Prosecutor v Musema*, ICTR Case no ICTR-96-13-T, Judgment and Sentence (27 January 2000) at para 247 [emphasis added]. See also L Zegveld, *Accountability of Armed Opposition Groups in International Law* (Cambridge: Cambridge University Press, 2002) at 136: "[I]nternal conflicts are distinguished from international armed conflicts by the parties involved rather than by the territorial scope of the conflict."

[43] Ash warns about overlooking state intent in interpreting international treaties, questioning "why States would desire to enter into future agreements if the terms they have agreed to in past treaties are to be stretched beyond recognition and applied in a manner inconsistent with what was agreed." See Ash, *supra* note 22 at 274, n 15.

In negotiations leading to the adoption of the *Rome Statute*, the issue of prosecuting grave breaches of IHL committed in NIAC was a subject of acute debate. The discussion focused, again, on the scope of, and threshold for, internal armed conflict. Threshold provisions were intended primarily to accommodate delegations that feared interference in their internal affairs.[44] The Bureau of the conference rephrased section D of Article 5 *quater* of the then draft statute so that it would apply to NIAC as defined in Article 1(1) of *Additional Protocol II*.[45] The high threshold set by this provision would require that rebels be in control of territory and conduct military operations and that a state necessarily be involved.[46] In the text of the *Rome Statute* finally adopted, breaches of IHL committed in NIAC are divided between violations of common Article 3[47] and violations of laws and customs applicable in armed conflicts not of an international character.[48]

Article 8(2)(e) of the *Rome Statute* relates to the latter category. Similar to violations of common Article 3, its threshold, enshrined in Article 8(2)(f), excludes situations of internal disturbance and tensions. However, this latter provision introduces a key novelty with respect to the definition of a NIAC. For the ICC to prosecute violations of laws and customs applicable to NIAC (other than violations of common Article 3), it must ascertain that those violations arise from "armed conflicts that take place in the territory of a State when there is protracted armed conflict between governmental authorities and organized armed groups or between such groups."[49]

Proposed by Sierra Leone,[50] this definition, in which "protracted armed violence" is replaced by "protracted armed conflict," derives

---

[44] Anthony Cullen, "The Definition of Non-International Armed Conflict in the Rome Statute of the International Criminal Court: An Analysis of the Threshold of Application Contained in Article 8(2)(f)" (2008) 12:3 J Confl & Sec L 419 at 428.

[45] See Proposal of the Bureau, UN Doc A/CONF.183/C.1/L.5 (10 July 1998) at 9, in UN Diplomatic Conference of Plenipotentiaries on the Establishment of an International Criminal Court, *Official Records of the United Nations Diplomatic Conference of Plenipotentiaries on the Establishment of an International Criminal Court (Reports and Other Documents)*, volume 3 (New York: United Nations, 2002) at 212.

[46] See Cullen, *supra* note 44 at 429.

[47] *Rome Statute*, *supra* note 8, art 8(2)(c), (d).

[48] *Ibid*, art 8(2)(e).

[49] *Ibid*, art 8(2)(f).

[50] See *Thirty-fifth Meeting of the Committee of the Whole*, UN Doc A/CONF.183/C.1/SR.35 (13 July 1998) at para 8, in UN Diplomatic Conference of Plenipotentiaries

from the 1995 *Tadić* decision.[51] In fact, Article 8(2)(f) of the *Rome Statute* inherited more than this novel definition of NIAC. The notion of "laws and customs applicable in armed conflicts not of an international character" is in itself new. While it is quite certain that laws applicable in NIAC may relate to either common Article 3 and *Additional Protocol II*, the notion of "customs applicable in armed conflicts not of an international character" is grounded in the finding of the Appeals Chamber in *Tadić* that state practice tends to extend rules applicable in international armed conflict to NIAC.[52] Moreover, it is said that the two bodies of law have crystallized into customary IHL.[53] However, it remains unclear just when and how a state practice of prosecuting war crimes committed in NSAC emerged. If no such evidence of a customary practice can be adduced, one must agree with those commentators who argue that Article 8(2)(f) of the *Rome Statute* provides for a new category of NIAC.[54]

In its first judgment of March 2012, the Trial Chamber of the ICC did not touch upon this issue, although the accused, Thomas Lubanga, was found guilty of conscription, enlistment, and the utilization of child soldiers in an armed conflict not of an international character opposing exclusively non-state armed groups.[55] At the confirmation of charges stage of the proceedings, the Pre-Trial Chamber first characterized the conflict as international in nature. This characterization was justified by the fact that Uganda had intervened indirectly to support rebel groups operating against

---

on the Establishment of an International Criminal Court, 35th Meeting of the Committee of the Whole, *Official Records of the United Nations Diplomatic Conference of Plenipotentiaries on the Establishment of an International Criminal Court (Summary records of the plenary meetings and of the meetings of the Committee of the Whole)* volume 2 (New York: United Nations, 2002) at 334.

51 Theodor Meron, "Crimes under the Jurisdiction of the International Criminal Court" in Ham von Hebel et al, eds, *Reflections on the ICC* (The Hague: TMC Asser Press, 1994) at 54.

52 *Tadić, supra* note 5 at para 97.

53 *Ibid* at para 98.

54 Marco Sassoli and Antoine Bouvier, eds, *How Does Law Protect in War*, 2nd edition, volume 1 (Geneva: ICRC, 2006) at 110; René Provost, *International Human Rights and International Humanitarian Law* (Cambridge: Cambridge University Press, 2002) at 268-69; William A Schabas, *An Introduction to the International Criminal Court*, 3rd edition (Cambridge: Cambridge University Press, 2007) at 116.

55 *Prosecutor v Thomas Lubanga Dyilo*, International Criminal Court Case (ICC) no ICC-01/04-01/06-2842, Public Judgment pursuant to Article 74 of the Statute (14 March 2012) (Trial Chamber I) [*Lubanga*].

the Democratic Republic of Congo (DRC) during one period of the war. Yet the Pre-Trial Chamber also found the conflict to be non-international at another period in time, given that it had involved various armed factions, including Lubanga's armed group, fighting each other for control of a gold-mining area of Ituri without the implication of the DRC or any other foreign state.[56]

The prosecution, which sought confirmation of the charges only with respect to this latter category of conflict, was denied leave to appeal the decision of the Pre-Trial Chamber. However, at trial, the Trial Chamber inquired into the nature of the conflict. It concluded that

the existence of a possible conflict that was "international in character" between the DRC and Uganda does not affect the legal characterisation of the UPC/FPLC's [Union of Congolese Patriot / Forces Patriotiques pour la libération du Congo] concurrent non-international armed conflict with the APC and FRPI [Congolese People's Army and Forces de Résistance Patriotique d'Ituri] militias, which formed part of the internal armed conflict between the rebel groups.[57]

It therefore decided to view the relevant conflict, in which the accused's alleged war crimes were committed, as an "armed conflict between the UPC/FPLC and other armed groups."[58] Although the Trial Chamber did not address the point, it is worth examining what

---

[56] *Prosecutor v Thomas Lubanga Dyilo*, ICC Case no ICC-01/04-01/06-803-tEN, Public Redacted Version with Annex I of the Decision on the Confirmation of Charges (29 January 2007) at paras 220, 236 (Pre-Trial Chamber I).

[57] *Lubanga*, *supra* note 55 at para 565.

[58] *Ibid* at para 567. It is to be noted that in the subsequent case of Mathieu Ngudjolo, acquitted on charges of conscripting, enlisting, and utilizing children in hostilities, although the Trial Chamber did not precisely touch upon the nature of the conflict, it nevertheless concluded that there had been an attack by Ngiti and Lendu militias on the Bogoro village in eastern DRC, which was under the control of the UPC (a Hema militia). See *Prosecutor v Mathieu Ngudjolo*, ICC Case no ICC-01/04-02/12-3-tENG, Public Judgment pursuant to Article 74 of the Statute (18 December 2012) (Trial Chamber II) at 120-25. However, in the case of Germain Katanga, after an extensive analysis of the nature of the conflict prevailing at the time of the attack on the Bogoro village, the same Chamber recharacterized the conflict, which pitted APC, Ngiti, and Lendu combatants (to whom the Ugandan army lent its support) against the UPC, as an NIAC and not an exclusively NSAC. See *Prosecutor v Germain Katanga*, ICC Case no ICC-01/04-01/07-3436, Public Judgment pursuant to Article 74 of the Statute (7 March 2012) (Trial Chamber II) at paras 1229-30.

implications this conception of a NIAC, crafted within an international criminal law context, entails for IHL.

IMPLICATIONS FOR IHL

IHL is the source of grave breaches prosecuted under international criminal law (ICL). One implication of the establishment of a system of offences in connection with NSAC is a reversal of this relationship, whereby ICL becomes a source of IHL obligations. This means that in 1998 states negotiating the *Rome Statute* did not only criminalize acts they considered contrary to the protection of human dignity, but they also, perhaps unconsciously, laid the groundwork for a law of armed conflict hitherto unknown in IHL. What is novel about this development is not that the protection scheme (IHL) and the enforcement regime (ICL) are mutually reinforcing. Rather, the major innovation lies in the fact that the two legal regimes are now under the sway of a common implementing mechanism.

ICL AS A SOURCE OF IHL

IHL and ICL share the common ideal of enhancing human security. Although they are distinct branches of law, in regard to their social functions, they are usually considered to aim at the same objective. Yet, for Rachel Kerr, IHL is "best viewed as having a preventative function, rather than as a basis for criminal prosecution."[59] Guénaël Mettraux concludes similarly that the *Geneva Conventions* are not and were not intended to be criminal codes.[60] However, one cannot ignore the fact that, with respect to the protection of human dignity, IHL embodies values that in most societies are protected through the criminal law. ICL and IHL indisputably complement each other. ICL consists of two elements, namely (1) the prohibition of conduct or definition of standards of behaviour (what some commentators have called IHL of a criminal nature[61]) and (2) sanctions for violation of such prohibitions or standards. IHL obligations only relate

---

[59] Rachel Kerr, *The International Criminal Tribunal for the Former Yugoslavia: An Exercise in Law, Politics, and Diplomacy* (Oxford: Oxford University Press, 2004) at 93-94.

[60] Guénaël Mettraux, "Dutch Courts' Universal Jurisdiction over Violations of Common Article 3 qua War Crimes" (2006) 4 J Int'l Criminal Justice 362 at 368.

[61] Andreas Paulus and Mindia Vashakmadze, "Asymmetrical War and the Notion of Armed Conflict: A Tentative Conceptualization" (2009) 91:873 Int'l Rev Red Cross 95 at 99.

to the first element of ICL, namely the prohibition of certain conduct.

Nevertheless, the dichotomy between prevention (IHL) and punishment (ICL), highlighted by Kerr and Mettraux, can be understood in the way IHL has developed. The *Geneva Conventions* set out standards of conduct expected in situations of armed conflict but do not provide for international enforcement mechanisms. Rather, they rely on national legal systems in this latter regard. In national law, IHL is indeed implemented in military codes that are, in large part, simply criminal law applicable to activities of armed forces. By way of illustration, while common Article 3 of the *Geneva Conventions* does not provide for prosecution of breaches of the law applicable to NIAC, as such, states have nevertheless taken legal action with respect to such breaches coming within their domestic jurisdiction.[62] Therefore, while Alexander Zahar and Göran Sluiter argue that, in the absence of an enforcement mechanism, the mere labelling of an act as prohibited is not criminal law,[63] the ICTY has been clear that violations of common Article 3 have been criminalized since 1949.[64]

This approach means that the imposition of a penalty on a reprehensible act is not a necessary condition for this conduct to be recognized as criminal. Further, from the ICTY's point of view, mere prohibition is sufficient since it seems obvious that some national legal order, as an extension of the international legal order, will provide for a sanction. It is not therefore indefensible to consider that IHL, when it dictates a standard, is criminal law. The humanitarian face of this criminal law simply derives from the objective it pursues, the protection of human dignity, and the circumstance in which this objective is pursued, namely armed conflict. To this extent, IHL is not only the substantive element of ICL. At least in its preventative dimension, it is ICL. This does not mean that ICL is composed primarily of IHL obligations. The sources of ICL are varied, and it is far from being a monolithic body of law. ICL draws its substantive content from different sources of law. It can even create entirely new obligations in its own right.

This analysis demonstrates that in encapsulating NSAC within its conception of NIAC, Article 8(2)(f) of the *Rome Statute* created more

---

[62] Zahar and Sluiter, *supra* note 36 at 113-17.

[63] *Ibid* at 117.

[64] *Prosecutor v Delalic et al*, ICTY Case no IT-96-21-A, Appeal Judgment (20 February 2001) at para 162 (Appeals Chamber).

than a system of offences. A genuine IHL regime, peculiar to NSAC, came into being. IHL should no longer be read only with reference to the *Geneva Conventions* and the *Hague Conventions*.[65] Certainly, since the inception of ad hoc UN criminal tribunals, a broader interpretation of these conventions has inevitably made ICL one of the sources of IHL. To illustrate, while omitted from the grave breaches listed in the *Geneva Conventions*, sexual crimes committed in the course of armed conflict are now prosecuted as war crimes by international criminal tribunals. Mere criminalization, even where it lacks an appropriate penalty, leads to the establishment of standards of conduct expected from combatants in the field. In this regard, the question arises as to whether, in including the category of NSAC within NIAC, the ICTY, the drafters of the *Rome Statute*, and the ICC have considered the legal effects of the concept extending beyond the confines of ICL. In other words, did the states parties to the *Rome Statute*, for example, agree to assume IHL obligations arising out of this new class of conflict? The next section analyzes this issue through the lens of the institutional relationships between ICL and IHL.

REINFORCEMENT OF IHL MECHANISMS

The institutional issue is important because, as ICL and IHL are mutually reinforcing, it would be preferable to have both legal regimes enforced in a coordinated manner. The implementation of these two systems naturally falls within the purview of states. However, with the blossoming of ICL, states' stranglehold on the application of IHL has been tempered, as international criminal courts and tribunals have also acquired the authority to sanction grave breaches of IHL. In particular, states parties to the *Rome Statute* are no longer able to determine the conditions in which IHL will be enforced. This is a dramatic shift, as for long time there was a blatant lack of independent authority (or a high degree of institutional coordination)[66] in deciding whether an internal armed conflict existed, effectively leaving such determinations to states.[67]

---

65 *Geneva Conventions, supra* note 3; *Hague Convention IV Respecting the Laws and Customs of War on Land*, BTS 1910 No 9, 1 Bevans 631 (in force 16 January 1910).

66 Natasha T Balendra, "Defining Armed Conflict" (2008) 26:6 Cardozo L Rev 2461 at 2486.

67 Lindsay Moir, *The Law of Internal Armed Conflict* (Cambridge: Cambridge University Press, 2002) at 45.

However, the scope of the power of international criminal tribunals to determine the scope of application of IHL should not be overstated. These courts are in fact only able to exercise influence within the limits of their punitive functions. In other words, they may compete with states in determining the existence of a conflict, but their determination is relevant only for the purpose of punishing war crimes. States, on the other hand, are required to recognize the existence of an armed conflict for the purpose of implementing their IHL obligations for the protection of war victims. There is room for concern regarding whether states (or other parties involved) will readily acknowledge the existence of a NSAC and apply IHL pertaining thereto. And even if they do, it is doubtful that they will have the objectivity and independence of an international judicial body.

Nevertheless, this doubt can be cleared away in the ICC framework, based on the complementarity principle.[68] In light of this principle, states parties will endeavour to align themselves with the provisions of the *Rome Statute* at the domestic level. To give any meaning to the principle of complementarity implies the translation into domestic law of the *Rome Statute* crimes at least. Given that the *Rome Statute* establishes offences committed in a NSAC as war crimes, states parties will necessarily introduce corresponding IHL provisions into their domestic law. If a state party fails to do so, the ICC may eventually pursue such a case on the basis of the unwillingness or inability of the state party to do so.[69] The principle of complementarity can therefore be said to constitute an incentive for states to recognize the existence of a NSAC and to trigger the application of the corresponding IHL regime on their own.

It is difficult to say whether in creating the category of NSAC during the Rome conference states had in mind the substantive regulation of humanitarian issues stemming therefrom. It is likely that they merely contemplated the attribution of jurisdiction to the ICC over crimes committed during a NIAC. They were likely focused on addressing the fact that, while prosecution of violations of the law of international armed conflict was well established, common Article 3 and *Additional Protocol II* contain no mention of individual criminal responsibility.[70] In other words, they likely approached the

---

[68] *Rome Statute, supra* note 8, arts 1, 17.

[69] *Ibid*, art 17.

[70] Roman Boed, "Individual Criminal Responsibility for Violations of Article 3 Common to the Geneva Conventions of 1949 and of Additional Protocol II

issue less in terms of humanitarian protection and more in terms of criminal responsibility. This is corroborated by the drafting history of Article 8(2)(f), which gained most support from countries either recovering from, or still plagued by, civil wars, such as Sierra Leone, Guinea-Bissau, Sudan, Uganda, Slovenia, and Bosnia-Herzegovina. The proposal received little discussion and was adopted in the final days of the conference. The consequence of this haste is obvious. The rules of IHL applicable in NSAC are far from being comprehensively defined, which raises the issue of the scope of IHL thereby created.[71]

THE SCOPE OF IHL APPLICABLE IN NSAC

At the outset, it is important to clarify the reasons for focusing on the scope of the IHL regime applicable in NSAC. If such a new category of armed conflict has indeed been defined, it goes without saying that it bears its own characteristics, which any substantive regulation applicable to it must take into account. Moreover, the limitations of Article 8(2)(f) of the *Rome Statute* are such as to cry out for scrutiny not only of its ICL significance but also of its IHL implications.

IHL APPLICABLE IN NSAC UNDER THE *ROME STATUTE*

Article 8(2)(e) of the *Rome Statute*, to which Article 8(2)(f) refers, lists a total of twelve offences punishable as war crimes in a NSAC. The prohibited acts are elements of IHL. The question arises whether these offences comprehensively address IHL issues that may arise from this particular type of conflict. The offences include attacks on civilians, attacks against protected persons and property of a non-military character, declaring that no quarter will be given, killing treacherously an adversary, sexual violence against persons, and conscription and enlisting of children.[72] In addition to protecting civilian populations and their property, which is at the core of IHL,[73] the rules embodied in Article 8(2)(e) of the *Rome Statute*

Thereto in the Case Law of the International Criminal Tribunal for Rwanda" (2002) 13 Crim LF 293 at 298. ICTR and ICTY jurisprudence has settled the issue. See *Tadić, supra* note 5 at para 128; *Akayesu, supra* note 41 at para 617.

[71] Fleck, *supra* note 38 at 610-11.

[72] *Rome Statute, supra* note 8, art 8(2)(e).

[73] Michael N Schmitt, "The Principle of Discrimination in Twenty-First Century Warfare" (1999) 2 Yale Human Rts & Dev LJ 143 at 144.

are limited to "Geneva law." Broadly speaking, this body of law shields those who are not directly participating in hostilities from their effects. In contrast, "Hague law" (limiting the means and methods of warfare) was missing from the NIAC framework until the Review Conference of the Rome Statute in Kampala, Uganda, in 2010. This omission was all the more regrettable since access by non-state groups to weapons is one of the contemporary humanitarian concerns of the international community. The review conference was the occasion to add supplementary provisions applicable in NIAC. Under the amendments adopted at Kampala, weapons already banned in international armed conflict are also banned in NIAC.[74] These prohibited means of warfare include the use of weapons incapable of discriminating between lawful and unlawful targets.[75]

However, one could argue that the principle of discrimination can be inferred from the principle of distinction, insofar as Article 8(2)(e) prohibits attacks against civilians, protected persons, and property. The principle of discrimination arguably covers the principles of distinction, proportionality, and limitation.[76] By the principle of distinction, attacks on protected targets are prohibited. Whereas proportionality requires that, whenever collateral civilian damage resulting from attacks against permissible targets exceeds the direct military advantage gained from such attacks, the military operation should not be conducted.

The principle of limitation, however, demonstrates how important it was to bring the principle of discrimination within the body of Article 8(2)(e) in itself. In effect, the principle of limitation touches upon the choice of means and methods of warfare, requiring that

---

[74] According to the amendment to Article 8(2)(e), it will be considered as war crimes the acts of "(xiii) Employing poison or poisoned weapons; (xiv) Employing asphyxiating, poisonous or other gases, and all analogous liquids, materials or devices; (xv) Employing bullets which expand or flatten easily in the human body, such as bullets with a hard envelope which does not entirely cover the core or is pierced with incisions." *Rome Statute, supra* note 8. See *Resolution RC/Res.5 on Amendments to Article 8 of the Rome Statute,* in *Review Conference of the Rome Statute of the International Criminal Court Official Records,* ICC Doc RC/11 (2010) 13 at 15, online: <http://www.icc-cpi.int/iccdocs/asp_docs/ASP9/OR/RC-11-ENG.pdf>. See also Roger S Clark, "Amendments to the Rome Statute of the International Criminal Court Considered at the First Review Conference on the Court, Kampala, 31 May-11 June 2010" (2010) 2:2 Goettingen J Int'l L 689.

[75] Schmitt, *supra* note 73 at 147.

[76] *Ibid* at 148.

means or methods least likely to cause collateral damage are to be preferred. As such, non-military targets and civilians are protected, as are combatants who should be spared unnecessary suffering. Happily, following the review conference, Article 8(2)(e) of the *Rome Statute* now embodies both the principles of distinction and of limitation.

THE INCOMPLETENESS OF THE IHL OF NSAC

However, it remains arguable that the *Rome Statute*'s provisions on NSAC are not sufficiently comprehensive. This insufficiency is mainly attributable to structural inadequacies in the way that this particular class of conflict has been codified. For instance, the principle of distinction rests on the premise that a clear line can be established between civilian and combatant. Yet, based on Article 8(2)(e), it would be extremely challenging to draw such a line in the context of NSAC. This difficulty may explain the absence of any provision on the treatment of persons who fall within the power of the enemy. More troublesome still is that nothing is said about humanitarian assistance.

On the distinction between civilians and combatants, the notion of direct participation in hostilities requires consideration of the point at which, in the particular case of NSAC, part of the civilian population is transformed into a fighting force,[77] thus losing the IHL protection against targeted attack. As a matter of principle, any person who participates directly in hostilities loses the protection afforded to members of the civilian population. This principle establishes a close link between direct participation and membership in the civilian population. In this sense, the two concepts are mutually exclusive.

Indeed, he or she who participates directly in hostilities is not entitled to protection as a civilian — hence, the importance of defining the latter concept. The notion of membership is central to the understanding of what a civilian is and also reflects the approach taken by the ICRC. In classic internal armed conflicts, a civilian is any person who is not a member either of the armed forces of the state or of the non-state armed group. The question that arises is how to identify a member of a non-state armed group. It is important to note here that non-state organizations, like states, may

---

[77] Nils Melzer, *Interpretative Guidance on the Notion of Direct Participation in Hostilities under International Humanitarian Law* (Geneva: ICRC, 2009) at 5.

consist of an army or military component and a civilian component. It becomes necessary, especially in a conflict in which two or more such groups are in conflict, to clarify what it means to be a member of a non-state armed group. In this regard, the ICRC's study has based membership in a non-state armed group on the concept of "continuous combat function."[78] In other words, non-state armed groups are composed of persons whose continuous function it is to take a direct part in hostilities.[79]

The structuring effect of this concept can be grasped at two levels. At one level, it determines the nature of the acts that qualify as direct participation in hostilities and, therefore, within the functions of a combatant. At the other level, this continuous combat function frames the belonging to an armed group as well as the applicability of IHL.

In effect, acts committed by a person who does not have a continuous combat function will not be considered as direct participation in hostilities. Such a person continues to be regarded as belonging to the civilian population even if his or her direct participation in hostilities is spontaneous, sporadic, or on an unorganized basis. Conversely, the continuous combat function involves a sustainable integration into an organized armed group acting as an armed force of a non-state group.[80] Clearly, the decisive criterion for determining membership in a non-state armed group is whether a person performs acts of direct participation in hostilities on behalf of the group. This criterion is important in that it determines the applicability of IHL.

Indeed, it is essential for the application of IHL that a group on which obligations are imposed be identified, even though in the field of criminal prosecution the prevailing principle is one of individual responsibility. NSAC does not depart from the traditional view of IHL to the effect that its obligations do not apply in circumstances of disorganized violence. Hence, the threshold according to which, under Article 8(2)(f), the provisions of the *Rome Statute* do not apply to internal tensions.

Moreover, the definition of NIAC, which includes a new category of NSAC, specifically refers to groups having a certain level of organization and engaged in protracted violence. These criteria of

[78] *Ibid* at 16.
[79] *Ibid.*
[80] *Ibid* at 34.

intensity and organization, developed by the ICTY,[81] make difficult the application of IHL to certain non-state conflicts, such as religious and ethnic conflicts, where opposing sides are not really organized around armed forces made up of persons whose continuous function is to engage in combat.[82] In this way, the criterion of "protracted violence" comes into play. The configuration proposed by the *Rome Statute* is better suited to political groups that, as in the DRC and Somalia, may be composed of administrative and military wings. In the latter case, it would not be incongruous to envisage a system of prisoners of war. It is regrettable in this connection that the provisions of Article 8(2)(e) of the *Rome Statute* do not criminalize ill-treatment that may be suffered by members of armed forces in the hands of the enemy during NSAC.

Article 8(2)(e) is similarly silent in regard to a failure to provide humanitarian assistance. It is clear that one can impose on two non-state warring factions a humanitarian obligation to provide medical aid without discrimination.[83] It would, however, be more problematic to require them to ensure access by humanitarian actors in the field[84] and to guarantee their freedom of movement.[85] They are, after all, entities devoid of sovereignty. Thus, only humanitarian organizations already in the country could be guaranteed access to territories controlled by such groups. For others coming from abroad, it is reasonable to question the status of the state in whose territory the two factions are fighting. One cannot claim to subject such a conflict to IHL without worrying about the role it can effectively play. The ICRC's proposal, during the negotiation of *Additional Protocol II*, consisted of applying IHL to NSAC only if the state had

---

[81] "[T]he determination of the existence of an armed conflict is based solely on two criteria: the intensity of the conflict and the organization of the parties." *Prosecutor v Limaj*, ICTY Case no IT-03-66-T, Judgment (30 November 2005) at para 170 (Trial Chamber); *Prosecutor v Haradinaj*, ICTY Case no IT-04-84-T, Judgment (3 April 2008) at paras 49, 60 (Trial Chamber).

[82] However, the Inter-American Commission on Human Rights has considered that "a mere thirty hours of intense and organized hostilities can be sufficient to justify invoking IHL." *Juan Carlos Abella v Argentina*, Inter-Am Comm HR, No 55/97, Doc OEA/Ser/L/V/II.98 (1997) at 38, cited by Carswell, *supra* note 13 at 151.

[83] *Additional Protocol II, supra* note 11, art 9; Jean-Marie Henckaerts and Louise Doswald-Beck, *Customary International Humanitarian Law*, Volume 1: *Rules* (Cambridge: ICRC, 2005), Rules 109-10.

[84] *Additional Protocol II, supra* note 11, art 18; Henckaerts and Doswald-Beck, *supra* note 83, Rules 55-56 at 193-202.

[85] *Ibid*, Rule 56 at 200.

disappeared or was too weak to intervene.[86] The *Rome Statute* is silent on this point.

In fact, it is difficult to conceive of NSAC outside the context of a failed state. In these circumstances, however, even if state failure can be factually ascertained, it would be difficult legally to negate such a state's statehood. Therefore, it may remain the sole entity representing the territory on the international plane. Consequently, it is likely that it may deny the existence of the conflict, hence denying humanitarian access to areas in which the conflict is taking place. In an extreme case, this could lead to the application of two separate legal orders to the same factual situation. On the one hand, the state could continue to treat the NSAC as a law enforcement matter, while, on the other hand, the warring parties would be subject to IHL obligations for their conduct of hostilities *inter se*.

EXCLUSIVELY NSAC AS A CASE OF LEGAL PLURALISM

The political configuration in which armed conflict takes place can substantially influence the applicable law. The following comments build on the premise that NSAC is most likely to occur in the context of a "failed state."[87] The relevant literature identifies three levels of state failure, which in fact constitute stages of the state's inability to perform key functions *vis-à-vis* its citizens.[88] The first stage is that of state weakness, characterized by poor political and socio-economic governance. At this stage, the state monopoly on legitimate force is not threatened. It is at the second and third stages, those of the "failing state" and "failed state" respectively, that the state's monopoly on legitimate force is compromised. The lack of a monopoly on legitimate force in essence means that the state is no longer capable of enforcing the law or at least ceases to be the only authority able to discharge that function. Depending on the roles still played by the state, NSAC may mobilize different legal relationships.

---

[86] Pilloud et al, *supra* note 30 at 1351.

[87] "Failed states" are often considered to be at the root of the phenomenon of human rights abuses. John Yoo, "Fixing Failed States" (2010) UC Berkeley Public Law Research Paper no 1552395 at 2-3, online: SSRN <http://ssrn.com/abstract =1552395>; Geiß, *supra* note 20 at 131. The absence of "effective fulfilment of state functions" is the benchmark of state failure. Kirsten Schmalenbach, "Preventing and Rebuilding Failed States" in Thomas Giegerich, ed, *A Wiser Century? Judicial Dispute Settlement, Disarmament and the Laws of War 100 Years after the Second Hague Peace Conference* (Berlin: Duncker and Humblot, 2009) 231 at 233.

[88] Geiß, *supra* note 20 at 129.

Let us consider scenarios in which the state can still enforce the law as well as situations in which state authority has partially or totally collapsed so that the state is no longer able to provide for any of its essential functions.[89]

NSAC AS A LAW ENFORCEMENT SITUATION

A state that retains its monopoly on legitimate force will claim to resolve a NSAC through domestic law enforcement mechanisms. According to Anthony Cullen, by making clear that its application has no effect on the legal status of non-state actors, common Article 3 does not prevent a *de jure* government from treating such actors as criminals.[90] Therefore, it seems that IHRL, which will regulate the use of the criminal law, and common Article 3 may apply concurrently, the former without derogation if the armed conflict does not amount to a public emergency.[91]

Even if the internal conflict reaches the level of a public emergency, thus justifying derogation from the enjoyment of certain human rights, it has been argued that the *American Convention on Human Rights* would still afford protections superior to those of common Article 3.[92] These protections would be further enhanced by virtue of the principle that derogations from IHRL must not be incompatible with other international obligations of the state.[93] Affected civilian populations may also claim respect for their rights since the state remains responsible for securing the safety and liberty of its citizens and for conducting investigations into murders.[94] Thus,

---

[89] As Geiß recognizes, state failure "is a gradual process." *Ibid.* Therefore, total loss of control over the entire territory is exceptional. What is important in this analysis is the loss of the *monopoly* on the legitimate use of force, which may open the door to protracted violence and, hence, armed conflict.

[90] Cullen, *supra* note 1 at 56.

[91] Hernan Montealegre, "The Compatibility of a State Party's Derogation under Human Rights Conventions with Its Obligations under Protocol II and Common Article 3" (1983) 42 Am UL Rev 41 at 43.

[92] *American Convention on Human Rights*, 1144 UNTS 123, 9 ILM 673 (1970) (in force 18 July 1978). See Lysaght, *supra* note 37 at 20.

[93] Lysaght, *supra* note 37 at 26; Paulus and Vashakmadze, *supra* note 61 at 103.

[94] *Civil Liberties Organisation v Chad*, African Commission on Human and Peoples' Rights, Communication no 74/92 (1995), 18th Ordinary Session, 9th Annual Activity Report at paras 21-22. Civilian victims may launch tort suits, but cannot complain against armed opposition groups under an international human rights regime because human rights law only binds governments. See Henckaerts and Doswald-Beck, *supra* note 83 at 299.

even though state practice in relation to the application of common Article 3 is relatively scarce,[95] one may argue that this scenario is not all that bad since states are nevertheless subject to heavier obligations under IHRL.

However, in the specific context of NSAC, the legal relationship between the state and the opposing entities is to be distinguished from the relationship between the warring groups themselves. While they may be seen as mere criminals by the state, the prevailing relationship between them is that of an armed conflict. Whereas the law enforcement relationship would be subject to human rights and possibly other international obligations,[96] the NSAC relationship would be governed by IHL. The submission of the latter relationship to IHL is advantageous in that IHL binds all of the parties to a conflict regardless of their status.[97] However, as a result, contrary to the findings of some international organs,[98] IHRL may cease to have any practical application in the NSAC relationship since the natural guarantor of human rights, the state, is not a party to the NSAC.[99]

In these circumstances, where both sets of legal relations co-exist, the state must comply with its human rights obligations in its law enforcement operations with regard to the NSAC, but it should also recognize the existence of the NSAC so as to perform certain of its IHL obligations, such as the obligation to provide access to its territory for humanitarian assistance[100] or the performance of certain

---

[95] Cullen, *supra* note 1 at 55, citing a survey conducted by Moir, *supra* note 67 at 67-68.

[96] Carswell, *supra* note 13 at 147.

[97] Henckaerts and Doswald-Beck, *supra* note 83 at 299. On the legal basis for imposing legal obligations on persons and entities other than the state under IHL, one commentator says, "when a government ratifies a convention, it does so on behalf of all its nationals, including those who may revolt against it." see Lysaght, *supra* note 37 at 12. See also Elder, *supra* note 25 at 55.

[98] *Legality of the Threat or Use of Nuclear Weapons*, Advisory Opinion [1996] ICJ Rep 226 at para 25; UN Human Rights Committee, "General Comment No. 29: States of Emergency (Article 4 of the *International Covenant on Civil and Political Rights*)," UN Doc CCPR/C/21/Rev.1/Add.11 (2001) at para 3.

[99] Unless the view of Christian Tomuschat, "The Applicability of Human Rights Law to Insurgent Movements" in Horst Fischer et al, eds, *Crisis Management and Humanitarian Protection* (Berlin: Berliner Wissenschefts-Verlag, 2004) 573, that human rights law applies also to armed opposition groups in time of war, is extended to the situation of failed states.

[100] For instance, according to Article 27 of *Geneva Convention (I)*, the state should be encouraged to give authorization to humanitarian societies of its nationality

functions of protecting powers[101] or neutral powers[102] (by way of analogy to IHL applicable in international armed conflict). Equally, it should be required of the state that it treat humanely any members of the non-state armed force who fall under its power[103] and that it not criminally charge such persons as medical personnel who bring assistance to wounded members of non-state armed groups.[104] It may also be required that state forces not attack medical units and personnel of non-state armed groups in their law enforcement operations.[105]

In addition, the issue of criminal accountability should be analyzed with caution. The question arises about what legal regime should govern the punishment of crimes committed in NSAC. This question can be thought of in two ways. On the one hand, there should be no suggestion that the government ignore serious violations of rules applicable in NSAC. Those violations should therefore be punished as war crimes or, in applicable circumstances, as crimes against humanity or genocide. The main challenge to this approach is the controversial view of some commentators that crimes of genocide and crimes against humanity necessarily require proof of a state policy as a constitutive element of the offence.[106]

On the other hand, the law enforcement paradigm commands that armed forces of non-state actors cannot claim any immunity

---

to assist wounded persons who are members of non-state armed groups. See *Geneva Convention (I), supra* note 3, art 27.

[101] *Ibid,* arts 8, 10, 11.

[102] *Ibid,* art 4.

[103] *Ibid,* art 12.

[104] *Ibid,* art 18(3).

[105] *Ibid,* ch III, IV.

[106] William A Schabas, "Crimes against Humanity: The State Plan or Policy Element" in Leila Nadya Sadat and Michael P Scharf, eds, *The Theory and Practice of International Criminal Law* (Leiden: Martinus Nijhoff, 2008) 347; Cherif Bassiouni, *The Legislative History of the International Criminal Court: Introduction, Analysis and Integrated Text* (Leiden: Martinus Nijhoff, 2005) at 151-52. But see, in contrast, Claire de Than and Edwin Shorts, *International Criminal Law and Human Rights* (London: Sweet and Maxwell, 2003) at 95; Institute of International Law, *The Application of International Humanitarian Law and Fundamental Human Rights in Armed Conflicts in Which Non-State Entities Are Parties* (1999) (resolution adopted 25 August 1999 at the Institute's Berlin session), online: <http://www.idi-iil.org/idiE/resolutionsE/1999_ber_03_en.PDF>: "Under Article 7 of the Rome Statute of the International Criminal Court, crimes against humanity can be committed by persons acting for States or non-state entities."

when they cause the death of members of the armed forces of the adversary non-state actor or when they attack the state's military or non-military interests. In such cases, these offences will be subject to the ordinary criminal law of the state. The situation will differ slightly if law enforcement operations rise to the level of an armed conflict between the warring non-state armed groups and the state's armed forces. The applicable IHL regime will plainly apply to this situation, namely common Article 3 and (for parties to it) *Additional Protocol II.* Therefore, in this type of NIAC, two types of conflict would have to be distinguished — that is, one between non-state armed groups and a state armed force and another between two or more non-state entities engaged in combat against each other.

THE ARMED CONFLICT PARADIGM

It is difficult to imagine that a breakdown of governance within a state would lead to its total extinction.[107] In any event, it is now international practice that the UN may step in to fulfil basic state functions and rebuild the state. In this particular circumstance, the nature of the applicable legal regime will depend on two principal factors — that is, whether the UN force is tasked with enforcing the law (the law enforcement paradigm) or whether the UN force engages actively in the conflict (the armed conflict paradigm).[108]

With regard to the law enforcement paradigm, if a UN Security Council resolution authorizes state forces to have recourse to "all necessary means" those forces may find themselves in a position of substituting for the failed state's law enforcement organs. Consequently, if the level of confrontation with non-state armed groups remains below the threshold of Article 8(2)(f) of the *Rome Statute* or of *Additional Protocol II,* IHRL should govern actions towards civilian populations as well as members of non-state armed groups.

---

[107] According to Geiß, "there seems to be widespread agreement that the only 'failed state' ... is Somalia." Geiß, *supra* note 20 at 130. Despite this, the UN Security Council has constantly reaffirmed "respect for the sovereignty, territorial integrity, political independence and unity of Somalia." See, for example, *Security Council Resolution 1816 (2008)*, UNSCOR, UN Doc S/RES/1816 (2008); *Security Council Resolution 1838 (2008)*, UNSCOR, UN Doc S/RES/1838 (2008); *Security Council Resolution 1846 (2008)*, UNSCOR, UN Doc S/RES/1846 (2008); *Security Council Resolution 1851 (2008)*, UNSCOR, UN Doc S/RES/1851 (2008).

[108] Rob McLaughlin, "The Legal Regime Applicable to Use of Lethal Force When Operating under a United Nations Security Council Chapter VII Mandate Authorising All Necessary Means" (2007) 12:3 J Confl & Sec L 389 at 391.

Conversely, if the use of force against those non-state warring entities reaches the level of an armed conflict, IHL should apply.

However, what is of concern here is what legal regime will apply in the event that no UN force is deployed to a failed state — that is, one that lacks a monopoly on legitimate violence. For the reasons stated earlier, it would surely be advantageous to place a NSAC arising out of this context under IHL. However, doing so raises the pertinent question of whether the application of IHL absolutely excludes the enforcement of IHRL due to the incapacity of the latter's natural guarantor, the state. In other words, is it possible to impose respect for IHRL on non-state armed groups in a NSAC?

In the context of classical NIAC, some commentators have answered this question in the affirmative. The jurisprudence of human rights bodies has developed a theory of effective control of territory by the state to define the scope of that state's obligation to respect human rights.[109] State responsibility in international law is grounded on the same theory — that is, the ability to exercise "all or some of the public powers normally to be exercised by [the] Government."[110] It could be argued that this theory should lead to imposing the obligation to respect human rights on non-state armed groups because they claim to replace the state. Human rights theories are indeed based on the idea that political power must be limited by the rights and liberties of individuals. However, the assumption of power is just one of the grounds for confrontation between non-state armed groups. They may also fight for other reasons, such as for control over natural resources or for ethnic, national, or racial domination. In such cases, because it is indifferent to the reasons of the conflict, IHL alone should apply.

CONCLUSION

In 1995, the ICTY introduced the category of NSAC as a subset of NIAC. Although the ICC has endorsed this innovation, the fact that this type of conflict was recognized in the context of ICL raises questions as to its legal implications, particularly for IHL. In this

---

109 *Loizidou v Turkey*, European Court of Human Rights (ECHR) Case no 15318/89, Preliminary Objections, Judgment (23 March 1995) at para 62; *Alejandre and Others v Cuba* (1999), Inter-Am Comm HR, No 86/99 at paras 24-25.

110 *Bankovic v Belgium, the Czech Republic, Denmark, France, Germany, Greece, Hungary, Iceland, Italy, Luxembourg, the Netherlands, Norway, Poland, Portugal, Spain, Turkey and the United Kingdom* (Dec), No 52207/99, [2001] XII ECHR 333 at para 71.

regard, it goes without saying that defining war crimes occurring in NSAC forms the basis for some minimum IHL obligations. This article has tried to analyze the scope of such rules. Upon reflection, it appears that these rules are limited to a few principles. Key issues such as the treatment of prisoners of war (or detainees) and humanitarian assistance are not covered. These limitations highlight the need to take into account the role of the territorial state in developing a system of IHL applicable to NSAC. Some legal obligations should be imposed on the territorial state in this regard. As a result of its attributes as a sovereign entity under international law, it is likely to influence the implementation of any sound system of IHL applicable in NSAC.

This article has also analyzed the legal framework of NSAC. It appears that multiple legal regimes may find application depending on the socio-political context of the conflict. Considering this type of conflict on its own, it is possible to identify several types of legal relations each of which calls for the application of a specific body of law. There is, first, the relationship of armed conflict that arises from the fact that two or more non-state groups confront one another on the territory of a state. When such a conflict has reached the threshold of Article 8(2)(f) of the *Rome Statute*, it should certainly be subject to IHL. Such groups should also be subjected to IHRL obligations if they control territory and exercise some sort of public powers in that territory.

Then there is the legal relationship between one or more non-state groups in conflict, on the one hand, and the armed forces of a state. This relationship is similar to conventional internal armed conflict. This essentially means that two types of law may be applicable. When the confrontation remains below the threshold of internal strife, the legal regime applicable to law enforcement operations, governed by IHRL, should prevail. When its intensity rises to the level of armed conflict, the law of traditional internal armed conflict should apply. We might therefore have an internal conflict with two sub-categories: on the one hand, the armed conflict of non-state groups fighting each other and, on the other hand, a conflict opposing the state to the fighting non-state groups. In any event, even when assuming law enforcement functions, it is important that the state recognize the existence of the NSAC to the extent that certain IHL obligations may be imposed on it. This multiplication of applicable legal regimes is grounded in the idea that legal pluralism characterizes the concept of NSAC.

Sommaire

Cet article soutient que depuis l'affaire *Tadić* devant le Tribunal pénal international pour l'ex-Yougoslavie, une nouvelle catégorie de conflit armé s'est glissée du droit pénal international au droit international humanitaire: celle des groupes armés qui se combattent à l'intérieur des frontières d'un État sans l'intervention des forcées armées de ce dernier. Toutefois, la mesure dans laquelle les règles de cette catégorie de conflit recouvrent les problématiques qui peuvent se poser dans une telle guerre n'a pas fait l'objet d'une étude approfondie. Il peut être déduit des crimes de guerre que le Statut de Rome de la Cour pénale internationale réprime dans ce type de conflit une douzaine de règles de droit international humanitaire. Après avoir dressé un historique de la consécration de cette catégorie de conflit armé, l'auteur soutient qu'il y a lieu de développer davantage ces règles pour un régime de droit humanitaire plus élaboré applicable aux conflits opposant exclusivement les groupes armées non étatiques. L'absence d'un tel régime ne devrait cependant pas être considérée comme établissant la preuve d'un vide juridique. L'auteur propose que soit appliqué aux relations entre les groupes armés concernés et l'État territorial le régime international des droits de la personne et aux rapports entre ces groupes entre eux le régime du droit des conflits armés, notamment les principales règles coutumières dont il est désormais admis qu'elles sont autant applicables à un conflit armé international qu'à un conflit armé non international.

Summary

This article argues that since the *Tadić* case before the International Criminal Tribunal for the Former Yugoslavia, a new category of armed conflict has migrated from international criminal law to international humanitarian law: that of armed groups fighting each other within the borders of a state without the intervention of the armed forces of the latter. However, the extent to which the rules of this category of conflict cover issues that may arise in such a conflict has not been comprehensively examined. One may infer, from the war crimes that the *Rome Statute of the International Criminal Court* criminalizes in this type of conflict, a dozen rules of international humanitarian law. After giving an historical account of the codification of this category of armed conflict, the author argues that there is a need to further develop these rules in order to provide a more comprehensive humanitarian law regime applicable to conflict exclusively between non-state armed groups. The absence of such a comprehensive regime should not, however, be taken as evidence of a legal vacuum. The author suggests that a law enforcement regime resting on international human rights law should be applied to relations between the armed groups and the territorial state, while the warring relationship between the armed groups should fall under the law of armed conflict, including those core customary rules that are now recognized as being equally applicable to international and non-international armed conflict.

Chronique de droit interaméricain en 2013 / Digest of Inter-American Law in 2013

Les développements en droit interaméricain pour l'année 2013

BERNARD DUHAIME ET ELISE HANSBURY

INTRODUCTION

Au sein de l'Organisation des États Américains,[1] la Commission et la Cour interaméricaines des Droits de l'Homme [respectivement la Commission et la Cour] sont les deux principaux organes chargés de veiller à la protection des droits de la personne dans les Amériques.[2] Ces instances sont habilitées à instruire des recours individuels intentés contre des États membres et portant sur des allégations de violations de la *Convention américaine relative aux droits*

Bernard Duhaime, professeur au Département de sciences juridiques de la Faculté de science politique et de droit de l'Université du Québec à Montréal. Elise Hansbury, doctorante au Département de sciences juridiques de la Faculté de science politique et de droit de l'Université du Québec à Montréal. Les auteurs tiennent à remercier Madame Myriam Cloutier qui a contribué à la préparation de cette chronique.

[1] L'Organisation des États Américains [ci-après *OÉA* ou *l'Organisation*] est une organisation internationale régionale au sens de l'article 52 de la *Charte des Nations Unies* (voir *Charte des Nations Unies,* 26 juin 1945, 59 Stat 1031, TS 993, 3 Bevans 1153), qui regroupe les États suivants: Antigua-et-Barbuda, Argentine, Les Bahamas, Barbade, Belize, Bolivie, Brésil, Canada, Chili, Colombie, Costa Rica, Cuba, Dominique, Équateur, El Salvador, États-Unis, Grenade, Guatemala, Guyana, Haïti, Honduras, Jamaïque, Mexique, Nicaragua, Panama, Paraguay, Pérou, République dominicaine, Saint-Kitts-et-Nevis, Saint-Vincent-et-les-Grenadines, Sainte-Lucie, Suriname, Trinité-et-Tobago, Uruguay, Venezuela.

[2] Voir à ce sujet Bernard Duhaime, "Le système interaméricain et la protection des droits économiques, sociaux et culturels des personnes et des groupes vivant dans des conditions particulières de vulnérabilité" (2006) 44 ACDI 95 aux pp. 96 et s.

319

de l'homme[3] et d'autres instruments interaméricains applicables.[4] La présente chronique portera sur certaines décisions rendues par la Cour en 2013.

Dans le cadre de cette période, la Cour interaméricaine des Droits de l'Homme a adopté treize jugements sur le fond, trois décisions sur l'interprétation de jugements antérieurs, de même que vingt-cinq décisions relatives à des mesures provisoires. La Commission interaméricaine des Droits de l'Homme a, pour sa part, adopté quarante-quatre résolutions relatives à la recevabilité d'affaires, huit relatives à l'irrecevabilité, six décisions de solutions à l'amiable, trois décisions sur le fond et vingt-six décisions portant sur des mesures conservatoires.

Les deux instances ont abordé plusieurs thèmes d'actualité et d'importance particulière pour les Amériques, entre autres en ce qui a trait aux droits des réfugiés, des déplacés internes, des enfants, des afrodescendants, des défenseurs des droits de la personne de même que sur les enjeux portant sur les services de santé, les conflits armés, la liberté d'expression, l'indépendance des tribunaux, la peine de mort et la lutte contre l'impunité.

AFFAIRE DE LA FAMILLE PACHECO TINEO (BOLIVIE) (2013), INTER-AM CT HR (SÉR C) NO 272

À l'occasion de ce jugement, la Cour eut l'occasion de se prononcer sur la portée des standards interaméricains applicables aux migrants[5] et aux demandeurs d'asile.[6] Dans le cadre de cette affaire,

---

[3] *Convention américaine relative aux Droits de l'Homme*, 1969, 1144 RTNU 123, OASTS n°36, [*Convention américaine*].

[4] Voir, par ex, *Charte de l'Organisation des États Américains*, 1948, 119 RTNU 3, modifiée par 721 RTNU 324, OASTS n°1-A, par OASTS n°66, 25 ILM 527, par 1-E Rev. Doc off OEA/Ser.A/2 Add. 3 (SEPF), 33 ILM 1005 et par 1-F Rev. Doc off OEA/Ser.A/2 Add.4 (SEPF), 33 ILM 1009 [*Charte*]; *Déclaration Américaine des Droits et Devoirs de l'Homme*, 1948, Res. XXX. Final Act, Ninth International Conference of American States, Doc off OEA/ Ser.L/V/II.23/Doc.21, rev 6 (1979) [*Déclaration américaine* ou *Déclaration*]; *Protocole additionnel à la Convention américaine relative aux Droits de l'Homme, traitant des droits économiques, sociaux et culturels* (*Protocole de San Salvador*), 1988, OASTS n°69 [*Protocole de San Salvador*]; *Convention interaméricaine pour la prévention et la répression de la torture*, 1985, OASTS n°67; *Convention interaméricaine sur la disparition forcée des personnes*, 1994, 33 ILM1429.

[5] Voir à ce sujet Bernard Duhaime et Catherine Lafontaine, "Equality Rights and Migrations in the Americas: Revisiting the *Dorzema et al. Vs. Dominican Republic* Case" (2013) Hors-série novembre 2013 RQDI 449 aux pp 452 et s.

[6] Voir généralement Leonardo Franco, *Asilo y la Proteccion Internacional de los Refugiados en America Latina*, Buenos Aires, Siglo XXI, 2013.

les victimes — membres d'une même famille ayant fui des persécutions au Pérou[7] — se virent refuser une demande de statut de réfugié alors qu'elles traversaient la Bolivie en route vers le Chili, où elles résidaient et avaient obtenu un tel statut. Les autorités boliviennes, qui avaient reçu des informations à cet effet de la part du gouvernement chilien, rejetèrent sommairement cette demande et expulsèrent les victimes qui furent remises aux autorités péruviennes.

Dans un premier temps, la Cour réitéra que les personnes en situation migratoire irrégulière constituent un groupe exposé à une situation de vulnérabilité particulière[8] et que les dispositions de la Convention américaine les concernant doivent être interprétées à la lumière des normes plus spécifiques du droit international public applicables en matière de droit des migrants et des réfugiés (aux para. 128-29, 139-43). Plus spécifiquement, le Tribunal interaméricain nota que le droit d'asile ou le droit de demander le statut de réfugié, de même que le principe de non-refoulement, étaient inclus aux articles 22.7 et 22.8 de la *Convention* (aux para. 135 et s) qui doivent être lus et compris à la lumière de la *Convention de 1951 relative au statut de réfugié*.[9] Ainsi, les États doivent apprécier individuellement chaque demande, de sorte qu'ils puissent évaluer le risque qu'un demandeur soit exposé à une violation de ses droits à la vie, à la liberté ou à l'intégrité s'il retourne dans son pays d'origine (au para. 157).

Conformément à sa jurisprudence passée,[10] la Cour indiqua que sont incompatibles avec la *Convention* les politiques migratoires qui criminalisent l'irrégularité du statut migratoire des personnes et qui prévoient alors la détention systématique de celles-ci sans procéder à une évaluation individualisée (au para. 131). Ainsi, dans le cadre de procédures pouvant mener à des expulsions ou à des

---

7 Il convient de noter que les demandeurs, accusés de terrorisme, avaient été victimes de violations de leurs droits dans le cadre de *l'Affaire du Pénitencier Castro Castro (Pérou)* (2006), Inter-Am Ct HR (Sér C) n°160. Voir aussi Bernard Duhaime et Ariel E. Dulitzky, "Chronique de la jurisprudence du système interaméricain en 2006" (2006) 19:2 RQDI 331 à la p 356 [Duhaime et Dulitzky 2006].

8 Voir à ce sujet *Nadege Dorzema (République dominicaine)* (2012), Inter-Am Ct HR (Sér C) n° 251 [*Affaire Dozema*]; voir aussi Bernard Duhaime et Christopher Campbell-Duruflé, "Defending the Human Rights of Migrants in the Americas: The Nadège Dorzema et al v Dominican Republic Case" (2013) Hors-série novembre 2013 RQDI 486; Duhaime, *supra* note 2 aux pp 121 et s.

9 *Convention de 1951 relative au statut de réfugié*, 28 juillet 1951, 189 RTNU 150.

10 Voir par ex. *Affaire Dorzema*, *supra* note 8; *Vélez Loor (Panama)* (2010), Inter-Am Ct HR (Sér C) n° 218 [*Affaire Vélez Loor*].

déportations, l'État doit évaluer individuellement la situation de chaque personne, tout en assurant à celle-ci des garanties judiciaires minimales, incluant (1) le droit d'être informée des accusations la concernant, des possibilités de recours permettant de s'opposer à une expulsion ou déportation, de la possibilité d'obtenir des services d'aide juridique, d'interprétation ou d'assistance consulaire; (2) le droit de demander la révision ou l'appel d'une décision la concernant; (3) le droit d'obtenir une décision motivée conformément au droit applicable; (4) le droit de rester dans le pays d'accueil en attendant que la décision portant sur sa demande de révision ou d'appel soit rendue (aux para. 133, 159). Dans le cas présent, la Bolivie avait violé les articles 8 (garanties judiciaires) et 25 (protection judiciaire) de la *Convention,* parce que les autorités migratoires n'avaient pas informé les victimes de leurs droits et avaient rejeté leur demande de statut de réfugié sans leur accorder d'audience ou d'entrevue et sans les informer de cette décision. Elles les avaient ensuite expulsées sommairement sans leur donner l'opportunité de présenter un recours visant à suspendre l'expulsion ou à réviser le rejet de leur demande.

De plus, comme il l'avait fait en 2001, dans le cadre de son *Avis consultatif nº 17 sur les droits et la condition juridique des enfants,*[11] le Tribunal interaméricain rappela que, lors de la détermination du statut migratoire d'enfants, les autorités doivent permettre à ceux-ci d'être entendus en toute confiance et de bénéficier de protections procédurales spéciales adaptées à leur statut de mineur (au para. 220), en conformité avec l'article 19 de la *Convention* lue à la lumière de la *Convention des Nations Unies sur les droits de l'enfant.*[12] Le Tribunal rappela que le rejet de la demande d'un parent ne doit pas emporter automatiquement le rejet de la demande de l'enfant et, qu'en principe, un enfant ne devrait pas être séparé de ses parents sauf si cela s'avérait être dans son intérêt supérieur (aux para. 224-26). Il indiqua, en effet, que les États ont l'obligation non seulement de protéger les enfants, mais aussi de favoriser le développement du noyau familial, en conformité avec l'article 17 de la *Convention* (au para. 226).

---

[11] *Les droits et la condition juridique des enfants* (2002), Avis consultatif OC-17/02, Inter-Am Ct HR (Sér A) nº 17 [*Avis consultatif nº 17*].

[12] *Convention des Nations Unies sur les droits des enfants,* Rés AG 44/25, Doc off AG NU, 44ᵉ sess, supp nº 49, Doc NU A/44/49 (1989) [*Convention relative aux droits des enfants*].

Enfin, la Cour précisa que lorsqu'une personne s'est vue reconnaître le statut de réfugié par un État, les autres États doivent tenir compte de cette reconnaissance lorsque cette personne entre sur leur territoire (au para. 150), en conformité avec les articles 8 et 25 de la *Convention*. Ainsi, dans le cas présent, la Bolivie avait une obligation de "protection, diligence et précaution" particulière dans le traitement des victimes, considérant que celles-ci avaient déjà vu leur statut de réfugié reconnu par un État tiers, à savoir le Chili (au para. 179).

Cette décision sera d'un grand intérêt pour les juristes canadiens considérant les modifications récentes apportées au régime canadien par l'adoption en 2012 de la *Loi C-31 visant à protéger le système d'immigration du Canada*[13] qui fut l'objet de vives critiques de la part de la société civile[14] et du Haut Commissariat des Nations unies pour les réfugiés,[15] parce que ces modifications restreindraient considérablement les droits et recours disponibles aux demandeurs d'asile. Rappelons qu'en 2000, la Commission interaméricaine avait déjà formulé une série de recommandations au Canada visant à remédier aux problèmes existant alors dans le régime canadien.[16]

AFFAIRE MENDOZA (ARGENTINE) (2013), INTER-AM CT HR (SÉR C) NO 260

En instruisant ce dossier, la Cour eut à se prononcer sur le cas de cinq mineurs condamnés à la prison à perpétuité pour des délits qu'ils avaient commis avant d'atteindre la majorité. Il fut démontré que, durant leur détention, certains d'entre eux furent soumis à des actes de torture et des traitements cruels, inhumains et dégradants. L'un des jeunes fut également retrouvé pendu dans sa cellule.

---

[13] Voir *Loi visant à protéger le système d'immigration du Canada*, LC 2012, c 17.

[14] Voir, par ex, Amnistie internationale, *Réfugiés : le droit d'asile au Canada* (2013), en ligne: Amnistie Internationale <http://www.amnistie.ca/sinformer/dossiers/canada/refugies-droit-dasile-Canada>; Conseil canadien pour les réfugiés, *Changements au système de détermination du statut de réfugié (C-31)* (2012), en ligne: Conseil canadien pour les réfugiés <http://ccrweb.ca/fr/la-reforme-refugies>.

[15] Haut Commissariat des Nations Unies pour les réfugiés, *Commentaires du HCR sur le projet de loi C-31* (2012), en ligne: HCNUR <http://www.unhcr.ca/resources/documents/RPT-2012-05-08-billc31-submission-f.pdf>.

[16] OÉA, Commission interaméricaine des Droits de l'Homme, *Report on the Situation of Human Rights of Asylum Seekers within the Canadian Refugee Determination System*, Doc off OEA/Ser.L/V/II.106/ Doc. 40, rev (2000)

Le Tribunal interaméricain rappela qu'en vertu de l'article 19 de la *Convention américaine* (lu à la lumière de l'article 3 de la *Convention relative aux droits de l'enfant*) ainsi que de l'*Avis consultatif n° 17*[17] précité, l'intérêt supérieur de l'enfant exige que l'État adopte des mesures spéciales de protection favorisant le développement du plein potentiel de l'enfant et la réalisation effective de ses droits. En l'espèce, l'État avait l'obligation de prendre en compte l'auto-nomie progressive de l'enfant de même que le degré de maturité et de vulnérabilité de celui-ci dans l'application de la législation pénale et administrative le concernant. Ainsi, conformément aux articles 8 et 25 de la *Convention*, de même qu'aux standards onusiens pertinents,[18] le principe du traitement différencié exige que l'État mette sur pied un système de justice juvénile, incluant des centres de détention, qui tienne compte du développement physique et psychologique de l'enfant, favorisé par la cellule familiale. Il est primordial que les autorités considèrent également les besoins émotifs et éducatifs de ce dernier dans l'application de la législation et des sanctions pertinentes. De plus, celles-ci doivent être destinées principalement à la réinsertion sociale de l'enfant (aux para. 139-51).

Le Tribunal interaméricain affirma que l'imposition d'une peine de prison à perpétuité sans possibilité de révision périodique de la sentence n'était justement pas proportionnelle à l'objectif de réin-sertion sociale des enfants. Cette peine favorisait, au contraire, l'exclusion de l'enfant de la société, poursuivant un but purement punitif, en contravention de l'article 5.6 de la *Convention* qui prévoit que "les peines privatives de liberté doivent avoir pour but essentiel l'amendement et le reclassement social des condamnés" (aux para. 165-67). De plus, elle était arbitraire et portait atteinte à l'article 7.3 de la *Convention* (aux para. 161-64). Tout en se référant au jugement dans l'*Affaire Harkins and Edwards c United Kingdom* rendu récem-ment par la Cour européenne des droits de l'homme,[19] le Tribunal conclut que la disproportion des peines imposées aux cinq mineurs

---

[17] *Avis consultatif n° 17, supra* note 11.

[18] *Convention relative aux droits des enfants, supra* note 12; Comité des droits de l'enfant, *Observation générale n° 10, Les droits de l'enfant dans le système de justice pour mineurs,* Doc off CRC NU, 44ᵉ sess, Doc NU CRC/C/GC/1025 (2007); *Ensemble des règles minima des Nations Unies concernant l'administration de la justice pour mineurs (Règles de Beijing),* Rés AG 40/33, Doc off AG NU, 96ᵉ sess, Doc NU A/Res/40/33 (1985).

[19] *Harkins and Edwards c United Kingdom,* n° 9146/07 et n° 32650/07, [2012] IV CEDH 45.

et l'impact psychologique de celles-ci constituaient un traitement cruel et inhumain, en contravention de l'article 5 de la *Convention* (au para. 172).

À la lumière du principe selon lequel l'État a une obligation accrue de protection des personnes, de surcroit mineures, sous sa garde,la Cour affirma que l'absence de contrôle périodique et régulier de l'état de santé de l'un des jeunes durant sa détention, sur une période de treize ans, malgré les recommandations des médecins à cet effet, portait atteinte aux articles 5 et 19 de la *Convention américaine* (aux para. 187-95). De plus, l'État viola le droit à l'intégrité de deux des victimes puisque les agents correctionnels avaient eu recours à la pratique de la *falanga* — de forts coups sur les pieds: une forme de torture dont l'interdiction est impérative. En effet, l'État ne put fournir d'explications satisfaisantes et crédibles quant aux lésions constatées sur le corps de ces jeunes et ne renversa pas, en conséquence, la présomption selon laquelle les autorités carcérales avaient causé ces blessures, en contravention de l'article 5 de la *Convention américaine* et des articles 1, 6 et 8 de la *Convention interaméricaine sur la prévention et la répression de la torture* (aux para. 199-211).[20]

Malgré le fait que l'État argentin ait reconnu sa responsabilité objective quant au décès de l'un des jeunes retrouvé pendu alors qu'il était sous sa garde, il contrevint néanmoins à son obligation d'ouvrir une enquête *ex officio* et de fournir une explication satisfaisante et convaincante des évènements. Puisqu'il fut établi que la victime souffrait d'une dépression dans les jours précédant sa mort, une enquête aurait dû être ouverte quant à la responsabilité individuelle des agents correctionnels afin de déterminer si tous les moyens avaient été pris pour prévenir la mort du jeune détenu. En outre, le défaut d'ouvrir une enquête criminelle relative à la mort d'une personne sous son contrôle ne dispense pas l'État de son obligation d'ouvrir toute autre enquête susceptible de déterminer les responsabilités disciplinaires, civiles et administratives des personnes et institutions impliquées dans le décès de la victime. La Cour conclut donc que l'État argentin avait contrevenu aux droits aux garanties judiciaires (art. 8) et à la protection judiciaire (art. 25) des parents de la victime (aux para. 217-24).

À ce propos, rappelons que le Canada a émis une réserve à la *Convention relative aux droits de l'enfant* selon laquelle il ne s'engage

---

[20] Voir à ce sujet *Affaire du Centre de réhabilitation des enfants (Paraguay)* (2004), Inter-Am Ct HR (Sér C) n⁰ 112 au para 152 [*Affaire du Centre de réhabilitation des enfants*]; *Convention interaméricaine pour la prévention et la répression de la torture*, 1997, OASTS no 67.

pas, en toute circonstance, à séparer les enfants des adultes en centres de détention.[21] En effet, le droit canadien, à l'instar de la législation de plusieurs pays du continent, autorise, selon les cas, la Couronne à poursuivre pénalement un mineur devant les tribunaux pour adultes, à lui imposer une peine habituellement réservée aux adultes et à le détenir dans des pénitenciers pour adultes.[22] La décision interaméricaine pourra informer le débat en droit canadien portant sur le système de justice juvénile qui, pour certains commentateurs, s'éloigne de la philosophie du droit des mineurs pour se rapprocher de celle du droit pénal classique.[23]

AFFAIRE LUNA LÓPEZ (HONDURAS) (2013), INTER-AM CT HR (SÉR C) NO 269

L'*Affaire Luna López* porte sur l'assassinat d'un militant écologiste élu au sein d'un conseil municipal au Honduras. La victime, qui occupait également des fonctions au sein de diverses agences chargées du respect de l'environnement, avait dénoncé à la justice et dans les médias plusieurs scandales portant sur des allégations de corruption et d'exploitation illégale des ressources impliquant des entreprises forestières. M. Luna López fit l'objet de menaces de mort, certaines anonymes, d'autres faites ouvertement par certains entrepreneurs forestiers, sans que les autorités judiciaires alertées n'interviennent de manière effective. En effet, la victime et une autre agente du conseil municipal furent subséquemment assassinées en public après une session du conseil.

Suivant sa jurisprudence constante sur le sujet,[24] la Cour conclut que l'État avait failli à son obligation de garantir le droit à la vie de la victime puisqu'il n'avait pas adopté avec la diligence requise les mesures nécessaires pour protéger M. Luna Lopez, y compris à l'encontre des actions de personnes privées (aux para. 117 et s). Il est intéressant de constater que, ce faisant, le Tribunal interaméricain prit en considération le fait que la victime était un militant

---

[21] *Convention relative aux droits des enfants*, supra note 12, réserve du Canada, en ligne: RTNU <https://treaties.un.org/pages/>.

[22] Voir *Loi sur le système de justice pénale pour les adolescents*, LC 2002, c-1.

[23] Voir, par ex, Jean Trépanier, "La transformation du régime canadien visant les jeunes contrevenants: les frontières de la justice des mineurs en mutation" (2005) 85 Rev dr pén 559 à la p 571.

[24] Voir, par ex, *Affaire Velásquez Rodríguez (Honduras)* (1988), Inter-Am Ct HR (Sér C) n° 4. Voir aussi Dinah Shelton, "Private Violence, Public Wrongs and the Responsibility of States" (1989-1990) 13 Fordman Int'l LJ 1.

écologiste et, assimilant celui-ci à un défenseur des droits de la personne, rappela que ces défenseurs, en raison de leurs activités, sont placés en situation particulière de vulnérabilité. Conséquemment, lorsque ceux-ci sont menacés en raison de leurs actions, les États doivent adopter des mesures spéciales pour leur permettre d'exercer librement leurs activités (aux para. 122 et s).[25] Notons à ce sujet que la Cour considéra que l'État avait eu connaissance de l'existence d'un risque réel d'atteinte à la vie de la victime puisque les menaces de mort avaient clairement été dénoncées aux autorités. La Cour conclut que, considérant notamment la connaissance du risque à l'encontre d'une personne en situation particulière de vulnérabilité, l'État avait failli à son obligation positive d'adopter des mesures de protection adéquate à son endroit (aux para. 124 et s)[26] Ce faisant, le Tribunal interaméricain semble suggérer que, lorsqu'il est établi que la victime est en situation particulière de vulnérabilité et qu'il est prouvé que les autorités étatiques avaient connaissance d'un risque réel d'atteinte aux droits de celle-ci, l'État a le fardeau de démontrer qu'il a adopté des mesures adéquates et effectives de protection pour empêcher que ce risque ne se matérialise (aux para. 138-139).[27]

Il convient cependant de mentionner que la Cour ne conclut pas à une violation du droit aux garanties judiciaires et à la protection judiciaire de la victime, malgré le fait que les enquêtes subséquentes à l'assassinat, menées par les autorités honduriennes, ne permirent pas d'identifier et de sanctionner tous les responsables (aux para. 159 et s). Ce faisant, la Cour prit note de la complexité de l'affaire, des diverses initiatives adoptées par les autorités, de même que des difficultés auxquelles celles-ci faisaient face (y compris l'assassinat de plusieurs suspects). La Cour interaméricaine rappela qu'en matière d'enquête et de sanction, l'État a une obligation de moyen

---

[25] Voir, de façon similaire, *Affaire Fleury (Haïti)* (2003), Inter-Am Ct HR (Sér C) n°162 mesures provisoires, Ordonnance du Président de la Cour interaméricaine des Droits de l'Homme du 18 mars 2003, 5ᵉ considérant se référant à la Résolution 1842 (XXXXII-O/02) de l'Assemblée Générale de l'Organisation des États Américains et la *Déclaration des Nations Unies sur le droit et la responsabilité des individus,* groupes et organes de la société de promouvoir et de protéger les Droits de l'Homme et les libertés fondamentales universellement reconnus AG Rés 53/144.

[26] Voir à ce sujet Duhaime, *supra* note 2 aux pp 148 et s.

[27] Voir aussi *Affaire du massacre de Pueblo Bello (Colombie)* (2006), Inter-Am Ct HR (Sér C) n° 140 aux para 123-35 et *Affaire Castillo González (Venezuela)* (2012), Inter-Am Ct HR (Sér C) n° 256 au para 128.

et non de résultat, et conclut donc que l'État ne pouvait être tenu responsable en l'espèce. Il est troublant de constater que le dossier indiquait pourtant très clairement que plusieurs témoins et certaines des autorités judiciaires chargées de l'affaire avaient également fait l'objet de menaces et n'avaient pas obtenu de protection adéquate (aux para. 171-74) — des omissions qui, à notre avis, auraient pu être imputées à l'État. Cette affaire met en exergue le défi que constitue pour la Cour l'évaluation *in concreto* de la qualité des enquêtes et procédures judiciaires visant la sanction de violations des droits de la personne dans le cadre de dossiers complexes.[28]

La Cour refusa également de conclure que l'État était responsable de la violation du droit à la participation politique de M. Luna López, garanti par l'article 23 de la *Convention*. Ce faisant, elle considéra que cette participation avait été limitée indirectement du fait du décès de la victime et n'était pas directement attribuable aux actions ou omissions de l'État (aux para. 141-44).[29] Enfin, bien que la Commission et les représentants des victimes ne présentèrent pas d'allégation à la Cour à ce sujet, il eut été intéressant que celle-ci se prononce également sur l'éventuelle responsabilité de l'État quant à l'exercice, par M. Luna López, du droit à la liberté d'expression.[30] En effet, celui-ci avait subi des menaces de mort et fut ultimement assassiné en raison des dénonciations faites auprès des médias et des autorités judiciaires relativement à des allégations de corruption et d'autres crimes qui auraient été commis par des entreprises forestières. Rappelons, en effet, que ce type d'expression est au cœur des activités des défenseurs des droits de la personne et contribue à exacerber leur vulnérabilité.[31]

---

[28] Voir par ex *Affaire Nogueira de Carvalho (Brésil)* (2006), Inter-Am Ct HR (Sér C) n° 161 portant également sur l'assassinat d'un défenseur des droits de la personne; Duhaime et Dulitzky 2006, *supra* note 7 aux pp 351 et s.

[29] Voir à ce sujet *Affaire Chitay Nech (Guatemala)* (2010), Inter-Am Ct HR (Sér C) n° 212, où l'État fut tenu responsable de la violation du droit à la participation politique d'un maire et leader autochtone enlevé et exécuté par les autorités étatiques pendant le conflit guatémaltèque. Voir aussi Pierre-Etienne Caza, "Au nom du Père," *Journal UQAM* (22 mars 2010) à la p 11, en ligne: Journal UQAM <http://www.journal.uqam.ca/archives/2009-2010/3613.pdf>.

[30] Voir, par ex, l'*Affaire Manuel Cepeda-Vargas (Colombie)* (2010), Inter-Am Ct HR (Sér C) n° 213, où la Cour conclut à la violation du droit à la liberté d'expression de la victime assassinée pour avoir exercé des fonctions politiques au sein du Parti communiste [*Affaire Manuel Cepeda-Vargas*].

[31] Voir à ce sujet OÉA, Commission interaméricaine des Droits de l'Homme, *Second Report on the Situation of Human Rights Defenders in the Americas*, OEA/Ser.L/V/II.Doc 66 (2011).

AFFAIRE DU TRIBUNAL CONSTITUTIONNEL (*CAMBA CAMPOS ET AL.*) (*ÉQUATEUR*) (2013), INTER-AM CT HR (SÉR C) NO 268[32] ET AFFAIRE DE LA COUR SUPRÊME DE JUSTICE (QUINTANA COELLO ET AL.) (ÉQUATEUR) (2013), INTER-AM CT HR (SÉR C) NO 266[33]

Ces deux décisions relatives aux tribunaux équatoriens participent aux efforts des instances interaméricaines visant à consolider les principes relatifs à la primauté du droit et à l'accès à la justice sur le continent, notamment au moyen de l'identification des composantes d'un système judiciaire indépendant et impartial garant des droits et libertés protégés par la *Convention*.[34] En novembre 2004, alors que régnait un contexte d'instabilité politique en Équateur où plusieurs présidents se succédèrent, le Congrès national vota par résolution en faveur de la destitution en bloc des magistrats du Tribunal constitutionnel et de la Cour suprême du pays, puis ouvrit à l'encontre de certains d'entre eux des procédures en jugement politique.[35]

Rappelant d'emblée sa jurisprudence antérieure relative à l'indépendance des juges et, plus particulièrement, sa décision rendue en 2001 dans l'*Affaire de la Cour constitutionnelle (Pérou),*[36] dont les faits sont similaires à ceux en l'espèce, la Cour interaméricaine affirma que la protection accordée par l'article 8 de la *Convention* s'étend à toute procédure au cours de laquelle une décision, action ou omission émanant de l'État est susceptible de porter atteinte aux droits d'un individu. En ce sens, toute décision adoptée par un organe étatique qui exerce une fonction à caractère matériellement juridictionnel doit respecter les garanties judiciaires. Qui plus est, le contenu de ces garanties et de la protection judiciaire (art. 25) applicables aux procédures concernant la personne des juges

---

[32] Ci-après TC.

[33] Ci-après CS.

[34] Voir notamment le plus récent rapport de la Commission interaméricaine, OÉA, Commission interaméricaine des Droits de l'Homme, *Towards strengthening access to justice and the rule of law in the Americas,* Doc off OEA/Ser. L/V/II.Doc.44 (2013).

[35] Sur la Constitution équatorienne, voir *Affaire du Tribunal constitutionnel (Camba Campos et al.) (Ecuador)* aux para. 48-54: l'article 130.9 de la Constitution équatorienne de 1998 prévoit la procédure de jugement politique, qui autorise le Congrès national à déterminer si un haut fonctionnaire a commis une infraction législative ou constitutionnelle dans l'exercice de ses fonctions.

[36] *Affaire de la Cour constitutionnelle (Pérou)* (2001), Inter-Am Ct HR (Sér C) n° 71. Voir également *Affaire Reverón Trujillo (Venezuela)* (2009), Inter-Am Ct HR (Sér C) n° 197; *Affaire Chocron Chocron (Venezuela)* (2011), Inter-Am Ct HR (Sér C) no 227.

doivent être analysés à la lumière des standards relatifs à l'indépendance judiciaire (TC aux para. 166, 197, 228-29; CS aux para. 144, 158). Ainsi, tel qu'établi dans les *Principes fondamentaux relatifs à l'indépendance de la magistrature des Nations Unies*[37] qu'elle fit siens, la Cour affirma que le principe de la séparation des pouvoirs exige que le système judiciaire en général, et ses magistrats en particulier, soient indépendants de toute pression indue et qu'il soit garanti à ces derniers un processus adéquat de nomination et l'inamovibilité de leur charge (TC aux para. 188-99; CS aux para. 144).

Sur l'inamovibilité des juges, une lecture conjointe des articles 8.1 et 23.1(c) de la *Convention* confirme le droit des magistrats d'accéder et d'occuper une charge publique dans des conditions générales d'égalité, c'est-à-dire que doivent exister des critères et procédures raisonnables et objectifs quant à la nomination, la promotion, la suspension et la destitution des juges, aux fins de garantir la stabilité de la fonction et du pouvoir judiciaire en général. Ils ne peuvent donc être destitués que pour une faute disciplinaire grave ou pour incompétence, selon un système gradué de sanctions qui tient compte de la gravité de la faute reprochée, laquelle ne peut jamais être liée au contenu d'une décision (TC aux para. 189-95; CS aux para. 145-51).

Notons que l'indépendance de la fonction judiciaire, favorisée par la protection spécifique accordée aux juges dans le cadre de procédures les concernant, comporte non seulement une dimension individuelle, liée à la personne même du juge exerçant ses droits, mais également une dimension institutionnelle.[38] Dans les limites de cette dernière, l'indépendance de la fonction judiciaire transcende la seule personne du juge et garantit le principe de la séparation des pouvoirs, la primauté du droit et le bon fonctionnement de la démocratie (TC au para. 197, 198; CS au para. 154).

En l'espèce, le Tribunal interaméricain soutint qu'il n'avait pas été démontré que le Congrès était compétent pour réviser la

---

[37] *Principes fondamentaux relatifs à l'indépendance de la magistrature des Nations Unies*, Rés AG 40/32 et 40/146, Doc Off AG NU, 40e sess, Doc NU A/Res/40/32 et A/Res/40/146.

[38] Selon la Cour, le droit à la liberté d'expression (art. 13) et les droits politiques (art. 23) ont également une dimension collective intimement liée au maintien de l'ordre démocratique. Voir *Compulsory membership in an association prescribed by law for the practice of journalism (art. 13 and 29 American Convention on Human Rights)* (1985), Avis consultatif OC-5/85, Inter-Am Ct HR (Sér A) no 5; *Affaire Manuel Cepeda-Vargas, supra* note 30; Amaya Úbeda de Torres, *Democracia y derechos humanos en Europa y en América*, Madrid, Reus, 2006.

nomination des juges du Tribunal constitutionnel. Ce faisant, il affirma qu'il n'existait pas d'explication raisonnable pour la destitution des juges une année et demie après leur nomination et que l'absence d'un délai de prescription pour la révision d'une nomination au sein du plus haut tribunal du pays portait atteinte à la garantie de stabilité de la fonction judiciaire (TC aux para. 178-80). Quant à la destitution des juges de la Cour suprême, la Constitution équatorienne de 1998 avait retiré au Congrès ladite compétence. La Cour suprême avait établi, par conséquent, une procédure de plainte pour faute disciplinaire grave ou incompétence à l'encontre de ses membres: il existait donc une procédure de destitution que le Congrès aurait décidé d'écarter, en contravention des garanties devant être assurées contre les pressions externes (CS aux para. 159-62).

De plus, durant le vote concernant leur destitution et les procédures de jugement politique ultérieures, les magistrats ne purent ni être entendus adéquatement, ni exercer leur droit à la défense, ni entreprendre de recours effectif pour contester la résolution du Congrès (TC aux para. 183; CS aux para. 168-69). En effet, les membres remplaçants nouvellement nommés au Tribunal constitutionnel rendirent, dans la foulée des évènements, une décision voulant que l'action en inconstitutionnalité devant ledit tribunal constituait le seul recours possible pour contester une résolution du Congrès. Or, ce recours, qui aurait été entendu par le Tribunal constitutionnel, ne présentait pas les garanties nécessaires d'impartialité en ce qu'une décision favorable aux juges destitués aurait eu pour effet d'invalider la nomination des nouveaux membres dudit Tribunal (TC aux para. 231-38; CS aux para. 189-93). La Cour conclut donc que l'État avait violé les droits aux garanties judiciaires et à la protection judiciaire des magistrats destitués.

Finalement, la Cour analysa plus avant le contexte de crise politique au sein duquel étaient survenus les faits des litiges. Lesdites destitutions et les évènements qui suivirent étaient motivés par la volonté d'une majorité de parlementaires du Congrès d'empêcher que des procédures pénales ne soient déclenchées contre un ancien président équatorien. Il en résulta un climat de crise au sein duquel une majorité parlementaire souhaitait exercer un plus grand contrôle sur les plus hauts tribunaux du pays, entrainant de ce fait une déstabilisation non seulement du pouvoir judiciaire, mais également de l'ordre démocratique et du principe de la séparation des pouvoirs, en contravention des articles 8 de la *Convention américaine* et 3 de la *Charte démocratique interaméricaine* (TC aux para. 207-21; CS aux para. 170-79).[39]

Les standards établis par le Tribunal interaméricain, de même que les nombreux rapports et décisions de la Commission interaméricaine sur la question de l'indépendance judiciaire, à la fois dans sa dimension individuelle et institutionnelle, pourront intéresser le juriste canadien en ce qui a trait au débat entourant la légalité de la récente nomination du Juge Nadon à la Cour suprême du Canada. Alors qu'elle fut contestée au motif qu'elle ne respecterait ni les termes ni l'esprit de la loi, cette nomination fut effectivement invalidée par la Cour suprême qui, dans une décision qualifiée d'historique, considéra que l'assermentation de l'un de ses propres membres était nulle *ab initio*.[40]

Affaire Peralta Suarez (Équateur) (2013), Inter-Am Ct HR (Sér C) no 261

Dans cette affaire, la faute professionnelle d'un médecin exerçant en pratique privée, recommandé par un organisme public à ses employés, entraina pour la victime une série de complications médicales et d'interventions chirurgicales, ultérieurement réalisées en clinique privée. Suite aux complications qui découlèrent de l'intervention du médecin, la mère de la victime déposa une plainte pénale contre ce dernier, laquelle fut finalement rejetée au motif qu'elle était prescrite, suite à une série de retards et d'omissions dans le processus judiciaire.

Bien qu'elle tint compte de l'indivisibilité et de l'interdépendance des droits civils et politiques et des droits économiques, sociaux et culturels, et bien qu'elle prit note des dispositions de la *Déclaration américaine*,[41] de la *Charte de l'OEA*[42] et du *Protocole de San Salvador*[43] garantissant le droit à la santé[44] (aux para. 131-32), la Cour interaméricaine choisit néanmoins d'analyser la présente affaire exclusive-

---

39 OÉA, Assemblée générale, Charte démocratique interaméricaine, Doc off OEA/Ser.P/AG/\Res.1 XXVIII-E/01 (2001).

40 Voir *Renvoi relatif à la Loi sur la Cour suprême, art. 5 et 6*, 2014 CSC 2. Voir notamment Micheal Plaxton et Carissima Mathen, "Purposive Interpretation, Quebec, and the Supreme Court Act" (2013) 22:3 Const Forum 15.

41 *Déclaration américaine, supra* note 4, art XI.

42 *Charte OEA, supra* note 4, art 45.

43 *Protocole de San Salvador, supra* note 4, art 10.

44 Notons également que, ce faisant, la Cour apprécia les précédents européens pertinents en la matière, les standards établis par le Comité des droits économiques, sociaux et culturels, de même que les travaux de l'Assemblée générale

ment à la lumière du droit à l'intégrité personnelle, garanti par l'article 5 de la *Convention*, un droit distinct, bien qu'intimement lié au droit à la santé. Ce faisant, la Cour ne retint pas l'approche proposée par le Juge Ferrer Mac-Gregor Poisot qui, dans son opinion séparée, se positionna en faveur de la "justiciabilité" d'un droit autonome à la santé, garanti par l'article 26 de la *Convention*.[45]

Ainsi, selon l'opinion majoritaire de la Cour, la protection de la santé humaine requiert la mise en place d'un cadre législatif règlementant la prestation de services de santé qui permet d'éviter tout risque d'atteinte à l'intégrité personnelle et répond aux principes de disponibilité, d'accessibilité, d'acceptabilité et de qualité des soins médicaux (au para. 152). Tel qu'établi dans l'*Affaire Alban Cornejo (Équateur)*,[46] lorsque les soins sont fournis par des établissements privés, l'État n'est pas relevé de son obligation de présider à la supervision de la qualité des soins de santé, incluant l'octroi des permis d'exercice de la profession, le contrôle continu des compétences des médecins en exercice et l'inspection des installations sanitaires (aux para. 143, 149, 152). Ce faisant, l'État doit également mettre en place les mécanismes de supervision nécessaires à la réalisation des objectifs législatifs ainsi que des procédures administratives et judiciaires qui permettent aux victimes d'obtenir, le cas échéant, réparation (au para. 132).

De plus, le Tribunal interaméricain rappela qu'en vertu des articles 8 et 25 de la *Convention*, et tel qu'établi précédemment dans l'*Affaire Ximenes Lopes (Brésil)*,[47] l'obligation de mener une enquête

de l'OÉA sur le sujet (voir notamment OÉA, Assemblée générale, *Progress indicators in respect of rights contemplated in the Protocol of San Salvador*, OEA/Ser.L/XXV/2.1, Doc 2/11, rev 2 (2011) aux para 72-73).

[45] Sur la justiciabilité des droits économiques, sociaux et culturels sur la base de l'article 26 de la Convention, voir généralement Laurence Burgogue-Larsen, "Economic and Social Rights" dans Laurence Burgogue-Larsen et Amaya Ubeda de Torres, dir, *The Inter-American Court of Human Rights : Case Law and Commentary*, Oxford, Oxford University Press, 2011. Voir aussi Duhaime, *supra* note 2; Bernard Duhaime, "L'OEA et le Protocole de San Salvador" dans Lucie Lamarche et Pierre Bosset, dir., *Donner droit de cité aux droits économiques, sociaux et culturels – La Charte des droits et libertés du Québec en chantier*, Yvon Blais, Cowansville (Qc), 2011 aux pp 363-405.

[46] *Affaire Alban Cornejo (Équateur)* (2007), Inter-Am Ct HR (Sér C) n°171 au para 119; voir aussi Bernard Duhaime et Ariel E Dulitzky, "Chronique de la jurisprudence du système interaméricain en 2007" (2007) 20:2 RQDI 299 à la p 316 [Duhaime et Dulitzky 2007].

[47] *Affaire Ximenes Lopes (Brésil)* (2006), Inter-Am Ct HR (Sér C) n°149; voir aussi Duhaime et Dulitzky 2006, *supra* note 7.

dans un délai raisonnable s'accroit lorsqu'une compensation dans le cadre d'une procédure civile dépend du résultat des procédures criminelles. La célérité de la procédure criminelle est d'autant plus importante lorsque l'état de santé de la personne concernée est en jeu. En effet, les retards indus ont pour effet d'empêcher la victime de reprendre une vie normale, notamment lorsque l'atteinte à l'intégrité personnelle affecte un retour au travail et requiert, en ce sens, une compensation financière (aux para. 102-4).

En l'espèce, malgré la mise en place d'un cadre législatif relatif aux soins de santé, l'État manqua à son obligation de supervision, en ce (1) qu'il avait créé une double situation de risque en permettant à un médecin de fournir des soins sans les permis nécessaires tout en faisant la promotion de ses services auprès de ses employés; et (2) qu'aucun contrôle de qualité n'avait été assuré par les autorités publiques quant aux services fournis par la clinique privée. La Cour nota également que les délais excessifs dans le traitement de la plainte contre le médecin, qui entraînèrent la prescription de celle-ci, ne résultaient pas de la complexité du dossier médical, mais du seul défaut des autorités judiciaires responsables de recueillir les expertises techniques nécessaires. La victime ne put intenter de procédures civiles en dommages et intérêts contre son médecin et ne disposait d'aucun recours effectif pour contester la prescription (aux para. 96-100). Le Tribunal interaméricain estima donc que l'État avait violé les droits à l'intégrité personnelle, aux garanties judiciaires et à la protection de la victime ainsi que les droits aux garanties judiciaires et à la protection judiciaire de la mère de la victime.

Dans la même veine que la jurisprudence interaméricaine relative au droit à une vie décente[48] et aux droits reproductifs[49] qui contribuent au développement du droit à la santé,[50] cette décision participe aux efforts interaméricains de réformes structurelles des services de santé à la lumière des droits protégés par la *Convention*. Rappelons

---

[48] Voir *Affaire de la communauté autochtone Yakye Axa (Paraguay)* (2005), Inter-Am Ct HR (Sér C) no125 [*Affaire Yakye Axa*]; *Affaire du Centre de réhabilitation des enfants*, *supra* note 20; *Affaire des enfants de la rue (Villagrán Morales et al.) (Guatemala)* (1999) Inter-Am Ct HR (Sér C) no63 [*Affaire des enfants de la rue*].

[49] Voir *Affaire Artavia Murillo et al. ("In vitro fertilization") (Costa Rica)* (2012), Inter-Am Ct HR (Sér C) no 257.

[50] Voir généralement Duhaime *supra* note 2; James L. Cavallaro et Emily J. Schaffer, "Less as More: Rethinking Supranational Litigation on Economic and Social Rights in the Americas" (2004) 56 Hastings LJ 217; Mónica Feria Tinta, "Justiciability of Economic, Social and Cultural Rights in the Inter-American System of Human Rights: Beyond Traditional Paradigms and Notions" (2007) 29 HRQ 431.

que ce jugement intervient la même année où les États parties au *Protocole de San Salvador*[51] sont invités à soumettre au Secrétaire général de l'OÉA un premier rapport sur la mise en œuvre progressive de certains droits protégés par le *Protocole*, dont le droit à la santé, conformément à l'article 19 de ce dernier. Ce faisant, les États suivront les indicateurs développés par le Groupe de travail sur l'étude des rapports nationaux présentés en vertu du Protocole de San Salvador puis adoptés par l'Assemblée générale de l'OÉA.[52]

AFFAIRE DES COMMUNAUTÉS AFRO-COLOMBIENNES DÉPLACÉES DU BASSIN DE LA RIVIÈRE CACARICA (OU L'AFFAIRE DE L'OPÉRATION GENESIS) (COLOMBIE) (2013), INTER-AM CT HR (SÉR C) NO 270

Une fois de plus, la Cour eut à traiter d'allégations de violations des droits de la personne dans le cadre du conflit armé colombien. Cette fois-ci, les victimes, membres de communautés afro-colombiennes du nord-ouest de la Colombie, avaient été contraintes de fuir leurs territoires traditionnels en raison de l'opération militaire "Genesis" menée par l'armée colombienne contre les Forces armées révolutionnaires de Colombie (FARC), de même qu'en raison des attaques et menaces perpétrées par des membres d'organisations paramilitaires qui opéraient également dans la région.

[51] Le Canada n'a pas adhéré au Protocole de San Salvador. Pour ce faire, il faudrait qu'il adhère premièrement à la Convention américaine, voir Bernard Duhaime, "Canada and the Inter-American Human Rights System – Time to become a full player" (2012) 67 Int'l J 639 aux pp 644 et s; Bernard Duhaime, "Strengthening the protection of human rights in the Americas: a role for Canada?" dans Monica Serrano dir, *Human Rights Regimes in the Americas*, Tokyo, United Nations University Press, 2010 aux pp 84-113.

[52] OÉA, Working Group for the analysis of national reports under the Protocol of San Salvador, *Progress Indicators for Measuring Rights Under the Protocol of San Salvador*, OEA/Ser.L/XXV/2.1 GT/PSS/Doc.2/11, rev 2 (2011); OÉA, Assemblée générale, 42e sess, *Adoption of progress indicators for measuring rights under the Protocol of San Salvador*, Doc off OEA/Ser.P/AG/ RES.2713 (XLII-O/12) (2012). Ces indicateurs sont inspirés de ceux qui avaient été préalablement développés par la Commission interaméricaine à la demande de l'Assemblée générale. Voir à ce sujet OÉA, Commission interaméricaine des Droits de l'Homme, *Guidelines for the preparation of progress indicators in the area of economic, social and cultural rights*, Doc off OEA/Ser.G/CP/Doc. 14, rev 1 (2008). La Commission interaméricaine a créé en 2012 l'Unité sur les droits économiques, sociaux et culturels actuellement présidée par la Commissaire Rose-Marie Belle Antoine, chargée de travailler en collaboration avec le Groupe de travail de l'OÉA sur les droits économiques, sociaux et culturels, voir en ligne: Inter-Am Comm HR <http://www.oas.org/en/iachr/desc/default.asp>. Voir généralement Duhaime, *supra* note 45; Andrew Clapham et Mary Robinson, *Realizing the Right to Health*, Zurich, Rüffer & Rub, 2009.

Dans un premier temps, le Tribunal interaméricain indiqua que les violations alléguées s'inscrivaient dans le cadre d'un conflit armé non international et que, par conséquent, il était nécessaire d'interpréter la *Convention américaine* à la lumière des normes de droit international humanitaire [*DIH*] applicables, à savoir l'article 3 commun aux quatre *Conventions de Genève*[53] et le *Protocole II additionnel aux Conventions de Genève*[54] ratifiés par la Colombie, de même que le droit international humanitaire coutumier[55] (aux para. 221-22). Rappelons que la Commission et la Cour ont souvent eu recours au *DIH* comme norme de *lex specialis* permettant d'interpréter la portée de la Convention américaine dans ce type de situation.[56]

Dans la présente affaire, la Cour considéra que les demandeurs n'avaient pas pu prouver que l'armée colombienne avait violé les principes du *DIH* relatifs à la distinction et à la proportionnalité dans le cadre de bombardements qui eurent lieu à proximité des communautés (aux para. 227-40). Par contre, le Tribunal déclara l'État responsable des incursions paramilitaires menées dans la région, qui causèrent la mort de personnes et le déplacement forcé des communautés (aux para. 248 et s). Ce faisant, la Cour réitéra sa jurisprudence relative aux règles d'attribution de responsabilité des États pour des actions de groupes ou personnes privées. Tel qu'établi dans l'*Affaire des dix-neufs marchands (Colombie)* et l'*Affaire du massacre de la Rochela (Colombie)*,[57] elle considéra qu'il existait bel et bien une collusion entre l'armée colombienne et les groupes

[53] *Convention de Genève pour l'amélioration du sort des blessés et des malades dans les forces armées en campagne*, 12 août 1949, 75 RTNU 31; *Convention de Genève pour l'amélioration du sort des blessés, des malades et des naufragés des forces armées sur mer*, 12 août 1949, 75 RTNU 85; *Convention de Genève relative au traitement des prisonniers de guerre*, 12 août 1949, 75 RTNU 135; *Convention de Genève relative à la protection des personnes civiles en temps de guerre*, 12 août 1949, 75 RTNU 287.

[54] *Protocole additionnel aux Conventions de Genève du 12 août 1949 relatif à la protection des victimes des conflits armés non internationaux (Protocole II)*, 8 juin 1977, 1125 RTNU 609.

[55] La Cour s'est notamment référée à Jean-Marie Henckaerts et Louise Doswald-Beck, *Droit international humanitaire coutumier*, Bruxelles, Bruylant, 2006.

[56] Voir généralement Bernard Duhaime, "Protecting Human Rights in the Americas: recent achievements and challenges" dans Gordon Mace, Jean-Philippe Thérien et Paul Haslam, dir, *Governing the Americas: Regional Institutions at the Crossroads*, Boulder, Lynne Rienner Publishers, 2007 aux pp 137 et s.

[57] *Affaire des dix-neuf marchands (Colombie)* (2004), Inter-Am. Ct HR (Sér. C) n° 109; *Affaire du massacre de La Rochela (Colombie)* (2007), Inter-Am Ct HR (Sér C) n° 163. Voir aussi Duhaime et Dulitzky 2007, *supra* note 46 à la p 316.

paramilitaires et que les opérations de ceux-ci n'auraient pu avoir lieu sans la collaboration ou l'acquiescement de l'État (aux para. 250-81).

Le Tribunal interaméricain conclut à la responsabilité de l'État non seulement en raison des opérations paramilitaires qui forcèrent les communautés à se déplacer de leurs territoires traditionnels, mais également du fait que l'État avait failli à son obligation de garantir le droit au déplacement et à la résidence (art. 22). En effet, en plus de devoir adopter des mesures préventives contre les déplacements forcés, l'État doit assurer le retour ou la relocalisation en toute sécurité des populations déplacées, de même que la pleine participation de ces populations à la planification et à la gestion des ces opérations (au para. 220). Par ailleurs, la Cour reconnut que la Colombie avait manqué à son obligation internationale d'assurer l'aide humanitaire nécessaire à ses populations pendant leurs déplacements, en particulier en ce qui a trait aux services de santé disponibles, à l'alimentation et à l'approvisionnement en eau potable (aux para. 323-24), en contravention des articles 5 et 22 de la *Convention*.[58] Rappelons que la Cour avait adopté une approche semblable relativement à ces droits économiques et sociaux dans le cadre de *l'Affaire Sawoyamaxa (Paraguay)*, portant sur les droits d'une communauté autochtone déplacée vivant dans des conditions infrahumaines.[59]

Enfin, la Cour déclara également que le droit des victimes à la propriété (art. 21) avait été violé puisque les opérations paramilitaires avaient occasionné la destruction de biens de caractère civil situés dans les communautés. Le Tribunal considéra que cette violation avait un caractère aggravé puisque la destruction de la propriété collective des victimes avait également compromis leurs "conditions de vie minimales" (aux para. 349-50). Ce faisant, la Cour prit en considération le fait que certaines communautés afrodescendantes colombiennes (tout comme les peuples autochtones)[60] entretiennent une relation particulière avec la terre. Ainsi,

---

[58] Il est intéressant de constater, à ce sujet, que la Cour semble avoir reconnu une obligation étatique d'assistance humanitaire bien plus exigeante que celle prévue à l'article 18 du *Protocole II additionnel aux Conventions de Genève* applicable en situation de conflit armé non international.

[59] *Affaire de la communauté autochtone Sawhoyamaxa (Paraguay)* (2006), Inter-Am Ct HR (Sér C) nº146 au para 155. Voir aussi Duhaime, *supra* note 2 aux pp 152 et s.

[60] Dans le cadre d'affaires traitant des droits territoriaux et des droits économiques, sociaux et culturels des afrodescendants, la Commission et la Cour ont souvent repris une approche semblable à celle adoptée quant aux droits des peuples

l'État doit garantir cette relation au moyen de mesures spéciales visant à protéger le droit de propriété et d'usage des communautés, de même que leur survie (aux para. 346).[61]

Il convient de noter que la Cour considéra que l'État avait failli à son obligation de protéger les communautés contre l'exploitation illégale de leurs terres traditionnelles par des entreprises forestières (aux para. 355-58). Ce faisant, la Cour ne tint compte que de l'inefficacité des recours judiciaires et administratifs prévus pour remédier à de telles situations, sans s'attarder aux allégations plus controversées présentées par les représentants des victimes voulant que ces entreprises aient agi en collusion avec les paramilitaires de façon à déposséder les victimes de leurs terres et à occasionner des dommages importants à l'environnement.[62]

AFFAIRE OSORIO RIVERA Y FAMILIARES (PÉROU) (2013), INTER-AM CT HR (SÉR C) NO 274 ET AFFAIRE GARCÍA LUCERO ET AL (CHILI) (2013), INTER-AM CT HR (SÉR C) NO 267

Dans ces deux affaires, la Cour fut confrontée à des pratiques de disparitions forcées et de torture perpétrée dans un contexte de

---

autochtones. Voir par exemple *Affaire du village Moiwana (Suriname)* (2005), Inter-Am Ct HR (Sér C) n°124. Voir aussi *Affaire López-Álvarez (Honduras)* (2006), Inter-Am Ct HR (Sér C) n°141 et *Garifuna Community of "Triunfo de la Cruz" c Honduras* (2006), Inter-Am Comm HR, n°29/06; OÉA, *Annual report of the Inter-American Commission on Human Rights*, Doc off OEA/Ser.L/V/II.127/Doc. 4, rev 1 (2006). Voir aussi Duhaime et Dulitzky 2006, *supra* note 7 aux pp 337 et s et aux pp 350 et s.

[61] Sur la position de la Cour relativement à la relation particulière que les peuples autochtones entretiennent avec la terre, voir *Affaire de la Communauté Mayagna (Sumo) Awas Tigni (Nicaragua)* (2001), Inter-Am Ct HR (Sér C) n° 79; *Affaire Yakye Axa*, *supra* note 48. Voir aussi, Duhaime, *supra* note 2 aux pp. 145 et s; Jo M. Pasqualucci, "International Indigenous Land Rights: A Critique of the Jurisprudence of the Inter-American Court of Human Rights in Light of the United Nations Declaration on the Rights of Indigenous Peoples" (2010) 27 Wis Int'l LJ 51.

[62] Voir à ce sujet Washington Office for Latin America, *Court's Ruling on Operation Genesis a Leap Forward for Justice for Afro-Colombian Victims* (2014), en ligne: Washington Office for Latin America, <http://www.wola.org/commentary/court_s_ruling_on_operation_genesis_a_leap_forward_for_justice_for_afro_colombian_victims>. À propos du crime de pillage commis par des entreprises privées dans le cadre de conflits armés non internationaux, voir James G. Stewart, *Crimes de guerre des sociétés*, New York, Open Society Institute, 2011, en ligne: Open Society Foundations <http://www.opensocietyfoundations.org/sites/default/files/crimes-de-guerre-des-societes-20120601.pdf>.

violations systématiques et généralisées des droits de la personne orchestrées par les États péruvien, pendant la lutte contre le Sentier lumineux, et chilien lors de la dictature du général Pinochet. Il est intéressant de constater que, dans les deux cas, la Cour admit en preuve les rapports des Commissions Vérité et Réconciliation (CVR) péruvienne et chilienne aux fins d'établir le contexte et le *modus operandi* de la perpétration des violations massives des droits de la personne existant alors au Pérou et au Chili. Ces décisions s'inscrivent dans le courant jurisprudentiel interaméricain relatif à la lutte contre l'impunité, incluant l'interdiction impérative des pratiques de disparitions forcées et de torture.[63]

La lutte contre l'impunité exige que soient déterminées la responsabilité générale de l'État, de même que la responsabilité pénale des agents étatiques, eu égard aux violations des droits de la personne, *a fortiori* lorsqu'elles sont massives, systématiques et généralisées (Rivera au para. 180; Lucero au para. 123). Ce faisant, la Cour réitéra dans les deux affaires les principes gouvernant l'effectivité des enquêtes, des poursuites, des sanctions et des réparations, en conformité avec les articles 8 et 25 de la *Convention*. Ainsi, l'enquête doit être ouverte sans délai, *ex officio* et réalisée de manière diligente, sérieuse, exhaustive, impartiale et effective, utilisant toutes les ressources juridiques ou autres disponibles (Rivera au para. 178; Lucero aux para. 121-23). Quant à l'obligation de sanctionner les responsables, la législation pénale doit inclure une qualification autonome du crime de disparition forcée et de torture conforme aux standards internationaux en la matière (Rivera aux para. 204-5). Les poursuites pénales contre les agents étatiques doivent se dérouler devant un tribunal ordinaire, la justice militaire ne constituant pas le forum approprié pour traiter des plaintes relatives aux violations des droits de la personne (Rivera au para. 189).[64] Une disposition législative interne ne saurait empêcher ni conditionner la mise en œuvre de

---

[63] Voir par ex. *Affaire Anzualdo-Castro (Pérou)* (2009), Inter-Am Ct HR (Sér C) n°202 [*Affaire Anzualdo-Castro*]; *Affaire Almonacid Arellano (Chili)* (2006), Inter-Am Ct HR (Sér C) n° 154 [*Affaire Almonacid Arellano*]; *Affaire Goiburu et al (Paraguay)* (2006), Inter-Am Ct HR (Sér C) n° 153; *Affaire Baldeoìn-Garcìia (Peru)* (2006), Inter-Am Ct HR (Sér C) n° 147; *Affaire De la Cruz-Flores (Pérou)* (2004), Inter-Am Ct HR (Sér C) n°115; *Affaire Maritza Urrutia (Guatemala)* (2003), Inter-Am Ct HR (Sér C) n° 103; *Affaire Baìmaca-Velaìsquez (Guatemala)* (2000), Inter-Am Ct HR (Sér C) n° 70; *Affaire Cantoral-Benavides (Pérou)* (2000), Inter-Am Ct HR (Sér C) n° 69.

[64] Voir à ce sujet l'*Affaire Durand y Ugarte (Pérou)* (2000), Inter-Am Ct HR (Sér C) n° 68; Duhaime, *supra* note 56 à la p 136.

ces obligations (Rivera au para. 149).[65] L'établissement de mécanismes institutionnels destinés aux réparations doit mettre fin aux violations, assurer la réparation intégrale du préjudice subi et ne pas empêcher la victime d'intenter un recours individuel devant une instance compétente, conformément au corpus juridique interaméricain et international en la matière.[66] L'existence de ces mécanismes ne relève pas l'État de son obligation d'enquêter, de poursuivre et de sanctionner les personnes responsables (Lucero aux para. 182-85).[67]

Ainsi, dans l'affaire péruvienne, le Tribunal interaméricain dut premièrement déterminer si la disparition de la victime était attribuable à l'État. Selon la preuve: (1) la privation de la liberté de la victime fut causée par des agents de l'État; (2) elle marqua le point de départ des éléments constitutifs du crime de disparition forcée (aux para. 125-26); (3) les éléments de preuve avancés par l'État quant à la remise en liberté de la victime n'étaient pas convaincants; (4) les agents étatiques agirent selon le *modus operandi* révélé par le Rapport de la CVR quant à la pratique des disparitions forcées (aux para. 153-54); (5) le refus de l'État de fournir à la famille, pendant plus de 22 ans, l'information pertinente relativement au sort de la victime constituait un élément du crime de disparition forcée (au para. 156). Sur la base de l'ensemble de ces éléments, le Tribunal attribua à l'État la responsabilité de la disparition forcée de Monsieur Osorio Rivera (au para. 157).

Ce faisant, l'État fut déclaré responsable de la violation des droits à la liberté (art. 7), à l'intégrité personnelle (art. 5) et à la vie (art. 4) de Monsieur Osorio Rivera. À la lumière des affaires récentes *Anzualdo-Castro (Pérou)*[68] et *Massacre du Río Negro (Guatemala)*,[69] l'État

---

[65] Voir *Affaire Barrios Altos (Pérou)* (2001), Inter-Am Ct HR (Sér C), n° 75 et *Almonacid Arellano, supra* note 63.

[66] Voir notamment *Déclaration des principes fondamentaux de justice relatifs aux victimes de la criminalité et aux victimes d'abus de pouvoir*, Rés AG NU 40/34, Doc off AG NU, 96ᵉ sess, Doc NU A/RES/40/34 (1985); *Principes fondamentaux et directives concernant le droit à un recours et à réparation des victimes de violations flagrantes du droit international des droits de l'homme et de violations graves du droit international humanitaire*, Rés AG NU 60/147, Doc off AG NU, 64ᵉ sess, Doc NU A/RES/60/147 (2005).

[67] Voir généralement, Elisabeth Lambert Abdelgawad et Kathia Martin-Chenut, *Réparer les violations graves et massives des droits de l'homme: La Cour interaméricaine, pionnière et modèle?*, Paris, Société de législation comparée, 2010.

[68] *Affaire Anzualdo-Castro, supra* note 63.

[69] *Affaire du massacre de Río Negro (Guatemala)* (2012), Inter-Am Ct HR (Sér C) n° 250.

fut également déclaré responsable de l'atteinte au droit à la personnalité juridique (art. 3) de la victime soustraite à la protection de la loi et placée dans une situation d'indétermination juridique (au para. 170).[70] De plus, les articles 8 et 25 de la *Convention américaine* furent également violés, en ce que (1) la mise en accusation d'un seul agent étatique était contraire au critère d'exhaustivité de l'enquête et de l'obligation d'établir l'ensemble des responsabilités; (2) l'enquête devant un forum militaire violait le droit au juge naturel; (3) les délais des procédures pénales étaient excessifs; (4) la qualification du délit de disparition forcée n'était pas conforme aux standards internationaux; (5) les lois d'amnistie avaient constitué un obstacle à l'obligation d'enquête et de sanction, à l'époque où elles étaient en vigueur (aux para. 218-21).

Dans l'affaire chilienne, la victime fut arrêtée, détenue et torturée par les forces armées, puis relâchée après plusieurs mois de détention. Elle s'exila au Royaume-Uni avec sa famille et entreprit ultérieurement les démarches pour être reconnue comme victime dans le cadre du mécanisme national de réconciliation et de compensation. La Cour interaméricaine déclara l'État responsable de la violation des droits aux garanties judiciaires (art. 8) et à la protection judiciaire (art. 25) de la victime et de sa famille, en raison du délai excessif de seize ans qui s'était écoulé depuis la première fois où il eut connaissance des allégations de torture en décembre 1994 et l'ouverture, en octobre 2011, de l'enquête s'y rapportant (au para. 127). Par contre, le Tribunal interaméricain conclut que l'État n'avait pas engagé sa responsabilité internationale depuis l'ouverture de l'enquête jusqu'à ce moment. La Cour jugea en effet que, dans le cadre de cette enquête portant sur des allégations de torture, même si l'État avait l'obligation d'ouvrir une enquête sans que la victime ne porte plainte, une certaine forme de collaboration de la victime était essentielle (aux para. 137-38). Or, il fut mis en preuve que les agents responsables de l'enquête ne réussirent pas à obtenir le témoignage de la victime, malgré plusieurs demandes à cet effet. Ainsi, puisque la victime conservait la possibilité d'exercer ses droits au cours de l'enquête qui était toujours ouverte, l'État ne manqua par conséquent pas à son obligation de diligence dans la poursuite de l'enquête (aux para. 137-40).[71] La Cour conclut par ailleurs que

---

[70] Voir Christopher Campbell-Duruflé, "The Right to Juridical Personality of Arbitrarily Detained and Unidentified Migrants after the Case of the Guyaubín Massacre" (2013) Hors-série novembre 2013 RQDI 429.

[71] Il convient de noter que, conformément à la jurisprudence de la Cour interaméricaine, l'État a l'obligation d'ouvrir une enquête *ex officio* dès qu'il a eu

le fait que la victime résidait au Royaume-Uni ne pouvait constituer un obstacle au dépôt d'une poursuite civile devant les instances chiliennes ordinaires pour obtenir réparation (au para. 206).

Notons aussi que, contrairement aux faits de *l'Affaire Almonacid Arellano (Chili)*,[72] il ne fut pas démontré que les lois d'amnistie chiliennes et les dispositions relatives à la prescription furent appliquées en l'espèce et qu'elles constituèrent un obstacle à l'ouverture de l'enquête. La Cour estima en ce sens qu'il n'était pas approprié de statuer sur la responsabilité internationale de l'État eu égard à la seule existence de ces lois au moment de la survenance des faits (aux para. 147-61).

Les standards interaméricains relatifs à la poursuite des enquêtes dans le cadre de violations structurelles des droits de la personne pourraient ici inspirer le juriste canadien qui s'intéresse à la question des disparitions non élucidées de femmes autochtones au Canada, alors qu'un rapport récent du Comité parlementaire spécial sur la violence faite aux femmes autochtones ne recommande pas la tenue d'une enquête publique.[73] Rappelons que la Commission interaméricaine envoya une délégation au Canada pour investiguer ce phénomène au mois d'août 2013, et que le Rapporteur spécial des Nations Unies sur les droits des peuples autochtones, M. James Anaya, en visite au Canada en octobre 2013, dénonça le phénomène inquiétant de la disparition de ces femmes et le manque de confiance des communautés autochtones quant à l'effectivité des enquêtes ouvertes.[74]

---

connaissance (ou aurait dû avoir connaissance) des allégations de torture, sans que la victime n'ait besoin de porter plainte. L'inaction de la victime dans la dénonciation des actes de torture ne saurait ainsi relever l'État de son obligation d'enquêter. Voir par ex. *Affaire Gutièrrez Soler (Colombia)* (2005), Inter-Am Ct HR (Sér C) n⁰ 132; *Affaire Velez Loor, supra* note 10; *Affaire Cabrera Garcìa et Montiel Flores (Mexico)* (2010), Inter-Am Ct HR (Sér C) n° 220 [*Affaire Cabrera Garcìa et Montiel Flores*].

[72] *Affaire Almonacid-Arellano, supra* note 63.

[73] Chambre des Communes, Comité spécial sur la violence faite aux femmes autochtones, *Femmes invisibles: un appel à l'action* (mars 2014); Lee-Anne Goodman, "Le rapport sur la violence faite aux femmes autochtones ne préconise pas d'enquête," *La Presse* (7 mars 2013), en ligne: La Presse <http ://www.lapresse.ca/ actualites/national/201403/07/01-4745606-le-rapport-sur-la-violence-aux -femmes-autochtones-ne-preconise-pas-denquete.php>.

[74] OÉA, Commission interaméricaine des Droits de l'Homme, *Communiqué de presse*, en ligne: Commission interaméricaine des Droits de l'Homme <http :// www.oas.org/en/iachr/activities/countries.asp>; ONU, United Nations Special Rapporteur on the rights of indigenous peoples, James Anaya, *Statement upon conclusion of the visit to Canada*, 15 October 2013, en ligne: James Anaya <http ://

AFFAIRE MÉMOLI *(ARGENTINE)* (2013), INTER-AM CT HR
(SÉR C) NO 265

Dans le cadre de l'Affaire *Mémoli,* la Cour eut à évaluer la compatibilité avec la *Convention* de diverses sanctions imposées par les autorités judiciaires argentines aux deux victimes en raison de propos considérés comme déshonorant ou dénigrant la réputation d'autrui.[75] Les victimes furent reconnues coupables de diffamation en vertu du Code pénal argentin et condamnées respectivement à un et cinq mois de prison avec sursis.

Il nous faut rappeler qu'au début du millénaire, la Commission interaméricaine et son Rapporteur spécial sur la liberté d'expression avaient développé une doctrine à l'effet que les sanctions subséquentes de nature pénale étaient difficilement réconciliables avec l'article 13 de la *Convention* et que des sanctions de natures civiles étaient préférables.[76] Dans la présente affaire, la Cour décida plutôt de développer un test annoncé dans sa décision antérieure portant sur l'*Affaire Kimel (Argentine)*[77] qui laissait entendre que de telles sanctions, dans certaines circonstances, pouvaient respecter le libellé de l'article 13 (au para. 126).

Ainsi, la Cour conclut que, dans le cas présent, les condamnations ne constituaient pas une violation de la liberté d'expression aux motifs suivants: (1) les condamnations résultaient de l'application d'une loi préalablement établie; (2) elles poursuivaient un but légitime et conforme à la *Convention* (soit la protection de l'honneur et de la réputation d'autrui, garantie par l'article 11 de la *Convention*

---

unsr.jamesanaya.org/statements/statement-upon-conclusion-of-the-visit-to
-Canada>; Isabelle Hachey, "Femmes autochtones : l'ONU lance une enquête
au Canada," *La Presse,* 14 décembre 2011, en ligne: La Presse <http ://www.
lapresse.ca/actualites/national/201112/14/01-4477645-femmes-autochtones
-lonu-lance-une-enquete-au-canada.php>.

[75] Les victimes avaient entre autre affirmé que des membres d'une association culturelle avaient commis des actes de fraude.

[76] Voir par exemple OÉA, Office du Rapport Spécial sur la liberté d'expression, *Annual Report of the Special Rapporteur on Freedom of Expression 2002,* Chapter V, en ligne: Commission interaméricaine des Droits de l'Homme <https ://www. oas.org/en/iachr/expression/showarticle.asp?artID=138&lID=1>; OÉA, Commission interaméricaine des Droits de l'Homme, 108ᵉ sess, *Declaration of Principles on Freedom of Expression approved by the Inter-American Commission on Human Rights* (2000), principe 10, en ligne: Commission interaméricaine des Droits de l'Homme <http://www.oas.org/en/iachr/expression/showarticle.asp?artID=26& lID=1>.

[77] *Affaire Kimel (Argentine)* (2008), Inter-Am Ct HR (Sér C) n°177 [*Affaire Kimel*].

elle-même); (3) les mesures étaient nécessaires, adéquates et pro-
portionnelles dans une société libre et démocratique; (4) les expres-
sions et les termes utilisés par les victimes pouvaient *a priori* entraîner
des poursuites judiciaires pour atteinte à l'honneur ou à la réputation des personnes concernées; (5) les autorités judiciaires argentines avaient soupesé de façon raisonnable et suffisante le droit à
la liberté d'expression des victimes et le droit à l'honneur ou à la
réputation des tiers; (6) les faits décrits par les victimes dans leur
propos n'étaient pas d'intérêt public; (7) les sanctions imposées
aux victimes n'étaient pas excessives ou disproportionnées (aux
para. 130-49).

En établissant cette conclusion, la Cour rappela qu'elle se gardait
bien d'agir comme un tribunal d'appel et qu'elle ne voulait pas réviser l'appréciation de la preuve faite par les tribunaux argentins, en
conformité avec la doctrine de la quatrième instance (aux para.
140, 147).[78] Ceci dit, il nous faut noter que même si la Cour se limita
à analyser la rigueur et la méthode employées par les autorités judiciaires nationales pour traiter des informations à l'étude lors du
procès (para. 141), il reste que le Tribunal interaméricain prit quand
même la peine d'évaluer si, à la lumière de la preuve déposée, il
était prévisible que les propos des victimes puissent donner lieu à
une poursuite en diffamation (au para. 137), ce qui pourrait s'appa-
renter, en somme, à une certaine appréciation de la preuve. Notons
que, dans le cadre de son évaluation de la gravité de la sanction
imposée par les autorités argentines et de l'impact de celle-ci sur
la liberté d'expression des victimes, la Cour tint compte du fait que
les peines d'emprisonnement avaient été suspendues. Toutefois,
cette appréciation ne permet pas de clore le débat entourant la
compatibilité des sanctions pénales effectivement imposées dans
le cadre de poursuites en diffamation.

Il est intéressant de noter que la disposition législative faisant
l'objet de ce litige avait été déclarée incompatible avec la *Convention*,
dans le cadre de l'*Affaire Kimel (Argentine)* précitée, parce que son
texte n'était pas assez précis pour permettre de déterminer si les
propos de la victime pouvaient être illégaux et, conséquemment,

---

[78] Voir à ce sujet Bernard Duhaime, "Standard of Review in the Practice of the
Inter-American Human Rights Institutions: Subsidiarity and the Struggle against
Impunity in the Americas: What Room Is There for Deference in the Inter-
American System?" dans Lukasz Gruszczynski et Wouter Werner, dir, *International
Law between Constitutionalization and Fragmentation: The Role of Law in the Post-
National Constellation*, Oxford, Oxford University Press, 2014, aux pp 289-315.

violaient le principe de légalité.[79] Ceci étant dit, la Cour interaméricaine prit la peine de différencier les deux situations en notant que cette même disposition était malgré tout suffisamment précise pour s'appliquer aux propos des victimes de la présente affaire et permettre de qualifier ceux-ci de diffamatoires (aux para. 132-37). Ce raisonnement peut surprendre puisqu'il semble conditionner l'analyse de la précision du texte de la norme (et donc sa conformité avec le principe de légalité) à une appréciation *in concreto* et non *in abstracto* comme la Cour semble l'avoir fait par le passé.[80]

Notons enfin que la Cour déclara que l'État avait violé le droit aux garanties judiciaires et à la propriété (respectivement aux art. 8 et 21) des victimes en raison des poursuites civiles et des saisies avant jugement qui perdurèrent pendant plus de quinze ans sans qu'un jugement final ne soit rendu (aux para. 167-85). Par contre, puisqu'elle avait déjà conclu que les sanctions pénales appliquées aux mêmes conduites ne constituaient pas une violation de la liberté d'expression, la Cour jugea qu'il serait inapproprié de déterminer si les procédures civiles avaient également violé ce droit (au para. 158). Cette retenue de la Cour est regrettable, il va sans dire, puisqu'une décision à ce sujet aurait permis de clarifier à quel point des poursuites civiles pour diffamation peuvent engendrer un effet dissuasif (la doctrine du *chilling effect*) sur l'expression des personnes et constituer une violation de l'article 13 de la Convention. Rappelons à ce sujet que la Cour avait déjà appliqué cette doctrine dans le cadre d'une affaire similaire.[81] Une telle analyse aurait été d'autant plus intéressante pour le lecteur canadien, considérant, entre autres, les débats qui occupent la communauté juridique du Québec et des autres provinces à propos des poursuites bâillons (aussi appelées les SLAPP ou *Strategic Lawsuits against Public Participation*) et leur compatibilité avec la liberté d'expression.[82]

---

[79] *Affaire Kimel, supra* note 77 aux para. 66-67, 128.

[80] Voir *Affaire Castillo Petruzzi et al. (Pérou)* (1999), Inter-Am Ct HR (Sér C) n° 52 aux para. 117 et s [*Affaire Castillo Petruzzi*]; OÉA, Commission interaméricaine des Droits de l'Homme, *Report on Terrorism and Human Rights*, OEA/Ser.L/V/II.116/Doc. 5, rev 1 corr (2002) au para. 225.

[81] Voir *Affaire Herrera-Ulloa (Costa Rica)* (2004), Inter-Am Ct HR (Sér C) n°107 aux para 133-36.

[82] Voir également généralement Lucie Lemonde et Gabrielle Ferland-Gagnon, "Les étapes de la mobilisation citoyenne et de l'adoption de la loi contre les poursuites-bâillons" (2010) 51:1 C de D 195; Lucie Lemonde, "Mobilisation contre les SLAPP : A-t-on débâillonné les luttes ?" (2012) 8 Nouveaux Cahiers du Socialisme; Normand Landry, *SLAPP. Bâillonnement et répression judiciaire du*

Affaire García Cruz et Sánchez Silvestre (Mexique) (2013), Inter-Am Ct HR (Sér C) no 273 et Affaire Gutiérez et famille (Argentine) (2013), Inter-Am Ct HR (Sér C) no 271

Les décisions *García Cruz et Sánchez Silvestre (Mexique)* et *Gutiérez et famille (Argentine)* ont respectivement trait (1) à la détention illégale et à la torture des victimes en vue d'obtenir des aveux visant leur condamnation et (2) à l'exécution extrajudiciaire d'un commissaire de police. Dans les deux affaires, les États reconnurent leur responsabilité internationale pour les violations alléguées.

Dans l'affaire mexicaine, la Cour félicita les efforts des parties puisque la solution à l'amiable prévoyait la reconnaissance totale de la responsabilité étatique quant aux faits et aux violations des droits de la personne établis dans le Rapport sur le fond de la Commission (incluant les faits survenus avant l'acceptation de la compétence de la Cour par l'État), ainsi que la détermination de mesures de réparation. Intervenue à une étape préliminaire du litige, la reconnaissance de responsabilité, en plus d'accélérer le processus judiciaire, témoignait de la volonté de l'État mexicain de réparer intégralement le préjudice subi, en plus d'apporter une solution aux problèmes structurels révélés par l'affaire (aux para. 22-23).

La Cour se limita ainsi à exposer les faits et les violations reconnus, en ce que la sentence constituait *per se* une mesure de réparation et de garantie de non-répétition (au para. 29). La détention illégale et la torture par des agents de l'État des victimes violèrent les articles 5 (droit à l'intégrité personnelle) et 7 (droit à la liberté) de la *Convention américaine* ainsi que les articles 1, 6, 8 et 10 de la *Convention interaméricaine pour la prévention de la torture* (aux para. 32-54). L'État avait l'obligation d'ouvrir une enquête indépendante suite à la dénonciation d'un acte de torture, de fournir, le cas échéant, une explication satisfaisante aux lésions occasionnées et de démontrer que la confession avait été obtenue de manière volontaire.[83] De plus, l'utilisation d'aveux obtenus sous la torture constitue une atteinte au droit à un procès équitable; ceux-ci doivent ainsi

---

discours, politique Montréal, Les Éditions Écosociété, 2012. Voir également les décisions récentes de la Cour suprême du Canada quant à l'effet dissuasif de la poursuite en diffamation sur l'exercice de la liberté d'expression: *Bou Malhab c. Diffusion Métromédia CMR*, 2011 CSC 9 [2011] 1 RCS 214 et *WIC Radio Ltd c Simpson*, 2008 CSC 40, [2008] 2 RCS 420.

[83] Voir également *Affaire des frères Gómez Paquiyauri (Pérou)* (2004), Inter-Am Ct HR (Sér C) n°110 aux para. 153-54.

être exclus de la preuve considérée au procès (au para. 58).[84] Les tribunaux mexicains procédèrent ultérieurement à un contrôle de conventionnalité de la législation pénale interne avec la *Convention*, confirmant la règle de l'exclusion de la preuve obtenue sous la torture.[85] Bien que ces jugements contribuèrent à la résolution de l'affaire en révoquant la condamnation pénale des victimes et en ordonnant leur libération immédiate, ils furent rendus quinze ans après la survenance des faits, privant ainsi illégalement les victimes de leur liberté durant autant d'années (aux para. 59-62). Les droits aux garanties judiciaires (art. 8) et à la protection judiciaire (art. 25) furent violés en raison de (1) l'absence d'une enquête sérieuse suite à la dénonciation des actes de torture; (2) la violation du droit à un avocat durant les procédures criminelles; et (3) la violation du principe de présomption d'innocence due à l'utilisation des aveux obtenus sous la torture (para. 55-56).

Cette décision du Tribunal interaméricain, qui homologua en quelque sorte l'entente à l'amiable convenue entre les victimes et l'État mexicain et qui permit de favoriser la célérité et l'économie des procédures, dans un contexte de surcharge et de sous-finance-ment de ses propres activités,[86] semble s'inscrire dans le virage amorcé par plusieurs États du continent en faveur de la déjudicia-risation des différends au profit des modes alternatifs de règlement des conflits, dont la médiation.[87] Ce phénomène est d'autant plus pertinent de nos jours, alors que plusieurs États membres de l'OÉA semblent avoir adopté une approche ou, du moins, un discours plus favorable à l'endroit des droits de la personne. De plus, il

---

[84] Voir, par ex, *Affaire Cabrera García et Montiel-Flores, supra* note 71.

[85] Sur le contrôle de conventionnalité, voir *Affaire Almonacid Arellano, supra* note 63; *Affaire La Cantuta (Pérou)* (2006), Inter-Am Ct HR (Sér C) n°162; Duhaime, *supra* note 78 à la p 299.

[86] Voir à ce sujet OÉA, Cour interaméricaine des Droits de l'Homme, *Annual Report 2012* (2012), en ligne: Cour interaméricaine des Droits de l'Homme <http://www.corteidh.or.cr/sitios/informes/docs/ENG/eng_2012.pdf>; Ariel Dulitzky, "The Inter-American Human Rights System Fifty Years Later: Time for a Change" (2011) Hors-série 2011 RQDI 127.

[87] Pensons ici, à titre d'exemple, à la réforme du *Code de procédure civile* du Québec récemment adoptée qui fait une plus grande place aux modes alternatifs de règle-ment des différends: *Loi instituant le nouveau code de procédure civile*, LQ 2014, c 1. Voir Barreau du Québec, Communiqué 2014, *Adoption du projet de loi 28, la Loi instituant le nouveau Code de procédure civile : Un pas vers un changement de culture* (21 février 2014), en ligne: Barreau du Québec <http://www.barreau.qc.ca/fr/actualites-medias/communiques/2014/02/21-pl28>.

convient de noter que la consolidation des acquis démocratiques, de même que les réformes apportées aux systèmes de justice de l'hémisphère ces deux dernières décennies semblent permettre aux États de mieux répondre à leurs obligations en matière de respect des droits de la personne, en comparaison avec les premières années d'opération de la Cour.

Nonobstant cette réalité, le Tribunal interaméricain ne renonce toutefois pas à son rôle de gardien du régime international des droits de la personne qui transcende la seule volonté des parties. Ainsi, dans l'affaire argentine, alors même que la Commission et les représentants des victimes se déclarèrent satisfaits de la reconnaissance de responsabilité de l'État, la Cour estima néanmoins nécessaire de procéder à une analyse sur le fond. Elle jugea, en effet, que la reconnaissance de responsabilité de l'État argentin ne permettait pas d'identifier tous les responsables de l'exécution de la victime, en contravention du droit des victimes à la vérité et des garanties de non-répétition. Elle rappela ainsi que son rôle ne se limitait pas à valider formellement ledit acte de reconnaissance effectué par l'État, mais consistait également à en évaluer la portée à la lumière de la nature et de la gravité des violations alléguées, ainsi que des exigences et de l'intérêt de la justice (aux para. 21-22).

Le Tribunal interaméricain se prononça ainsi sur l'exécution extrajudiciaire de la victime, un commissaire de police de la province de Buenos Aires qui, au moment des faits, enquêtait sur des allégations de corruption, de contrebande, de fraude, de narcotrafic et d'association illicite perpétrées par des fonctionnaires publics, connues en Argentine sous le nom de l'affaire de la "douane parallèle" (*Caso de la aduana paralela*). L'enquête criminelle sur l'exécution de la victime mena à la mise en accusation d'un policier de la Police fédérale argentine, qui fut subséquemment innocenté et remis en liberté. Réitérant sa jurisprudence constante sur le rôle fondamental du droit à la vie pour la jouissance des autres droits de la Convention,[88] la Cour conclut que la preuve circonstancielle, incluant le témoignage des témoins oculaires, et la rétractation des déclarations de culpabilité de deux mineurs obtenues sous la menace, démontraient que l'exécution extrajudiciaire de la victime avait été perpétrée par des agents de l'État (aux para. 76-92).

Il est intéressant de noter, au final, que tout en soulevant plusieurs irrégularités et omissions dans l'enquête, le Tribunal interaméricain

---

[88] Voir notamment *Affaire des enfants de la rue*, *supra* note 48 au para 144.

affirma qu'il ne lui appartenait pas de se prononcer sur la teneur des pistes d'enquête privilégiées par les responsables étatiques au cours de l'enquête. Il jugea néanmoins que certaines d'entre elles, qui auraient pu permettre d'identifier et de sanctionner les responsables de l'assassinat de la victime, avaient été négligées aux dépens du droit aux garanties judiciaires et à la protection judiciaire des proches de la victime. Enfin, se défendant d'intervenir dans les enquêtes réalisées par les agents de l'État, la Cour identifia certaines pistes qui auraient dû, selon elle, être poursuivies afin de faire la lumière sur les circonstances entourant l'exécution de la victime (aux para. 96-100).

CONCLUSION

L'année 2013 aura permis à la Cour d'adopter une série de décisions importantes qui ont su faire progresser le droit interaméricain des droits de la personne dans différents domaines. En plus des décisions abordées dans la présente chronique, le Tribunal a également rendu jugement dans l'*Affaire J (Pérou)*,[89] portant sur les droits à la liberté, aux garanties judiciaires et à l'intégrité d'une femme victime de nombreuses violations dans le cadre de la lutte des autorités péruviennes contre le terrorisme du Sentier lumineux dans les années 1980-2000. Cette décision, bien qu'intéressante, reprend essentiellement des principes déjà établis par la Cour et la Commission dans leurs jurisprudences respectives sur le sujet.[90]

La Commission, pour sa part, adopta également des décisions importantes. Pensons entre autres aux affaires *Ivan Teleguz c États-Unis*,[91] *Clarence Allen Lackey et al. c États-Unis, Miguel Ángel Flores c États-Unis* et *James Wilson Chambers c États-Unis*,[92] dans le cadre

---

[89] *Affaire J (Pérou)* (2013), Inter-Am Ct HR (Sér C) n° 275.

[90] Voir, par ex, *Affaire Loyaza Tamayo (Pérou)* (1997), Inter-Am Ct HR (Sér C) n° 33; *Affaire Castillo Petruzzi, supra* note 80. Voir aussi *Raquel Martín de Mejía c Peru* (1995), Inter-Am Comm HR, No 5/96, *Annual Report of the Inter-American Commission on Human Rights: 1995*, OEA/Ser.L./V/II.91/Doc. 7, rev.

[91] *Ivan Teleguz c États-Unis* (2013), Inter-Am Comm HR, No 53/13, *Annual report of the Inter-Am Commission on Human Rights: 2013*, en ligne: Inter-American Commission on Human Rights <http://www.oas.org/en/iachr/decisions/merits.asp>

[92] *Clarence Allen Lackey et al, Miguel Ángel Flores, James Wilson Chambers c États-Unis* (2013), Inter-Am Comm HR, No 52/13, *Annual report of the Inter-Am Commission on Human Rights: 2013*, en ligne: Inter-American Commission on Human Rights <http://www.oas.org/en/iachr/decisions/merits.asp>.

desquelles elle déclara contraire à la *Déclaration américaine* l'imposition de la peine de mort à des personnes en situation de handicap mental. Ces décisions sont intéressantes en ce qu'elles interviennent au moment où la Cour suprême américaine est amenée à se prononcer sur la même question, à savoir si les personnes souffrant d'une déficience intellectuelle peuvent néanmoins être condamnées à mort si elles obtiennent plus de 70 au test de quotient intellectuel, selon le seuil établi par la Cour suprême de Floride.[93]

Pour ce qui est de l'année 2014, on peut s'attendre à ce que la Cour rende sa décision dans l'*Affaire Benito Mendez*, soumise à la Cour en 2012, qui a trait à la privation arbitraire de liberté et l'expulsion vers Haïti de Dominicains d'origine haïtienne, par l'État dominicain.[94] Cette décision est importante en ce qu'elle interviendra dans le contexte de la dénationalisation de plusieurs milliers de Dominicains d'origine haïtienne, ordonnée par le Tribunal constitutionnel dominicain, dans un jugement de septembre 2013 qui est ouvertement en opposition avec la décision de la Cour interaméricaine dans l'*Affaire Yean et Bosico (République dominicaine)*[95] sur la question de l'interprétation de la Constitution dominicaine, relativement au droit à la nationalité.[96]

Il est par ailleurs possible qu'au cours de l'année 2014, la Cour développe davantage les principes et standards élaborés dans l'*Affaire Pacheco* commentée dans la présente chronique. En effet, certains pays membres du Marché commun du Sud [MERCOSUR], à savoir l'Argentine, le Brésil, l'Uruguay et le Paraguay, ont déposé en juillet 2011 une demande d'avis consultatif auprès du Tribunal

---

[93] Voir, par ex, John H. Blum, "Hall v Florida: Florida's Attempt to Limit Atkins' Constitutional Protection" American Constitution Society Blog, 20 février 2014, en ligne: American Constitution Society for Law and Policy <http://www.acslaw.org/acsblog/hall-v-florida-florida's-attempt-to-limit-atkins'-constitutional-protection>.

[94] OÉA, Commission interaméricaine des Droits de l'Homme, Communiqué n° 91/12, "IACHR Takes Case Involving Dominican Republic to the IA Court HR" (18 juillet 2012), en ligne: Commission interaméricaine des Droits de l'Homme <http://www.oas.org/en/iachr/media_center/PReleases/2012/091.asp>.

[95] *Affaire Yean et Bosico (République dominicaine)* (2005), Inter-Am Ct HR (Sér C) n° 130.

[96] Sur la situation prévalant en République dominicaine, voir OÉA, Commission interaméricaine des Droits de l'Homme, Communiqué 97/13, "IACHR Wraps Up Visit to the Dominican Republic" (6 décembre 2013), en ligne: Commission interaméricaine des Droits de l'Homme <http://www.oas.org/en/iachr/media_center/PReleases/2013/097.asp>.

interaméricain concernant l'identification des obligations incombant aux États quant aux procédures et garanties applicables aux enfants et adolescents migrants non-accompagnés, à la lumière de la *Convention* et des autres standards de droit international pertinents.[97]

---

[97] Voir la demande déposée auprès de la Cour, MERCOSUR, Institut de politiques publiques en droits de la personne, *Demande d'avis consultatif à la Cour interaméricaine des Droits de l'Homme portant sur les enfants migrants* (2011), en ligne: Cour interaméricaine des Droits de l'Homme <http://joomla.corteidh.or.cr:8080/joomla/solicitudoc/solicitud_fr.pdf>.

Chronique de droit international économique en 2013 / Digest of International Economic Law in 2013

I. Commerce

HERVÉ A. PRINCE

I. Introduction

Si l'on devait résumer en quelques mots la politique économique et commerciale du Canada au cours de l'année 2013, on pourrait sans risque de se tromper, parler d'action pour un régionalisme économique plus accru. En effet, s'il y a un domaine dans lequel l'action publique s'est exprimée avec efficacité et constance au cours de l'année écoulée, c'est bien celui de l'intégration économique où le gouvernement fédéral a mobilisé toutes les ressources disponibles pour mener à terme les négociations en vue de la conclusion d'accords économiques régionaux d'importance.

En ce sens, la signature de l'entente de principe[1] le 18 octobre 2013 entre le premier ministre Stephen Harper et le président de la Commission européenne, José Manuel Barroso, portant sur l'*Accord économique et commercial global entre le Canada et l'Union européenne* (*AECG*) constituera l'une des principales victoires du gouvernement fédéral. À cela, s'ajoute l'*Accord de libre-échange Canada – Corée du*

Hervé Agbodjan Prince est docteur en droit et professeur de droit international économique à la Faculté de droit de l'Université de Montréal. Il est chercheur régulier et directeur de l'axe de recherche "Relations économiques internationales et droit" au Centre de droit des affaires et du commerce international (CDACI) de l'Université de Montréal. L'auteur tient à remercier ses assistantes de recherche, Abikè Yacoubou, Sarah Barrere et Angéline Couvreur dont les recherches lui ont permis de rédiger cette chronique.

[1] Affaires étrangères, Commerce et Développement Canada, "Le Canada conclut un accord commercial historique avec l'Union européenne," en ligne: <http://www.actionplan.gc.ca/fr/nouvelles/ceta-aecg/canada-conclut-accord-commercial-historique-lunion>.

Sud (*ALECC*)[2] sur lequel le gouvernement fédéral fonde beaucoup d'espoir pour redynamiser les exportations canadiennes en direction de la quinzième puissance économique mondiale. Actuellement la balance commerciale entre la Corée et le Canada est plutôt défavorable au Canada. On estime les exportations canadiennes de marchandises à un peu plus de trois milliards de dollars en 2012 alors que le commerce bilatéral des marchandises entre les deux pays était estimé à plus de dix milliards pour la même année.[3] En signant cet accord de large portée, le Canada espère ainsi combler son retard avec l'une des économies les plus dynamiques de l'Asie Pacifique.

Ces succès de la diplomatie économique du pays cachent à peine l'échec du gouvernement Harper à faire valoir ses arguments dans les contentieux qui l'opposent à ses partenaires commerciaux dans le cadre de l'Organisation mondiale du commerce (OMC).

À partir d'une analyse critique de la politique commerciale du gouvernement fédéral, nous tenterons dans cette chronique de revenir sur les actions menées au cours de l'année écoulée.

II. Le commerce canadien sur les plans bilatéral et régional

A. L'intégration économique à l'échelle mondiale

1. L'intégration nord-américaine

Avec 583 notifications d'accords commerciaux régionaux (ACR) à l'OMC, dont une vingtaine pour la seule année 2013,[4] on craint l'effet de l'accentuation du régionalisme économique sur le système multilatéral. L'impasse du cycle de Doha amorcé depuis 2001 et qui tarde toujours à être conclu est un facteur aggravant de cette prolifération. Parmi les nombreux motifs de ce blocage, on réfère surtout à l'incapacité des États à faire converger des intérêts

---

[2] Pour un aperçu complet de l'Accord, voir, Affaires étrangères, Commerce et Développement Canada, "Accord de libre-échange Canada – Corée du Sud (*ALECC*) – Aperçu," en ligne: <http://international.gc.ca/trade-agreements -accords-commerciaux/agr-acc/korea-coree/overview-apercu.aspx?lang=fra>.

[3] Gouvernement du Canada, "Relations Canada-Corée," en ligne: <http://www. canadainternational.gc.ca/korea-coree/bilateral_relations_bilaterales/index. aspx?lang=fra&menu_id=35>.

[4] OMC, "Accords commerciaux régionaux," en ligne: <http://www.wto.org/ french/tratop_f/region_f/region_f.htm>.

extrêmement divergents dans un cadre multilatéral qui ne cesse de s'élargir.

Mais cette difficulté de négociations n'est pas simplement l'apanage du cadre multilatéral. Il apparaît aussi dans des cercles plus restreints, qu'ils soient bilatéraux ou plurilatéraux, où l'incapacité des États à modifier des accords existants va les amener à s'engager dans de nouvelles négociations qui déboucheront sur des accords dont certaines dispositions remettront en cause des engagements pris dans le cadre d'autres accords. N'est-ce pas là une tactique en cours d'essai dans le cadre de l'*Accord de libre-échange nord-américain* (*ALENA*)? L'engagement du Canada, des États-Unis et du Mexique dans les négociations du libre-échange du Partenariat transpacifique (PTP)[5] pose en effet la question d'une modification déguisée de l'*ALÉNA*. Alors que la modification de cet accord dont plusieurs dispositions mériteraient d'être remaniées est difficile à réaliser,[6] il va sans dire que la possibilité pour les États de négocier de nouveaux engagements correspondant à leurs besoins plus actuels constitue une voie de contournement facile à emprunter. Il n'y a pas de doute que le Canada s'empressera de se prévaloir de dispositions plus avantageuses contenues dans ces nouveaux accords plutôt que de se complaire dans un statu quo imposé par certaines dispositions de l'*ALENA*. En se joignant aux négociations du PTP, le Canada espère tirer profit à la fois d'un vaste marché en Asie Pacifique, mais aussi, élargir ses marges de manœuvre en termes d'accès aux marchés qu'il considère comme prioritaires pour son économie.

Le Canada ne néglige pas pour autant ses relations privilégiées avec les États-Unis. Misant sur sa position géographique par rapport à la première puissance économique mondiale, le Canada a conclu au cours de l'année 2013 un important accord économique avec son voisin du sud pour accroître ses échanges commerciaux. On pense ici à l'accord devant mener à la construction d'un pont public qui reliera Windsor en Ontario et Détroit au Michigan. L'accord encadre les rôles et les responsabilités des deux parties en ce qui a trait à la construction, au financement, à l'exploitation et à l'entretien du

---

5 Sont parties à ces négociations, l'Australie, Brunei, le Chili, les États-Unis, le Japon, la Malaisie, le Mexique, la Nouvelle-Zélande, le Pérou, Singapour et le Vietnam. Le Canada s'est joint aux négociations en 2012.

6 Voir à ce propos l'article 2202 de l'*ALÉNA*.

nouveau passage international.[7] Il s'agit là d'un accord d'importance commerciale pour le Canada et les États-Unis puisque le corridor Windsor-Détroit constitue le plus important passage frontalier terrestre international d'Amérique du Nord. Il compte près de 30 % des échanges commerciaux effectués par camions entre les deux pays.[8] Le projet dont la réalisation se fera sur la base d'un partenariat public-privé, mobilisera 631 millions de dollars sur deux ans.[9] Le projet de loi visant à officialiser la mise en œuvre du projet a été sanctionné à la fin de l'année 2012.[10] On ne devrait pas tarder à observer les effets concrets de ce nouvel accord.

2. *Le commerce canadien dans les Amériques*

Au plan régional, la politique commerciale canadienne au cours de l'année écoulée s'est surtout traduite par la conclusion d'accords de libre-échange avec ses partenaires latino-américains. Trois pays de l'Amérique latine pourront ainsi bénéficier d'un régime préférentiel pour l'accès au marché canadien de leurs biens et services. Ce sera le cas pour le Panama[11] dont l'accord visant à établir une zone de libre-échange avec le Canada est entré en vigueur le 1er avril 2013. Cet accord élargit la portée de l'*Accord sur la promotion et la protection des investissements étrangers* (*APIE*) en existence depuis 1998 entre les deux parties puisqu'il est désormais remplacé par un accord de libre-échange qui inclut à la fois un chapitre sur les investissements étrangers et des dispositions portant sur la libéralisation du commerce des marchandises et des services, y compris les services financiers et les marchés publics.[12]

L'*Accord de libre-échange conclu avec le Chili* (*ALECC*)[13] est entré en vigueur le 30 septembre 2013. Il élargit la portée d'un accord

---

7   Premier ministre du Canada, communiqué, en ligne: <http://www.pm.gc.ca/ fra/nouvelles/2012/06/15/pm-annonce-la-signature-dun-accord-la-construction -du-nouveau-passage>.

8   Plan d'action économique du Canada, en ligne: <http://actionplan.gc.ca/fr/ initiative/passage-international-de-la-riviere-detroit> consulté le 18 avril 2014.

8   *Ibid.*

10 *Loi concernant un pont destiné à favoriser le commerce* LC 201, ch 31, art 179.

11 *Accord de libre-échange Canada – Panama*, en ligne: <http://www.international.gc. ca/trade-agreements-accords-commerciaux/agr-acc/panama/panama-toc -panama-tdm.aspx?lang=fra>.

12 *Accord de libre-échange Canada-Panama*, en ligne: <http://www.international.gc.ca/ trade-agreements-accords-commerciaux/agr-acc/panama/panama-toc-panama -tdm.aspx?lang=fra>.

13 On estime que depuis l'entrée en vigueur de l'*ALECC* en 1997, les échanges commerciaux entre le Canada et le Chili ont triplé et le Canada est devenu la

conclu en juillet 1997 entre le Canada et ce pays. Compte tenu des retombées économiques substantielles générées par l'*ALECC*, il était dans l'intérêt des deux partenaires commerciaux de le moderniser en étendant son champ d'application à de nouveaux secteurs, tels que les services financiers ou les marchés publics, et de redéfinir notamment les règles d'origine applicables aux marchandises en provenance de chacun des deux pays.[14]

Le Canada a également signé le 5 novembre 2013 avec le Honduras un accord de libre-échange ainsi que deux accords parallèles portant sur le travail et la coopération en matière environnementale.[15] Même si le Honduras ne fait pas partie des marchés prioritaires du Canada dans les Amériques,[16] la conclusion d'un accord de libre-échange avec ce pays permet de renforcer des liens commerciaux et d'offrir de nouvelles occasions d'affaires et un accès préférentiel aux entreprises des deux États. Il en sera de même pour le commerce bilatéral avec les pays membres de l'Union européenne une fois que l'AECG rentrera en vigueur.

3. *Le bilatéralisme commercial avec l'Europe*

Plusieurs fois annoncée, la signature d'une entente de principe sur l'*Accord économique et commercial global entre le Canada et l'Union européenne* a fini par se concrétiser le 18 octobre 2013.[17] Sans qu'il soit encore possible de se prononcer précisément sur le réel contenu de cet accord étant donné l'opacité dans laquelle se sont déroulées

---

plus importante source d'investissement direct étranger au Chili. Voir Affaires étrangères, Commerce et Développement Canada, en ligne: <http://www.international.gc.ca/trade-agreements-accords-commerciaux/agr-acc/chile-chili/index.aspx?lang=fra>.

[14] *Accord de libre-échange entre le Canada et le Chili*, en ligne: <http://www.international.gc.ca/trade-agreements-accords-commerciaux/agr-acc/chile-chili/menu.aspx?lang=fr>.

[15] *Accord de libre-échange Canada-Honduras*, en ligne: <http://www.international.gc.ca/trade-agreements-accords-commerciaux/agr-acc/honduras/toc-tdm.aspx?lang=fra>.

[16] Ont été identifiés comme marches prioritaires du Canada en Amérique centrale et du Sud les pays suivants: Costa Rica, Panama, Colombie, Pérou, Chili, Uruguay, Paraguay, Brésil. Voir Affaires étrangères, Commerce et Développement Canada, "La stratégie commerciale mondiale pour assurer la croissance et la prospérité du Canada," en ligne: <http://www.international.gc.ca/commerce/strategy-strategie/full-report_rapport-complet.aspx?lang=fra&view=d>.

[17] Premier ministre du Canada, "Le Canada conclut un accord commercial historique avec l'Union européenne," en ligne: <http://pm.gc.ca/fra/nouvelles/2013/10/18/canada-conclut-accord-commercial-historique-lunion-europeenne>.

les négociations, on peut affirmer toutefois, que l'*AECG* une fois ratifié, constituera l'accord de coopération économique le plus ambitieux de toute l'histoire du Canada.

Cela peut se comprendre puisque le régime juridique des relations économiques et commerciales entre le Canada et l'Union européenne est plutôt marqué par un certain "*informalisme*" et un éclatement de régime. *Informalisme* d'abord, parce qu'en dehors de l'*Accord-cadre de coopération commerciale et économique* signé en 1976,[18] l'essentiel des instruments juridiques qui régissent les relations commerciales et économiques entre le Canada et l'Union européenne sont constitués de déclarations,[19] de plans d'action[20] et de programmes divers.[21] Tous ces instruments qui n'ont pas la valeur juridique d'un traité international signé en bonne et due forme peuvent donner le sentiment qu'en dehors du cadre multilatéral de l'OMC, le Canada ne bénéficie pas de relations commerciales et économiques privilégiées avec l'Europe.

Régime éclaté ensuite parce que les seuls accords économiques et commerciaux qui existent entre les deux partenaires se limitent à des secteurs particuliers de l'économie.[22] Certes, le Canada dispose d'un accord de libre-échange avec les pays de l'Association

---

18 *Accord-cadre de coopération commerciale et économique entre le Canada et les communautés européennes* (1976), en ligne: <http://www.canadainternational.gc.ca/eu-ue/commerce_international/agreements-accords.aspx?lang=fra>.

19 Déclaration sur les relations transatlantiques Canada-Communauté européenne (1990), en ligne: <http://www.canadainternational.gc.ca/eu-ue/commerce_international/transatlantic-transatlantique.aspx?lang=fra>; Déclaration conjointe de l'Union Européenne et du Canada, en ligne: <http://www.ic.gc.ca/eic/site/ecic-ceac.nsf/fra/gv00386.html>.

20 Déclaration politique et Plan d'action commun Canada-Union européenne, en ligne: <http://www.canadainternational.gc.ca/eu-ue/commerce_international/joint_political-politique_conjointe.aspx?lang=fra>.

21 Voir par ex., "Programme de partenariat Canada-Union européenne," en ligne: <http://www.canadainternational.gc.ca/eu-ue/commerce_international/partnership-partenariat.aspx?lang=fra>.

22 À titre d'exemple, "Accord sur les vins et spiritueux entre le Canada et l'Union européenne," en ligne: <http://www.agr.gc.ca/fra/industrie-marches-et-commerce/politiques-commerciales-agroalimentaires/accords-commerciaux-en-vigueur/accord-sur-les-vins-et-spiritueux-entre-le-canada-et-l-union-europeenne/?id=1383943512933>; *Accord sur le transport aérien entre le Canada et la Communauté européenne et ses États membres*, en ligne: <http://archives.gouvernement.fr/fillon_version2/gouvernement/accord-sur-le-transport-aerien-entre-le-canada-et-la-communaute-europeenne-et-ses-etats.html>.

européenne de libre-échange (*AELE*).[23] Mais l'*AELE* n'est pas l'Union européenne et la portée matérielle de cet accord est bien mince par rapport à ce que semble offrir l'*AECG*.

Malgré l'accueil enthousiaste que réservent à l'*AECG* aussi bien les provinces canadiennes[24] que le milieu des affaires des deux côtés de l'Atlantique, sa ratification et sa mise en œuvre éventuelles soulèvent déjà de nombreuses interrogations. Certains États européens semblent profiter de l'occasion pour faire avancer certains dossiers, notamment la question des visas exigibles au Canada pour certains ressortissants européens. De plus, l'arbitrage investisseur-État prévu dans l'*AECG* semble rebuter certaines chancelleries européennes qui y voient un danger pour l'exercice effectif des pouvoirs de règlementation des États ou de l'Union. Alors que l'arbitrage investisseur-État existe depuis bien longtemps dans de nombreux traités bilatéraux d'investissement (TBI), la perspective pour les États européens d'être trainés devant des juges privés et de se faire condamner notamment pour expropriation indirecte ne semble enchanter ni les opinions publiques européennes, ni leurs dirigeants. Au surplus, la ratification au sens du droit européen d'un accord dit "mixte,"[25] tel que l'*AECG*, pose des difficultés particulières. Toutes choses qui peuvent légitimement faire douter de l'imminence d'une ratification de l'*AECG*.

En attendant, le Canada poursuit sa politique de conquête du marché européen en se lançant dans des négociations tous azimuts avec plusieurs pays européens non membres de l'Union.[26] Même

---

[23] Islande, Liechtenstein, Norvège et Suisse. Voir Affaires étrangères, Commerce et Développement Canada, "Le Canada et l'Association européenne de libre-échange (*AELE*)," en ligne: <http://www.international.gc.ca/trade-agreements-accords-commerciaux/agr-acc/eu-ue/efta.aspx?lang=fra>.

[24] Compte tenu des règles relatives au partage des compétences dans le cadre de la fédération canadienne et du processus de ratification des traités prévu par la Constitution canadienne, la mise en œuvre d'un tel accord nécessitera l'adhésion des provinces.

[25] Les accords mixtes sont des accords internationaux entre l'Union européenne et les États tiers et qui couvrent des secteurs qui relèvent de la double compétence de l'Union européenne et de ses États membres (compétence partagée) et pour la ratification desquels la procédure ordinaire ne suffit pas. Leur adoption requiert en outre, la ratification par chacun des États membres de l'Union. Pour plus de détails sur les accords mixtes, voir Eleftheria Neframi, *Les accords mixtes de la Communauté européenne : Aspects communautaires et internationaux*, 1re éd, Bruxelles, Bruylant, 2007.

[26] Serbie, Moldavie, Turquie et Macédoine.

si ces négociations, excluant la Turquie, sont au stade préliminaire, elles s'inscrivent dans l'offensive commerciale canadienne décrite dans sa stratégie commerciale mondiale adoptée en 2007.

4. *L'offensive commerciale canadienne dans le reste du monde*

Cette offensive commerciale canadienne ne se limite pas aux frontières de l'Europe, et l'année 2013 donnera largement l'occasion d'en juger. Admis à la fin de l'année 2012 aux négociations de libre-échange du Partenariat transpacifique (PTP), le Canada ne manquera pas tout au long de l'année écoulée de s'y impliquer, espérant ainsi profiter du grand marché régional en construction. Il faut rappeler que douze pays participent à ces négociations.[27] La réunion des ministres des pays participants aux négociations du PTP qui s'est tenue à Singapour en décembre 2013 visait à planifier des travaux sur des sujets de négociation, tels que la propriété intellectuelle, la règlementation applicable aux sociétés d'État, l'enjeu environnemental, la régulation des services financiers, l'investissement étranger, les mesures sanitaires et phytosanitaires et les questions juridiques et institutionnelles.

Même si la participation du Canada au PTP n'était pas acquise dès le départ,[28] l'enjeu pour le Canada dans ces négociations est surtout de pouvoir participer à la construction d'un des plus importants blocs commerciaux régionaux du XXIe siècle avec un marché d'environ 658 millions de personnes et un PIB qui tournerait autour de 20,7 milliards de dollars.

De plus, la conclusion du PTP auquel participent les trois pays membres de l'*ALÉNA* pourrait également induire la modification *de facto* de certaines dispositions du traité nord-américain dont certaines dispositions ne sont plus adaptées aux besoins actuels de ses États membres.

Au-delà de ce grand marché en construction, le Canada s'intéresse à d'autres partenaires asiatiques tel que le Japon avec lequel le Canada négocie en ce moment un accord de libre-échange économique, mais aussi la Thaïlande avec laquelle des discussions explo-

---

[27] Australie, Brunei, Chili, États-Unis, Japon, Malaisie, Mexique, Nouvelle-Zélande, Pérou, Singapour, Vietnam et Canada.

[28] L'idée du PTP est née en 2005 à la suite de l'accord de libre-échange conclu entre le Chili, Brunei, la Nouvelle-Zélande et Singapour. Le Canada s'est joint au groupe des participants aux négociations à la fin 2012, alors que les États-Unis y participaient déjà depuis 2008.

ratoires dans l'optique d'établir un accord de libre-échange ont eu lieu en mars 2013. Dans la même veine, en 2013, s'est déroulée en Inde la huitième série de négociations pour conclure un accord de libre-échange.

Parallèlement, l'année 2013 marquera la fin des négociations en vue de la conclusion d'un accord de libre-échange avec la Corée. Premier accord d'intégration économique conclu avec un pays asiatique, cette entente donne accès à la quinzième économie mondiale dont le taux de croissance annuel moyen se situe autour de 6 % avec une population de cinquante millions de personnes. Sur le fond, il s'agit d'un accord de large portée qui envisage la libéralisation des échanges de biens et de services, des marchés publics, de la propriété intellectuelle et des investissements étrangers. Cet accord avec la Corée, septième partenaire commercial du Canada, ne fera que renforcer la coopération bilatérale et les liens que les deux partenaires entretiennent au sein d'autres forums internationaux comme la Coopération économique Asie-Pacifique (APEC), l'Organisation de coopération et de développement économiques (OCDE) ou le G-20.

C'est donc avec cette même détermination que le gouvernement fédéral s'intéresse au marché africain. Conscient de la croissance économique en Afrique et du potentiel africain en termes d'occasions d'affaires,[29] le Canada ne néglige pas ses relations avec le continent noir. Et c'est dans le secteur des ressources naturelles que le bilatéralisme commercial afro-canadien va s'exprimer de manière plus marquante. C'est très certainement ce qui explique le choix du Canada de privilégier des accords de promotion et de protection des investissements[30] plutôt que des accords de libre-échange économique. Au demeurant, malgré son implication grandissante dans le commerce mondial, le Canada n'a pas souvent été impliqué dans les contentieux commerciaux internationaux.

B.   LES DIFFÉRENDS LIÉS À L'*ALENA* AU COURS DE L'ANNÉE 2013

Au cours de l'année 2013, sept affaires ont été portées devant les groupes spéciaux établis sur la base de l'article 1904 de l'*ALÉNA*, dont seulement deux sont allées jusqu'au bout de la procédure

---

[29] On estime à près de trois milliards le commerce bilatéral de marchandises entre le Canada et le Nigéria pour la seule année 2011 et celui avec le Ghana à environ 322 millions de dollars pour la même année.

[30] Voir la chronique portant sur les investissements étrangers.

arbitrale et se sont soldées par une sentence des groupes spéciaux.[31] Il convient de noter que les sept affaires concernaient des différends entre les États-Unis et le Mexique. Les cinq autres affaires ont été réglées à l'amiable conformément à l'article 71.2 des règles de procédure relatives aux révisions des groupes spéciaux. Le Canada n'ayant été impliqué dans aucune de ces affaires, nous avons décidé aux fins de la chronique de commenter les deux décisions rendues par le tribunal binational de l'*ALÉNA* opposant le Mexique et les États-Unis.

1.   Light-Walled Rectangular Pipe and Tube from Mexico Final Results of the 2008-2009 Antidumping Duty Administrative Review[32]

Reeder a très bien identifié le cœur de l'histoire en cause: "*In recent years the conflict over zeroing, a controversial methodology the Department of Commerce uses in the calculation of dumping margins, has garnered increasing attention in both United States courts and international dispute resolution fora.*"[33] En effet, la *réduction à zéro* est une méthode appliquée par les organismes d'enquête de certains États dans le calcul des marges de dumping. Elle consiste à "écarter ou à réduire à zéro cette marge dans les cas où le prix à l'exportation est supérieur au prix sur le marché intérieur."[34] Le recours à cette pratique, notam-

---

[31] *Light-Walled Rectangular Pipe and Tube from Mexico, Final Results of 2008-2009 Antidumping Duty Administrative Review,* USA-MEX-2011-1904-02, 6 août 2013; *Final Determination of the Administrative and Sunset Review of the Antidumping Duty on the Imports of Certain Type of Stearic Acid from the United States of America, Irrespective of the Country of Shipment,* MEX-USA-2011-1904-01, 10 octobre 2013; *Stainless Steel Sheet and Strip in Coils from Mexico,* USA-MEX-2011-1904-01, 18 mars 2013; *Stainless Steel Sheet and Strip in Coils from Mexico: Final Results of AD Duty Administrative Review,* USA-MEX-2010-1904-01, 12 février 2013; *New Shipper Review of Antidumping Duty Order on Seamless Refined Copper Pipe and Tube from Mexico,* USA-MEX-2012-1904-03, 3 juillet 2013; *Feuille d'acier inoxydable et feuillard d'acier inoxydable en rouleaux provenant du Mexique,* USA-MEX-2009-1904-02, 18 janvier 2013; *Feuille et feuillards d'acier inoxydable en rouleau en provenance du Mexique (résultats finals de l'examen administratif en matière de droits antidumping),* USA-MEX-2008-1904-01, 8 février 2013.

[32] *Light Walled Rectangular Pipe and Tube from Mexico, Final Results of 2009-2010 Antidumping Duty Administrative Review,* USA-MEX-2012-1904-01, *ALÉNA,* ch 19, art 1904.

[33] Casey Reeder, "Zeroing in on *Charming Betsy*: How an Antidumping Controversy Threatens to Sink the Schooner," 36 Stetson Law Review à la p 256. Trouvable en ligne: <http://heinonline.org/HOL/Page?handle=hein.journals/stet36&div=15&collection=journals&set_as_cursor=0&men_tab=srchresults#267>.

[34] Dictionnaire de l'OMC, en ligne: <http://www.wto.org/french/thewto_f/glossary_f/zeroing_f.htm>.

ment aux États-Unis, est controversé, car elle peut se traduire par l'application de droits antidumping plus élevés que ceux qui devraient normalement être appliqués. À ce titre, les États-Unis ont été considérés en situation de violation de l'*Accord sur les mesures antidumping* à plus de dix reprises par l'OMC.[35] En 2004, un premier rapport de l'OMC avait jugé que les États-Unis avaient violé l'*Accord sur les mesures antidumping* (*Accord antidumping*) pour avoir utilisé la réduction à zéro.[36] Ce sera la première décision d'une longue série de condamnations de la pratique américaine puisqu'à l'heure actuelle, une douzaine de rapports ont déclaré les États-Unis en violation de l'*Accord antidumping*, et trois affaires sont actuellement pendantes devant l'Organe de règlement des différends (ORD).[37] Si les raisons invoquées par l'Organe d'appel peuvent différer selon les affaires, l'incompatibilité de cette pratique avec le droit international économique a été confirmée de manière générale, que ce soit dans le cadre des enquêtes préliminaires ou des examens administratifs.[38]

[35] Organe d'appel, États-Unis, *Détermination finale de l'existence d'un dumping concernant certains bois d'œuvre résineux en provenance du Canada*, DS264, 11 août 2004; Organe d'appel, États-Unis, *Lois, réglementations et méthode de calcul des marges de dumping (réduction à zéro)*, DS294, 18 avril 2006; Organe d'appel, États-Unis, *Mesures relatives à la réduction à zéro et aux réexamens à l'extinction*, DS322, 9 janvier 2007; Groupe spécial, États-Unis, *Mesures antidumping visant les crevettes en provenance de l'Équateur*, DS335, 30 janvier 2007; Organe d'appel, États-Unis, *Mesures antidumping finales visant l'acier inoxydable en provenance du Mexique*, DS344, 30 avril 2008; Organe d'appel, États-Unis, *Maintien en existence et application de la méthode de réduction à zéro*, DS350, 4 février 2009; Groupe spécial, États-Unis, *Réexamens administratifs antidumping et autres mesures concernant les importations de certains jus d'orange en provenance du Brésil*, DS382, 25 mars 2011; Groupe spécial, États-Unis, *Mesures antidumping visant les sacs en polyéthylène pour le commerce de détail en provenance de Thaïlande*, DS383, 22 janvier 2010; Groupe spécial, États-Unis, *Utilisation de la réduction à zéro dans les mesures antidumping concernant des produits en provenance de Corée*, DS402, 18 janvier 2011; Groupe spécial, États-Unis, *Mesures antidumping visant certaines crevettes en provenance du Vietnam*, DS404, 11 juillet 2011.

[36] Organe d'appel, États-Unis, *Détermination finale de l'existence d'un dumping concernant certains bois d'œuvre résineux en provenance du Canada*, DS264, 11 août 2004.

[37] Organe d'appel, États-Unis, *Mesures antidumping visant les produits plats en acier au carbone résistant à la corrosion en provenance de Corée*, DS420, 31 janvier 2011; Organe d'appel, États-Unis, *Mesures antidumping visant les crevettes et les lames de scie au diamant en provenance de Chine*, DS422, 8 juin 2012; Organe d'appel, États-Unis, *antidumping visant certaines crevettes en provenance du Vietnam*, DS429, 20 février 2012; Organe d'appel, États-Unis, *Certaines méthodes et leur application aux procédures antidumping visant la Chine*, DS471, 3 décembre 2013.

[38] Tania Voon, "NAFTA Chapter 19 Panel Follows WTO Appellate Body in Striking Down Zeroing," ASIL Insights, 23 septembre 2010 à la p 2.

De la même manière, plusieurs décisions de groupes spéciaux établis sur la base de l'article 1904.2 de l'*ALENA* sont venues sanctionner l'utilisation de la réduction à zéro par le Département américain du commerce. Dans l'affaire, *Certain Softwood Lumber Products*,[39] un groupe spécial avait déclaré que le Département du commerce ne pouvait pas utiliser la méthode de la réduction à zéro dans le calcul des marges de dumping, notamment sur la base de la doctrine *Charming Betsy*.[40] De la même façon, dans un rapport sur le fil machine,[41] le groupe spécial a demandé au Département du commerce de recalculer les marges antidumping appliquées à des entreprises canadiennes sans réduire à zéro les marges de dumping négatives et ce, toujours sur la base de la doctrine *Charming Betsy* et de l'arrêt *Chevron*.[42] Enfin, dans l'affaire *Stainless Steel Sheet*,[43] où un groupe spécial avait été constitué sur la base de l'article 1904.2 de l'*ALENA*, on avait demandé au Département du commerce de recalculer les marges de dumping sans réduction à zéro.[44]

Comme dans la présente affaire, l'organisme d'enquête avait appliqué cette méthode dans le cadre des examens administratifs, et les entreprises visées avaient intenté un recours devant le groupe spécial. Celui-ci avait estimé que les principes posés dans l'arrêt *Chevron* et par la doctrine *Charming Betsy* rendaient cette pratique incompatible avec le droit américain.[45]

Dans les faits, il semble que la méthode de la réduction à zéro n'est pas prévue en tant que telle par la loi américaine. Le Congrès américain ne s'étant pas prononcé sur la question, il apparaît que c'est à l'organisme d'enquête qu'il incombe de "s'autoréguler" sur cette question. Ainsi, en 2006, le Département américain du

[39] Article 1904 *Binational Panel Review, pursuant to the NAFTA, In the Matter of Certain Softwood Lumber Products from Canada: Final Affirmative Antidumping Determination*, USA-CDA- 2002-1904-02, 9 juin 2005.

[40] Jeffrey L. DUNOFF, "Less than Zero, the Effect of Giving Domestic Effect to WTO Law," 6:1 Loyola University Chicago International Law Review 2008 à la p 293.

[41] Article 1904, *Binational Panel Review pursuant to the NAFTA, In the Matter of Carbon and Certain Alloy Steel Wire Rod from Canada*, USA-CDA-2006-1904-04, 28 novembre 2007.

[42] *Supra* note 41 à la p 295.

[43] Article 1904 *Binational Panel pursuant to the NAFTA, Stainless Steel Sheet and Strip in Coils From Mexico: Final Results of 2004/2005 Antidumping Review*, USA-MEX-2007-1904-01, 14 avril 2010.

[44] *Supra* note 39 à la p 1.

[45] *Ibid* à la p 3.

commerce avait annoncé qu'il n'utiliserait plus la réduction à zéro dans le cadre de la méthode de comparaison de moyenne à moyenne utilisée dans les enquêtes initiales. Toutefois, il continuera à l'utiliser dans le cadre des examens administratifs.[46]

La présente affaire intervient dans ce contexte après que le Département du commerce ait une fois de plus appliqué la réduction à zéro dans le calcul des marges de dumping d'une entreprise mexicaine.

a. Retour sur les faits de la cause

Le 5 août 2008, à la suite de son enquête initiale, l'Administration du commerce international[47] a adopté une mesure antidumping sur les tubes et tuyaux rectangulaires à paroi mince en provenance de plusieurs pays, dont le Mexique.[48] Le 13 septembre 2010, le Département du commerce a publié ses résultats préliminaires de l'examen administratif portant sur les ventes réalisées par deux entreprises entre le 30 janvier et le 31 juillet 2009, dont Maquilacero,[49] une entreprise productrice et exportatrice mexicaine.[50] Après avoir reçu les commentaires des différentes entreprises concernées, le Département du commerce a publié ses déterminations finales le 18 février 2011. D'après ses calculs, la marge moyenne pondérée du dumping pratiqué par Maquilacero doit être fixée à 3,11 % pour la période visée.[51]

---

[46] Federal Register, Notice of Final Modification, 27 décembre 2006, en ligne: <https://www.federalregister.gov/articles/2006/12/27/E6-22178/antidumping -proceedings-calculation-of-the-weighted-average-dumping-margin-during -an-antidumping>.

[47] L'*International Trade Administration* est l'agence responsable de déterminer l'existence d'un dumping aux États-Unis, en ligue: <https://www.nafta-sec-alena. org/Default.aspx?tabid=137&language=fr-CA>.

[48] Article 1904 *Binational Panel Review pursuant to NAFTA, Light-Walled Rectangular Pipe and Tube from Mexico, Final Results of the 2008-2009 Antidumping Duty Administrative Review*, USA-MEX-2011-1904-02, 5 décembre 2012 à la p 2. En ligne: <http://www.worldtradelaw.net/naftadatabase/nafta19.asp?table1=s:-2>.

[49] Federal Register, *Light-Walled Rectangular Pipe and Tube from Mexico: Preliminary Results of Antidumping Duty Administrative Review*, 13 septembre 2010, en ligne: <https://www.federalregister.gov/articles/2010/09/13/2010-22777/light-walled -rectangular-pipe-and-tube-from-mexico-preliminary-results-of-antidumping -duty>.

[50] *Ibid* à la p 1.

[51] *Ibid* aux pp 3-4.

Un mois plus tard, l'entreprise Maquilacero a déposé un recours en révision de ces résultats, demandant la constitution d'un groupe spécial sur la base de l'article 1904.2 de l'*ALENA*. Pour contester ces résultats, l'entreprise remet en cause la méthodologie adoptée par le Département du commerce consistant à continuer d'appliquer la réduction à zéro dans le cadre des examens administratifs alors qu'il a renoncé à l'utiliser dans le cadre des enquêtes préliminaires. L'entreprise invoque au soutien de son allégation deux arguments.[52] Premièrement, l'entreprise allègue qu'il s'agit d'une politique arbitraire contraire à la loi américaine. Selon la plaignante, la loi américaine ne fait pas de différence entre les enquêtes préliminaires et les examens administratifs. L'entreprise invoque au soutien de son argumentation deux décisions du Circuit fédéral qui font état de l'insuffisance d'explication du Département du commerce quant à cette politique de différenciation.[53] À cet argument, le Département du commerce répond simplement qu'étant donné que l'entreprise n'a pas exercé son recours administratif, sa requête ne pouvait être considérée comme recevable.

Deuxièmement, l'entreprise considère que l'interprétation du Département du commerce placerait les États-Unis en situation de violation de leurs obligations internationales. En effet, l'absence de mise en conformité de l'action de l'organisme par rapport aux décisions de l'OMC serait contraire à la doctrine *Charming Betsy*.[54] La décision de l'OMC à laquelle l'entreprise fait référence ne saurait avoir d'effet avant d'être exécutée selon les prescriptions légales,[55] c'est-à-dire selon la procédure établie dans l'acte adopté par le Congrès lors de la ratification des traités de l'OMC en 1994. À ce stade de l'affaire, la principale question juridique à laquelle le groupe spécial devrait répondre serait donc de savoir si la politique de calcul du dumping adoptée par l'autorité d'enquête est cohérente et légitime, d'un point de vue à la fois national et international.

---

[52] *Ibid* aux pp 11-12.

[53] *Dongbu Steel Co, Ltd c United States*, 635 F 3d 1363, 1371 (2011); *JTEKT Corp and Koyo Corp c United States*, 642 F 3d 1378 (2011).

[54] Casey Reeder, *supra* note 34 aux pp 275-76: la doctrine *Charming Betsy*, ayant évolué depuis la décision *Murray c The Schooner Charming Betsy*, 6 US 64 (US 1804), pose le principe selon lequel une loi doit être interprétée de façon à ne pas violer le droit international.

[55] Binational Panel Review, *supra* note 50 à la p 13.

b. Le raisonnement du panel quant à la détermination
de la conformité de la politique de calcul adopté par le
Département du commerce

Le raisonnement du groupe spécial s'est fait en plusieurs étapes. Dans un premier temps, le groupe spécial commence par rappeler les règles qui encadrent son contrôle sur les déterminations anti-dumping réalisées par les organismes nationaux compétents, c'est-à-dire, les paragraphes 2 et 3 de l'article 1904, ainsi que l'annexe 1911 de l'*ALENA*. Il résulte de ces dispositions que le groupe spécial doit notamment appliquer "les principes juridiques généraux qu'un tribunal de la Partie importatrice appliquerait."[56] En l'espèce, en raison du contexte de common law, il incombe au groupe spécial d'appliquer le principe du *stare decisis*. La Cour compétente pour juger de la conformité de la détermination antidumping est la Cour du commerce international, dont les décisions peuvent faire l'objet d'un appel devant le Circuit fédéral. Ainsi, dans un premier temps, le groupe spécial passe en revue les principes qui doivent guider sa décision, conformément aux décisions rendues par ces deux juridictions.[57] Ces principes sont les mêmes que ceux qui guideront le groupe spécial dans sa décision ultime.

Le groupe spécial contextualise la question soulevée par la plaignante qui consiste à savoir s'il était possible d'appliquer le principe de l'arrêt *Charming Betsy* pour considérer que l'utilisation de la réduction à zéro par le Département du commerce viole les obligations internationales des États-Unis.[58]

Il faut rappeler que depuis 2004, l'utilisation de la réduction à zéro par les États-Unis a fait l'objet de plusieurs rapports défavorables par l'OMC, déclarant systématiquement la pratique de la réduction à zéro incompatible avec l'Accord antidumping et ce, que ce soit pendant les enquêtes préliminaires ou les examens administratifs.[59] Toutefois, le groupe spécial note ici que les traités du cycle d'Uruguay doivent être transposés dans la législation interne. Or, la Cour Suprême a posé le principe selon lequel dans une telle situation, les dispositions du traité "ne peuvent être

---

[56] Traité de l'*ALENA*, ch 19, art 1904 (3), Binational Panel Review, *supra* note 50 à la p 4.

[57] Binational Panel Review, *supra* note 50 aux pp 4-11.

[58] *Ibid* à la p 13.

[59] *Ibid* aux pp 14-15.

appliquées que conformément à la législation qui les a mises en vigueur."[60] De plus, la loi adoptée par le Congrès dans ce contexte met en place une procédure précise et exclusive quant à la mise en œuvre des rapports de l'OMC.[61] Il doit notamment y avoir une consultation du Congrès, comme cela a été le cas pour le changement de méthodologie effectué en 2006.[62] Le groupe spécial note finalement que le Département du commerce peut être considéré ici comme le représentant des États-Unis et charge la scène internationale de fustiger les États-Unis pour leur application controversée de la réduction à zéro.[63]

Au terme du raisonnement du groupe spécial, il apparaît que la doctrine *Charming Betsy* n'appelle pas à une interprétation différente de la loi de celle qu'a adoptée le Département du commerce.[64]

Le second argument invoqué par la plaignante est celui de la différence injustifiée et arbitraire consistant à continuer d'appliquer la réduction à zéro à certaines marges de dumping pendant les examens administratifs, alors que le Département du commerce ne l'applique plus pendant les enquêtes préliminaires. Cette interprétation donnée par l'organisme d'enquête serait contraire à la législation américaine.

Le groupe spécial, en se basant sur les deux décisions rendues par le Circuit fédéral,[65] établit que "*Commerce had not supplied a reasonable interpretation why U.S. antidumping law supports the inconsistent application of zeroing to administrative reviews, but not to investigations.*" Or, en l'espèce, le Département du commerce n'a pas apporté d'explications supplémentaires[66] permettant de satisfaire le principe d'explication raisonnable posé par l'arrêt *Chevron*.[67]

---

[60] *Ibid* à la p 18.

[61] *Ibid* à la p 15.

[62] *Ibid* à la p 16.

[63] *Ibid* à la p 19, il y est précisé que: "*the same party that will face potential abjuration in the international forum for an interpretation of its obligations that offends the law of nations to which the Charming Betsy doctrine responds.*"

[64] Binational Panel Review, *supra* note 50 à la p 20.

[65] *Dongbu Steel Co Ltd c United States*, 635 F 3d 1363, 1371 (2011); *JTEKT Corp and Koyo Corp c United States*, 642 F 3d 1378 (2011).

[66] Il convient de noter ici que Maquilacero a soulevé cet argument après le rendu des déterminations finales du Département du commerce, ce qui n'a pas permis à l'organisme d'enquête d'y répondre.

[67] Binational Panel Review, *supra* note 50 aux pp 36-37. Précisons que la décision du Circuit fédéral pose plusieurs principes d'interprétation, et notamment la

Dans sa décision initiale en date du 5 décembre 2012, le groupe spécial a demandé au Département du commerce de justifier sa politique de calcul et d'évaluation du dumping et, notamment, la différence d'application de la méthode controversée de la réduction à zéro selon que l'évaluation a lieu au stade de l'enquête ou au stade de l'examen administratif.

Au moyen d'une communication en date du 4 mars 2013, le Département du commerce a présenté ses explications au groupe spécial ainsi qu'à la partie adverse relativement à son utilisation de la réduction à zéro dans le cadre des examens administratifs.[68] La plaignante a pu soumettre ses commentaires le 1er mai 2013, auxquels le Département du commerce a répondu par une communication le 17 juin 2013.[69]

c.   L'influence du système de common law sur la décision ultime du groupe spécial

La décision ultime du groupe spécial apparaît en décalage par rapport à la décision initiale. En effet, la survenance d'une nouvelle décision du Circuit fédéral va venir modifier la question juridique posée au groupe spécial.

Rappelons une fois de plus que le groupe spécial est lié par la jurisprudence américaine. Or, entre le rendu de la décision initiale en décembre 2012 et la décision sans appel rendue en août 2013, la situation jurisprudentielle américaine a évolué. De cette manière, les deux décisions rendues en 2011 par le Circuit fédéral ont influencé dans une large mesure le raisonnement du panel quant à savoir si le Département du commerce "avait fourni une explication suffisante de son application de la réduction à zéro aux examens administratifs et non aux enquêtes préliminaires."[70]

On se souvient qu'en 2011, le Circuit fédéral avait renvoyé l'affaire devant la Cour du commerce international, qui a alors validé les

---

règle selon laquelle en l'absence de détermination claire de la loi sur une question litigieuse, la juridiction saisie de l'affaire doit déterminer si l'autorité administrative responsable pour combler ce vide juridique l'a fait en accord avec le sens général de la loi.

[68] Binational Panel Review, *Light-Walled Rectangular Pipe And Tube from Mexico Final Results of the 2008-2009 Antidumping Duty Administrative Review, Final Decision*, USA-MEX-2011-1904-02, 11 août 2013 à la p 1.

[69] Binational Panel Review, *supra* note 50 à la p 2.

[70] *Ibid.*

explications données par le Département du commerce.[71] Grâce
à l'appel des plaignantes, le Circuit fédéral a pu se prononcer de
nouveau sur la question et a alors confirmé le jugement rendu par
la Cour du commerce international.

De la sorte, lorsque l'affaire revient devant le groupe spécial, les
deux décisions sur lesquelles il s'était basé pour rendre sa décision
initiale étaient en décalage par rapport à l'état actuel de la jurisprudence. Les explications initialement contestées du Département
du commerce ont été validées par la juridiction à laquelle le groupe
spécial doit se référer pour rendre sa décision. De cette façon, la
question à laquelle le groupe spécial doit désormais répondre n'est
plus celle de la conformité de la politique de calcul adoptée par le
Département du commerce, mais plutôt celle consistant à déterminer l'applicabilité de la décision *Union Steel* au cas d'espèce.[72]

Le principe du *stare decisis*, l'une des règles fondamentales régissant les systèmes de common law, prévoit que sous réserve de certaines exceptions, les juridictions confrontées à un problème de
droit sont liées par les décisions précédemment rendues sur la
question. L'une des exceptions notables à ce principe est le *distinguishing* qui permet aux juridictions de diverger des précédents
lorsque les circonstances de l'espèce diffèrent du précédent. C'est
pourquoi la démarche du groupe spécial a d'abord consisté à déterminer s'il était lié à la décision *Union Steel* pour le cas d'espèce
soulevé devant lui en vertu du principe du *stare decisis* avant de rejeter
l'application du *distinguishing* et toute forme de contestation de la
réduction à zéro.

d. De l'application du principe du *stare decisis* au rejet de
    l'exception du *distinguishing* ainsi que de toute allégation
    contestant l'application de la réduction à zéro lors des
    examens administratifs

Le panel rappelle dans un premier temps que sa constatation
d'explications insuffisantes de la part du Département du commerce
ne faisait qu'abonder dans le sens des deux décisions du Circuit
fédéral. Il prend ensuite acte de la décision *Union Steel* et note que
les explications avancées par le Département du commerce dans
l'affaire *Union Steel* ont été entièrement confirmées par la Cour du
commerce international.

---

[71] Binational Panel Review, *supra* note 66 à la p 3.
[72] *Ibid* à la p 2.

Le raisonnement du Département du commerce peut ainsi se décliner en trois volets.[73] Tout d'abord, il rappelle sa position selon laquelle la réduction à zéro est utile pour recalculer les marges de moyenne pondérée qui rendent la valeur normale inférieure aux prix des produits exportés, et empêchent donc l'application de droits antidumping. Ensuite, il rappelle que son changement de pratique ne s'est pas fait arbitrairement, mais de façon à se conformer à la décision de l'OMC. Enfin, son interprétation serait justifiée en raison des différences inhérentes aux méthodes de comparaison.

Ces justifications peuvent sembler quelque peu équivoques. Par exemple, ce changement de pratique s'est certes fait de façon conforme à une décision de l'OMC, mais qu'en est-il du respect des autres décisions de l'OMC ? En effet, depuis 2006, de nouveaux rapports de l'OMC sont venus condamner la réduction à zéro également dans le cadre des examens administratifs, mais le Département du commerce en a complètement fait abstraction. Le fait que celui-ci choisisse d'appliquer seulement l'un des rapports démontre au contraire l'arbitraire de sa démarche.

Pourtant les deux juridictions nationales américaines ont tour à tour approuvé les explications données par le Département du commerce, laissant au groupe spécial le seul choix de les approuver à son tour. Ainsi, le groupe spécial retient les éléments du raisonnement de la Cour et du Circuit fédéral qui lui apparaissent les plus pertinents. Par exemple, la Cour du commerce international a retenu que l'organisme d'enquête possède une marge discrétionnaire lui permettant d'adapter ses méthodes afin de se conformer au droit international.[74] De plus, la différence d'application de la réduction à zéro lui apparaît logique en raison des caractéristiques propres à chaque méthode de comparaison, appliquées dans différents contextes.[75]

---

[73] Binational Panel Review, *supra* note 66 aux pp 3-4.

[74] *Ibid* à la p 4.

[75] *Ibid* à la p 5. *United States Court of Appeals for the Federal Circuit, Union Steel, LG Hausys, LTD, LG Hausys America, Inc, and Dongbu Steel Co, LTD c États-Unis and Nucor Corporation and United States Steel Corporation*, 2012-1248, 1315, 16 avril 2013 aux pp 13-14: apparemment, le Département utilise généralement la comparaison de moyenne à moyenne dans le cadre des enquêtes initiales, alors qu'il estime la comparaison de transaction à moyenne plus appropriée au contexte des examens administratifs. Selon l'organisme, la comparaison de moyenne à moyenne permettrait d'apprécier une vue globale de la politique de prix d'une entreprise, alors que la comparaison de transaction à moyenne permettrait

Au terme de l'énumération des différentes constatations établies par le Circuit fédéral et la Cour du commerce international, le groupe spécial finit donc par rejeter l'allégation de Maquilacero visant à faire réexaminer la pratique de la réduction à zéro. Il estime que l'entreprise cherche ici à débattre de la même question ayant fait l'objet de discussions devant les deux juridictions nationales, notant que les arguments qu'elle invoque pour soutenir son allégation sont les mêmes que ceux invoqués par les plaignantes dans l'affaire *Union Steel* et que les explications fournies par le Département du commerce au groupe spécial sont les mêmes que celles fournies au Circuit fédéral. En conséquence, l'allégation de Maquilacero est redondante par rapport à celle des plaignantes dans l'affaire *Union Steel*. La Cour du commerce international, comme le Circuit fédéral, ayant confirmé la position du Département du commerce, la question de sa conformité ne peut pas être réexaminée devant le groupe spécial.[76]

Dans une certaine mesure, le principe du *distinguishing* aurait pu permettre d'empêcher l'application du *stare decisis*, mais cette exception a été rejetée par le groupe spécial. La plaignante soutient que les faits de l'affaire *Union Steel* sont différents des faits de la présente affaire. Dans l'affaire *Union Steel*, le Département du commerce avait appliqué la méthode de la réduction à zéro à la fois pendant l'enquête et pendant l'examen administratif. Compte tenu de la modification apportée en 2006, le Département du commerce avait appliqué la réduction à zéro seulement pendant l'examen administratif. Selon la plaignante, le raisonnement et la solution des juridictions américaines dans l'affaire *Union Steel* ne seraient donc pas applicables au cas de l'espèce, et le groupe spécial ne serait pas tenu par le principe du *stare decisis*. Le Département du

---

d'apprécier plus précisément les prix pratiqués lors de transactions individuelles. Cette différence de méthodologie serait alors justifiée, car l'enquête vise à évaluer l'importance du dumping et conséquemment le montant des droits antidumping, alors que l'examen administratif doit évaluer un droit antidumping déjà en place. Cette explication a été validée à la fois par la Cour du commerce international et par le Circuit fédéral. Selon ces deux juridictions, la spécificité est moins importante dans le cadre des enquêtes que dans le cadre des examens administratifs. Selon le Circuit fédéral, la réduction à zéro ne serait pas nécessaire dans le cadre des comparaisons de moyenne à moyenne, car les prix élevés compensent automatiquement les prix bas à l'intérieur de chaque groupe moyen. Au contraire, dans le cadre des comparaisons de transaction à moyenne, les prix ne sont pas pondérés et la réduction à zéro permettrait de révéler les dumpings masqués.

[76] Binational Panel Review, *supra* note 66 à la p 5.

commerce, même s'il reconnaît ce changement dans ses méthodes, considère toutefois que cela ne constitue pas une raison suffisante pour écarter toute référence à la décision *Union Steel.*

Le groupe spécial devra alors déterminer si les faits des deux affaires sont assez similaires pour que le premier serve de précédent au second. Pour le groupe spécial, la question se pose plutôt en ces termes: "quelles raisons fondaient la solution du premier cas et dans quelle mesure ces raisons peuvent-elles être appliquées à la seconde affaire"?[77] On voit ici que le groupe spécial transforme la question du *distinguishing* relative aux faits en une question de fond. Ainsi, si le groupe spécial relève une différence factuelle entre les deux affaires, il estime toutefois que la question dans l'affaire *Union Steel* était de savoir si le raisonnement adopté par le Département du commerce pour justifier son changement de pratique était acceptable ou non. Il s'agissait d'un problème d'ordre général, détaché des considérations pratiques et factuelles.

Deux arguments principaux viennent soutenir cette constatation. Le premier argument est celui de la généralité, caractéristique que l'on retrouve à la fois dans le langage utilisé par les États-Unis, par les plaignants et par la juridiction américaine elle-même.[78] Le deuxième argument est celui de l'absence totale de référence à la situation précédant le changement de politique du Département du commerce par la juridiction américaine. Ainsi, le groupe spécial estime que le raisonnement adopté par la juridiction américaine pour confirmer la politique du Département du commerce *"have been entirely unaffected by the factual distinction noted here by complainant."*[79] Les seules différences relevées par la Cour dans le rendu de sa décision sont celles qui existent entre les types de comparaison utilisés par le Département du commerce.

Il apparaît en effet que les faits propres à cette affaire, et notamment la différence de politique du Département avant et après 2006, n'avaient pas leur place dans le raisonnement délivré par la Cour du commerce international. Son raisonnement s'est au contraire focalisé sur la légitimité de la distinction faite par le Département du commerce entre les enquêtes et les examens administratifs.

---

[77] Binational Panel Review, *supra* note 66 à la p 7.

[78] *Ibid,* "the operative language in the brief of the US is generic and non-specific to the case" (p 8); "the brief of the Korean steel producers is to similar effect" (à la p 8); "the Court continue throughout its opinion to use the general language" (à la p 9).

[79] *Ibid* à la p 10.

Toutefois, c'est également l'angle adopté par le groupe spécial qui permet d'écarter l'application du principe du *distinguishing*.

De cette façon, le groupe spécial conclut que la différence factuelle entre les deux cas n'est pas propre à empêcher la prise en compte de l'affaire *Union Steel*. En conséquence, le *distinguishing* ne pouvant faire œuvre d'exception, le principe du *stare decisis* s'applique et le groupe spécial se trouve lié aux décisions de la Cour du commerce international et du Circuit fédéral.

Dans ses commentaires, Maquilacero faisait également valoir que si le Département du commerce estimait la compensation inhérente à la comparaison de moyenne à moyenne, il devrait également l'examiner dans le cadre de la comparaison de transaction à moyenne, notamment dans les cas où des variations importantes de prix surviennent dans le marché intérieur de l'entreprise exportatrice. En réponse, le Département du commerce soutient que cette allégation doit être rejetée, car Maquilacero n'aurait pas effectué son recours administratif devant l'agence, ce qui est une condition essentielle et préalable à l'exercice d'un recours devant le groupe spécial. Selon l'agence, il s'agit de la première fois que la plaignante soutient cette prétention, qui est donc irrecevable à ce stade de la procédure.[80]

Selon le groupe spécial, il ne s'agit pas là d'un nouvel argument invoqué par la plaignante, mais d'un exemple visant à démontrer que les explications fournies par le Département du commerce ne sont pas convaincantes. Suivant le raisonnement adopté précédemment, le groupe spécial va donc rejeter cet argument, considérant qu'il n'importe pas en l'espèce de déterminer si celui-ci était susceptible de démontrer l'incohérence des explications de l'organisme d'enquête ou non.[81]

Le groupe spécial considèrera qu'au vu de la décision *Union Steel*, l'interprétation adoptée par le Département du commerce doit être considérée comme conforme avec la législation américaine.[82] Logiquement, les déterminations de l'organisme d'enquête adoptées sur la base de cette interprétation, c'est-à-dire comprenant l'utilisation de la réduction à zéro, doivent elles aussi être approuvées.[83]

À la suite de la conclusion à laquelle parvient le groupe spécial dans la présente affaire, on peut se demander pourquoi, dans sa

---

[80] Binational Panel Review, *supra* note 66 à la p 10.

[81] *Ibid* à la p 13.

[82] *Ibid.*

[83] *Ibid* à la p 14.

décision initiale, le groupe spécial avait estimé que la doctrine *Charming Betsy* n'était pas suffisante pour considérer que la réduction à zéro pratiquée par le Département du commerce était incompatible avec les engagements internationaux des États-Unis. Différentes raisons peuvent expliquer le raisonnement du groupe spécial. Tout d'abord, les décisions précédemment évoquées avaient provoqué certaines tensions et critiques chez des panélistes de l'*ALENA*.[84] De plus, les groupes spéciaux de l'*ALENA* ne sont pas des organes permanents, mais des panels *ad hoc* établis à chaque conflit. La structure générale des groupes spéciaux ne semble pas propre à développer une cohérence dans leurs décisions.

Quant à l'application du principe *stare decisis* par le groupe spécial, il convient de noter que l'indépendance des groupes spéciaux est remise en question par le rapport qui les lie aux décisions des juridictions nationales. Dans sa décision ultime, le groupe spécial ne semble pas développer sa propre argumentation, et il se contente de reprendre les éléments principaux du raisonnement de la juridiction nationale. Le principe du *stare decisis* rend les groupes spéciaux tributaires des institutions nationales des États membres. Dans un cas tel que la réduction à zéro où l'État ne semble pas prêt à remettre en cause sa politique, le poids des groupes spéciaux de l'*ALENA* semble bien léger.

Il est toutefois important de mentionner qu'au moment où nous rédigeons cette chronique, le Département du commerce a complètement abandonné la méthode de la réduction à zéro.[85] Cette nouvelle politique met donc un terme à cette controverse longue de plus de dix ans sur la méthode de calcul des marges de dumping adoptée par les États-Unis. La réduction à zéro apparaît désormais comme une pratique obsolète, les États-Unis étant l'un des derniers États à l'avoir utilisée.

2. *Final Determination of the Administrative and Sunset Review of the Antidumping Duty on the Imports of Certain Type of Stearic Acid from the United States of America, Irrespective of the Country of Shipment, du 10 octobre 2013 (MEX-USA-2011-1904-01)*

La présente décision a été adoptée le 13 octobre 2013 par le groupe spécial établi sur la base de l'article 1904 de l'*ALENA*, en règlement

---

84 Tania Voon, *supra* note 39 à la p 3.

85 Federal Register, *Notice of Final Modification*, 14 février 2012, en ligne: <https://www.federalregister.gov/articles/2012/02/14/2012-3290/antidumping-proceedings-calculation-of-the-weighted-average-dumping-margin-and-assessment-rate-in>.

d'un différend entre l'entreprise mexicaine Quimic et l'Unité des pratiques commerciales internationales du Mexique [ci-après organisme d'enquête]. Il s'agissait d'une demande en révision de la détermination finale de l'organisme concernant des importations d'acide stéarique en provenance des États-Unis.

a.   Les faits de la cause

Le 8 avril 2005, l'Unité des pratiques commerciales internationales du Mexique a publié sa détermination finale concernant les droits antidumping imposés aux importations d'acide stéarique. Cinq années plus tard, l'organisme d'enquête a notifié sa décision de réexaminer les droits antidumping au cours d'un examen administratif ainsi que d'un examen d'extinction, la période d'enquête s'étendant de janvier à décembre 2009. Dans sa détermination finale, adoptée le 29 septembre et publiée le 7 octobre 2011, l'organisme d'enquête constatait que la révocation des droits antidumping entraînerait un maintien de la pratique de concurrence déloyale. Par conséquent, les droits antidumping seront fixés à un taux de 17,38 % pour une période de cinq ans supplémentaires. Toutefois, l'organisme d'enquête a décidé de révoquer l'ensemble des droits antidumping applicables à l'entreprise exportatrice américaine Vantage, même s'il maintient une période d'examen pour trois années supplémentaires.

Pendant les audiences, Quimic, une entreprise de production mexicaine, avait fait valoir que Vantage n'était pas une partie intéressée à la procédure administrative puisqu'elle n'avait pas fait l'objet de l'enquête originelle de 2005. À l'époque, les droits antidumping avaient été imposés à d'autres entreprises, dont une entreprise appelée Uniquema. Pour cette raison, l'entreprise Quimic estimait que l'organisme d'enquête ne pouvait pas procéder à une fixation individuelle des marges de dumping pratiquées par Vantage sur l'année 2009 dans le cadre d'un réexamen puisque les marges de dumping de cette entreprise n'avaient pas été examinées en premier lieu dans le cadre de l'enquête originelle en 2005.

La détermination finale de l'organisme d'enquête allant à l'encontre de ses intérêts, le 4 novembre 2011, l'entreprise Quimic déposait une demande de révision, demandant la constitution d'un groupe spécial sur la base de l'article 1904 de l'*ALENA*. Le 15 décembre 2011, l'entreprise Vantage déposait un avis de comparution "à titre de précaution". Le lendemain, l'organisme d'enquête faisait également savoir qu'il souhaitait participer à la procédure de révision de sa détermination finale. Les parties au différend ont ensuite déposé tour à tour leur mémoire afin de présenter leurs arguments respectifs, dont il convient à présent d'examiner le détail.

b. Les arguments des parties quant à la détermination finale

Dans ses mémoires en date du 5 mars 2012 et du 21 mai 2012, l'entreprise Quimic a fait valoir que l'organisme d'enquête n'avait pas choisi la bonne procédure d'examen pour fixer les droits antidumping applicables à l'entreprise Vantage, ce qui rendrait sa décision ultime illégale. Plusieurs arguments sont invoqués au soutien de cette allégation.

Tout d'abord, et de manière générale, l'article 11.2 de l'Accord antidumping, l'article 68 de la *Loi sur le Commerce extérieur* (*LCE*), et les articles 99 et 100 du Règlement de la *Loi sur le Commerce extérieur* (*RLCE*) n'autoriseraient pas l'organisme d'enquête à modifier les droits antidumping au cours d'un examen. En dehors de cette impossibilité générale de modification, la plaignante fait valoir qu'il était de toute façon impossible de modifier les droits antidumping de Vantage dans le cadre de l'examen administratif. En effet, il apparaît que Vantage était un "nouvel expéditeur," une entreprise récente qui n'avait pas exporté pendant la période de l'examen original. Selon la plaignante, cela signifie que l'entreprise ne pouvait être considérée comme une partie intéressée à participer à la procédure d'examen administratif et il était donc illégal de déterminer une marge de dumping applicable seulement à Vantage dans le cadre de cette procédure.

En conséquence, la procédure applicable à la situation de Vantage serait la seule procédure établie par l'article 9.5 de l'Accord antidumping, l'article 89-D de la *LCE* et l'article 101 de la *RLCE*. Ces articles établiraient une procédure spéciale pour les entreprises n'ayant pas exporté durant la période d'examen original. Ainsi, Vantage aurait dû demander l'ouverture d'un examen concernant un nouvel expéditeur et non se manifester pendant l'examen administratif. L'organisme d'enquête aurait par ailleurs dû réorienter la demande de l'entreprise vers la procédure d'examen concernant un nouvel expéditeur. De plus, pendant l'audience tenue à Mexico le 11 avril 2013, Quimic a ajouté que l'organisme avait déterminé un droit antidumping au cours de la procédure établie par l'article 68 de la *LCE* alors que cet article n'autorisait que la confirmation, la modification ou la révocation.

L'organisme d'enquête estime au contraire que la loi l'autorise à réexaminer les droits antidumping et à les modifier ou les révoquer si besoin est, et ce, conformément à l'article 11.2 de l'*Accord sur les mesures antidumping*.

Par ailleurs, l'organisme d'enquête considère que, conformément à l'article 51 de la *LFPCA*, tout exportateur, importateur ou producteur national doit être considéré comme une partie intéressée. En conséquence, il importe peu de savoir si Vantage était une entreprise récente ou si elle avait exporté pendant la période d'examen originel, du moment que l'entreprise exportait au moment de la période d'examen administratif. Refuser d'intégrer l'entreprise dans le processus d'examen au motif qu'elle n'était pas une partie intéressée serait, au sens de l'organisme d'enquête, contraire à la loi.

Enfin, l'organisme d'enquête considère qu'il n'y a pas eu création d'un droit antidumping au cours de l'examen administratif, mais qu'il s'agissait d'une simple modification, conformément à l'article 68 de la *LCE*.

Quant à l'entreprise Vantage, sa participation à la procédure devant le panel a été autorisée, car les griefs de la plaignante sont centrés sur le droit antidumping (0 %) que lui a attribué l'organisme d'enquête dans la décision contestée. Toutefois, ses arguments ne peuvent être pris en compte ici, parce que notamment l'entreprise a choisi la juridiction mexicaine comme étant compétente pour connaître de ses plaintes.

c.   Les questions juridiques posées au groupe spécial

On peut demander tout d'abord si l'organisme d'enquête pouvait modifier un droit antidumping spécifique sur la base du mécanisme établi par les articles 11.2 de l'Accord antidumping, 68 de la *LCE*, 99 et 100 de la *RLCE* au cours de l'examen administratif. Deuxièmement, il s'agit de savoir si l'organisme d'enquête avait l'obligation d'utiliser la procédure établie par les articles 9.5 de l'*Accord sur les mesures antidumping* et 89-D de la *LCE* pour déterminer le droit antidumping applicable à un nouvel expéditeur.

Conformément à l'article 1904.2, le groupe spécial doit apprécier la conformité de la détermination finale de l'organisme d'enquête au regard de la législation de la partie importatrice. Le groupe spécial commence donc par passer en revue les règles encadrant son contrôle, et qui doivent le guider dans le rendu de sa décision avant de s'intéresser aux problèmes de fond soulevés dans cette affaire. Il faut préciser au passage que le groupe spécial a dû limiter son contrôle à certaines des déterminations réalisées par l'organisme d'enquête, mais c'est surtout la question de la détermination des critères d'examen et de leur application qui retient l'attention du lecteur.

Même si l'organisme d'enquête a entamé à la fois un examen administratif et un examen à l'expiration, les contestations du plaignant portent sur le seul examen administratif. En conséquence, le groupe spécial devra limiter son contrôle à la conformité de la détermination finale de l'organisme d'enquête adoptée suite à l'examen administratif.

Le groupe spécial se contente de fonder sa décision sur les règles de l'*ALENA* d'une manière générale, sans préciser sur quelle disposition il se fonde. On peut supposer que l'article 1904.14 de l'*ALENA* constitue un élément de réponse, celui-ci prévoyant que les Parties à l'accord devront établir des règles de procédures limitant "l'examen du groupe spécial aux erreurs que font valoir les Parties ou des personnes privées." Cette limitation du contrôle du groupe spécial au seul examen administratif apparaît légitime puisque d'une manière générale, il n'est pas nécessaire d'aller au-delà des prétentions des parties.

Le critère d'examen établi par l'annexe 1911 quant aux litiges émanant de la partie mexicaine est l'article 238 du Code fiscal fédéral. Toutefois, celui-ci a été remplacé par l'article 51 de la loi fédérale sur la procédure contentieuse administrative (*LFPCA*) et c'est donc cet article que le groupe spécial doit prendre en compte comme critère d'examen. Au regard de ce critère d'examen, le groupe spécial a dû déterminer la recevabilité de la demande de la plaignante avant d'envisager d'autres articles que celui expressément prévu à l'annexe 1911.

L'article 51 de la *LFPCA* énonce les cas dans lesquels une décision de l'administration pourra être déclarée illégale. Il s'agit notamment de motifs d'incompétence de l'agent à l'origine de la décision, de l'inaccomplissement des formalités, d'erreurs de procédure affectant entre autres la défense des intérêts privés ou de la mauvaise interprétation des faits. L'entreprise plaignante invoque une violation générale de cette disposition. Ainsi, l'organisme d'enquête et Vantage font valoir que la plainte telle qu'elle a été présentée ne remplit pas les exigences posées par l'article 51 de la *LFPCA* en ce sens que la plaignante ne démontre pas précisément un lien entre les motifs d'illégalité et ses prétentions.

En dépit du manque de clarté des critères d'examen présentés par la plaignante, le groupe spécial considèrera que l'organisme d'enquête a été capable de répondre à toutes les prétentions de la plaignante et de défendre ses intérêts de manière appropriée. En ce sens, la plainte n'est pas viciée et l'examen de la conformité par le groupe spécial est légalement fondé. Le groupe spécial rappelle toutefois que la recevabilité de la demande de la plaignante est liée aux circonstances précises de l'espèce et que cela ne doit pas être vu comme une dérogation à la responsabilité de la plaignante d'exposer avec précision ses revendications fondées sur l'article 51 de la *LFPCA*.

Le groupe spécial s'appuie ici sur le raisonnement qu'adopteraient les juridictions mexicaines dans une situation d'imprécision de la plainte. Selon une décision de la Cour fédérale de justice fiscale et administrative, il appartient au juge d'évaluer si l'essence et la pertinence de la demande sont en conformité avec les exigences posées par la loi, sans toutefois que ces exigences procédurales prennent le pas sur le fond de la demande. Le juge doit donner la préférence à la vérité factuelle et réelle de la demande plutôt qu'à la procédure. Même s'il est vrai que la plaignante ne semble pas soulever un motif d'illégalité en particulier, il conteste la détermination finale de l'organisme d'enquête au titre de l'article 51 de manière générale, ce qui suffit à établir le bien-fondé de sa requête.

Au-delà de cette question procédurale, le groupe spécial devait aussi se prononcer sur la possibilité de prendre en considération l'article 50 de la *LFPCA* qui n'était pas expressément cité comme critère d'examen afin d'interpréter l'article 51 de cette même loi. Le groupe spécial va toutefois rejeter cette allégation de la plaignante.

La plaignante faisait valoir que l'article 50 de la *LFPCA* devait servir de contexte d'interprétation de l'article 51 de la même loi. L'organisme d'enquête estimait en réponse que l'article 50 de la *LFPCA* n'était pas visé par l'annexe 1911 de l'*ALENA* établissant les critères d'examen sur lesquels les groupes spéciaux peuvent se fonder. En l'espèce, le groupe spécial se rallie à ce dernier argument, considérant qu'il ne peut fonder son examen sur des dispositions qui ne sont pas expressément visées par l'annexe 1911, car cela serait contraire aux articles 1904.3, 1904. 8 et à l'annexe 1911 de l'*ALENA*. Il se réfère ensuite à certaines décisions précédemment rendues par les groupes spéciaux, seulement à titre informatif étant donné qu'il n'est pas lié par le principe du *stare decisis* par rapport à ces décisions.

La question de l'extension des critères d'examen a en effet déjà été traitée à de multiples reprises et une majorité de groupes spéciaux semblent avoir conclu qu'il était impossible d'étendre les critères d'examen à des articles non expressément visés par l'annexe 1911. Toutefois, les dispositions que le groupe spécial invoque au soutien de son argumentation ne semblent pas spécialement pertinentes et propres à empêcher sinon une "extension" des critères d'examen, au moins une interprétation des critères d'examen dans le contexte législatif de la partie importatrice. Cela peut même sembler pertinent, y compris au sens du traité de l'*ALENA*. Par exemple, l'article 1904.2 énonce que les examens de conformité doivent se baser sur la législation antidumping, réputée comprendre entre autres "les lois (et) le contexte législatif ... dans la mesure où un tribunal de la Partie importatrice tiendrait compte de ces facteurs." Même si cet article s'applique à la législation antidumping et non pas aux critères d'examen en tant que tel, il semble qu'il puisse servir de base à une interprétation plus souple des règles encadrant le contrôle des groupes spéciaux. Ainsi, bien que le groupe spécial ne se réfère ici qu'aux décisions qui ont tranché dans le même sens que lui, on peut trouver certaines décisions divergentes au sein des rapports rendus par les groupes spéciaux. Entre autres, un groupe spécial avait notamment décidé de prendre en compte les articles 237 et 239, dans l'interprétation de l'article 238 du Code fiscal fédéral, estimant qu'il n'y avait pas d'intention démontrée par les membres de l'*ALENA* d'exclure ces articles de toute considération. Le groupe spécial invoquait avec pertinence la nécessité d'une application harmonieuse des critères d'examen par les groupes spéciaux et les cours nationales, et d'une interprétation uniforme de dispositions liées entre elles.

La présente décision du groupe spécial s'inscrit au contraire dans la lignée des décisions rejetant toute "extension" ou interprétation plus large des critères d'examen. Cela semble problématique, car non seulement le contrôle des groupes spéciaux est limité aux lois et aux jurisprudences de la partie importatrice, mais si son contrôle doit se limiter aux seuls articles inscrits dans le traité, il devient extrêmement restreint. Il s'agit à notre sens d'une forte limitation instaurée par le traité, mais également d'une autolimitation des groupes spéciaux. En effet, les organes de règlement des différends établis par les traités ont souvent recours à une interprétation souple du traité pour tenter d'étendre leurs compétences. Il ne leur incombe pas plus de les réduire drastiquement tel que le poursuit la présente décision.

Bien que non négligeable en importance, cette question d'extension des critères d'examen n'était pas au cœur de la présente affaire et il convient à présent de s'intéresser aux solutions adoptées par le groupe spécial quant aux problèmes de fond.

d. L'analyse des solutions adoptées par le groupe spécial quant au fond de l'affaire

Par rapport aux deux principaux problèmes de droit soulevés par cette affaire, le groupe spécial a tranché en faveur de la possibilité de modification d'un droit antidumping dans le cadre de l'examen administratif, estimant qu'il n'était pas démontré que les dispositions antidumping invoquées instauraient une procédure obligatoire et spéciale pour les nouveaux expéditeurs. Ayant résolu l'ensemble des questions juridiques, il s'est également prononcé en faveur de l'application du principe d'économie jurisprudentielle pour les demandes accessoires présentées par les plaignantes.

En guise de rappel, examinons l'allégation de la plaignante selon laquelle les articles 11.2 de l'*Accord sur les mesures antidumping*, 68 de la *LCE*, et 99 et 100 de la *RLCE* mettent en place une procédure d'examen administratif qui n'est pas appropriée pour la modification d'un droit antidumping particulier.

Tout d'abord, le groupe spécial note que l'article 11.1 de l'*Accord sur les mesures antidumping* pose le principe général selon lequel un droit antidumping ne doit être maintenu que dans la mesure où il est toujours nécessaire pour neutraliser le dommage causé par le dumping. Le paragraphe deux de cet article invoqué par la plaignante consiste en une modalité d'application de ce principe général, précisant que l'examen peut avoir lieu, soit à la demande de toute partie intéressée, soit de l'initiative de l'organisme d'enquête. Le groupe spécial retient que cette disposition habilite l'organisme d'enquête à modifier ou à révoquer le droit afin de s'assurer que celui-ci est maintenu uniquement dans la mesure où il est nécessaire au sens de l'article 11.1 de l'accord précité.

De la même façon, l'article 68 de la *LCE* établit que les droits antidumping peuvent être réévalués annuellement à la demande d'une partie intéressée ou par l'organe d'enquête à tout moment. Le groupe spécial retient que cet article confère de larges pouvoirs à l'organisme d'enquête, qui peut amorcer un examen à tout moment et que celui-ci peut conduire à une confirmation, à une modification ou à une révocation des droits antidumping, dépendamment des résultats de l'enquête. Quant aux articles 99 et 100 de la *RLCE*, ils contiennent tous deux une référence expresse aux examens *ex officio.*

Après examen de l'ensemble de ces dispositions, le groupe spécial considère comme inexistantes les limites évoquées par la plaignante, selon lesquelles l'organisme d'enquête ne pouvait ni intervenir de sa propre initiative, ni dans le cadre d'un examen administratif, aussi bien dans les dispositions de la loi mexicaine que de l'Accord antidumping. Le groupe spécial estime que non seulement ces dispositions n'interdisaient pas à l'organisme d'enquête de prendre de telles mesures, mais elles l'y invitaient explicitement.

Par ailleurs, le groupe spécial considère comme irrecevable l'argument soulevé par la plaignante durant l'audience et selon lequel l'article 68 de la *LCE* n'autorise pas la détermination d'un droit antidumping pendant un examen administratif. Il estime que l'organisme d'enquête a appliqué une révocation du droit antidumping, et non une modification, ce qui est conforme à l'article invoqué. Il est intéressant de noter ici l'absence de débat concernant la nature de la décision de l'organisme d'enquête à l'égard de Vantage. Pourtant, cette "nature" de la décision semble cruciale: s'agissait-il d'une détermination, d'une modification ou d'une révocation? Les parties ne semblaient pas d'accord sur le terme, qui était susceptible de déterminer l'issue du différend. Durant l'audience, l'entreprise plaignante avait qualifié cette démarche de "détermination," tandis que selon l'organisme d'enquête, il s'agissait d'une simple "modification." Finalement, le groupe spécial qualifie cette mesure de "révocation," sans apporter d'arguments solides.

Quoi qu'il en soit, à ce stade, le groupe spécial a établi la possibilité pour l'organisme d'enquête de modifier ou de révoquer un droit antidumping de façon *ex officio,* c'est-à-dire de sa propre initiative. Toutefois, l'article 68 de la *LCE* pose une autre condition et il doit maintenant déterminer si l'entreprise Vantage pouvait être qualifiée de "partie intéressée" et donc, avoir le droit de participer à la procédure d'examen administratif.

La notion de partie intéressée est définie par l'article 51 de la *LCE.* Ainsi, les producteurs ayant soumis des demandes, les importateurs et les exportateurs, dont le produit est évalué, ainsi que toute personne morale étrangère ayant un intérêt direct dans l'enquête en cours doivent être considérés comme des parties intéressées. Le groupe spécial considère que rien ne permet d'interpréter l'article 51 comme limitant l'acception de la notion de "partie intéressée" aux seuls producteurs et exportateurs étrangers qui ont effectivement exporté le produit pendant la période d'enquête originelle. Ainsi, même en présumant que Vantage était un nouvel expéditeur, il n'est pas possible de considérer que l'organe d'enquête ne pouvait pas traiter l'entreprise comme une partie intéressée au terme des articles 68 de la *LCE* et 99 et 100 de la *RLCE*. Considérant donc que Vantage peut être qualifiée de partie intéressée et que les modifications des droits antidumping sont autorisées par les articles susmentionnés, le groupe spécial conclut que l'organisme d'enquête avait la possibilité de modifier le droit antidumping de Vantage au cours de l'examen administratif. Il rejette donc cette première allégation et valide la conformité de la détermination finale sur ce point.

Le groupe spécial devait également se prononcer sur la question de savoir si les articles 9.5 de l'*Accord sur les mesures antidumping* et 89-D de la *LCE* prévoyaient une procédure spéciale obligatoire pour la détermination des droits antidumping applicables aux nouveaux expéditeurs.

L'article 9.5 de l'*Accord sur les mesures antidumping* prévoit qu'un examen doit être effectué afin de déterminer rapidement "les marges de dumping individuelles pour les exportateurs ou les producteurs du pays exportateur qui n'ont pas exporté le produit vers le membre importateur pendant la période couverte par l'enquête". Selon le groupe spécial, cet article requiert des États la mise en place d'un processus d'examen accéléré pour les nouveaux expéditeurs qui veulent obtenir un droit antidumping spécifique. Il n'établit aucune exigence procédurale spécifique, mise à part celle d'un "calendrier" accéléré et une interdiction d'imposition de droits spécifiques avant la fin de l'enquête. Il appartient ainsi aux États membres d'établir leurs propres procédures, du moment qu'elles respectent les conditions posées par l'article 9.5 de l'Accord antidumping. De la même façon, l'article 89-D de la *LCE* définit la notion de "nouvel expéditeur" et donne le droit aux entités pouvant être qualifiées comme tel d'avoir accès à une procédure spéciale.

Après l'examen de ces deux articles, le groupe spécial estime que ces dispositions ne mettent pas en place un mécanisme exclusif et obligatoire d'examen concernant les nouveaux expéditeurs. La mise en place d'un processus d'examen accéléré constitue un droit propre aux nouveaux expéditeurs et non une obligation de l'organisme d'enquête. Bien au contraire, l'organisme d'enquête ne peut pas amorcer cet examen *ex officio*, car la demande doit obligatoirement émaner de l'entreprise. En l'absence d'une telle demande, l'organisme d'enquête peut à tout moment procéder à un examen via les procédures "normales." Ainsi, en l'absence de demande émanant de Vantage, l'organisme d'enquête pouvait procéder à la fixation des marges de dumping de l'entreprise dans le cadre de l'examen administratif et n'était pas tenu de réorienter la demande de Vantage vers la procédure d'examen concernant un nouvel expéditeur.

Le groupe spécial ajoute avec justesse que l'interprétation donnée par la plaignante est susceptible de conduire à un blocage en l'absence de demande d'examen émanant du nouvel expéditeur, l'organisme d'enquête n'ayant alors aucun moyen de fixer un droit antidumping spécifique pour une entreprise ayant des marges manifestement différentes des autres entreprises. Une telle situation résulterait alors en une situation de violation de l'Accord antidumping, qui n'autorise le maintien d'un droit antidumping que dans la mesure où celui-ci est nécessaire pour compenser le dommage causé par le dumping. En résumé, il apparaît nécessaire que lorsque l'organisme d'enquête considère que les circonstances requièrent l'examen d'un nouvel expéditeur, il puisse l'amorcer *ex officio* en vertu de la compétence que lui confère l'article 68 de la *LCE* et la *RLCE*, à moins que le nouvel expéditeur ne le requière lui-même en vertu de l'article 89-D.

Ce raisonnement du groupe spécial nous paraît logique et conforme au sens de l'*Accord sur les mesures antidumping*. En effet, le but de l'Accord est de procurer aux entreprises le moyen le plus rapide possible d'obtenir la détermination d'un droit antidumping ajusté à leurs marges de dumping de façon précise et spécifique. Le droit antidumping se doit d'être le plus juste possible, c'est-à-dire limité à la compensation du dommage causé par le dumping. Or, si les marges de dumping sont plus faibles que le droit antidumping imposé, il s'agit d'une situation inappropriée à laquelle il convient de remédier rapidement. En l'espèce, il semblait plus rapide pour Vantage de demander une détermination spécifique dans le cadre de l'examen administratif plutôt que dans le cadre de l'examen concernant un nouvel expéditeur, en accord avec la rapidité exigée par l'article 9.5 de l'Accord antidumping. Le groupe spécial semble adopter ici une décision complètement conforme aux dispositions énoncées.

S'étant prononcé sur ces deux questions de fond, le groupe spécial va rejeter les motions accessoires en application du principe d'économie jurisprudentielle. D'une manière générale, ce principe constitue un pouvoir discrétionnaire des juridictions et des groupes arbitraux pour refuser d'examiner chaque allégation des parties lorsque ce refus n'influence pas la solution finale. Sur la base de ce principe, le groupe spécial va rejeter les demandes accessoires présentées par Vantage et Quimic. L'entreprise Vantage faisait valoir qu'elle devait être considérée comme "l'héritière" des intérêts de l'entreprise Uniquema. Celle-ci ayant reçu des droits antidumping suite à l'enquête initiale, Vantage devait être considérée comme succédant à l'entreprise et non comme une nouvelle expéditrice. Toutefois, le groupe spécial considère que la question de savoir si Vantage était ou non une entreprise nouvellement expéditrice est sans importance en l'espèce. Il apparaît en effet que la question de la nouveauté de l'entreprise n'a pas influé sur le raisonnement du groupe spécial et l'application du principe d'économie juris-prudentielle semble donc justifiée. L'entreprise Quimic, quant à elle, contestait une communication de l'organisme d'enquête quant à une décision de l'OMC. Considérant que cette décision n'a pas fondé son raisonnement, le groupe spécial va également rejeter cette allégation.

En guise de propos conclusifs concernant cette affaire, il convient de remarquer que le Mexique est un pays moniste qui ne requiert donc pas de transposition des traités internationaux dans sa législation interne. Dès que le traité est ratifié, il devient applicable au même titre qu'une loi, voire de façon supérieure. L'*Accord sur les mesures antidumping* fait donc partie intégrante de la législation mexicaine sur le dumping. Cela est particulièrement intéressant, car les groupes spéciaux deviennent compétents pour évaluer la conformité des déterminations finales, non seulement au regard des dispositions législatives nationales, mais également par rapport aux traités internationaux pertinents, et notamment ceux de l'OMC. Ce type de système constitutionnel favorise une meilleure application et un plus grand respect des traités internationaux. Comme on le voit en l'espèce, les dispositions législatives mexicaines semblent en parfaite conformité avec l'*Accord sur les mesures anti-dumping*. On peut ici faire un parallèle avec la première décision soumise à l'étude sur la méthode de la réduction à zéro,[86] dans laquelle il avait fallu à l'organisme d'enquête américain plus d'une dizaine d'années pour rendre ses procédures d'examen conformes au droit de l'OMC.

---

[86] *Supra* note 50.

III. LE COMMERCE CANADIEN ET L'ORGANISATION MONDIALE DU COMMERCE (OMC)

A. LES DÉVELOPPEMENTS DANS LE SYSTÈME COMMERCIAL MULTILATÉRAL

Si la désignation du Brésilien Roberto Cavalho de Azevêdo[87] à la tête de l'OMC pour succéder au Français Pascal Lamy peut s'expliquer par l'influence grandissante des pays émergents dans les négociations multilatérales, les résultats de la Conférence ministérielle de l'OMC dite, "Conférence de Bali"[88] constituent une autre marque du nouvel équilibre qui se dessine; une sorte de "transformation géopolitique" faisant des économies émergentes à la fois "des instigatrices et actrices"[89] de l'évolution des relations commerciales multilatérales.

Alors que le dernier cycle de négociations commerciales multilatérales piétine[90] et que l'ancien directeur général de l'OMC aura cherché en vain à rapprocher des positions des États pour faire déboucher les négociations, l'arrivée d'un nouveau directeur de l'OMC aura pour le moment fait son effet puisque le "paquet de Bali"[91] a permis quelques avancées notables. Celles-ci se résument à travers les trois piliers suivants:

Le premier pilier concerne la facilitation des échanges. L'accord sur la facilitation des échanges constitue une réelle avancée des négociations menées dans le cadre du cycle de Doha. En ce sens, il étend son champ d'application au-delà des secteurs déjà couverts que sont les services financiers et les technologies. Une fois entré en vigueur, l'accord devrait contribuer à réduire les formalités administratives, assurer la clarté, l'efficacité et la transparence des procédures en plus de rendre les échanges plus rapides

---

[87] OMC, Conseil général, "Le Conseil général désigne M. Azevêdo comme nouveau directeur général, M Lamy promet une transition en douceur," en ligne: <http://www.wto.org/french/news_f/news13_f/gc_14may13_f.htm>.

[88] OMC, Conférence ministérielle, jours 3, 4 et 5: "Un 'Paquet de Bali' voit le jour à l'issue de consultations-marathon," en ligne: <http://www.wto.org/french/news_f/news13_f/mc9sum_07dec13_f.htm>.

[89] OMC, Allocution du DG Pascal Lamy, en ligne: <http://www.wto.org/french/news_f/sppl_f/sppl271_f.htm>.

[90] OMC, Programme de Doha, en ligne: <http://www.wto.org/french/tratop_f/dda_f/dda_f.htm>.

[91] OMC, "Déclaration ministérielle de Bali et les décisions," en ligne: <https://mc9.wto.org/fr/projet-de-declaration-ministerielle-de-bali>.

et moins chers. L'accord contient également des dispositions relatives aux marchandises en transit et une assistance aux pays en développement.

Le deuxième pilier concerne l'agriculture. L'accord sur le volet agricole maintient le régime intérimaire dont bénéficiaient les programmes de détention de stocks publics à des fins de sécurité alimentaire dans les pays en développement. Cette solution intérimaire sera maintenue en attendant qu'une solution définitive soit trouvée avec notamment l'établissement d'un programme de travail pour parvenir à une solution d'ici quatre ans. Quant à la question des subventions à l'exportation ou des mesures ayant des effets similaires, les négociateurs se sont contentés d'une déclaration politique dite "ferme" visant à les limiter. Il faut rappeler que lors de la Conférence ministérielle de Hong Kong, les États avaient déjà pris des engagements visant à les éliminer d'ici 2013.[92] À cet égard, cette déclaration politique dite "ferme" s'apparente plus à un recul qu'à une réelle avancée. Les pays prendront toutefois des engagements visant à améliorer l'accès aux marchés des produits du coton provenant des pays en développement.

Le dernier pilier porte sur les questions de développement. Il n'y a pas d'éléments nouveaux par rapport à ce qui était convenu à Genève en 2011.[93] Il s'agit principalement d'assurer l'accès aux marchés des pays développés, en franchise de droits et sans contingent des exportations des pays les moins avancés, de permettre à ces pays de bénéficier de règles d'origine préférentielles simplifiées ainsi que de dérogations en matière de commerce des services. Signe d'une certaine attention portée aux pays en développement, c'est au cours de la Conférence ministérielle de Bali que les ministres vont adopter les modalités et les conditions d'accession du Yémen à l'OMC. Le Yémen devient ainsi le trente-cinquième pays de la catégorie des PMA à devenir membre de l'OMC après treize ans de procédure.[94] Le pays avait présenté sa demande d'accession à l'OMC en 2000.

---

[92] Voir, OMC, Déclaration ministérielle, Programme de travail de Doha, OMC Doc WT/MIN/(05)/DEC, 22 décembre 2005.

[93] OMC, Conférence ministérielle, Déclaration finale du président, OMC Doc WT/MIN(11)/11, 17 décembre 2011.

[94] OMC, "La Conférence ministérielle approuve l'accession du Yémen à l'OMC," en ligne: <http://www.wto.org/french/news_f/news13_f/acc_yem_03dec13_f.htm>.

L'OMC connaitra plusieurs autres adhésions au cours de cette année 2013. Il en sera ainsi du Laos qui devient le 158e membre de l'OMC après ratification de l'ensemble des textes relatifs à son accession.[95] La Russie est également devenue membre de l'OMC après dix-neuf ans de procédure.[96] Le Tadjikistan devient le 159e membre de l'OMC en 2013 alors que le Groupe de travail de l'accession du pays à l'OMC a été établi le 18 juillet 2001.[97]

Au cours de l'année 2013, l'Organe de règlement des différends de l'OMC n'aura pas non plus manqué d'activités. Un groupe spécial publiera pas moins de trois rapports en 2013.[98] Quant à l'Organe d'appel, il a rendu ses rapports dans les affaires *Canada – Certaines mesures affectant le secteur de la production d'énergie renouvelable* et *Canada – Mesures relatives au programme de tarifs de rachat garantis.*[99]

---

[95] OMC, *Protocole d'accession de la République démocratique populaire Lao à l'Accord de Marrakech instituant l'Organisation mondiale du commerce fait le 26 octobre 2012, Notification d'acceptation et d'entrée en vigueur*, OMC Doc WLI/101, 9 janvier 2013.

[96] OMC, *Conférence ministérielle, Accession de la Fédération de Russie, Décision du 16 décembre 2011*, OMC Docs WT/MIN(11)/24 et WT/L/839, 17 décembre 2011. Concernant l'adhésion de la Russie en tant que membre observateur de l'accord sur les marchés publics, voir OMC, "Le Comité des marchés publics accueille la Russie en tant qu'observateur," en ligne: <http://www.wto.org/french/news_f/news13_f/gpro_29may13_f.htm>.

[97] OMC, *Protocole d'accession de la République du Tadjikistan à l'accord de Marrakech instituant l'Organisation mondiale du commerce fait à Genève le 10 décembre 2013, Notification d'acceptation et d'entrée en vigueur*, OMC Doc WLI/100, 7 février 2013; Voir également, OMC, Nouvelle, "Le Tadjikistan deviendra le 159ème Membre de l'OMC," en ligne: <http://www.wto.org/french/news_f/news13_f/acc_tjk_31jan13_f.htm>.

[98] Chine, *Droits antidumping définitifs visant les appareils à rayons x utilisés pour les inspections de sécurité en provenance de l'Union européenne*, OC Doc. WT/DS425/R (Rapport du groupe spécial), 26 février 2013; Chine, *Mesures antidumping et compensatoires visant les produits à base de poulet de chair en provenance des États-Unis*, OMC Doc. WT/DS427/R (Rapport du groupe spécial), 2 août 2013; Communautés européennes, *Mesures prohibant l'importation et la commercialisation des produits dérivés du phoque*, OMC Docs WT/DS400/R et WT/DS401/R (Rapport du groupe spécial), 25 novembre 2013.

[99] *Canada – Certaines mesures affectant le secteur de la production d'énergie renouvelable* et *Canada – Mesures relatives au programme de tarifs de rachat garantis*, OMC Docs WT/DS412/AB/R et WT/DS426/AB/R (Rapport de l'Organe d'appel), 6 mai 2013.

B.   LES DIFFÉRENTS DEVANT L'OMC IMPLIQUANT LE CANADA

*1.   Canada – Certaines mesures affectant le secteur de la production
     d'énergie renouvelable et Canada – Mesures relatives au programme
     de tarifs de rachat garantis*[100]

La présente décision fait suite à l'appel déposé respectivement par
le Canada, le Japon et l'Union européenne de certaines questions
de droit et interprétations du droit figurant dans les rapports du
groupe spécial dans les affaires *Canada – Certaines mesures affectant
le secteur de la production d'énergie renouvelable* et *Canada – Mesures
relatives au programme de tarifs de rachat garantis.*[101] Ces deux différends
posaient la question de la compatibilité avec le droit de l'OMC de
certaines mesures étatiques visant à favoriser le recours aux énergies
renouvelables.

a.   Les faits de la cause

En 2009, la province de l'Ontario met sur pied un programme de
tarifs de rachat garantis (programme TRG) qui permet aux producteurs d'énergie éolienne et solaire photovoltaïque de recevoir
un prix garanti par kilowattheure à condition que leurs installations contiennent un certain niveau d'éléments d'origine nationale.
Ce niveau devrait se situer entre 20 et 60 % et les contrats conclus,
couvrent une durée de vingt ans ou quarante ans. Le programme
de TRG[102] est un dispositif mis en place par les pouvoirs publics pour
augmenter la fourniture d'électricité produite à partir de certaines
sources d'énergie renouvelable dans le réseau d'électricité ontarien
et, par le fait même, pour réduire progressivement la part du charbon
et de l'énergie nucléaire. Le programme lancé en 2009 par l'Office
de l'électricité de l'Ontario (OEO) a été établi conformément à la

---

[100] *Canada – Certaines mesures affectant le secteur de la production d'énergie renouvelable*
     et *Canada – Mesures relatives au programme de tarifs de rachat garantis*, OMC Docs
     WT/DS412/AB/R et WT/DS426/AB/R (Rapport de l'Organe d'appel), 6
     mai 2013.

[101] *Canada – Certaines mesures affectant le secteur de la production d'énergie renouvelable*
     et *Canada – Mesures relatives au programme de tarifs de rachat garantis*, OMC Docs
     WT/DS412/R et WT/DS426/R (Rapport du groupe spécial), 19 décembre 2012.

[102] Les plaignants contestent la compatibilité avec les règles de l'OMC du pro-
     gramme TRG, des contrats TRG individuels pour l'utilisation des sources
     d'énergie éolienne ou solaire photovoltaïque et des contrats microTRG indivi-
     duels pour l'utilisation des sources d'énergie solaire photovoltaïque, exécutés
     par l'OEO depuis le début du programme TRG.

directive du ministre de l'Énergie et de l'Infrastructure de l'Ontario[103] (directive TRG de 2009 du ministre) agissant en vertu de la *Loi de 1998 sur l'électricité*, modifiée par la *Loi de 2009 sur l'énergie verte*. La participation au programme TRG est ouverte aux installations implantées en Ontario qui produisent de l'électricité à partir des sources d'énergie renouvelable, telles que l'éolien, le solaire photovoltaïque, la biomasse renouvelable, le biogaz, le gaz d'enfouissement et l'énergie hydraulique.[104] Dans le cadre du programme TRG, les installations électriques doivent respecter des niveaux minima requis de teneur en éléments nationaux.[105] Ce calcul se fait en fonction d'activités désignées et un pourcentage admissible associé[106] doit être atteint.

Le Japon et l'Union européenne contestent la conformité du programme TRG par rapport aux engagements internationaux du Canada. Les plaignants considèrent en effet que les mesures en cause violent la règle du traitement national[107] en ce sens qu'elles accordent un traitement moins favorable aux produits japonais et européens qu'aux produits canadiens. Les plaignants considèrent également que les mesures visées sont constitutives de mesures d'investissement liées au commerce contraires à l'obligation du traitement national.[108] Selon le Japon, le programme TRG impose un "minimum requis de teneur en éléments nationaux" ce qui constitue une MIC. Enfin, le Canada accorde par ce programme des subventions subordonnées à l'utilisation de production nationale de préférence aux produits étrangers.[109] Ces subventions seraient prohibées au sens des articles 3.1 et 3.2 de l'*Accord SMC*.

Dans son rapport rendu le 19 décembre 2012, le groupe spécial a reconnu que le Canada a violé les articles III.4 du *GATT* de 1994

---

[103] Directive datée du 24 septembre 2009 enjoignant à l'OEO d'élaborer un programme de tarifs de rachat garantis (TRG) (pièce JPN-102 présentée au Groupe spécial) et d'inclure une prescription imposant aux requérants de présenter un plan pour la réalisation des objectifs concernant la teneur en éléments nationaux (c'est-à-dire ontariens) énoncés dans les règles TRG.

[104] Les règles TRG et microTRG exposent, entre autres choses: (i) les prescriptions en matière d'admissibilité des projets et de candidature; (ii) les critères de raccordement du projet au réseau d'électricité.

[105] Rapport du Groupe spécial, *supra* note 102 au para 7.9.

[106] *Ibid* au para 7.159.

[107] Art III: 4 du *GATT* de 1994.

[108] Art 2.1 de l'*Accord sur les mesures d'investissement et liées au commerce* (*Accord MIC*).

[109] Art 1.1 de l'*Accord sur les subventions et les mesures compensatoires* (*Accord SMC*).

considérant que l'acquisition de l'électricité par les pouvoirs publics était réalisée pour une revente sur le marché, une condition de non-application de l'exception prévue à l'article III.4 du *GATT*. Le groupe spécial juge incompatibles à l'article 2.1 de l'*Accord MIC* les mesures canadiennes, mais rejette la violation au titre de l'*Accord SMC*. Le groupe spécial considère en effet que les plaignants n'ont pas démontré l'existence d'une subvention parce qu'ils n'ont pas fait la preuve de l'existence d'un avantage conféré. Par conséquent, on ne saurait considérer que le Canada a violé les articles 3.1 et 3.2 de l'*Accord SMC*.

C'est en interjetant appel de cette décision du groupe spécial que les plaignants demandent à l'Organe d'appel de déterminer d'une part, la relation juridique qui existe entre les articles III.8 du *GATT* de 1994 et 2.2 de l'*Accord MIC*. D'autre part, ils demandent de clarifier les conditions de l'existence d'une subvention au sens de l'article 1.1 de l'*Accord SMS*.

b.   Le raisonnement de l'Organe d'appel

L'Organe d'appel s'est d'abord évertué à déterminer les conditions d'applicabilité de l'article III.8 du *GATT* de 1994 aux mesures d'investissement liées au commerce afin de déterminer jusqu'à quel point les mesures canadiennes échapperaient à l'obligation du traitement national.

À titre préliminaire, rappelons qu'il n'existe pas de définition précise d'une mesure d'investissement liée au commerce. L'*Accord MIC* se contente d'en dresser simplement une liste exemplative. D'après la liste exemplative, toute mesure étatique de caractère obligatoire qui soumet l'engagement d'un investissement étranger dans le pays d'accueil à des conditions qui ont des effets sur le commerce international des marchandises est une mesure d'investissement liée au commerce. Les mesures d'investissement liées au commerce doivent toutefois être conformes au traitement national ainsi qu'à l'article XI du *GATT* de 1994.

Quant à la relation entre l'article 2.2 de l'*Accord MIC* et l'article III.8, rappelons également que celle-ci avait déjà été établie dans l'affaire *Indonésie-Automobile* où le groupe spécial avait reconnu l'existence d'un lien entre les MIC et l'article III du *GATT* de 1994 dans son ensemble.[110] Dans le cas qui nous concerne, l'Organe

---

[110] Indonésie, *Certaines mesures affectant l'industrie automobile*, OMC Docs WT/DS54/R; WT/DS55/R; WT/DS59/R; WT/DS64/R (Rapport du groupe spécial), 2 juillet 1998.

d'appel devra se prononcer plus précisément sur la relation entre l'article III.8 du *GATT* de 1994 et l'article 2.2 de l'*Accord MIC.*

Pour l'Organe d'appel, le programme TRG doit être considéré comme une MIC. Les prescriptions relatives à la teneur en éléments nationaux pour le matériel de production des énergies renouvelables sont des conditions visant à satisfaire les producteurs qui utilisent ces types d'énergie. Ces prescriptions "régissent" l'acquisition d'électricité par les pouvoirs publics de l'Ontario. Il existe donc une relation étroite entre le matériel de production d'énergie renouvelable et le produit acquis, c'est-à-dire l'électricité.

Pour l'Organe d'appel, l'article III.8 du *GATT* de 1994 s'applique de manière générale aux MIC, mais n'impose pas d'obligations additionnelles aux États. L'article III:8 du *GATT* de 1994 prévoit en effet ce qui suit:

Les dispositions du présent article ne s'appliqueront pas aux lois, règlements et prescriptions régissant l'acquisition, par des organes gouvernementaux, de produits achetés pour les besoins des pouvoirs publics et non pas pour être revendus dans le commerce ou pour servir à la production de marchandises destinées à la vente dans le commerce.

Les mesures visées par l'article III.8 du *GATT* de 1994 sont constituées de lois, de règlements ou de prescriptions régissant l'acquisition de produits achetés par les pouvoirs publics. En outre, cette acquisition ne doit pas être destinée à la revente dans le commerce. Pour l'Organe d'appel, les produits achetés "pour les besoins des pouvoirs publics" doivent être interprétés comme ce qui est consommé par les pouvoirs publics ou ce qui est fourni par eux dans l'exercice de leur fonction publique. Le mot "pour" se rapporte aux produits achetés "aux fins des pouvoirs publics"; l'article III: 8 exige donc un lien rationnel entre le produit et la fonction gouvernementale qui est exercée. Une revente doit être entendue comme un profit et pour savoir si une transaction constitue une revente dans le commerce, il faut l'évaluer dans son ensemble. S'il existe un but lucratif, il y a revente, et, dans le cas contraire, il y a vente à perte.

De plus, l'article III.8 constitue une dérogation au champ d'application du traitement national. Pour l'Organe d'appel, l'électricité, et non la production de l'électricité, est un produit visé par la réglementation de l'Ontario, et peut être considérée comme un produit acheté par les pouvoirs publics. En l'occurrence, l'électricité n'est pas le produit traité moins favorablement. La discrimination entre produits nationaux et étrangers ne concernant pas les produits achetés par les pouvoirs publics, la prescription de l'article III.8 du *GATT* de 1994 selon laquelle les lois, règlements ou prescriptions doivent régir l'acquisition de produits achetés par les pouvoirs publics n'est donc pas remplie. L'Organe d'appel en déduit que les mesures canadiennes ne peuvent pas être visées par l'article III.8 du *GATT* de 1994. Elles sont donc incompatibles avec l'article III.4 du *GATT* de 1994 et l'article 2.1 de l'*Accord MIC*. On peut déplorer que cette interprétation restrictive de l'Organe d'appel sanctionne d'une certaine manière la politique de protection de l'environnement voulue par Ontario.

En ce qui concerne la qualification des mesures ontariennes au titre de l'accord SMC, l'Organe d'appel a considéré que le programme TRG et les contrats TRG constituent des achats publics au sens de l'article 1.1(a)(1)(iii) de l'*Accord SMC*.[111] Quant au critère de l'avantage, l'Organe d'appel considère qu'en l'absence de programme TRG, les producteurs n'auraient pas obtenu "la rémunération assurée par le programme sur la base des conditions existantes du marché en Ontario." Si le programme TRG n'existait pas, les nouveaux arrivants sur le marché devraient négocier un prix pour l'électricité utilisant des énergies renouvelables. L'Organe d'appel a commencé par l'étude du critère juridique afin de savoir s'il existe un avantage au titre de l'article 1.1(b) de l'*Accord SMC*.

Il s'agit d'examiner si, d'après le point de repère prévu à l'article 14(d) de l'*Accord SMC*, la rémunération obtenue par les producteurs qui utilisaient les technologies éolienne et solaire photovoltaïques dans le cadre du programme TRG était "plus qu'adéquate" par rapport à la rémunération que ces mêmes producteurs recevraient sur le "marché" pertinent de l'électricité en Ontario, compte tenu des "conditions existantes du marché." Le groupe spécial avait noté que le marché pertinent n'avait pas besoin d'être un marché qui soit "non faussé par l'intervention des pouvoirs publics" ou qui soit exempt du moindre degré d'intervention des pouvoirs publics. L'Organe d'appel a indiqué dans des différends antérieurs que, pour déterminer si un avantage avait été conféré, il fallait évaluer si le bénéficiaire avait reçu une "contribution financière" à des conditions plus favorables que celles auxquelles il avait accès sur le marché.

L'Organe d'appel a également contesté la définition du marché pertinent sur laquelle repose l'analyse de l'avantage faite par le

---

[111] Organe d'appel, *supra* note 101 au para 5.124-5.127.

groupe spécial. Les marchés de l'électricité éolienne et solaire photovoltaïque existent en Ontario uniquement en raison de l'intervention des pouvoirs publics. Le point de repère pertinent doit être issu non pas du marché de gros de l'électricité produite à partir de toutes les sources d'énergie, mais plutôt des marchés de l'électricité éolienne et solaire photovoltaïque, qui sont définis par le choix des pouvoirs publics de l'Ontario concernant l'approvisionnement diversifié en énergie. La question pertinente est donc de savoir si les fournisseurs d'électricité éolienne et solaire photovoltaïque seraient entrés sur les marchés de l'électricité éolienne et solaire photovoltaïque en l'absence du programme TRG, et non s'ils seraient entrés sur le marché de gros de l'électricité mélangée. Le simple fait de participer au programme TRG ne constitue pas un avantage en soi. Il faut comparer les rémunérations des produits d'énergie renouvelable avec celles du même marché concurrentiel de ce type d'énergie.

L'Organe d'appel rejette donc le raisonnement du groupe spécial en précisant que l'Union européenne et le Japon n'avaient pas établi que les mesures contestées conféraient un avantage selon l'article 1.1(b) de l'*Accord SMC.*

IV. Conclusion

Au total, on peut considérer que le Canada poursuit de manière aussi fidèle que possible les priorités qu'il s'est données en 2007 dans le cadre du document fédéral sur la Stratégie commerciale mondiale. Il s'agit principalement de conquérir de nouveaux marchés à fort potentiel à travers la conclusion d'accords de libre-échange. Il s'agit aussi de poursuivre l'engagement du pays dans les négociations commerciales internationales. De ce point de vue, l'année 2013 aura donné toute satisfaction. Il n'en demeure pas moins vrai qu'en termes de contentieux commerciaux, le dispositif canadien doit être renforcé pour mieux faire face aux nouveaux enjeux, qui naitront de la prolifération des accords commerciaux et des conflits que leur mise en œuvre peut générer, mais également, les conflits actuels dans lesquels le Canada est impliqué et dont les issues ne nous sont pas toujours favorables.

II. Investissement

CHARLES-EMMANUEL CÔTÉ

I. LE CANADA ET LE DROIT INTERNATIONAL DE L'INVESTISSEMENT EN 2013

Un développement majeur du droit international de l'investissement retient tout particulièrement l'attention en 2013, avec la ratification par le Canada de la *Convention pour le règlement des différends relatifs aux investissements entre États et ressortissants d'autres États (Convention CIRDI)*, près de cinquante ans après sa signature à Washington.[1] Ce développement récent fait l'objet d'une analyse plus approfondie, après un tour d'horizon des principaux faits marquants de l'année pour le Canada.

A. PRATIQUE CONVENTIONNELLE DU CANADA EN MATIÈRE D'INVESTISSEMENT ÉTRANGER

De nombreuses négociations bilatérales sur l'investissement ont été menées à terme par Ottawa en 2013. L'entente de principe intervenue avec Bruxelles sur l'*Accord économique et commercial global Canada-Union européenne (AECG)* est de toute première importance, compte tenu des flux de capitaux potentiels entre les parties. Bien que le texte de l'accord ne soit pas encore signé, les informations rendues publiques indiquent qu'il comportera un chapitre sur l'investissement.[2] Ce premier exercice par l'Union européenne de

---

Charles-Emmanuel Côté est vice-doyen aux études de premier cycle et à la formation continue et professeur agrégé à la Faculté de droit de l'Université Laval.

[1] *Convention pour le règlement des différends relatifs aux investissements entre États et ressortissants d'autres États*, 575 RTNU 160, RT Can 2013 n° 24 (entrée en vigueur: 14 octobre 1966) [*Convention CIRDI*].

[2] Canada, *Résumé technique des résultats finaux de la négociation. Accord économique et commercial global Canada-Union européenne. Accord de principe*, 2013 aux pp 13-16,

7 brbr

sa nouvelle compétence en la matière, legs du traité de Lisbonne,[3] donnera un aperçu de l'approche qu'elle entend privilégier, poursuivant celle de ses États membres, ou embrassant plutôt celle de l'Amérique du Nord. Ottawa est aussi parvenu à conclure d'autres négociations bilatérales en Europe au sujet d'accords sur la promotion et la protection de l'investissement étranger (APIE) avec l'Albanie, la Moldavie et la Serbie.[4] Le redéploiement en Afrique du programme de négociations d'APIE a connu beaucoup de succès en 2013, avec la conclusion des négociations avec le Bénin, la Côte d'Ivoire, la Guinée, le Nigeria et la Zambie, ainsi que l'entrée en vigueur de l'APIE conclu avec la Tanzanie.[5] Les négociations d'un nouvel accord de libre-échange avec le Honduras ont aussi été couronnées de succès, tandis que l'accord de libre-échange avec le Panama est entré en vigueur, chaque accord comportant un chapitre sur l'investissement.[6] L'APIE Canada-Panama de 1996 a été suspendu lors de l'entrée en vigueur du nouvel accord de libre-échange, conformément à la pratique habituelle du Canada.[7]

B.   DIFFÉRENDS RELATIFS AUX INVESTISSEMENTS IMPLIQUANT
     LE CANADA OU DES INVESTISSEURS CANADIENS

Trois notifications d'intention d'attraire le Canada devant un tribunal arbitral pour violation du chapitre 11 de l'*Accord de libre-échange*

---

en ligne: MAECD <http://plandaction.gc.ca/sites/default/files/pdfs/aecg-resumetechnique.pdf>.

[3] *Traité sur le fonctionnement de l'Union européenne (version consolidée)*, 25 mars 1957 [2012] JO C 326 à la p 47, art 206-7. Voir Marc Bungenberg, "EU Investment Treaty-Making after Lisbon" dans Kurt Hübner, dir, *Europe, Canada and the Comprehensive Economic and Trade Agreement*, Oxford, Routledge, 2011.

[4] Canada, ministère des Affaires étrangères, du Commerce et du Développement, *Accords sur la promotion et la protection des investissements étrangers (APIE)*, 18 décembre 2013 en ligne: MAECD <http://www.international.gc.ca/trade-agreements-accords-commerciaux/agr-acc/fipa-apie/index.aspx?lang=fra>.

[5] *Accord entre le gouvernement du Canada et le gouvernement de la République-Unie de Tanzanie sur la promotion et la protection réciproque des investissements*, 16 mai 2013, RT Can 2013 n° 26 (entrée en vigueur: 9 décembre 2013).

[6] Canada, ministère des Affaires étrangères, du Commerce et du Développement, *Les Accords de libre-échange du Canada*, 18 décembre 2012 en ligne: MAECD <http://www.international.gc.ca/trade-agreements-accords-commerciaux/agr-acc/fta-ale.aspx?lang=fra>; *Accord de libre-échange entre le Canada et la République du Panama*, 14 mai 2010, RT Can 2013 n° 9 (entrée en vigueur: 1er avril 2013) [*ALÉ Canada-Panama*].

[7] *ALÉ Canada-Panama, ibid*, art 9.38.

nord-américain (ALÉNA)[8] se sont concrétisées en 2013 avec le dépôt formel de trois plaintes de la part d'investisseurs américains, au titre du règlement d'arbitrage de la Commission des Nations Unies pour le droit commercial international (CNUDCI). Une société pharmaceutique réclame 500 millions de dollars CAN en dommages dans l'affaire *Ely Lilly c Canada*,[9] au motif que la déclaration d'invalidité de ses brevets par les tribunaux canadiens violerait la clause du traitement juste et équitable et constituerait une expropriation directe de son investissement au Canada. Les deux autres affaires visent l'imposition par deux provinces de moratoires sur l'exploitation de certaines ressources naturelles. D'une part, le moratoire imposé par l'Ontario sur l'exploitation de l'énergie éolienne dans la province, dans le contexte de sa politique énergétique verte et de son programme de tarifs de rachat garantis d'électricité, fait l'objet d'une réclamation de 475 millions de dollars CAN dans l'affaire *Windstream Energy c Canada*.[10] La demanderesse, une société qui développe des technologies vertes pour le secteur énergétique, estime avoir été traitée de façon discriminatoire, contraire au traitement juste et équitable et d'une manière équivalant à une expropriation. Les faits entourant cette affaire ont déjà soulevé une première réclamation de la part d'un autre investisseur américain dans l'affaire *Mesa Power Group c Canada*.[11] D'autre part, le moratoire imposé par le Québec sur l'exploration et l'exploitation des gisements gaziers et pétroliers du golfe Saint-Laurent soulève une réclamation de 250 millions de dollars CAN de la part d'une société pétrolière qui détenait des permis d'exploration dans

---

[8] *Accord de libre-échange nord-américain entre le gouvernement du Canada, le gouvernement des États-Unis mexicains et le gouvernement des États-Unis d'Amérique*, 17 décembre 1992, RT Can 1994 n° 2 (entrée en vigueur: 1er janvier 1994) [*ALÉNA*].

[9] *Ely Lilly c Canada*, "Notification d'arbitrage" (chapitre 11 *ALÉNA*, 12 septembre 2013).

[10] *Windstream Energy c Canada*, "Notification d'arbitrage" (chapitre 11 *ALÉNA*, 20 janvier 2013). Le programme de tarifs de rachat garantis de l'Ontario a été contesté avec succès à l'Organisation mondiale du commerce (OMC), en raison des contraintes d'exploitation illicites qu'il impose afin de favoriser les fabricants locaux de matériel nécessaire à la production d'énergies vertes. Voir *Canada – Certaines mesures affectant le secteur de la production d'énergie renouvelable (plainte du Japon)* (2013), OMC DocWT/DS412/AB/R (Rapport de l'Organe d'appel); *Canada – Mesures relatives au programme de tarifs de rachat garantis (plainte de l'Union européenne)* (2013), OMC Doc WT/DS426/AB/R (Rapport de l'Organe d'appel).

[11] *Mesa Power Group c Canada*, "Notification d'arbitrage" (chapitre 11 *ALÉNA*, 4 octobre 2011).

ce secteur de la province, dans l'affaire *Lone Pine Resources c Canada*,[12] au motif qu'il s'agit d'une violation du traitement juste et équitable et d'une expropriation.

En plus de ces nouvelles réclamations introduites contre le Canada, trois autres arbitrages fondés sur le chapitre 11 de l'*ALÉNA* étaient toujours pendants en 2013.[13] Une dernière réclamation contre le Canada a connu un dénouement surprenant dans l'affaire *St. Marys VCNA c Canada*,[14] puisque les parties se sont entendues pour mettre fin aux procédures par un règlement amiable consigné dans une sentence arbitrale. L'investisseur étranger s'est finalement rendu aux arguments du Canada, qui invoquait la clause de refus des avantages du chapitre 11 au motif que la société américaine n'avait pas suffisamment d'activités réelles aux États-Unis. Il semble que St. Marys VCNA était en réalité détenue par le géant brésilien Votorantim Cimentos afin de servir de coquille pour placer son investissement canadien sous la protection de l'*ALÉNA*. L'investisseur reconnaît qu'il n'a jamais eu l'intérêt juridique pour agir au titre du chapitre 11 de l'*ALÉNA*.[15] Il s'agit d'un rare cas d'application de la clause de refus des avantages que le Canada insère maintenant systématiquement dans ses accords d'investissement, afin d'empêcher le recours abusif à l'arbitrage par un investisseur provenant en réalité d'un État tiers.[16] La simple existence de la clause a offert un rapport de force utile au Canada, lui permettant d'écarter une réclamation illégitime, avant même que son utilisation ne soit avalisée par le tribunal arbitral.

Alors que le Canada fait face à un flot stable mais continu de réclamations de la part d'investisseurs américains, les réclamations d'investisseurs canadiens contre des États étrangers demeurent beaucoup plus rares, surtout à l'extérieur de l'Amérique du Nord.

---

[12] *Lone Pine Resources c Canada*, "Notification d'arbitrage" (chapitre 11 *ALÉNA*, 6 septembre 2013).

[13] Voir *Detroit International Bridge Company c Canada*, "Notification d'arbitrage" (Chapitre 11 *ALÉNA*, 29 avril 2011); *Mesa Power Group c Canada*, "Notification d'arbitrage" (Chapitre 11 *ALÉNA*, 4 octobre 2011); *Mercer International c Canada*, "Requête," CIRDI Aff nº ARB(AF)/12/3 (chapitre 11 *ALÉNA*, 30 avril 2012).

[14] *St. Marys VCNA c Canada*, sentence (chapitre 11 *ALÉNA*, 12 avril 2013). Voir ALÉNA, *supra* note 8, art 1113(2).

[15] *Ibid*, para 7.

[16] Voir Charles-Emmanuel Côté, "Le Canada et l'investissement direct étranger : entre ouverture et inquiétude" dans Mathieu Arès et Éric Boulanger, dir, *L'investissement et la nouvelle économie mondiale. Trajectoires nationales, réseaux mondiaux et normes internationales*, Bruxelles, Bruylant, 2012 à la p 299.

Dans une affaire *Infinito Gold c Costa Rica*, un investisseur canadien a notifié le Costa Rica de son intention de porter une réclamation en arbitrage sur la base de son APIE avec le Canada.[17] L'investisseur canadien détenait depuis 1993 une concession pour l'exploitation du gisement aurifère Las Crucitas, mais la chambre administrative de la Cour suprême du Costa Rica a annulé la concession en 2010, alors que sa chambre constitutionnelle en confirmait la validité en 2011. Infinito Gold allègue que ces jugements contradictoires de la plus haute juridiction costaricaine violent les clauses de l'APIE sur l'expropriation, le traitement juste et équitable et la non-discrimination. Parmi les investissements réalisés depuis 1993, l'investisseur canadien comptabilise les montants investis au titre de la responsabilité sociale de l'entreprise dans le développement local des communautés voisines du projet minier. Cette nouvelle réclamation n'est pas la première à se fonder sur l'APIE Canada-Costa Rica, puisque deux réclamations ont déjà été soumises sans succès sur ce fondement.[18]

La dernière réclamation introduite en 2013 par un investisseur canadien soulève des questions de droit international complexes sur la succession d'États en matière de traités. La société World Wide Minerals a annoncé la présentation d'une réclamation contre le Kazakhstan concernant la suspension des opérations et la confiscation de l'usine de traitement d'uranium qu'elle exploite dans l'ancienne république socialiste soviétique, après y avoir investi des sommes importantes avec la bénédiction d'Astana.[19] L'investisseur canadien fonde sa réclamation sur l'APIE conclu en 1989 entre le Canada et l'Union des républiques socialistes soviétiques (URSS), en alléguant que le Kazakhstan a succédé à l'URSS pour ce traité.

---

[17] *Accord entre le gouvernement de la République du Costa Rica et le gouvernement du Canada pour l'encouragement et la protection des investissements*, 18 mars 1998, RT Can 1999 n° 43 (entrée en vigueur: 29 septembre 1999); *Infinito Gold c Costa Rica*, "Notification d'intention" (APIE Canada-Costa Rica, 4 avril 2013).

[18] Voir *Quadrant Pacific Growth Fund c Costa Rica*, ordonnance du tribunal mettant fin à l'instance, CIRDI Aff n° ARB(AF)/08/1 (APIE Canada-Costa Rica, 27 octobre 2010); *Alasdair Ross Anderson c Costa Rica*, sentence, CIRDI Aff n° ARB(AF)/07/3 (APIE Canada-Costa Rica, 19 mai 2010). Dans la première affaire, le tribunal arbitral a mis fin à l'instance en raison de la suspension des procédures pendant plus de six mois pour défaut de paiement de l'avance sur les frais du tribunal. Dans la seconde affaire, le tribunal a décliné compétence en raison de l'absence d'un investissement au sens de l'APIE.

[19] World Wide Minerals Ltd, "World Wide Minerals Initiates Investor-State Arbitration against Kazakhstan," (16 décembre 2013) en ligne: Yahoo! Finance <http://finance.yahoo.com>.

Or Ottawa négocie depuis 2011 un APIE avec Astana, laissant entendre que le Canada et le Kazakhstan ne sont pas encore liés par un accord d'investissement![20] Cette impression est renforcée par une note du gouvernement canadien qui indique que la Russie est l'État successeur à l'APIE Canada-URSS de 1989.[21] Quelques éléments de solution du problème peuvent être dégagés de la *Convention de Vienne sur la succession d'États en matière de traités*,[22] bien que ni le Canada, ni le Kazakhstan n'y soient parties, puisqu'elle se fonde sur la pratique des États et quelques principes indiscutables.[23] Un principe qui la sous-tend est celui de l'intransmissibilité des traités "personnels," c'est-à-dire conclus *intuitu personæ*, comme les traités d'établissement, par opposition aux traités "réels" fixant le régime applicable à l'utilisation d'un territoire donné.[24] Les accords d'investissement appartiennent vraisemblablement à la première catégorie, puisqu'ils sont fondés sur la confiance mutuelle entre les parties quant au traitement des investissements étrangers effectués sur leur territoire. Certaines règles particulières s'appliquent au cas de l'État successeur issu d'une séparation, que l'État prédécesseur continue ou non d'exister, comme en l'espèce avec la disparition de l'URSS en 1991. Ces règles posent le principe de la transmission du traité à l'État successeur, sauf incompatibilité avec l'objet et le but du traité, ou encore en cas de changement radical des conditions d'exécution du traité.[25] La transmission de l'APIE Canada-URSS au Kazakhstan est-elle contraire à son objet et à son but? La confiance réciproque entre Ottawa et Moscou à la base de l'accord de 1989 était-elle exclusive ou peut-elle s'étendre automatiquement à Astana? Le consentement de l'URSS à l'arbitrage en

---

[20] Canada, ministère des Affaires étrangères, du Commerce et du Développement, "Négociation de l'accord sur la promotion et la protection des investissements étrangers (APIE) entre le Canada et le Kazakhstan," (27 juin 2013) en ligne: MAECD <http://www.international.gc.ca/trade-agreements-accords-commerciaux/agr-acc/fipa-apie/kazakhstan.aspx?lang=fra>.

[21] Canada, ministère des Affaires étrangères, du Commerce et du Développement, *Accords sur la promotion et la protection des investissements étrangers (APIE)*, (18 décembre 2013), en ligne: MAECD <http://www.international.gc.ca/trade-agreements-accords-commerciaux/agr-acc/fipa-apie/index.aspx?lang=fra>.

[22] 23 août 1978, 1946 RTNU 3 (entrée en vigueur: 6 novembre 1996).

[23] Patrick Daillier, Mathias Forteau et Alain Pellet, *Droit international public*, 8ᵉ éd, Paris, LGDJ, 2009 au nᵒ 353.

[24] *Ibid* au nᵒ 361.

[25] *Convention de Vienne sur la succession d'États en matière de traités*, 1946 RTNU 3, art 34(2)b).

1989 peut-il lier le Kazakhstan en 2013? L'institution de l'arbitrage repose sur le consentement des parties, ce qui semble devoir faire des APIE des traités *intuitu personæ* par excellence. Il est permis de douter que le Kazakhstan a bien succédé à l'URSS pour l'APIE de 1989.

La seule sentence arbitrale rendue en 2013 concernant le Canada rejette sur le fond la réclamation d'une société minière canadienne dans l'affaire *Vannessa Ventures c. Venezuela*,[26] fondée sur l'APIE entre le Canada et la république bolivarienne.[27] Les différends fondés sur un autre accord que l'*ALÉNA* demeurent relativement peu nombreux et celui le plus invoqué par les investisseurs canadiens est justement l'APIE entre le Canada et le Venezuela.[28] Vannessa Ventures a soumis à l'arbitrage une réclamation de plus de 1 000 millions de dollars US contre le Venezuela en 2004, en raison de la résiliation de son contrat d'investissement en 2001 et de la reprise de toutes ses installations dans le gisement aurifère de Las Cristinas. Elle avait acquis ses parts dans le projet de Placer Dome Inc, une autre société canadienne avec laquelle la société d'État Corporación Venezolana de Guayana avait conclu un contrat en 1991 pour développer ce projet. Ce transfert de propriété a été fait sans le consentement du partenaire vénézuélien et en contravention du contrat d'investissement. La majorité du tribunal arbitral juge qu'il est compétent pour connaître du litige, mais un des arbitres est d'avis qu'il ne l'est pas en raison de la mauvaise foi avec laquelle a été effectué l'investissement de Vannessa Ventures.[29] Le tribunal arbitral

---

[26] Sentence, CIRDI Aff n° ARB(AF)/04/6 (APIE Canada-Venezuela, 16 janvier 2013).

[27] *Accord entre le gouvernement du Canada et le gouvernement de la République du Venezuela concernant la promotion et protection des investissements*, 1er juillet 1996, RT Can 1998 n° 20 (entrée en vigueur: 28 janvier 1998).

[28] *Rusoro Mining c Venezuela*, "Requête introductive d'instance," CIRDI Aff n° ARB(AF)/12/5 (APIE Canada-Venezuela, 1er août 2012) [non publiée]; *Crystallex International Corporation c Venezuela*, "Requête introductive d'instance," CIRDI Aff n° ARB(AF)/11/2 (APIE Canada-Venezuela) [non publiée]; *Nova Scotia Power Incorporated c Venezuela*, sentence, CIRDI Aff n° ARB(AF)/11/1 (APIE Canada-Venezuela, 30 avril 2014) [non publiée]; *Quadrant Pacific Growth Fund, supra* note 18; *Alasdair Ross Anderson, supra* note 18; *Frontier Petroleum Services c République tchèque*, sentence finale (APIE Canada-Tchécoslovaquie, 12 novembre 2010); *Ulemek c Croatie*, sentence (APIE Canada-Croatie, 25 mai 2008) [non publiée]; *EnCana Corporation c Équateur*, sentence (APIE Canada-Équateur, 3 février 2006).

[29] *Vannessa Ventures Ltd c Venezuela*, sentence, CIRDI Aff n° ARB (AF)/04/6 (APIE Canada-Venezuela, 16 janvier 2013) aux para 113, 168-69.

juge qu'au regard du contrat, le Venezuela était justifié de le résilier et de reprendre les installations de l'investisseur canadien, et qu'il ne saurait s'agir d'une expropriation illicite ou d'une violation du traitement juste et équitable ou de la garantie de protection et de sécurité complètes des investissements étrangers.[30]

C. JURISPRUDENCE CANADIENNE SUR L'INVESTISSEMENT ÉTRANGER

Un recours judiciaire inusité a été intenté par une bande autochtone de Colombie-Britannique contre la ratification imminente de l'APIE Canada-Chine de 2012, dans l'affaire *Première Nation des Hupacasath c Canada (ministre des Affaires étrangères).*[31] La Première Nation des Hupacasath a tenté sans succès d'obtenir un jugement déclaratoire de la Cour fédérale, qui aurait empêché Ottawa de ratifier le traité sans l'avoir au préalable consultée à ce sujet. Cette affaire rappelle la contestation infructueuse du chapitre 11 de l'*ALÉNA* entreprise par une organisation non gouvernementale il y a une dizaine d'années.[32] Dans cette dernière affaire, un argument fondé sur la protection constitutionnelle de la compétence des cours supérieures avait échoué. La présente affaire met de l'avant de nouveaux arguments constitutionnels découlant des obligations de la Couronne envers les peuples autochtones du Canada. Dans un jugement très étoffé et bien motivé, le juge en chef Crompton rejette la demande au motif que les effets préjudiciables potentiels de la ratification de l'APIE sur les droits ancestraux que revendique la bande sur l'Île de Vancouver ne sont pas importants et sont de nature hypothétique. Selon le juge en chef, les faits ne donnent pas naissance à l'obligation de la Couronne de consulter la bande et Ottawa peut donc librement exercer sa prérogative afin de confirmer le consentement du Canada à être lié à l'accord. L'appel de ce jugement est toujours pendant à la Cour d'appel fédérale, ce qui freine la ratification par le Canada de l'APIE Canada-Chine de 2012.

---

[30] *Ibid* aux para 112, 209, 214, 222-32.

[31] 2013 CF 900, pourvoi de plein droit à la CAF, A-324-13 (30 septembre 2013); *Accord entre le gouvernement du Canada et le gouvernement de la République populaire de Chine concernant la promotion et la protection réciproque des investissements*, 9 septembre 2012 (non en vigueur), en ligne: MAECI <http://www.international. gc.ca/trade-agreements-accords-commerciaux/agr-acc/fipa-apie/china-text -chine.aspx?lang=fra&view=d>. Pour une analyse de l'APIE Canada-Chine, voir cette chronique dans l'*Annuaire* de 2012.

[32] *Council of Canadians c Canada (AG)*, 2005 CanLII 28428 (CS Ont), conf par 2006 CanLII 40222 (CA Ont); Côté, *supra* note 17 aux pp 289-90.

II. La ratification de la *Convention CIRDI* par le Canada

Le 1er novembre 2013, le Canada a finalement déposé son instrument de ratification de la *Convention CIRDI* auprès de la Banque internationale pour la reconstruction et le développement (Banque mondiale).[33] Conformément à ses dispositions, le traité est formellement entré en vigueur pour le Canada le 1er décembre 2013.[34] Avec le Mexique et la Pologne, le Canada demeurait le seul pays membre de l'Organisation de coopération et de développement économiques (OCDE) à ne pas adhérer à la *Convention CIRDI*.[35]

Les raisons précises de cette ratification tardive sont multiples. Il faut tout de même rappeler qu'Ottawa était assez hostile au droit international de l'investissement au cours des années 1960 et 1970, en raison de la dépendance chronique de l'économie canadienne envers les capitaux américains et des inquiétudes que cela soulevait pour le maintien de la souveraineté du Canada.[36] Le virage complet opéré à cet égard par Ottawa à partir du milieu des années 1980 aurait pu être l'occasion pour le Canada d'adhérer à la *Convention CIRDI*, surtout avec la conclusion de l'*ALÉNA*. La priorité aura toutefois été de doter le Canada d'un système complet d'arbitrage civil et commercial, au moyen de la mise en œuvre de la *Convention pour la reconnaissance et l'exécution des sentences arbitrales étrangères*[37] (*Convention de New York*).[38] Des difficultés propres au fédéralisme canadien sont aussi souvent invoquées, concernant le refus de certaines provinces de coopérer pour mettre en œuvre la *Convention*

---

[33] *Convention CIRDI, supra* note 1, art 73; CIRDI, Communiqué, "Canada [*sic*] ratifie la Convention du CIRDI" (1er novembre 2013); Canada, Communiqué, "Le Canada ratifie un important traité international sur les différends relatifs aux investissements" (1er novembre 2013). Le Canada avait signé le traité le 15 décembre 2006.

[34] *Convention CIRDI, supra* note 1, art 68(2).

[35] CIRDI, *Contracting States, including dates of entry into force for each of them of the Convention on the Settlement of Investment Disputes between States and Nationals of Other States (Art 68 of the Convention)*, Doc no ICSID/8-A à la p 1 (Février 2014).

[36] Côté, *supra* note 16 aux pp 269-87.

[37] 10 juin 1958, 330 RTNU 39, RT Can 1986 no 43 (entrée en vigueur pour le Canada: 10 août 1986).

[38] Frédérique Sabourin, "Une perspective québécoise sur la *Convention pour le règlement des différends relatifs aux investissements entre États et ressortissants d'autres États*," dans Sylvette Guillemard, dir, *Mélanges en l'honneur du professeur Alain Prujiner. Études de droit international privé et de droit commercial international*, Cowansville (Qc), Yvon Blais, 2011 à la p 321.

CIRDI.[39] En définitive, la décision de ratifier ce traité en 2013 s'explique probablement par la pression combinée de plusieurs facteurs: la politique commerciale extérieure du Canada qui soutient l'expansion du droit international de l'investissement; les pressions exercées par les milieux d'affaires canadiens; les pressions de la part de l'Union européenne dans le contexte des négociations de l'AECG; le déblocage de la machine administrative fédérale-provinciale; l'anomalie — voire l'embarras — que constituait l'absence du Canada du CIRDI (alors que sa Secrétaire générale est elle-même une Canadienne depuis 2009).

L'opportunité de la ratification de la *Convention CIRDI* par le Canada pourrait être remise en question, à l'heure où le CIRDI est fortement contesté.[40] La Bolivie, l'Équateur et le Venezuela ont dénoncé le traité avec fracas au cours des dernières années, essentiellement parce que le CIRDI serait biaisé en faveur des investisseurs étrangers.[41] Les limites du système CIRDI se font aussi sentir pour ces derniers. Par exemple, l'accès au CIRDI demeure plus restreint qu'à d'autres forums d'arbitrage en raison du double test de compétence des tribunaux arbitraux, qui doivent vérifier la satisfaction des critères de la *Convention CIRDI* en plus de ceux de l'accord sur l'investissement sur lequel se fonde la réclamation.[42] Pourtant, il ne faut pas exagérer non plus la portée de cette ratification, qui a d'abord une valeur symbolique pour le Canada. Dans tous ses accords sur l'investissement,[43] le Canada consent déjà unilatéralement à l'arbitrage suivant le règlement d'arbitrage de

---

[39] Voir Conférence pour l'harmonisation des lois au Canada, *Loi sur le règlement des différends internationaux relatifs aux investissements. Rapport* par Philippe Lortie, Whitehorse, 1997 au para 12 [CHLC, *Rapport sur le CIRDI*].

[40] Voir généralement Leon E. Trakman, "The ICSID under Siege" (2012) 45 Cornell Int'l LJ 603.

[41] CIRDI, Communiqué, "Le Venezuela adresse une communication en vertu de l'article 71 de la Convention CIRDI" (26 janvier 2012); CIRDI, Communiqué, "Ecuador Submits a Notice Under Article 71 of the ICSID Convention" (9 juillet 2009); CIRDI, Communiqué, "Bolivia Submits a Notice under Article 71 of the ICSID Convention" (16 mai 2007). La dénonciation de la *Convention CIRDI* prend effet six mois après la réception par la Banque mondiale d'une notification à cette fin de la part d'un État contractant. *Convention CIRDI, supra* note 1, art 71.

[42] Voir Dieudonné Édouard Onguene Onana, *La compétence en arbitrage international relatif aux investissements. Les conditions d'investissement et de nationalité devant le CIRDI*, Bruxelles, Bruylant, 2012 aux pp 41-44.

[43] Côté, *supra* note 16 aux pp 281, 286, 297 et 302. Voir par ex. *ALÉNA, supra* note 8, art 1120; Canada, *APIE-type du Canada (2012)*, art 25 [archivé par l'auteur].

la CNUDCI[44] ou le mécanisme supplémentaire du CIRDI.[45] Ces procédures d'arbitrage sont déjà fréquemment utilisées par les investisseurs étrangers contre le Canada et par les investisseurs canadiens contre des États étrangers, pour connaître de leurs réclamations fondées sur la violation de ces accords. La ratification de la *Convention CIRDI* par le Canada ouvre simplement aux investisseurs une troisième voie procédurale pour soumettre à l'arbitrage leurs réclamations fondées sur ses accords sur l'investissement, qui prévoient déjà le consentement unilatéral du Canada à l'arbitrage CIRDI.[46] Elle permet en outre aux investisseurs canadiens d'insérer une clause CIRDI dans leurs contrats d'investissement avec des États étrangers avec lesquels le Canada n'a pas conclu d'accord sur l'investissement, afin de bénéficier quand même de cette procédure d'arbitrage, sans pour autant bénéficier de la protection matérielle d'un tel accord.

L'origine et le fonctionnement de la *Convention CIRDI* sont bien connus et il suffit de se rapporter à la littérature abondante sur le sujet.[47] Il convient plutôt de s'attarder aux conséquences juridiques particulières pour le Canada de l'ajout de cette nouvelle procédure d'arbitrage pour le règlement des différends relatifs aux investissements. Contrairement à l'arbitrage CNUDCI ou au mécanisme supplémentaire du CIRDI, l'arbitrage CIRDI est totalement rattaché au droit international public, qui devient la seule loi du for.[48] Le tribunal CIRDI n'élisant son for dans aucun droit national, peu

---

44 CNUDCI, *Règlement d'arbitrage de la CNUDCI (version révisée de 2010)*, NewYork, NU, 2011.

45 CIRDI, *Règlement du mécanisme supplémentaire*, Doc n° CIRDI/11, Washington (DC), CIRDI, 2006.

46 Voir *supra* note 41 et le texte correspondant.

47 Voir généralement Christoph H Schreuer et al, *The ICSID Convention: A Commentary*, 2e éd, Cambridge, Cambridge University Press, 2009; Moshe Hirsh, *The Arbitration Mechanism of the International Center for the Settlement of Investment Disputes*, Dordrecht, Martinus Nijhof, 1993; Georges R. Delaume, "Le Centre international pour le règlement des différends relatifs aux investissements (CIRDI)" (1982) 109 JDI 755; Aron Broches, "The Convention on the Settlement of Investment Disputes between States and Nationals of Other States" (1972) 136 Rec Cours 331; *Investissements étrangers et arbitrage entre États et personnes privées. La Convention BIRD du 18 mars 1965*, Paris, Pedone, 1969; Nigel S Rodley, "Some Aspects of the World Bank Convention on the Settlement of Investment Disputes" (1966) 4 ACDI 43.

48 Alain Prujiner, "Aspects fondamentaux du droit international de l'investissement: perspective de droit international privé," cours donné à l'Université d'été sur le

importe le lieu physique où il choisit de se réunir (que ce soit à Washington ou ailleurs), la sentence CIRDI n'est soumise au contrôle judiciaire d'aucun juge national. De plus, puisque les sentences CIRDI sont exécutoires dans tout État contractant comme un "jugement définitif d'un tribunal fonctionnant sur le territoire dudit État," l'adhésion au CIRDI suppose l'abolition du contrôle judiciaire au stade de la reconnaissance et de l'exécution des sentences CIRDI.[49] Enfin, la *Convention CIRDI* envisage la possibilité pour un État contractant de reconnaître la capacité de ses collectivités publiques d'agir comme partie dans un arbitrage CIRDI.[50] Avant d'examiner plus en détail ces aspects particuliers de la *Convention CIRDI* au regard des mesures de mise en œuvre prises par le Canada, la question de la portée *ratione temporis* de son adhésion au CIRDI se pose d'emblée.

A.   LA PORTÉE *RATIONE TEMPORIS* DE L'ADHÉSION DU CANADA
     AU CIRDI

Le principe de base posé par le droit des traités est celui de leur non-rétroactivité, à moins qu'une intention différente ne ressorte du traité ou ne soit ailleurs établie.[51] Deux hypothèses peuvent être envisagées en ce qui concerne le consentement à l'arbitrage CIRDI par le Canada. La première hypothèse est celle où le CIRDI serait ouvert seulement aux différends relatifs aux investissements nés après le 1er décembre 2013, date d'entrée en vigueur de la *Convention CIRDI* pour le Canada. La ratification du Canada n'aurait qu'une portée prospective et son consentement unilatéral à l'arbitrage CIRDI, exprimé antérieurement dans ses accords sur l'investisse-

---

droit international de l'investissement, présentée à la Faculté de droit de l'Université Laval, 17 mai 2011 [non publié]. Voir Alain Prujiner, « Le droit international privé : un droit du rattachement » dans Christian Dominicé, Robert Patry et Claude Raymond, dir, *Études de droit international en l'honneur de Pierre Lalive*, Bâle, Helbing & Lichtenhahn, 1993, 161.

[49] *Convention CIRDI*, *supra* note 1, art 54(1). Techniquement, seules les obligations pécuniaires imposées par la sentence CIRDI doivent être exécutoires comme un jugement définitif d'un tribunal national, mais cette distinction a peu de conséquences pratiques puisque la quasi-totalité des sentences CIRDI se limitent à imposer de telles obligations. Schreuer et al, *supra* note 47 à la p 1137.

[50] *Ibid*, art 25(1).

[51] *Convention de Vienne sur le droit des traités*, 23 mai 1969, 1155 RTNU 354, RT Can 1980 n° 37, art 28 (entrée en vigueur: 27 janvier 1980). "[L]es dispositions d'un traité ne lient pas une partie en ce qui concerne un acte ou un fait antérieur à la date d'entrée en vigueur de ce traité au regard de cette partie."

ment, ne pourrait être utilisé par un investisseur étranger qu'à l'égard de faits postérieurs à son adhésion au CIRDI. La seconde hypothèse est celle de l'ouverture du CIRDI aux différends nés avant le 1er décembre 2013. La ratification du Canada aurait une portée rétrospective et son consentement unilatéral à l'arbitrage CIRDI exprimé antérieurement dans ses accords sur l'investissement pourrait être utilisé par un investisseur étranger à l'égard de faits survenus avant son adhésion au CIRDI.

Le texte de la *Convention CIRDI* n'offre aucune réponse claire à cette question, l'article 68 se contentant de dire qu'elle entre en vigueur 30 jours après sa ratification. Comme un auteur l'a noté, la question de la compétence *ratione temporis* des tribunaux CIRDI demeure relativement peu étudiée comparée à leur compétence *ratione personæ* ou *rationæ materiæ*.[52] Les quelques affaires qui ont porté sur la question concernaient la compétence du tribunal CIRDI sur un différend né avant l'entrée en vigueur du traité bilatéral sur l'investissement applicable, plutôt qu'avant celle de la *Convention CIRDI*. Cette dernière question ne semble avoir été abordée par aucun tribunal CIRDI à ce jour. Le cas original du Canada la soulève véritablement pour la première fois, lui qui a ratifié la *Convention CIRDI* plus de vingt ans après avoir conclu des accords sur l'investissement où il a exprimé son consentement unilatéral à l'arbitrage CIRDI.

Bien que la première hypothèse envisagée ci-dessus semble correspondre au principe de la non-rétroactivité des traités, une interprétation de l'article 68 dans son contexte et à la lumière de l'objet et du but de la *Convention CIRDI* semble aussi permettre de concilier la seconde hypothèse avec le principe de non-rétroactivité.[53] La *Convention CIRDI* ne prévoit pas de règles de fond applicables aux investissements étrangers, mais seulement des règles de procédure au cœur desquels se trouvent la condition du consentement à l'arbitrage CIRDI et l'obligation d'assurer la reconnaissance du caractère exécutoire des sentences CIRDI sur son territoire. C'est donc le consentement à l'arbitrage qui devrait être postérieur au 1er décembre 2013, consentement qui se parachève et devient obligatoire

---

[52] John P Gaffney, "The Jurisdiction *Ratione Temporis* of ICSID Tribunals" (2007) 22:7 Mealey's Int'l Arb Rep 1 à la p 1. Voir aussi Stanimir A Alexandrov, "The 'Baby Boom' of Treaty-Based Arbitrations and the Jurisdiction of ICSID Tribunals: Shareholders as 'Investors' and Jurisdiction *Ratione Temporis*" (2005) 4 Law & Prac Int'l Cts & Tribunals 19 aux pp 49-57.

[53] *Convention de Vienne sur le droit des traités, supra* note 51, art 31(1).

lors de la réunion du consentement du Canada et de celui de l'investisseur étranger. Au regard de la *Convention CIRDI*, l'acte ou le fait postérieur à l'entrée en vigueur serait ainsi la réunion du consentement des parties et non la survenance du différend, qui relèverait des règles de fond fixées par l'accord sur l'investissement applicable. Cette interprétation est soutenue par les travaux préparatoires de la Commission du droit international (CDI) sur le droit des traités, qui concluaient que l'idée de différend dans une clause juridictionnelle d'un accord renvoie à tout différend existant après son entrée en vigueur et que cela ne confère pas à l'accord un effet rétroactif.[54] La CDI précise aussi que l'application d'un traité à une situation née avant son entrée en vigueur, mais se poursuivant après celle-ci, ne lui confère pas d'effet rétroactif pour autant. De même, c'est la demande de reconnaissance et d'exécution d'une sentence CIRDI qui devrait être postérieure au 1er décembre 2013 et qui serait le fait postérieur à l'entrée en vigueur de la *Convention CIRDI* auquel l'obligation d'assurer la reconnaissance du caractère exécutoire des sentences CIRDI serait applicable. Les travaux préparatoires de la *Convention CIRDI* demeurent silencieux sur la question et n'éclairent pas le sens de la portée *ratione temporis* de l'adhésion au CIRDI.[55]

La loi uniforme de mise en œuvre de la *Convention CIRDI* proposée en 1997 par la Conférence pour l'harmonisation des lois au Canada (CHLC) prévoit une disposition sur la portée *ratione temporis* de la loi.[56] Elle prévoit que la loi s'applique aux sentences CIRDI rendues antérieurement à son entrée en vigueur, ce qui permet aux investisseurs étrangers d'obtenir l'exécution au Canada d'une sentence CIRDI rendue avant le 1er décembre 2013 contre un État étranger. La loi prévoit en outre qu'elle s'applique aux "accords portant le consentement à une procédure d'arbitrage [CIRDI]" conclus avant son entrée en vigueur. Cette disposition semble viser

54 CDI, "Projet d'articles sur le droit des traités et commentaires," dans *Annuaire de la Commission du droit international*, 1966, vol 2, New York, NU, 1967 (A/CN.4/SER.A/1966/Add.1), 203 à la p 231 aux para 2-3; Alexandrov, *supra* note 52 aux pp 49-50.

55 *Convention de Vienne sur le droit des traités*, *supra* note 51, art 32. Voir Antonio R Parra, "Participation in the ICSID Convention" (2013) 28 ICSID Rev 169 aux pp 170-71; Schreuer et al, *supra* note 47 à la p 1270; Banque internationale pour la reconstruction et le développement, *Rapport des administrateurs sur la convention pour le règlement des différends relatifs aux investissements entre États et ressortissants d'autres États* (18 mars 1965) au para 46.

56 CHLC, *Loi uniforme sur le règlement des différends internationaux relatifs aux investissements* (1997), art 4 [CHLC, *Loi uniforme sur le CIRDI*].

au premier chef les accords sur l'investissement du Canada ou les contrats d'État dans lesquels une clause CIRDI a été prévue avant l'entrée en vigueur de la loi, mais elle ne dit rien sur le moment où le différend doit être né. Ces dispositions proposées dans la loi uniforme sont reprises systématiquement dans les lois de mise en œuvre de la *Convention CIRDI* adoptées à ce jour.[57] La pratique législative canadienne soutient ainsi la seconde hypothèse de l'ouverture du CIRDI aux différends nés avant le 1er décembre 2013, ainsi que du caractère exécutoire au Canada des sentences CIRDI rendues avant cette date.

Cette question de la portée *ratione temporis* de l'adhésion du Canada au CIRDI n'est pas que théorique puisqu'elle a déjà failli se poser dans l'affaire *Mercer International c Canada*, concernant un différend né avant le 1er décembre 2013.[58] Dans sa requête introductive d'instance présentée suivant le mécanisme supplémentaire du CIRDI, l'investisseur américain a aussi donné son consentement à l'arbitrage suivant la *Convention CIRDI*, dans l'éventualité où le Canada dépose sa ratification avant le début des procédures. Or le tribunal arbitral a été constitué avant celle-ci, ce qui signifie que l'affaire ne sera pas soumise au CIRDI, mais demeure dans le cadre de son mécanisme supplémentaire.

B. LA MISE EN ŒUVRE DE LA *CONVENTION CIRDI* AU REGARD DU PARTAGE DES COMPÉTENCES LÉGISLATIVES

Les États contractants ont l'obligation expresse de prendre les mesures d'exécution nécessaires afin de donner effet à la *Convention CIRDI* sur leur territoire, qu'il s'agisse de mesures législatives ou d'autres types de mesures.[59] La mise en œuvre du traité comporte essentiellement deux aspects: un aspect institutionnel et un aspect procédural.[60] Au plan institutionnel, l'État contractant doit assurer sa participation aux travaux du CIRDI (déléguer un représentant au Conseil administratif, désigner des personnes qualifiées pour figurer sur la liste de conciliateurs et la liste d'arbitres, contribuer au financement du Centre), ainsi que reconnaître les privilèges et

---

57 Voir, par ex, *Loi sur le règlement des différends internationaux relatifs aux investissements*, LC 2008, c 8, art 4 (*Loi fédérale sur le CIRDI*); *Loi de 1999 sur le règlement des différends internationaux relatifs aux investissements*, LO 1999, c 12, ann. D, art 4.

58 *Mercer International c Canada*, "Requête," CIRDI Aff n° ARB(AF)/12/3 au para 110 (chapitre 11 *ALÉNA*, 30 avril 2012).

59 *Convention CIRDI*, *supra* note 1, art 69.

60 Voir Schreuer et al, *supra* note 47 à la p 1274.

immunités du Centre dans son droit national.[61] Au plan procédural, l'État contractant peut choisir de désigner des collectivités publiques ou des organismes dépendant de lui afin de leur donner la capacité d'agir comme partie dans un différend soumis au CIRDI, mais il doit surtout reconnaître le caractère exécutoire des sentences CIRDI sur son territoire comme s'il s'agissait d'un jugement définitif de ses propres tribunaux.[62]

Huit lois de mise en œuvre de la *Convention CIRDI* ont été adoptées et sont entrées en vigueur à ce jour au Canada, au fédéral,[63] dans cinq provinces[64] et deux territoires.[65] Un projet de loi de mise en œuvre déposé par un député de l'opposition est par ailleurs à l'étude à l'Assemblée législative du Manitoba.[66] Ces lois de mise en œuvre s'inspirent largement de la loi uniforme préparée par la CHLC.[67] Au Québec, la *Convention CIRDI* a été approuvée par une résolution de l'Assemblée nationale, ce qui constitue l'étape préalable à sa mise en œuvre législative, puisqu'il s'agit d'un engagement international important selon le droit québécois des relations internationales.[68] Cette approbation permet au gouvernement de prendre un décret par lequel le Québec se déclare lié par la *Convention CIRDI*, ce qui est logiquement la prochaine étape à franchir avant l'adoption d'une loi québécoise de mise en œuvre.

---

[61] *Convention CIRDI, supra* note 1, art 4(1), 13(1), 17, 19-24.

[62] *Ibid,* art 25(1), 54.

[63] *Loi fédérale sur le CIRDI, supra* note 57.

[64] *Settlement of International Investment Disputes Act,* SA 2013, c S-7.8 (Alberta); *Settlement of International Investment Disputes Act,* SBC 2006, c 16 (Colombie-Britannique); *Loi sur le règlement des différends internationaux relatifs aux investissements,* LS 2006, c S-47.2 (Saskatchewan); *Settlement of International Investment Disputes Act,* SNL 2006, c S-13.3 (Terre-Neuve-et-Labrador); *Loi de 1999 sur le règlement des différends internationaux relatifs aux investissements, supra* note 57 (Ontario).

[65] *Loi sur le règlement des différends internationaux relatifs aux investissements,* LNun 2006, c 13 (Nunavut); *Loi sur le règlement des différends internationaux relatifs aux investissements,* LTN-O 2009, c 15 (Territoires-du-Nord-Ouest).

[66] PL 207, *Loi sur le règlement des différends internationaux relatifs aux investissements,* 3ᵉ sess, 40ᵉ lég, Manitoba, 2013 (première lecture le 26 novembre 2013).

[67] CHLC, *Loi uniforme sur le CIRDI, supra* note 55.

[68] Québec, Assemblée nationale, *Journal des débats,* 40ᵉ lég, 1ʳᵉ sess, vol 43 nᵒ 83 (24 octobre 2013) à la p 5188. Voir *Loi sur le ministère des Relations internationales,* LRQ c M-25.1.1, art 22.2-22.4; Daniel Turp, "Le consentement de l'État du Québec aux engagements internationaux et sa participation aux forums internationaux" dans Jacques-Yvan Morin et Sienho Yee (dir), *Multiculturalism and International Law: Essays in Honour of Edward McWhinney,* Leyde, Martinus Nijhoff, 2009.

La mise en œuvre des traités est une compétence partagée en droit constitutionnel canadien selon la matière visée par le traité.[69] La *Convention CIRDI* apparaît comme un traité mixte interpellant à la fois le législateur fédéral et les législateurs provinciaux.[70] Ses aspects institutionnels relèvent essentiellement de la compétence fédérale sur les immunités des organisations internationales et sur la représentation du Canada dans les organisations internationales.[71] Sans surprise, la loi fédérale de mise en œuvre de la *Convention CIRDI* règle entièrement ces questions institutionnelles, sans le concours des provinces.[72] Bien que la position traditionnelle du Québec en matière de relations internationales soit de maximiser sa participation aux forums internationaux, force est de constater que le CIRDI offre peu de marge de manœuvre à cet égard.[73] Son Conseil administratif est composé d'un seul représentant par État contractant et ses attributions demeurent limitées aux questions de régie interne.[74] Les véritables activités du CIRDI s'exercent en réalité devant ses tribunaux arbitraux, ce qui signifie que la désignation du Québec comme collectivité publique ayant la capacité d'agir dans un arbitrage CIRDI serait une réponse satisfaisante à ses demandes. Une autre réponse intéressante serait la conclusion d'arrangements entre le CIRDI et un centre d'arbitrage situé au Québec, afin que des arbitrages CIRDI puissent s'y dérouler, idée dont Ottawa a promis dans le passé de faciliter la réalisation.[75]

---

[69] *Canada (AG) c Ontario (AG)*, 1937 UKPC 7 [1937] AC 326, 351 (Conseil privé).

[70] Voir Sabourin, *supra* note 38 à la p 321; Yves L. Fortier, "The Canadian Approach to Investment Protection: How Far We Have Come!" dans Christina Binder et al, dir, *International Investment Law for the 21st Century: Essays in Honour of Christoph Schreuer*, Oxford, Oxford University Press, 2009 à la p 527.

[71] CHLC, *Rapport sur le CIRDI*, *supra* note 39 aux para 27, 41-42. Voir *Loi concernant les privilèges et immunités des missions étrangères et des organisations internationales*, LRC 1985, c F-29.4; *Loi sur les accords de Bretton Woods et des accords connexes*, LRC 1985, c B-7. La désignation du représentant du Canada au Conseil administratif du CIRDI ne nécessite aucune mesure législative et le gouvernement fédéral peut y procéder en vertu de sa prérogative sur les affaires étrangères.

[72] *Loi fédérale sur le CIRDI*, *supra* note 57, art 5, 11.

[73] Voir Québec, *La politique internationale du Québec – La force de l'action concertée*, Québec, Gouvernement du Québec, 2006 aux pp 28-30; Ministère des Relations internationales, *L'action internationale du Québec: Le Québec dans les forums internationaux*, Québec, Gouvernement du Québec, 2005; Sabourin, *supra* note 38 à la p 331.

[74] *Convention CIRDI*, *supra* note 1, art 4, 6.

[75] *Ibid*, art 63(a); CHLC, *Rapport sur le CIRDI*, *supra* note 39 au para 28; Sabourin, *supra* note 39 à la p 330. Il pourrait s'agir par exemple du Centre canadien d'arbitrage commercial (CCAC) situé à Montréal.

Le partage des compétences concernant les aspects procéduraux de la *Convention CIRDI* est moins évident, c'est pourquoi l'adoption d'une loi de mise en œuvre uniforme par le fédéral et les provinces a été envisagée afin de limiter les contestations constitutionnelles.[76] L'élément central de la mise en œuvre de la *Convention CIRDI* en droit interne consiste à abolir le contrôle judiciaire de la demande de reconnaissance et d'exécution des sentences CIRDI.[77] Ces dernières sont nécessairement des sentences arbitrales étrangères au regard de l'ordre juridique canadien, en raison de leur rattachement au droit international public. Or, la Cour suprême du Canada rappelait récemment dans son arrêt *Yugraneft Corp c Rexx Management Corp*[78] que la reconnaissance et l'exécution des sentences arbitrales relèvent de la compétence provinciale sur la propriété et les droits civils ainsi que sur l'administration de la justice dans la province.[79] Ainsi seules les provinces apparaîtraient compétentes pour assurer la mise en œuvre des aspects procéduraux de la *Convention CIRDI* au Canada, en abolissant le contrôle judiciaire des demandes de reconnaissance et d'exécution des sentences CIRDI par leur cour supérieure. Par exemple, la procédure de reconnaissance et d'exécution des sentences arbitrales étrangères au Québec est prévue par le *Code de procédure civile*, qui vise à mettre en œuvre la *Convention de New York*.[80] Pourtant, la législation fédérale prévoit aussi que la Cour fédérale et les cours supérieures provinciales sont compétentes pour connaître des demandes de reconnaissance et d'exécution des sentences arbitrales étrangères, toujours dans le but de mettre en œuvre la *Convention de New York*.[81] Cette mise en œuvre conjointe par le fédéral et les provinces a été souhaitée par le milieu de l'arbitrage dans les années 1980 au moment de la ratification de la *Convention de New York* par le Canada.[82]

---

[76] Dominique D'Allaire, "Loi sur le règlement des différends internationaux relatifs aux investissements étrangers et commentaires" (2009) 22 RQDI 87 à la p 96.

[77] *Convention CIRDI, supra* note 1, art 54(1); Schreuer et al, *supra* note 48 à la p 1117.

[78] 2010 CSC 19 [2010] 1 RCS 649.

[79] *Ibid* para 32; Sabourin, *supra* note 38 à la p 321, n 5. Voir *Loi constitutionnelle de 1867* (R-U), 30 & 31 Vict, c 3, reproduite dans LRC 1985, app II, n⁰ 5, art 92(13) et 92(14).

[80] *Code de procédure civile*, LRQ c C-25, art 948-951.1.

[81] *Loi sur la Convention des Nations Unies concernant les sentences arbitrales étrangères*, LRC 1985, c 16 (2e supp), art 6; *Loi d'interprétation*, LRC 1985, c I-21, art 35.

[82] Voir William C Graham, "The New York Convention of 1958: A Canadian Perspective," dans Nabil Antaki et Alain Prujiner, dir, *L'arbitrage commercial*

La compétence du Parlement fédéral pour légiférer sur la compétence des cours supérieures provinciales en matière de contrôle des demandes de reconnaissance et d'exécution des sentences arbitrales étrangères semble discutable, au regard du principe dégagé par l'arrêt *Yugraneft Corp.* Quant à la Cour fédérale, elle n'est pas une cour supérieure au sens de la Constitution du Canada, ce qui signifie qu'elle n'a aucune compétence inhérente et qu'elle n'est compétente que pour appliquer les lois fédérales qui lui donnent une telle fonction.[83] De surcroît, sa compétence demeure généralement concurrente à celle des cours supérieures provinciales, notamment lorsque la responsabilité civile de la Couronne fédérale est en jeu. La question qui se pose est celle de savoir si le Parlement fédéral peut confier cette compétence à la Cour fédérale, comme la législation fédérale le fait actuellement.[84] Cette situation doit être distinguée de celle où la Cour fédérale exerce le contrôle judiciaire de sentences arbitrales rendues au Canada sur la base de la loi fédérale sur l'arbitrage, concernant les litiges où le Canada est une partie, ou les litiges de droit maritime, où sa compétence semble indubitable.[85]

La loi fédérale de mise en œuvre de la *Convention CIRDI* prétend abolir le contrôle judiciaire des "juridictions supérieures" sur les demandes de reconnaissance et d'exécution des sentences CIRDI, ce qui vise à la fois la Cour fédérale et les cours supérieures provinciales.[86] Le législateur fédéral légifère ainsi sur la propriété et les droits civils et l'administration de la justice dans les provinces, ce

---

international, Montréal, Wilson and Lafleur, 1986 aux pp 212-13. Les participants au colloque de Québec sur l'arbitrage commercial international ont adopté une résolution en 1985 appelant le fédéral et les provinces à adopter une loi uniforme en matière d'arbitrage. Nabil Antaki et Alain Prujiner, "Avant-propos," dans *L'Arbitrage commercial international, ibid* à la p 8.

83 *Loi constitutionnelle de 1867, supra* note 79, art 101; *Loi sur la Cour fédérale,* LRC 1985 c F-7, art 17(1). Henri Brun, Guy Tremblay et Eugénie Brouillet, *Droit constitutionnel,* 5e éd, Cowansville (Qc), Yvon Blais, 2008 aux pp 810-12.

84 Graham, *supra* note 82 à la p 189. La Cour fédérale pourrait connaître des demandes de reconnaissance et d'exécution de certaines sentences arbitrales étrangères en vertu de sa compétence en matière d'amirauté.

85 Voir *Loi sur l'arbitrage commercial,* LRC 1985, c 17 (2e supp), art 5; Henri C. Alvarez, "Judicial Review of NAFTA Chapter 11 Arbitral Awards," dans Frédéric Bachand et Emmanuel Gaillard, dir, *Fifteen Years of NAFTA Chapter 11 Arbitration,* Huntington (NY), JurisNet, 2011 aux pp 123-27.

86 *Loi fédérale sur le CIRDI, supra* note 57, art 8(1); *Loi d'interprétation, supra* note 82, art 35.

qui semble à première vue devoir échapper à sa compétence constitutionnelle.[87] S'il s'était limité à abolir le contrôle judiciaire de la
Cour fédérale sur les demandes de reconnaissance et d'exécution
des sentences CIRDI, sa compétence aurait été plus plausible,
concernant par exemple les sentences arbitrales rendues à l'étranger
contre le Canada.[88] Une auteure a même avancé que le Parlement
fédéral serait compétent pour abolir le contrôle judiciaire des demandes de reconnaissance et d'exécution des sentences CIRDI
rendues contre le Canada ou contre un État étranger, alors que la
compétence provinciale se limiterait aux (éventuelles) sentences
CIRDI rendues contre une province.[89] Cette lecture du droit constitutionnel canadien est problématique et il aurait sans doute été
préférable que les lois de mise en œuvre collent davantage au partage des compétences législatives, ce qui aurait mieux garanti la
sécurité juridique de la mise en œuvre de la *Convention CIRDI* au
Canada.[90] Il apparaît indispensable que les provinces abolissent
également le contrôle judiciaire des demandes de reconnaissance
et d'exécution des sentences CIRDI, afin que les obligations pécuniaires qu'elles imposent puissent être exécutées comme un jugement de leur cour supérieure, non seulement à l'égard des sentences
CIRDI rendues contre la province, mais pour les sentences CIRDI
rendues contre un État étranger et peut-être aussi celles rendues
contre le Canada.

Il faut noter qu'une disposition de la *Convention CIRDI* autorise
les États fédéraux à "assurer l'exécution" des sentences CIRDI
par l'entremise de leurs tribunaux fédéraux, qui doivent les considérer comme des jugements définitifs des tribunaux d'une entité
fédérée.[91] Cela pourrait laisser entendre que le contrôle judiciaire
des demandes de reconnaissance et d'exécution des sentences
CIRDI demeure possible par les tribunaux fédéraux, ce qui est

---

[87] *Contra* D'Allaire, *supra* note 76 aux pp 96-97.

[88] Le Parlement fédéral est compétent pour légiférer sur la propriété publique
fédérale. *Loi constitutionnelle de 1867*, *supra* note 79, art 91(1A).

[89] D'Allaire, *supra* note 76 aux pp 96-97.

[90] Voir par ex. *Loi sur la responsabilité civile de l'État et le contentieux administratif*, LRC
1985 c C-50, art 20.1-20.4. Cette loi reconnaît le caractère exécutoire des décisions
rendues par les groupes spéciaux constitués en vertu de certains traités du Canada
sur le travail et l'environnement, comme s'il s'agissait d'ordonnance rendue par
la Cour fédérale.

[91] *Convention CIRDI*, *supra* note 1, art 51(1) *in fine*.

naturellement contraire à l'objet et au but de la *Convention CIRDI*.[92] Cette disposition problématique a été prévue à la demande des États-Unis et colle davantage à leur système judiciaire partagé qu'au système judiciaire intégré du Canada. Le fédéral ne saurait de toute façon s'approprier la compétence sur la propriété et les droits civils et l'administration de la justice dans les provinces sur la base d'un traité, puisque la mise en œuvre des traités ne constitue pas un chef de compétence au Canada.

Dans l'hypothèse où certaines provinces devaient refuser d'adopter une loi de mise en œuvre, le Canada pourrait être tenté d'utiliser la clause territoriale de la *Convention CIRDI*, qui prévoit qu'un État contractant peut exclure un territoire qu'il représente sur le plan international de son champ d'application.[93] Cette clause ne semble cependant pas avoir été prévue pour jouer le rôle d'une clause fédérale, mais plutôt pour répondre aux besoins des États européens qui possédaient toujours des colonies et des territoires outre-mer lors de la conclusion du traité.[94] La *Convention CIRDI* utilise d'ailleurs l'expression "collectivité publique" ("*constituent subdivision*") lorsqu'elle se réfère aux entités fédérées.[95] Les provinces canadiennes constituent l'assise territoriale du Canada, plutôt que des territoires dont il assurerait la représentation sur le plan international.

C. LA MISE EN ŒUVRE DE LA *CONVENTION CIRDI* AU REGARD DE LA PROTECTION CONSTITUTIONNELLE DES COURS SUPÉRIEURES

La question de la constitutionnalité des lois de mise en œuvre de la *Convention CIRDI* au regard du partage des compétences est délicate, mais elle peut aisément se résoudre au moyen d'une action législative concertée des provinces et du fédéral et d'une interprétation atténuée de leurs dispositions par les tribunaux. Une seconde question constitutionnelle se pose, mais elle soulève des difficultés d'un autre ordre. Elle touche cette fois à l'étendue de la protection constitutionnelle des cours supérieures par l'article 96 de la *Loi*

---

[92] Schreuer et al, *supra* note 47 à la p 1143-44.

[93] *Convention CIRDI*, *supra* note 1, art 70.

[94] Schreuer et al, *supra* note 47 à la p 1276-77; Sabourin, *supra* note 38 à la p 324.

[95] *Convention CIRDI*, *supra* note 1, art 25(1).

constitutionnelle de 1867.[96] Cette protection constitutionnelle a pour effet d'empêcher le législateur fédéral et les législateurs provinciaux de porter atteinte à certains attributs fondamentaux des cours supérieures au Canada. La question qui se pose est celle de savoir si le contrôle judiciaire des demandes de reconnaissance et d'exécution de sentences CIRDI fait partie des attributs des cours supérieures. Les conséquences juridiques d'une réponse affirmative sont considérables, puisque cela empêcherait le Canada de mettre complètement en œuvre la *Convention CIRDI* sans une modification constitutionnelle.

La Cour suprême du Canada a développé un critère en trois volets dans le *Renvoi relatif à la loi de 1979 sur la location résidentielle*[97] afin de déterminer si une compétence ou un pouvoir d'une cour supérieure peuvent être transférés à un tribunal inférieur ou à un tribunal administratif. Elle a repris ce critère et l'a développé davantage dans son arrêt *MacMillan Bloedel Ltd c Simpson*,[98] qui demeure l'arrêt de principe sur la protection des cours supérieures par l'article 96 de la *Loi constitutionnelle de 1867*. Il est par ailleurs acquis que cette protection constitutionnelle s'impose tant aux lois fédérales qu'aux lois provinciales.[99] Le premier volet du critère consiste à vérifier si la compétence ou le pouvoir transférés correspondent à ceux qui étaient exercés par les cours supérieures lors de la Confédération.[100] Cette recherche historique vise à vérifier s'il s'agit bien du transfert d'une compétence ou d'un pouvoir des cours supérieures qui sont protégés par la Constitution. Dans l'affirmative, les deux autres volets du critère visent à vérifier si ce transfert est néanmoins acceptable. Le deuxième volet consiste à déterminer si la compétence ou le pouvoir transférés demeurent de nature judiciaire dans leur nouveau cadre institutionnel ou s'ils prennent une coloration administrative.[101] Le troisième volet consiste à examiner la fonction

---

[96] La question de l'incidence de l'article 96 de la *Loi constitutionnelle de 1867* a été brièvement abordée par un auteur dans le contexte de la ratification de la *Convention de New York* par le Canada, concernant l'attribution aux arbitres du pouvoir d'imposer des mesures conservatoires. Graham, *supra* note 82 à la p 200.

[97] *Renvoi relatif à la loi de 1979 sur la location résidentielle*, [1981] 1 RCS 714, 734-36.

[98] *MacMillan Bloedel Ltd c Simpson*, [1995] 4 RCS 725.

[99] *McEvoy c Nouveau-Brunswick (PG)* [1983] 1 RCS 704, 721.

[100] *MacMillan Bloedel Ltd c Simpson*, *supra* note 98 aux para 738 (jc Lamer, motifs maj), 765 (j McLachlin, motifs conc sur ce point).

[101] *Ibid.*

globale du tribunal afin d'évaluer dans tout son contexte institutionnel la compétence ou le pouvoir transférés.[102] Le tribunal inférieur ou le tribunal administratif ne peuvent exercer de pouvoirs
ou de fonctions qui appartenaient historiquement aux cours supérieures que s'ils sont simplement complémentaires ou accessoires
à leurs fonctions administratives générales. Une étape préalable à
l'application du critère consiste à qualifier la compétence ou le
pouvoir transférés selon la nature du différend plutôt que selon le
recours exercé, puisque plusieurs recours actuels n'existaient pas
en 1867.[103] Les cinq juges de la majorité ont ajouté une étape complémentaire au critère, avec laquelle les quatre juges dissidents
n'étaient pas d'accord. Elle consiste à examiner si la compétence
ou le pouvoir transférés relèvent des compétences ou des pouvoirs
"inhérents" ou "fondamentaux" des cours supérieures.[104] Dans un
tel cas, la compétence ou le pouvoir ne peuvent être retirés aux
cours supérieures, puisqu'ils font partie de leur caractère essentiel
ou de leurs attributs immanents. Cette étape finale vise à répondre
à la question fondamentale de savoir s'il est légal de "dépouiller"
une cour supérieure de cette compétence ou de ce pouvoir.[105]

Dans l'affaire *Council of Canadians*, ce critère a été appliqué aux
tribunaux arbitraux institués en vertu du chapitre 11 de l'*ALÉNA*.
La conclusion principale de la Cour supérieure de l'Ontario était
que la protection constitutionnelle des cours supérieures garantie
par l'article 96 de la *Loi constitutionnelle de 1867* ne concerne pas
l'*ALÉNA* en tant que traité ne faisant pas partie du droit en vigueur
au Canada.[106] La Cour d'appel n'a pas confirmé ce raisonnement,
afin de ne pas décider s'il convenait d'ajouter une étape concernant
l'applicabilité du critère de l'article 96.[107] Elle a toutefois endossé
l'application du critère faite en *obiter dictum* par la juge Pepall.[108]
Cette dernière avait qualifié avec justesse la compétence ou le pouvoir de ces tribunaux comme étant de connaître des différends de

---

102 *Ibid* aux para 739 (jc Lamer, motifs maj), 765 (j McLachlin, motifs conc sur ce
point).

103 *Ibid* aux para 740 (jc Lamer, motifs maj), 765 (j McLachlin, motifs min).

104 *Ibid* aux para 747-49 (jc Lamer, motifs maj).

105 René Pepin, "Les parlements peuvent-ils vider les cours supérieures de leur
juridiction? Ont-elles des pouvoirs "inhérents," "inaliénable"?" Réflexions sur
la décision *MacMillan Bloedel Ltd*, (1996-97) 22 Queen's LJ 487 à la p 497.

106 *Council of Canadians, supra* note 32 au para 44 (CS Ont).

107 *Ibid* aux para 26-29 (CA Ont).

108 *Ibid* au para 36 (CA Ont).

droit international public, c'est-à-dire de déterminer si le Canada viole les obligations prévues par le chapitre 11 de l'*ALÉNA*. Comme de tels différends ne faisaient pas partie de la compétence ou des pouvoirs des cours supérieures en 1867, le premier volet du critère n'a pas été rempli.[109] Quant au nouveau critère de l'arrêt *MacMillan Bloedel*, la Cour supérieure a jugé que la compétence des tribunaux arbitraux n'est pas exclusive en ce qui concerne les faits à la base du différend, puisque l'article 1121 de l'*ALÉNA* prévoit que les tribunaux canadiens conservent leur compétence ou leurs pouvoirs sur les procédures d'injonction, les procédures déclaratoires et les autres recours extraordinaires ne supposant pas le paiement de dommages-intérêts.[110] La Cour d'appel a jugé encore plus simplement qu'aucune compétence ou aucun pouvoir n'était retiré aux cours supérieures, puisque les investisseurs étrangers conservent la liberté d'exercer un recours devant les tribunaux canadiens plutôt que devant un tribunal arbitral.[111] Cette affaire semble toutefois devoir être distinguée de la question de l'abolition du contrôle des demandes de reconnaissance et d'exécution des sentences CIRDI, puisque la nature du différend concerné n'est pas la même. L'affaire *Council of Canadians* portait plutôt sur les différends relatifs à la violation par le Canada de ses obligations internationales au titre du chapitre 11 de l'*ALÉNA*. La Cour d'appel de l'Ontario elle-même a fait la distinction entre ces différends et ceux qui peuvent en découler concernant la reconnaissance et l'exécution des sentences arbitrales.[112]

Afin d'évaluer si la mise en œuvre de la *Convention CIRDI* est compatible avec la protection constitutionnelle des cours supérieures au Canada, il convient d'abord de définir la compétence ou le pouvoir qui sont transférés ou retirés, selon la nature du différend en cause. Le contrôle judiciaire de la demande de reconnaissance et d'exécution des sentences CIRDI, qui sont des sentences arbitrales étrangères, est enlevé aux cours supérieures pour être remplacé par le contrôle exercé par un comité *ad hoc* d'annulation institué sur la base de la *Convention CIRDI*.[113] Ce contrôle est actuellement

---

[109] *Ibid* aux para 52 (CS Ont), 51 (CA Ont).

[110] *Ibid* au para 53 (CS Ont).

[111] *Ibid* au para 53 (CA Ont).

[112] *Ibid* au para 48 (CA Ont).

[113] *Convention CIRDI, supra* note 1, art 52. Les motifs d'annulation de la sentence arbitrale au regard de la *Convention CIRDI* sont: vice dans la constitution du

exercé par les cours supérieures provinciales et la Cour fédérale en vertu de lois basées sur la loi-type de la CNUDCI, qui donne effet aux dispositions de la *Convention de New York*.[114] Malgré quelques différences, une étude récente conclut à la similitude des principes qui sous-tendent le contrôle judiciaire effectué aux termes de la *Convention de New York* et le contrôle fait par le comité *ad hoc* d'annulation aux termes de la *Convention CIRDI*.[115]

Sans prétendre vider la question, des doutes peuvent être soulevés quant à la compatibilité des lois de mise en œuvre de la *Convention CIRDI* avec l'article 96 de la *Loi constitutionnelle de 1867*. Si le contrôle judiciaire des demandes de reconnaissance et d'exécution des sentences arbitrales étrangères n'existait sans doute pas au Canada en 1867, puisque l'institution de l'arbitrage était alors inconnue en droit canadien,[116] le contrôle des demandes concernant

---

tribunal arbitral; excès de pouvoir manifeste du tribunal arbitral; corruption d'un membre du tribunal arbitral; inobservance grave d'une règle fondamentale de procédure; défaut de motifs.

[114] CNUDCI, *Loi-type de la CNUDCI sur l'arbitrage commercial international, 1985, avec les amendements adoptés en 2006*, Vienne, NU, 2008, art 34; *Convention de New-York*, *supra* note 37, art V. Voir *Loi sur la Convention des Nations Unies concernant les sentences arbitrales étrangères*, *supra* note 81, art 6; *Loi sur l'arbitrage commercial*, LRC 1985, c 17 (2ᵉ supp), art 5; *Code de procédure civile*, *supra* note 80, art 949, 950. Les motifs d'annulation de la sentence arbitrale au regard de la *Convention de New York* et de la *Loi-type* sont: incapacité des parties ou invalidité de la convention d'arbitrage; impossibilité pour une partie de faire valoir ses moyens dans la procédure d'arbitrage; sentence portant sur un différend non visé par le compromis ou la clause compromissoire; défaut dans la constitution du tribunal arbitral ou la procédure d'arbitrage; sentence non obligatoire ou annulée ou suspendue par une autorité compétente; non-arbitrabilité de l'objet du différend; reconnaissance ou exécution de la sentence contraire à l'ordre public.

[115] Armand de Mestral, "L'annulation des sentences arbitrales 'investisseur-État' en vertu de la *Loi-type* au Canada et du régime du CIRDI," dans Frédéric Bachand et Fabien Gélinas, dir, *D'une réforme à une autre. Regards croisés sur l'arbitrage au Québec*, Cowansville (Qc), Yvon Blais, 2013 à la p 189. Il faut toutefois noter que le motif de la contravention à l'ordre public n'existe pas dans le régime du CIRDI.

[116] John E.C. Brierley, "Overview of International Commercial Arbitration in Quebec and in the Canadian Common Law Provinces," dans Nabil Antaki et Alain Prujiner, dir, *L'arbitrage commercial international*, Montréal, Wilson & Lafleur, 1986 aux pp 276-78. Les provinces de common law ont toutes calqué leur première loi sur l'arbitrage sur la loi anglaise de 1889, tandis que la validité des clauses compromissoires n'a été reconnue en droit civil québécois qu'en 1983, dans un arrêt de la Cour suprême du Canada. Voir *Arbitration Act, 1889* (R-U), 52 & 53 Vict, c 49; *Zodiak International c Polish People's Republic*, [1983] 1 RCS 529.

les jugements étrangers existait.[117] L'étape préalable au critère de l'article 96 consiste à qualifier la compétence ou le pouvoir transférés selon la nature du différend, plutôt que selon le recours exercé, afin de pallier l'inexistence de certains recours en 1867. Dans la mesure où les demandes de reconnaissance et d'exécution de sentences étrangères peuvent être assimilées aux demandes de reconnaissance et d'exécution des jugements étrangers, la mise en œuvre de la *Convention CIRDI* transférerait une compétence ou un pouvoir appartenant historiquement aux cours supérieures en faveur des comités *ad hoc* d'annulation du CIRDI. La nature similaire de ces différends pourrait résider dans le recours commun qui est fait à l'appareil judiciaire étatique afin de rendre exécutoire une décision de justice (arbitrale ou judiciaire) étrangère.[118] Ces différends soulèvent la même question de "[l]'équilibre délicat entre les besoins contradictoires de la protection des patrimoines et du respect des décisions susceptibles de les affecter."[119] Ce transfert aux comités *ad hoc* d'annulation du CIRDI serait difficilement justifiable au regard des deuxième et troisième volets du critère de l'article 96, puisque le contrôle exercé par le comité *ad hoc* sur les sentences CIRDI demeure de nature judiciaire et qu'il s'agit de la seule fonction exercée par le comité. En somme, si le contrôle judiciaire des demandes de reconnaissance et d'exécution des sentences arbitrales étrangères devait être assimilé à celui des demandes concernant les jugements étrangers, il semble que la mise en œuvre

[117] Voir Ethel Groffier, *Précis de droit international privé québécois*, 4ᵉ éd, Cowansville (Qc), Yvon Blais, 1990 à la p 284; Édouard Fabre-Surveyer, "La conception du droit international privé d'après la doctrine et la pratique au Canada" (1935) 53 Rec Cours 177 aux pp 244-56; Eugène Lafleur, *The Conflict of Laws in the Province of Quebec*, Montréal, Théorêt, 1898 aux pp 239-47.

[118] Voir Alain Prujiner, "L'exécution des sentences arbitrales internationales au Québec," dans Nabil Antaki et Alain Prujiner, dir, *L'arbitrage commercial international*, Montréal, Wilson & Lafleur, 1986, 289 aux pp 289-91. La Cour fédérale soumet les demandes de reconnaissance et d'exécution des sentences arbitrales et des jugements étrangers aux mêmes règles de procédure. *Règles de la Cour fédérale*, DORS/98-106, art 326-34. L'approche traditionnelle de la jurisprudence québécoise considérait aussi les sentences arbitrales étrangères comme des jugements étrangers, mais ils sont maintenant soumis à des dispositions distinctes par le *Code de procédure civile*, sauf en ce qui concerne la règle sur la défense orale de la contestation des demandes de reconnaissance et d'exécution. Groffier, *supra* note 117 à la p 331; Prujiner, *ibid* à la p 300; *Code de procédure civile*, *supra* note 80, art 175.2(6), 785-86, 948-52.1.

[119] Prujiner, *ibid* à la p 289.

complète de la *Convention CIRDI* puisse être problématique au regard de l'article 96 de la *Loi constitutionnelle de 1867*.

Puisque le contrôle judiciaire des cours supérieures est aboli à l'égard des demandes de reconnaissance et d'exécution des sentences CIRDI, il est nécessaire d'examiner aussi l'incidence du critère complémentaire élaboré par la majorité dans l'arrêt *MacMillan Bloedel* concernant les pouvoirs inhérents des cours supérieures. La jurisprudence anglaise et canadienne a rejeté l'idée que le contrôle judiciaire des sentences arbitrales rendues au Royaume-Uni ou au Canada fait partie des pouvoirs inhérents des cours supérieures, ce qui signifie qu'elles ne peuvent pas prétendre exercer leur contrôle sur ces sentences au-delà de ce que leur permet la législation sur l'arbitrage.[120] La Cour suprême du Canada a par ailleurs exclu la soumission de l'arbitrage conventionnel au pouvoir de surveillance et de contrôle des tribunaux inférieurs, ce qui confirme que les cours supérieures n'ont pas de pouvoirs inhérents à l'égard des arbitrages se déroulant au Canada.[121] Ce rejet serait fondé sur la nécessaire séparation entre l'arbitrage conventionnel qui relève de la sphère privée et l'appareil judiciaire étatique qui relève de la sphère publique.[122]

Il semble néanmoins qu'il faille distinguer le contrôle judiciaire de l'arbitrage conventionnel se déroulant au Canada du contrôle judiciaire des demandes de reconnaissance et d'exécution de sentences arbitrales étrangères. S'il est clairement établi que le premier ne fait pas partie des pouvoirs inhérents des cours supérieures, la question demeure ouverte quant au second. La nature de ces différends, où l'appareil judiciaire étatique est sollicité afin de rendre exécutoire la sentence arbitrale rendue à l'étranger, fait en sorte qu'un rattachement plus direct existe entre la sphère privée et la sphère publique. Ce rattachement s'impose d'autant plus que les différends soumis au CIRDI ne sont pas purement privés mais bien mixtes, opposant une partie privée à un État et ayant généralement le droit international public comme droit applicable. Au vu des

---

[120] Frédéric Bachand, *L'intervention du juge canadien avant et durant un arbitrage commercial international*, Cowansville (Qc), Yvon Blais, 2005 aux pp 119-24. Voir *Bremer Vulkan Schiffbau Und Maschinenfabrik c South India Shipping Corporation Ltd*, [1981] AC 909 (Chambre des Lords); *Berthout c IC2C Communications Inc*, [1998] RJQ 1263 (CS Qué).

[121] *Desputeaux c Éditions Chouette (1987) inc*, 2003 CSC 17 [2003] 1 RCS 178; Bachand, *ibid* à la p 127.

[122] Bachand, *supra* note 120 aux pp 124 et 126.

balises dégagées par la Cour suprême du Canada concernant la notion évanescente de pouvoirs inhérents des cours supérieures, il ne semble pas exclu que le contrôle des demandes de reconnaissance et d'exécution des sentences arbitrales étrangères en fasse partie. Le fondement de la notion est que les cours supérieures ont besoin de ces pouvoirs pour maintenir leur autorité en tant que cours supérieures, ainsi que pour empêcher qu'on fasse obstacle à leur procédure ou que l'on en abuse.[123] La majorité de la Cour suprême juge qu'ils comprennent "les pouvoirs essentiels à l'administration de la justice et au maintien de la primauté du droit."[124] Le contrôle par les cours supérieures des demandes de reconnaissance et d'exécution des sentences arbitrales étrangères leur permet d'empêcher que l'on abuse de l'appareil judiciaire canadien pour exécuter ces sentences, ce qui assure l'équilibre entre la protection des droits de propriété au Canada et le respect des décisions étrangères, et contribue au maintien de la primauté du droit. Il ne semble donc pas exclu que l'on puisse juger que le contrôle judiciaire de ces demandes de reconnaissance et d'exécution des sentences arbitrales étrangères relève des pouvoirs inhérents des cours supérieures. L'abolition de ce pouvoir inhérent à l'égard des sentences CIRDI violerait dès lors l'article 96 de la *Loi constitutionnelle de 1867*. Face à cette incertitude juridique et compte tenu des contestations judiciaires antérieures de la constitutionnalité du chapitre 11 de l'*ALÉNA* et de l'éventuelle ratification de l'APIE Canada-Chine, le risque que les lois de mise en œuvre de la *Convention CIRDI* soient contestées à leur tour est réel.

D.   VERS LA RECONNAISSANCE DE LA CAPACITÉ DES PROVINCES
      CANADIENNES AU CIRDI?

Un aspect original de la *Convention CIRDI* est qu'elle permet à l'État contractant de désigner les "collectivités publiques" et les "organismes dépendant de lui" auxquels il accepte de reconnaître la capacité d'agir comme partie dans un arbitrage CIRDI.[125] Cette reconnaissance permet aux collectivités publiques de consentir à l'arbitrage CIRDI dans la mesure où l'État contractant approuve ce

---

123 *MacMillan Bloedel, supra* note 100, 749-50; IH Jacob, "The Inherent Jurisdiction of the Court" (1970) 23 CLP 23 à la p 27.

124 *MacMillan Bloedel, supra* note 100, 754.

125 *Convention CIRDI, supra* note 1, art 25(1).

consentement, ou s'il a renoncé à cette condition d'approbation.[126] La notion de collectivité publique se veut la plus flexible possible, afin d'englober toute collectivité territoriale existant au sein de l'État contractant, ce qui comprend notamment les entités fédérées des États fédéraux, comme l'exprime plus clairement l'expression "*constituent subdivision*" employée dans la version anglaise du traité.[127] L'Australie demeure à ce jour le seul État fédéral ayant reconnu la capacité de ses entités fédérées par une désignation formelle transmise au CIRDI, tout en renonçant à la condition d'approbation de leur consentement à l'arbitrage.[128] Les seules autres collectivités publiques ayant été désignées par un État contractant sont les territoires insulaires dépendants du Royaume-Uni, ainsi que la région administrative du Kutai occidental, située en Indonésie dans la province du Kalimantan oriental.

Ces désignations n'altèrent pas du tout les règles du droit international général sur la responsabilité de l'État pour le fait de ses collectivités publiques.[129] Peu importe qu'un État contractant ait fait une telle désignation ou non, les actions ou omissions de ses collectivités publiques qui violent ses obligations internationales lui sont attribuables et constituent un fait internationalement illicite qui engage pleinement sa responsabilité internationale. En revanche, la violation par une collectivité publique d'un contrat auquel elle est partie et qui ne contreviendrait à aucune obligation internationale de l'État contractant n'engage aucunement la responsabilité internationale de ce dernier.[130] Une telle hypothèse peut se présenter si aucune clause parapluie existe dans les accords sur

---

[126] *Ibid* au 25(3).

[127] *Gouvernement de la province du Kalimantan oriental c PT Kaltim Prima Coal*, Sentence, CIRDI Aff n° ARB/07/3 au para 191 (28 décembre 2009); Schreuer et al, *supra* note 47 aux pp 152-53.

[128] CIRDI, *Designation by Contracting States Regarding Constituent Subdivisions or Agencies (Art 25(1) and (3) of the Convention)*, Doc n° ICSID/8-C (Février 2014).

[129] CDI, "Projet d'articles sur la responsabilité de l'État pour fait internationalement illicite et commentaires y relatifs," dans *Annuaire de la Commission du droit international*, 2001, vol. 2, 2ᵉ partie, New York, NU, 2007 (A/CN.4/SER.A/2001/Add.1), 26, art 4 et para 9-10; Schreuer et al, *supra* note 47 aux pp 150-52. Voir généralement Charles-Emmanuel Côté, "Les difficultés d'application du principe d'unité de l'État fédéral dans le droit de la responsabilité de l'État : retour sur le(s) livre(s) d'André Momméja et Maurice Donot " (2013) 117 RGDIP 769.

[130] *Salini Costruttori SpA c Maroc*, Sentence sur la compétence, CIRDI Aff n° ARB/00/4, 129 JDI 196, aux para 60-62 (TBI Italie-Maroc, 23 juillet 2001).

l'investissement conclus par l'État contractant, ou encore si aucun accord existe avec l'État d'origine de l'investisseur étranger. Dans un tel cas, la violation d'un contrat conclu entre un investisseur étranger et une collectivité publique pourrait néanmoins être soumise à l'arbitrage CIRDI, si la collectivité publique a été dûment désignée au CIRDI et si son consentement à l'arbitrage a reçu l'approbation par son État contractant, si cette condition n'a pas été levée. Un tel arbitrage ne serait pas fondé sur un traité d'investissement, mais plutôt sur le contrat.

La rare jurisprudence du CIRDI sur ces questions montre que la désignation de la collectivité publique par son État contractant est indispensable pour que le tribunal CIRDI soit compétent. Dans l'affaire *Cable Television of Nevis Ltd c Fédération de Saint-Kitts-et-Nevis*,[131] l'absence de désignation de l'Île de Nevis par l'État fédéral a empêché l'investisseur étranger d'utiliser la clause CIRDI pourtant prévue dans le contrat qu'il avait conclu avec l'entité fédérée. En outre, l'investisseur étranger avait tenté d'attraire devant un tribunal CIRDI non pas l'entité fédérée, mais plutôt l'État fédéral qui n'était pas partie au contrat d'investissement. La *Convention CIRDI* n'impose aucune exigence formelle concernant la désignation d'une collectivité publique; la désignation peut être générale ou *ad hoc*, transmise officiellement au CIRDI ou non. L'intention de l'État contractant de désigner la collectivité publique doit néanmoins être claire et ne peut être inférée de documents équivoques, *a fortiori* si l'État contractant manifeste explicitement son opposition à cette désignation.[132]

La ratification de la *Convention CIRDI* par le Canada ouvre des perspectives nouvelles pour la participation des entités fédérées à l'arbitrage des différends relatifs aux investissements. Aucun État australien n'a été partie à un arbitrage CIRDI à ce jour et la politique récente de l'Australie rejette désormais l'arbitrage entre investisseur étranger et État.[133] Aucune entité fédérée n'a été partie à un arbitrage CIRDI fondé sur un traité; seule l'affaire *Cable Television*

131 Sentence, CIRDI Aff n° ARB/95/2, 13 ICSID Rev 328 aux pp 345-52 et 391 (13 janvier 1997). Voir *Gouvernement de la province du Kalimantan oriental, supra* note 127 au para 202.

132 *Gouvernement de la province du Kalimantan oriental, supra* note 127 aux para 192, 198, 200-1; Schreuer et al, *supra* note 47 à la p 156.

133 Jürgen Kurtz, "Australia's Rejection of Investor-State Arbitration: Causation, Omission and Implication" (2012) 27 ICSID Rev 65. Le nouveau gouvernement australien semble toutefois avoir tempéré la politique de son prédécesseur avec la signature le 5 décembre 2013 d'un accord de libre-échange avec la Corée du

of Nevis Ltd a impliqué une entité fédérée, mais elle était fondée sur un contrat d'investissement et l'entité fédérée n'était pas partie à l'arbitrage. Le Canada demeure l'un des États les plus actifs dans le contentieux de l'investissement et sa politique commerciale extérieure soutient la poursuite de la conclusion d'accords prévoyant l'arbitrage entre investisseur étranger et État. Au surplus, le premier ministre du Canada a publiquement fait part de son mécontentement face à la situation actuelle, où le fédéral doit indemniser les investisseurs étrangers lésés par les agissements des provinces qui contreviennent aux obligations internationales du Canada.[134] Cette annonce a été faite dans le contexte de l'affaire *AbitibiBowater Inc c Canada*,[135] où le fédéral a dû se résoudre à verser plus de 130 millions de dollars US dans un règlement amiable avec l'investisseur américain lésé par une expropriation directe et sans indemnisation faite par la province de Terre-Neuve-et-Labrador. Des investisseurs étrangers continuent par ailleurs à présenter régulièrement des réclamations contre des mesures de provinces canadiennes.

Le gouvernement fédéral a fait part de son intention de désigner les provinces qui le souhaiteront au CIRDI et de renoncer comme l'Australie à la condition d'approbation préalable du consentement des provinces à l'arbitrage CIRDI.[136] Compte tenu de la politique du Québec sur sa place dans les forums internationaux, il semble probable qu'il demandera à Ottawa sa désignation au CIRDI.[137] Quelles seraient les conséquences d'une telle désignation? Elle ne changerait rien à la responsabilité actuelle du Canada pour les mesures québécoises qui sont contraires aux APIE et aux accords de libre-échange du Canada, puisque la désignation d'une collectivité publique n'altère en rien les règles du droit international général sur la responsabilité de l'État fédéral pour le fait de son

---

Sud, qui prévoit un système d'arbitrage pour les différends entre investisseur étranger et État. Luke Nottage, "Arbitration Rights Back for the South Korea-Australia FTA," en ligne: EastAsiaForum <http://www.eastasiaforum.org/2014/01/01/arbitration-rights-back-for-the-south-korea-australia-fta/>.

[134] "Provinces Should Pay for NAFTA Losses: PM," *CBC News* (26 août 2010), en ligne: CBC <http://www.cbc.ca/news/canada/newfoundland-labrador/provinces-should-pay-for-nafta-losses-pm-1.881721>; Bertrand Marotte et John Ibbitson, "Provinces on Hook for Future Trade Disputes: Harper," *Globe and Mail* (26 août 2010).

[135] Sentence d'accord des Parties (chapitre 11 *ALÉNA*, 15 décembre 2010); Côté, *supra* note 16 aux pp 288-89.

[136] CHLC, *Rapport sur le CIRDI*, *supra* note 39 au para 15.

[137] Voir *supra* note 73 et le texte correspondant.

entité fédérée. La ratification de la *Convention CIRDI* permettra donc la contestation de mesures québécoises au CIRDI, mais le Canada sera la partie visée par ces réclamations. À cet égard, les propos tenus par le ministre des Relations internationales du Québec dans les débats à l'Assemblée nationale sur l'approbation de la *Convention CIRDI* sont équivoques, dans la mesure où ils laissent entendre qu'une mesure québécoise ne peut pas être contestée au CIRDI sans le consentement du Québec.[138] Ce qui est vrai par contre, c'est que le Québec ne pourra pas être attrait devant un tribunal CIRDI sans son consentement, et ce, même s'il est désigné au CIRDI par le Canada.[139]

Deux hypothèses de consentement à l'arbitrage CIRDI par une province sont envisageables. D'une part, une province désignée au CIRDI pourrait vouloir consentir à l'arbitrage CIRDI concernant les réclamations d'investisseurs étrangers fondées sur les APIE et les accords de libre-échange du Canada. Une telle participation des provinces n'est cependant pas prévue par ces accords, ce qui soulève de nombreuses difficultés juridiques, mais elle pourrait répondre au souhait du gouvernement fédéral de ne plus payer la note pour les provinces. À supposer que cela soit possible, le consentement d'une province n'écarterait pas celui du Canada, mais s'y ajouterait, ce qui ne manquerait pas de soulever à nouveau des difficultés pratiques réelles.[140] Il faut rappeler que le Québec a formellement souscrit aux principes et aux règles du chapitre 11 de l'*ALÉNA* au moyen d'une loi, mais cette approbation législative ne vaut sans doute pas consentement à l'arbitrage CIRDI.[141] D'autre part, une province désignée au CIRDI pourrait stipuler une clause CIRDI dans un contrat conclu avec un investisseur étranger. Dans la mesure où la violation du contrat ne suffirait pas à engager la responsabilité du Canada au regard de ses accords sur l'investissement, cette stipulation offrirait une protection juridique accrue aux investisseurs étrangers, qui jouiraient d'un recours à l'arbitrage CIRDI contre la province sur le fondement de ce contrat, en plus d'un recours à l'arbitrage commercial international. Ceci pourrait contribuer à rendre la province plus attrayante pour les investissements étrangers.

[138] *Journal des débats, supra* note 68 à la p 5183.

[139] Voir Sabourin, *supra* note 38 à la p 325.

[140] Voir Schreuer et al, *supra* note 47 à la p 152.

[141] *Loi concernant la mise en œuvre des accords de commerce international,* LRQ c M-35.2, art 2, 6.

Canadian Practice in International Law / Pratique canadienne en matière de droit international

At the Department of Foreign Affairs, Trade and Development in 2013 / Au ministère des Affaires étrangères, Commerce et Développement en 2013

compiled by / préparé par

BILL CROSBIE

LAW OF THE SEA

United Nations Convention on the Law of the Sea — Commemoration of the Thirtieth Anniversary of Opening for Signature

On 10 December 2013, the Canadian Representative to the Western Europe and Others Group (WEOG) of the United Nations delivered the following statement:

Mr. Chairman,

I have the honour, and I am personally delighted, to speak on behalf of Member States of the Western Europe and Others Group.

Bill Crosbie, The Legal Adviser, Department of Foreign Affairs, Trade and Development, Ottawa, Canada. The extracts from official correspondence contained in this survey have been made available by courtesy of the Department of Foreign Affairs, Trade and Development. Some of the correspondence from which extracts are given was provided for the general guidance of the enquirer in relation to specific facts that are often not described in full in the extracts within this compilation. The statements of law and practice should not necessarily be regarded as definitive.

We are here to mark the 30th anniversary of the opening for signature of the United Nations Convention on the Law of the Sea on December 10, 1982 at Montego Bay in Jamaica, at the conclusion of the Third United Nations Conference on the Law of the Sea. This Conference was an enormous and highly complex endeavour and the Convention is the culmination of many years of effort by more than 150 States. We especially recognize the crucial role played by Ambassador Arvid Pardo of Malta and, in particular, his visionary speech delivered on 1 November 1967.

The Convention is exceptional for its scope and the comprehensiveness of the legal regime that it established for the use of the world's oceans and seas. The Convention provides a framework for many aspects of oceans governance — ranging from navigation to marine pollution and from dispute settlement to the management of living and non-living marine resources.

Of particular note is the Convention's successful blend of zonal and functional approaches and its balance of rights and obligations, its gathering of Coastal States, flag States and landlocked States under one overarching instrument. This was achieved by recognizing that ocean issues are interrelated, like the oceans themselves.

Of enduring and fundamental importance is the system of maritime zones established by the Convention, with distinctive legal features. In that regard, I note that the creation of the exclusive economic zone clarified the scope of Coastal states' rights and jurisdiction under international law.

Those were some of the key elements to the Convention's undeniable contribution to peace, security and the rule of law. In that regard, we also note the significant contribution made by the International Tribunal for the Law of the Sea, and the International Court of Justice, to the peaceful settlement of disputes for law of the sea-related issues, and by the Commission on the Limits of the Continental Shelf to the orderly process of defining the interface between the continental shelf and the Area. The work of these bodies, along with that of the International Seabed Authority, contributes to predictability and clarity in the maritime domain and the preservation of a stable world order.

The Convention also provided focus and impetus to existing international organizations such as the International Maritime Organization. Building on the principles laid down in UNCLOS, the IMO has since tackled among other issues dumping, ballast waters and invasive species, using its specialized expertise to improve maritime safety and shipping standards, an essential task given the importance of shipping to our global prosperity.

While we can be proud of the achievements of Montego Bay, the intervening years have demonstrated that the full and effective implementation of the Convention has not yet been achieved and that we still have work ahead of us. For example, as evidence of illegal, unreported and unregulated fishing shows, we must do a better job as flag states to complement actions taken by Coastal states and Port states. And preservation and protection of the marine environment will undoubtedly figure as one of the main priorities of the years to come.

We must also support efforts by institutions to better coordinate in accordance with their respective mandates given by Member States. Given the broad-based, wide-ranging and interconnected nature of ocean activities, not only is international coordination needed but also coordination at the bilateral, regional and global levels. Better integration among a wide range of actors constitutes a valuable objective to move the collective oceans governance agenda forward.

As we face the next 30 years — and beyond — it is inevitable that new challenges will arise. However, we are hopeful that the importance of the issues will spur us to find consensus on the best way to address them successfully and preserve the oceans for future generations.

In closing, with the goal of universal participation in sight, we call on States that have not yet done so to become parties to UNCLOS.

INTERNATIONAL LAW COMMISSION (ILC)

ILC — Draft Articles on the Expulsion of Aliens

On 31 December 2013, the Mission of Canada to the ILC delivered the following written comments on the *Draft Articles on the Expulsion of Aliens.*

1. Canada has reviewed the *Draft Articles on the Expulsion of Aliens* and wishes to share the following comments and views on definitions, language and scope; non-refoulement; grounds for expulsion; disguised expulsion and extradition; detention; and the rights conferred in the Draft Articles.

2. Firstly, the legal status and purpose of the Draft Articles merits clarification. Given existing and inconsistent State practice, precedent and doctrine in this area, Canada does not view the Draft Articles as either a progressive development or a formulation and systematization of rules of international law. Canada encourages the Commission to include a clear statement at the beginning of the Draft Articles that the

Articles neither codify existing international law nor re-interpret long-standing and well understood treaties.

3. The Commentary to Article 3 suggests legal force by stating that, "the right of expulsion is regulated by the present Draft Articles and by other applicable rules of international law." Canada would replace this statement with, "A State may only expel an alien in accordance with its international legal obligations."

4. Similarly, the Draft Articles cannot "set out" human rights since they do not constitute a human rights agreement. Thus Canada recommends the removal of the phrase, "including those set out in the present draft articles" in Article 14(2).

5. Several references are made to obligations under "general international law." These references should clarify whether this term includes customary international law and treaty law.

6. Several references to the Declaration on the Human Rights of Individuals Who are not Nationals of the Country in which They Live appear in the Commentary to these Draft Articles. Canada objects to any suggestion that this Declaration represents customary international law.

7. Finally, given the overlap and connections between the Articles, Canada has chosen to respond thematically (rather than Article by Article).

Definitions, linguistic changes, and scope

8. Canada would remove "refugee" from the definition of "expulsion" in Article 2(a) (Definitions). As drafted, it remains unclear whether "refugee" in this context is meant to apply to "protected persons", "refugee claimants", or others. The definition of "expulsion" in the Draft Articles needs to be clarified as multiple interpretations are possible with varying potential implications.

9. Article 6(2) (Prohibition of the expulsion of refugees) refers to a "refugee... who has applied for recognition of refugee status". For greater clarity, if the intention of the Draft Articles is to safeguard against the expulsion of a person whose refugee status determination application is pending, then paragraph (2) should therefore refer to "alien", rather than "refugee".

10. The definition of "alien" includes stateless persons, according to the Commentary to Article 2 (Definitions). Article 7 (Prohibition on the expulsion of stateless persons), which distinctly regards stateless persons,

is thus unnecessary unless the Draft Articles advocate separate, additional protection for stateless persons.

11. Canada recommends that the grounds for discrimination listed in Article 15 (Obligation not to discriminate) include sexual orientation.

Non-refoulement

12. Canada recommends that Article 6 (Refugees), Article 23 (Right to life) and Article 24 (Prohibition on expulsion to torture) be grouped and re-worked to better reflect existing norms of international law. The prohibition on the expulsion of aliens to torture or cruel or unusual treatment is addressed in each of Articles 6(3), 23 and 24, with an important distinction. Article 6(3) allows for expulsion in such circumstances if there are reasonable grounds for regarding the person as a danger to the security of the asylum country or the person is convicted of a serious crime, posing a danger to the community of the asylum country. Conversely, Articles 23 and 24 provide an unconditional prohibition against refoulement to torture or cruel or unusual treatment.

13. Canada agrees with the formulation in Article 6(3) in respect of the expulsion of refugees absent a risk of death or torture.

14. Article 23(1) (Obligation not to expel an alien to a State where his or her life or freedom would be threatened) would prevent expulsion to a State where the alien's freedom would be threatened. This is not Canada's understanding of the current scope of international law. States may expel to a situation of detention in another State. States Parties to the Convention relating to the Status of Refugees may not expel to persecution on grounds named in that Convention. More generally, States may not expel to a foreseeable real and personal risk of being subjected to torture or other similarly serious violations of human rights. A State that retains the death penalty may expel to the death penalty.

15. Canada agrees with the obligation not to expel an alien to a real risk of torture as described in Article 24, as this is also contained in the Convention against Torture (CAT). However, Canada does not agree with the expanded scope of Article 24, in particular the inclusion of "degrading" treatment. This term is an overbroad interpretation of the obligation of non-refoulement implicit in Article 7 of the International Covenant on Civil and Political Rights (ICCPR). It fails to capture the essence of non-refoulement, which is the obligation not to return someone to serious violations of human rights such as torture.

Grounds for expulsion

16. Canada notes the comparison between Article 5(2) (Grounds for Expulsion) and Article 6(1) (Prohibition on the Expulsion of Refugees). Article 5(2) limits the expulsion of aliens to grounds provided by law, including national security and public order. Article 6(1) provides national security and public order as the only permissible grounds for expulsion of refugees. Canada would also allow expulsion of aliens, including individuals recognized as Convention refugees by other countries, found to have committed gross or systematic human rights violations, war crimes, or crimes against humanity. As the Commentary notes, Article 6(2) is derived not from the Convention relating to the Status of Refugees but from the Organisation for African Unity's Convention Governing the Specific Aspects of Refugee Protection in Africa. Canada prefers to see the paragraphs of Article 6 remain consistent with the Refugee Convention, noting that expulsion under Draft Article 6(1) cannot be limited to national security and public order.

17. Canada suggests that Article 5(3) (Grounds for expulsion) state only: "The grounds for expulsion shall be assessed in good faith and reasonably." Expulsion decisions are based on different processes depending on context (e.g. tourist visa, permanent resident application, refugee claimant, etc.). Many expulsion decisions are administrative in nature (such as the routine refusal to extend a tourist visa) and quite legitimately would not take into account the gravity of the facts or the conduct of the alien in question.

18. Regarding the process of expulsion decisions, Canada requests that the Commentary to Article 5 clarify that the grounds for expulsion be considered at the time of the decision rather than the time of removal.

19. Canada has difficulties with Article 7 (Prohibition on the expulsion of stateless persons), which limits the grounds for expulsion of lawfully present stateless persons to national security and public order. The use of "lawfully" in this context is odd. Once an individual is subject to an expulsion, they are no longer lawfully in the country; expulsions must be according to law. If "lawfully" is removed, the grounds are too narrow. Canada does not understand its obligations in respect of statelessness to include limitations on the removal of stateless persons that are more limited than those faced by persons with a nationality.

Disguised expulsion and extradition

20. Canada wishes to clarify the meaning of "expulsion" in Article 2(a) (Definitions), which is defined as, "a formal act, or conduct consisting of an action or omission, attributable to a State, by which an alien is compelled to leave the territory of that State." Canada understands this definition to thus include expulsion by the State and expulsion attributable to the State in accordance with the principles of State responsibility. Canada wishes to emphasize that the scope of "conduct attributable to a State" should incorporate the same threshold for attribution as described in the *Draft Articles on State Responsibility for Internationally Wrongful Acts.*

21. Article 11 (Prohibition of disguised expulsion) states that, "disguised expulsion means the forcible departure of an alien from a State resulting indirectly from actions or omissions of the State, including where the State supports or tolerates acts committed by its nationals or other persons, with the intention of provoking the departure of aliens from its territory" (emphasis added). Framed as such, Draft Article 11 suggests a lower threshold for State responsibility where the conduct of private actors is not attributable to the State and does not amount to a breach of an international obligation. Since Articles 2 and 11 both regard attributable expulsion, these provisions should incorporate the same threshold for attribution described in the *Draft Articles on State Responsibility for Internationally Wrongful Acts.*

22. Article 13 (Prohibition of the resort to expulsion) regards the use of expulsion to "circumvent" extradition procedures. Canada is concerned that the word "circumvent" does not adequately capture the improper purpose or bad faith standard suggested by this provision. That is, States cannot use deportation procedures for the sole purpose of avoiding an extradition process where there is not otherwise a legitimate immigration purpose. Canada would prefer the following wording: "A State shall not resort to expulsion in the absence of a legitimate immigration purpose solely to avoid extradition."

Detention

23. In Article 19 (Detention conditions), Canada is concerned about the obligation to detain aliens subject to expulsion separately from incarcerated persons, except under "exceptional circumstances." As separation of these two groups is occasionally unfeasible, Canada would prefer

that Article 19(1) (b) stipulate, "When possible, an alien subject to expulsion should be detained separately from persons sentenced to penalties involving deprivation of liberty"....

24. Canada agrees that the duration of detention should not be unrestricted or excessive. For greater certainty, Canada suggests that Article 19(2) (a) prohibit "indefinite" detention rather than "excessive" detention. Similarly, detention review should be conducted on defined or prescribed intervals, rather than restricted to "regular" intervals. Canada prefers that Article 19(3) (a) reflect this language.

25. Furthermore, Article 19(2) (b) should not restrict detention decisions to courts only. Administrative decision-makers have the power to extend the duration of detention under Canadian legislation. Thus, such decisions are not exclusively taken by a "court or person authorized to exercise judicial power." Canada suggests that Article 19(2)(b) include "judicial or quasi-judicial decision-making power" (emphasis added).

Rights conferred

26. Canada respects the importance of the family unit, as enshrined in its ICESCR and ICCPR commitments. However, "right to family life" as articulated in Article 20 (Obligation to respect the right to family life) merits clarification. Canada maintains that a State may expel an alien in situations which would interfere with the right to the protection of family life. Further, Canada notes that this is an unsettled area of law. Caution should be taken not to overstate the limitation on the right of States to remove aliens. The prohibition on interference with family life, "on the basis of a fair balance between the interests of the State and the alien", gives undue deference to the alien's right. This Article should reflect the entitlement of a State to expel aliens who are serious criminals or who pose a serious risk to public safety or national security.

27. Canada has noted the proposal to limit certain procedural rights to aliens unlawfully in a State's territory for less than six months, as described in Article 26(4) (Procedural Rights). Canada is not aware of any basis in international law that would support such a temporal limitation.

28. Furthermore, Canada is unable to agree with Article 27 (Suspensive effect of an appeal against an expulsion decision). Since an appeal under Canadian law does not necessarily suspend an expulsion decision[,] Canada would suggest, "An appeal lodged by an alien subject

to expulsion who is lawfully present in the territory of the expelling State may suspend an expulsion decision, as provided by law"....

29. At international law, aliens have no right of admission to a State. Aliens who are removed are not entitled to re-admission. Canada cannot agree with Article 29 on the right to readmission should an alien's removal be later established as unlawful. Instead, an unlawful expulsion decision cannot be used to prevent the alien from requesting or re-applying for admission.

30. Article 30 (Protection of the property of an alien subject to expulsion) requires an expelling State to take "appropriate measures" to protect the property of an alien subject to expulsion. The Commentary explains the purpose of this provision is to provide a reasonable amount of time before or after expulsion to allow for the repatriation of property. The Article itself should reflect this purpose.

Parliamentary Declarations in 2013 / Déclarations parlementaires en 2013

compiled by / préparé par

ALEXANDRA LOGVIN

STATEMENTS MADE ON THE INTRODUCTION OF LEGISLATION /
DÉCLARATIONS SUR L'INTRODUCTION DE LA LÉGISLATION

Alexandra Logvin is a lawyer at Fasken Martineau DuMoulin LLP in Ottawa / Alexandra Logvin est avocate au bureau de Fasken Martineau DuMoulin LLP à Ottawa. This compilation covers parliamentary declarations made during the first and second sessions of the 41st Parliament (28 January – 10 December 2013) / Cette compilation contient les déclarations faites au cours des 1re et 2e sessions parlementaires de la 41e législature (28 janvier – 10 décembre 2013).

Bill C-61 (C-5):   *Offshore Health and Safety Act / Loi sur la santé et la sécurité dans la zone extracôtière*
Bill C-3:   *Safeguarding Canada's Seas and Skies Act / Loi visant la protection des mers et ciel canadiens*
Bill C-4:   *Economic Action Plan 2013 Act No. 2 / Loi no 2 sur le plan d'action économique de 2013*

STATEMENTS IN RESPONSE TO QUESTIONS / DÉCLARATIONS EN RÉPONSE AUX QUESTIONS

ENVIRONMENT / ENVIRONNEMENT

Greenhouse Gases / Gazes à effet de serre
Convention to Combat Desertification in Those Countries Experiencing Serious Drought and/or Desertification, Particularly in Africa / Convention des Nations Unies sur la lutte contre la désertification dans les pays gravement touchés par la sécheresse et/ou la désertification, en particulier en Afrique

FOREIGN AFFAIRS / AFFAIRES ÉTRANGÈRES

Arctic Council / Conseil de l'Arctique
Great Britain / Grande-Bretagne
Inauguration of Pope / Intronisation du pape
International Civil Aviation Organization (ICAO) / Organisation de l'aviation civile internationale (OACI)
Iran
Jordan / Jordanie
Nelson Mandela
Peru / Pérou
Ukraine
United States / États-Unis

HEALTH / SANTÉ

Energy Drinks / Boissons énergisantes
Global Fund to Fight AIDS, Tuberculosis and Malaria / Fonds mondial de lutte contre le sida, la tuberculose et le paludisme
Polio

HUMAN RIGHTS / DROITS DE LA PERSONNE

China / Chine
Forced Marriage / Mariage forcé
Funding: Office of Religious Freedom / Financement : Bureau de la liberté de religion

BILL S-7: COMBATING TERRORISM ACT / LOI S-7: LOI SUR LA LUTTE
CONTRE LE TERRORISME[1]

Mr. Robert Goguen (Parliamentary Secretary to the Minister of
Justice):

---

[1] Editor's note: *An Act to Amend the Criminal Code, the Canada Evidence Act and the
Security of Information Act / Loi modifiant le Code criminel, la Loi sur la preuve au*

Bill S-7 is targeted criminal law reform [... and] is designed to re-enact the investigative hearings and recognizance with conditions in the *Criminal Code* that expired in March 2007, with additional safeguards over those that existed in the original legislation. The bill would also create new offences of leaving or attempting to leave Canada for the purpose of committing certain terrorist offences, would respond to recommendations made during the parliamentary review of the *Anti-terrorism Act* and includes further improvements to the *Criminal Code*, the *Canada Evidence Act* and the *Security of Information Act*.

The investigative hearing is designed to facilitate the gathering of information by a judge, which may be relevant to the investigation of past or future terrorist offences following an application made by a peace officer ...

The committee had the benefit of hearing from Maureen Basnicki, a co-founder of the Canadian Coalition Against Terror. She disagreed with those who characterized the original introduction of the investigative hearing and recognizance provisions of 2001 as an example of legislators having hit the panic button after 9/11. Instead, she stated, "Far from being an overreaction to 9/11, these provisions were, in fact, a sober and responsible recognition of the danger posed by terrorism to the future of the international community." As a result, she urged all members to have in mind the security of Canadians when considering and voting on Bill S-7. As Ms. Basnicki put it: "Canada should not be removing reasonable tools for fighting terrorism while terrorists are busy sharpening their tools for use against Canadians and other innocent victims. While the provisions of Bill S-7 can always be revisited at a later date, the lives shattered by a future terrorist attack that may have been prevented cannot be reconstituted by any act of Parliament."

The bill also proposes the creation of new offences for leaving or attempting to leave Canada for the purpose of committing certain terrorist offences. These offences are specifically designed to prevent persons from leaving Canada in order to participate abroad in the activity of a terrorist group, for example, receiving training, or to commit certain other terrorist acts abroad. These offences have received the support of certain witnesses. For example, Mr. Rob Alexander, a member of and spokesman for the Air India 182 Victims Families Association, asserted during the hearing that the proposed new offences are necessitated by the globalization of terrorism-related activities, given reports of persons leaving Canada to receive terrorist

---

Canada et la Loi sur la protection de l'information; introduced in the Senate on February 15, 2012 and first read in the House of Commons on 5 June 2012. The Bill received Royal Assent on 25 April 2013 (SC 2013, c 9).

training abroad. He argued that these potential Canadian offenders may pose a potentially mortal threat and danger to members of the Canadian armed forces on duty abroad. In his view, these proposed offences would help minimize this dilemma.

The horrific nature of terrorism requires a proactive and preventive approach. These new offences would allow law enforcement to intervene at an early stage in the planning process to prevent terrorist acts from being carried out. The proposed new offences would send a strong deterrent message potentially to assist in mitigating the threat of terrorism and would provide an appropriate maximum penalty.

In the course of debates on Bill S-7, some have alleged that the bill fails to protect human rights. To the contrary, the bill contains numerous human rights safeguards. I think we can all agree that counterterrorism measures must protect security, while respecting human rights.

Consider, for example, the investigative hearings. Under the investigative hearing provisions, the court would be empowered to compel persons who are reasonably believed to have information about past or future terrorism offences to appear in court and provide information. Without a doubt, the government has gone to great lengths to ensure that witnesses would be protected during the hearing from unintended consequences. First, the Attorney General must consent before the investigative hearing process could be initiated ... Second, a judge would have to agree that an investigative hearing is in fact warranted for it to be held ... As a third safeguard, I direct the members' attention to the fact that under the original 2001 legislation, there was the power to arrest a person without warrant in certain limited circumstances, such as when the person was about to abscond, in order to ensure his or her attendance before a judge. However, the original legislation was silent as to how long the period of detention could be after such an arrest. Bill S-7 would remedy this defect by stating that section 707 of the Criminal Code, which sets out the maximum period of time an arrested person can be detained at a criminal trial, would also apply to a person arrested to attend an investigative hearing. Section 707 allows the detention of a witness for up to a maximum of 90 days, with judicial review for the detentions within each 30-day period. Fourth, as a fundamental principle of our legal system in this country, the person named in the investigative hearing order would have the right to retain and instruct counsel at any stage of the proceedings ...

In 2004, the Supreme Court of Canada took note of this robust provision and rejected the argument that the investigative hearing violated an individual's right to silence and the right against self-incrimination. The court also extended the use and derivative use immunity procedural safeguards found in section 83.28 of the Criminal Code to extradition and deportation proceedings. On this last point ... Bill S-7 would be read in the context of the judgment of the Supreme Court of Canada to ensure that protections built into this section for use and derivative use immunity would be extended to extradition or deportation hearings. In summary, Bill S-7 incorporates appropriate and balanced safeguards.

The issue of review and accountability also arose during the debate and discussion of the bill. Let there be no mistake; Bill S-7 contains multiple reporting, parliamentary review and sunset provisions. The bill requires that Parliament review the investigative hearing and recognizance with conditions provisions prior to the date they sunset. These measures would be subject to another sunset clause, which would result in their expiry after five years, unless they were renewed by parliamentary resolution.

The proposals in the bill also include, as was the case with the original legislation, annual reporting requirements by the federal government and the provinces on the use of these provisions ...

To conclude, the measures proposed in the Bill S-7 are necessary, proportionate and balanced, and they are replete with safeguards.

(*House of Commons Debates, 28 March 2013, pp. 15336-37*)
(*Débats de la Chambre des Communes, le 28 mars 2013, pp. 15336-37*)

BILL S-9: NUCLEAR TERRORISM ACT / LOI S-9: LOI SUR LE
TERRORISME NUCLÉAIRE[2]

Mr. Robert Goguen (Parliamentary Secretary to the Minister of Justice):

Bill S-9, the ... important counterterrorism bill ... will put Canada into a position to ratify and become a state party to the 2005 Amendment to the *Convention on [the] Physical Protection of Nuclear Materials*, the CPPNM amendment,[3] and the 2005 *International Convention for the Suppression of Acts of Nuclear Terrorism*, the ICSANT.[4]

---

2 Editor's note: *An Act to Amend the Criminal Code / Loi modifiant le Code criminel*; introduced in the Senate on 27 March 2012 and first read in the House of Commons on 25 September 2012. The Bill received Royal Assent on 19 June 2013 (SC 2013, c 13).

3 Editor's note: The convention was signed at Vienna and at New York on 3 March 1980, and entered into force 8 February 1987. Canada signed the convention on 23 March 1980 and ratified it on 21 March 1986. Canada ratified the amendment to the convention on 3 December 2013.

4 Editor's note: The convention was signed at New York on 13 April 2005, and entered into force 7 July 2007. Canada signed the convention on 14 September 2005 and ratified it on 21 November 2013.

Let me begin by quoting former United Nations secretary Kofi Annan, who warned that if nuclear terrorism attacks were to occur, "it would not only cause widespread death and destruction, but would stagger the world economy and thrust tens of millions of people into dire poverty."

In my remarks today, I will describe the four offences proposed in Bill S-9. I will also outline how these offences fit within the existing Criminal Code counterterrorism operations with the intent to cause death, serious bodily harm, or substantial damage to property or the environment.

The penalty proposed for a conviction under section 82.3 is a maximum term of life imprisonment. This offence captures the distinct criminalization requirements of both the CPPNM amendment and the ICSANT. It is important to note that in seeking to ratify international agreements, dualist countries like Canada can rely on existing domestic law to achieve compliance with the treaty requirements. In this regard, for the unlawful export or import of nuclear materials where no specific intent is called for by the CPPNM amendment, Canada will be relying on a number of offences which directly target this activity, notably under the Export and Import Permits Act, the Nuclear Safety and Controls Act and the Customs Act.

Second, the bill proposes, at section 82.4, an offence for using or altering nuclear or radioactive material, or a nuclear or radioactive device, with the intent to compel a person, government, or international organization to do or refrain from doing any act. The proposed offence also criminalizes the commission of an act against a nuclear facility or its operations, also with the intent to compel a person, government, or international organization to do or refrain from doing an act.

Common to all the criminal acts in this offence is the intent to compel or influence the behaviour of others. This intent requirement is a characteristic of terrorism. Given the seriousness of these nefarious acts, this offence would carry a maximum punishment of life imprisonment.

The third offence in Bill S-9 addresses the commission of an indictable offence for the purpose of obtaining nuclear or radioactive material, or nuclear or radio active device, or to obtain access to a nuclear facility. If convicted under this section, offenders would be liable to a maximum of life imprisonment.

Both the CPPNM amendment and the ICSANT specifically reference criminal conduct such as theft and robbery committed for the purposes of obtaining nuclear or radioactive materials or devices. However, the treaties also specifically prohibit the "use of force or any other form of intimidation," at article 9(f) of the CPPNM amendment and "use of force," at article 2(2) of the ICSANT to obtain these materials.

By prohibiting the use of force, the treaties contemplate prohibiting conduct beyond the specified conducts. The notion of use of force is quite broad and could include any acts of violence or force and therefore any number of existing indictable offences could be contemplated as falling within that conduct, such as murder. It is for this reason that the present formulation of section 82.5 has been used. The scope of this offence is comparable to the requirement of the treaties, although formulated differently.

The final offence set out in Bill S-9 proposes a specific offence to threaten to commit any of the other offences in Bill S-9. The proposed punishment is a maximum term of 14 years of imprisonment. The 14-year maximum penalty in the new offence recognizes the heightened seriousness of a threat in a nuclear context, with a sentence proportionate to the potential chaos that such a threat could create ...

These four offences that I have just described, combined with the general provisions of the Criminal Code that address different forms of party liability, such as attempts and conspiracies as well as existing Canadian law outside of the Criminal Code, would put Canada in a position to ratify both of the treaties.

When we look at the proposed level of punishment for the offences in Bill S-9, I think members would agree that they are appropriate given the grave nature of the prohibited conduct. They are also consistent with other terrorism acts in the Criminal Code, for example, section 83.2, commission of an offence for a terrorist group, and subsection 83.21, instructing others to carry out terrorist activities. Both of these carry maximum terms of life imprisonment.

Some of the other areas of Bill S-9 that warrant mention are, first, that it would provide for concurrent prosecutorial jurisdiction over the offences between the provincial and federal attorneys general, an arrangement which is consistent with other terrorism offences in the Criminal Code. Second, the bill would provide for new offences to be added to both the wiretap and the DNA provisions of the Criminal Code. Third, by adding the CPPNM amendment and the ICSANT to the definition of terrorism activities under section 83.01(1)(a) of the Criminal Code, a number of existing powers and procedures would apply to the new offences, including reverse onus at bail and one-year wiretap authorizations, to name a few. These offences were designed in such a way so as to fit within the existing terrorism provisions of the Criminal Code.

In addition, these treaties require a sentence to assume extraterritorial prosecutorial jurisdiction over these offences. In this regard, Bill S-9 would give Canadian courts the jurisdiction to try these new offences in situations, for example, where the offence was committed outside Canada by a Canadian citizen or when the person who committed the act or omission outside Canada was, after the commission of the offence, present in Canada.

Canada can already assume similar jurisdiction to prosecute other terrorism acts in the Criminal Code.

The final technical aspect of the bill that I will note is, as called for by both the CPPNM amendment and the ICSANT, these offences would specifically not apply to a lawful act that is committed during an armed conflict or to activities undertaken by military forces of a state in the exercise of their official duties to the extent that those activities were governed by other rules of international law.

The military exclusion language used in Bill S-9 is similar to that which is present as set out in subsection 431.2(3) and subsection 80.3(1) of the Criminal Code. Notably, the Supreme Court of Canada in the December 2012 *Khawaja* decision provided guidance on the application of the military exclusion clause used in the definition of terrorist activities in the Criminal Code. In rejecting the application of military exclusion to the defendant, the court found: first, the military exclusion clause functioned as a defence and therefore it was for the defence to raise an error of reality to the claim that it applied; and second, the conduct in question must otherwise be in accordance with applicable international law such as the Geneva Convention.

Over the course of Bill S-9 moving through the legislative process, much has been said about the impetus for Bill S-9 from both a domestic and international perspective. The context in which the bill has been brought forward has been debated and continues to be of vital importance.

The original CPPNM, which was negotiated in 1980, is presently the only legally binding international instrument in the area of physical protection of nuclear material. Canada signed it in September 1980 and ratified it in March 1986. Canada achieved ratification in 1986 through amendments to a range of statutes, including the Criminal Code.

Twenty-five years later the international community, through the International Atomic Energy Agency, recognized the need to revisit the original CPPNM. In this regard, in July 2005, state parties to the CPPNM, including Canada, adopted the CPPNM amendment. One of the key additions to the original treaty is a requirement for state parties to protect nuclear facilities and materials in peaceful domestic use, storage and transport.

Also, in 2005 under the guidance of the United Nations General Assembly, the ICSANT was negotiated and adopted. The purpose of the ICSANT was to cover a broad range of nuclear terrorism acts and possible targets.

Canada is not alone in seeking to become a state party with these two important nuclear security treaties. At a second world leaders nuclear summit held last year in Seoul, Republic of Korea, 53 heads of state, including the Prime Minister of Canada, recognized the importance of multilateral instruments that addressed nuclear security such as the CPPNM amendment and the ICSANT.

The world leaders committed to work together through a universal assurance of a CPPNM amendment and the ICSANT. If Bill S-9 is passed, Canada will be in a position to report this accomplishment at the next world leaders nuclear summit in 2014. The CPPNM amendment at last count has 64 state parties while the ICSANT has 83 state parties.

Some of our closest allies have recently taken important domestic steps in this area. The United Kingdom became a state party to the ICSANT in 2009 and the CPPNM amendment in April 2010. In addition, Australia modified its laws to achieve ratification of the CPPNM amendment in 2008 and the ICSANT in 2012.

Let me conclude my remarks by heightening what Belfer Center for Science and International Affairs at Harvard University said in its 2011 report entitled "U.S.-Russia Joint Threat Assessment on Nuclear Terrorism." In a short yet powerful statement it warned that of all the varieties of terrorism, nuclear terrorism poses the gravest threat to the world. Bill S-9 is balanced and timely and, most important, it is designed to target this new reality.

(*House of Commons Debates, 7 March 2013, pp. 14707-8*)
(*Débats de la Chambre des Communes, le 7 mars 2013, pp. 14707-8*)

BILL S-10: PROHIBITING CLUSTER MUNITIONS ACT / LOI S-10: LOI INTERDISANT LES ARMES À SOUS-MUNITIONS[5]

Mr. Deepak Obhrai (Parliamentary Secretary to the Minister of Foreign Affairs):

Canada has long recognized that explosive remnants of war, such as those caused by cluster munitions, are a serious humanitarian concern. They maim and kill innocent civilians around the world. They have a detrimental economic impact, and they hinder access to essential infrastructure ...

Canada has long played a leading international role in the protection of civilians from the use of conventional weapons that are prone to indiscriminate effects because we have seen the devastating impacts of that use. Since 2006, our government has contributed to more than 250 projects in this global effort, making us one of the world's top contributors. More

---

5　Editor's note: *An Act to Implement the Convention on Cluster Munitions / Loi de mise en oeuvre de la Convention sur les armes à sous-munitions;* introduced in the Senate on 25 April 2012 and first read in the House of Commons on 6 December 2012.

recently, in February of this year, the Minister of State of Foreign Affairs, Americas and Consular Affairs, while in Colombia, announced an additional $2.93 million over four years, to assist landmine survivors, including children and youth, with their recovery and reintegration into society ...

Bill S-10 ... would fully implement our legislative requirements under the Convention on Cluster Munitions. Canada was a key participant throughout the negotiations of the convention. We are proud to have been among its first 94 signatories in December 2008.

From the beginning, Canada's goal was to strike a balance between a commitment to the elimination of cluster munitions and effective, legitimate and important security considerations. Bill S-10 would do just that.

During negotiations, we committed to the eventual elimination of these weapons, but we also had to recognize the reality that not all countries were participating in the negotiations or were ready to commit to a convention. A compromise was needed to allow countries that wanted to renounce cluster munitions and ratify the convention to be able to engage in military co-operation and operations with countries that intended to retain these weapons for the time being.

The compromise that was reached set out that these military activities would be permitted on the basis that the state parties would engage in diplomatic advocacy to urge non-state parties to reconsider. That compromise, found in article 21, was critical to allowing Canada and its allies to join the convention. Canada had a clear mandate in negotiations. We have always been open and transparent in exactly what we wanted to accomplish. It is important to note that this was not just the Canadian position but was shared by other countries. The provision of article 21 was necessary to bring others on board.

Bill S-10, when enacted, would prohibit the use, development, making, acquisition, possession, movement, import, and export of cluster munitions. It would also prohibit the stockpiling of cluster munitions in Canada, through the proposed offence of possession. This offence would cover any form of possession, including stockpiling, and would easily be enforced and, if necessary, prosecuted in Canada's criminal justice system.

Bill S-10 would also prohibit anyone from aiding or abetting another person in the commission of a prohibited activity. This would capture a number of potential cross-border scenarios where people or organizations subject to Canadian law engage in activities that are prohibited by the convention. It would also ensure that those who are subject to Canadian law could be prosecuted for the offences in Canada. For example, the convention does not require state bodies to criminalize investment. However, liability for aiding and abetting, as set out in the bill, would include investment scenarios in which there is sufficient intention and connection between the investment and the prohibited activity to meet Canadian charter and criminal law requirements.

We recognize that one of the most discussed aspects of the convention relates to article 29, which specifically allows state parties to engage in military co-operation and operations with states that are not party without breaching their obligations. As the convention allows this, the proposed legislation also contains exceptions that would allow Canada to engage in combined military operations and co-operation with states that are not party to the convention. Bill S-10 would preserve Canada's ability to work alongside our allies, and it would provide Canadian Forces members and civilians with them assurances that they would not face criminal liability when doing their jobs.

For Canada, military co-operation and operations with other states that currently do not intend to ratify the convention, such as the United States, are of central importance to our security and defence policy. Again, it is vital that our men and women in uniform are not unjustly accused of criminal conduct and are in no way compromised in doing their jobs or what we ask of them in the interest of national security and defence.

Even in the context of military co-operation, the convention reiterates that state parties shall not engage in specified activities that are fully within their control. Under Bill S-10, Canadian Armed Forces members would be prohibited from using cluster munitions in their operations. They would not be able to request their use if the choice of munitions was under exclusive Canadian control, even in the context of joint military operations. In addition, and going beyond what is required by the convention, as a matter of policy, the Canadian Forces would prohibit personnel on exchange, secondment or attachment with allied forces from themselves using cluster munitions and from training and instructing in the direct use of cluster munitions. The Canadian Forces would also prohibit, as a matter of policy, the transportation of any cluster munitions aboard Canadian assets.

As the prohibiting cluster munitions act makes its way through the legislative process, our government has already taken concrete steps to fulfill its commitment under the Convention on Cluster Munitions. The Canadian Armed Forces has removed its remaining stockpiles of cluster munitions from active service and has already begun the process of destroying them. We are confident that the destruction will be completed within the timeframe required by the convention. It is important to note that Canada has never produced or used cluster munitions in its operations ...

Knowing the humanitarian devastation caused by the explosive remnants of war, Canada is fully committed to the goals of the Convention on Cluster Munitions and to implementing our requirements under the convention.

We are proud to have tabled this legislation, and we are particularly proud of the important role played in Canada to get us here today.

(*House of Commons Debates, 29 May 2013, pp. 17323-24*)
(*Débats de la Chambre des Communes, le 29 mai 2013, pp. 17323-24*)

BILL S-12: INCORPORATION BY REFERENCE IN REGULATIONS ACT /
LOI S-12: LOI SUR L'INCORPORATION PAR RENVOI DANS LES
RÈGLEMENTS[6]

Mr. Robert Goguen (for the Minister of Justice):

La technique de l'incorporation par renvoi est actuellement utilisée dans un vaste éventail de règlements fédéraux. En effet, peu nombreux sont les domaines réglementés où elle n'apparaît pas. Avec ce projet de loi, le gouvernement veut s'assurer qu'il peut avoir recours à cette technique rédactionnelle, qui est devenue essentielle dans la façon dont il réglemente. Il veut également être un chef de file sur le plan international pour ce qui est de la modernisation de la réglementation.

Plus précisément, le projet de loi S-12 donne suite aux préoccupations que le Comité mixte permanent d'examen de la réglementation a exprimées sur l'utilisation de cette technique. Le projet de loi créerait la sécurité juridique requise pour répondre à ces préoccupations.

L'incorporation par renvoi est déjà devenue un outil essentiel largement utilisé pour atteindre les objectifs du gouvernement. En effet, l'incorporation par renvoi est une façon efficace d'atteindre un grand nombre des objectifs de la Directive du Cabinet sur la gestion de la réglementation, une directive qui vise à améliorer l'efficacité et le rendement des règlements.

Par exemple, les règlements qui utilisent cette technique favorisent la coopération et l'harmonisation intergouvernementale, un objectif clé du Conseil de coopération en matière de réglementation, établi par notre premier ministre et le président Obama.

L'incorporation par renvoi de textes législatifs d'autres administrations aux fins d'harmonisation, ou de normes élaborées à l'échelle internationale, permet de réduire les chevauchements, un important objectif de la Commission sur la réduction de la paperasse, qui a déposé son rapport plus tôt cette année.

[6] Editor's note: *An Act to Amend the Statutory Instruments Act and to Make Consequential Amendments to the Statutory Instruments Regulations / Loi modifiant la Loi sur les textes réglementaires et le Règlement sur les textes réglementaires en conséquence*; introduced in the Senate on 17 October 2012 and first read in the House of Commons on 12 December 2012.

L'incorporation par renvoi est aussi un important outil à la disposition du gouvernement afin de permettre au Canada de s'acquitter de ses obligations internationales. L'incorporation de documents internationalement acceptés, plutôt que leur reproduction dans les règlements, permet aussi de réduire les différences techniques qui nuisent au commerce, qui est par ailleurs une obligation du Canada aux termes de l'Accord sur les obstacles techniques au commerce, adopté dans le cadre de l'Organisation mondiale du commerce.

L'incorporation par renvoi est également un moyen efficace de bénéficier du savoir-faire des organismes de normalisation canadiens. Le Canada a un Système national de normes qui est reconnu mondialement. L'incorporation dans la réglementation de normes, élaborées au Canada ou à l'échelle internationale, permet de tenir compte des meilleures données scientifiques et de l'approche la plus acceptée dans les domaines touchant la vie courante. En fait, il est primordial qu'on puisse se fier à cette expertise technique afin de pouvoir avoir accès aux connaissances techniques au Canada et à l'étranger.

Les témoignages des représentants du Conseil canadien des normes devant le Comité sénatorial permanent des affaires juridiques et constitutionnelles ont clairement fait ressortir le fait que les normes nationales et internationales sont très largement utilisées au Canada. En s'assurant que les autorités réglementaires peuvent continuer d'utiliser l'incorporation par renvoi pour réaliser leurs objectifs réglementaires, on contribue ainsi à protéger les Canadiens par l'accès aux technologies les plus récentes.

L'incorporation par renvoi permet d'intégrer à la réglementation l'expertise qu'offrent le Système national de normes du Canada et les normes internationales. Cette technique fait partie des choix qui s'offrent aux autorités réglementaires en matière de réglementation.

(*House of Commons Debates, 13 February 2013, pp. 14091-92*)

(*Débats de la Chambre des Communes, le 13 février 2013, pp. 14091-92*)

BILL S-13: PORT STATE MEASURES AGREEMENT IMPLEMENTATION ACT / LOI S-13: LOI DE MISE EN OEUVRE DE L'ACCORD SUR LES MESURES DE L'ÉTAT DU PORT[7]

Mr. Randy Kamp (Parliamentary Secretary to the Minister of Fisheries and Oceans and for the Asia-Pacific Gateway):

---

[7] Editor's note: *An Act to Amend the Coastal Fisheries Protection Act / Loi modifiant la Loi sur la protection des pêches côtières*; introduced in the Senate on 8 November 2012 and first read in the House of Commons on 8 March 2013.

The purpose of Bill S-13 is to enable Canada to ratify the international agreement on port state measures to prevent, deter and eliminate illegal, unreported and unregulated fishing ... The port state measures agreement negotiations focused on illegal fishing and transshipping on the high seas, what we call IUU fishing or illegal, unreported and unregulated fishing. IUU fishing is an issue of grave concern. The agreement deals with the worldwide problem of IUU fishing, which has deep economic and environmental consequences. The committee heard that the estimated economic loss from IUU fishing averages between $10 billion and $23 billion every year.

The international agreement ensures that there is a cohesive and collaborative effort to sustainably manage the resources contained in our oceans. On November 22, 2009, the member countries of the Food and Agriculture Organization of the UN reached an agreement on it. Canada was one of the countries that played a leadership role in that effort. Canada signed the port state measures agreement in 2010 and now needs to follow through with this commitment by ensuring that our legislation is amended to fulfill our international commitments.

Some of the most important stipulations in the port state measures agreement include: establishing standards for information to be provided by vessels seeking entry to port; continuing to deny port entry and service to vessels that are implicated in pirate fishing or IUU fishing unless entry is for enforcement purposes; and, setting minimum standards for vessel inspections and the training of inspectors ...

Fish is a highly traded food commodity and as such illegal, unreported and unregulated fishing rapidly becomes a global problem with significant economic, social and environmental consequences. IUU fishing operators gain economic advantage over legitimate fish harvesters through lower cost of operations by circumventing national laws and regulations. They also undermine conservation and management measures of regional fisheries management organizations and other international standards.

Once IUU fish enter the market, it is very difficult if not impossible to distinguish them from legally caught fish. IUU fishing will remain a lucrative business if the benefits of landing and selling such products continue to outweigh the costs associated with being caught. IUU fish in the market can depress prices for fish products to unprofitable levels for legitimate fish harvesters. Canadian fish harvesters are susceptible to price fluctuations in international markets, as approximately 85% of fish caught in Canadian waters are exported, representing more than $4 billion annually.

Illegal, unreported and unregulated fishing, often referred to as pirate fishing, puts the livelihoods of legitimate fishermen around the world at risk and has an impact on the conservation and protection of our fisheries.

Pirate fishing is a global problem that undermines responsible fishing and has consequences on food security, safety at sea, marine environmental protection and the stability of prices for fish products in some markets. IUU fishing also poses serious potential threats to marine ecosystems and fish stocks. Therefore, by strengthening the *Coastal Fisheries Protection Act* we will protect this vital resource and support the international fight against pirate fishing. Canadian fishermen feel the impacts of pirate fishing, including the depletion of stocks from overfishing, unfair competition with illegal fish products and price fluctuations created by illegal fish products in foreign markets. Therefore, we need to continue to be leaders in the fight against threats to our fishery in order to maintain a fair and stable market environment for our high quality fish and our seafood exports.

The proposed amendments to Canada's *Coastal Fisheries Protection Act* would help us to do that. The amendments represent the next steps in our effort to combat illegal, unreported and unregulated fishing. There are some loopholes now where fish can be caught illegally and then moved to another vessel, which can then legitimately say that it did not catch those fish illegally.

Bill S-13 proposes a new definition of fishing vessel that includes container vessels and any type of transshipment vessels so that transshipment at sea of fish that has not already been landed would be caught under the act. Also, if a country is fishing outside of the authority or the control of a regional fish management organization, if it is just fishing without any compliance with the international norms, then fish caught by that vessel would also be subject to intervention under the act.

The amendments to the *Coastal Fisheries Protection Act* would expand our capacity to deal with illegally caught fish from other jurisdictions. We would have the ability to deal with illegal fish product imports in the efficient way required by the port state measures agreement to which we are a signatory.

Canadians can be proud of our already strong port access regime for foreign fishing vessels. Among other measures, Canada does not allow entry to vessels on the illegal, unreported and unregulated fishing vessel list of the Northwest Atlantic Fishing Organization, or the International Commission for the Conservation of Atlantic Tunas, usually called ICCAT. The IUU vessel lists are a key tool for combating pirate fishing globally. These lists include not only the fishing vessels, but also any vessel that helps fishing vessels engaged in illegal acts. For example, if they provide fuel or transshipping products or packing materials, all of these activities would be covered and included in the list. Arrangements have already been undertaken among several regional fisheries management organizations to share their lists so that members can take the necessary action to deny port entry or services to listed vessels. This makes IUU fishing more and more difficult and expensive.

The proposed changes to the *Coastal Fisheries Protection Act* set out even tougher prohibitions against the importation of illegally caught fish and other living marine organisms. Contravention of these provisions would be an offence under the amended *Coastal Fisheries Protection Act*, with penalties specified under the act. Together these measures would help dry up the profits from illegal fishing activities. Fisheries and Oceans Canada, in close collaboration with the Canada Border Services Agency, would carry out monitoring and enforcement with a view to minimizing impacts on legitimate cross-border trade of fish and seafood products.

Canada has a large stake in the fisheries and a lot of the stocks we fish are straddling stocks, stocks of fish that move from one area to another in the ocean. This means that to protect our fisheries we have to protect them inside and outside of our exclusive economic zone. When we combat illegal fishing that takes place elsewhere in the world it has a far-reaching positive effect here in Canada.

Preventing illegally taken fish and seafood products from entering Canadian markets is also a priority for Canada's major trading partners. Stronger controls at the border would help maintain our reputation as a responsible fishing nation and trading partner. The amendments to the Coastal Fisheries Protection Act that are before us would strengthen and clarify Canada's domestic rules and reinforce our leadership role in the global fight against pirate fishing.

(*House of Commons Debates, 24 May 2013, pp. 16991-92*)
(*Débats de la Chambre des Communes, le 24 mai 2013, pp. 16991-92*)

BILL S-14: FIGHTING FOREIGN CORRUPTION ACT / LOI S-14 : LOI VISANT À COMBATTRE LA CORRUPTION TRANSNATIONALE[8]

Mr. Bob Dechert (Parliamentary Secretary to the Minister of Foreign Affairs):

Canada has long played a prominent role on the international stage in combatting corruption. Bill S-14 signals our commitment to further deter and prevent Canadian companies from bribing foreign public officials.

---

[8] Editor's note: *An Act to Amend the Corruption of Foreign Public Officials Act / Loi modifiant la Loi sur la corruption d'agents publics étrangers*; introduced in the Senate on 5 February 2013 and first read in the House of Commons on 27 March 2013. The Bill received Royal Assent on 19 June 2013 (SC 2013, c 26).

The amendments proposed in Bill S-14 are intended to ensure that Canadian companies continue to act in good faith in the pursuit of freer markets and expanded global trade. They also signal our commitment and our expectation that other countries do the same.

The CFPOA [Corruption of Foreign Public Officials Act] has been in force since 1999 and was first introduced to implement our international obligations under the OECD anti-bribery convention and two more anti-corruption conventions through the OAS and the UN.

In essence, the CFPOA makes it a crime in Canada to bribe a foreign public official to gain a business advantage abroad. It also makes it possible to prosecute a conspiracy to commit or an attempt to commit such a bribery. It covers aiding and abetting the commission of bribery, an intention in common to commit bribery and counselling others to commit bribery.

Laundering property and the proceeds of crime, including the proceeds of bribery offences, as well as the possession of property and proceeds, are already offences under the Criminal Code. The new offences being created in the CFPOA would also be captured by these Criminal Code provisions once they were in force.

The six proposed amendments included in Bill S-14 are intended to answer the call for enhanced vigilance. They demonstrate a comprehensive approach to fighting bribery and signal our government's strong and un-wavering commitment to that fight ...

The first amendment, the introduction of nationality jurisdiction, would allow us to prosecute Canadians or Canadian companies on the basis of their nationality, regardless of where the bribery takes place in the world. Currently, we can only do so after providing a substantial link between the offence and Canadian territory.

The second amendment would provide exclusive authority to the RCMP to lay charges under the act. This would ensure that a uniform approach is taken across Canada and would raise awareness of Canadian businesses regarding the RCMP's primary role in the CFPOA investigations.

The third amendment, the elimination of the words "for profit" from the definition of "business," would ensure that bribery applies to all, not just those paid by businesses that make a profit.

The fourth amendment would increase the maximum jail term to 14 years. It is currently punishable by a maximum of five years' imprisonment and unlimited fines. The possibility of unlimited fines will remain as it is.

The fifth amendment creates a new books and records offence specific to foreign bribery. International anti-corruption treaties to which Canada is a party require that measures be put in place to ensure that individuals and companies do not "cook the books." The penalties for the new offence would mirror those of the foreign bribery offence; that is, a maximum of 14 years of imprisonment and unlimited fines.

The sixth and final amendment would eliminate the facilitation payments exception. Currently, the act states that payments made "to expedite or secure the performance by a foreign public official of any act of a routine nature" do not constitute bribes for the purposes of the CFPOA. The CFPOA also provides for an inclusive list of acts of a routine nature.

[A] facilitation payment is a payment made to a foreign public official to do something that he or she is already obligated to do, such as deliver the mail on time. Conversely, payments that are made to receive a business advantage constitute bribes, which are already illegal under the CFPOA. As a result of the elimination of the facilitation payments defence, this would not create a competitive disadvantage for Canadian companies in international markets. Bribes are illegal under the legislation of every OECD country.

In order to ensure a level playing field for all businesses, Bill S-14 provides for the delay of the coming into force of the elimination of the facilitation payments exception to allow Canadian companies to adjust their own practices and internal policies, if they have not already done so, to ban the use of facilitation payments in their day-to-day operations. This time to adjust is all the more important given that some other countries continue to allow facilitation payments.

With Bill S-14, our government has taken a proactive role in raising awareness of its zero-tolerance position, and we are taking a proactive role in raising awareness of the risks of engaging in corruption abroad.

(*House of Commons Debates, 24 May 2013, pp. 16963-65*)
(*Débats de la Chambre des Communes, le 24 mai 2013, pp. 16963-65*)

BILL S-16: TACKLING CONTRABAND TOBACCO ACT / LOI S-16: LOI VISANT À COMBATTRE LA CONTREBANDE DE TABAC[9]

Mr. Robert Goguen (Parliamentary Secretary to the Minister of Justice):

The bill proposes amendments to the Criminal Code to create a new offence of trafficking in contraband tobacco and to provide minimum penalties for imprisonment for persons who are convicted for a second or subsequent time of this offence.

---

[9] Editor's note: *An Act to Amend the Criminal Code (Trafficking in Contraband Tobacco) / Loi modifiant le Code criminel (contrebande de tabac)*; introduced in the Senate on 5 March 2013 and first read in the House of Commons on 5 June 2013.

To help reduce the problem of trafficking in contraband tobacco, the government committed to establish mandatory jail time for repeat offenders of trafficking in contraband tobacco in its 2011 election platform. The bill would fulfill that commitment.

There are no offences in the Criminal Code dealing with contraband tobacco at the present time. While there exists an offence of selling contraband tobacco in the Excise Act, 2001, that offence exists in support of our fiscal policy in the area of tobacco. This government believes that something more is required to deal with the problem that has become trafficking in contraband tobacco.

The proposed bill prohibits the sale, offer for sale, transportation, delivery, distribution or possession for the purpose of sale of tobacco product or raw leaf tobacco that is not packaged, unless it is stamped. The terms "tobacco product," "raw leaf product," "packaged" and "stamped" have the same meaning as in section 2 of the Excise Act, 2001.

The penalty for a first offence is up to six months imprisonment on summary conviction and up to five years imprisonment if prosecuted on indictment. Repeat offenders convicted of this new offence and where 10,000 cigarettes or more, or 10 kilograms or more of any tobacco product, or 10 kilograms or more of raw leaf tobacco is involved would be sentenced to a minimum of 90 days on a second conviction, a minimum of 180 days on a third conviction and a minimum of two years less a day on subsequent convictions ...

[T]he contraband tobacco market first became a significant issue in Canada in the late 1980s and early 1990s. During that period, more and more legally manufactured Canadian cigarettes destined for the duty-free market began making their way back into the Canadian underground economy. The high retail price of legitimate cigarettes made smuggling them back across the border a lucrative illicit business.

The Royal Canadian Mounted Police and Canada Customs seized record quantities of contraband tobacco. The RCMP was also engaged in investigating this illegal activity at its source. These investigations eventually led to negotiated settlements involving several tobacco companies paying more than $1.5 billion in criminal fines and civil restitution.

However, the illicit tobacco market in Canada has rebounded in recent years and once again has become an acute problem.

Tobacco is not just a Canadian problem. The illicit trafficking of tobacco is a multi-billion dollar business worldwide today, fuelling organized crime and corruption and spurring addiction to a deadly product.

Last year smuggling experts, customs officials and diplomats of nearly 160 countries, including Canada, gathered in Geneva, Switzerland to finalize the development of what had eluded governments for decades, and that was an international instrument allowing for a global crackdown on the black market in tobacco.

Under the auspices of the World Health Organization Framework Convention on Tobacco Control, a global treaty to curb tobacco use, delegates worked to complete protocol to stop cigarette smuggling.

Illicit tobacco feeds an underground economy that supports many of the most violent actors on the world stage. Organized crime syndicates and terrorist groups facilitate global distribution and use the profits to finance their activities.

Perhaps even more troubling is the impact that smuggling has on the public health crisis caused by tobacco. Worldwide, one out of 10 adults dies prematurely from tobacco-related diseases such as lung cancer, emphysema, cardiovascular disease and stroke. If the trend continues to hold, tobacco will kill about 500 million people.

By 2030, that figure will reach eight million deaths a year and with cigarettes being heavily marketed in poor countries, 80% of those deaths will be in the developing world. Over the 21st century, an estimated one billion people could die from tobacco use.

In Canada today, illegal tobacco activity is primarily connected to illegal manufacture and not to the diversion of legally manufactured products as it was in the past. [It also] includes, to a lesser degree, the illegal importation of counterfeit cigarettes and other forms of illicit tobacco from overseas ...

Transnational crime of the type found in contraband tobacco smuggling is considered a threat to public safety and national security and has a direct impact on individual Canadians, small businesses and the economy. It also has implications for relationships with our international partners, especially the United States ... Canada and the United States share a long history of law enforcement co-operation across the border. Recent and ongoing threat assessments have identified that organized crime is the most prevalent threat encountered at the shared border. This includes significant levels of contraband trafficking, ranging from illicit drugs and tobacco to firearms, notably handguns, and human smuggling. In this regard, Canada and the United States have explored the concept of integrated cross-border maritime law enforcement operations. Joint maritime law enforcement vessels, manned by specially trained and designated Canadian and U.S. law enforcement officers, have been authorized to enforce the law on both sides of the international boundary line in the course of integrated cross-border operations.

The contraband tobacco market is driven largely by illegal operations in both Canada and the United States. The provinces of Ontario and Quebec have the highest concentration of contraband tobacco manufacturing operations, the majority of the high-volume smuggling points and the largest number of consumers of contraband tobacco ...

Protecting society from criminals is a responsibility the government takes seriously. Accordingly, this bill is part of the government's continued commitment to take steps to protect Canadians and make our streets and communities safer. Canadians want a justice system that has clear and strong law that denounces and punishes serious crimes, including illicit activities involving contraband tobacco. They want laws that impose penalties that adequately reflect the serious nature of these crimes. This bill would do that.

(*House of Commons Debates, June 11, 2013, pp. 18100-2*)
(*Débats de la Chambre des Communes, le 11 juin 2013, pp. 18100-2*)

BILL S-17: TAX CONVENTIONS IMPLEMENTATION ACT, 2013 / LOI
S-17: LOI DE 2013 POUR LA MISE EN OEUVRE DE CONVENTIONS
FISCALES[10]

Mr. Corneliu Chisu (Pickering — Scarborough East):

For those wondering why this bill started in the Senate first, I should note that, going back to 1976, the convention has been to bring tax convention legislation to the Senate first. In fact, there have been 30 different pieces of tax convention legislation in front of Parliament since 1976.

Bill S-17 proposes to implement tax conventions or tax treaties, either new or updated, with Canada and the following countries: Namibia, Serbia, Poland, Hong Kong, Luxembourg and Switzerland. These new and updated treaties would augment Canada's strong network of tax treaties. Indeed, currently Canada has comprehensive tax treaties in place with 90 countries, one of the world's largest networks of bilateral tax treaties. This is an important feature of Canada's international tax system, a feature that is key to promoting our ability to compete.

---

[10] Editor's note: *An Act to Implement Conventions, Protocols, Agreements and a Supplementary Convention, Concluded between Canada and Namibia, Serbia, Poland, Hong Kong, Luxembourg and Switzerland, for the Avoidance of Double Taxation and the Prevention of Fiscal Evasion with Respect to Taxes / Loi mettant en oeuvre des conventions, des protocoles, des accords, un avenant et une convention complémentaire conclus entre le Canada et la Namibie, la Serbie, la Pologne, Hong Kong, le Luxembourg et la Suisse en vue d'éviter les doubles impositions et de prévenir l'évasion fiscale en matière d'impôts*; introduced in the Senate on 6 March 2013 and first read in the House of Commons on 9 May 2013. The Bill received Royal Assent on 19 June 2013 (SC 2013, c 27).

What is more, we continue to work on agreements with other jurisdictions, as demonstrated in today's legislation. As part of Canada's ongoing effort to update and modernize our network of income tax treaties, Bill S-17 would achieve two important objectives. First, it would help combat tax evasion by ensuring Canada works with other countries to stop tax cheats. Second, it would help encourage global trade by preventing double taxation. Clearly, I would hope that all parliamentarians and all Canadians would agree that everyone should pay their fair share of taxes.

[It] is not appropriate that some corporations would take advantage of Canada's tax rules to avoid paying their fair share, or that some wealthy individuals would use an offshore account to hide income tax or evade tax. We are against tax cheats because those tax cheats are essentially hiking taxes on honest Canadians. Honest, hard-working Canadians and small-business owners are left having to pay more taxes when cheats do not pay their fair share, and that is simply not fair.

However, to detect and deter those tax cheats, the Canada Revenue Agency needs to work with and share information with foreign tax agencies around the world. To this end, Canada supports the international consensus to work through the Organisation for Economic Co-operation and Development, or OECD, to set an international tax information exchange standard. That standard is implemented under bilateral tax treaties and tax information exchange agreements like those new and updated treaties included in Bill S-17.

The second objective I mentioned referenced encouraging global trade by preventing double taxation. Here at home, our government has worked hard to cut taxes. In fact, we have done it 150 times, in every way government collects taxes, from the GST to personal tax to business tax and much more. We firmly believe that a more competitive tax system helps create an environment that enables Canada's entrepreneurs to excel, not a tax system that punishes entrepreneurs and stands in the way of their success, both here in Canada and abroad.

(*House of Commons Debates, 3 June 2013, p. 17609*)
(*Débats de la Chambre des Communes, le 3 juin 2013, p. 17609*)

BILL C-51: SAFER WITNESSES ACT / LOI C-51: LOI AMÉLIORANT
LA SÉCURITÉ DES TÉMOINS[11]

[11] Editor's note: *An Act to Amend the Witness Protection Program Act and to Make a Consequential Amendment to Another Act / Loi modifiant la Loi sur le programme de protection des témoins et une autre loi en conséquence*; introduced in the House of Commons on December 11, 2012. The Bill received Royal Assent on 26 June 2013 (SC 2013, c 29).

Ms. Candice Bergen (Parliamentary Secretary to the Minister of Public Safety):

One of our top priorities is to help build safer communities for all Canadians. One of the ways we are doing that is by providing law enforcement officials with the tools they need to do their job more efficiently and effectively ... The legislation before us today strengthens our track record and will go a long way to enhancing our collective efforts to combat organized crime. Crimes committed by organized crime networks present a serious concern to both police and Canadians. Many organized crime groups are involved with the illicit drug trade, which we all know is growing.

According to Statistics Canada, for example, cocaine trafficking, production and distribution in Canada has grown nearly 30% over the last decade. Today we also know that organized crime is becoming more global, more transnational and more pervasive. We know that organized crime groups are becoming more sophisticated to avoid detection and arrest ...

Public safety is the cornerstone of the witness protection program as it offers protection, including new identities, for certain individuals whose testimony or co-operation can be so vital to the success of law enforcement operations.

Although witness protection was informally available since 1970, Canada's federal witness protection program was officially established in 1996 with the passage of the *Witness Protection Program Act*. Today, the federal program, which is administered by the RCMP, can provide emergency protection to witnesses under threat, offering such services as permanent relocation and Since provincial governments are also responsible for the administration of justice, many provinces, including Quebec, Ontario, Manitoba, Saskatchewan and Alberta, have established their own witness protection programs, which differ from the federal program.

The federal program has a legislated mandate to provide national protection services to all law enforcement agencies in Canada, as well as to international courts and tribunals.

Legislation governing the federal witness protection program, however, has not been substantially changed since it first came into force, despite the constantly changing nature of organized crime and some calls for reform.

The safer witnesses act would help to strengthen the current federal witness protection program, a program that, as I have mentioned, is often vital to effectively combatting crime, particularly organized crime.

As the hon. Shirley Bond, Minister of Justice and Attorney General of British Columbia, noted when commenting on Bill C-51, in the fight against crime, protecting witnesses is essential. Bill C-51 would enhance the protection offered to key witnesses who wish to co-operate with law enforcement officials in the fight against serious organized crime ...

Bill C-51 would also help to protect individuals and front-line officers involved in administering and delivering witness protection ...

The safer witnesses act would also promote greater integration between federal and provincial witness protection programs and will help to ensure that individuals can access federal identity documents more quickly and easily.

Bill C-51 proposes important changes in five main areas ... First, the changes will allow provincial and territorial governments to request that their programs be designated under the federal *Witness Protection Program Act.* This designation will facilitate their witnesses receiving a secure identity change without needing to be admitted into the federal program, which is the case today ... Under these changes proposed by the legislation before us today, federal organizations would be required to assist the RCMP in obtaining identity changes not only for witnesses in the federal program but also for witnesses in designated provincial programs. Provincial governments have been requesting an expedited process for obtaining federal identity documents, and we are acting on their request. These two changes, which our government has introduced, would help meet these demands from provinces such as Quebec, Ontario, Manitoba, Saskatchewan and Alberta ... A third area of reform proposed by Bill C-51 concerns the protection and disclosure of information about people within provincial and municipal witness protection programs. Under the existing federal Witness Protection Program Act, the prohibition against disclosure of information is limited to only information about the change of name and location of federal protectees. The bill would broaden the type of information to be protected and include information about the change of identity and location of provincial witnesses in designated programs as well as information about the federal and designated programs, including those who administer both the federal and provincially designated programs, which is so important ...

The fourth set of changes in the safer witnesses act would mean that the federal witness protection program would be able to accept referrals of persons assisting organizations with a mandate related to national security, national defence or public safety rather than only from law enforcement and international courts and tribunals, as is currently the case. Such organizations include the Canadian Security Intelligence Service and National Defence ...

Finally, Bill C-51 would also address a number of operational issues, based on experiences gained in administering the current program over the past

15 years. For example, this would include permitting voluntary termination from the federal program and extending the amount of time emergency protection could be provided to candidates being considered for admission into the federal program. The change would be to extend the current 90-day availability of emergency protection to a maximum of 180 days. These changes have been recognized as important as the program has been used and administered over the last several years.

(*House of Commons Debates, 11 February 2013, pp. 13970-72*)
(*Débats de la Chambre des Communes, le 11 février 2013, pp. 13970-72*)

BILL C-56: COMBATING COUNTERFEIT PRODUCTS ACT / LOI C-56:
LOI VISANT À COMBATTRE LA CONTREFAÇON DE PRODUITS[12]

Ms. Kellie Leitch (Parliamentary Secretary to the Minister of Human Resources and Skills Development and to the Minister of Labour):

Last year our government welcomed the final passage and coming into force of the *Copyright Modernization Act*, which gave new rights and new tools for copyright owners and users, giving them the certainty and tools they need to fully engage in the online world. As part of the overall balance of the bill, the copyright modernization act introduced specific provisions to deal with the issue of online piracy.

With the *Combating Counterfeit Products Act*, we would be taking the next step in putting in place the legislative changes that are needed to deal with counterfeiting and piracy in the physical marketplace and at our borders. This bill would protect Canadians from harmful counterfeit products. It would help our creative businesses and workers, and law enforcement and border officers confront the increasing threat of trademark counterfeiting and copyright piracy. It would also bring Canada's laws in line with international standards ...

Commercial counterfeiting and piracy are growing issues in Canada and around the world. As with illicit activities, the scope of counterfeiting and piracy is difficult to track and measure. However, this is what we do know. The RCMP investigated over 4,500 cases of IP crimes in Canada between 2005 and 2012. In 2005, the RCMP seized over $7 million worth of counterfeit and pirated goods. In 2012, this number had grown to $38 million, a fivefold increase.

---

[12] Editor's note: *An Act to Amend the Copyright Act and the Trade-marks Act and to Make Consequential Amendments to Other Acts / Loi modifiant la Loi sur le droit d'auteur, la Loi sur les marques de commerce et d'autres lois en conséquence;* introduced in the House of Commons on 1 March 2013.

Canada is not alone. Other developed countries are signalling a rise in the prevalence of counterfeit and pirated goods in the marketplace.

This increase in the value of seizures in Canada is also consistent with what we have heard from Canadian businesses. They have been telling us for years now that counterfeiting and piracy have an impact on innovation and economic growth across the country.

Over the last six years, organizations such as the Canadian Intellectual Property Council and the Canadian Anti-Counterfeiting Network have issued reports calling for legislative changes to deal with counterfeiting and piracy. Most recently, we heard the same calls from several witnesses at a study before the Standing Committee on Industry, Science and Technology.

The measures proposed in the bill are crucial if we are to keep creating high-tech jobs in the future.

Businesses have been overwhelmingly vocal in their support of the bill. For example, Mr. Kevin Spreekmeester, vice-president of global marketing at Canada Goose Inc. and co-chair of the Canadian Intellectual Property Council, said, on March 1: "Canadians have long been victims to the illicit counterfeit trade and the new measures announced today should be welcome news for consumers, businesses and retailers alike." Mr. Jayson Myers, president and CEO of the Canadian Manufacturers & Exporters, explained that counterfeiting "has been a longstanding priority issue for manufacturers ... [they] punish legitimate businesses. They are a drain on our economy and on jobs — and they put the health, safety and environment of every Canadian at risk."

Counterfeiting and piracy hurt our economy. However, beyond their economic impact, there are serious criminality and health and safety issues that we simply cannot overlook. The commercial production and distribution of counterfeit and pirated goods has been associated with organized crime. This is just another line of business for them and it may help them fund other types of activities, such as drug smuggling and illegal firearm sales.

As for health and safety, there are numerous examples of counterfeit goods that could expose Canadians to danger. Think of the counterfeit batteries or car parts, medicines or baby food.

In 2005, 11% of counterfeiting and piracy cases examined by the RCMP involved harmful products. In 2012, this number grew to 30% ...

In July 2012, Canada Border Services Agency officers referred a shipment to the RCMP for investigation. This shipment contained 476 counterfeit wheel bearings, with a commercial value of $45,000, which were to be used by the Canadian mining industry.

What this illustrates is the fact that these goods have not been subjected to Canadian safety standards and may cause harm as a result. Who knows whether these pieces of equipment would have actually functioned to the standard of levels that we expect in Canadian equipment.

With the new provisions in this bill, we will start to get a fuller picture of the threat that commercial counterfeiting and piracy pose to the Canadian economy and to address it within Canada and at its borders ...

First, the bill would strengthen Canada's intellectual property rights enforcement regime at the border. Currently, border officers are not allowed to search for and detain counterfeit and pirated goods without a court order obtained by the trademark or copyright owner, which has proven to be onerous for businesses overall.

Bill C-56 introduces a process that would allow rights holders to submit to the CBSA a request for assistance, which would enable border officers to share information with rights holders regarding suspect commercial shipments.

The request for assistance would allow rights holders to record details about their trademark or copyright at the border, and to provide contact information. It would also contain practical information about how to identify legitimate versus counterfeit or pirated goods. The request for assistance would be an effective tool to enable rights holders to defend their private rights in civil court.

Let me be clear. Bill C-56 would not allow border officers to seize goods for copyright or trademark infringement. It would provide the authority for border officers to temporarily detain goods suspected of being counterfeit or pirated, and then provide limited information to rights holders regarding those detained goods.

This information could only be used to determined if the goods were counterfeit or pirated, or to assist the rights holders in pursuing remedies in the courts. The courts would remain the only competent authority to determine whether goods detained at the border infringed intellectual property rights and to apply appropriate remedies.

The bill would also amend the *Trade-marks Act* and the *Copyright Act* to allow border officers to temporarily detain shipments suspected of containing commercial counterfeit and pirated goods. Border officers would be able to act either following a request for assistance or on their own initiative ...

The bill would provide a specific exception at the border for individual consumers importing goods intended for personal use, as part of their personal baggage.

Goods that were made legitimately in the country where they were produced would be excluded from the new border measures.

With this bill, we would send a clear message. We understand the threats that counterfeiting and piracy represent for our businesses, for the economy and for the health and safety of Canadians, and we are acting accordingly.

(*House of Commons Debates, 30 May 2013, pp. 17445-47*)
(*Débats de la Chambre des Communes, le 30 mai 2013, pp. 17445-47*)

BILL C-60: ECONOMIC ACTION PLAN 2013 ACT, NO. 1 / LOI C-60: LOI NO 1 SUR LE PLAN D'ACTION ÉCONOMIQUE DE 2013[13]

Mrs. Shelly Glover (Parliamentary Secretary to the Minister of Finance):

Bill C-60 would implement key measures from the recent federal budget, economic action plan 2013, which is a positive and forward-looking blueprint to help grow the Canadian economy today and into tomorrow. This plan would make our economy stronger by helping our manufacturers buy new equipment with tax relief, help small businesses create more jobs with a hiring credit, help rebuild our roads and bridges with record new support for infrastructure and much more. Today's legislation, along with the standard second budget implementation bill, which will be introduced in the fall, will help implement that ambitious and positive plan ...

[O]ver 1.4 million net new jobs have been created since January 2006 ... We have also seen that as the best job creation in the entire G7 during that entire time period ... Both the independent International Monetary Fund and the Organisation for Economic Co-operation and Development are projecting that Canada will have among the strongest growth in the G7 in years ahead. Even better, here is what the IMF had to say about Canada only a few weeks ago, "Canada is in an enviable position." For the fifth straight year, the World Economic Forum has ranked Canada's banking system the soundest in the world. Canada has the lowest overall tax rate on new business investment in the G7.

All major credit rating agencies, like Moody's, Fitch, and Standard and Poor's, have affirmed Canada's rock-solid AAA credit rating. Our net debt to GDP ratio remains the lowest in the G7 by far ...

Some big global economic challenges from beyond our borders remain, especially in the United States and Europe. These are among our most important trading partners. Even though these are not made in Canada

---

[13] Editor's note: *An Act to Implement Certain Provisions of the Budget Tabled in Parliament on March 21, 2013 and Other Measures / Loi portant exécution de certaines dispositions du budget déposé au Parlement le 21 mars 2013 et mettant en œuvre d'autres mesures;* introduced in the House of Commons on 29 April 2013. The Bill received Royal Assent on 26 June 2013 (SC 2013, c 33).

problems, they will continue to negatively impact Canada. Like any smart person would in any situation like this, if a problem is out there, we protect ourselves against it. That is exactly what we are doing in economic action plan 2013 by staying squarely focused on what matters when facing a challenging global economy: jobs and economic growth, keeping taxes low and balancing the budget by 2015 ...

In an uncertain global economic economy, the best way for government to build confidence is to maintain its own sound fiscal position, not engage in reckless deficit spending ... I want to read a great quote by one of the most respected newspaper columnists in Canada, Peter Worthington. He said: "The federal budget ... is one of those things that should please every thinking Canadian ... it's reality ... Think for a moment ... When you look at Cyprus, Europe, the U.S. and the rest of the world, this should be a huge relief to Canadian taxpayers ... jobs are more or less secure as are pensions and health-care costs. Working Canadians will continue to be the blessed of the developed world." [... With this Bill,] Canadians can [be] rest assured that this ... government will maintain a low-tax plan, we will maintain a plan for job creation and we will look to prosperity for our country for years and years to come.

(*House of Commons Debates, 1 May 2013, pp. 16149-50*)
(*Débats de la Chambre des Communes, le 1 mai 2012, pp. 16149-50*)

BILL C-61 (C-5): OFFSHORE HEALTH AND SAFETY ACT / LOI C-61 (C-5): LOI SUR LA SANTÉ ET LA SÉCURITÉ DANS LA ZONE EXTRACÔTIÈRE[14]

Hon. Joe Oliver (Minister of Natural Resources):

There is no question the offshore oil and gas industries have made an enormous economic contribution to Newfoundland and Labrador, and Nova Scotia. Indeed, it is not an exaggeration to say that these industries have transformed the economy of eastern Canada. Not long ago the province of Newfoundland and Labrador was receiving the highest per capita equalization payments in the country.

---

[14] Editor's note: *An Act to Amend the Canada-Newfoundland Atlantic Accord Implementation Act, the Canada-Nova Scotia Offshore Petroleum Resources Accord Implementation Act and Other Acts and to Provide for Certain Other Measures / Loi modifiant la Loi de mise en œuvre de l'Accord atlantique Canada — Terre-Neuve et la Loi de mise en œuvre de l'Accord Canada — Nouvelle-Écosse sur les hydrocarbures extracôtiers et d'autres lois, et comportant d'autres mesures*; introduced in the House of Commons on 2 May 2013, reintroduced as Bill C-5 on 24 October 2013.

Today it is among our strongest provincial economies and now contributes to the equalization program. Newfoundland and Labrador's GDP has performed at or above the national average in 9 of the past 13 years. A large part of that success comes from offshore oil and gas, which accounted for 33% of Newfoundland and Labrador's GDP in 2011.

Resource revenues, again primarily from the offshore, have allowed the province to steadily pay down its debt. The total provincial debt was almost $7.7 billion in 2012, down from a high of $12 billion just eight years ago.

Simply put, offshore energy development has given Newfoundland and Labrador more jobs, lower taxes and new investments in services and infrastructure that play such an important role in building stronger communities. These benefits will continue to grow ...

Hibernia was the largest project of any kind ever undertaken in Newfoundland and Labrador. As valuable as Hibernia has been, the Hebron project may be even bigger. Hebron represents a capital investment of as much as $14 billion. It could deliver $20 billion in taxes and royalties to the province over the 30-year life of the project.

Just a few months ago, the Canada-Newfoundland and Labrador Offshore Petroleum Board announced its latest calls for bids for exploration licences in offshore Newfoundland and Labrador, netting $117 million in work commitments by major players in the oil industry.

Nova Scotia's offshore area also offers enormous potential. The Play Fairway Analysis undertaken by the Government of Nova Scotia estimates that the offshore area may contain 8 billion barrels of oil and 3.3 trillion cubic feet of natural gas.

The Atlantic offshore is a major gas producer with three gas fields serving Atlantic Canada and the U.S. northeast. In the past two years, the Nova Scotia offshore area has seen the largest bids ever for offshore parcels in Atlantic Canada with more than a total of $2 billion bid for 12 parcels of land. Shell Canada and BP Exploration clearly see the potential that exists in the Nova Scotia offshore.

Meanwhile, there is an estimated 120 trillion cubic feet of natural gas, and production continues to grow. Sable Island's 270 million cubic feet a day will soon be joined by 200 million cubic feet a day from Deep Panuke ...

The changes we intend to make need to be mirrored by provincial legislation in order for the amendments to come into force. Our government has been working closely with the governments of Newfoundland and Labrador and Nova Scotia to achieve this. Both provinces introduced their legislation in May, and both have given royal assent to their respective bills. At this time, they must wait for the legislation to pass our federal Parliament for the new regime to come to fruition.

The proposed amendments will address gaps in the current legislation. They will vest authority for offshore occupational health and safety in the accord acts.

There are two safety regimes that apply to workers in the offshore. Occupational health and safety pertains to the workers, in the sense of the hazards they may face, their protective equipment, and the safeguards on the equipment they use in their functions. It also pertains to three essential worker rights: the right to refuse dangerous work, the right to information, and the right to participate in taking decisions on workplace health and safety.

Under the current regime, occupational health and safety is a jurisdiction of the provinces. Operational safety pertains to the workplace systems, facilities and equipment, as well as the risk management and integrity of those systems, facilities and equipment. Examples of this are the prevention of gas blowout, ability of a facility to withstand storms, and fire suppression systems. This was included in the accord acts and provided that the offshore petroleum boards be responsible on behalf of both levels of government.

Following a tragic accident where a worker was killed due to an improperly installed door, the overlap of occupational health and safety and operational safety created a grey area. It was not clear whether the door's installation fell under one jurisdiction or the other. The lack of clarity prevented any party from being liable, as it was unclear under whose jurisdiction the incident should be regulated. The provinces and federal government agreed that the best course of action was to eliminate the grey area and incorporate the power for occupational health and safety directly in the accord acts.

For the section on occupational health and safety, which typically would fall under the purview of the Minister of Labour, the legislation specifies that the Minister of Natural Resources may receive advice from the Minister of Labour, and any regulations related to occupational health and safety must be made on the recommendation of both ministers.

(House of Commons Debates, 7 June 2013, pp. 17934-35)
(Débats de la Chambre des Communes, le 7 juin 2013, pp. 17934-35)

BILL C-3: SAFEGUARDING CANADA'S SEAS AND SKIES ACT / LOI C-3: LOI VISANT LA PROTECTION DES MERS ET CIEL CANADIENS[15]

Hon. Lisa Raitt (Minister of Transport):

---

[15] Editor's note: *An Act to Enact the Aviation Industry Indemnity Act, to Amend the Aeronautics Act, the Canada Marine Act, the Marine Liability Act and the Canada*

This proposed legislation focuses on five key initiatives. The first, amendments to the *Canada Shipping Act, 2001*; the second, amendments to the *Marine Liability Act*; the third, amendments to the *Canada Marine Act*; the fourth, amendments to the *Aviation Industry Indemnity Act*; and fifth, amendments to the *Aeronautics Act.*

[A]ll these initiatives [are] important ... because they support [the] commitment to provide long-term economic growth, jobs and prosperity[,] red tape reduction action plan, which will save businesses time and money, and will make government regulations clearer and more predictable [, the] plan for responsible resource development to ensure timely and efficient reviews of proposed resource projects, while strengthening world-class environmental standards [, and] the economic action plan 2012, which focused on the drivers of growth and job creation: innovation, investment, education, skills and communities.

The economic action plan is giving Canada the ability to meet the challenges of the current global economy, to emerge from this period stronger, and to enable our economy and public finances to remain sustainable for many years to come ...

[With respect to the] *Canada Shipping Act, 2001* ... the principal legislation that governs safety and protection of the environment in marine transportation and in recreational boating. It applies to Canadian vessels in all waters, and it applies to all vessels in Canadian waters. The objectives of this act include protecting the marine environment, reducing the impact of marine pollution incidents in Canadian waters, and ensuring the safety of the general public. The amendments our government is proposing today would increase marine environmental protection by strengthening provisions pertaining to pollution prevention and response. To accomplish these objectives the amendments aim to strengthen requirements for spill prevention and preparedness at oil handling facilities by requiring that certain facilities submit both prevention and emergency plans to the Minister of Transport.

The *Canada Shipping Act, 2001* provides civil and criminal liability to certified response organizations responding to a ship-source oil spill or environmental emergency. However, the act does provide such immunity to these organizations if they are responding to spills that take place when a vessel is either loading or unloading at an oil handling facility. Consequently, these responders are reluctant to respond to such an incident ...

Shipping Act, 2001 and to Make Consequential Amendments to Other Acts / Loi édictant la Loi sur l'indemnisation de l'industrie aérienne et modifiant la Loi sur l'aéronautique, la Loi maritime du Canada, la Loi sur la responsabilité en matière maritime, la Loi de 2001 sur la marine marchande du Canada et d'autres lois en conséquence; introduced in the House of Commons on 18 October 2013.

Spill responders, including our international partners, tell us that they are reluctant to help in such emergencies without this sort of immunity. Given that the immediate response is crucial to minimize the impact of these such incidents, if we provide better assurance of immunity for these agents, the amendments would enhance Canada's access to international resources for spill response.

Canada and the United States have a long history of helping each other in times of distress, including responding together to oil spills and other environmental incidents involving our waterways. Although Canada does not rely solely upon the assistance of our American neighbours in such matters, we have been fortunate to have it. We expect that these amendments would ensure it for the future. It is worth noting that these proposed amendments would not change the partnership but it would build upon it. By introducing these proposed amendments to the *Canada Shipping Act, 2001,* our government is reiterating its commitment to ensure marine safety, to protect our marine environment, and to support the crucial role of shipping to Canada's trade and economy ...

[With respect to] the *Marine Liability Act,* [p]rotecting our waterways from pollution is a priority of our government and we take it very seriously. The potential for a chemical spill in Canadian waters requires appropriate mechanisms to responsibly address the potential consequences of such an event. Therefore, we will continue to take action to ensure Canada has the most stringent tanker safety regime in the world.

Given the importance of trade to Canada's continuing prosperity, we must recognize that this involves the transportation of hazardous and noxious substances. Indeed, almost 400 million metric tonnes of cargo carried by ships in Canada annually, which is really only 3.5%, would be considered hazardous or noxious substances. These substances consist of a very broad range of marine cargo, such as chemicals, liquefied natural gas, propane or other materials. Now while it is only a small percentage, 3.5%, this wide variety of substances can cause an array of environmental damage should there be an accident or incident. Therefore, the Marine Liability Act, being the principal legislation we have to address this matter, deals with the liability of ship owners and operators in relation to passengers, cargo, pollution and property damage.

In building on our current robust system, the amendments that our government is proposing to the act will introduce a comprehensive liability and compensation regime that really is in step with our other international conventions that we have already ratified ... The amendments would accomplish two main objectives. First, they would enhance our pollution liability and compensation regime, which would enable Canada to ratify an international convention that would significantly increase the amount of compensation available for pollution and other damages caused by hazardous and noxious substances from ships. Second, the amendments would implement the provisions of the *2010 Hazardous and Noxious Substances Convention* in Canadian law ...

[With respect to] the *Aviation Industry Indemnity Act* ... the Canadian air industry requires insurance coverage to operate. In addition to general risks, this coverage must address risks for acts of war, terrorism, or civil unrest. Indeed, the attacks of September 11, 2011, caused instability in the insurance market, specifically for war risks to third parties; in other words, people and property on the ground which could be affected by aviation incidents.

In response, the Government of Canada developed a program to indemnify aviation businesses against liability they may face from third parties, such as property owners on the ground who experienced loss caused by extreme events such as war. This coverage is known as the "aviation war risk liability program," and it has addressed the matter. However, without permanent authority to enable federal support related to war-risk insurance, it must be renewed repeatedly.

Therefore, our government is now proposing new legislation, the aviation industry indemnity act, that would repeal aviation-related provisions of the Marine and Aviation War Risks Act and give the Minister of Transport permanent authority to provide indemnities in emergency situations and allow air-industry operators to get coverage in the case of continuing market instability. In short, it would allow the same kind of coverage, but would eliminate the need to regularly renew it. As well, to ensure transparency, the minister would report to Parliament within 90 days of an indemnity being authorized and every two years if there was no change ...

Finally, the safeguarding Canada's seas and skies act also includes proposed amendments to the *Aeronautics Act* concerning civilian involvement in military aviation accident investigations. [... The Bill] would give our military flight safety investigators the tools they need to fully investigate flight safety occurrences involving civilians by giving them the power to search premises, seize documents and take statements. These tools are parallel to those available to the investigators working for the Transportation Safety Board which investigates aviation occurrences not related to military aviation safety. The changes would also permit access to on-board flight recordings by a board of inquiry convened under the *National Defence Act*. This access would only arise in the appropriate circumstances and for military administrative purposes only. Most important, these tools would ensure that civilians would contribute their expertise to military aviation safety. As a result, we would continue to develop effective aviation safety measures for all the Canadian Forces and all Canadians.

(House of Commons Debates, 21 October 2013, pp. 144-47)
(Débats de la Chambre des Communes, le 21 octobre 2013, pp. 144-47)

BILL C-4: ECONOMIC ACTION PLAN 2013 ACT NO. 2 / LOI C-4: LOI NO 2 SUR LE PLAN D'ACTION ÉCONOMIQUE DE 2013[16]

Mr. Andrew Saxton (Parliamentary Secretary to the Minister of Finance):

Economic action plan 2013 builds on the strong foundation that was laid last year. In addition to the portfolio of initiatives we have introduced since 2006 with affordable measures to create jobs, promote growth, and generate long-term prosperity, it will help to further unleash potential for Canadian businesses and entrepreneurs to innovate and thrive in the modern economy.

Let us revisit the facts. Today Canada has the strongest job growth among G7 countries since the recession. Our unemployment rate is at its lowest level in four years. It is significantly lower than that of the U.S., which is a phenomenon that has not been seen in nearly three decades. Meanwhile, we have created over one million net new jobs, nearly 80% of which are in the private sector, and our government continues to make new opportunities for Canadians to find employment. Today's legislation does little to detract from this goal.

Both the independent International Monetary Fund, IMF, and the Organisation for Economic Co-operation and Development, OECD, are projecting that Canada's growth will be among the strongest performances in the G7 in the years ahead. Real GDP is significantly above pre-recession levels and is the best performance in the G7.

While other countries continue to struggle with debt that is spiralling out of control, Canada is in the best fiscal position in the G7. Canada still remains on track to return to balanced budgets in 2015.

---

16 Editor's note: *A Second Act to Implement Certain Provisions of the Budget Tabled in Parliament on March 21, 2013 and Other Measures / Loi no 2 portant exécution de certaines dispositions du budget déposé au Parlement le 21 mars 2013 et mettant en oeuvre d'autres mesures*; introduced in the House of Commons on 22 October 2013. The Bill received Royal Assent on 12 December 2013.

However, our government has been very clear that we will not raise taxes on Canadians to balance the budget. [The] government believes that keeping taxes low means more money in the pockets of hard-working Canadians, and that in turn helps keep our economy strong.

A recent study by KPMG concluded that Canada's total business tax cost, which includes corporate income tax, capital taxes, sales taxes, property taxes, and wage-based taxes is more than 40% lower than it is in the United States. In short, our government has created an environment that encourages new investment, growth, and job creation, and one that ensures Canada has the strongest fiscal position and the lowest business tax costs in the G7.

Having the lowest overall tax rate on new business investment in the G7 translates into Canada having a competitive business tax system, one that plays a key role in supporting businesses in all sectors of the Canadian economy to invest, grow, and thrive ...

Canada's system of international taxation was strengthened in order to better support cross-border trade and investment and to improve fairness ...

[There are] three key aspects of the bill today: a continued focus on job creation and support for job creators, a firm response to tax loopholes and tax evasion, and an overall respect for taxpayers' dollars.

While we believe in the benefits of lower taxes, our government fully understands that sustaining an effective tax system also rests on the foundation of tax fairness. That is why economic action plan 2013 is committed to closing tax loopholes that allow a select few businesses and individuals to avoid paying their fair share. Broadening and protecting the tax base supports our government's effort to return to balanced budgets, responds to provincial governments' concerns about protecting provincial revenues on our shared tax bases, and helps give Canadians confidence that the tax system is indeed fair.

Since 2006, and including measures proposed in economic action plan 2013, the government has introduced over 75 measures to improve the integrity of the tax system. Today's legislation takes additional steps in support of this objective.

Two examples include further extending the application of Canada's thin capitalization rules — which limit the amount of Canadian profits that can be distributed to certain non-resident shareholders as deductible interest payments — to Canadian resident trusts and non-resident entities, and introducing stiff administrative monetary penalties and criminal offences to deter the use, possession, sale, and development of electronic suppression-of-sales software designed to falsify records for the purpose of tax evasion.

We are also providing the Canada Revenue Agency, the CRA, with new tools to enforce the tax rules to combat international tax evasion and aggressive tax avoidance, all while we are taking immediate action to improve the integrity and neutrality of the tax system. Specifically, economic action plan 2013 does this by streamlining the process for the CRA to obtain information concerning unnamed persons from third parties, such as banks; requiring certain financial intermediaries, including banks, to report to the CRA clients' international electronic fund transfers of $10,000 or more; and introducing a new program to stop international tax evasion that would pay rewards to individuals who report major international tax non-compliance ...

Lowering taxes is not the only way our government is furthering taxpayers' dollars. Canadians deserve streamlined services and efficient programs. Today's legislation contains several measures fully in line with our government's respect for taxpayers' dollars. A few examples include modernizing the Canada student loans program by moving to electronic service delivery, improving the efficiency of the temporary foreign worker program by expanding electronic service delivery, phasing out the labour-sponsored venture capital corporations tax credit, and modernizing service delivery for Canadians by accelerating the move from paper-based to automated passport application e-services ...

The legislation ... introduces some new ways our government can support job creation in this country. Examples include extending and expanding the hiring credit for small business, which would benefit an estimated 560,000 employers; increasing and indexing the lifetime capital gains exemption to make investing in small business more rewarding; expanding the accelerated capital cost allowance to further encourage investments in clean energy generation; freezing employment insurance premium rates for three years, leaving $660 million in the pockets of job creators and workers in 2014 alone.

Let me elaborate on one of these measures that I think will have a big impact for small businesses. Among the many ways that Canada's income tax system supports small business owners, farmers and fishermen is the lifetime capital gains tax exemption, the LCGE. In order to increase the potential rewards of investing in small business, farming and fishing, economic action plan 2013 proposes to increase the LCGE from $750,000 to $800,000 in 2014. The exemption helps these entrepreneurs better ensure their financial security for retirement and facilitates the intergenerational transfer of their businesses. In 2007 our government increased the LCGE to $750,000 from $500,000, the first increase in the exemption since 1988.

In addition, to ensure the real value of the LCGE is not eroded over time, economic action plan 2013 proposes to index the $800,000 LCGE limit to inflation for the first time ever. The first indexation adjustment will occur for the 2015 taxation year. This is added security for the small business owner and provides financial freedom to create new jobs ...

With a comprehensive and forward-looking agenda, these initiatives will deliver high quality jobs, economic growth and sound public finances. Economic action plan 2013 would allow Canada to meet these challenges and emerge from them stronger than ever today and in the future.

(House of Commons Debates, 23 October 2013, pp. 304-7)
(Débats de la Chambre des Communes, le 23 octobre 2013, pp. 304-7)

Statements in Response to Questions / Déclarations en réponse aux questions

Environment / Environnement

Greenhouse Gases / Gazes à effet de serre

M. Peter Julian (Burnaby — New Westminster):

Le ministre va-t-il enfin reconnaître que les changements climatiques sont réels et prouvés par la science, oui ou non?

L'hon. Joe Oliver (ministre des Ressources naturelles):

J'accepte la science ... Nous allions nos cibles de gaz à effet de serre à celles des États-Unis, qui visent une réduction de 17 % d'ici à 2020. Nous sommes à mi-chemin quant à l'atteinte de nos engagements.

(House of Commons Debates, April 15, 2013, p. 15406)
(Débats de la Chambre des Communes, le 15 avril 2013, p. 15406)

Convention to Combat Desertification in Those Countries Experiencing Serious Drought and/or Desertification, Particularly in Africa / Convention des Nations Unies sur la lutte contre la désertification dans les pays gravement touchés par la sécheresse et/ou la désertification, en particulier en Afrique[17]

Mme Hélène Laverdière (Laurier-Sainte-Marie):

Le Canada se retire de la convention des Nations Unies pour lutter contre la sécheresse et la désertification, notamment en Afrique. C'est vraiment

---

[17] Editor's note: *United Nations Convention to Combat Desertification in Those Countries Experiencing Serious Drought and/or Desertification, Particularly in Africa,* signed in Paris on 14 October 1994 (drafted 17 June 1994), entered into force 26 December 1996. Canada ratified the convention on 1 December 1995, and issued its notification of withdrawal on 28 March 2013.

incroyable. Le Canada devient le seul pays au monde à ne pas participer à cet effort collectif. En octobre dernier, à Dakar, le premier ministre a dit qu'on n'abandonnerait pas l'Afrique. Pourquoi revient-il sur sa promesse? Pourquoi abandonne-t-il certaines des personnes les plus vulnérables sur cette planète?

Mr. Paul Dewar (Ottawa Centre):

Will the [Government] reinstate Canada's involvement in this important UN Convention?

Ms. Lois Brown (Parliamentary Secretary to the Minister of International Cooperation):

Canada does play a leadership role in advancing global food security and nutrition. Membership in this convention was costly for Canadians and showed few results. [L]ess than 20% of this agency's dollars actually funds projects. We are focusing Canadian tax dollars where they can provide real results. For example, Canada has helped almost four million farming households in eleven African countries to access better seed varieties for these climates ... We are making Canada's aid dollars more effective, focused and accountable. We are focused on results to deal with drought, rather than paying for conferences and salaries for UN bureaucrats. Recognizing the urgency of the situation in Africa in the last two years, Canada responded quickly and generously to both the drought in East Africa and in the Sahel region. We will continue to focus our assistance dollars on those who need it most.

(House of Commons Debates, 28 March 2013, p. 15348)
(Débats de la Chambre des Communes, le 28 mars 2013, p. 15348)

FOREIGN AFFAIRS / AFFAIRES ÉTRANGÈRES

Arctic Council / Conseil de l'Arctique

Mr. Dennis Bevington (Western Arctic):

The effects of climate change and the massive loss of Arctic sea ice are creating urgent issues in the Arctic, which require international co-operation. [L]ast week in Norway the Arctic minister said Canada's focus will be on business. Why is the government ... using this important forum to advance corporate interests?

Mr. Greg Rickford (Parliamentary Secretary to the Minister of Aboriginal Affairs and Northern Development, for the Canadian

Northern Economic Development Agency and for the Federal Economic Development Initiative for Northern Ontario):

Canada's north is home to world-class reserves of natural resources. This represents tremendous economic potential, not just for northerners but for all Canadians. That is why we are working with aboriginal groups, the territorial governments and the private sector to ensure those resources are developed in a sustainable manner. We have strong laws and regulatory frameworks to protect our environment in the north. We want northerners to be able to benefit today and for generations to come from jobs and economic growth in the north.

(*House of Commons Debates, 1 February 2013, p. 13568*)
(*Débats de la Chambre des Communes, le 1 février 2013, p. 13568*)

Great Britain / Grande-Bretagne

Mr. Robert Sopuck (Dauphin — Swan River — Marquette):

Today our Prime Minister, alongside Her Majesty The Queen and with many other dignitaries from around the world, is among the many mourners in London remembering and honouring the life of a truly inspiring leader, Margaret Thatcher. [H]ow [will] Margaret Thatcher be remembered and honoured in Canada?

Hon. James Moore (Minister of Canadian Heritage and Official Languages):

Today we do remember the life of Margaret Thatcher, who rose from humble beginnings as a grocer's daughter to become the first female prime minister of Great Britain. Margaret Thatcher was a true leader who had a strong vision for her country and was proud of her values and her principles. During her three terms as prime minister, Margaret Thatcher was a true champion of freedom and liberty and of fighting Communism around the world. She inspired millions around the world to the cause of freedom. On behalf of the Prime Minister, I join all Canadians in saluting the life and legacy of Lady Thatcher.

(*House of Commons Debates, 17 April 2013, p. 15539*)
(*Débats de la Chambre des Communes, le 17 avril 2013, p. 15539*)

Mr. Ed Holder (London West):

[What are] the Canada-U.K. relationship and ways in which it might be strengthened in the near future.

Hon. James Moore (Minister of Canadian Heritage and Official Languages):

The Canada-U.K. relationship is broad and deep and, of course, has survived through profound international change. In recent years, our relationship has grown even stronger with the celebration of Her Majesty's Golden and Diamond Jubilees, as well as successful visits of the Prince of Wales as well as the Duke and Duchess of Cambridge. On June 13 of this year, for the first time since Prime Minister Mackenzie King had the privilege in 1942, our Prime Minister will be speaking to both Houses of the U.K. Parliament to advance Canada's interests in Europe and work together with the U.K. on our prosperity and security together.

(*House of Commons Debates, 22 May 2013, p. 16801*)
(*Débats de la Chambre des Communes, le 22 mai 2013, p. 16801*)

Mr. Joe Daniel (Don Valley East):

Earlier this year, our government and our High Commissioner in London, Gordon Campbell, announced an exciting plan to consolidate Canada's diplomatic presence in London by revitalizing and renovating historic Canada House in the heart of London, Trafalgar Square. At the same time, in order to finance this revitalization, we announced a plan to sell the Macdonald House at Grosvenor Square and move all of Canada's team in London to Canada House. Could the Minister of Foreign Affairs please update the House on this development?

Hon. John Baird (Minister of Foreign Affairs):

We are very excited. We have been in Macdonald House for only 50 years. Canada House has been sitting vacant, by and large, since we left more than 50 years ago. We have an exciting plan to revitalize Canada House in Trafalgar Square to make it the face of Canada in one of the most exciting places in the world. Through the leadership of Gordon Campbell, our High Commissioner, we have obtained more than half a billion dollars for this property. We have bought another building right beside Canada House and we will be able to integrate the two, get the entire Canadian team working together. It is a good deal for taxpayers and a great face in Trafalgar Square for Canada.

(*House of Commons Debates, 29 November 2013, p. 1551*)
(*Débats de la Chambre des Communes, le 29 novembre 2013, p. 1551*)

Inauguration of Pope / Intronisation du pape

Mr. Bryan Hayes (Sault Ste. Marie):

An estimated 14 million Catholics in Canada, along with the rest of the world, have been watching today as Jorge Mario Bergoglio was installed as Pope Francis, Supreme Pontiff of the Catholic Church and 265th successor to Saint Peter. He is the first pontiff from Latin America. [What is] Canada's representation at this historic event?

L'hon. Denis Lebel (ministre des Transports, de l'Infrastructure et des Collectivités et ministre de l'Agence de développement économique du Canada pour les régions du Québec):

Le Canada était représenté par une délégation dont faisaient partie le gouverneur général ainsi que plusieurs représentants de la Chambre, notamment le ministre de la Citoyenneté, de l'Immigration et du Multiculturalisme et la ministre d'État à la diversification de l'économie de l'Ouest. Ils ont rencontré plusieurs dirigeants mondiaux aussi présents lors de cette occasion. Le Canada partage l'engagement du Saint-Siège à défendre la dignité de la personne ainsi que la liberté de conscience et de religion. Au nom de tous les Canadiens, nous tenons à féliciter le pape François au moment où il prend de nouvelles responsabilités à titre de chef de l'Église catholique, de pasteur et de guide pour les chrétiens fidèles aux diverses traditions dans le monde. *Ad multos annos.*

(*House of Commons Debates, 19 March 2013, p. 14926*)
(*Débats de la Chambre des Communes, le 19 mars 2013, p. 14926*)

International Civil Aviation Organization (ICAO) / Organisation de l'aviation civile internationale (OACI)

M. Alexandre Boulerice (Rosemont — La Petite-Patrie):

Lundi, le Qatar a présenté un plan pour déménager à Doha l'Organisation de l'aviation civile internationale, actuellement basée à Montréal. L'OACI est une institution internationale forte et vitale pour Montréal ... Quel est le plan des conservateurs pour garder l'OACI chez nous, à Montréal, au Québec, au Canada?

Mr. Deepak Obhrai (Parliamentary Secretary to the Minister of Foreign Affairs):

[O]ur government is working very hard to keep the ICAO in Montreal. The minister is personally ready, willing and keen to work with the

Government of Quebec and the City of Montreal to keep ICAO in such a world-class city as Montreal. We have reached an agreement with ICAO that is good for all involved. That is why it was supported by the ICAO council. We believe the presence of its headquarters in Montreal represents an economic benefit of more than $100 million each year ... [T]he presence of the headquarters in Montreal is very important for Canada ... [T]he Minister of Foreign Affairs has spoken to the Prime Minister of Qatar twice in the last two days on this issue. We will continue working very hard to keep ICAO in Montreal.

(*House of Commons Debates, 24 April 2013, p. 15839*)
(*Débats de la Chambre des Communes, le 24 avril 2013, p. 15839*)

Iran

Mr. Scott Reid (Lanark — Frontenac — Lennox and Addington):

[What is] the government [doing] to bear pressure on the Iranian regime while at the same time supporting the people of Iran in their pursuit of freedom?

Hon. John Baird (Minister of Foreign Affairs):

Just two days ago, we strengthened our actions against Iran by adding another 30 people and 82 entities to our sanction list. We have never had any confidence that the regime will act in good faith when it comes to the people of Iran. On May 10, I took part in the Global Dialogue on the Future of Iran. It was an opportunity to speak to those behind the regime's firewalls. To date, I am pleased to say that more than 360,000 users inside Iran have accessed content from the event we hosted at the Munk School at the University of Toronto. We stand with the courageous activists who are working for freedom in Iran.

(*House of Commons Debates, 31 May 2013, p. 17469*)
(*Débats de la Chambre des Communes, le 31 mai 2013, p. 17469*)

Jordan / Jordanie

Mr. Paul Dewar (Ottawa Centre):

[T]he ambassador's position in Jordan is critical, given the key role this country plays in the Middle East. Canadians are simply left scratching their heads at [the] appointment of [Bruno Saccomani as Canada's ambassador to Jordan]. [I]s this just another Conservative patronage appointment?

Mr. Deepak Obhrai (Parliamentary Secretary to the Minister of Foreign Affairs):

Mr. Saccomani is a very distinguished individual with a strong record as a professional public servant. Our government, this House and all Canadians can be proud of the work he has done and continues to do.

(*House of Commons Debates, 18 April 2013, p. 155606*)
(*Débats de la Chambre des Communes, le 18 avril 2013, p. 155606*)

Nelson Mandela

Mr. Dave Van Kesteren (Chatham-Kent — Essex):

Canada and the world is deeply saddened to learn of the passing of Nelson Mandela yesterday. The son of a tribal chief, Nelson Mandela sought an education, went on to actively participate in politics, and became a leading symbol in the fight against apartheid ... Could the parliamentary secretary to the Minister of Foreign Affairs please remind the House of some of Nelson Mandela's most impressive accomplishments?

Hon. Deepak Obhrai (Parliamentary Secretary to the Minister of Foreign Affairs and for International Human Rights):

Nelson Mandela's fight to end apartheid had a tremendous impact on me when I was growing up in Tanzania, when apartheid dominated southern Africa. Canadians were touched deeply by his life and his active pursuit of equality, justice, and freedom for all people. Nelson Mandela was also a passionate crusader against AIDS. He received the Nobel Peace Prize, became an honorary Canadian citizen, and was made a Companion of the Order of Canada. Canada joins South Africa and the world in mourning and celebrating a unique and special leader. Our thoughts and prayers are with his family.

(*House of Commons Debates, 6 December 2013, p. 1876*)
(*Débats de la Chambre des Communes, le 6 décembre 2013, p. 1876*)

Peru / Pérou

Mr. James Lunney (Nanaimo — Alberni):

Today Peru's Minister of Defence is in Ottawa. [W]hat [does Canada's minister] expect to accomplish in his meetings with his counterpart today?

Hon. Peter MacKay (Minister of National Defence):

Today we are welcoming to Canada Peru's minister of national defence, Pedro Cateriano Bellido, and the commander of the Peruvian navy as well, admiral Carlos Roberto Tejada Mera. Canada enjoys a strong relationship with Peru based on shared values, including democracy. [L]ater today we will be signing a defence co-operation memorandum of understanding that will help guide our future defence relations in areas such as policy, peace, humanitarian operations, disaster response and military education and training. This agreement strongly supports the growing ties between Canada and Peru and our government's leadership in the Americas.

(*House of Commons Debates, 1 March 2013, p. 14502*)
(*Débats de la Chambre des Communes, le 1 mars 2013, p. 14502*)

Ukraine

Mr. Ed Komarnicki (Souris — Moose Mountain):

Our Minister of Foreign Affairs is ... in Ukraine on behalf of Canada. Yesterday he met with the foreign ministry of Ukraine, as well as with more than a dozen civil society representatives, a broad group of religious leaders, business people and opposition leaders. [W]hat messages [did] the minister deliver to these important stakeholders and what [will] he be doing in Ukraine today?

Hon. Deepak Obhrai (Parliamentary Secretary to the Minister of Foreign Affairs and for International Human Rights):

Yesterday the Minister of Foreign Affairs expressed Canada's grave concerns with Ukraine government's crackdown on mass protests against its decision to suspend negotiations with the European Union. Today he will visit the Holodomor monument to pay his respects to those who perished under Soviet tyranny. He will also be visiting Independence Square in support of Canada and Ukraine's shared values of democracy and human rights. We are proud of our principled approach in these matters. This government continues to stand with the people of Ukraine.

(*House of Commons Debates, 5 December 2013, p. 1826*)
(*Débats de la Chambre des Communes, le 5 décembre 2013, p. 1826*)

United States / États-Unis

Hon. Thomas Mulcair (Leader of the Opposition):

Canadians reacted with shock and sadness yesterday as we witnessed the horrific acts of violence committed in Boston. Could the government update Canadians on its response to this tragedy and specifically the steps taken to provide assistance and consular services to the 2,000 Canadians and their families who were at yesterday's Boston Marathon?

Hon. James Moore (Minister of Canadian Heritage and Official Languages):

[W]e stand with [all those in Boston] in this most difficult time for the city of Boston, indeed for the United States. It appears that no Canadians were seriously injured or killed in yesterday's attack, but that does not affect the fact that we are heartbroken as Canadians. Our hearts, our thoughts and our prayers are with those who are affected by this terrible tragedy. [O]ur government stand[s] shoulder to shoulder with President Obama, the mayor of Boston and governor of Massachusetts as they try to find those cowards who are responsible for this terrible attack.

(*House of Commons Debates, 16 April 2013, p. 15490*)
(*Débats de la Chambre des Communes, le 16 avril 2013, p. 15490*)

HEALTH / SANTÉ

Energy Drinks / Boissons énergisantes

Hon. Hedy Fry (Vancouver Centre):

The U.S. is investigating deaths linked to energy drinks. Mexico banned the sales for anyone under age 18 ... Will the minister ... do her duty to protect the health of Canadians?

Hon. Leona Aglukkaq (Minister of Health, Minister of the Canadian Northern Economic Development Agency and Minister for the Arctic Council):

Health Canada has been very clear that caffeinated energy drinks are not recommended for children. Our government announced a new approach to regulating energy drinks and would include limits on the level of caffeine in these products. It also includes improved labelling in order to support the consumers and parents in making informed choices. The new measures will help all Canadians make informed decisions about the amount of caffeine they consume.

(*House of Commons Debates, 6 February 2013, p. 13789*)
(*Débats de la Chambre des Communes, le 6 février 2013, p. 13789*)

Global Fund to Fight AIDS, Tuberculosis and Malaria / Fonds mondial de lutte contre le sida, la tuberculose et le paludisme

Mme Hélène Laverdière (Laurier — Sainte-Marie):

Le Fonds mondial de lutte contre le sida, la tuberculose et le paludisme contribue plus que n'importe quel autre organisme à réduire le nombre de nouvelles infections dans les pays en développement. Aujourd'hui, on est à un point tournant où on pourrait enfin contrôler ces maladies. C'est pour cela que le fonds a demandé aux donateurs de redoubler leur effort. Les États-Unis et la Suisse se sont déjà engagés à augmenter substantiellement leur contribution. Est-ce que le Canada va faire la même chose?

Ms. Lois Brown (Parliamentary Secretary to the Minister of International Cooperation):

Our government is committed to ensuring that our development is focused and effective. Canadians expect accountability with that. This is why we have untied our food aid and at the same time we have doubled our aid to Africa. Our contributions to the global fund to fight TB, AIDS and malaria are at unprecedented levels. Canada is paid up on all of its contributions to the funds that we have designated. In fact, the minister contributed an extra $20 million just last week.

(*House of Commons Debates, 7 June 2013, p. 17919*)
(*Débats de la Chambre des Communes, le 7 juin 2013, p. 17919*)

Polio

Mr. Wladyslaw Lizon (Mississauga East — Cooksville):

This week is World Immunization Week ... [What has been] Canada's latest contribution to end polio?

Ms. Lois Brown (Parliamentary Secretary to the Minister of International Cooperation):

Today at the Global Vaccine Summit, the Minister of International Cooperation announced that Canada will remain a leader in polio eradication. Bill Gates said Canada's increased support will help ensure that we can end polio and help all children live healthy and productive lives. However, to accomplish this, violence against vaccine workers must end.

Canada calls on all parties to denounce acts of violence against immunization workers. We also need everyone to continue to promote scientific facts about vaccination. Canada remains committed to making polio history.

(*House of Commons Debates, 25 April 2013, p. 15920*)
(*Débats de la Chambre des Communes, le 25 avril 2013, p. 15920*)

HUMAN RIGHTS / DROITS DE LA PERSONNE

China / Chine

Mme Rosane Doré Lefebvre (Alfred-Pellan):

Il semble que l'Agence des services frontaliers du Canada invite les représentants du gouvernement chinois à des réunions derrière des portes closes, lors desquelles le Canada approuve des demandes de déportation de dissidents recherchés par le gouvernement chinois. On connaît toutes les préoccupations de la communauté internationale et du Canada quant au traitement des dissidents en Chine. Comment le gouvernement peut-il permettre une telle collaboration?

Hon. Vic Toews (Minister of Public Safety):

Our government is committed to removing foreign criminals who have no right to be in Canada, something that the member opposes. Individuals who are in Canada illegally are removed only after officials have determined that they can be removed without undue risk. Our government has never shied away from raising human rights issues with China, and we will conduct ourselves lawfully in every respect.

(*House of Commons Debates, 14 February 2013, p. 14155*)
(*Débats de la Chambre des Communes, le 14 février 2013, p. 14155*)

Forced Marriage / Mariage forcé

Mrs. Stella Ambler (Mississauga South):

Every year around the world, millions of girls as young as eight or nine years old are forced into marriage. Some suggest the number could be as high as 14 million a year ... Through the maternal, newborn, and child health initiative, Canada has committed nearly $3 billion over five years to help women and children lead longer, healthier lives. This is in addition to the almost $14 million in support the country has provided toward ending sexual violence and encouraging the full participation of women in emerging democracies. [What are] this government's [other] efforts to halt the practice of early, child, and forced marriage around the world?

Hon. John Baird (Minister of Foreign Affairs):

Our government has made it a priority to fight the scourge of child, early, and forced marriage. This is why Canada, today, will introduce the first-ever stand-alone resolution at the United Nations General Assembly against child, early, and forced marriage. This resolution calls for the protection of these children and calls on the General Assembly to take action to bring an end to this barbaric practice. I am also pleased to announce today that Canada will contribute an additional $5 million to fight early and child marriage around the world.

(House of Commons Debates, 24 October 2013, p. 357)
(Débats de la Chambre des Communes, le 24 octobre 2013, p. 357)

Funding: Office of Religious Freedom / Financement: Bureau de la liberté de religion

Ms. Joyce Murray (Vancouver Quadra):

Today we learned that the [government is] cutting $270 million from foreign affairs, including human rights programs. That is on top of eliminating $11 million for Rights and Democracy, protecting human rights abroad. However, it has increased $5 million to create a new bureaucracy for only religious rights ... What about other human rights [such as] ... women and the LGBTQ community ... ?

Hon. John Baird (Minister of Foreign Affairs):

This government has made human rights the cornerstone of our foreign policy. Promoting Canadian values is something that is tremendously important. No country has spoken more loudly on human rights, religious freedom, or on the important rights that women and gays have right around the world, than this government. We are very proud of our Office of Religious Freedom. It is a fundamental freedom. It promotes pluralism, which is a fundamental Canadian value, and we make no apologies for standing up for this important human right.

(House of Commons Debates, 26 February 2013, p. 14323)
(Débats de la Chambre des Communes, le 26 février 2013, p. 14323)

Sexual Minorities / Minorités sexuelles

Mr. Randall Garrison (Esquimalt — Juan de Fuca):

It is less than 100 days until the Olympic Games open in Sochi, but Canadians are very concerned about the impact of Russia's new anti-gay laws. Russia has already arrested and expelled non-Russians under these so-called "gay propaganda" laws. Will the Minister of Foreign Affairs appoint a special consular officer to assist LGBT athletes and spectators in Sochi to ensure that all Canadians can take part, freely and fully, in these Olympic Games?

Hon. Deepak Obhrai (Parliamentary Secretary to the Minister of Foreign Affairs and for International Human Rights):

Canada has very much made its position very clear in reference to athlete participation in Russia, and the Russian authorities have agreed that nobody will be discriminated against when they go to the Olympics in Russia. We will keep an eye on it and we will make our representation to the Russian authority should anything else happen.

(*House of Commons Debates, 31 October 2013, p. 646*)
(*Débats de la Chambre des Communes, le 31 octobre 2013, p. 646*)

GENDER EQUALITY / ÉGALITÉ DES SEXES

Royal Succession / Succession au trône

Mr. James Lunney (Nanaimo — Alberni):

The Crown is particularly relevant as we mark the final days of Her Majesty Queen Elizabeth II's Diamond Jubilee. Like all institutions, the Canadian Crown has evolved over time and today our government is introducing legislation to formally assent to the next step in this evolution. Can the Minister of Canadian Heritage please tell the House more about his legislation?

Hon. James Moore (Minister of Canadian Heritage and Official Languages):

Today we have tabled legislation that will ensure that gender equality will indeed be in place for all successors to the throne.[18] This modernization

---

[18] Editor's note: *Succession to the Throne Act, 2013* (Bill C-53) — *An Act to Assent to Alterations in the Law Touching the Succession to the Throne / Loi de 2013 sur la succession au trône* (Loi C-53) — *Loi d'assentiment aux modifications apportées à la loi*

makes good sense. The Prime Minister told Canadians that we would put this reform forward and we are. Given what we know the legislation to be about in the near future, on behalf of the government and I think indeed all members of Parliament I want to say that we wish the Duke and Duchess of Cambridge all the best in the coming months and indeed many years.

(*House of Commons Debates, 31 January 2013, p. 13524*)
(*Débats de la Chambre des Communes, le 31 janvier 2013, p. 13524*)

IMMIGRATION

Citizenship / Citoyenneté

Mr. Kevin Lamoureux (Winnipeg North):

In 2005 the ... government allocated some $69 million to reduce processing times for citizenship applications. Today ... the processing time has increased and waiting times are over four, five, six years and beyond. Now there is a record high of over 300,000 residents waiting for their citizenship applications to be processed ... When will the [Government] take concrete actions to decrease the processing times for citizenship applications?

Mr. Rick Dykstra (Parliamentary Secretary to the Minister of Citizenship and Immigration):

Canadians should actually [be] proud that there is such a high demand for Canadian citizenship. After all, who would not want to be a citizen of the greatest country in the world. Part of the increase in wait times has resulted from the fact that our government has maintained and sustained the highest levels of immigration in Canadian history. We welcome approximately 30,000 more newcomers each year than [before]. [W]e are fixing [the wait time].

(*House of Commons Debates, 4 March 2013, p. 14556*)
(*Débats de la Chambre des Communes, le 4 mars 2013, p. 14556*)

Newcomers / Nouveaux arrivants

Mr. Parm Gill (Brampton — Springdale):

[What is the government doing] to help immigrants succeed?

---

concernant la succession au trône; introduced in the House of Commons on 31 January 2013, Royal assent given on 27 March 2013 (SC 2013, c 6).

Hon. Jason Kenney (Minister of Citizenship, Immigration and Multiculturalism):

It is unacceptable that new Canadians have an unemployment rate twice as high as that of the general population. That is why this government has tripled our investment in settlement services. We are reforming our immigration system to ensure that people who arrive here have the skills to succeed upon arrival, but we have also invested significantly in pre-arrival orientation. Through the Canadian immigration integration project, today we have graduated 20,000 newcomers from abroad, people who have a much better chance to get settled, find good jobs and succeed in their new Canadian lives. We are investing in the success of newcomers.

(*House of Commons Debates, 12 February 2013, p. 14040*)
(*Débats de la Chambre des Communes, le 12 février 2013, p. 14040*)

Refugees / Réfugiés

Mr. Kevin Lamoureux (Winnipeg North):

Today the Canadian Doctors for Refugee Care and the Canadian Association of Refugee Lawyers went to Federal Court to challenge the Minister of Citizenship and Immigration's reckless health cuts to the most marginalized and vulnerable people in Canada. They are arguing that the cuts are unconstitutional, illegal and a breach of obligations under international law. The cuts were announced last June without consultation. Will the minister listen to the front-line health care workers and fix his mess?

Hon. Jason Kenney (Minister of Citizenship, Immigration and Multiculturalism):

We have listened to Canadians. Canadian taxpayers have no obligation to provide gold-plated health insurance to illegal immigrants who have been deemed by our fair and generous legal system not to be refugees. It is interesting to note that we brought in the initial part of this change on July 1 and we immediately saw a 90% reduction in the number of asylum claims being filed by nationals of the democracies of the European Union.

(*House of Commons Debates, 25 February 2013, p. 14253*)
(*Débats de la Chambre des Communes, le 25 février 2013, p. 14253*)

Mme Sadia Groguhé (Saint-Lambert):

Lorsque les Canadiens d'origine syrienne ont demandé l'aide du gouvernement pour qu'ils puissent être réunis avec leur famille qui vit dans la terreur en Syrie, le ministre de l'Immigration a bêtement refusé de les rencontrer. Il leur a aussi dit que la Turquie ne permettait pas aux réfugiés syriens de sortir du pays, sauf que l'ambassadeur turc a démenti ces accusations sans fondement. Maintenant que le ministre ne peut plus se réfugier dans de fausses excuses, peut-il nous dire comment il compte favoriser la réunification familiale pour les Canadiens d'origine syrienne?

Mr. Rick Dykstra (Parliamentary Secretary to the Minister of Citizenship and Immigration):

The Minister of Immigration has met and spoken with Syrian Canadians across the country on many occasions about the crisis in Syria. The fact is that Turkey does not allow potential refugees to even leave the country until the UNHCR has made a decision on their case and refers their case to a country for resettlement. We are focused on this and we are doing what we can. The minister has worked extremely hard to assist those in Syria.

(*House of Commons Debates, 20 March 2013, p. 14965*)
(*Débats de la Chambre des Communes, le 20 mars 2013, p. 14965*)

Ms. Jinny Jogindera Sims (Newton — North Delta):

15 years ago Jose Figueroa came to Canada from war-ravaged El Salvador to start a new life. Now he has a family with three children and a supportive community. However, the government is deporting Mr. Figueroa because he was affiliated with the FMLN in the eighties. The FMLN is the internationally-recognized democratically-elected government of El Salvador, and Conservative ministers attended its inauguration. The contradiction makes no sense. Will the minister stop separating Mr. Figueroa from his family in Canada?

Mr. Rick Dykstra (Parliamentary Secretary to the Minister of Citizenship and Immigration):

We have a fair and just immigration system ... Typically, failed refugee claimants have as many as seven negative judicial, quasi-judicial and administrative decisions before they face deportation. This means that our independent IRB has found no merit to the claim that has been put forward in terms of seeking asylum in our country.

(*House of Commons Debates, 24 May 2013, p. 16983*)
(*Débats de la Chambre des Communes, le 24 mai 2013, p. 16983*)

Persons with Disabilities / Personnes handicapées

Mme Manon Perreault (Montcalm):

Cela fait plus d'un an que le Canada doit faire un rapport à l'ONU sur la mise en oeuvre de la Convention relative aux droits des personnes handicapées. Pourquoi les conservateurs n'ont-ils toujours pas fait ce rapport? ... Quand vont-ils mettre en oeuvre la convention, afin de créer un Canada plus accessible et plus inclusif?

L'hon. Jason Kenney (ministre de l'Emploi et du Développement social et ministre du Multiculturalisme):

[Aujourd'hui, c'est] la Journée internationale des personnes handicapées. J'étais très heureux de voir les militants pour les Canadiens handicapés appuyer les politiques et les mesures de notre gouvernement qui faciliteront l'accès des gens ayant des habilités différentes au marché du travail. Nous allons continuer à travailler ensemble pour en arriver à une meilleure inclusion de tous les Canadiens, peu importe leurs habiletés.

(*House of Commons Debates, 3 December 2013, p. 1695*)
(*Débats de la Chambre des Communes, le 3 décembre 2013, p. 1695*)

Protecting Canadians Abroad / Protection des Canadiens à l'étranger

Mr. Kyle Seeback (Brampton West):

Prabh Srawn [a Canadian Forces reservist] has been missing for a little over two weeks [in Australia], and the family feels that not enough is being done to find him. [W]hat has been done and what will be done to find Prabh Srawn?

Hon. Diane Ablonczy (Minister of State of Foreign Affairs (Americas and Consular Affairs)):

Earlier today, I spoke with Australia's High Commissioner to Canada. I thanked her for their authority's dedicated efforts and relayed Canada's request that the search for Mr. Srawn not be reduced at this time. Canada has been actively working with Australian authorities to discuss the search mission and to convey the family's concerns ... We join Canadians in praying for his safe return ... Our engagement with Australian authorities at all levels will definitely continue.

(*House of Commons Debates, 28 May 2013, p. 17157*)
(*Débats de la Chambre des Communes, le 28 mai 2013, p. 17157*)

Mr. Paul Dewar (Ottawa Centre):

Earlier today we heard the disturbing news that CBC reporters Derek Stoffel and Sasa Petricic were detained in Istanbul. [Can] the government update us on their status, what is happening and what the government is doing to help them[?]

Hon. Diane Ablonczy (Minister of State of Foreign Affairs (Americas and Consular Affairs)):

The Minister of Foreign Affairs has spoken personally with the Turkish ambassador to express his concern about the arrest of these two journalists and also about the ongoing situation in Turkey. Canadian officials are in touch with the CBC and have met with the two detained journalists. The Turkish ambassador has assured us that the two journalists are safe and well treated. We will continue to liaise at the highest levels until this matter is resolved.

(House of Commons Debates, 12 June 2013, p. 18178)
(Débats de la Chambre des Communes, le 12 juin 2013, p. 18178)

Mr. Wayne Marston (Hamilton East — Stoney Creek):

[T]wo Hamilton men, Nick Miele, and his 18-year-old cousin, Ben Constantini ... have been behind bars in a Dominican jail since the early morning hours of May 28. Close family members are gravely concerned that these men are in ill health, and that they have not been afforded due process. [What] efforts are being made on behalf of these men?

Mr. Deepak Obhrai (Parliamentary Secretary to the Minister of Foreign Affairs):

Consular assistance is being provided to the two Canadians who have been arrested in the Dominican Republic for allegedly injuring another Canadian citizen. Although the Government of Canada cannot exempt them from local laws, consular officials are advocating for fair treatment and due process, and will remain in contact with the families.

(House of Commons Debates, 14 June 2013, p. 18377)
(Débats de la Chambre des Communes, le 14 juin 2013, p. 18377)

Right to Food / Droit à l'alimentation

Mr. Dean Allison (Niagara West — Glanbrook):

[What is] Canada's commitment to food security?

Ms. Lois Brown (Parliamentary Secretary to the Minister of International Cooperation):

Canada is a global leader in providing food to those people in developing countries who need it most. We are committed to achieving long-term results that improve the lives of women, men and children living in poverty. That is why the Minister of International Cooperation announced today more Canadian support for the world's hungry under the new food assistance convention. From untying food assistance to being the first G8 country to deliver on its L'Aquila food security commitment, our government has stood up for those most in need.

(House of Commons Debates, 5 February 2013, p. 13706)
(Débats de la Chambre des Communes, le 5 février 2013, p. 13706)

Sri Lanka

Hon. Bob Rae (Toronto Centre):

In the light of increasing evidence with respect to the activities of the government of Sri Lanka, its failure to reconcile with the minority Tamil population in Sri Lanka, its failure to deal with the human rights crisis, which is seen as increasingly deep, there being groups and observers across the board including the UN Human Rights Council that are challenging what the government of Sri Lanka is saying, can the Government of Canada state what it is doing to make sure that the next meeting of the Commonwealth heads of states will not in fact take place in Colombo but will be located elsewhere and that the Government of Canada has a clear position with respect to which meetings it will attend and which it will not?

Mr. Bob Dechert (Parliamentary Secretary to the Minister of Foreign Affairs):

The Prime Minister has spoken out, loudly and clearly, on this very important issue of human rights. He voiced our concerns on the lack of accountability for the serious allegations of war crimes and the lack of reconciliation with the Tamil community, and said the events that have taken place since the end of the civil war are unacceptable. We have relayed the Government of Canada's position both to the high commissioner and directly to the minister of foreign affairs for Sri Lanka. Canada will continue to speak loudly and clearly on behalf of human rights around the world, especially in Sri Lanka.

Right Hon. Stephen Harper (Prime Minister):

I have indicated that unless changes occur in Sri Lanka, I will not attend the Commonwealth summit there. I am concerned with further developments since I made that statement, which are taking that country in a worse direction.

(House of Commons Debates, 25-26 February 2013, pp. 14248, 14319)
(Débats de la Chambre des Communes, le 25 et 26 février 2013, pp. 14248, 14319)

United Nations Human Rights Council / Conseil des droits de l'homme des Nations unies

Mr. Larry Miller (Bruce — Grey — Owen Sound):

Richard Falk [Special Rapporteur to the UNHRC] is once again attacking UN Watch, an NGO led by Canadian Hillel Neuer, and has called for it to be investigated ... [Does] the government agree with Mr. Falk or not?

Hon. Jason Kenney (Minister of Citizenship, Immigration and Multiculturalism):

Richard Falk is an embarrassment to the United Nations Human Rights Council. He has praised 9/11 conspiracy theorists repeatedly. He has suggested that the United States provoked terrorist attacks against it. He is now attacking a Canadian-led UN Watch. We call on Richard Falk to be fired as a special rapporteur of the United Nations Human Rights Council. He is a disgrace to that body and the United Nations.

(House of Commons Debates, 11 June 2013 p. 18088)
(Débats de la Chambre des Communes, le 11 juin 2013, p. 18088)

INTERNATIONAL CRIMINAL LAW / DROIT PÉNAL INTERNATIONAL

Chemical Weapons / Armes chimiques

Mme Hélène Laverdière (Laurier-Sainte-Marie):

[Nous sommes] extrêmement préoccupé[s] par les allégations d'utilisation d'armes chimiques en Syrie ... Est-ce que le gouvernement va ... se joindre au reste du monde afin de demander que les Nations Unies mènent une enquête sur ces allégations?

Mr. Bob Dechert (Parliamentary Secretary to the Minister of Foreign Affairs):

Our government is providing real leadership on this issue through a credit of up to $2 million to the Organisation for the Prohibition of Chemical Weapons to conduct just such a study ... We are very concerned about these reports and remain in close contact with our allies. The use of chemical weapons on the people of Syria would be heinous and contrary to international law.

(*House of Commons Debates, 26 April 2013, p. 15969*)
(*Débats de la Chambre des Communes, le 26 avril 2013, p. 15969*)

Corruption

Hon. John McKay (Scarborough — Guildwood):

When Dr. Porter was chair of SIRC, he was in possession of some of Canada's most sensitive information. He is now languishing in one of Panama's most notorious prisons in the presence of pimps, drug dealers and organized crime. [W]hat steps [has] the government taken to get Dr. Porter out of his Panamanian jail in order to face justice and in order to be put into a secure Canadian facility?

Hon. Vic Toews (Minister of Public Safety):

[O]ur government has been following this issue very closely. We are very pleased that there was an arrest in this matter. We congratulate the authorities on a successful arrest. While I cannot comment on a specific case, I can say that anyone involved in corruption must face the full force of the law, and our government will take the steps necessary to ensure that happens.

(*House of Commons Debates, 2 June 2013, p. 17523*)
(*Débats de la Chambre des Communes, le 2 juin 2013, p. 17523*)

International Criminal Court (Syria) / Cour pénale internationale (Syrie)

Hon. Irwin Cotler (Mount Royal):

When over 50 countries called on the UN Security Council to refer the criminality in Syria to the International Criminal Court, Canada was absent. The Minister of Foreign Affairs announces the matter should be left up to the Syrian people, contradicting the government's former and correct position that Assad must be held accountable for his actions. When will the government reconsider its position and join this urgent international call for justice on behalf of the Syrian people under assault and pursuant to our international legal responsibilities?

Hon. John Baird (Minister of Foreign Affairs):

Last month, 50 countries did call for Assad to face justice at the International Criminal Court. I am pleased that they join me, because I did it six months ago when I said, "What Assad needs to be facing is the International Criminal Court to face charges for committing crimes against humanity." I did that on July 6, 2012.

(*House of Commons Debates, 1 February 2013, p. 13573*)
(*Débats de la Chambre des Communes, le 1 février 2013, p. 13573*)

Iran

Hon. Irwin Cotler (Mount Royal):

The government has listed Iran as a state sponsor of terrorism and Iranian footprints are reported in yesterday's aborted terror attack, but while the government removed Iran's immunity from civil suit from victims of Iranian terror, allowing Iran to be held civilly accountable, the government is now invoking that very diplomatic immunity to protect Iran against civil suits by victims of Iranian terror. Why is the government standing up for Iran in Canadian courts? Why is the government undermining the very recently enacted civil remedies for victims of terror act? Why are we defending the rights of Iran against the victims of Iranian terror?

Mr. Deepak Obhrai (Parliamentary Secretary to the Minister of Foreign Affairs):

Canada condemns the aggressive and destabilizing action of the Iranian regime, including the blatant support that Iran provides to terrorist groups. Canada views the regime in Iran as the biggest threat to international peace and security in the world today. The Government of Canada in no way condones the actions of the Iranian regime.

(*House of Commons Debates, 23 April 2013, p. 15797*)
(*Débats de la Chambre des Communes, le 23 avril 2013, p. 15797*)

Landmines and Cluster Bombs / Mines terrestres et bombes à fragmentation

Mr. Paul Dewar (Ottawa Centre):

The International Committee of the Red Cross is voicing strong warnings about the huge gaps in the Conservatives' bill to ratify the Convention on Cluster Munitions. There are gaps that show that if this legislation goes forward, it would mean that Canadian Forces would be in joint operations using cluster munitions, if we can imagine that. Why is the government proposing flawed legislation with huge loopholes, instead of honouring Canada's commitment to ban cluster munitions?

Mr. Deepak Obhrai (Parliamentary Secretary to the Minister of Foreign Affairs):

Our legislation fully implements Canada's commitment to the convention and is in line with our key allies, including Australia and the United Kingdom. The Canadian Forces will make its policy to prohibit its members from using cluster munitions. This legislation preserves Canada's ability to work alongside our allies.

(*House of Commons Debates, 18 June 2013, p. 18543*)
(*Débats de la Chambre des Communes, le 18 juin 2013, p. 18543*)

Nuclear Non-Proliferation / Non-prolifération des armes nucléaires

Mr. Joe Daniel (Don Valley East):

North Korea continues to thumb its nose at the world. Today, the regime in Pyongyang confirmed it conducted a third nuclear test, in direct contravention of the global will and North Korea's international obligations. [What is] Canada's reaction to [this issue]?

Hon. John Baird (Minister of Foreign Affairs):

This reckless and provocative test marks a serious, misguided threat to regional peace and security. What makes it even more unconscionable is that many North Korean people are starving to death while their government misallocates resources on a nuclear weapons program. We are disappointed that North Korea's leaders have continued along this irresponsible path of placing nuclear weapons above the well-being and health of their own people. Canada will work with our international partners to pursue all appropriate actions and sanctions against this rogue regime.

(*House of Commons Debates, 12 February 2013, p. 14041*)
(*Débats de la Chambre des Communes, le 12 février 2013, p. 14041*)

Ukraine

Mr. Bob Zimmer (Prince George — Peace River):

At this time each year Canadians gather in solemn commemoration of the Holodomor, perpetuated by the Soviet regime on the Ukrainian people 80 years ago. In 2008, our Parliament passed an act to establish a Holodomor memorial day, and to officially recognize the Ukrainian Famine of 1932 to 1933 as an act of genocide. [W]hy [is] it important that all Canadians remember the atrocities that took place during the Holodomor?

Hon. Tim Uppal (Minister of State (Multiculturalism)):

On the fourth Saturday of November we join Ukrainian communities across Canada in commemorating Holodomor Memorial Day. Holodomor was a horrific act of genocide carried out by Joseph Stalin's soviet regime through the deliberate starvation of millions of Ukrainians. Our government has been committed to raising awareness of Holodomor through the establishment of a monument to the victims of communism in Ottawa. We have an obligation to ensure future generations of Canadians learn about and remember the Holodomor. We will always remember them.

(*House of Commons Debates, 22 November 2013, p. 1264*)
(*Débats de la Chambre des Communes, le 22 novembre 2013, p. 1264*)

Violence against Women / Violence faite aux femmes

Mrs. Joy Smith (Kildonan — St. Paul):

[What are] Canada's ... efforts to combat violence against women?

Hon. Rona Ambrose (Minister of Public Works and Government Services and Minister for Status of Women):

Canada ... is committed to ending violence against women and girls at home and abroad. Just this week, at the United Nations, we have taken a leadership role to take our message from Canada to the world that engaging men and boys is an important part in ending violence against women. While men are the perpetrators of violence against women and girls, the majority of men are good and want to help; so we ask them to take a stand and not be bystanders and work with us and women across this country to end violence against women and girls.

(*House of Commons Debates, 8 March 2013, p. 14783*)
(*Débats de la Chambre des Communes, le 8 mars 2013, p. 14783*)

War Crimes (Sri Lankan Civil War) / Crimes de guerre (guerre civile au Sri Lanka)

Mr. Wayne Marston (Hamilton East — Stoney Creek):

International pressure continues to grow for an independent investigation into the very serious allegation of war crimes that were committed in the final days of the Sri Lankan civil war. Yesterday, the United Nations Human Rights Council passed a resolution that, once again, underscores the need for accountability. Today, Conservative senator Hugh Segal is in Sri Lanka. [W]ill the senator be pushing the Sri Lankan government for an immediate independent inquiry into those reprehensible actions during that civil war?

Hon. John Baird (Minister of Foreign Affairs):

No other government in the world has worked harder, has pushed harder to ensure that there is accountability, meaningful reconciliation and a return to human rights in Sri Lanka. No other leader in the world has been more outspoken, more morally clear, on this issue than the Prime Minister of Canada. All Canadians can be tremendously proud of that. We will continue to work through the Commonwealth, through the United Nations, to ensure that there is real accountability, meaningful reconciliation and a return to decent human rights in that country.

(*House of Commons Debates, 21 March 2013, p. 15058*)
(*Débats de la Chambre des Communes, le 21 mars 2013, p. 15058*)

INTERNATIONAL HUMANITARIAN LAW / DROIT INTERNATIONAL HUMANITAIRE

Humanitarian Intervention and Aid / Aide et intervention humanitaire

Haiti / Haïti

Mme Hélène Laverdière (Laurier-Sainte-Marie):

Ce dernier gèle l'aide financière à Haïti ... Quand les conservateurs prendront-ils la coopération internationale au sérieux?

Ms. Lois Brown (Parliamentary Secretary to the Minister of International Cooperation):

[W]e are concerned for the people of Haiti. While the results of projects have largely met expectations, progress toward a self-sustaining Haiti has been limited. Projects to which we previously committed are making progress, and we stand ready to help should a humanitarian crisis arise. But future commitments will be dependent on greater leadership, accountability and transparency from the government of Haiti.

(*House of Commons Debates, 28 January 2013, p. 13302*)
(*Débats de la Chambre des Communes, le 28 janvier 2013, p. 13302*)

Mme Hélène Laverdière (Laurier — Sainte-Marie):

Le Tribunal constitutionnel de la République dominicaine a rendu un verdict qui a pour effet de retirer la nationalité dominicaine à bon nombre de personnes nées dans ce pays et notamment à beaucoup de personnes d'origine haïtienne. Ce jugement va à l'encontre du droit international et suscite un tollé partout dans le monde ... Les Haïtiens de Montréal ont créé un groupe de pression pour attirer l'attention. Le gouvernement va-t-il les appuyer?

Hon. John Baird (Minister of Foreign Affairs):

Obviously, we are following this issue tremendously closely. I am very committed to working with my colleague and friend opposite on what we might do to provide that support and assistance to these individuals.

(*House of Commons Debates, 5 November 2013, p. 774*)
(*Débats de la Chambre des Communes, le 5 novembre 2013, p. 774*)

Mali

Hon. Thomas Mulcair (Leader of the Opposition):

[What is] Canada's involvement in the ongoing mission in Mali?

Right Hon. Stephen Harper (Prime Minister):

[T]he government has been very clear that it will not undertake a Canadian combat mission in Mali. At the same time, we are providing technical assistance to the French and other military forces who are there. We have committed heavy lift aircraft to that engagement, which is being done under a United Nations mandate.

Hon. John Baird (Minister of Foreign Affairs):

As we speak, the Minister of International Cooperation is in Ethiopia at meetings of the African Union. Earlier today he pledged $13 million to support the people of Mali in their humanitarian needs during this crisis.

Depuis l'année dernière, le Canada a donné plus de 75 millions de dollars en assistance humanitaire. La population du Mali peut continuer à compter sur le soutien du Canada en cette période difficile pour assurer une voie vers la stabilité, la sécurité et la prospérité.

(*House of Commons Debates, 28-29 January 2013, pp. 13296, 13394*)
(*Débats de la Chambre des Communes, le 28 et 29 janvier 2013, pp. 13296, 13394*)

L'hon. Mauril Bélanger (Ottawa — Vanier):

Lorsque le Mali et son gouvernement ont subi un coup d'État au printemps de 2012, plusieurs pays, dont le Canada, ont suspendu leur programme d'aide bilatérale. Un peu plus tard, lorsqu'un gouvernement provisoire fut instauré, quelques pays seulement ont rétabli leur programme. Cependant, à la suite des élections présidentielles de cet été et de l'assermentation du président Ibrahim Boubacar Keïta, le 5 septembre, la plupart des pays ont rétabli leur programme d'aide, mais pas le Canada. Pourquoi?

Ms. Lois Brown (Parliamentary Secretary to the Minister of International Development):

Canada is a leader in helping Malians through humanitarian crises. Our assistance provides emergency health care and access to water and food for displaced persons and refugees. Canada will continue to work with other donors, Canadian non-governmental organizations, and multilateral organizations such as the World Food Programme to provide stability to the people of Mali. The ambassador of Mali to Canada called Canada's assistance "exemplary."

(*House of Commons Debates, 24 October 2013, p. 360*)
(*Débats de la Chambre des Communes, le 24 octobre 2013, p. 360*)

Palestine

Mr. Paul Dewar (Ottawa Centre):

On Sunday, U.S. Secretary of State John Kerry announced a $4-billion plan to invest in the Palestinian private sector to help restart the peace process. In contrast, Canada's aid commitment to the Palestinian authority expired in March, and the Minister of Foreign Affairs has taken a "wait and see" approach in terms of renewal ... Will the Minister of Foreign Affairs actually confirm that he will advance the cause of the Palestinian people and renew the funds?

Hon. John Baird (Minister of Foreign Affairs):

About eight weeks ago, I travelled to Ramallah and met with President Abbas and Prime Minister Fayyad. I met with my counterpart, Mr. al-Malki, the Minister of Foreign Affairs. [O]ur aid for the Palestinian authority has not lapsed. In fact, there have been some construction delays, issues that are no fault of Canada, or frankly, of the Palestinian Authority. Aid has been extended to complete the commitments we have made. It was $300 million over five years, and we will take the sixth year to get the job done. I did consult about what their priorities are. They identified economic development, health, education and security. We are currently reviewing what we heard in Ramallah.

(*House of Commons Debates, 31 May 2013, pp. 17469*)
(*Débats de la Chambre des Communes, le 31 mai 2013, p. 17469*)

Phillipines / Philippines

Hon. Thomas Mulcair (Leader of the Opposition):

12 days ago, Typhoon Haiyan struck the Philippines, creating one of the greatest humanitarian crises in the world's history. [What have been] Canada's plans to help?

Right Hon. Stephen Harper (Prime Minister):

Obviously, this is a massive humanitarian crisis. [T]he Government of Canada has been there. Obviously, we are supporting this crisis financially. We provided a matching fund that we encourage our citizens to donate to. I know, particularly, our Filipino Canadian friends across the country are raising money and sending their support. We are providing some flexibility in immigration. [T]here are now hundreds of members of the Canadian Armed Forces and other Canadian officials who are present on the ground. Obviously, we are very proud of the work they are doing to assist.

(*House of Commons Debates, 19 November 2013, p. 1051*)
(*Débats de la Chambre des Communes, le 19 novembre 2013, p. 1051*)

Syria / Syrie

Mr. David Sweet (Ancaster — Dundas — Flamborough — Westdale:

It has been 22 months since the beginning of the crisis in Syria and Canadians, along with the international community, continue to be horrified by the violence inflicted on Syrian people. [What is] our government's most recent announcement to help the people of Syria?

Hon. John Baird (Minister of Foreign Affairs):

All Canadians, this government and all members of the House remain gravely concerned about the situation in Syria and the ever growing potential of the violence spilling into the neighbouring countries. That is why today the Government of Canada has announced that significant additional humanitarian assistance to provide food, water, housing and safety for people inside Syria and in the neighbouring countries will be provided to assist them in their time of need. Our government has and will continue to support the efforts of the international community to bring about an end to this violence. We stand by the people of Syria in their time of need.

(*House of Commons Debates, 30 January 2013, p. 13444*)
(*Débats de la Chambre des Communes, le 30 janvier 2013, p. 13444*)

Global Poverty / Pauvreté mondiale

Mr. Joe Daniel (Don Valley East):

Yesterday, World Bank President Dr. Jim Yong Kim called for the end of extreme global poverty by 2030. He said, "We cannot reach our goal without the private sector." [W]hat [is] Canada doing to help encourage private sector-led development?

Hon. Julian Fantino (Minister of International Cooperation):

Our government has announced three new initiatives to encourage private sector-led growth, including support for a World Bank facility that would provide insurance for projects that help support economic growth and reduce poverty. Canadians can be very proud of these initiatives and investments. In fact, World Bank President Dr. Jim Yong Kim said that these investments will "help rebuild fragile economies, which creates good jobs and helps people lift themselves out of poverty." He also said, "We are very grateful to our Canadian partners ..." [W]e will continue to help create jobs and growth for those who are most in need in impoverished countries.

(*House of Commons Debates, 12 June 2013, p. 18178*)
(*Débats de la Chambre des Communes, le 12 juin 2013, p. 18178*)

Refugees / Réfugiés

Mme Hélène Laverdière (Laurier-Sainte-Marie):

Au lieu de l'augmentation promise dans le rétablissement des réfugiés, le gouvernement a admis 25 % moins de réfugiés que l'année dernière ... Pourquoi le ministre a-t-il rompu sa promesse d'offrir une terre d'accueil à plus de réfugiés?

L'hon. Jason Kenney (ministre de la Citoyenneté, de l'Immigration et du Multiculturalisme):

Nous sommes en train d'augmenter le nombre de réfugiés réétablis au Canada afin de renforcer notre tradition humanitaire en immigration pour la protection des réfugiés. Juste hier, j'étais en Irak. Nous accueillons à peu près 4 000 réfugiés irakiens par année. Cela dit, la guerre civile en Syrie a entraîné la fermeture de notre bureau à Damas et cela a affecté le traitement de ce rétablissement de réfugiés irakiens. Nous sommes en train de régler ce problème là-bas.

(*House of Commons Debates, 7 March 2013, p. 14731*)
(*Débats de la Chambre des Communes, le 7 mars 2013, p. 14731*)

Ms. Elizabeth May (Saanich — Gulf Islands):

There are over one million refugees in camps in Turkey, Jordan and Lebanon, and there is inadequate help for those people who are caught up in the conflict. Acknowledging that the government has increased financial contributions to the UN High Commissioner for Refugees, what more can the government do? Is there a possibility of providing emergency assistance to those refugees with connections to Canada?

Right Hon. Stephen Harper (Prime Minister):

We are obviously all deeply troubled by the humanitarian situation in Syria, which just gets progressively worse. We are not only worried about the situation in Syria, but, frankly, the wider instability that threatens the rest of the region. That is why ... the government has brought forward some specific help to Syria and to some of its neighbours as well. We continue, through various agencies of the government and through working with our allies, to look at ways that we can help further.

(*House of Commons Debates, 1 May 2013, p. 16145*)
(*Débats de la Chambre des Communes, le 1 mai 2013, p. 16145*)

TRADE AND ECONOMY / COMMERCE ET ÉCONOMIE

Aerospace / Industrie aérospatiale

Air Travel / Transport aérien

Mr. Bruce Hyer (Thunder Bay — Superior North):

Our Canadian economy loses $2.3 billion every year and thousands of jobs due to Canada's uncompetitive airline ticket prices. More and more Canadians are crossing the border for lower American airfares. Unlike the U.S.A., [Canada's] government profits from exorbitant airport rents and high security fees on top of various other taxes. When will the [government] stop overtaxing airports and killing our Canadian airline and tourism industries?

Hon. Steven Fletcher (Minister of State (Transport)):

Canada works on a user-pay system. The people who use our airports pay for the use of the airports. There is a dividend that the federal government receives from airports each year and that is because the airports lease the land from the federal government. This is very different than the U.S. model, where U.S. airports are heavily subsidized by the taxpayer. We will not have the taxpayer subsidize air travel. People who use air travel will pay for their trips.

(*House of Commons Debates, 24 May 2013, p. 16984*)
(*Débats de la Chambre des Communes, le 24 mai 2013, p. 16984*)

Foreign Workforce / Main-d'œuvre étrangère

Mr. Mike Sullivan (York South — Weston):

Why is Transport Canada rubber-stamping wet leases and letting potentially unqualified foreign pilots fly Canadian flights?

Hon. Steven Fletcher (Minister of State (Transport)):

Canada has one of the safest transportation systems in the world. It gets stronger every year. The number of aviation accidents has fallen by 25% since 2000 while air travel has increased significantly. Foreign pilots, just like Canadian pilots, go through a rigorous selection process in order to ensure that they are fully qualified. Officials are currently reviewing this policy to see if reform is needed.

(*House of Commons Debates, 28 February 2013, p. 14452*)
(*Débats de la Chambre des Communes, le 28 février 2012, p. 14452*)

Space and Satellites / Espace et satellites

Mme Laurin Liu (Rivière-des-Mille-Îles):

Que vont faire les conservateurs pour conserver l'expertise des employés de l'agence [spatiale canadienne] au Canada? Laisseront-ils le commandant Hadfield en apesanteur?

L'hon. Christian Paradis (ministre de l'Industrie et ministre d'État (Agriculture)):

Nous avons annoncé la participation du Canada à la très importante mission RADARSAT Constellation. C'est une mission de pointe. Nous sommes les leaders dans le monde par rapport aux satellites. On est très fier d'avoir Chris Hadfield, cet astronaute canadien qui est le premier commandant de la Station spatiale internationale. [O]n a annoncé dans notre Plan d'action économique de 2012 la participation du Canada à la Station spatiale internationale jusqu'à 2020. C'est ce qui permet d'avoir des commandants tels que Chris Hadfield, dont nous sommes très fiers.

(*House of Commons Debates, 8 February 2013, p. 13914*)
(*Débats de la Chambre des Communes, le 8 février 2013, p. 13914*)

Africa / Afrique

Mr. Ed Holder (London West):

Africa is one of the most dynamic regions in the world. According to the International Monetary Fund, 5 of the world's 20 fastest-growing economies are in sub-Saharan Africa. [What is Canada doing to] open up markets in this region?

Mr. Gerald Keddy (Parliamentary Secretary to the Minister of International Trade, for the Atlantic Canada Opportunities Agency and for the Atlantic Gateway):

This week the Minister of International Trade is leading a trade mission to Ghana and Nigeria. He is accompanied by representatives from 28 Canadian companies, promoting industries in high demand in developing countries. Canadian companies are creating jobs and prosperity throughout Africa. This is yet another example of how deeper trade is a win-win for Canadians and for our trading partners around the world.

(*House of Commons Debates, 29 January 2013, p. 13392*)
(*Débats de la Chambre des Communes, le 29 janvier 2013, p. 13392*)

Arts and Culture / Arts et culture

Hon. Laurie Hawn (Edmonton Centre):

Today Rush, one of the most influential rock bands in Canadian history, is being inducted into the Rock and Roll Hall of Fame. The trio, composed of leader singer and bassist Geddy Lee, guitar player Alex Lifeson and drummer Neil Peart, has sold more than 40 million records worldwide. Their album sales place them third behind The Beatles and the Rolling Stones for the most consecutive gold or platinum studio albums sold by a rock band. [H]ow [has] this influential band impacted and shaped the music scene in Canada?

Hon. James Moore (Minister of Canadian Heritage and Official Languages):

Formed in 1968 in Toronto and still selling out concerts to this very day, Rush has become one of the most influential bands in Canada's history. Songs like Freewill, Tom Sawyer and Closer to the Heart are known and loved by all Canadians. The band's fame extends well beyond Canada. Rush's international popularity will have indeed been recognized and will be formally recognized today as Rush is inducted in the Rock and Roll Hall of Fame. On behalf of all Canadians and I think all members of the House, we want to wish Rush àll the best and congratulations on their success and their recognition today.

(House of Commons Debates, 18 April 2013, p. 15607)
(Débats de la Chambre des Communes, le 18 avril 2013, p. 15607)

Canada–US Border / Frontière canado-américaine

Mme Rosane Doré Lefebvre (Alfred-Pellan):

[L]es États-Unis ont frappé un mur budgétaire et ont annoncé des compressions de près de 85 milliards de dollars. Les services frontaliers seront les premiers touchés ... Quel est le plan du gouvernement pour s'assurer que les voyageurs, nos commerces et nos entreprises ne feront pas les frais des compressions de l'autre côté de la frontière?

Hon. John Baird (Minister of Foreign Affairs):

[W]e have been working very closely with our counterparts in the United States to ensure the free flow of travel and of goods. [T]he efforts and leadership shown by [Canada's government] with the beyond the border plan have already had a favourable impact on the Canadian economy. As the sequestration process goes forward, we are going to keep a close eye on it and will take the necessary actions.

(*House of Commons Debates, 6 March 2013, p. 14670*)
(*Débats de la Chambre des Communes, le 6 mars 2013, p. 14670*)

Mr. Brian Masse (Windsor West):

What [is the government] doing to put a stop to [a new travel] tax on trade on Canadians?

Mr. Deepak Obhrai (Parliamentary Secretary to the Minister of Foreign Affairs):

We believe that any fee on travellers crossing the Canada-U.S. border would be bad for jobs and bad for the economy. There is $1.6 billion in cross-border trade supporting jobs and growth in both countries. Canadian officials will strongly lobby against this proposal. This kind of fee had been proposed before and not enacted ... We value our trade relations with the U.S.A. Canadian travellers contribute approximately $20 billion annually, roughly $2 billion crosses the U.S.-Canada border each year, and over eight million U.S. jobs depend on trade with Canada.

(*House of Commons Debates, 22 April 2013, p. 15714*)
(*Débats de la Chambre des Communes, le 22 avril 2013, p. 15714*)

Canada's Economy / Économie du Canada

Mr. Mark Adler (York Centre):

[What is] the state of the Canadian economy?

Hon. Christian Paradis (Minister of Industry and Minister of State (Agriculture)):

Today Statistics Canada announced another month of positive economic growth in November, along with the creation of over 900,000 net new jobs since July 2009. It is no wonder both the IMF and the OECD project that Canada will continue to be among the G7 economic leaders in the years ahead.

(*House of Commons Debates, 31 January 2013, p. 13522*)
(*Débats de la Chambre des Communes, le 31 janvier 2013, p. 13522*)

Corporate Social Responsibility / Responsabilité sociale des entreprises

Ms. Niki Ashton (Churchill):

This week a delegation representing the citizens of northern Greece came to Canada to raise their opposition to the actions of the Canadian gold mining company Eldorado. The two projects this company is undertaking in Greece risk creating serious environmental degradation and have already led to major social unrest ... Does the Conservative government believe that Canadian mining companies, especially those that receive government support, like Eldorado, should follow the same standards of corporate social responsibility abroad as we have here in Canada?

Mr. Gerald Keddy (Parliamentary Secretary to the Minister of International Trade, for the Atlantic Canada Opportunities Agency and for the Atlantic Gateway):

Canadian mining and oil and gas companies employ thousands of people abroad and create economic growth and development in countries where they operate. Our government is committed to working with our trading partners to pursue policies that support a responsible and sustainable investment environment. The reality is we provide jobs in Canada and we provide jobs abroad. Those are dollars in the pockets of workers in both countries.

(*House of Commons Debates, 30 May 2013, p. 17367*)
(*Débats de la Chambre des Communes, le 30 mai 2013, p. 17367*)

Intellectual Property / Propriété intellectuelle

Anti-Counterfeiting Trade Agreement (ACTA) / Accord commercial anti-contrefaçon (ACAC)

Ms. Charmaine Borg (Terrebonne — Blainville):

Last July the European Parliament rejected the anti-counterfeiting trade agreement over serious concerns about the regressive changes it would impose on intellectual property in the digital age, yet on Friday, [this Government] introduced a bill in the House that would pave the way for the ACTA without question ... Are the Conservatives planning to ratify ACTA, yes or no? ... Le projet de loi C-56 n'est-il pas simplement une façon d'appuyer l'ACTA par la porte arrière?

L'hon. Christian Paradis (ministre de l'Industrie et ministre d'État (Agriculture)):

Nous sommes très heureux d'avoir déposé à la Chambre un projet de loi de lutte contre la contrefaçon [le projet de loi C-56]. Au pays, la contrefaçon est un problème grandissant. La contrefaçon trompe les Canadiens et est liée à des enjeux entourant la sécurité. C'était donc notre devoir de moderniser les lois, pour veiller à ce qu'on puisse cesser cette contrefaçon afin que les Canadiens ne soient pas trompés, et d'assurer une meilleure sécurité ... Le projet de loi C-56 est une façon d'appuyer et de protéger les familles canadiennes ... Il faut veiller à ce que les lois soient modernisées et qu'elles soient appropriées, et ce, afin de doter les autorités d'outils efficaces pour lutter contre la contrefaçon.

(*House of Commons Debates, 4 March 2013, p. 14556*)
(*Débats de la Chambre des Communes, le 4 mars 2013, p. 14556*)

Mining / Mines

Mr. Brian Storseth (Westlock — St. Paul):

[W]hat [is] our government doing to support [the mining] sector?

Mr. David Anderson (Parliamentary Secretary to the Minister of Natural Resources and for the Canadian Wheat Board):

Today the Minister of Natural Resources is speaking to the Prospectors and Developers Association of Canada conference about Canada's open, transparent and efficient environment for mining investment. The PDAC conference is the largest in the world and it showcases Canada's international strength in mining. Through our responsible resource development initiative, low corporate taxes and red tape reduction initiatives, our government is creating jobs and economic growth across Canada in mining communities.

(*House of Commons Debates, 4 March 2013, p. 14557*)
(*Débats de la Chambre des Communes, le 4 mars 2013, p. 14557*)

Sealing Industry / Industrie du phoque

Mrs. Tilly O'Neill Gordon (Miramichi):

[What has been done in relation to] our government's continued fight against the European Union seal ban?

Hon. Leona Aglukkaq (Minister of Health, Minister of the Canadian Northern Economic Development Agency and Minister for the Arctic Council):

Our government commends Canadian sealers and industry groups for bringing this challenge forward through the European General Court ...

The ban on seal products adopted by the European Union was a political decision that has no basis in fact or science. We will continue to stand up for the seal hunters and their families and defend a way of life in Canada's remote coastal communities.

(*House of Commons Debates, 25 April 2013, p. 15921*)
(*Débats de la Chambre des Communes, le 25 avril 2013, p. 15921*)

Steel Industry / Industrie de l'acier

Mr. Wayne Marston (Hamilton East — Stoney Creek):

Yesterday almost 1,000 steelworkers were locked out of the U.S. Steel plant in Nanticoke. This is the third time this has happened since U.S. Steel has been allowed to come into the country ... Bill Ferguson, president of USW Local 8782, said that the gates were now closed on one of the most productive and efficient steel mills in North America. When will the Conservatives ... enforce the *Investment Canada Act*? ... When will the government admit it was a mistake to allow U.S. Steel to come to Canada to take over Stelco and admit, as well, that it sold out Canadians workers?

Hon. Christian Paradis (Minister of Industry and Minister of State (Agriculture)):

Our thoughts are with the workers and their families. [T]his is a labour dispute under provincial laws. [W]e did not hesitate to take actions in the past to ensure it was compliant with its requirements. It is a shame to see that the opposition would block all forms of foreign investment. What it would rather propose, as we heard at its convention, is the nationalization of steel companies. This is way off base and irresponsible.

(*House of Commons Debates, 29 April 2013, p. 16026*)
(*Débats de la Chambre des Communes, le 29 avril 2013, p. 16026*)

Taxation / Fiscalité

Mr. Murray Rankin (Victoria):

The first step to addressing tax evasion is to figure out just how much money we are losing ... That is what [the] governments [of the United States, the U.K., Australia] have already done. [W]hen the Parliamentary Budget Officer is asked to run the numbers for Parliament, the [government] refuse[d] to release to him the data he needs to do his job. Why will [the government] not release the data we need to take action on tax evasion?

Hon. Gail Shea (Minister of National Revenue and Minister for the Atlantic Canada Opportunities Agency):

In a recent appearance at the finance committee, even the OECD acknowledged that the tax gap is almost impossible to calculate. That is why the OECD says that all countries should have robust auditing, and that is exactly what we are doing. Our record speaks for itself. Since 2006, we have audited thousands of cases and have identified over $4.5 billion of unpaid tax.

(*House of Commons Debates, 6 March 2013, p. 14673*)
(*Débats de la Chambre des Communes, le 6 mars 2013, p. 14673*)

Tourism / Tourisme

M. François Lapointe (Montmagny — L'Islet — Kamouraska — Rivière-du-Loup):

L'industrie du tourisme s'inquiète de la baisse constante, depuis des années, des dépenses des visiteurs internationaux au Canada. Quelles mesures les conservateurs vont-ils adopter dans le prochain budget, afin de corriger cette situation?

L'hon. Christian Paradis (ministre de l'Industrie et ministre d'État (Agriculture)):

[L]e Canada est très concurrentiel en matière de tourisme. C'est pourquoi notre gouvernement a lancé la Stratégie fédérale en matière de tourisme. Malgré le ralentissement économique, on peut voir que les dépenses liées au tourisme ont augmenté au pays pendant 13 trimestres de suite. De plus en plus d'emplois liés au secteur touristique sont créés et on continue d'accueillir de plus en plus de touristes de la Chine, de l'Inde et du Brésil, ce qui montre que ça va bien en matière de tourisme. Nous allons continuer sur cette voie.

(*House of Commons Debates, 8 February 2013, p. 13915*)
(*Débats de la Chambre des Communes, le 8 février 2013, p. 13915*)

Hon. Stéphane Dion (Saint-Laurent — Cartierville):

The government will step down from the Bureau International des Expositions, and in doing so, will kill any success of Toronto's potential bid to host World Expo 2025, an event that could attract up to 40 million visitors. This defection was made without consideration of Toronto City Council's upcoming feasibility report. Why is the government wasting this exceptional opportunity to boost Toronto's economy, job market, and tourism and to promote Canada's accomplishments to the world?

L'hon. Maxime Bernier (ministre d'État (Petite Entreprise et Tourisme, et Agriculture)):

Nous faisons la promotion de ce pays, ici même au Canada, mais surtout à l'extérieur du Canada. J'étais en Chine récemment, avec la Commission canadienne du tourisme, pour m'assurer que nos amis de la Chine pourront venir au Canada. Comme chacun le sait, nous avons signé une entente de coopération avec le gouvernement chinois. Cela fait en sorte que nous avons encore plus de touristes venant de ce pays, ce qui est très bon pour l'économie canadienne.

(*House of Commons Debates, 8 November 2013, p. 932*)
(*Débats de la Chambre des Communes, le 8 novembre 2013, p. 932*)

Trade Agreements / Accords commerciaux

The Americas / Les Amériques

Hon. Ron Cannan (Kelowna — Lake Country):

This week the Prime Minister and the Minister of International Trade are in South America, working to deepen our trading relationships and create new opportunities for Canada's exporters. [What is] our government's ... trade plan [in this region]?

Mr. Gerald Keddy (Parliamentary Secretary to the Minister of International Trade, for the Atlantic Canada Opportunities Agency and for the Atlantic Gateway):

Our government continues to expand Canada's role in the Americas ... Canada has signed trade agreements with Peru, Colombia, Honduras and Panama ... Our ... government continues to develop new opportunities to grow Canadian exports and create Canadian jobs.

(*House of Commons Debates, 23 May 2013, p. 16894*)
(*Débats de la Chambre des Communes, le 23 mai 2013, p. 16894*)

China / Chine

Ms. Elizabeth May (Saanich — Gulf Islands):

[A]n investor state agreement ... with the west African country of Benin ... was tabled with the House in February.[19] Benin has a gross domestic product of $7 billion. We can compare and contrast it to the People's Republic of China, which is $7 trillion, yet this tiny West African country

[19] Editor's note: On 13 February 2013, the government tabled in the House of Commons the *Agreement between the Government of Canada and the Government of the Republic of Benin for the Promotion and the Reciprocal Protection of Investments* done at Ottawa on 8 January 2013.

has negotiated far better terms that are much more protective of domestic health, environment and labour legislation in an investor state conflict than what Canada negotiated. Why is this? Why could we not negotiate as good a deal as Benin got from us?

Right Hon. Stephen Harper (Prime Minister):

Canada's economic relationship with China is very important. China is the second-largest economy in the world and growing. I note that Canadian businesses, Canadian investors and Canadians generally have welcomed the fact that we will have legal protections in our dealings with China.

(*House of Commons Debates, 21 March 2013, p. 15060*)
(*Débats de la Chambre des Communes, le 21 mars 2013, p. 15060*)

Mr. Don Davies (Vancouver Kingsway):

[W]ith the [Canada-China] FIPA, Conservatives want to lock Canadians into a 31-year deal with China ... Will Conservatives ... fix the serious deficiencies in FIPA before it is too late?

Mr. Gerald Keddy (Parliamentary Secretary to the Minister of International Trade, for the Atlantic Canada Opportunities Agency and for the Atlantic Gateway):

Canadians are protected in Canada ... Canadian exporters and Canadian investors in China need protection. That is what this FIPA does. That is why we are supporting it.

(*House of Commons Debates, 18 April 2013, p. 15600*)
(*Débats de la Chambre des Communes, le 18 avril 2013, p. 15600*)

European Union / Union européenne

Mme Mylène Freeman (Argenteuil — Papineau — Mirabel):

Le gouvernement s'engagera-t-il à consulter les Canadiens au sujet des conditions de cette entente?

Hon. Ed Fast (Minister of International Trade and Minister for the Asia-Pacific Gateway):

These negotiations are the most open and transparent that Canada has ever undertaken. In fact, the provinces are at the negotiating table when it comes to matters within their jurisdiction. Our government is committed to keeping Canadians informed and to consulting extensively on this agreement. [T]his agreement will be Canada's most comprehensive ever, one that will open up new opportunities for Canada's exporters and manufacturers. It is expected to increase our GDP by $12 billion a year, which is the equivalent of 80,000 new jobs in Canada, or $1,000 for each Canadian in extra income per year ... We have made it clear time and again that the standard we have set is that we will only sign an agreement that is in the best interests of Canadians.

(*House of Commons Debates, 7 June 2013, p. 17917*)
(*Débats de la Chambre des Communes, le 7 juin 2013, p. 17917*)

Mr. David Christopherson (Hamilton Centre):

Today's announcement [of Canada on reaching an agreement in principle] contains a lot of hype, but not the actual text of the agreement ... Why will this government not just release the text of this deal and let Canadians judge it for themselves?

Hon. Pierre Poilievre (Minister of State (Democratic Reform)):

[O]ur position has always been clear: 80,000 net new jobs, half a billion new customers for Canadian job creators, $1,000 in additional income for the average family of four in this country. This is a good deal, it is the right thing to do, and we are proud of the Prime Minister for delivering it.

Mr. Erin O'Toole (Parliamentary Secretary to the Minister of International Trade):

This is an exciting opportunity for Canada, with 500 million new consumers and a 20% increase in trade with the European Union ... Today the Prime Minister signed the agreement in Brussels. A sector-by-sector overview is being released, and Canadian stakeholders from coast to coast are excited. This is a win for Canada ... Once CETA is fully implemented, approximately 99% of EU tariff lines will be duty free. That includes 100% of non-agricultural lines and over 95% of agricultural tariff lines. It is truly a game changer for Canada.

(*House of Commons Debates, 18 October 2013, pp. 104, 109*)
(*Débats de la Chambre des Communes, le 18 octobre 2013, pp. 104, 109*)

Japan / Japon

Mr. Kevin Sorenson (Crowfoot):

[The Government] consistently made representations to Japan, seeking expanded access for Canadian beef derived from animals under 30 months of age. [What is] the status of these negotiations?

Hon. Gerry Ritz (Minister of Agriculture and Agri-Food and Minister for the Canadian Wheat Board):

I am pleased to announce today that Japan has expanded access and is now accepting Canadian beef from animals under 30 months of age. This is expected to double the value of Canadian exports by some $150 million annually.

(*House of Commons Debates, 28 January 2013, p. 13304*)
(*Débats de la Chambre des Communes, le 28 janvier 2013, p. 13304*)

Trade in Weapons / Ventes d'armes

Hon. Mark Eyking (Sydney — Victoria):

Negotiations for the global Arms Treaty[20] resume on March 18. [Will these receive the] government's support ...?

Mr. Deepak Obhrai (Parliamentary Secretary to the Minister of Foreign Affairs):

Canada already has some of the highest global standards in the export control of munitions. We believe that any treaty regarding the sale of munitions helps move the international community closer to our world-leading standards. That said, the legitimate civilian use of firearms for sporting, hunting and collecting purposes should not be the target of the arms trade treaty. [... T]his government has an excellent record of working hard to ensure that the arms treaty is moving forward and that we work to ensure that there is legitimate civilian use of firearms for sporting, hunting and collecting purposes and not for civilian unrest. We will continue to work with others to determine how to move forward. On the ATT, Canada continues to support the arms treaty.

(*House of Commons Debates, 8 March 2013, p. 14782*)
(*Débats de la Chambre des Communes, le 8 mars 2013, p. 14782*)

Mme Ève Péclet (La Pointe-de-l'Île):

67 pays ont signé le traité international sur le commerce des armes. Parmi eux, il y a l'Australie, le Brésil, l'Italie, la France, l'Allemagne, le Mexique et le Royaume-Uni. Ils ont tous signé le premier jour où c'était possible de le faire, soit hier ... Pourquoi le Canada ne s'engage-t-il pas maintenant à signer ce traité?

---

[20] Editor's note: *The Arms Trade Treaty*, signed at New York on 3 June 2013, not yet in force. Canada has not signed the treaty.

Hon. John Baird (Minister of Foreign Affairs):

[W]e would consult Canadians, firearms owners, provinces and territories and industry before the government would act, and that is exactly what we intend to do.

(*House of Commons Debates, 4 June 2013, p. 17644*)
(*Débats de la Chambre des Communes, le 4 juin 2013, p. 17644*)

World Trade Organization (WTO) / Organisation Mondiale du Commerce (OMC)

Rules of Origin / Règles d'origine

Hon. Laurie Hawn (Edmonton Centre):

Our government ... stood with our livestock industry, including opposing the United States' discriminatory country of origin labelling. After a successful WTO challenge by our government, the U.S. was forced to review its country of origin labelling to make it fair to Canadian livestock producers. Today, the U.S. released its latest version of the rule. [What is] government's view of today's developments?

Mr. Pierre Lemieux (Parliamentary Secretary to the Minister of Agriculture):

The ministers of agriculture and international trade have been clear that our government is extremely disappointment with the regulatory changes put forward by the U.S. with respect to the country of origin labelling. These changes will not bring the U.S. into compliance with its WTO obligations. We will consider all options at our disposal, including, if necessary, the use of retaliatory measures. Our government will continue to aggressively defend the interests of our Canadian livestock producers and we will not stop until we succeed.

(*House of Commons Debates, 24 May 2013, p. 16983*)
(*Débats de la Chambre des Communes, le 24 mai 2013, p. 16983*)

Ban on Seal Products / Interdiction de la commercialisation des produits du phoque

Mr. Scott Simms (Bonavista — Gander — Grand Falls — Windsor):

The World Trade Organization did indeed uphold the ban on seal products, one that flies in the face of what is fair trade ... When will [the government] lift the veil of the inhumane animal harvesting practices in Europe?

Hon. Ed Fast (Minister of International Trade):

This government has committed to appeal the decision of the World Trade Organization ... Canada and the European Union have made it very clear that this issue is quite separate from the negotiations of the free trade agreement between Canada and the European Union. This EU ban on virtually all Canadian seal products is clearly inconsistent with the EU's international trade obligations. This ... government is firmly committed to defending the legitimate, economic activities of Canadians. That includes Canada's sealing industry and the coastal and northern communities that depend on the seal harvest.

(*House of Commons Debates, 25 November 2013, p. 1318*)
(*Débats de la Chambre des Communes, le 25 novembre 2013, p. 1318*)

SPORTS

Mr. Ed Holder (London West):

Today marks one year to go until the kickoff of the 2014 Sochi winter games. [H]ow [is] Canada excelling in sport from the grassroots to the world stage [?]

Hon. Bal Gosal (Minister of State (Sport)):

Last Friday the Minister of Industry and I were happy to light the 2013 Canada Summer Games torch before it makes its way to Sherbrooke, Quebec. I am proud to say our Special Olympians set a new record, winning 44 gold, 44 silver and 21 bronze medals at the World Winter Games. Those are the results of which we are proud.

(*House of Commons Debates, 7 February 2013, p. 13866*)
(*Débats de la Chambre des Communes, le 7 février 2013, p. 13866*)

Mr. Dan Albas (Okanagan — Coquihalla):

[We] were surprised to hear that the IOC has announced that wrestling will not be included on the list of core sports for the 2020 Olympics. [What is] the government's stance on this decision?

Hon. Bal Gosal (Minister of State (Sport)):

Many people were shocked by this decision, including Wrestling Canada's president Don Ryan, who was "deeply surprised by the recent recommendation." The Canadian Olympic Committee says it is disappointing to potentially lose this important sport from the Canadian Olympic games roster in 2020, and Olympic medallist Carol Huynh says it is hard to think of the Olympic games without wrestling. [O]ur government will continue to support our wrestlers through our record level funding to amateur athletics as they prepare for the important upcoming events.

(House of Commons Debates, 13 February 2013, p. 14083)
(Débats de la Chambre des Communes, le 13 février 2013, p. 14083)

Mr. John Weston (West Vancouver — Sunshine Coast — Sea to Sky Country):

With just 59 days to go until the 2014 Sochi Winter Olympics, could the Minister of State for Sport please tell the House what our government is doing to ensure Team Canada is well prepared for these upcoming games?

Hon. Bal Gosal (Minister of State (Sport)):

Our government is proud to be the single largest contributor to sport in our country. In fact, our winter athletes have benefited from a 112% increase in funding from the previous ... government. This support has allowed Canada to emerge as a leading sport nation and provide our athletes with cutting-edge science and research, a world-class training environment and the best coaching in the world. The 2014 Sochi winter games is an occasion to come together as Canadians to support our athletes in their pursuit of excellence.

(House of Commons Debates, 10 December 2013, p. 2019)
(Débats de la Chambre des Communes, le 10 décembre 2013, p. 2019)

Treaty Action Taken by Canada in 2013 / Mesures prises par le Canada en matière de traités en 2013

compiled by/ préparé par

GARY LUTON

BILATERAL

Austria
Second Protocol amending the Convention between Canada and the Republic of Austria for the Avoidance of Double Taxation and the Prevention of Fiscal Evasion with Respect to Taxes on Income and on Capital, done at Vienna on 9 December 1976, as amended by the Protocol done at Vienna on 15 June 1999.
Signed: Vienna, 9 March 2012
Entered into force: 1 October 2013
CTS: 2013/18

Bahrain
Agreement between the Government of Canada and the Government of the Kingdom of Bahrain for the Exchange of Information on Tax Matters.
Signed: Ottawa, 4 June 2013

Barbados
Protocol amending the Agreement between Canada and Barbados for the Avoidance of Double Taxation and the Prevention of Fiscal Evasion with Respect to Taxes on Income and on Capital, done at Bridgetown on 22 January 1980.
Signed: Bridgetown, 8 November 2011
Entered into force: 17 December 2013
CTS: 2013/29

Benin
Agreement between the Government of Canada and the Government of the Republic of Benin for the Promotion and Reciprocal Protection of Investments.
Signed: Ottawa, 8 January 2013

Brunei Darussalam
Agreement between the Government of Canada and the Government of His

Gary Luton is the Director of the Treaty Law Division in the Legal Affairs Bureau of the Department of Foreign Affairs, Trade and Development / Gary Luton est le Directeur de la Direction du droit des traités du ministère des Affaires étrangères, du Commerce et du Développement. The Treaty Law Division of the Department of Foreign Affairs, Trade and Development is part of the Department's Legal Affairs Bureau. The division is responsible for providing legal advice to the federal government on international treaty law (and for arrangements not intended to give rise to binding obligations). It is also responsible for procedures related to the making of treaties. This requires ensuring that the form and substance of international agreements into which Canada may enter conforms to international law and Canadian practice. The division is also responsible for the preparation of formal instruments relating to the signature and ratification of international treaties by the

Majesty the Sultan and Yang Di-Pertuan of Brunei Darussalam for the Exchange of Information on Tax Matters.
Signed: Bandar Seri Begawan, 9 May 2013

China (People's Republic of)
Protocol to the Agreement between the Government of Canada and the Government of the People's Republic of China for Cooperation in the Peaceful Uses of Nuclear Energy.
Signed: Beijing, 19 July 2012
Entered into force: 1 January 2013
CTS: 2013/4

European Union
Agreement between Canada and the European Union on Customs Cooperation with Respect to Matters Related to Supply-Chain Security
Signed: Brussels, 4 March 2013
Entered into force: 1 November 2013
CTS: 2013/22

France
Agreement between the Government of Canada and the Government of the French Republic Concerning Youth Mobility
Signed: Ottawa, 14 March 2013

Agreement between the Government of Canada and the Government of the French Republic on Social Security
Signed: Ottawa, 14 March 2013

Implementing Agreement concerning the Agreement between the Government of Canada and the Government of the French Republic on Social Security
Signed: Ottawa, 14 March 2013

Protocol amending the Convention between the Government of Canada and the Government of the French Republic for the Avoidance of Double Taxation and the Prevention of Fiscal Evasion with Respect to Taxes on Income and on Capital signed on 2 May 1975, as amended by the Protocol signed on 16 January 1987 and as further amended by the Protocol signed 30 November 1995.
Signed: Paris, 2 February 2010

---

government of Canada. The Treaty Law Division maintains the original text or a certified copy of treaties signed by Canada and publishes on an annual basis in the Canada Treaty Series the texts of agreements that have come into force for Canada. This information is available online at <http://www.treaty-accord.gc.ca>. / La Direction du droit des traités du ministère des Affaires étrangères, du Commerce et du Développement fait partie de la Direction générale des affaires juridiques du Ministère. Elle est chargée de fournir des avis juridiques concernant le droit international des traités (ainsi que les instruments n'ayant pas pour objet de créer des obligations contraignantes) au gouvernement fédéral. Elle est également responsable de la procédure liée à la conclusion des traités, et doit notamment s'assurer que la forme et le fond des accords internationaux qui pourraient être conclus par le Canada sont conformes au droit international et à la pratique canadienne. La Direction du droit des traités s'occupe en outre de la préparation des instruments officiels se rapportant à la signature et à la ratification des traités internationaux par le Gouvernement du Canada. La Direction du droit des traités conserve le texte original ou une copie certifiée des traités signés par le Canada, et elle publie chaque année dans le Recueil des traités du Canada les textes des accords qui sont entrés en vigueur pour le Canada. Cette information est disponible sur l'internet à l'adresse suivante <http://www.treaty-accord.gc.ca>.

Entered into force: 27 December 2013
CTS: 2013/31

Greece
Agreement between Canada and the Hellenic Republic Concerning Youth Mobility.
Signed: Athens, 28 May 2011
Entered into force: 1 February 2013
CTS: 2013/7

Honduras
Free Trade Agreement between Canada and the Republic of Honduras
Signed: Ottawa, 5 November 2013

Agreement on Environmental Cooperation between Canada and the Republic of Honduras.
Signed: Ottawa, 5 November 2013

Agreement on Labour Cooperation between Canada and the Republic of Honduras *Signed:* Ottawa, 5 November 2013

Hong Kong
Agreement between the Government of Canada and the Government of the Hong Kong Special Administrative Region of the People's Republic of China for the Avoidance of Double Taxation and the Prevention of Fiscal Evasion with Respect to Taxes on Income.
Signed: Hong Kong, 11 November 2012.
Entered into force: 29 October 2013
CTS: 2013/20

India
Agreement between the Government of Canada and the Government of the Republic of India for Cooperation in Peaceful Uses of Nuclear Energy.
Signed: Toronto, 27 June 2010
Entered into force: 20 September 2013
CTS: 2013/17

International Civil Aviation Organization
Supplementary Agreement between the Government of Canada and the International Civil Aviation Organization Regarding the Headquarters of the International Civil Aviation Organization.
Signed: Montreal, 27 May 2013
Entered into force: 23 October 2013
CTS: 2013/19

Israel
Mutual Recognition Agreement between the Government of Canada and the Government of the State of Israel for Conformity Assessment of Telecommunications Equipment.
Signed: Tel Aviv, 24 June 2012
Entered into force: 18 January 2013
CTS: 2013/5

Agreement between the Government of Canada and the Government of the State of Israel on Mutual Assistance in Customs Matters.
Signed: Ottawa, 11 December 2012
Entered into force: 24 July 2013
CTS: 2013/15

Kazakhstan
Agreement between the Government of Canada and the Government of the Republic of Kazakhstan for Cooperation in the Peaceful Uses of Nuclear Energy.
Signed: Astana, 13 November 2013

Liechtenstein
Agreement between Canada and the Principality of Liechtenstein for the Exchange of Information on Tax Matters.
Signed: Vaduz, 31 January 2013

Luxembourg
Protocol amending the Convention between the Government of Canada

and the Government of the Grand Duchy of Luxembourg for the Avoidance of Double Taxation and the Prevention of Fiscal Evasion with Respect to Taxes on Income and on Capital, done at Luxembourg on 10 September 1999.
Signed: Montreal, 8 May 2012
Entered into force: 10 December 2013
CTS: 2013/27

Exchange of Notes concerning the Convention between the Government of Canada and the Government of the Grand Duchy of Luxembourg for the Avoidance of Double Taxation and the Prevention of Fiscal Evasion with Respect to Taxes on Income and on Capital, done at Luxembourg on 10 September 1999.
Signed: Luxembourg, 8 May 2012 and Brussels, 11 May 2012
Entered into force: 10 December 2013
CTS: 2013/28

Panama
Free Trade Agreement between Canada and the Republic of Panama.
Signed: Ottawa, 14 May 2010
Entered into force: 1 April 2013
CTS: 2013/9

Agreement on the Environment between Canada and the Republic of Panama.
Signed: Ottawa, 13 May 2010
Entered into force: 1 April 2013
CTS: 2013/10

Agreement on Labour Cooperation between Canada and the Republic of Panama.
Signed: Ottawa, 13 May 2010
Entered into force: 1 April 2013
CTS: 2013/11

Agreement between Canada and the Republic of Panama for Tax Cooperation and the Exchange of Information Relating to Taxes.

Signed: Panama, 17 March 2013
Entered into force: 6 December 2013
CTS: 2013/25

Poland
Convention between Canada and the Republic of Poland for the Avoidance of Double Taxation and the Prevention of Fiscal Evasion with Respect to Taxes on Income.
Signed: Ottawa, 14 May 2012
Entered into force: 30 October 2013
CTS: 2013/21

Serbia
Agreement on Social Security between Canada and the Republic of Serbia.
Signed: Belgrade, 12 April 2013

Tanzania
Agreement between the Government of Canada and the Government of the United Republic of Tanzania for the Promotion and the Reciprocal Protection of Investments. *Signed:* Dar es Salaam, 16 May 2013
Entered into force: 9 December 2013
CTS: 2013/26

United Arab Emirates
Agreement between the Government of Canada and the Government of the United Arab Emirates for Cooperation in the Peaceful Uses of Nuclear Energy.
Signed: Ottawa, 18 September 2012
Entered into force: 10 June 2013
CTS: 2013/14

United Kingdom of Great Britain and Northern Ireland (British Virgin Islands)
Agreement between the Government of Canada and the Government of the British Virgin Islands under Entrustment from the Government of the United Kingdom of Great Britain and Northern Ireland for the Exchange of Information on Tax Matters.
Signed: London, 21 May 2013

United States

Agreement between the Government of Canada and the Government of the United States of America for the Sharing of Visa and Immigration Information.
Signed: Ottawa, 13 December 2012
Entered into force: 21 November 2013
CTS: 2013/23

Exchange of Notes between the Government of Canada and the Government of the United States of America concluding Amendments to the Treaty between the Government of Canada and the Government of the United States of America on Pacific Coast Albacore Tuna Vessels and Port Privileges.
Signed: Washington, 18 June 2013
Provisional Application: 18 June 2013

Exchange of Notes between the Government of Canada and the Government of the United States of America constituting an Agreement amending Chapter 4 of Annex IV of the Treaty between the Government of Canada and the Government of the United States of America Concerning the Pacific Salmon.
Signed: Washington, 13 and 23 December 2013

Protocol amending the Agreement between Canada and the United States of America on Great Lakes Water Quality, 1978, as amended on 16 October 1983 and on 18 November 1987.
Signed: Washington, 7 September 2012
Entered into force: 12 February 2013
CTS: 2013/8

Uruguay

Agreement between Canada and the Oriental Republic of Uruguay for the Exchange of Information on Tax Matters.
Signed: Montevideo, 5 February 2013

MULTILATERAL

Arctic

Agreement on Cooperation on Aeronautical and Maritime Search and Rescue in the Arctic, Nuuk, 12 May 2011.
Signed by Canada: 12 May 2011
Entered into force for Canada: 19 January 2013
CTS: 2013/6

Agreement on Cooperation on Marine Oil Pollution Preparedness and Response in the Arctic, Kiruna, 15 May 2013
Signed by Canada: 15 May 2013

Aviation

Convention on International Interests in Mobile Equipment, Cape Town, 16 November 2001.
Signed by Canada: 31 March 2004
Entered into force for Canada: 1 April 2013
CTS 2013/12

Protocol to the Convention on International Interests in Mobile Equipment on Matters Specific to Aircraft Equipment, Cape Town, 16 November 2001.
Signed by Canada: 31 March 2004
Entered into force for Canada: 1 April 2013
CTS: 2013/13

Commerce

Protocol amending the Agreement on Government Procurement, Geneva, 30 March 2012.
Deposit of the Instrument of Acceptance by Canada: 18 November 2013

Customs

Protocol of Amendment to the International Convention on the Simplification and Harmonization of Customs Procedures (Specific Annexes: Chapters A-1, B-1, B-3, C-1, E-1, E-2, E-3, F-2, F-3, F-4, H-1, J-1, J-3, J-4, J-5).

Entered into force for Canada: 26 September 2013

Environment
United Nations Convention to Combat Desertification in those Countries Experiencing Serious Drought and/or Desertification, Particularly in Africa, Paris, 14 October 1994.
Notification of withdrawal by Canada: 28 March 2013

Exhibitions
Convention relating to International Exhibitions, Paris, 22 November 1928
Notification of withdrawal by Canada: 19 December 2012.
Withdrawal by Canada: 19 December 2013 *(entry into effect)*

Fisheries
Convention on the Conservation and Management of High Seas Fisheries Resources in the North Pacific Ocean, Tokyo, 24 February 2012.
Signed by Canada: 27 March 2013

Food Assistance
Food Assistance Convention, London, 25 April 2012.
Signed by Canada: 6 September 2012
Entered into force for Canada: 1 January 2013
CTS: 2013/3

Health
Minamata Convention on Mercury, Kumamoto, 10 October 2013.
Signed by Canada: 10 October 2013

Investment Protection
Agreement Establishing the Inter-American Investment Corporation.
Signed by Canada: 11 October 2013

Convention on the Settlement of Investment Disputes between States and Nationals of Other States, Washington, 18 March 1965.

Signed by Canada: 15 December 2006
Entered into force for Canada: 1 December 2013
CTS: 2013/24

Labour
Maritime Labour Convention, 2006, Geneva, 23 February 2006.
Entered into force for Canada: 20 August 2013
CTS: 2013/16

Narcotics
Amendments to Annex I of the International Convention against Doping in Sport, Paris, 12 November 2012.
Entered into force for Canada: 1 January 2013
CTS: 2013/2

Nuclear
Amendment to the Convention on the Physical Protection of Nuclear Material, Vienna, 8 July 2005.
Deposit of the Instrument of Ratification by Canada: 3 December 2013

Convention on Supplementary Compensation for Nuclear Damage, Vienna, 12 September 1997.
Signed by Canada: 3 December 2013

Science
Agreement Establishing an International Science and Technology Center, Moscow, 27 November 1992.
Notification of withdrawal by Canada: 6 May 2013
Withdrawal by Canada: 6 November 2013 (entry into effect)

Agreement to Establish a Science and Technology Center in Ukraine, Kiev, 25 October 1993.
Notification of withdrawal by Canada: 6 May 2013
Withdrawal by Canada: 6 November 2013 (entry into effect)

Telecommunications
Final Acts of the World Radiocommunication Conference of the International Telecommunication Union (WRC-2012), Geneva, 17 February 2012.
Signed by Canada: 17 February 2012
Entered into force for Canada: 15 March 2013

Terrorism
International Convention for the Suppression of Acts of Nuclear Terrorism, New York, 13 April 2005.
Signed by Canada: 14 September 2005
Entered into force for Canada: 21 December 2013
CTS: 2013/30

Tropical Timber
International Tropical Timber Agreement, 2006, Geneva, 27 January 2006.
Notification of withdrawal by Canada: 14 April 2013
Withdrawal by Canada: 14 April 2013 (entry into effect)

BILATÉRAL

Autriche
Deuxième protocole modifiant la Convention entre le Canada et la République d'Autriche tendant à éviter les doubles impositions et à prévenir l'évasion fiscale en matière d'impôts sur le revenu et sur la fortune, faite à Vienne le 9 décembre 1976 et modifiée par le Protocole fait à Vienne le 15 juin 1999.
Signé: Vienne, le 9 mars 2012
Entrée en vigueur: le 1er octobre 2013
RTC : 2013/18

Bahreïn
Accord entre le gouvernement du Canada et le gouvernement du Royaume de Bahreïn sur l'échange de renseignements en matière fiscale.
Signé: Ottawa, le 4 juin 2013

Barbade
Protocole amendant l'Accord entre le Canada et la Barbade tendant à éviter les doubles impositions et à prévenir l'évasion fiscale en matière d'impôts sur le revenu et sur la fortune, fait à Bridgetown le 22 janvier 1980.
Signé: Bridgetown, le 8 novembre 2011
Entrée en vigueur: le 17 décembre 2013
RTC : 2013/29

Bénin
Accord entre le gouvernement du Canada et le gouvernement de la République du Bénin concernant la promotion et la protection réciproque des investissements.
Signé: Ottawa, le 8 janvier 2013

Brunéi Darussalam
Accord entre le gouvernement du Canada et le gouvernement de Sa Majesté le Sultan et Yang Di-Pertuan de Brunéi Darussalam sur l'échange de renseignements en matière fiscale.
Signé: Bandar Seri Begawan, le 9 mai 2013

Chine (République populaire de)
Protocole relatif à l'Accord de coopération entre le gouvernement du Canada et le gouvernement de la République populaire de Chine en matière d'utilisations pacifiques de l'énergie nucléaire.
Signé: Beijing, le 19 juillet 2012
Entrée en vigueur: le 1er janvier 2013
RTC : 2013/4

Émirats arabes unis
Accord entre le gouvernement du Canada et le gouvernement des Émirats arabes unis concernant les utilisations pacifiques de l'énergie nucléaire.
Signé: Ottawa, le 18 septembre 2012
Entrée en vigueur: le 10 juin 2013
RTC: 2013/14

États-Unis

Accord entre le gouvernement du Canada et le gouvernement des États-Unis d'Amérique concernant l'échange de renseignements sur les visas et l'immigration.
Signé: Ottawa, le 13 décembre 2012
Entrée en vigueur: le 21 novembre 2013
RTC: 2013/23

Échange de notes entre le gouvernement du Canada et le gouvernement des États-Unis d'Amérique concluant les amendements au Traité entre le gouvernement du Canada et le gouvernement des États-Unis d'Amérique concernant les thoniers (thon blanc) du Pacifique et leurs privilèges portuaires.
Signé: Washington, le 18 juin 2013
Application provisoire: le 18 juin 2013

Échange de notes entre le gouvernement du Canada et le gouvernement des États-Unis d'Amérique constituant un accord amendant le chapitre 4 de l'Annexe IV du Traité entre le gouvernement du Canada et le gouvernement des États-Unis d'Amérique concernant le saumon du Pacifique.
Signé: Washington les 13 et 23 décembre 2013

Protocole amendant l'Accord de 1978 entre le Canada et les États-Unis d'Amérique relatif à la qualité de l'eau dans les Grands Lacs, tel qu'il a été modifié le 16 octobre 1983 et le 18 novembre 1987.
Signé: Washington, le 7 septembre 2012
Entrée en vigueur: le 12 février 2013
RTC: 2013/8

France

Accord entre le gouvernement du Canada et le gouvernement de la République française relatif à la mobilité des jeunes.
Signé: Ottawa, le 14 mars 2013

Accord entre le gouvernement du Canada et le gouvernement de la République française sur la sécurité sociale.
Signé: Ottawa, le 14 mars 2013

Accord d'application concernant l'Accord entre le gouvernement du Canada et le gouvernement de la République française sur la sécurité sociale.
Signé: Ottawa, le 14 mars 2013

Avenant à la Convention entre le gouvernement du Canada et le gouvernement de la République française tendant à éviter les doubles impositions et à prévenir l'évasion fiscale en matière d'impôts sur le revenu et la fortune, signée le 2 mai 1975 et modifiée par l'avenant du 16 janvier 1987 puis par l'avenant du 30 novembre 1995.
Signé: Paris, le 2 février 2010
Entrée en vigueur: le 27 décembre 2013
RTC: 2013/31

Grèce

Accord entre le Canada et la République hellénique concernant la mobilité des jeunes.
Signé: Athènes, le 28 mai 2011.
Entrée en vigueur: le 1er février 2013
RTC: 2013/7

Honduras

Accord de libre-échange entre le Canada et la République du Honduras.
Signé: Ottawa, le 5 novembre 2013

Accord de coopération dans le domaine de l'environnement entre le Canada et la République du Honduras.
Signé: Ottawa, le 5 novembre 2013

Accord de coopération dans le domaine du travail entre le Canada et la République du Honduras.
Signé: Ottawa, le 5 novembre 2013

Hong Kong

Accord entre le gouvernement du Canada et le gouvernement de la Région administrative spéciale de Hong Kong de la République populaire de Chine en vue d'éviter les doubles impositions et de prévenir l'évasion fiscale en matière d'impôts sur le revenu.
Signé: Hong Kong, le 11 novembre 2012
Entrée en vigueur: le 29 octobre 2013
RTC: 2013/20

Inde

Accord entre le gouvernement du Canada et le gouvernement de la République de l'Inde sur la coopération en matière d'utilisation de l'énergie nucléaire à des fins pacifiques.
Signé: Toronto, le 27 juin 2010
Entrée en vigueur: le 20 septembre 2013
RTC: 2013/17

Israël

Accord de reconnaissance mutuelle entre le gouvernement du Canada et le gouvernement de l'État d'Israël concernant l'évaluation de la conformité du matériel de télécommunication.
Signé: Tel-Aviv, le 24 juin 2012
Entrée en vigueur: le 18 janvier 2013
RTC: 2013/5

Accord entre le gouvernement du Canada et le gouvernement de l'État d'Israël concernant l'assistance mutuelle en matière douanière.
Signé: Ottawa, le 11 décembre 2012
Entrée en vigueur: le 24 juillet 2013
RTC: 2013/15

Kazakhstan

Accord de coopération entre le gouvernement du Canada et le gouvernement de la République du Kazakhstan concernant les utilisations pacifiques de l'énergie nucléaire.
Signé: Astana, le 13 novembre 2013

Liechtenstein

Accord entre le Canada et la Principauté de Liechtenstein sur l'échange de renseignements en matière fiscale.
Signé: Vaduz, le 31 janvier 2013.

Luxembourg

Avenant amendant la Convention entre le gouvernement du Canada et le gouvernement du Grand-Duché de Luxembourg en vue d'éviter les doubles impositions et de prévenir la fraude fiscale en matière d'impôts sur le revenu et sur la fortune, faite à Luxembourg le 10 septembre 1999.
Signé: Montréal, le 8 mai 2012
Entrée en vigueur: le 10 décembre 2013
RTC: 2013/27

Échange de notes concernant la Convention entre le gouvernement du Canada et le gouvernement du Grand-Duché de Luxembourg en vue d'éviter les doubles impositions et de prévenir la fraude fiscale en matière d'impôts sur le revenu et sur la fortune, faite à Luxembourg le 10 septembre 1999.
Signé: Luxembourg, le 8 mai 2012 et Bruxelles, le 11 mai 2012
Entrée en vigueur: le 10 décembre 2013
RTC: 2013/28

Organisation de l'aviation civile internationale

Accord supplémentaire entre le gouvernement du Canada et l'Organisation de l'aviation civile internationale relatif au siège de l'Organisation de l'aviation civile internationale.
Signé: Montréal, le 27 mai 2013
Entrée en vigueur: le 23 octobre 2013
RTC: 2013/19

Panama

Accord de libre-échange entre le Canada et la République du Panama.
Signé: Ottawa, le 14 mai 2010
Entrée en vigueur: le 1er avril 2013
RTC: 2013/9

Accord sur l'environnement entre le Canada et la République du Panama.
Signé: Ottawa, le 13 mai 2010
Entrée en vigueur: le 1er avril 2013
RTC: 2013/10

Accord de coopération dans le domaine du travail entre le Canada et la République du Panama.
Signé: Ottawa, le 13 mai 2010
Entrée en vigueur: le 1er avril 2013
RTC: 2013/11

Accord entre le Canada et la République du Panama sur la coopération et l'échange de renseignements en matière fiscale.
Signé: Panama, le 17 mars 2013
Entrée en vigueur: le 6 décembre 2013
RTC: 2013/25

Pologne
Convention entre le Canada et la République de Pologne en vue d'éviter les doubles impositions et de prévenir l'évasion fiscale en matière d'impôts sur le revenu.
Signée: Ottawa, le 14 mai 2012
Entrée en vigueur: le 30 octobre 2013
RTC: 2013/21

Royaume-Uni de Grande-Bretagne et d'Irlande du Nord (îles Vierges britanniques)
Accord entre le gouvernement du Canada et le gouvernement des îles Vierges britanniques, agissant en vertu d'un mandat du gouvernement du Royaume-Uni de Grande-Bretagne et d'Irlande du Nord, sur l'échange de renseignements en matière fiscale.
Signé: Londres, le 21 mai 2013

Serbie
Accord de sécurité sociale entre le Canada et la République de Serbie.
Signé: Belgrade, le 12 avril 2013

Tanzanie
Accord entre le gouvernement du

Canada et le gouvernement de la République-Unie de Tanzanie sur la promotion et la protection réciproque des investissements.
Signé: Dar es Salaam, le 16 mai 2013
Entrée en vigueur: le 9 décembre 2013
RTC: 2013/26

Union européenne
Accord entre le Canada et l'Union européenne sur la coopération douanière concernant les questions liées à la sécurité de la chaîne d'approvisionnement.
Signé: Bruxelles, le 4 mars 2013
Entrée en vigueur: le 1er novembre 2013
RTC: 2013/22

Uruguay
Accord entre le Canada et la République orientale de l'Uruguay sur l'échange de renseignements en matière fiscale.
Signé: Montevideo, le 5 février 2013

MULTILATÉRAL

Arctique
Accord de coopération en matière de recherche et de sauvetage aéronautiques et maritimes dans l'Arctique, Nuuk, 12 mai 2011.
Signé par le Canada: le 12 mai 2011
Entrée en vigueur pour le Canada: le 19 janvier 2013
RTC: 2013/6

Accord de coopération sur la préparation et la lutte en matière de pollution marine par les hydrocarbures dans l'Arctique, Kiruna, 15 mai 2013.
Signé par le Canada: le 15 mai 2013

Assistance alimentaire
Convention relative à l'assistance alimentaire, Londres, 25 avril 2012.
Signée par le Canada: le 6 septembre 2012
Entrée en vigueur pour le Canada: le 1er janvier 2013
RTC: 2013/3

Aviation
Convention relative aux garanties internationales portant sur des matériels d'équipement mobiles, Le Cap, 16 novembre 2001.
Signée par le Canada: le 31 mars 2004
Entrée en vigueur pour le Canada: le 1er avril 2013
RTC: 2013/12

Protocole portant sur les questions spécifiques aux matériels d'équipement aéronautiques à la Convention relative aux garanties internationales portant sur des matériels d'équipement mobiles, Le Cap, 16 novembre 2001.
Signé par le Canada: le 31 mars 2004
Entrée en vigueur pour le Canada: le 1er avril 2013
RTC: 2013/13

Bois tropicaux
Accord international de 2006 sur les bois tropicaux, Genève, 27 janvier 2006.
Notification de dénonciation par le Canada: le 14 avril 2013
Dénonciation par le Canada: le 14 avril 2013 (prise d'effet)

Commerce
Protocole portant Amendement de l'Accord sur les marchés publics, Genève, 30 mars 2012.
Depôt de l'Instrument d'acceptation par le Canada: le 18 novembre 2013

Douanes
Protocole d'amendement à la Convention internationale pour la simplification et l'harmonisation des régimes douaniers (annexes spécifiques: chapitres A-1, B-1, B-3, C-1, E-1, E-2, E-3, F-2, F-3, F-4, H-1, J-1, J-3, J-4, J-5).
Entrée en vigueur pour le Canada: le 26 septembre 2013

Environnement
Convention des Nations Unies sur la lutte contre la désertification dans les pays gravement touchés par la sécheresse et/ou la désertification, en particulier en Afrique, Paris, 14 octobre 1994.
Notification de dénonciation par le Canada: le 28 mars 2013

Expositions
Convention concernant les expositions internationales, Paris, 22 novembre 1928.
Notification de dénonciation par le Canada: le 19 décembre 2012
Dénonciation par le Canada: le 19 décembre 2013 (prise d'effet)

Nucléaire
Amendement à la Convention sur la protection physique des matières nucléaires, fait à Vienne le 8 juillet 2005.
Depôt de l'Instrument de ratification par le Canada: le 3 décembre 2013

Convention sur la réparation complémentaire des dommages nucléaires, Vienne, 12 septembre 1997.
Signée par le Canada: le 3 décembre 2013

Pêche
Convention sur la conservation et la gestion des ressources halieutiques hauturières du Pacifique Nord, Tokyo, 24 février 2012.
Signée par le Canada: le 27 mars 2013

Protection des investissements
Accord constitutif de la Société interaméricaine d'investissement.
Signé par le Canada: le 11 octobre 2013

Convention pour le règlement des différends relatifs aux investissements entre États et ressortissants d'autres États, Washington, 18 mars 1965.
Signée par le Canada: le 15 décembre 2006
Entrée en vigueur pour le Canada: le 1er décembre 2013
RTC: 2013/24

Santé
Convention de Minamata sur le mercure, Kumamoto, 10 octobre 2013.
Signée par le Canada: le 10 octobre 2013

Science
Accord portant création d'un Centre international pour la science et la technologie, Moscou, 27 novembre 1992.
Notification de dénonciation par le Canada: le 6 mai 2013
Dénonciation par le Canada: le 6 novembre 2013 (prise d'effet)

Accord instituant un centre pour la science et la technologie en Ukraine, Kiev, 25 octobre 1993.
Notification de dénonciation par le Canada: le 6 mai 2013
Dénonciation par le Canada: le 6 novembre 2013 (prise d'effet)

Stupéfiants
Amendements à l'annexe I de la Convention internationale contre le dopage dans le sport, Paris, 12 novembre 2012.
Entrée en vigueur pour le Canada: le 1er janvier 2013

RTC: 2013/2

Télécommunications
Actes finals de la Conférence mondiale des radiocommunications de l'Union internationale des télécommunications (CMR-2012), Genève, 17 février 2012.
Signé par le Canada: le 17 février 2012
Entrée en vigueur pour le Canada: le 15 mars 2013

Terrorisme
Convention internationale pour la répression des actes de terrorisme nucléaire, New York, 13 avril 2005.
Signée par le Canada: le 14 septembre 2005
Entrée en vigueur pour le Canada: le 21 décembre 2013
RTC: 2013/30

Travail
Convention du travail maritime, 2006, Genève, 23 février 2006.
Entrée en vigueur pour le Canada: le 20 août 2013
RTC : 2013/16

Canadian Cases in Public International Law in 2013 / Jurisprudence canadienne en matière de droit international public en 2013

compiled by / préparé par

GIB VAN ERT, GREG J. ALLEN, AND REBECCA ROBB

Refugee protection — human smuggling — constitutionality of section 117 of Immigration and Refugee Protection Act

R v Appulonappa, 2013 BCSC 31 (11 January 2013) (British Columbia Supreme Court)

In a *voir dire,* Silverman J heard an application by four accused charged under section 117 of the *Immigration and Refugee Protection Act (IRPA)*[1] for an order declaring section 117 to be in violation of section 7 of the *Canadian Charter of Rights and Freedoms* and to be of no force or effect pursuant to section 52 of the *Constitution Act, 1982.*[2] The accused argued the provision's criminalization of human smuggling was overly broad and thus inconsistent with the principles of fundamental justice.[3]

This proceeding arose from the arrival in Canada of a freight ship in 2009 with seventy-six Sri Lankan Tamils on board who lacked proper documentation. The four accused were allegedly in charge of the smuggling operation. They did not pay for their voyage, and their accommodation on the ship was superior to that of the other refugee claimants. Defence counsel intended to argue at trial that while the accused may have been engaged in the practice of aiding

Gib van Ert, Counsel, Hunter Litigation Chambers, Vancouver. Greg J Allen, Associate, Hunter Litigation Chambers, Vancouver. Rebecca Robb, Associate, Hunter Litigation Chambers, Vancouver.

[1] *Immigration and Refugee Protection Act,* SC 2001, c 27 [*IRPA*].

[2] *Canadian Charter of Rights and Freedoms,* Part I of the *Constitution Act, 1982,* being Schedule B to the *Canada Act (UK),* 1982, c 11 [*Charter*].

[3] *R v Appulonappa,* 2013 BCSC 31 at para 38 [*Appulonappa*].

other refugees in their flight, the accused were also themselves refugees.[4]

At the time of the alleged offences, section 117 of the *IRPA* read in relevant part:[5]

117. (1) No person shall knowingly organize, induce, aid or abet the coming into Canada of one or more persons who are not in possession of a visa, passport or other document required by this Act.	117. (1) Commet une infraction quiconque sciemment organise l'entrée au Canada d'une ou plusieurs personnes non munies des documents — passeport, visa ou autre — requis par la présente loi ou incite, aide ou encourage une telle personne à entrer au Canada.

The Crown defended the constitutionality of the provision, arguing that it was consistent with Canada's legitimate goals and international obligations.

Silverman J began his analysis by reviewing the international community's approach to the issue of refugees in order to shed light on the meaning and scope of "human smuggling." He noted that the international community generally exempts refugees from criminal liability for the steps they take to flee persecution. This prohibition on criminalizing illegal entry by refugees is found in Article 31 of the *Convention Relating to the Status of Refugees* (*Refugee Convention*)[6] and is codified under section 133 of the *IRPA*. However, this prohibition is limited in scope—it does not also protect those who organize, induce, aid, or abet the arrival of refugees.

Silverman J noted that under the *Protocol against Smuggling of Migrants by Land, Sea and Air, supplementing the United Nations Convention against Transnational Organized Crime* (*Smuggling Protocol*),[7] human smuggling is defined to include a motive for a financial or

---

[4] *Ibid* at paras 42-43.

[5] This provision was amended on 15 December 2012. *Immigration and Refugee Protection Act*, SC 2012, c 17, section 41.

[6] *Convention Relating to the Status of Refugees*, 189 UNTS 150, Can TS 1969 No 6, in force 22 April 1954 [*Refugee Convention*].

[7] *Protocol against Smuggling of Migrants by Land, Sea and Air, supplementing the United Nations Convention against Transnational Organized Crime*, 2241 UNTS 507 (ratified by Canada 13 May 2002) [*Smuggling Protocol*].

other material benefit. While states parties are required to implement domestic legislation creating the offence of human smuggling, they are entitled to adopt legislation that defines the offence more broadly.[8] Silverman J observed that the Canadian definition of human smuggling went well beyond the minimum standard set out in the protocol.[9] Whether or not the scope of this provision is lawful has been the subject of divided judicial opinion. Silverman J noted that the Federal Court reached different conclusions in *Boio v Canada (Citizenship and Immigration)*[12] and *Hernandez v Canada (Minister of Public Safety and Emergency Preparedness)*[11] on whether the crime of human smuggling in section 117 dictated the proper meaning of "people smuggling" under section 37(1)(*b*) of the *IRPA* and whether, properly construed, people smuggling required an element of profit.[12]

Despite these contradictions in the law, Silverman J found it was clear that certain categories of persons and conduct are not intended to be prosecuted for human smuggling: (1) those who provide support to migrants for humanitarian reasons and (2) those who provide support to migrants on the basis of familial relations.[13] In drawing this conclusion, Silverman J relied in part on the *Refugee Convention* and the *travaux préparatoires* for the *United Nations Convention against Transnational Organized Crime*.[14]

While nothing prohibited their prosecution, Silverman J was of the view that it was clear from the Crown's expert, the defence's expert, and the Crown's submissions that these categories of persons technically fell within the scope of section 117 of the *IRPA*. Silverman J was easily satisfied that section 117 of the *IRPA* infringed section 7 of the *Charter* and was overly broad — it captured the actions of persons who the government did not intend to proceed against and whose prosecution did not further the government's objective.[15] Silverman J further held the impugned provision was,

---

8   *Appulonappa, supra* note 3 at paras 65-69.

9   *Ibid* at para 75.

10   *Boio v Canada (Citizenship and Immigration)*, 2012 FC 569 [*Boio*].

11   *Hernandez v Canada (Minister of Public Safety and Emergency Preparedness)*, 2012 FC 1417.

12   *Appulonappa, supra* note 3 at paras 76-81.

13   *Ibid* at paras 83-85.

14   *United Nations Convention against Transnational Organized Crime*, 2225 UNTS 209 (ratified by Canada on 13 May 2002).

15   *Appulonappa, supra* note 3 at paras 137, 140.

for the same reason, inconsistent with the principles and purposes of the governing international instruments.[16]

The Crown had argued that the provision's overbreadth was saved by subsection 117(4) of the *IRPA*, which provides that no proceeding for an offence under section 117 may be instituted except by or with the consent of the Attorney General of Canada. Silverman J was unconvinced as it was not clear on the face of the provision and from the Crown's explanation how the provision actually worked to protect categories of persons that the government does not intend to prosecute. Section 117 was therefore not saved by subsection 117(4). Nor was it saved by section 1 of the *Charter*. Silverman J declared section 117 of the *IRPA* to be of no force or effect.

In light of this judgment, the subsequent decision of the Federal Court of Appeal in *B010 v Canada (Minister of Citizenship and Immigration)*[17] (summarized later in this article) is of particular interest. There, the Federal Court of Appeal considered section 117 to be in compliance with Canada's international obligations and held it proper to interpret the meaning of "people smuggling" under section 37(1) (*b*) by referring to section 117 of the *IRPA*. No mention was made of *Appulonappa*.

Two other federal decisions since *Appulonappa* are also of note. In *B006 v Canada (Citizenship and Immigration)*,[18] the Federal Court observed that the Federal Court of Appeal in *B010* was aware of *Appulonappa* but elected not to refer to it. The court in *B006* was satisfied that the question of whether section 117 was overbroad did not relate to the issue of whether the Immigration and Refugee Board could rely on section 117 to interpret people smuggling under section 37(1)(*b*) of the *IRPA*.[19]

In *Canada (Public Safety and Emergency Preparedness) v JP*,[20] the Federal Court of Appeal observed that *Appulonappa* was under appeal to the British Columbia Court of Appeal and that the effect of the British Columbia Supreme Court's constitutional declaration had been suspended pending determination of the appeal.[21] The appellants had urged the Federal Court of Appeal not to follow *B010* on the

---

[16] *Ibid* at para 155.

[17] *B010 v Canada (Minister of Citizenship and Immigration)*, 2013 FCA 87 (Federal Court of Appeal) [*B010* FCA].

[18] *B006 v Canada (Citizenship and Immigration)*, 2013 FC 1033 at para 82.

[19] *Ibid* at para 132.

[20] *Canada (Public Safety and Emergency Preparedness) v JP*, 2013 FCA 262.

[21] *Ibid* at para 9.

basis that it had not considered *Appulonappa* and that, even if it was bound by *Boro*, too many issues remained unresolved pending the appeal of *Appulonappa*. The Federal Court of Appeal was not dissuaded and followed *Boro* in rendering its decision, satisfied that its task was limited to resolving whether section 37(1)(*b*) of the *IRPA* was constitutionally valid. Clearly there is significant controversy around the question. The decision of the Court of Appeal for British Columbia will be of great interest, although it may not be the final word on the matter.

State Immunity Act — exceptions — hostage taking and torture

Steen v Islamic Republic of Iran, 2013 ONCA 30 (21 January 2013) (Court of Appeal for Ontario)

The appellants asked the Ontario Court of Appeal to consider whether the Islamic Republic of Iran was immune from judgment enforcement pursuant to the *State Immunity Act* (*SIA*).[22] Between 1982 and 1988, Iran directed Hezbollah to undertake kidnappings of American citizens. The hostages were only released after the United States transferred money, assets, and weapons to Iran.[23] Among those hostages were two American citizens, Alann Steen and David Jacobsen, who were kidnapped, detained, and tortured in Beirut, Lebanon, by Hezbollah at the direction of Iran.

In 2003 and 2006, Steen and his wife as well as Jacobsen's family (the appellants) each obtained significant damage awards from the United States District Court for the District of Columbia for the kidnapping, confinement, and torture of Steen and Jacobsen. Iran did not respond to either action and it did not pay any money to satisfy those judgments.

Subsequently, the appellants sought to enforce the judgments in Canada. Iran, the Iranian Ministry of Information and Security and the Iranian Revolutionary Guard (the respondents) moved to dismiss the appellants' actions pursuant to Rule 21.01 (determination of an issue before trial)[24] on the basis that Iran is a foreign state immune from the jurisdiction of any court in Canada. The two issues before the Ontario Superior Court of Justice were (1) whether the commercial activity exception to state immunity under section 5 of

---

[22] *State Immunity Act*, RSC 1985, c S-18.

[23] *Steen v Islamic Republic of Iran*, 2011 ONSC 6464 at paras 14-18 (Motions Court) [*Steen* MC].

[24] *Rules of Civil Procedure*, RRO 1990, Reg 194, Rule 21.01(3).

the *SIA* applied or, alternatively, (2) whether the acts were subject to a common law exception to immunity as non-sovereign acts.[25]

On 1 November 2011, the motions judge, Corrick J, declined to enforce the American judgments on the basis of the *SIA*.[26] Corrick J was of the view that the true nature of the impugned sovereign acts was criminal, not commercial, an outcome consistent with the Ontario Court of Appeal's decision in *Bouzari v Iran*,[27] in which Goudge JA held that kidnapping and torture are not commercial activity.[28] Corrick J was also of the view that the *SIA* was a complete code, following *Bouzari* — no common law exception to the act was available.[29] She nevertheless awarded costs of the motion against the respondents for their pre-litigation conduct, being the brutal and reprehensible acts committed against Steen and Jacobsen as well as the respondents' failure to satisfy the judgment debts owed to the appellants, which ultimately prompted the Canadian proceedings.[30]

The appellants applied for a stay of Corrick J's judgment since, at that time, legislation was before Parliament that, if implemented, would amend the *SIA* to prevent certain listed foreign states from claiming immunity. However, as the legislation was not yet enacted, Corrick J declined to grant the stay.[31]

The appellants raised three issues on appeal: (1) whether kidnapping for a ransom amounted to "commercial activity," bringing Iran within the *SIA* section 5 exception to immunity; (2) whether a common law exception to state immunity applied; and (3) whether the respondents lost the benefit of state immunity by committing acts in violation of peremptory norms of international law. The respondents cross-appealed the costs award by Corrick J.

Armstrong JA, writing for the Ontario Court of Appeal, discussed at the outset of his reasons the implications of the new *Justice for Victims of Terrorism Act* (*JVTA*), which had come into force after Corrick J's decision.[32] The *JVTA* provides that a court of competent jurisdiction can only recognize a judgment of a foreign court against

---

[25] *Steen MC, supra* note 23 at para 13.

[26] *Ibid* at para 55.

[27] *Bouzari v Iran,* (2004), 71 OR (3d) 675 (CA).

[28] *Steen MC, supra* note 23 at para 43.

[29] *Ibid* at paras 44-52.

[30] *Ibid* at para 58.

[31] *Ibid* at paras 53-54.

[32] *Justice for Victims of Terrorism Act,* SC 2012, c 1 [*JVTA*].

a foreign state if that state is set out on the list referred to in section 6.1 of the *SIA*.[33] At the time the appeal was heard, counsel for the appellants had known that Iran would be listed under the *SIA*. The Court of Appeal queried whether there was any need to pursue the appeal on that basis. Counsel for the appellants submitted that at that point in time that it was uncertain whether Iran would be added to the list, so the appeal was not yet moot. Armstrong JA proceeded to determine the appeal and cross-appeal as, in his view, it was not a foregone conclusion that the addition of Iran to the list would result in a successful proceeding to enforce the two American judgments.[34]

With respect to the first ground of appeal, the appellants argued that their case was distinguishable from *Bouzari* as Mr Bouzari had been kidnapped, imprisoned, and tortured for refusing to pay a bribe in the context of an oil and gas transaction. The *Steen* case instead involved the systematic exchange of hostages for money and guns. Human beings, the appellants submitted, could be treated like a commodity in these circumstances. Armstrong JA rejected that rather unattractive submission and confirmed that the exchange of hostages for money and guns is not a commercial act within the meaning of the *SIA*.

Armstrong JA also rejected the appellants' argument that the Supreme Court of Canada's decision in *Kuwait Airways Corp v Iraq* left open the question of whether there is a common law exception to state immunity.[35] In *Kuwait*, LeBel J, writing for the Court, observed:

[T]he *SIA* represents a clear rejection of the view that the immunity of foreign states is absolute. It reflects a recognition that there are now exceptions to the principle of state immunity and in so doing reflects the evolution of that principle at the international level. But I need not determine here whether the *SIA* is exhaustive in this respect or whether the evolution of international law and of the common law has led to the development of new exceptions to the principles of immunity from jurisdiction and immunity from execution (on this issue and the controversies it has generated, see F. Larocque, "La *Loi sur l'immunité des États* canadienne et la torture" (2010), 55 *McGill L.J.* 81). It will suffice to determine whether the commercial activity exception applies in the case at bar.[36]

---

[33] *Ibid*, s 4(5).
[34] *Steen v Islamic Republic of Iran*, 2013 ONCA 30 at para. 15 [*Steen* CA].
[35] *Kuwait Airways Corp v Iraq*, 2010 SCC 40 [*Kuwait*].
[36] *Ibid* at para 24.

Armstrong JA agreed with Corrick J that *Bouzari* had settled the issue.[37] He also noted that *Bouzari* was followed by the Quebec Court of Appeal in *Islamic Republic of Iran v Hashemi*.[38]

Finally, Armstrong JA found the appellants could not rely on peremptory norms to defeat the right to state immunity, relying on *Bouzari* and *Hashemi*, in the latter of which Morissette JA had held that customary international law has not developed an exception to state immunity for state acts that violate peremptory norms.[39] In reaching this conclusion, Morissette JA had relied on the International Court of Justice's decision in *Jurisdictional Immunities of the State (Germany v Italy)*,[40] a case that involved a request by Germany that the ICJ find that Italy had failed to respect Germany's jurisdictional immunities by allowing civil claims to be brought against it in the Italian courts for injuries caused by violations of international humanitarian law by the German Reich during the Second World War. The ICJ explained the relationship between *jus cogens* norms and the rule of state immunity as follows (as cited by Armstrong JA):

This argument therefore depends upon the existence of a conflict between a rule, or rules, of *jus cogens*, and the rule of customary law which requires one State to accord immunity to another. In the opinion of the Court, however, no such conflict exists ... The two sets of rules address different matters. The rules of State immunity are procedural in character and are confined to determining whether or not the courts of one State may exercise jurisdiction in respect of another State. They do not bear upon the question whether or not the conduct in respect of which the proceedings are brought was lawful or unlawful.[41]

Morissette JA had been of the view that *Germany v Italy* refuted the argument against jurisdictional immunity based on customary international law and on the *jus cogens* protection of human rights.[42] Armstrong JA agreed. Despite the respondents' success on the merits, Armstrong JA refused leave to appeal Corrick J's costs order, finding there to be no strong grounds to do so.

---

[37] *Steen* CA, *supra* note 34 at para 26.

[38] *Islamic Republic of Iran v Hashemi*, 2012 QCCA 1449.

[39] *Steen* CA, *supra* note 34 at para 31.

[40] *Jurisdictional Immunities of the State (Germany v Italy: Greece Intervening)*, [2012] ICJ Rep 99 [*Germany v Italy*].

[41] *Steen* CA, *supra* note 34 at para 33.

[42] *Ibid* at para 35.

Extradition — statut de réfugié — Convention relative aux droits de l'enfant

Savu c Canada (Ministre de la Justice), 2013 QCCA 554 (20 mars 2013) (Cour d'appel du Québec)

Le demandeur, M. Savu, a demandé la révision judiciaire de la décision du ministre de la Justice du Canada ordonnant son extradition vers la Roumanie pour y purger une peine de cinq ans et demi de prison à la suite d'une condamnation pour fraude. Selon l'article 49 de la *Loi sur l'extradition,*[43] une telle demande est entendue par la cour d'appel de la province où la décision a été rendue, en l'espèce, la Cour d'appel du Québec. Savu a obtenu le statut de réfugié au Canada en 2002, sa revendication ayant été fondée sur sa crainte de persécution à titre de membre de la minorité gitane (Rom). À l'époque il avait déjà été condamné en Roumanie à la suite d'accusations de fraude et d'emploi de documents contrefaits, mais sa condamnation a été annulée par la Cour d'appel de Roumanie. Suivant un deuxième procès *in absentia,* Savu a été déclaré coupable et condamné à nouveau. À partir de juillet 2005, la Roumanie demanda l'extradition de Savu du Canada. Le ministre a ordonné son extradition en 2009, mais a offert à Savu l'opportunité de soumettre des observations additionnelles suite aux décisions de la Cour suprême du Canada dans les affaires *Németh* et *Gavrila* de 2010.[44] En février 2012, le ministre de la Justice, ayant consulté le ministre de la Citoyenneté et de l'Immigration sur les risques pour Savu s'il était extradé en Roumanie, a confirmé sa décision d'ordonner son extradition.

À la Cour d'appel, Savu a contesté la conclusion du ministre que l'exclusion en vertu de l'alinéa (1)(F)(b) de la *Convention relative au statut des réfugiés*[45] s'appliquait à lui. Cette exclusion vise "les personnes dont on aura des raisons sérieuses de penser qu'elles ont commis un crime grave de droit commun en dehors du pays d'accueil avant d'y être admises comme réfugiés." Le juge Jacques (avec la concurrence des juges Morissette et Kasirer) rejette cet argument et suit la décision de la Cour suprême dans l'affaire *Németh* où le juge Cromwell pour la cour était d'avis qu'une infraction punissable d'une peine d'emprisonnement d'au moins dix ans constituait un

---

[43] *Loi sur l'extradition,* LC 1999, c 18.

[44] *Németh c Canada (Justice),* 2010 CSC 56; *Gavrila c Canada (Justice),* 2010 CSC 57 [*Németh*].

[45] *Refugee Convention, supra* note 6.

"crime grave de droit commun." Les infractions pour lesquelles Savu a été trouvé coupable en Roumaine sont passibles au Canada de peines d'emprisonnement de 10 et 14 ans. Ayant trouvé que la norme de contrôle applicable en l'espèce était celle de la raisonnabilité,[46] le juge Jacques refuse d'intervenir.[47]

Le deuxième motif avancé par Savu contre la décision du ministre était que celui-ci avait tort quant à son évaluation de la situation actuelle des Roms en Roumanie. Eu égard à l'article 44(1) de la *Loi sur l'extradition* — qui exige que le ministre refuse l'extradition s'il est convaincu qu'elle serait injuste ou tyrannique, ou que la demande d'extradition est discriminatoire — le ministre a conclu que la Roumaine "est une démocratie constitutionnelle qui a fait des progrès considérables depuis le départ de M. Savu en 2001," par exemple de par son accession à l'Union européenne.[48] Le juge Jacques affirme que cette conclusion est raisonnable, eu égard aux faits et aux règles de droits applicables.[49]

Le troisième motif avancé par Savu impliquait ses deux filles de 8 et 13 ans. Savu a souligné que, selon l'art 3 de la *Convention relative aux droits de l'enfant*,[50] l'intérêt supérieur de l'enfant doit être une considération primordiale dans toutes les décisions qui les concernent, et que la décision du ministre ne laissait pas voir qu'il avait été "réceptif, attentif et sensible" aux intérêts de ses enfants: *Baker c Canada (ministre de la Citoyenneté et de l'Immigration).*[51] À ce sujet le juge Jacques s'est exprimé ainsi:

La *Convention relative aux droits de l'enfant* n'a pas d'application directe au Canada, puisqu'elle n'a pas été mise en vigueur par le Parlement. Malgré ce fait, les valeurs qui y sont exprimées devraient tout de même être prises en compte par le décideur.

En l'espèce, la décision du ministre vise avant tout le demandeur, bien qu'elle emporte aussi des effets incidents sur ses enfants.

Même s'il s'agit d'une considération pertinente, le seul fait d'avoir des enfants ne constitue pas en soi un motif de refuser l'extradition demandée par un pays lié au Canada par un traité. Si tel était le cas, ce seul fait d'avoir

---

[46] *Savu c Canada (Ministre de la Justice)*, 2013 QCCA 554 aux para 49-55 [*Savu*].

[47] *Ibid* aux para 56-73.

[48] Cité *ibid* au para 82.

[49] *Ibid* aux para 74-91.

[50] *Convention relative aux droits de l'enfant*, 1577 RTNU 3, RT Can 1992 n⁰ 3, 28 ILM 1457 (entrée en vigueur: 2 septembre 1990.

[51] *Baker c Canada (ministre de la Citoyenneté et de l'Immigration)*, [1992] 2 RCS 817.

des enfants empêcherait toute extradition, indépendamment de sa justification.

Les conséquences sur les enfants du demandeur ne peuvent empêcher son extradition que si elles la rendent injuste ou tyrannique, choquante pour la conscience ou simplement inacceptable, et ce, compte tenu de tous les facteurs, incluant ceux qui penchent en faveur de l'extradition.[52]

Par conséquent, le juge a rejeté la demande de révision judiciaire.

Le poids à accorder à l'intérêt supérieur de l'enfant dans de tels cas est souvent troublant. La plupart des gens seront d'accord qu'il est profondément regrettable de séparer un enfant de son père dans le cas où les crimes du père ne sont pas de nature violente. Et pourtant, la *Convention relative aux droits de l'enfant* n'a clairement pas été conçue comme moyen pour les criminels de s'en sortir à bon compte. Si l'on peut sympathiser avec la décision du juge Jacques sur ce point, il est regrettable qu'il a répété la déclaration — énoncé pour la première fois par la Cour suprême du Canada dans l'affaire *Baker*— que la *Convention* n'est pas mise en œuvre en droit canadien. Alors que la *Convention* n'est pas expressément mise en œuvre, comme le sont certains autres traités canadiens, l'historique législatif révèle que le droit canadien (fédéral et provincial) a été examiné en profondeur, et a été jugé conforme à la *Convention*, avant sa ratification par le Canada. Ce n'est pas la pratique au Canada de ratifier des traités qui ne peuvent être respectés en raison de conflits avec le droit interne. Il est donc un peu facile, dans ces circonstances, de conclure que la *Convention* n'est pas mise en œuvre en droit canadien. La mise en œuvre de traités prend plusieurs formes.[53]

Refugee protection — human smuggling — constitutionality of section 117 of the Immigration and Refugee Protection Act

B010 v Canada (Minister of Citizenship and Immigration), 2013 FCA 87 (22 March 2013) (Federal Court of Appeal); leave to appeal to SCC refused 3 October 2013.

---

[52] *Savu, supra* note 46 aux para 96-99.

[53] Voir Elisabeth Eid et Hoori Hamboyan, "La mise en œuvre par le Canada des obligations découlant de traités internationaux de droits de la personne: créer du sens au-delà de l'absurde" dans Oonagh Fitzgerald, dir, *Règle de droit et mondialisation: Rapports entre le droit international et le droit interne* (Cowansville, QC: Yvon Blais, 2006) 555.

In this case, the Federal Court of Appeal heard and considered two appeals of judicial review decisions. The appellants, "B010" and "B072," were Sri Lankan nationals found on board the *MV Sun Sea*, along with 490 other Sri Lankan migrants who landed in Canada on 13 August 2010. The Immigration Division of the Immigration and Refugee Board declared both B010 and B072 inadmissible to Canada pursuant to section 37(1)(b) of the *IRPA*, which provides:

37.(1) A permanent resident or a foreign national is inadmissible on grounds of organized criminality for ... (b) engaging, in the context of transnational crime, in activities such as people smuggling, trafficking in persons or money laundering.	37.(1) Emportent interdiction de territoire pour criminalité organisée les faits suivants: ... (b) se livrer, dans le cadre de la criminalité transnationale, à des activités telles le passage de clandestins, le trafic de personnes ou le recyclage des produits de la criminalité.[54]

Their inadmissibility rested on their involvement in the organization and operation of a people smuggling operation.

B010 was a Tamil who left Sri Lanka when the Sri Lankan government gained control of territory formerly controlled by the Liberation Tigers of Tamil Eelam. B010 was smuggled first to Thailand and then to Canada by ship. He was asked to monitor the ship engine for the duration of the trip. He denied ever receiving any compensation or differential treatment for his work.[55] B072 appeared to have assumed a more important role in the organization of the human smuggling expedition to Canada, although he maintained he was always operating under the instruction of the smugglers.[56]

The board in each decision interpreted the meaning of people smuggling under section 37(1)(b) by way of the definition of human smuggling under section 117 of the *IRPA*. Under a protocol to the *Convention against Transnational Organized Crime*,[57] "smuggling of migrants" is defined as "the procurement, in order to obtain, directly or indirectly, a financial or other material benefit, of the illegal

---

[54] *IRPA, supra* note 1, s 37(1)(b).

[55] *B010* FCA, *supra* note 17 at paras 10-11.

[56] *Ibid* at paras 12-13.

[57] *Convention against Transnational Organized Crime, supra* note 14; *Smuggling Protocol, supra* note 7.

entry of a person into a State Party of which the person is not a national or a permanent resident."[58] The definition of human smuggling under section 117 of the *IRPA* is broader as it does not require proof that the smuggler engaged in the impugned acts for the purpose of material benefit.

The appellants were unsuccessful in their judicial review applications. In B010's case,[59] Noël J was of the view that Canada was not in breach of the protocol or the convention for defining human smuggling to extend beyond merely those persons that derive financial or other material benefit. Noël J also found, however, that the board had erred in determining that B010 was not compensated, as he had clearly received preferable treatment.[60]

The following serious question of general importance was certified by Noël J:

For the purposes of paragraph 37(1)(*b*) of the *Immigration and Refugee Protection Act*, is it appropriate to define the term "people smuggling" by relying on section 117 of the same statute rather than a definition contained in an international instrument to which Canada is a signatory?

In short reasons, Hughes J reached the same result in the case of B072 and certified the same question of general importance.[61]

The two appeals were heard together on consent. The issue before the Federal Court of Appeal was whether material benefit was an element of people smuggling.[62] The appellants argued that the definition of people smuggling under the *IRPA* must conform to the protocol's definition of "smuggling of migrants," as section 3(3)(f) provides that the *IRPA* must be construed in a manner that complies with Canada's international human rights obligations. The appellants also referred the Federal Court of Appeal to other decisions where the Federal Court had interpreted the phrase "people smuggling" to require evidence of profit.[63]

---

58 *Smuggling Protocol, supra* note 7, art 3(a).

59 *B010, supra* note 10.

60 *Ibid* at paras 48-49, 64.

61 *B072 v Canada (Citizenship and Immigration)*, 2012 FC 899.

62 *B010 FCA, supra* note 17 at para 7.

63 *Ibid.* The appellants referred to *Hernandez v Canada (Minister of Public Safety and Emergency Preparedness)*, 2012 FC 1417 and *JP v Canada (Minister of Public Safety and Emergency Preparedness)*, 2012 FC 1466.

The appellants further relied on Article 2 of the protocol, which requires that states parties protect the rights of smuggled migrants, and Article 6, which requires that states parties adopt legislation to establish the criminal offence of intentionally smuggling migrants for the purpose of obtaining directly or indirectly a financial or other material benefit.[64]

The appellants submitted that by not requiring evidence of material benefit, the definition of human smuggling will result in absurd decisions, such as family members being rendered inadmissible simply for assisting one another in their flight to Canada.[65] Finally, the appellants argued that a finding of inadmissibility under section 37(1)(b) would place Canada in violation of its *non-refoulement* obligations.[66]

Dawson JA, writing for the court, first addressed the question of whether Noël J had erred in finding that B010 had received material benefit.[67] Dawson JA reversed Noël J on the point, finding it apparent from the record before the Board that the minister had not adduced evidence on the conditions of B010's accommodation. Dawson JA then turned to consider the scope of the definition of "person smuggling" under the *IRPA*.[68]

Dawson JA agreed with Noël J that the appropriate standard of review was reasonableness, not correctness. She was satisfied that the nature of the issue, the interpretation of the phrase "people smuggling" in a home statute, did not raise a constitutional question, a question of law of general importance to the legal system as a whole or a true question of jurisdiction. Dawson JA was also unconvinced that the importance of the issue in and of itself was sufficient to justify imposing a correctness standard.[69]

Applying a reasonableness standard to the decisions below, Dawson JA upheld the conclusions reached by Noël J and Hughes J. She found that nothing in the Convention or the Protocol:

(i) prohibited a signatory state from enacting legislation that renders those persons who contribute to, but do not profit from, people smuggling inadmissible;

---

[64] *B010* FCA, *supra* note 17 at para 74.

[65] *Ibid* at para 92.

[66] *Ibid.*

[67] *Ibid* at para 51.

[68] *Ibid* at paras 55, 57.

[69] *Ibid* at paras 65-70.

(ii) required a signatory state to enact legislation that tracks the language of the Protocol, noting that the legislative guide for implementing the Protocol instructs that the language of the Protocol "was not intended for enactment or adoption verbatim"; or

(iii) prevented a signatory from enacting legislation that criminalized a broader range of conduct.[70]

Dawson JA noted that other states had implemented similarly broad provisions to criminalize human smuggling.[71] She was of the view that section 117 conformed to Canada's international obligations.

Dawson JA observed that *IRPA* section 3(3)(f) requires that the act be interpreted in a manner that complies with the international human rights instruments to which Canada is a party. The relevant human rights instrument, in Dawson JA's view, was the *Refugee Convention*. She observed that Article 33 of the *Refugee Convention* was potentially applicable, for under this article Canada is prohibited from returning an individual to a territory where their life or freedom would be threatened on one of the grounds established under the *Refugee Convention*. Dawson JA was satisfied, nonetheless, that declaring a person inadmissible was not equivalent to removal or *refoulement*,[72] relying on the Supreme Court of Canada's decision in *Németh v Canada (Justice)*.[73] On this basis, Canada was not in breach of the *Refugee Convention*.

In answer to the appellants' argument that the scope of the definition of people smuggling would result in absurd decision making, Dawson JA found that the language of the provision was a sufficiently clear expression of parliamentary intent. To interpret it otherwise would render the absurd result that persons convicted of human smuggling might not also be found inadmissible.[74] Dawson JA was also content that the reporting process for inadmissibility was discretionary. For instance, it might be apparent to the minister's delegate that the person was simply assisting other family members in their flight to Canada. The delegate could exercise their discretion to not prepare a report.[75] Dawson JA distinguished the Federal Court cases that had interpreted the phrase "people smuggling" to require

---

[70] *Ibid* at paras 76-78.

[71] *Ibid* at para 79.

[72] *Ibid* at paras 87-90.

[73] *Németh, supra* note 44 at para 50.

[74] *B010* FCA, *supra* note 17 at para 92.

[75] *Ibid* at para 93.

evidence of profit on the basis that those decisions had applied a correctness standard of review.

Dawson JA therefore answered the certified question as follows:

> Yes, it is reasonable to define inadmissibility under paragraph 37(1)(b) by relying upon subsection 117(1) of the *Immigration and Refugee Protection Act*, which makes it an offence to knowingly organize, induce, aid or abet the coming into Canada of one or more persons who are not in possession of a visa, passport or other document required by the Act. To do so is not inconsistent with Canada's international legal obligations.

It is very much to be regretted that the Supreme Court of Canada declined leave to appeal from this decision. The national import-ance of the questions raised can hardly be doubted. Furthermore, the result is inconsistent with *Appulonappa* (summarized earlier) as well as previous Federal Court decisions. Yet another reason for the Supreme Court of Canada to have considered the case is Dawson JA's application of a deferential standard of review to a question of law touching Canada's international human rights obligations — an interpretive stance that is bound to result in inconsistent and mis-taken approaches to Canada's international legal obligations.[76]

International treaties — Charter analysis — right to strike

Saskatchewan v Saskatchewan Federation of Labour, 2013 SKCA 43 (26 April 2013) (Saskatchewan Court of Appeal); leave to appeal to SCC granted (17 October 2013).

In this case, the Saskatchewan Court of Appeal was tasked with assessing the constitutional validity of two sets of provincial legisla-tion: the *Public Service Essential Services Act* (*Essential Services Act*)[77] as well as the *Trade Union Amendment Act, 2008* and *Trade Union Amendment Act, 2008 (No. 2).*[78] The *Essential Services Act,* in particular, had imposed restrictions on the ability of public sector workers in Saskatchewan to strike. The trial judge held that the right to strike

---

[76] In *Febles v Canada (Minister of Citizenship and Immigration),* 2012 FCA 324 at para 24, Evans JA for the majority of the Federal Court of Appeal rightly insisted on a correctness standard of review in a case where the meaning of Article 1(F)((b) of the *Refugee Convention, supra* note 6, was in issue, observing that the provisions of an international convention should be interpreted as uniformly as possible.

[77] *Public Service Essential Services Act,* SS 2008, c P-42.2.

[78] *Trade Union Amendment Act,* SS 2008, cc 26-27.

was protected by section 2(d) of the *Charter* and that the restrictions imposed by the *Essential Services Act* were breaches of section 2(d), which could not be justified under section 1 of the *Charter*.[79] The trial judge reached this conclusion, in part, by looking to various international treaties and instruments to which Canada was a party that recognize and protect the freedom of workers to organize, engage in collective bargaining, and strike.[80]

On appeal, the respondents again argued that the right to strike is enshrined in international law. The respondents relied in particular on *ILO Convention no. 87 Concerning Freedom of Association and Protection of the Right to Organise*,[81] the *International Covenant on Economic, Social and Cultural Rights* (*ICESCR*),[82] and the *International Covenant on Civil and Political Rights* (*ICCPR*).[83] The respondents also referenced a report from the ILO Committee on Freedom of Association that was critical of the *Essential Services Act*.

In his reasons, Richards JA held that the starting point of the right to strike analysis was a trilogy of the Supreme Court of Canada cases from the 1980s (Labour Trilogy),[84] which held that section 2(d) did not extend to a right to strike.[85] He acknowledged that the Supreme Court of Canada had broadened its approach to section 2(d) following the Labour Trilogy, most notably in *Health Services and Support — Facilities Subsector Bargaining Association v British Columbia*[86] and *Ontario (Attorney General) v Fraser*,[87] but held that none of these cases had overturned the ratio from the Labour Trilogy that the freedom of association protection in section 2(d) does not include a right

79 *Charter, supra* note 2, ss 1, 2(d).

80 See *Saskatchewan v Saskatchewan Federation of Labour*, 2012 SKQB 62 at paras 107-14.

81 *ILO Convention no. 87 Concerning Freedom of Association and Protection of the Right to Organise*, 68 UNTS 17, Can TS 1973 No 14, in force 4 July 1950.

82 *International Covenant on Economic, Social and Cultural Rights*, 993 UNTS 3, Can TS 1976 No 46, (1967) 6 ILM 360 (in force 3 January 1976) [*ICESCR*].

83 *International Covenant on Civil and Political Rights*, 999 UNTS 171, Can TS 1976 No. 47, (1967) 6 ILM 368 (in force 23 March 1976) [*ICCPR*].

84 *Reference Re Public Service Employee Relations Act (Alta)*, [1987] 1 SCR 313 [*Alberta Reference*]; *PSAC v Canada*, [1987] 1 SCR 424; *RWDSU v Saskatchewan*, [1987] 1 SCR 460 [collectively, Labour Trilogy].

85 *Saskatchewan v Saskatchewan Federation of Labour*, 2013 SKCA 43 at para 46 [*Sask Labour*].

86 *Health Services and Support — Facilities Subsector Bargaining Association v British Columbia*, 2007 SCC 27, [2007] 2 SCR 391 [*Health Services*].

87 *Ontario (Attorney General) v Fraser*, 2011 SCC 20, [2011] 2 SCR 3 [*Fraser*].

to strike.[88] He further noted that in *Health Services* and *Fraser*, the Supreme Court of Canada had expressly stated that their decision did not address the right to strike.[89]

When assessing the respondent's argument that Canada's international obligations supported an interpretation of section 2(d), which included a right to strike, Richards JA acknowledged that *Charter* rights are to be interpreted in context, including the context provided by Canada's international obligations. However, he ultimately held that there was nothing in the international instruments cited by the respondents that would lead the court to depart from the Labour Trilogy's interpretation of section 2(d) of the *Charter* with respect to the right to strike.[90] He concluded that the international law considerations raised by the respondent could not have "any meaningful impact" on the question of whether the court was entitled to depart from the Labour Trilogy.[91]

On its face, the decision of Richard JA is a straightforward application of the Labour Trilogy's ratio with respect to the right to strike. His reasons reveal his opinion that he remains bound to apply this ratio by application of *stare decisis*. This view is surprising given the recent criticism of the Labour Trilogy by the Supreme Court of Canada in *Health Services* — which overruled the Labour Trilogy and held that its exclusion of collective bargaining from the ambit of section 2(d) should be rejected, in part due to Canada's international labour law obligations.

It is particularly surprising that Richards JA held that international law could not have "any meaningful impact" on the application of the ratio from the Labour Trilogy, given that the majority in *Health Services* was implicitly critical of the majority reasons in the *Alberta Reference* for overlooking international instruments when engaging in a contextual analysis of section 2(d). The majority in *Health Services* preferred the analysis of Dickson CJC in dissent in the *Alberta Reference*. Dickson CJC had concluded that the *ICESCR* and *ICCPR* contain explicit protection of the formation and activities of trade

---

[88] *Sask Labour, supra* note 85 at paras 40-46.

[89] See *Health Services, supra* note 86 at para 19. Richards JA cites *Fraser, supra* note 87 at para 25 for this same proposition, but in that paragraph of their reasons McLachlin CJC and LeBel J merely note that the majority in the Labour Trilogy, *supra* note 84 held that section 2(d) does not create a right to strike; they do not expressly remove the right to strike from the ambit of their reasons. That being said, *Fraser* does not address the right to strike.

[90] *Sask Labour, supra* note 85 at paras 70-71.

[91] *Ibid.*

unions, subject to reasonable limits. Further, he noted that the International Labour Organization's adjudicative bodies had formed a clear consensus that *Convention no. 87* contained protection for collective bargaining and the right to strike.[92] Leave has been granted in this case by the Supreme Court of Canada, and the appeal is tentatively set to be heard on 16 May 2014.

Refugee protection — Exclusion from refugee status — complicity in international crimes

Ezokola v Canada (Minister of Citizenship and Immigration), 2013 SCC 40 (19 July 2013) (Supreme Court of Canada)

Ezokola was a Congolese diplomatic envoy to the United Nations in New York who sought asylum in Canada for himself and his family in January 2008. He claimed he could no longer work for the Kabila government of the Democratic Republic of the Congo (DRC), which he objected to as corrupt, anti-democratic, and violent. He feared he would be regarded as a traitor for having resigned his post and fled to Canada. He alleged that the Congolese intelligence service had harassed and threatened him for alleged links to an opponent of the government. He sought asylum for himself, his wife, and their eight children.

Ezokola's claim was heard by the Immigration and Refugee Board. The board concluded that Ezokola was excluded from refugee protection under Article 1(F)(a) of the *Refugee Convention*[93] on the ground of his supposed complicity in crimes against humanity committed by members of the Congolese government he had served. The board considered that Ezokola had "personal and knowing awareness" of his government's crimes and had, by remaining in his post, helped to sustain the Congolese government.[94]

Mainville J (then of the Federal Court) allowed Ezokola's application for judicial review and quashed the board's decision as imposing guilt by association, there being no evidence that Ezokola had in fact committed or contributed to the commission of crimes by members of the DRC's government.[95] Mainville J considered that

---

[92] *Alberta Reference, supra* note 84 at paras 57-72.

[93] *Refugee Convention, supra* note 6.

[94] *Ezokola v Canada (Minister of Citizenship and Immigration)*, 2013 SCC 40 at paras 15-19 [*Ezokola*].

[95] *Ibid* at paras 20-23.

criminal responsibility for crimes against humanity required personal participation in the crime alleged or personal control over the events leading to the crime alleged.

The Federal Court of Appeal (Noël, Nadon and Pelletier JJA) disagreed with Mainville J and restored the board's decision. Noël JA for the court affirmed that a senior government official could be complicit in the crimes of his or her government simply by remaining in his or her position without protest and continuing to defend the government's interests despite knowledge of the government's crimes.[96]

The Supreme Court of Canada allowed Ezokola's appeal. It called the Federal Court of Appeal's approach "guilt by association" and expressly departed from a long-standing Federal Court of Appeal precedent[97] in order to "rein in the Canadian approach to complicity under art. 1F(a)" and bring Canadian law into line with the *Refugee Convention* (the international law to which Article 1(F)(a) expressly refers) and the approach to complicity taken by other states parties.[98] LeBel and Fish JJ, for the court, reviewed at length the applicable international legal norms, including the *Vienna Convention on the Law of Treaties,*[99] the *Refugee Convention,* and the *Rome Statute of the International Criminal Court,*[100] as interpreted both by international authorities and foreign courts.[101] The learned judges reformulated the test for complicity under Article 1(F)(a) of the *Refugee Convention* as follows:

[A]n individual will be excluded from refugee protection under art. 1F(a) for complicity in international crimes if there are serious reasons for considering that he or she voluntarily made a knowing and significant contribution to the crime or criminal purpose of the group alleged to have committed the crime. The evidentiary burden falls on the Minister as the party seeking the applicant's exclusion.[102]

---

96   *Ibid* at paras 24-7.

97   *Ramirez v Canada (Minister of Employment and Immigration),* [1992] 2 FC 306.

98   *Ezokola, supra* note 94 at para 30.

99   *Vienna Convention on the Law of Treaties,* 1155 UNTS 331, Can TS 1980 No 37 (in force 27 January 1980).

100 *Rome Statute of the International Criminal Court,* 2187 UNTS 3, Can TS 2002 No 13 (in force 1 July 2002) [*Rome Statute*].

101 *Ezokola, supra* note 94 at paras 31-36, 42-77.

102 *Ibid* at para 29.

Under the heading, "The Board Must Rely on International Law to Interpret Article 1F(a)," LeBel and Fish JJ noted that Article 1(F)(a) expressly refers to crimes "as defined in the international instruments" and therefore requires the board to "consider international criminal law to determine whether an individual should be excluded from refugee protection."[103] The learned judges regarded the *Rome Statute* as "the best place to start"[104] but also noted that that treaty "cannot be considered as a complete codification of international criminal law"[105] and therefore went on to consider jurisprudence both from international and foreign courts.

The court's review of this jurisprudence led it to conclude that even the broadest modes of commission recognized under international criminal law, namely common purpose liability and joint criminal enterprise, require a link between the individual and the crime or criminal purpose of a group.[106] Thus, complicity under Article 25(3)(d) of the *Rome Statute* (common purpose liability) is based on intentionally or knowingly contributing to a group's crime or criminal purpose.[107] Similarly, joint criminal enterprise liability, as recognized in the jurisprudence of the ad hoc international criminal tribunals, does not, even in its broadest form, capture individuals merely based on rank or association within an organization or institution.[108] These conclusions about the scope of complicity under international criminal law are supported by foreign jurisprudence interpreting Article 1(F)(a) of the *Refugee Convention*.[109] The court therefore concluded that the Canadian approach to complicity, as represented by the Federal Court of Appeal's decision in Ezokola's case, was out of step with international criminal law. The court allowed Ezokola's appeal and remitted his case to the board for redetermination.

This case is an admirable illustration of how Canadian courts should give effect to international legal norms directly implemented in domestic law. Unlike many other Canadian cases touching upon international law, the norms at issue were not given effect through

[103] *Ibid* at para 42.
[104] *Ibid* at para 48.
[105] *Ibid* at para 51.
[106] *Ibid* at paras 52-3.
[107] *Ibid* at paras 54-61.
[108] *Ibid* at paras 62-7.
[109] *Ibid* at paras 69-77.

the interpretive presumption of conformity with international law. There was no need to apply that doctrine for the simple reason that Article 1(F)(a) of the *Refugee Convention* is "directly incorporate[d] into Canadian law"[110] by section 98 of the *IRPA*, which reads: "A person referred to in section E or F of Article 1 of the Refugee Convention is not a Convention refugee or a person in need of protection." This provision requires a Canadian court interpreting it to determine and apply the international legal position, as LeBel and Fish JJ did so cogently here.

Customary international law — corporate social responsibility — direct negligence of parent corporation

Choc v Hudbay Minerals Inc, 2013 ONSC 1414 (22 July 2013) (Ontario Superior Court of Justice)

The plaintiffs, indigenous Mayan Q'echi' from Guatemala, brought three actions against a Canadian mining company (Hudbay) and its subsidiaries in negligence arising out of alleged human rights abuses that were undertaken by security personnel employed by Hudbay's subsidiary in Guatemala. The plaintiffs claimed that Hudbay was liable both in direct negligence and by way of vicarious liability. The defendants sought to strike each action as disclosing no reasonable cause of action, with Hudbay, in particular, arguing that the plaintiffs' case relied on the untenable proposition that Hudbay owed a duty of care to local indigenous peoples in Guatemala to ensure that the commercial activities of Hudbay's subsidiary in Guatemala were carried out in such a way as to protect those people with whom the subsidiary came into contact.

On the motion to strike, Amnesty International Canada intervened to make submissions on international norms and authorities, which, in its submission, established that a company owes a duty of care to the victims of human rights abuses carried out by or at the direction of its subsidiary. Amnesty International cited a variety of international instruments,[111] which it argued evidenced an emerging

---

[110] *Ibid* at para 15.

[111] Notably, the *Voluntary Principles on Security and Human Rights*, online: Foley Hoag LLP <http://www.voluntaryprinciples.org/>; OECD, *OECD Guidelines for Multinational Enterprises, 2011 Edition* (Paris: OECD Publishing, 2011), online: <http://dx.doi.org/10.1787/9789264115415-en>; UN Global Compact, online: UN <http://www.unglobalcompact.org/>; John Ruggie, *Promotion and Protection of All Human Rights, Civil, Political, Economic, Social and Cultural Rights, Including*

norm of international corporate conduct standards.[112] Amnesty International further argued that Canada had endorsed the main relevant standards, and Canadian courts should therefore recognize these principles and permit them to inform the analysis of when and to whom a Canadian corporation operating internationally owes a duty of care.[113]

In reasons on the motion to strike, Brown J assessed whether it was "plain and obvious" that the claim of direct negligence disclosed no reasonable cause of action and would fail. The submissions of Amnesty International with respect to international norms of corporate conduct standards were referenced solely with respect to the policy implications of recognizing a duty of care. There, Brown J noted that recognizing a duty of care would support the Canadian government's efforts to encourage Canadian companies to meet a high standard of corporate social responsibility both in Canada and abroad.[114] With respect to the second stage of the *Anns* analysis, the existence of policy reasons both in favour of and against the imposition of a duty of care led Brown J to hold that it was not "plain and obvious" that the direct negligence claim against Hudbay would fail.

Bribery Convention — conspiracy to bribe foreign public official

R v Karigar, 2013 ONSC 5199 (15 August 2013) (Ontario Superior Court of Justice)

The accused was charged under the *Corruption of Foreign Public Officials Act* (*CFPOA*)[115] for conspiring to offer bribes to Air India officials and India's minister of civil aviation in an attempt to obtain a contract from Air India. Section 3 of the *CFPOA* states as follows:

---

the Right to Development: Protect, Respect and Remedy: A Framework for Business and Human Rights, UNHRC, 8th Sess, UN Doc A/HRC/8/5 (2008); UN OHCHR, United Nations Guiding Principles on Business and Human Rights (New York and Geneva: OHCHR, 2011), online: OHCHR <http://www.ohchr.org/Documents/Publications/GuidingPrinciplesBusinessHR_EN.pdf>; and the work of the International Standards Organization with respect to corporate responsibility (see, for example, ISO 26000: Social Responsibility, online: ISO <http://www.iso.org/iso/home/standards/iso26000.htm>).

[112] *Choc v Hudbay Minerals Inc*, 2013 ONSC 1414 at paras 33-35.

[113] *Ibid* at para 36.

[114] *Ibid* at para 73.

[115] *Corruption of Foreign Public Officials Act*, SC 1998, c 34.

Bribing a foreign public official	*Corruption d'agents publics étrangers*
3. (1) Every person commits an offence who, in order to obtain or retain an advantage in the course of business, directly or indirectly gives, offers or agrees to give or offer a loan, reward, advantage or benefit of any kind to a foreign public official or to any person for the benefit of a foreign public official	3. (1) Commet une infraction quiconque, directement ou indirectement, dans le but d'obtenir ou de conserver un avantage dans le cours de ses affaires, donne, offre ou convient de donner ou d'offrir à un agent public étranger ou à toute personne au profit d'un agent public étranger un prêt, une récompense ou un avantage de quelque nature que ce soit:
(a) as consideration for an act or omission by the official in connection with the performance of the official's duties or functions; or	(a) en contrepartie d'un acte ou d'une omission dans le cadre de l'exécution des fonctions officielles de cet agent;
(b) to induce the official to use his or her position to influence any acts or decisions of the foreign state or public international organization for which the official performs duties or functions.	(b) pour convaincre ce dernier d'utiliser sa position pour influencer les actes ou les décisions de l'État étranger ou de l'organisation internationale publique pour lequel il exerce ses fonctions officielles.

The accused argued that by referencing an agreement to give a bribe, section 3(1) required both the agreement of the accused to give the bribe and the agreement of the official to receive the bribe. In circumstances where the Crown could not prove that a bribe was both offered and paid to a foreign public official, the accused argued that the constituent elements of the offence were not established. In the accused's case, the evidence established that two sums of money were transferred to the accused's bank account in India by his company, but there was no evidence as to what became of these sums or whether they were offered or paid to any foreign public official as a bribe.

In interpreting Parliament's intention in enacting section 3(1) of the *CFPOA*, Hackland RSJ noted that there was no existing jurisprudence interpreting the *CFPOA*.[116] To place the legislation in its proper context, he looked to the terms of the Organisation for Economic Co-operation and Development's *Convention on Combating Bribery of Foreign Public Officials in International Business Transactions* (*Bribery Convention*), to which Canada is a party.[117] The *Bribery Convention* is referenced in the preamble to the *CFPOA*.

Article 1 of the *Bribery Convention* states as follows:

2. Each Party shall take any measures necessary to establish that complicity in, including incitement, aiding and abetting, or authorisation of an act of bribery of a foreign public official shall be a criminal offence. Attempt and conspiracy to bribe a foreign public official shall be criminal offences to the same extent as attempt and conspiracy to bribe a public official of that Party.

Given the wording of the *Bribery Convention*, Hackland RSJ was satisfied that a conspiracy or agreement to bribe a foreign public official was a violation of the *CFPOA*.[118] This was supported by both the plain wording of the *CFPOA*, which specified that agreement is an element of the offence, and the terms of the *Bribery Convention*. By criminalizing a conspiracy or agreement to bribe a foreign public official, the *CFPOA* was in step with Canada's obligation under Article 1 of the *Bribery Convention* to criminalize conspiracies to give or offer bribes to foreign public officials.[119] The court proceeded to convict the accused.

Mobility rights — transfer of offenders — presumption of conformity in Charter *interpretation*

Divito v Canada (Public Safety and Emergency Preparedness), 2013 SCC 47 (19 September 2013) (Supreme Court of Canada)[120]

Divito, a Canadian citizen, was extradited to the United States where he pleaded guilty to serious drug offences and was sentenced to

---

[116] *R v Karigar*, 2013 ONSC 5199 at para 27 [*Karigar*].

[117] *Convention on Combating Bribery of Foreign Public Officials in International Business Transactions*, 37 ILM 1 (entered into force 15 February 1999).

[118] *Karigar, supra* note 116 at para 28.

[119] *Ibid.*

[120] One of the authors, Gib van Ert, appeared as counsel for the intervener, the British Columbia Civil Liberties Association, in this appeal.

seven-and-a-half years in prison. He submitted a request under the *International Transfer of Offenders Act* to be transferred to Canada to serve the remainder of his American sentence.[121] Divito's request was approved by the US authorities but refused by the Canadian federal minister of public safety on the basis that the nature of his offence and his affiliations with criminal organizations suggested that his return to Canada would constitute a potential threat to the safety of Canadians and the security of Canada. In reaching this decision, the minister relied on the discretion granted him by sections 8(1), 10(1)(a), and 10(2)(a) of the act.

Divito initially sought judicial review of the minister's decision before the Federal Court. This court concluded that the minister's decision was reasonable and dismissed Divito's application. Divito appealed to the Federal Court of Appeal where his only argument was that the act's provisions granting the minister discretion to refuse the transfer request were unconstitutional on the ground that they unjustifiably infringed his right under section 6(1) of the *Charter* ("Every citizen of Canada has the right to enter, remain in and leave Canada" / "Tout citoyen canadien a le droit de demeurer au Canada, d'y entrer ou d'en sortir").[122] The Federal Court of Appeal dismissed the appeal. The majority of that court found that the impugned provisions did not infringe section 6(1) at all, while the minority opinion of Mainville JA was that the provisions did infringe Divito's mobility rights, but the infringements were justifiable under section 1 of the *Charter*.

The Supreme Court of Canada dismissed the appeal. Abella J, writing for six members of the Court, held that the impugned provisions did not infringe the *Charter* at all. LeBel and Fish JJ, for themselves and McLachlin CJC, concurred in the result but found the impugned provisions to be an infringement of Divito's right to enter Canada. The majority reasons looked to "Canada's international obligations and relevant principles of international law" as "instructive in defining the right" to enter and remain in Canada. Abella J quoted approvingly Dickson CJC's well-known declaration, in the *Alberta Reference*,[123] that the *Charter* "should generally be presumed to provide protection at least as great as that afforded by similar provisions in international human rights documents which Canada

---

[121] *International Transfer of Offenders Act*, SC 2004, c 21.

[122] *Charter, supra* note 2, s 6(1).

[123] *Alberta Reference, supra* note 84 at 349.

has ratified."[124] Abella J also quoted the Court's more recent invocation of this principle in *Health Services*,[125] saying that the presumption "helps frame the interpretive scope of section 6(1)."[126]

Abella J noted that the "international law inspiration" for section 6(1) of the *Charter* "is generally considered to be art. 12 of the *International Covenant on Civil and Political Rights* [ICCPR]."[127] "As a treaty to which Canada is a signatory," said Abella J, "the ICCPR is binding. As a result, the rights protected by the ICCPR provide a minimum level of protection in interpreting the mobility rights under the *Charter*."[128] While this statement ought hardly to come as a surprise given the Court's previous affirmations of Dickson CJC's dissent in the *Alberta Reference*, it is nevertheless an admirably strong and clear affirmation of the presumption of minimum protection in *Charter* interpretation. Abella J proceeded to quote *ICCPR* Article 12 in full and to consider the UN Human Rights Committee's General Comment no. 27 on the meaning of Article 12(4)'s elusive statement that "[n]o one shall be arbitrarily deprived of the right to enter his own country." In particular, Abella J noted that while Article 12(4) protects against arbitrary interference with the right to enter, the Human Rights Committee in General Comment no. 27 was of the view that there are "few, if any" limitations on the right to enter that would be considered reasonable.[129] "The right to enter protected by section 6(1) of the *Charter*," said Abella J, "should therefore be interpreted in a way that is consistent with the broad protection under international law."[130]

Abella J then turned to the *Treaty between Canada and the United States of America on the Execution of Penal Sentences*[131] and its implementing legislation. Pursuant to the treaty (and subject to certain

---

[124] *Divito v Canada (Public Safety and Emergency Preparedness)*, 2013 SCC 47 at para 22 [*Divito*].

[125] *Health Services*, *supra* note 86 at para 70.

[126] *Divito*, *supra* note 124 at para 23.

[127] *Ibid* at para 24.

[128] *Ibid* at para 25.

[129] UN Human Rights Committee, *General Comment No 27, Article 12: Freedom of Movement*, UN Doc CCPR/C/21/Rev.1/Add.9 (1999) at para 21, reprinted in *Compilation of General Comments and General Recommendations made by Human Rights Treaty Bodies*, UN Doc HRI/GEN/1/Rev.9 (2008), vol 1 at 223.

[130] *Divito*, *supra* note 124 at paras 26-27.

[131] *Treaty between Canada and the United States of America on the Execution of Penal Sentences*, Can TS 1978 No 12.

exceptions), offenders sentenced to imprisonment in either state may be transferred to their state of citizenship if both states and the offender all consent. In implementation of the treaty, Canada enacted the federal *Transfer of Offenders Act* in 1978[132] and the *International Transfer of Offenders Act* in 2004. The relevant provisions of the latter act at the time of Divito's transfer request were as follows:

8. (1) The consent of the three parties to a transfer — the offender, the foreign entity and Canada — is required.

10. (1) In determining whether to consent to the transfer of a Canadian offender, the Minister shall consider the following factors:

   (a) whether the offender's return to Canada would constitute a threat to the security of Canada ...

(2) In determining whether to consent to the transfer of a Canadian or foreign offender, the Minister shall consider the following factors:

   (a) whether, in the Minister's opinion, the offender will, after the transfer, commit a terrorism offence or criminal organization offence within the meaning of section 2 of the Criminal Code ...

8. (1) Le transfèrement nécessite le consentement des trois parties en cause, soit le délinquant, l'entité étrangère et le Canada

10. (1) Le ministre tient compte des facteurs ci-après pour décider s'il consent au transfèrement du délinquant canadien:

   (a) le retour au Canada du délinquant peut constituer une menace pour la sécurité du Canada ...

(2) Il tient compte des facteurs ci-après pour décider s'il consent au transfèrement du délinquant canadien ou étranger:

   (a) à son avis, le délinquant commettra, après son transfèrement, une infraction de terrorisme ou une infraction d'organisation criminelle, au sens de l'article 2 du Code criminel.[133]

Divito contended that by giving the minister a discretion to consent or not to the transfer of a Canadian offender to a Canadian prison once the incarcerating state has consented to the transfer, these

---

[132] *Transfer of Offenders Act*, RSC 1985, c T-15, as repealed by *International Transfer of Offenders Act, supra* note 121, section 42.

[133] *International Transfer of Offenders Act, supra* note 121, s 8.

provisions unjustifiably infringed a Canadian offender's right to enter his or her own country. In essence, said Abella J, Divito argued that *Charter* section 6(1) includes an automatic right to serve a foreign prison sentence in Canada if the foreign state consents.[134]

Abella J rejected this interpretation of section 6(1), saying that in international law, to require the return of an offender to his or her home state "infringes the doctrine of state sovereignty" and that, as a matter of international law, Canada "has no legal authority to *require* the return of a citizen who is lawfully incarcerated by a foreign state."[135] This seems at least partly overstated. While Canada likely could not compel a foreign state to return its foreign-incarcerated national, the mere act of purporting to require a foreign state to return an offender is probably not, without more, an infringement of state sovereignty. Similarly, it is exaggerated to call the act and the treaties it implements as providing "an exception to the doctrine of state sovereignty in international law."[136] There is a tendency in Canadian judgments since *R v Hape* to throw around notions of state sovereignty, and allegations of its infringement, rather too freely.[137] Yet Abella J is right to say that underlying the Canada–US treaty and similar agreements is "the understanding that, absent a treaty, Canada was without a meaningful legal mechanism to administer the sentences imposed upon Canadian citizens who are lawfully incarcerated in a foreign state."[138]

Coming to Divito's constitutional challenge, Abella J held as follows:

In the case of extradition, the Canadian government permits the removal from Canada of a Canadian citizen who has not been convicted, to face charges in a foreign jurisdiction. Yet *Cotroni* found this to be only at the outer edges of the s. 6(1) right. In the case of a prisoner transfer, the Canadian citizen has been convicted in a foreign jurisdiction, is lawfully incarcerated there, and is seeking the Canadian government's permission to serve his or her foreign sentence in Canada. If the forcible removal of a presumed innocent Canadian citizen by extradition is at the outer edges of the core values sought to be protected by s. 6(1), the request of a convicted one to serve a foreign sentence in Canada falls off the edge. I have difficulty seeing

---

[134] *Divito, supra* note 124 at paras 31-39.

[135] *Ibid* at para 40.

[136] *Ibid* at para 44.

[137] *R v Hape*, 2007 SCC 26.

[138] *Divito, supra* note 124 at para 43.

how legislative provisions which facilitate the possibility of re-entry for a Canadian citizen lawfully convicted in a foreign jurisdiction, are analogous to the forced removal of a Canadian citizen by the state.

The mobility rights in section 6(1) should be construed generously, not literally, and, absent a literal interpretation, I am unable to see how section 6(1) is breached in the circumstances of this case. Canadian citizens undoubtedly have a right to enter Canada, but Canadian citizens who are lawfully incarcerated in a foreign jurisdiction cannot leave their prison, let alone leave to come to Canada. What makes the entry to Canada possible is the [Act]. But this possibility does not thereby create a constitutionally protected right to leave a foreign prison and enter Canada whenever a foreign jurisdiction consents to the transfer. Nor does it impose a duty on the Canadian government to permit all such citizens to serve their foreign sentences in Canada. The impugned provisions of the [Act], which make a transfer possible, do not, as a result, represent a breach of section 6(1).[139]

This argument is, with respect, difficult to follow. The impugned provisions were the legislative implementation of Canada's treaty right to refuse to admit foreign-imprisoned Canadian citizens into Canada. By conferring a discretion on the minister to refuse a Canadian (imprisoned or not) entry into Canada, the legislation clearly infringed section 6(1). As the concurring judges observed:

Parliament has crafted a regime whereby once the foreign state has consented to a transfer — thus removing the practical restrictions on an incarcerated citizen's ability to return to Canada — the sole impediment to the exercise of the citizen's section 6(1) right is the Minister's discretion. A statutory regime that grants a Minister the discretion to determine whether or not citizens can exercise their Charter-protected right to enter Canada constitutes, *prima facie*, a limit on the section 6(1) right of the citizens in question.[140]

The concurring judges went on to find, however, that sections 8(1), 10(1)(a), and 10(2)(a) of the act were justifiable infringements of Divito's mobility rights.[141]

139 *Ibid* at paras 47-48.
140 *Ibid* at para 64.
141 *Ibid* at paras 68-84.

The *Divito* decision is, in its *dicta* at least, encouraging for proponents of an interpretive presumption that the *Charter* protects rights to at least the same extent as international human rights law. The place of this presumption (which must be regarded as a close cousin of the general presumption of conformity with international law) in *Charter* jurisprudence has been uncertain ever since Dickson CJC first enunciated it. In *Divito*, Abella J for the majority of the Court strongly endorses the presumption — in principle. One may wonder, however, whether the majority's reasons in fact apply it. Article 12(4) of the *ICCPR* is far from clear. What does the qualification "arbitrarily" signify in the phrase: "No one shall be arbitrarily deprived of the right to enter his own country"? The question is, admittedly, hard. However, Abella J does not wrestle with it at all. By not doing so, she and her colleagues missed an opportunity to develop international mobility rights through a thoughtful, thorough consideration of the right to enter one's own country. Moreover, her conclusion that the impugned provisions do not infringe section 6(1) in the first place is hard to square with the Human Rights Committee statements she relies upon. *Divito* is a strangely mixed blessing for Canadian international human rights advocates: important in theory but disappointing in practice.

Castonguay Blasting Ltd v Ontario (Environment), 2013 SCC 52 (17 October 2013) (Supreme Court of Canada)

The appellant was a subcontractor hired to conduct blasting operations on a highway construction project commissioned by the Ontario Ministry of Transportation. In the course of the appellant's blasting operations, a section of rock was propelled 90 metres into the air, landing on the roof of a nearby home and causing significant damage. The appellant reported the incident to the contract administrator, who then reported it to the Ministry of Transportation. The appellant did not report the incident to the Ministry of Environment and was subsequently charged with failing to report the discharge of a contaminant into the natural environment per section 15(1) of the *Environmental Protection Act (EPA)*.[142] Section 15(1) states that every person who discharges a contaminant into the natural environment shall notify the Ministry of the Environment if the discharge is out of the normal course of events and causes or is likely to cause an adverse effect.[143]

[142] *Environmental Protection Act*, RSO 1990, c E-19.
[143] *Ibid* at s 15(1).

At issue before the Supreme Court of Canada was the proper interpretation of section 15(1) of the *EPA*. The Ministry of the Environment urged a purposive reading of the impugned section that would trigger an obligation to report discharges to the Ministry if those discharges caused, or were likely to cause, any of the eight definitions of "adverse effect" contained in section 1(1) of the *EPA*. The ministry argued that the notification requirement permitted it to respond in a timely way to the discharge of a contaminant into the natural environment by allowing for an investigation and subsequent remedial efforts.

In her reasons, Abella J noted that the reading of section 15(1) urged by the ministry was consistent with the precautionary principle, which she described as an "emerging international law principle":

[20] As the interveners Canadian Environmental Law Association and Lake Ontario Waterkeeper pointed out in their joint factum, section 15(1) is also consistent with the precautionary principle. This emerging international law principle recognizes that since there are inherent limits in being able to determine and predict environmental impacts with scientific certainty, environmental policies must anticipate and prevent environmental degradation (O. McIntyre and T. Mosedale, "The Precautionary Principle as a Norm of Customary International Law" (1997), 9 *J. Envtl. L.* 221, at pp. 221-22; *114957 Canada Ltée (Spraytech, Société d'arrosage) v. Hudson (Town)*, 2001 SCC 40, [2001] 2 S.C.R. 241, at paras. 30-32). Section 15(1) gives effect to the concerns underlying the precautionary principle by ensuring that the Ministry of the Environment is notified and has the ability to respond once there has been a discharge of a contaminant out of the normal course of events, without waiting for proof that the natural environment has, in fact, been impaired.[144]

The statements of Abella J in *Castonguay* with respect to the precautionary principle do not appear to have greatly influenced the outcome of the case, nor do they extend beyond similar statements made by L'Heureux-Dubé J in *114957 Canada Ltée (Spraytech, Société d'arrosage) v Hudson (Town)*,[145] but they are notable as a second

---

[144] *Castonguay Blasting Ltd v Ontario (Environment)*, 2013 SCC 52 at para 20 [*Castonguay*].

[145] *114957 Canada Ltée (Spraytech, Société d'arrosage) v Hudson (Town)*, 2001 SCC 40, [2001] 2 SCR 241 at paras 30-32.

endorsement by the Supreme Court of Canada of the precautionary principle as an emerging norm of customary international law.

International organizations — immunity — wrongful dismissal

Northwest Atlantic Fisheries Organization v Amaratunga, 2013 SCC 66 (29 November 2013) (Supreme Court of Canada)

This was a claim against the Northwest Atlantic Fisheries Organization (NAFO), an international organization with headquarters in Dartmouth, Nova Scotia, by a former senior employee, Mr Amaratunga, for breach of an employment contract. NAFO asserted immunity from the claim. The Nova Scotia Supreme Court denied NAFO immunity. The Nova Scotia Court of Appeal overturned this decision. LeBel J for the unanimous Supreme Court of Canada allowed the appeal in part but generally upheld NAFO's claim to immunity.

NAFO was created by the *Convention on Future Multilateral Co-operation in the Northwest Atlantic Fisheries* with the objective of contributing "through consultation and cooperation to the optimum utilization, rational management and conservation of the fishery resources" of the Northwest Atlantic.[146] The convention provides that NAFO has legal personality and that Canada and NAFO will agree on what immunities and privileges NAFO will have in Canada. This agreement is set out in the *Northwest Atlantic Fisheries Organization Privileges and Immunities Order* of 1980.[147] The relevant portions of the order are as follows:

3. (1) The Organization shall have in Canada the legal capacities of a body corporate and shall, to such extent as may be required for the performance of its functions, have the privileges and immunities set forth in Articles II and III of the Convention for the United Nations.

3. (1) L'Organisation possède, au Canada, la capacité juridique d'un corps constitué et possède, dans la mesure où ses fonctions l'exigent, les privilèges et les immunités prévus pour les Nations Unies aux Articles II et III de la Convention.

---

[146] *Convention on Future Multilateral Co-operation in the Northwest Atlantic Fisheries*, Can TS 1979 No 11.

[147] *Northwest Atlantic Fisheries Organization Privileges and Immunities Order*, SOR/80-64.

(2) Representatives of states and governments that are members of the Organization shall have in Canada, to such extent as may be required for the performance of their functions, the privileges and immunities set forth in Article IV of the Convention for representatives of members.

(3) All officials of the Organization shall have in Canada, to such extent as may be required for the performance of their functions, the privileges and immunities set forth in Article V of the Convention for officials of the United Nations.

(4) All experts performing missions for the Organization shall have in Canada, to such extent as may be required for the performance of their functions, the privileges and immunities set forth in Article VI of the Convention for experts on missions for the United Nations.

(2) Les représentants d'États et de gouvernements membres de l'Organisation possèdent, au Canada, dans la mesure où leurs fonctions l'exigent, les privilèges et les immunités prévus pour les représentants de membres de l'Article IV de la Convention.

(3) Tous les fonctionnaires de l'Organisation possèdent, au Canada, dans la mesure où leurs fonctions l'exigent, les privilèges et les immunités prévus pour les fonctionnaires des Nations Unies à l'Article V de la Convention.

(4) Tous les experts accomplissant des missions pour l'Organisation possèdent, au Canada, dans la mesure où leurs fonctions l'exigent, les privilèges et les immunités prévus à l'Article VI de la Convention à l'égard des experts en mission pour l'Organisation des Nations Unies.

Amaratunga was a long-time senior employee of NAFO who was dismissed in 2005. NAFO offered him a payout of a little over $150,000, composed of various elements including a so-called separation indemnity due under the NAFO Staff Rules and payable in two instalments. Amaratunga refused to cash a second cheque from NAFO, including the second instalment of the separation indemnity, for fear that doing so might preclude his claim against NAFO in the Nova Scotia courts. Amaratunga's claim sought damages for breach of contract, general damages, and punitive or aggravated damages. NAFO responded with its immunity plea, which was determined prior to trial.

The motions judge, Wright J, rejected NAFO's immunity claim.[148] The learned judge interpreted "required" in section 3(1) of the order to mean "necessary" or "essential" and found that immunity against Amaratunga's claim was not necessary or essential for the performance of NAFO's functions. Wright J added that to find NAFO immune would leave Amarantunga with no recourse to pursue his claims, a result inconsistent with the right to a fair hearing under Article 14 of the *ICCPR*.[149]

MacDonald CJ, for the Court of Appeal, held that Wright J had read section 3(1) too narrowly.[150] The correct approach was one that preserved NAFO's autonomy as an international organization. MacDonald CJ emphasized that Amarantuga's claims for wrongful dismissal, punitive damages, and solicitor-client costs were allegations of misconduct by NAFO that the appellant was asking the Nova Scotia Supreme Court to review and condemn.

LeBel J for the Supreme Court of Canada identified the main question on appeal as whether section 3(1) of the order granted NAFO immunity against Amaratunga's claim. The learned judge began with a discussion of jurisdictional immunities of states and international organizations in international law. The immunity of organizations, unlike states, derives from conventional international law, not custom. Since international organizations must, of necessity, operate on the territory of foreign states and through individuals having nationality, they are vulnerable to interference — hence, the need to grant immunities and privileges to international organizations.[151]

LeBel J noted that regulations and orders in council are interpreted according to the modern principle of statutory interpretation, but with consideration of the words granting the authority to make the regulation in question in addition to the other interpretive factors. Thus, the words "to such extent as may be required for the performance of its functions" found in section 3(1) of the order must be read in their entire context, in their grammatical and ordinary sense, harmoniously with the scheme and object of the parent

148 *Northwest Atlantic Fisheries Organization v Amaratunga*, 2010 NSSC 346.

149 *ICCPR, supra* note 83.

150 *Northwest Atlantic Fisheries Organization v Amaratunga*, 2011 NSCA 73.

151 *Northwest Atlantic Fisheries Organization v Amaratunga*, 2013 SCC 66 at para 29 [*Amaratunga*].

act and in light of the grant of authority and the intention of Parliament.[152] Approaching the interpretive question in this way, LeBel J rejected what he acknowledged as the "admittedly common" definition of "required" adopted by the judge at first instance, agreeing instead with the Court of Appeal that a broader interpretation was called for. Turning to the parent legislation,[153] LeBel J determined, from a consideration of Hansard, that Parliament sought to modernize the rules respecting the immunities and privileges of international organizations "both to reflect recent trends in international law and to make Canada an attractive location for such organizations to establish headquarters or offices."[154] A narrow interpretation of section 3(1) would run counter to these objectives. LeBel J added that "immunity is essential to the efficient functioning of international organizations," for without it "an international organization would be vulnerable to intrusions into its operations and agenda by the host state and that state's courts."[155]

LeBel J then turned to section 3 of the NAFO immunity order, with its invocations of the *Convention on the Privileges and Immunities of the United Nations*.[156] He held that the Governor in Council did not grant NAFO the absolute immunity conferred on the United Nations in the 1946 convention but, rather, "a functional immunity, that is, the immunity required to enable NAFO to perform its functions without undue interference."[157] LeBel J agreed with the parallel drawn by the Court of Appeal between this degree of immunity and the Supreme Court of Canada's discussion of parliamentary privilege in *Canada (House of Commons) v Vaid*.[158] Adopting the same approach, LeBel J held that "NAFO's autonomy to conduct its business and the actions it takes in performing its functions must be shielded from undue interference" and that "[w]hat is necessary for the performance of NAFO's functions, or what constitutes undue interference, must be determined on a case-by-case basis."[159]

---

[152] *Ibid* at paras 36-37.

[153] Formerly the *Privileges and Immunities (International Organizations) Act*, RSC 1985, c P-23, now the *Foreign Missions and International Organizations Act*, SC 1991, c 41.

[154] *Amaratunga, supra* note 151 at para 44.

[155] *Ibid* at para 45.

[156] *Convention on the Privileges and Immunities of the United Nations*, Can TS 1948 No 2.

[157] *Amaratunga, supra* note 151 at para 49.

[158] *Canada (House of Commons) v Vaid*, 2005 SCC 30.

[159] *Amaratunga, supra* note 151 at para 53.

Applying such an approach to the case before him, LeBel J held that to permit Amaratunga's claim, which asked the Nova Scotia Supreme Court to pass judgment on NAFO's management of its employees, "would constitute interference with NAFO's internal management, which goes directly to its autonomy."[160] In response to Amarantunga's denial of justice argument, LeBel J purported to distinguish certain European cases on an unclear basis[161] and went on to note that even the UN Human Rights Committee has observed that a limitation on *ICCPR* Article 14 based on an immunity derived from international law would not violate that article.[162]

LeBel J therefore largely upheld NAFO's immunity claim. He allowed the appeal in part, however, to permit Amarantunga to proceed with his claim for the unpaid portion of his separation indemnity. The learned judge reasoned that this claim related solely to a provision of NAFO's staff rules, which required payment of the indemnity to all departing employees regardless of the reason for their termination and that to enforce that rule against NAFO "would not amount to submitting NAFO's managerial operations to the oversight of Canadian courts."[163] NAFO had in fact conceded that its immunity did not protect it from a lawsuit seeking only payment of entitlements under its staff rules.

Family and children's rights — prisoner rights — Charter *interpretation*

Inglis v British Columbia (Minister of Public Safety), 2013 BCSC 2309 (16 December 2013) (British Columbia Supreme Court)

The plaintiffs were mothers who had given birth while incarcerated at a provincial jail. In 2008, the provincial government cancelled a

---

160 *Ibid* at para 58.

161 *Ibid* at para 60. LeBel J says only that these European cases "arose in a different legal context," namely that of the European Convention on Human Rights (*Convention for the Protection of Human Rights and Fundamental Freedoms*, 213 UNTS 221, ETS No 5 (in force 3 September 1953)). How that treaty is relevantly different from Article 14 of the ICCPR, a treaty to which Canada is a party and upon which Amaratunga relied, is left unexplained.

162 *Amaratunga, supra* note 151 at para 62, citing UN Human Rights Committee, *General Comment No 32, Article 14: Right to Equality Before Courts and Tribunals and to a Fair Trial*, UN Doc CCPR/C/GC/32 (2007) at para 18, reprinted in *Compilation of General Comments and General Recommendations made by Human Rights Treaty Bodies*, UN Doc HRI/GEN/1/Rev.9 (2008), vol 1 at 248.

163 *Amaratunga, supra* note 151 at para 65.

program that had previously allowed mothers to keep infants with them while serving sentences at provincial correctional facilities. The plaintiffs challenged the constitutionality of the province's decision to cancel the program under sections 7, 12, and 15 of the *Charter*.[164]

In her reasons, Ross J noted that analysis of *Charter* rights is contextual and that Canada's international obligations inform the meaning and scope of rights under the *Charter* and the principles of fundamental justice.[165] When assessing the context provided by Canada's international obligations, Ross J noted the protection given to mothers and the family unit by the *Universal Declaration of Human Rights*[166] and the *ICESCR*.[167] She further cited the special protection given to children in the *Convention on the Rights of the Child*,[168] the *Declaration on Social and Legal Principles relating to the Protection and Welfare of Children, with Special Reference to Foster Placement and Adoption Nationally and Internationally*,[169] the *United Nations Declaration on the Rights of Indigenous Peoples*,[170] and the *Declaration of the Rights of the Child*,[171] the latter of which states at Article 6:

The child, for the full and harmonious development of his personality, needs love and understanding. He shall, wherever possible, grow up in the care and under the responsibility of his parents, and, in any case, in an atmosphere of affection and of moral and material security; a child of tender years shall not, save in exceptional circumstances, be separated from his mother.[172]

---

[164] *Charter, supra* note 2, ss 7, 12, 15.

[165] *Inglis v British Columbia (Minister of Public Safety)*, 2013 BCSC 2309 at paras 359-60 [*Inglis*], citing *Victoria (City) v Adams*, 2009 BCCA 563 at para 35 and *Divito, supra* note 124.

[166] *Universal Declaration of Human Rights*, GA Res 217(III), reprinted in UN GAOR, 3d Sess, Part 1 at 71-77, UN Doc A/810 (1948).

[167] *ICESCR, supra* note 82.

[168] *Convention on the Rights of the Child, supra* note 50.

[169] *Declaration on Social and Legal Principles relating to the Protection and Welfare of Children, with Special Reference to Foster Placement and Adoption Nationally and Internationally*, GA Res 41/85, UNGAOR, 41st Sess, UN Doc A/RES/41/85 (1986).

[170] *United Nations Declaration on the Rights of Indigenous Peoples*, GA Res 61/295, UNGAOR, 61st Sess, Supp No 49, UN Doc A/RES/61/295 (2007).

[171] *Declaration of the Rights of the Child*, GA Res 1386 (XIV), UNGAOR, 14th Sess, Supp No 16, UN Doc A/4354 (1959) at 19.

[172] *Ibid*, art 6.

Lastly, Ross J cited the Basic Principles for the Treatment of Prisoners,[173] which had been cited as a relevant international norm in *Bacon v Surrey Pretrial Services Centre.*[174] At Article 5, the basic principles state that,

[e]xcept for those limitations that are demonstrably necessitated by the fact of incarceration, all prisoners shall retain the human rights and fundamental freedoms set out in the Universal Declaration of Human Rights, and, where the State concerned is a party, the International Covenant on Economic, Social and Cultural Rights ... as well as such other rights as are set out in other United Nations covenants.[175]

Ross J held that a number of themes were common to the above-noted instruments. Notably, the instruments acknowledged that special protection should be afforded to mothers before and after childbirth; the best interests of the child are paramount in any state action concerning children; a child should not be separated from his or her parents except with due process and when it is in the child's best interests to do so; and the state's responsibilities towards prisoners should be discharged in a manner in keeping with its fundamental responsibility to promote the well-being and development of all members of society.[176]

Ross J concluded that the program at issue, which placed infants with their incarcerated mothers if such placement was in the best interests of the infant, was consistent with the themes she had identified in Canada's international obligations and the various United Nations declarations cited.[177] In the result, she held that the cancellation of the program was a breach of the section 7 and 15 of the *Charter* rights of the incarcerated mothers and that the infringement could not be justified under section 1.[178]

Briefly noted / Sommaire en bref

Hupacasath First Nation v Canada (Minister of Foreign Affairs), 2013 FC 900 (26 August 2013) (Federal Court)

---

173 Basic Principles for the Treatment of Prisoners, GA Res 45/111, UNGAOR, 45th Sess, UN Doc A/RES/45/111 (1990) [Basic Principles].

174 *Bacon v Surrey Pretrial Services Centre*, 2010 BCSC 805 at para 272.

175 Basic Principles, *supra* note 173, art 5.

176 *Inglis*, *supra* note 165 at para 364.

177 *Ibid* at para 611.

178 *Ibid* at paras 633, 651.

This was an application by the Hupacasath First Nation (HFN) for judicial review of the federal government's pending ratification of the *Agreement between the Government of Canada and the Government of the People's Republic of China for the Promotion and Reciprocal Protection of Investments*, a bilateral investment treaty.[179] Neither HFN nor any other First Nations were consulted by Canada prior to, or in the course of, negotiating the agreement. HFN sought a declaration that Canada was required to engage in a process of consultation and accommodation with First Nations, including HFN, prior to ratifying or taking other steps that would bind Canada under the agreement.

Crampton CJ admitted opinion evidence from an associate professor at Osgoode Hall Law School and an international trade lawyer on a wide variety of issues relating to international investment protection, decided cases involving Canada, and the meaning of the agreement's provisions. Crampton CJ concluded that the potential adverse impacts of the agreement on HFN's Aboriginal rights and potential for self-government were non-appreciable and speculative in nature. Ratification of the agreement by Canada would not contravene the principle of the honour of the Crown or Canada's duty to consult with HFN before taking any action that might adversely impact upon its asserted aboriginal rights. HFN has appealed. The Federal Court of Appeal's decision will be addressed, if warranted, in a future issue of the *Yearbook*.

---

[179] *Agreement between the Government of Canada and the Government of the People's Republic of China for the Promotion and Reciprocal Protection of Investments*, 9 September 2012, online: <http://www.international.gc.ca/trade-agreements-accords-commerciaux/agr-acc/fipa-apie/china-text-chine.aspx?lang=eng> [not yet in force].

Canadian Cases in Private International Law in 2013 / Jurisprudence canadienne en matière de droit international privé en 2013

compiled by / *préparé par*

JOOST BLOM

JURISDICTION / COMPÉTENCE DES TRIBUNAUX

Common Law and Federal

Jurisdiction *in personam*

General principles — jurisdiction simpliciter *— presumptive connecting factors*

2249659 Ontario Ltd v Sparkasse Siegen, 2013 ONCA 354, 115 OR (3d) 241

Rohwedder Canada (RCI), then a subsidiary of a German company, agreed to supply assembly lines for an Ontario plant to manufacture solenoids for automobile transmissions. The plant was to be set up by a German corporation, TMG, through an affiliated Canadian company, TMC. The contract for the assembly lines was a purchase order to RCI from TMC, replacing an earlier one from TMG in identical terms. The purchase order referred to TMG's standard terms, previously communicated, which stated that the contract was governed by German law and that the place of jurisdiction was Herdorf, Germany. Both German parent companies subsequently encountered financial difficulties, the result of which was that TMC went out of business and RCI, which had new owners, was not paid. RCI brought the present action against TMG and the German financial institution that had provided financing for the Canadian plant, claiming they had guaranteed, or made negligent misstatements about, the financial viability of TMC. The defendants

Joost Blom is in the Faculty of Law at the University of British Columbia.

575

applied for a dismissal of the action because the court lacked jurisdiction *simpliciter* (the power, as a matter of law, to hear the case) or a stay of the proceedings based on the forum selection clause in the purchase order.

The motion judge held[1] the Ontario court lacked jurisdiction *simpliciter* and, in any event, should decline jurisdiction on the basis of the forum selection clause. The Court of Appeal reversed on both grounds. The judge had erred in the first place by treating the forum selection clause as a ground for saying the court lacked jurisdiction *simpliciter*; the latter question logically had to be answered before deciding what the effect of the clause might be. The court had jurisdiction based on two presumptive connecting factors, according to the methodology laid down in the *Van Breda* case.[2] One was that the claim rested on a tort committed in Ontario because the alleged misrepresentations were made there. The other was that the contract relied upon by RCI was also made in Ontario. It was unnecessary to decide whether a third presumptive connecting factor, that of carrying on business in Ontario, was made out, although TMC's status as a fully controlled subsidiary of TMG supported the argument that TMG was carrying on business in the province.

The forum selection clause was held not to apply to RCI's claims. It appeared only as a term of the purchase orders, whereas the claims were based, not on those orders, but on guarantees of TMC's obligations given by TMG and the German financial institution. That left the question of *forum non conveniens*. On the material before the motion judge the defendants had shown that the German court was an appropriate forum but had not shown that it was a clearly more appropriate forum than Ontario, as the test required.

Note. The implications of the *Van Breda* methodology for pleading practice were examined in *Newfoundland and Labrador (A.G.) v Rothmans Inc.*[3] The court stated: "The plaintiff should set out the

---

[1] *2249659 Ontario Ltd v Sparkasse Siegen*, 2012 ONSC 3128, noted (2012) 50 Can YB Int'l L 586.

[2] In the absence of statutory rules for jurisdiction *simpliciter*, Canadian courts must base jurisdiction on the presence of one or more common law presumptive connecting factors that satisfy the requirement of a real and substantial connection with the province: *Club Resorts Ltd v Van Breda*, 2012 SCC 17, [2012] 1 SCR 572 [*Van Breda*].

[3] *Newfoundland and Labrador (AG) v Rothmans Inc*, 2013 NLTD(G) 180.

presumptive connecting factor(s) relied upon to support an assumption of jurisdiction, and should clearly identify by way of pleading or otherwise the supporting jurisdictional facts."[4] A presumptive connecting factor in the usual sense has been held not to be necessary if the action is to enforce a foreign judgment: see *Yaiguaje v Chevron Corp*, noted below under Foreign Judgments; Common law and federal; Jurisdiction of the enforcing court; *Jurisdiction* simpliciter *in action to enforce foreign judgment*.

Resident defendant — corporate residence

Note. In a wrongful dismissal action, *Patterson v EM Technologies Inc*,[5] a Barbados company and its principal, who lived mainly in the United Arab Emirates, were both held to be resident in Ontario by virtue of carrying on business there. If jurisdiction *simpliciter* could not be based on that ground, it could be based on the presumptive connecting factor that the contract at issue was executed in Ontario.

Non-resident defendant — claim essentially financial —jurisdiction simpliciter *found to exist*

Kilderry Holdings Ltd v Canpower International BV, 2013 BCCA 82, 360 DLR (4th) 500

In 1996, Canpower, a Netherlands Antilles company controlled by Houston, a resident of British Columbia, borrowed funds from Kilderry, a company incorporated in the Bahamas whose directing mind lived in Bermuda. Canpower was to use the funds to acquire an Arizona mining property by buying its owner, Addwest Kentucky (AK). Kilderry would receive a 5 percent share in AK or a public company set up to hold the shares in AK. The funds were used to acquire Addwest International (AI), a publicly traded British Columbia company, which in turn acquired AK. In a subsequent slump in the gold mining industry, work on the mining property ceased and AI was delisted. By the time of the present action, the mining property had ended up in the hands, not of AI, but of Mojave, an Arizona company also controlled by Houston. Kilderry brought an action in British Columbia against Houston, who had long since moved to California, and against Canpower and AI,

---

4 *Ibid* at para 329, point 4.
5 *Patterson v EM Technologies Inc*, 2013 ONSC 5849 (Master).

claiming that the defendants had broken the 1996 lending agreement by manipulating the ownership of the mining property so
as to deprive Kilderry of its agreed interest in the mining property.
The non-resident defendants, which were all the defendants except
(the now inactive) AI, argued that the court lacked jurisdiction
simpliciter in respect of the claims against them. The question was
whether the court had "territorial competence," according to the
Court Jurisdiction and Proceedings Transfer Act (*CJPTA*),[6] which codi-
fies the grounds for jurisdiction *simpliciter* for British Columbia.[7]
For a non-resident defendant that does not attorn to the jurisdiction,
territorial competence depends upon the existence of a real and
substantial connection with the province.[8]

The Court of Appeal, reversing the chambers judge, held that the
Supreme Court of British Columbia lacked jurisdiction *simpliciter*.
The case did not fall under any of the presumed real and substantial
connections listed in the act. In particular, it could not be said that
the contractual obligations in question, to a substantial extent, were
to be performed in the province;[9] that the claim concerned a tort
committed in the province;[10] or that the claim concerned a business
carried on there,[11] given that AI was dormant and incapable of
carrying on any enterprise.

Nor, in the absence of any applicable presumption, was there a
real and substantial connection on the pleaded facts. The chambers
judge had wrongly focused on the connections with British
Columbia at the time the original deal was made, when Houston
was resident in the province and AI, a British Columbia public
company, was an active participant in the transactions. If the factual
connections were as they appeared in 1996 and 1997 there might
be grounds for jurisdiction. However, at the present time, there
was no real and substantial connection between the litigation and
British Columbia. Houston, the person said to be chiefly responsible
for the wrongs, was now based in California and had no presence
in British Columbia. The mine and its current owner were connected to Arizona. AI remained a British Columbia company but

---

[6] *Court Jurisdiction and Proceedings Transfer Act*, SBC 2003, c 28 [*CJPTA (BC)*].

[7] This uniform act is also law (with minor variations) in Saskatchewan (SS 1997,
c C-41.1 [*CJPTA (SK)*]) and Nova Scotia (SNS 2003 (2d Sess), c 2 [*CJPTA (NS)*]).

[8] *CJPTA (BC)*, *supra* note 6 at s 3(e).

[9] *Ibid* at s 10(e)(i).

[10] *Ibid* at s 10(g).

[11] *Ibid* at s 10(h).

was inactive and in no position to do anything with the mine. It would not accord with the principles of order and fairness for the court to take jurisdiction.

Note 1. After the chambers judge's decision, the Supreme Court of Canada's decision in *Club Resorts Ltd v Van Breda*[12] came down. The Court of Appeal held, in essence, that the new "presumptive connecting factor" approach adopted in *Van Breda* did not affect the principles to be applied under the *CJPTA*. The statutory tests for territorial competence, like the common law set forth in *Van Breda*, were based on the real and substantial connection test and so there was no need to reinterpret them.[13]

Note 2 — contract and trust claims. A number of cases involved the application of the *Van Breda*[14] methodology of common law presumptive connecting factors to contract claims. One group involved employment contracts, and in each case the place of making the employment contract was found to be a presumptive connecting factor. In *Pavilion Financial Corp v Highview Financial Holdings Inc,*[15] an employer's claims against a non-resident employee were based on breaches of non-competition covenants. The action was held to satisfy either of two presumptive connecting factors, namely that the contract was made in the province or that it was governed by the law of the province.

In *Jones v Raymond James Ltd,* a Manitoba employer sued a former employee, now working for a new employer in Ontario, for breach of confidentiality and non-solicitation covenants.[16] The new employer was also sued as being liable for the employee's wrongs on various grounds. Common law presumptive connecting factors were held to exist in that the new employer carried on business in Ontario and the original employment contract had been made in Ontario. In *Schram v Nunavut,*[17] the fact that the employment contract was made in New Brunswick was held to be a common law presumptive

---

12 *Van Breda, supra* note 2.

13 *Kilderry Holdings Ltd v Canpower International B.V.,* 2013 BCCA 82, 360 DLR (4th) 500 at para 9.

14 *Van Breda, supra* note 2.

15 *Pavilion Financial Corp v Highview Financial Holdings Inc,* 2013 MBQB 95, 292 Man R (2d) 40 (Master).

16 *Jones v Raymond James Ltd,* 2013 ONSC 4640.

17 *Schram v Nunavut,* 2013 NBQB 190, 406 NBR (2d) 168.

connecting factor where a New Brunswick resident brought a wrongful dismissal action in that province against the government of Nunavut.

The claim being based on a contract made in Ontario was held to be a common law presumptive connecting factor where an Ontario company sued California-resident defendants for breach of a contract to transfer Canadian wireless spectrum licences to the plaintiff. Alternatively, the wireless spectrum licences were property situated in Ontario, which would supply another presumptive connecting factor: *Inukshuk Wireless Partnership v 4253311 Canada Inc*.[18] Another case that used the place of making a commercial contract as a presumptive connecting factor was *Patterson v EM Technologies Inc*.[19]

Leone v Scaffidi[20] found jurisdiction *simpliciter* in a breach of contract claim against the estate of parents who had been resident in Italy, based on a failure to divide immovable property in Ontario among their children. Presumptive connecting factors were held to exist in that the alleged contract was made, to be performed, and broken in Ontario.

Bedford v Abushmaies[21] found jurisdiction *simpliciter* in Ontario in respect of claims by the defendant's former wife and his stepdaughter, both resident in the United States, against a Michigan resident for breach of trust obligations relating to immovable property in Ontario. The presumptive connecting factors were that the property was situated in Ontario and the trust was created there.

The *CJPTA* does not include the place of making the contract as one of its presumed real and substantial connections. The main presumption relating to contractual claims is that the obligations under the contract were, to a substantial extent, to be performed in the province. This was applied in *Original Cakerie Ltd v Renaud*.[22] An employee's obligations under the confidentiality provisions of his contract were held to be performed to a substantial extent in British Columbia, although the employee worked mainly in Ontario.[23]

---

[18] *Inukshuk Wireless Partnership v 4253311 Canada Inc*, 2013 ONSC 5631, 117 OR (3d) 206.

[19] *Patterson v EM Technologies Inc*, 2013 ONSC 5849 (Master).

[20] *Leone v Scaffidi*, 2013 ONSC 1849, 87 ETR (3d) 93.

[21] *Bedford v Abushmaies*, 2013 ONSC 1352.

[22] *Original Cakerie Ltd v Renaud*, 2013 BCSC 755.

[23] *CJPTA (BC)*, *supra* note 6 at s 10(e)(i).

Alberta in 2010 codified the principles for jurisdiction, not by adopting the *CJPTA*, but by reframing the rules of court along similar lines. See *Greenbuilt Group of Companies Ltd v RMD Engineering Inc,*[24] in which the new provisions are analyzed at length in the context of a contractual claim by an Alberta purchaser of industrial machinery against the Saskatchewan supplier. A presumed real and substantial connection with Alberta was held to have been shown, either because the claim related to a contract made, performed, or breached in Alberta or because the claim was governed by Alberta law.[25]

Note 3 — tort claims. In two cases, jurisdiction *simpliciter* was found on the basis that the alleged tort was committed in Ontario, one of the common law presumptive connecting factors approved in *Van Breda* itself.[26] One was *Greta Inc v de Lange,*[27] in which an international conspiracy to defraud the plaintiff was held to have been committed as much in Ontario as anywhere else. The other was *Re Ghana Gold Corp,*[28] an insolvency case, including various related claims, in which the debtor was involved in a mining joint venture carried out in Ghana. Some of the claims were based on misrepresentations made by the other party to the joint venture, a non-resident company, in Ontario. The place of the tort supplied the presumptive connecting factor for those claims. The court in the *Ghana Gold* case also dismissed an argument that the court lacked jurisdiction to grant protection to one of the companies against foreign creditors. The court held that presumptive connecting factors existed, namely that centralized cash management of the debtor company, and the rest of the corporate group to which it belonged, was in Ontario and the principal creditor was resident there.

Non-resident defendant — claim essentially financial — jurisdiction simpliciter found not to exist

Note. No presumptive connecting factor was found to exist in two cases in which foreign lawyers were sued in Ontario by their clients for wrongs committed in the conduct of foreign legal proceedings:

---

[24] *Greenbuilt Group of Companies Ltd v RMD Engineering Inc,* 2013 ABQB 297, 82 Alta LR (4th) 349, amended statement of claim approved, 2013 ABQB 346.

[25] *Alberta Rules of Court,* Alta Reg 124/2010, r 11.25(3)(b) and (c), respectively.

[26] *Van Breda, supra* note 2.

[27] *Greta Inc v De Lange,* 2013 ONSC 3086, aff'd 2014 ONCA 107.

[28] *Re Ghana Gold Corp,* 2013 ONSC 3284, 3 CBR (6th) 220.

582   *Annuaire canadien de droit international 2013*

Thinh v Philippe[29] (French lawyer allegedly mishandled an estate in France) and *West Van Inc v Daisley*[30] (North Carolina lawyers allegedly negligently represented client in North Carolina commercial litigation). In *Brown v Spagnuolo*,[31] defamation and conspiracy claims were brought in Ontario by two members of the government of Bermuda against a Bermudan public servant and an Ontario accomplice who had allegedly planted fake cheques in Bermudan government files to make it look like the plaintiffs took kickbacks. No presumptive connecting factor with Ontario was held to be present.

Non-resident defendant — claim arising out of personal injury or damage to property or reputation — jurisdiction simpliciter found to exist

Ontario v Rothmans Inc, 2013 ONCA 353, 363 DLR (4th) 506[32]

Ontario brought this action against numerous defendants who were engaged in manufacturing and distributing tobacco products, under the *Tobacco Damages and Health Care Costs Recovery Act*.[33] The legislation provided that any "Lead Company" within a corporate group that was the source of tobacco products was a "manufacturer" as broadly defined. Six non-resident companies that were "manufacturers" by virtue of this provision contended that the claims against them should be dismissed for want of jurisdiction *simpliciter*, since the claims lacked a real and substantial connection with Ontario.

The Court of Appeal, affirming the motion judge's decision, held that a presumptive connecting factor existed with Ontario, as required by *Van Breda*.[34] The tobacco manufacturers' liability under the act is triggered by a "tobacco related wrong," which is defined as either a tort committed in Ontario that causes or contributes to tobacco-related disease, or a breach of a common law, equitable or statutory duty or obligation owed by a manufacturer to persons in Ontario who have been exposed or might become exposed to a tobacco product.[35] Thus, the act creates, in effect, a statutory tort claim

---

29   *Thinh v Philippe*, 2013 ONSC 7395.
30   *West Van Inc v Daisley*, 2013 ONSC 1988, aff'd 2014 ONCA 232, 119 OR (3d) 481.
31   *Brown v Spagnuolo*, 2013 ONSC 5178.
32   Leave to appeal to SCC refused, 35497 (19 December 2013).
33   *Tobacco Damages and Health Care Costs Recovery Act, 2009*, SO 2009, c 13 [*Tobacco Act (Ont.)*].
34   *Van Breda, supra* note 2.
35   *Tobacco Act (Ont), supra* note 33 at s 1(1).

founded on a tort or tortious conduct. In this case, the tort alleged was conspiracy. It was well established that a conspiracy occurs in the jurisdiction where the harm is suffered regardless of where the wrongful conduct occurred. If a tort committed in Ontario is a presumptive connecting factor entitling Ontario courts to assume jurisdiction, a statutory tort with all of the same trappings, committed in Ontario, should be one, too.

Note. The same reasoning was used in *Saskatchewan v Rothmans, Benson & Hedges Inc*[36] to conclude that a claim under a similar statute fell under the presumed real and substantial connection of a "tort committed in the province" under the *CJPTA*.[37]

Non-resident defendant — claim arising out of personal injury or damage to property or reputation — jurisdiction simpliciter *found not to exist*

Note. The insistence in *Van Breda*[38] that jurisdiction *simpliciter* must be supported by a common law presumptive connecting factor has made it more difficult for plaintiffs to sue in their home province for injuries suffered in accidents that occurred elsewhere. The fact that damages were suffered in the province is not a presumptive connecting factor and other such factors may be difficult to establish. Thus, no jurisdiction *simpliciter* was held to exist in *Jefferson v Macklem*[39] (plaintiff injured in motor vehicle accident in Ontario; her subsequent residence in Newfoundland and Labrador was no presumptive connecting factor), *Mitchell v Jeckovich*[40] (plaintiff injured in motor vehicle accident in Niagara Falls, New York; the plaintiff's own underinsured motorist coverage with an Ontario insurer was insufficient to be a presumptive connecting factor with Ontario), and *Haufler v Hotel Riu Palace Cabo San Lucas*[41] (plaintiff injured while staying at hotel in Mexico; claim against hotel had no presumptive connecting factor with Ontario because there was no contract made in Ontario with the hotel and the hotel did not carry on business in Ontario).

---

[36] *Saskatchewan v Rothmans, Benson & Hedges Inc*, 2013 SKQB 357, 368 DLR (4th) 474.

[37] *CJPTA (SK)*, *supra* note 7 at s 9(g).

[38] *Van Breda*, *supra* note 2.

[39] *Jefferson v Macklem*, 2013 NLTD(G) 106, 38 Nfld & PEIR 273.

[40] *Mitchell v Jeckovich*, 2013 ONSC 7494, [2014] ILR I-5537.

[41] *Haufler v Hotel Riu Palace Cabo San Lucas*, 2013 ONSC 6044, 117 OR (3d) 275.

Non-resident defendant — matrimonial property claim — jurisdiction simpliciter found not to exist

Note. See *Aleong v Aleong,* noted below under Matrimonial causes; *Matrimonial property.*

Declining jurisdiction *in personam*

Forum selection clause

Aldo Group Inc v Moneris Solutions Corp, 2013 ONCA 725, 118 OR (3d) 81[42]

This litigation arose out of fraudulent use made of MasterCard credit cards at stores operated by Aldo. MasterCard determined that the losses were made possible by Aldo's stores failing to observe agreed protocols. It assessed a $4 million penalty on the firm, Moneris, that provided processing services for Aldo, which in turn debited Aldo's account for the amount. Aldo sued Moneris and MasterCard to recover the amount on the basis that the penalty had been wrongfully imposed. MasterCard applied to stay Aldo's claim against it on the basis of an exclusive forum selection clause in favour of New York that was contained in MasterCard's contracts with banks higher up the processing chain and with Moneris. The argument was that Aldo's claim was ultimately based on the terms of these agreements and so Aldo should be bound by the clause.

The Court of Appeal upheld the motion judge's dismissal of the application. Aldo, as a stranger to the agreements, pleaded direct claims against MasterCard. These claims, which included negligence, interference with the contractual relations, conspiracy, unlawful interference with economic relations and conversion, were not contractual and were not made by way of subrogation to Moneris's rights.

It was true that, according to the Canadian cases, where a plaintiff has accepted a forum selection clause it will not necessarily escape its bargain by pleading causes of action other than in contract or making claims against multiple parties only some of which are subject to the clause. However, those authorities did not compel the conclusion that a plaintiff is bound by a forum selection clause to which it did not agree simply because its claim arose in the context of another party's contractual relationship that included that

---

[42] Leave to appeal to SCC refused, 35700 (1 May 2014).

clause. There was American authority that non-signatories can be so "closely related" to the dispute that they should be bound by the clause on the basis that they could foresee their claims might come to be subject to it. Even if that line of cases might be followed in Ontario, the present case fell outside its scope because Aldo's interests were not completely derivative from or directly related to the interests of any signatory to the clause.

Note. In *Kim v APK Holdings Ltd,*[43] two investors resident in Saskatchewan sued a company that was managed in Saskatchewan for claims under Saskatchewan securities legislation and common law claims relating to their investment. The court refused to enforce an exclusive choice of a British Columbia forum on two grounds. One was that the clause, on its proper construction, did not apply to the claims, which were non-contractual. The other was that the case was so much more connected to Saskatchewan than to British Columbia that there was strong cause not to enforce the clause. In *Armadale Holdings Ltd v Synergize Int'l Inc.,*[44] a forum selection clause was not enforced because it was held not to be part of the agreement on which the claims were based. However, in *Kozicz v Preece,*[45] the court held that the clause should be enforced with respect to the non-contractual as well as the contractual claims; the former were too intertwined with the latter to treat them as distinct. See also *2249659 Ontario Ltd v Sparkasse Siegen,* noted above under Jurisdiction *in personam; General principles — jurisdiction* simpliciter *— presumptive connecting factors.*

Non-resident defendant — claim essentially financial — jurisdiction not declined

Quadrangle Holdings Ltd v Coady, 2013 NSSC 416, 339 NSR (2d) 85

Quadrangle pledged shares in Rally, a company engaged in oil exploration in Prince Edward Island, with Shannon, a company controlled by Coady, as security for Quadrangle's payment for shares in Shannon. The contract by which Quadrangle subscribed for the Shannon shares was governed by Alberta law. Coady caused the Rally shares to be sold and the proceeds received by another of

[43] *Kim v APK Holdings Ltd,* 2013 SKQB 382, 431 Sask R 291.
[44] *Armadale Holdings Ltd v Synergize Int'l Inc,* 2013 SKQB 308, 428 Sask R 209.
[45] *Kozicz v Preece,* 2013 ONSC 2823.

Coady's companies. Quadrangle claimed this was done without authority and sought damages from Shannon in contract and from Coady in tort in a Nova Scotia action. Shannon and Coady obtained a stay of these proceedings on the basis that Nova Scotia was *forum non conveniens*, Alberta being a clearly more appropriate forum. The Alberta court, however, held that the claims against both defendants were statute-barred, irrespective of whether the claims were in contract or tort and irrespective of whether Alberta or Nova Scotia law (which provided a longer limitation period) governed the claim.[46]

Quadrangle now applied to the Nova Scotia court to lift the stay that was previously granted on *forum non conveniens* grounds. The court granted the application. There would be no point in doing so if Quadrangle's tort claim was governed by Alberta law, because a Nova Scotia court would have to hold the claim statute-barred just as the Alberta court had done. But on the pleaded facts and the evidence submitted the tort claim was governed by Nova Scotia law, since the conversion of the shares took place in Nova Scotia, where the certificates were located and where Shannon gave them to a dealer with instructions to sell them. The Nova Scotia limitation period therefore applied to the claim against Coady (Shannon by this time was no longer active). The Alberta court's being precluded from hearing the case, as a result of a provision in the Alberta limitations statute,[47] cut the ground from under the previous decision that Alberta was clearly a more appropriate forum than Nova Scotia.

Note. In *Petrook v Natuzzi Americas Inc*,[48] although the plaintiff's employment contract with an Italian concern was governed by the law of North Carolina, where the employer's North American headquarters were, the action for wrongful dismissal was not stayed in favour of North Carolina. The plaintiff had worked mainly in Ontario and a stay would deprive her of the advantage of Ontario employment standards legislation.

---

[46] The *Limitations Act*, RSA 2000, c L-12, s 12(1), requires the Alberta limitation period to be applied to any Alberta proceeding in which a claimant seeks a remedial order, unless (as provided in s 12(2)) the claim is governed by a foreign law and that law provides for a shorter period than does Alberta law. Section 12(2) was added to reflect the result in *Castillo v Castillo*, 2005 SCC 83, [2005] 3 SCR 870.

[47] See the previous footnote.

[48] *Petrook v Natuzzi Americas Inc*, 2013 ONSC 4508, 10 CCEL (4th) 317.

Non-resident defendant — claim essentially financial — jurisdiction declined

Wenngatz v 371431 Alberta Ltd, 2013 BCCA 225, 362 DLR (4th) 356

The plaintiff, a resident of British Columbia, sued his sister and her company in the courts of both Alberta and British Columbia. The Alberta action was *in rem* in the sense that it sought a declaration that land owned by the sister's company was held on trust for the plaintiff. The British Columbia action included claims based on trust obligations relating to the same property, but also claims based on the sister's breach of various contracts. The Court of Appeal held the chambers judge had been wrong to let the claims based on trust proceed in the face of the sister's stay application based on *forum non conveniens*. The judge had attached too much weight to differences in remedy as between the two actions, given that the substance of the claims was the same. The judge had also overemphasized the weight of giving effect to the plaintiff's choice of forum. A stay should have been granted in respect of the claims based on a long-standing trust agreement, but the other claims that did not depend on that trust arrangement could proceed.

Note. Ontario was held to be *forum non conveniens* for claims against a national law firm whose alleged negligence had caused the plaintiff client to settle an action in Quebec: *Lixo Investments Ltd v Gowling Lafleur Henderson.*[49] Ontario was likewise *forum non conveniens* for a wrongful dismissal action by an employee of a hotel chain who had started with the employer in Canada but had transferred to New York, where she had worked for the last four years and where the witnesses and evidence relating to her claim were more readily available: *Sullivan v Four Seasons Hotels Ltd.*[50]

Non-resident defendant — injury to person, property or reputation — jurisdiction not declined

Central Sun Mining Inc v Vector Engineering Inc, 2013 ONCA 601, 117 OR (3d) 313[51]

This case involved tort claims against non-resident professional advisors for breaches of duty leading to an accident at a mine in

---

[49] *Lixo Investments Ltd v Gowling Lafleur Henderson,* 2013 ONSC 4862, aff'd 2014 ONCA 114.
[50] *Sullivan v Four Seasons Hotels Ltd,* 2013 ONSC 4622, 116 OR (3d) 365.
[51] Leave to appeal to SCC refused, 35640 (13 Mar. 2014).

Costa Rica. The advisers were said to have provided negligent advice to the plaintiff's Vancouver office, and it was on this basis that the motion judge held there was no presumptive connecting factor with Ontario because the misrepresentation was not made there. The Court of Appeal reversed this decision, holding that the pleaded facts showed the misrepresentations as having been received from the defendants in Toronto as well as Vancouver. Even if they had been received only by the Vancouver office, the tort was still committed in Ontario. Defendants should not escape liability simply because they send their studies to an office of the plaintiff outside Ontario with the clear understanding that it will be acted on in Ontario. The motion judge had also erred in holding that, if the presumptive connecting factor of a tort in Ontario existed it had been rebutted. Rebutting this presumptive connecting factor was a high bar that required showing that only a minor part of the tort was connected with the province. The evidence before the motion judge did not support such a conclusion.

Bouzari v Bahremani, 2013 ONSC 6337

The plaintiffs claimed to have been tortured in Iran by agents of the Iranian government. An earlier action against the Iranian state failed on the ground of state immunity.[52] The present proceeding was an action against Hashemi, an individual said to have been a party to the torture. Hashemi moved to have the Ontario court decline jurisdiction on *forum non conveniens* grounds, arguing that he lived in England and the courts of that country were therefore clearly more appropriate for hearing the action.[53]

Hashemi had lived in England for more than three years immediately after the alleged torture took place, derived his only income

---

[52] *Bouzari v Iran* (2004), 243 DLR (4th) 406 (CA).

[53] Jurisdiction *simpliciter* was not contested in this proceeding. The court refers to the plaintiffs' reliance on "forum of necessity": *Bouzari v Bahremani*, 2013 ONSC 6337 at para 29. The plaintiffs may have been relying in part on the *Justice for Victims of Terrorism Act*, SC 2012, c 1, s 2, which came into force in 2012 and gives Canadian courts jurisdiction to entertain civil actions for damages suffered in or outside Canada on or after 1 January 1985 as a result of an act or omission that is, or had it been committed in Canada would be, punishable under Part II.1 of the *Criminal Code*, RSC 1985, c C-46. Part II.1 makes punishable the funding of or participating in "terrorist activity" as defined in s 83.01. The definition of "terrorist activity" is broad enough that it might encompass at least some of the plaintiffs' claims.

from a business there, and was enrolled as a graduate student at an English university. However, he was currently in Iran, having been released on bail after a period in prison there. He argued he had previously been refused entry into Canada and could not travel to Canada to conduct a defence of the action. The plaintiffs argued that there was no evidence that Hashemi would be granted a visa to resume his studies in England or that he was currently employed in England.

The motion judge held there was no evidence on which to conclude that if Hashemi were able to leave Iran, he would be refused entry into Canada. Nor was there evidence that he would be admitted into the United Kingdom. The onus was on Hashemi to show that he could not properly defend himself in an Ontario court and he had not done so. It was true that a trial in England might make it easier for Hashemi to obtain his witnesses, but on the other hand it would deprive the plaintiffs of the application of Canadian law based on international covenants entered into by Canada. Hashemi had not shown that England was clearly a more appropriate forum.

Note. In *Kazi v Qatar Airlines*,[54] the plaintiff, a Muslim, was imprisoned in Qatar for three months, fined and lashed for having consumed alcohol and being verbally abusive on the Qatar Airlines flight to Doha, which was a stop on his way to Bangladesh. He sued the airline for failing to warn him about the strictness of Qatar law on the consumption of alcohol by Muslims. The motion judge denied a stay because, although Qatar was a marginally more appropriate forum for the action, it was not clearly so.

Lis alibi pendens — *jurisdiction not declined*

Ruloff Capital Corp v Hula, 2013 BCCA 514, 53 BCLR (5th) 117

Ruloff Capital sued Hula and his company in British Columbia for having broken an agreement to conduct jointly litigation in California. The action would be against a major media corporation, NBCU, for having misused confidential information that Hula had given it in relation to Hula's streaming video technology. Ruloff was to finance the litigation in return for a portion of any money judgment obtained. Hula, allegedly in breach of this agreement, had begun his own action against NBCU in California. Hula also commenced an action in California against Ruloff for a declaration that

---

[54] *Kazi v Qatar Airlines*, 2013 ONSC 1370.

their litigation agreement was terminated. A challenge by Ruloff to the court's jurisdiction in the action against it failed. Hula now sought a stay of Ruloff's British Columbia action on the basis that the matter was already before the court in California, which had positively asserted jurisdiction. Hula also said it could not afford to litigate in British Columbia but could in California because its law firm there was acting on a contingency fee.

The chambers judge refused the stay on the basis that California was not clearly a more appropriate forum. As was held in the leading Canadian precedent on parallel proceedings,[55] the existence of a parallel action in the United States should not deprive the plaintiff of access to the British Columbia forum when the latter was much the most closely connected to the action. The only connection with California was the focus of the impugned agreement to bring legal proceedings against NBCU. All other factors weighed overwhelmingly in favour of conducting the litigation in British Columbia, which was the jurisdiction in which the agreement and alleged breach of it arose and where all of the parties and witnesses resided. The Court of Appeal held there was no error in the chambers judge's analysis.

Note. Two insurance companies began separate proceedings in Ontario claiming that they were not liable, as liability insurers, to cover claims for pollution caused decades earlier by the insured's mines in Manitoba. The insured attorned to the Ontario court's jurisdiction in one of the actions but moved for a stay of the other the ground that Manitoba was clearly a more appropriate forum. The motion was dismissed, mainly because to have the two insurance disputes heard in different provinces would be inefficient and create a risk of inconsistent decisions: *Century Indemnity Co v Viridian Inc.*[56]

Class Actions

Jurisdiction simpliciter *found to exist in respect of the class action claim*

Kaynes v BP plc, 2013 ONSC 5802, 117 OR (3d) 685

The plaintiff brought a proposed class action in Ontario on behalf of purchasers of certain of BP's securities on the secondary market, claiming BP was liable under the Ontario *Securities Act* for misrepre-

---

55 *Teck Cominco Metals Ltd v Lloyd's Underwriters*, 2009 SCC 11, [2009] 1 SCR 321.

56 *Century Indemnity Co v Viridian Inc*, 2013 ONSC 4412.

sentations concerning its business. The relevant provision attaches civil liability to a "reporting issuer" or "any other issuer with a real and substantial connection to Ontario, any securities of which are publicly traded."[57] The proposed plaintiff class included all Canadian residents who had purchased the relevant BP securities, irrespective of the exchange on which they had been acquired. BP argued it did not carry on business in Ontario and the only possible presumptive connecting factor to support jurisdiction *simpliciter* over the claims was if a tort had been committed in Ontario. Even if a claim under the securities legislation was considered a tort, BP argued, the tort would be committed in Ontario only if the shares were purchased on the Toronto Stock Exchange. BP conceded the court had jurisdiction in respect of those purchasers, but sought to have excluded from the class all purchasers who had acquired the shares on exchanges in New York or Europe.

The motion judge considered the jurisdictional question on the basis that each purchaser of the securities was resident in Ontario; the action had not yet been certified and so it was not yet decided whether the class would include non-residents of the province. The claim for misrepresentation under the *Securities Act* was equivalent to one for a tort committed in Ontario, which was a presumptive connecting factor. The act did not restrict the cause of action to investors who had bought the securities on an Ontario exchange. The tort of misrepresentation is committed where the misrepresentation is relied upon, and since the act deems reliance on the misrepresentation, the statutory tort was committed in Ontario.

The judge also refused to stay the proceeding at this stage on *forum non conveniens* grounds. There was no forum that was clearly more appropriate. It made sense to have all the purchasers' claims decided in one court rather than in three different courts depending on which exchange was involved. A similar class action had been begun against BP in the United States, but it would be premature to stay on the basis of that proceeding, since it had not yet been certified.

Note. Given that jurisdiction over the claims in a class action depends on who is included in the plaintiff class as well as who are defendants, a decision on jurisdiction *simpliciter* or on declining jurisdiction may be made either before or at the time of the certification proceeding. Courts, as in *Kaynes*, have decided it before certification

---

57 *Securities Act*, RSO 1990, c S.5, s 138.1.

if that allowed one or more jurisdictional issues to be resolved at that time. The same was done in *Miller v Purdue Pharma Inc.*,[58] in which a claim for failure to warn against a corporate group of drug companies was held within the jurisdiction of the Saskatchewan court because the alleged tort was committed in the province, where the plaintiffs used the drug, thus providing a presumed real and substantial connection under the *CJPTA*.[59] The issue of *forum non conveniens* was deferred until the certification stage. In *Trillium Motor World Ltd v General Motors of Canada Ltd*,[60] jurisdiction *simpliciter* in a class action by car dealers in various provinces against General Motors (GM) was based on the presumptive connecting factor that Ontario law governed all the dealership contracts out of which the claims arose. In *Silver v IMAX Corp*,[61] the purchasers of securities on US exchanges were excluded from the plaintiff class at the certification stage, mainly because their claims were already the subject of a class action in the United States, which had been settled.

One phenomenon that has developed as a way to coordinate class actions in different provinces, is for the judges of the various courts to hold joint hearings on applications to approve global settlements that cover all the proceedings. One question this raises is whether the judge of one province can hold a court hearing outside the boundaries of the province. An Ontario court has said yes.[62] More recently, the British Columbia Court of Appeal has said no.[63]

Subject Matter Jurisdiction

Corporations and partnerships — application to dissolve extra-provincial partnership — court's jurisdiction

Swain v MBM Intellectual Property LLP, 2013 BCSC 1050

MBM was a law firm with its principal office in Ontario and an extra-provincially registered office in Vancouver, British Columbia. It was constituted as a limited liability partnership (LLP) under the Ontario

---

[58] *Miller v Purdue Pharma Inc*, 2013 SKQB 193, 421 Sask R 71.

[59] *CJPTA (SK), supra* note 7 at s 9(g).

[60] *Trillium Motor World Ltd v General Motors of Canada Ltd*, 2013 ONSC 2289.

[61] *Silver v IMAX Corp*, 2013 ONSC 1667, 36 CPC (7th) 254, leave to appeal to Div. Ct. refused, 2013 ONSC 6751.

[62] *Parsons v Canadian Red Cross Society*, 2013 ONSC 3053, 363 DLR (4th) 352.

[63] *Endean v British Columbia*, 2014 BCCA 61.

Limited Partnerships Act[64] and the Ontario *Partnership Act.*[65] Differences over the management of the firm created friction between the Vancouver and Ontario offices, to the point where the general manager of the firm told the petitioner, who was managing partner of the Vancouver office, that all of her privileges would be cut off and her name would be removed from the firm's website. The petitioner commenced this proceeding in British Columbia seeking dissolution of the limited liability partnership under the Ontario *Partnerships Act.* The respondent firm sought dismissal or a stay of the proceedings on the ground that a British Columbia court lacked jurisdiction to grant remedies provided by Ontario legislation.

The judge held the court had jurisdiction. A distinction was to be drawn in this context between a partnership and a corporation. The latter is a creature of statute, and it followed that the province under whose statute the corporation is formed necessarily desires to deal with the internal governance and status of the corporation. Thus, the Ontario *Business Corporations Act* states that the only court with jurisdiction to make orders under the act is the Superior Court of Justice of Ontario,[66] and similar provisions are found in other provinces' legislation. On the other hand, a partnership is created by contract. The Ontario *Partnerships Act* defines "court" as "every court and judge having jurisdiction in the case."[67] The British Columbia court had jurisdiction *simpliciter,* or territorial competence, because both the petitioner and the respondent LLP were ordinarily resident in the province. The dispute as to the dissolution of the LLP was a civil dispute arising in the province and so within the court's subject matter jurisdiction under the province's *Supreme Court Act.*[68] The fact that the LLP was governed by Ontario law did not take the dispute out of the court's jurisdiction.

Matrimonial Causes

Divorce

Wang v Lin, 2013 ONCA 33, 358 DLR (4th) 452

The husband and wife and their two children immigrated to Canada in 2005. The husband subsequently lost his permanent resident

---

[64] *Limited Partnerships Act,* RSO 1990, c L.16.
[65] *Partnerships Act,* RSO 1990, c P.5.
[66] *Business Corporations Act,* RSO 1990, c B.16, s 1(1) "court."
[67] *Partnerships Act, supra* note 65 at s 1(1) "court".
[68] *Supreme Court Act,* RSBC 1996, c 443, s 9(1).

Annuaire canadien de droit international 2013

status because he spent too little time in Canada, but the wife and the two children lived mainly in Ontario and obtained Canadian citizenship. In 2010, the wife and children, on visitors' visas, re-entered China and lived there with the husband. The wife claimed her intention was to return to Canada in two years. The family home in Toronto was retained, and the mother and children returned to visit relatives in 2011. In April 2012, the wife travelled to Toronto and commenced a divorce proceeding, together with applications for support and for a share of matrimonial property. The husband applied to stay the proceedings for lack of jurisdiction.

The Court of Appeal, reversing in part the motion judge's decision, held there was no jurisdiction *simpliciter* over the divorce proceeding or the support and property claims. To found jurisdiction under the *Divorce Act*, either spouse must have been ordinarily resident in the province for at least one year immediately preceding the commencement of the proceeding.[69] The wife had not been ordinarily resident in Ontario for that period, notwithstanding retention of the home in Toronto. She had been living and carrying on the customary mode of life in China. Her real home was there.

Jurisdiction *simpliciter* in respect of the support and property claims under the *Family Law Act*[70] depends on there being a presumptive connecting factor between those claims and Ontario. The real home or ordinary residence of the claimant should be considered a presumptive connecting factor for such claims, but in this case that factor was not present and there was therefore no real and substantial connection between the wife's claims and Ontario. Custody jurisdiction under the *Children's Law Reform Act*[71] required that the child be habitually resident in Ontario or, in certain circumstances, present in Ontario. The children here were neither habitually resident in the province nor present there when proceedings were commenced. They were subsequently brought to Canada and were now in school. Under the act,[72] the court had jurisdiction to make interim orders pending a decision on whether the children should be returned to the country of their habitual residence, and the matter was remitted to the motion judge to consider where orders, if any, should be made in that respect.

69 *Divorce Act*, RSC 1985 (2nd Supp), c 3, s 3(1).

70 *Family Law Act*, RSO 1990, c F.3.

71 *Children's Law Reform Act*, RSO 1990, c C.12.

72 *Ibid* at s 40.

Armoyan v Armoyan, 2013 NSCA 99, 334 NSR (2d) 204[73]

This was a case of parallel divorce proceedings, both of them protracted and bitterly fought. The wife petitioned for divorce in Florida and the husband, in Nova Scotia. In the first instance proceeding, the Nova Scotia judge made certain orders as to jurisdiction that were now appealed.[74]

The Court of Appeal held in the first place that the judge had been wrong to attach a condition to an adjournment of the jurisdictional proceeding before him, that the wife must not take any further step in the Florida proceeding pending the outcome of the jurisdictional decision in Nova Scotia. Even if it was in form a condition of an adjournment, it was in substance an interlocutory injunction against the wife's taking any further steps in a foreign proceeding. Such an order did not meet the conditions set out for anti-suit injunctions in the *Amchem* case.[75] In particular, the Florida court itself had not yet decided on whether it was *forum non conveniens*; on the facts it could not be said to be *forum non conveniens* for the divorce proceeding, given the extensive connections the family had with Florida; and it could not be said that to allow the Florida proceeding to continue would result in an injustice to the husband.

On the question of jurisdiction *simpliciter* in the husband's divorce proceeding and related claims, the background was that the family, after living for some time in Toronto, had lived together in Florida for the better part of two years, until the wife petitioned for divorce in Florida and the husband returned to Nova Scotia where he had bought a house for the family. A little more than a year after returning to Nova Scotia, he filed his divorce petition. The Court of Appeal agreed with the trial judge that jurisdiction *simpliciter* was established by the husband's ordinary residence in Nova Scotia during that last year.

However, the court disagreed with the trial judge on the issue of *forum non conveniens*. In holding that the wife had not shown that Florida was clearly a more appropriate forum, the judge had misapplied the relevant law, which was the relevant section of the *CJPTA*.[76]

---

[73] Leave to appeal to SCC refused, 35611 (6 February 2014).

[74] The first instance decision is noted (2012), 50 Can YB Int'l L 594.

[75] *Amchem Products Inc v British Columbia (Workers Compensation Board)*, [1993] 1 SCR 897.

[76] *CJPTA (NS)*, *supra* note 7 at s 12.

On the factors enumerated there, the Nova Scotia court should have deferred to the jurisdiction of the Florida court. The Florida proceeding had been commenced first, and the Florida court was reasonably entitled to conclude that its forum was more appropriate than Nova Scotia. To have the Nova Scotia proceeding continue also raised the prospect of conflicting decisions. A divorce granted by the Florida court must be recognized in Canada because, on the facts before the trial judge, the wife was ordinarily resident in Florida for a year before she commenced her proceeding.[77] The claims for corollary relief in the Nova Scotia proceeding would of necessity fail if the parties were divorced in Florida.

The husband's application for a division of matrimonial property stood on a different footing. Although procedurally, such claims could be pleaded in a divorce petition, they were legally distinct. Only a Nova Scotia court could deal with the validity of the conveyance of the husband's home and the wife's claim to title of that home, which was worth about $3 million and was integral to any division of matrimonial assets as a whole. The division of property would be more fairly and efficiently accomplished in the Nova Scotia court than in the court in Florida.

The issues of child support and spousal support, to the extent that they were framed independently of the divorce proceeding, should also be heard in Florida as the fairer and more efficient forum.

Lastly, the court turned to the trial judge's alternative ground for holding that the Nova Scotia court should not decline jurisdiction, which was that the wife was bound by an exclusive forum selection clause, in favour of Nova Scotia, in the parties' marital agreement. As part of the divorce proceeding in Florida, the court had held the clause was invalid because the entire agreement was void on account of the husband's fraud. Issue estoppel applied to this finding by the Florida court. The husband had proper notice of the proceeding but elected not to participate in the hearing, presumably because, had he appeared, he would have had to remedy his defaulted arrears on support and costs orders previously made by the Florida court. The circumstances did not support an exercise of the discretion not to apply issue estoppel; the husband should not be allowed to disregard the Florida court's decision on the issue of the validity of the forum selection clause.

---

[77] *Divorce Act*, RSC 1985 (2nd Supp), c 3, s 22(1).

Matrimonial property

Aleong v Aleong, 2013 BCSC 1428, [2014] 2 WWR 290

The husband and wife had married in British Columbia, lived there for twenty-four years, and raised their children there. In 1994, they cut their ties with British Columbia and moved back to Trinidad, from which both originally came. They lived together there until 2005 when the wife returned to British Columbia. The husband remained in Trinidad. The wife now brought an action for a division of the parties' matrimonial property, most of which, including the immovables, were outside British Columbia. The court, applying the *CJPTA*,[78] held that the court lacked territorial competence in relation to the claims. It was true that the claim concerned movable property located in the province, which was a presumed real and substantial connection supporting jurisdiction,[79] but the presumption was rebutted. The value of the property in British Columbia was dwarfed by the value of the assets located elsewhere. The judge went on to reject an argument that even if the wife's claim did not benefit from any of the presumed real and substantial connections in the act, she was entitled to show a real and substantial connection based on "other circumstances," namely the length of time over which the assets were accumulated and the location where the foundation for those assets was laid.

Note. In his decision on the last point, the judge relied upon the presumptive connecting factor methodology of the *Van Breda* case,[80] saying that none of the "other circumstances" the wife referred to amounted to a presumptive connecting factor according to the standards of that case. At this point, it is an open question whether the notion of a presumptive connecting factor ought to be applied in the context of the *CJPTA*. The presumptive connecting factors described in *Van Breda* are the judge-made analogue to the statutorily presumed real and substantial connections in the *CJPTA*. The *CJPTA* expressly permits a real and substantial connection to be shown even if none of the statutory presumptions applies. By contrast, *Van Breda* left no room for such a "residual" real and substantial connection — if no presumptive connecting factor is present, there is no jurisdiction. To restrict the "residual" test in the *CJPTA* to

---

[78] *CJPTA (BC), supra* note 6.

[79] *Ibid,* s 10(a).

[80] *Van Breda, supra* note 2.

presumptive connecting factors as in *Van Breda* is to pile a common law presumptive connecting factor test on top of the statutory presumed real and substantial connection test. That seems contrary to the structure of the statute, the most natural reading of which would allow a "residual" real and substantial connection to be shown ad hoc on the facts of the individual case if none of the statutory presumptions applies. Although that is probably what the statute intended, it admittedly has the drawback that it can leave territorial competence largely dependent on the sense of justice of the individual judge. It was to put the brakes on such "discretionary" decisions that the Supreme Court in *Van Breda* insisted that judges must in every case, without exception, set out a presumptive connecting factor on which jurisdiction *simpliciter* can be based.

Support obligations

Note. In *Gavriluke v Mainard,*[81] jurisdiction *simpliciter* in child support was based on the residence of the custodial parent and the children in Ontario. See also *Wang v Lin,* noted above under *Divorce*.

Infants and Children

Custody — jurisdiction

Applying the *CJPTA,*[82] a Nova Scotia court held that it had territorial competence to decide on the custody of children now resident in St. Pierre and Miquelon, but should decline jurisdiction as there were custody proceedings under way in that jurisdiction: *Detcheverry v Herritt.*[83] Similarly, a Saskatchewan court held it had jurisdiction under custody legislation but should decline it in favour of the courts of North Carolina: *Hamilton v Hamilton.*[84] An Ontario court held that it lacked jurisdiction under custody legislation because the child, though present in Ontario, was still habitually resident in the United States: *Mohammed v Hitram.*[85]

The choice between parallel custody proceedings in British Columbia and Alberta was made by simultaneous decisions of the

---

[81] *Gavriluke v Mainard,* 2013 ONSC 2337, 32 RFL (7th) 111.

[82] *CJPTA (NS), supra* note 7.

[83] *Detcheverry v Herritt,* 2013 NSSC 315, 336 NSR (2d) 150.

[84] *Hamilton v Hamilton,* 2013 SKQB 190, 421 Sask R 45.

[85] *Mohammed v Hitram,* 2013 ONSC 7239.

two courts in *Naibkhil v Qaderi*.[86] See also *Giesbrecht v Giesbrecht*,[87] in which judicial cooperation was used to resolve custody jurisdiction as between Manitoba and Alberta. A joint hearing of courts in Manitoba and Florida was used to coordinate a proceeding in Manitoba to order children returned to Florida, and a proceeding in Florida to determine whether the court there would exercise custody jurisdiction: *Cohen v Cohen*.[88] See also, on custody jurisdiction, *Wang v Lin*, noted above under Matrimonial causes; *Divorce*.

Child abduction

M.(R.) v S.(J.), 2013 ABCA 441, 369 DLR (4th) 421

A mother, resident in Israel, sought return of her son under the *Hague Convention*[89] on the basis that the Alberta-resident father's retention of the son was in violation of the mother's rights of custody in Israel. The lower court judge had refused to order the return, mainly on the basis that the son, who had just turned ten years old, had objected to being returned. Article 13 of the convention says that return may be refused if the court "finds that the child objects to being returned and has attained an age and degree of maturity at which it is appropriate to take account of its views." The Court of Appeal reversed this decision on the basis that there was no useful evidence before the lower court to support the proposition that the child had attained the required "age and degree of maturity." Even if there was sufficient evidence before the court to allow the judge to consider the boy's views, it was unreasonable to treat the child's objections as controlling and give them inordinate weight in the particular circumstances of the case, thereby defeating the purpose of the convention.

Note. See also *H.(A.) v H.(F.S.)(C)*,[90] in which the child's habitual residence in Australia was established, although the mother and child had lived there with the father for only two months before

---

[86] *Naibkhil v Qaderi*, 2013 BCSC 1433; the Alberta decision is 2013 ABQB 458.

[87] *Giesbrecht v Giesbrecht*, 2013 MBQB 115, 292 Man R (2d) 122.

[88] *Cohen v Cohen*, 2013 MBQB 292, 300 Man R (2d) 144.

[89] *Hague Convention on the Civil Aspects of Child Abduction*, 25 October 1980 (entered into force 1 December 1983) [*Hague Convention*], implemented in Alberta by the *International Child Abduction Act*, RSA 2000, c I-4.

[90] *H(A) v H(FS)(C)*, 2013 ONSC 1308.

they returned, initially for a visit but subsequently for good, to Ontario. The child was ordered returned to Australia under the *Hague Convention*.[91]

Québec

Règles générales de compétence juridictionnelle ‹

Forum non conveniens — *article 3135 CcQ*[92]

Stormbreaker Marketing & Productions Inc c World Class Events Ltd, 2013 QCCA 269[93]

Weinstock a présenté un moyen d'exception déclinatoire dans le cadre d'une réclamation par Stormbreaker contre World Class Events Ltd (WCEL). Weinstock est l'avocat américain de WCEL. Il maintient ses bureaux et réside en Géorgie, aux États-Unis. Poursuivi au Québec, il demande que le tribunal se déclare non-compétent pour trancher le litige. Subsidiairement, il demande au tribunal de décliner sa compétence puisque les tribunaux de l'État de Géorgie sont mieux placés pour trancher le litige.

WCEL avait offert à Stormbreaker la possibilité de participer à la promotion d'un tournoi de poker. En février 2009, Stormbreaker et WCEL signent une entente selon laquelle WCEL désigne Stormbreaker comme seul commanditaire officiel du tournoi en ligne. Pour obtenir ce privilège, Stormbreaker s'est engagée à défrayer pas moins de 3 000 000 $ USD en frais de publicité pour promouvoir le tournoi. De plus, elle a acheté, pour le compte d'une cliente, 30 droits de participation ayant une valeur de 300 000 $ USD. Le tournoi n'a pas eu lieu. Stormbreaker intente alors une poursuite en recouvrement des sommes payées contre WCEL. Weinstock confirme à Stormbreaker que les fonds qu'il détenait ont été remis à sa cliente, WCEL. Stormbreaker modifie alors sa requête pour demander la condamnation de Weinstock à lui payer la somme de 300 000 $ USD.

Le juge de première instance affirme que le litige se résume en trois questions: Weinstock est-il lié par la clause d'élection de for contenue au contrat conclu entre Stormbreaker et WCEL? La Cour supérieure est-elle compétente pour disposer du litige en vertu de

---

[91] *Supra* note 89, implemented in Ontario by the *Children's Law Reform Act,* RSO 1990, c C.12, s 46(2).

[92] *Code civil du Québec,* LQ 1991, ch 64 [*CcQ*].

l'article 3148(3) *CcQ?* Si oui, y a-t-il lieu de décliner compétence en vertu de l'article 3135 *CcQ?* Le juge répond par la négative à la première question et par l'affirmative aux deux autres questions.

La Cour d'appel accueille l'appel. Les deux seules parties au contrat sont Stormbreaker et WCEL. Aucun élément de preuve ne contredit l'affirmation de Weinstock à l'effet qu'il n'a jamais consenti à être lié par la clause d'élection de for contenue dans ce contrat. Le juge a également correctement répondu à la seconde question en concluant à la compétence des tribunaux québécois mais a omis de motiver son analyse subséquente. Le tribunal de Géorgie n'est pas "nettement plus approprié." La requête de Weinstock doit être rejetée. Si l'action en cours se poursuit, on peut prévoir dans un premier temps la condamnation des autres défendeurs. Par la suite, le tribunal tranchera si Weinstock doit lui aussi être condamné à rembourser la somme de 300 000 $ USD qu'il avait reçue en dépôt. Si tel est le cas, il sera subrogé dans le jugement contre les autres défendeurs, et il lui sera loisible de le faire reconnaître et le rendre exécutoire contre eux.

Litispendance — article 3137 CcQ

Note. Veuillez voir *CBS Canada Holdings Co c Canadian National Railway Company*[94] (conditions de litispendance satisfaites).

Actions personnelles à caractère patrimonial

Compétence — personne morale non domiciliée au Québec — activité au Québec — article 3148(2) CcQ — recours collectif

Chabot c WestJet, 2013 QCCS 5297

Requête de Chabot, tant personnellement qu'en sa qualité de tutrice de son fils X, afin d'être autorisée à exercer contre la compagnie aérienne WestJet un recours collectif pancanadien pour le compte des personnes handicapées ou ayant une déficience fonctionnelle en raison de leur obésité qui ont dû payer à WestJet ou à un de ses mandataires des frais additionnels pour le siège d'un accompagnateur. Elle soumet qu'à deux reprises, WestJet lui a fait payer un billet d'avion alors qu'elle exerçait des fonctions d'accompagnatrice de son fils handicapé. S'inspirant de la *Loi canadienne*

---

[93] Autorisation d'appeler à la CSC refusée, 35312 (25 juillet 2013).

[94] *CBS Canada Holdings Co c Canadian National Railway Company,* 2013 QCCS 471.

sur les droits de la personne[95] et de la *Charte canadienne des droits et libertés*,[96] elle estime qu'elle et son fils font l'objet de discrimination ayant pour effet de les restreindre dans leurs déplacements. Elle réclame une indemnité pour les frais payés par l'accompagnateur de même que des dommages moraux et punitifs. WestJet soutient notamment que le recours ne présente aucune apparence sérieuse de droit, que le groupe visé est trop disparate, et que les questions proposées par Chabot ne sont pas communes à tout le groupe.

La Cour accueille la requête en partie. La question de droit soulevée par Chabot paraît sérieuse. Étant donné que WestJet a son domicile en Alberta et que les facteurs de rattachement prévus à l'article 3148 *CcQ* quant à des passagers résidents dans une province autre que le Québec ne sont pas présents, le Tribunal limite le groupe proposé aux résidents de la province de Québec. Un simple comptoir dans un aéroport ne constitue pas un établissement au Québec au sens de l'article 3148(2) *CcQ.*

Compétence — faute commise au Québec — article 3148(3) CcQ

Note. Veuillez voir *Hofmann Plastics inc c Tribec Metals Ltd.*[97] La défenderesse, domiciliée en Ontario, n'a pas donné un avis suffisant à la demanderesse au Québec pour mettre fin à leur relation commerciale; la faute est commise au Québec.

Compétence — préjudice subi au Québec — article 3148(3) CcQ *— recours collectif*

Infineon Technologies AG c Option consommateurs, 2013 CSC 59, [2013] 3 RCS 600

Les appelantes sont des sociétés qui fabriquent la DRAM, une micro puce qui permet de stocker électroniquement de l'information et de la récupérer rapidement. La DRAM est couramment utilisée dans une grande variété d'appareils électroniques. Les appelantes vendent la DRAM, par l'intermédiaire d'un certain nombre de canaux de distribution, à des fabricants d'équipement d'origine (FEO), comme Dell inc. Les FEO incorporent les puces dans divers

---

[95] *Loi canadienne sur les droits de la personne,* LRC 1985, ch H-6, art 2 et 5.

[96] *Charte canadienne des droits et libertés, Loi Constitutionnelle de 1982,* Partie I, art 6 et 15.

[97] *E Hofmann Plastics inc c Tribec Metals Ltd,* 2013 QCCA 2112.

produits électroniques qu'ils fabriquent, qui sont ensuite vendus soit à des intermédiaires au sein du canal de distribution, soit directement aux consommateurs finaux. Les appelantes ont reconnu leur participation à un complot international en vue de supprimer et d'éliminer la concurrence en fixant les prix de la DRAM devant être vendue à des FEO. Elles ont été condamnées aux États-Unis et en Europe à de lourdes amendes pour leur rôles respectifs dans le complot.

Option consommateurs présente une requête devant la Cour supérieure afin d'obtenir l'autorisation d'exercer un recours collectif en dommages-intérêts au nom des membres du groupe touché contre les appelantes. Le groupe est composé d'acheteurs directs et indirects qui ont subi des pertes en payant, en tout ou en partie, la portion gonflée du prix de la DRAM vendue au Québec. Sa demande se fonde sur des allégations selon lesquelles les appelantes n'ont pas rempli les obligations que leur imposait la *Loi sur la concurrence*[98] et que leur conduite équivalait à une faute entraînant la responsabilité civile sous le régime du *Code civil du Québec*. Dans sa requête pour autorisation d'exercer un recours collectif, Option consommateurs désigne C à titre de membre du groupe. C, une résidente de Montréal, avait acheté un ordinateur personnel équipé de DRAM par l'entremise du site Web de Dell et l'avait payé par carte de crédit. Le juge saisi de la requête décide que la Cour supérieure n'a pas compétence territoriale pour entendre le recours collectif. Quoi qu'il en soit, il aurait rejeté la requête pour autorisation sur le fond, estimant que les exigences des alinéas 1003*b*) et 1003*d*) et de l'article 1048 du *Code de procédure civile*[99] n'avaient pas été respectées. La Cour d'appel infirme cette décision et accueille la requête en autorisation d'exercer le recours collectif.

La Cour suprême rejette le pourvoi. En raison des faits allégués, les tribunaux québécois ont compétence pour décider si le recours collectif devrait été autorisé sur le fondement de l'article 1003 *Cpc*. Le paragraphe 3148(3) *CcQ* donne compétence aux autorités québécoises dans les actions personnelles à caractère patrimonial lorsqu' "une faute a été commise au Québec, un préjudice y a été subi, un fait dommageable s'y est produit ou l'une des obligations découlant d'un contrat devait y être exécutée." Le préjudice subi au Québec constitue un facteur de rattachement indépendant: il n'est pas nécessaire que le préjudice soit lié à l'endroit où le fait

---

98 *Loi sur la concurrence*, LRC 1985, ch C-34.

99 *Code de procédure civile*, LRQ, ch C-25 [*Cpc*].

dommageable a été subi ou la faute commise. De plus, le libellé clair du paragraphe 3148(3) n'empêche pas le préjudice économique de servir de facteur de rattachement, et le droit civil québécois n'interdit pas non plus l'indemnisation de la perte purement économique.

En l'espèce, le préjudice économique aurait été subi par C — et non simplement comptabilisé — au Québec. Plus précisément, il découlerait du contrat intervenu entre elle et Dell. Bien que ce contrat ne soit pas, en fait, à l'origine de la cause d'action dans la présente affaire, qui est de nature extracontractuelle, il constitue un fait juridique établissant le lieu où le préjudice économique allégué s'est produit : la conclusion du contrat représente l'événement qui fixe le *situs* du préjudice matériel subi au Québec. En conséquence, le contrat s'avère pertinent pour décider si les tribunaux québécois ont compétence en l'espèce, sans égard au fait qu'aucune des appelantes n'y était partie. La perte financière de C découlait directement de son contrat intervenu avec Dell, qui est réputé, aux termes de la *Loi sur la protection du consommateur* du Québec,[100] avoir été conclu dans cette province. Le préjudice économique causé par ce contrat n'a pas simplement entraîné un effet à distance sur le patrimoine de C au Québec, mais il a été subi au Québec lors de la conclusion du contrat dans cette province, d'où l'application du paragraphe 3148(3) *CcQ* à la demande de cette dernière.

Quant aux exigences pour un recours collectif, la Cour décide que la requête en autorisation allègue des faits suffisants pour établir les éléments requis à l'article 1003 *Cpc*.

Compétence — préjudice subi au Québec — article 3148(3) CcQ

Entreprises Steve de Montbrun inc c CVS Caremark Corporation, 2013 QCCA 2103

Montbrun en appelle d'un jugement accueillant une exception déclinatoire soulevée par CVS et rejetant en conséquence la requête introductive d'instance amendée de Montbrun. Montbrun est une compagnie de transport qui a sa place d'affaires à Dorval. Elle aurait expédié des marchandises qui feraient l'objet de connaissements émis par l'expéditeur, Encore Gourmet Foods, de Plattsburgh, New-York, lesquels connaissements, selon Montbrun, désigneraient CVS,

---

[100] *Loi sur la protection du consommateur*, LRQ, ch P-40.1, anciens art 20 et 21 (abrogés LQ 2006, ch 56, art 3, mais en vigueur au moment de la conclusion du contrat entre C et Dell).

en Floride, en tant que consignataire. Les services de transport rendus par Montbrun auraient été rendus entièrement aux États-Unis, pour le bénéfice exclusif de CVS. Les contrats de transport auraient été négociés et conclus à Montréal. Le paiement du fret en vertu du contrat aurait également été effectué à Montréal. CVS n'a pas d'établissement ni de place d'affaires au Québec.

Après avoir considéré les prétentions respectives des parties, examiné une partie de la jurisprudence soumise et s'être prononcé sur l'interprétation de l'article 3148 *CcQ* et de l'article 2 de la *Loi sur les connaissements*,[101] le juge déclare que le moyen déclinatoire était bien fondé et que les tribunaux québécois ne sont pas compétents pour entendre le recours. Même si Montbrun soutient que le préjudice a été subi au Québec parce que, selon elle, l'une des obligations du contrat était que le paiement devait y être fait et que le défaut de paiement y est survenu, le juge est d'avis qu'il ne suffit pas qu'il y ait eu appauvrissement de Montbrun pour conclure que le préjudice a été subi au Québec. En outre, l'affirmation que le paiement devait être effectué au Québec n'est pas soutenue par la preuve; les connaissements émis ne désignaient aucun lieu spécifique de paiement. Dans la mesure où c'est CVS et non Encore Gourmet Foods qui est débitrice d'une obligation quelconque de paiement, cette obligation de paiement devrait être exécutée au domicile de CVS aux États-Unis.

La Cour d'appel rejette le pourvoi. De toute évidence, CVS n'a pas commis de faute susceptible d'entraîner sa responsabilité extra-contractuelle entre les parties. Le juge n'a pas erré en concluant que le principe de la territorialité fait en sorte que la *Loi sur les connaissements* ne s'applique pas à CVS. Vu l'absence de lien de droit entre les parties, aucune des conditions mentionnées au premier alinéa de l'article 3148 *CcQ* n'était remplie, ce qui laissait le tribunal sans compétence pour entendre l'action intentée par Montbrun. Dans les circonstances, le juge était justifié d'accueillir l'exception déclinatoire.

Note. In *Lacroix v Cassels Brock & Blackwell LLP*,[102] Quebec clients sued an Ontario law firm for failing to perform the terms of a settlement agreement relating to a legal proceeding in Ontario; no damage held to be suffered in Quebec. Similarly, in *Services Jade*

---

101 *Loi sur les connaissements*, LRC 1985, c B-5.

102 *Lacroix c Cassels Brock & Blackwell LLP*, 2013 QCCS 2986, autorisation d'appeler à la CA refusée, 2013 QCCA 1820.

ABL inc v Focus Lenders Services Group,[103] no damage was held to have been suffered in Quebec when United States clients of the plaintiff Quebec-based consultants allegedly conducted a smear campaign against the plaintiffs outside Quebec.

Compétence — une des obligations découlant d'un contrat devait être exécutée au Québec — article 3148(3) CcQ

Green Planet Technologies Ltd c Corporation Pneus OTR Blackstone / OTR Blackstone Tire Corporation, 2013 QCCA 56

In late 2011 Blackstone, a company based in Quebec, initiated discussions with Green Planet, based in Wales, about the possibility of purchasing Bridgestone "off the road" (OTR) tires for sale by it to one of its customers operating a mine in Brazil. According to Blackstone, the deal was limited to the purchase of seventy-two tires. It caused an advance of US $504,000 to be transferred to Green Planet in partial satisfaction of a signed purchase order for seventy-two tires at a total price of US $2,520,000. Green Planet said it would not deliver the seventy-two tires until Blackstone paid a deposit for 104 more tires that Green Planet said Blackstone had ordered and that Green Planet had reserved with its Chinese supplier. Blackstone initiated proceedings in the Superior Court of Montreal claiming cancellation of the purchase order and the return of the deposit by Green Planet. Green Planet filed a declinatory exception on the ground that none of the conditions of Article 3148(3) were satisfied and the Quebec court therefore lacked territorial competence to hear the action.

The Court of Appeal held, reversing the motion judge, that the declinatory exception should have been granted. The motion judge had erred in finding that the transfer from Blackstone's bank in Montreal to Green Planet's bank in the United Kingdom was itself evidence of an obligation arising from the contract to be executed in Quebec. None of the documentation supported the conclusion that Blackstone was contractually bound to pay the deposit in Quebec. Blackstone in fact paid in Quebec, but it was not bound to do so. The motion judge had rightly held that no damage was suffered in Quebec. The *situs* of Blackstone's loss in connection with the deposit was either in the United Kingdom, where the money was sent for the purchase, or in China, where the goods were to be shipped FOB by Green Planet's supplier. Nor did a loss of profit

---

[103] *Services Jade ABL inc v Focus Lenders Services Group,* 2013 QCCS 5546.

Blackstone claimed to suffer as a result of Green Planet's breach of contract amount to damage in Quebec. This loss was claimed as arising from Blackstone's inability to sell OTR tires to its customer in Brazil. Hence, the loss occurred in Brazil.

Note. Voir aussi *Taiko Trucking c SLT Express Way Inc*[104] (contrat de vente devait être exécutée au Québec; le préjudice de l'acheteur est subi au Québec).

Compétence — clause d'attribution de for — article 3148, alinéa 2 CcQ

Note. Voir *PIRS sa c Compagnie d'arrimage de Québec ltée*[105] (choix de for français; exception déclinatoire accueillie); et *André R Dorais, Avocats c Saudi Arabian General Investment Authority*[106] (choix de for dans projets de contrat mais convention écrite n'a jamais été signée).

PROCEDURE / PROCÉDURE

Common Law and Federal

Commencement of Proceedings

Service of process — Hague Convention

Khan Resources v Atomredmetzoloto JSC, 2013 ONCA 189, 361 DLR (4th) 446

Khan Resources (Khan), an Ontario corporation, entered into a joint venture with ARMZ, a subsidiary of the Russian State Atomic Energy Corporation, and other companies to develop a uranium mining property in Mongolia. Khan brought the present action against ARMZ in Ontario, claiming that the Russian government, through ARMZ, sought to deprive it of its interest in the Mongolian mining property. Khan sought to effect service on ARMZ in Russia through the Russian central authority designated pursuant to the *Hague Convention on Service.*[107] Rule 17.05(3) of the Ontario *Rules of*

---

104 *Taiko Trucking c SLT Express Way Inc*, 2013 QCCS 75.

105 *PIRS s.a. c Compagnie d'arrimage de Québec ltée*, 2013 QCCA 31.

106 *André R. Dorais, Avocats c Saudi Arabian General Investment Authority*, 2013 QCCS 3369, autorisation d'appeler à la CA refusée, 2013 QCCA 941.

107 *Hague Convention on the Service Abroad of Judicial and Extrajudicial Documents in Civil or Commercial Matters*, 15 November 1965 (entered into force for Canada 1 May 1989).

Civil Procedure[108] says that "in a contracting state" (referring to a party to the convention) service of an originating process must be through the central authority in the contracting state or in a matter permitted by the convention and that would be permitted under the usual rules for service in Ontario. The Russian central authority refused to serve ARMZ, relying on article 13 of the convention, which allows refusal to comply only if the state deems that compliance would infringe its sovereignty or security. Khan did not appeal that decision in Russia but brought a motion in the Ontario court for an order substituting or dispensing with service, or validating service by an alternative means.[109]

The Court of Appeal, reversing a decision of a Master, held there was no discretion to substitute, dispense with, or validate service if the convention applies. To admit such a discretion would undermine one of the purposes of the convention, which was to establish a uniform procedure for service in all contracting states. Rule 17.05(3) had to be read as a complete code for service in a contracting state. It implemented an international convention and so must be interpreted in the light of the legal obligations Canada undertook under the convention. Ontario case law also established that where service must be effected through the convention, a plaintiff cannot circumvent the requirement even if the defendant has received actual notice of the proceeding. In *obiter dicta*, the court left open the possibility that it might be possible to validate service other than in accordance with the convention in an extreme case where the plaintiff has exhausted all avenues available under the convention and where, if service is impossible, access to justice in relation to basic human rights would be denied.[110]

Evidence Obtained Locally for Use in Foreign Proceedings

Letters rogatory

Lantheus Medical Imaging Inc v Atomic Energy of Canada Ltd, 2013 ONCA 264, 361 DLR (4th) 711

---

[108] Ontario, *Rules of Civil Procedure*, RRO 1990, Reg 194.

[109] *Ibid*, r 16.04 and 16.08, respectively.

[110] *Khan Resources v Atomredmetzoloto JSC*, 2013 ONCA 189, 361 DLR (4th) 446 at paras 57-60, distinguishing rather than overruling *Zhang v Jiang* (2006) 82 OR (3d) 306 (SC), which involved an action against persons in China by Falun Gong members who claimed to have been tortured there.

Lantheus, an American pharmaceutical company, suffered large losses as a result of an interruption in the supply to it of medical isotopes by Atomic Energy of Canada Limited (AECL) when the reactor that produced the isotopes was shut down for a period. Lantheus' insurer denied coverage of the losses on the ground that they arose from an excluded peril. Lantheus began an action against the insurer in federal court in New York. It obtained a letter of request from the US court seeking the assistance of the Ontario Superior Court in securing documents and *viva voce* testimony from AECL for use at the trial of the US action. The court held that the evidence was "vital" because the cause of the water leak that led to the shutdown of AECL's reactor was a significant, if not determining, factor in Lantheus's ability to obtain insurance.

Lantheus applied to the court in Ontario under section 60 of the *Ontario Evidence Act*,[111] seeking an order giving effect to the letter of request. The application judge refused the order on the ground that the court did not have jurisdiction to enforce the letter of request against a federal Crown agency, which AECL is. He also held in the alternative that Lantheus had not met the standard for enforcement of letters rogatory in Ontario.

The Court of Appeal held that letters rogatory could be enforced against the federal Crown. This conclusion turned on the construction of the federal legislation on Crown liability, the details of which are not material in the present context.[112] The court also held that the application judge was wrong to refuse enforcement of the letter of request on the basis that Lantheus had not demonstrated that the evidence was to be used at trial rather than at pre-trial proceedings, and that Lantheus, as a result of a previous freedom of information application to AECL, had already received evidence of the same value as what it now sought to obtain. It was not a precondition of enforcement that the evidence be for use at trial as distinct from pre-trial proceedings. In any event, the evidence here was in fact required for trial. And the redacted documentary evidence already obtained from AECL was not of the same value as the *viva*

---

111 *Ontario Evidence Act*, RSO 1990, c E.23.

112 The *Crown Liability and Proceedings Act*, RSC 1985, c C-50, s 27 provides that in actions against the federal Crown, the "rules of practice and procedure" of the court in which the action is brought apply. The application judge held that the provision in the *Ontario Evidence Act* for enforcing letters rogatory was a "rule of evidence", which does not *per se* apply to actions against the federal Crown. The Court of Appeal held it was more properly characterized as a rule of practice and procedure and so did apply by virtue of s 27.

voce evidence being sought. Enforcement of the letter of request should have been ordered.

FOREIGN JUDGMENTS / JUGEMENTS ÉTRANGERS

Common Law and Federal

Jurisdiction of the Enforcing Court

Jurisdiction simpliciter *in action to enforce foreign judgment*

Yaiguaje v Chevron Corp, 2013 ONCA 758, 118 OR (3d) 1[113]

This was an action to enforce against Chevron, an American corporation, and its primary Canadian subsidiary, Chevron Canada, a judgment from Ecuador for US $18 billion for damage done to the plaintiffs, people living near Chevron's oil operations in Ecuador. Chevron was resisting enforcement of the judgment in the United States on the basis that it was obtained by fraud. The defendants entered no defence in the Ontario proceeding but moved to have service *ex juris* set aside and the action dismissed or permanently stayed on the ground of want of jurisdiction. One argument made in support of the motions was that the action out of which the judgment arose had no real and substantial connection with Ontario. The motion judge rejected this argument and held that Chevron had been properly served *ex juris* and Chevron Canada properly served at its place of business in Ontario. The motion judge nevertheless stayed the action on the basis that Chevron itself had no assets or business in Ontario and that Chevron Canada was not liable for Chevron's judgment.

The Court of Appeal held the stay should not have been granted. No party had sought the stay. The defendants had chosen not to attorn to the jurisdiction of the Ontario court and could not at the same time seek to uphold a stay on the basis of issues that were not the subject of evidence and to which the plaintiffs had no chance to respond.

For the rest, the Court of Appeal agreed with the motion judge that jurisdiction *simpliciter* to enforce a judgment in Ontario did not require that the litigation out of which the judgment arose have a real and substantial connection with Ontario. The territorial limits to a province's legislative authority meant that its courts could not take jurisdiction over matters that lacked a real and substantial connection with the province. However, in an action to enforce,

---

[113] Leave to appeal to SCC granted, 35682 (3 April 2014).

there is no constitutional issue because the decision of the court is limited to the enforceability of the judgment in Ontario. This is clearly within the constitutional authority of the court and does not offend against any obligation of comity to other states. Jurisdiction as against Chevron was therefore supported by the rule of court that authorized service *ex juris* if the action was to enforce a foreign judgment against the defendant.[114]

That did not extend to the claim against Chevron Canada, which was not the entity against which the judgment was granted. However, given the economically significant relationship between Chevron and Chevron Canada, and given that Chevron Canada had a place of business in Ontario, an Ontario court had jurisdiction to adjudicate a recognition and enforcement action against Chevron Canada's indirect corporate parent that also named Chevron Canada as a defendant and sought the seizure of the latter's shares and assets to satisfy a judgment against the former. Chevron Canada was entitled to dispute that its assets are exigible for the parent company's debts, but that would be an argument on the merits, which was not open at this stage because only jurisdiction was in issue.

Note. The same conclusion, that an action to enforce a foreign judgment does not require that the litigation giving rise to the judgment must have a real and substantial connection with the province, was reached in *CSA8-Garden Village LLC v Dewar*.[115] It seems plainly correct.

Conditions for Recognition or Enforcement

Nature of judgment — non-monetary order

Van Damme v Gelber, 2013 ONCA 388, 363 DLR (4th) 250[116]

Van Damme claimed that he had bought for 2 million euros a Gerhard Richter painting from a gallery in Palm Beach, Florida, that sold it on Gelber's behalf. Gelber refused to deliver the picture and took the position that there was no valid sale. Van Damme sued Gelber in state court in New York, but the picture was in Toronto, so Van Damme obtained an order from the Ontario court in 2007 enjoining Gelber from moving or dealing with the picture until the

---

114 Ontario, *Rules of Civil Procedure*, RRO 1990, Reg 194, r 17.02(m).

115 *CSA8-Garden Village LLC v Dewar*, 2013 ONSC 6229, 369 DLR (4th) 125.

116 Leave to appeal to SCC refused, 35517 (12 December 2013).

New York process was concluded. The purchase price was in the meantime held in escrow by the Ontario court. The New York court eventually granted Van Damme specific performance and ordered Gelber to deliver the picture in return for release of the purchase price less Van Damme's New York counsel fees as assessed by the New York court.

The Ontario Court of Appeal upheld the trial judge's decision that the order of the New York court should be enforced in Ontario. The New York court had jurisdiction because Gelber had attorned to its jurisdiction by making a motion for summary judgment that addressed the merits of the claim. Gelber made an argument on appeal that the trial judge had wrongly exercised the discretion as to whether to enforce a foreign non-monetary order,[117] because specific performance was not a remedy an Ontario court would have granted. The Court of Appeal held this argument had not been made at trial and so could not be raised now as an objection to the judge's decision. The argument was also wrong as a matter of law; in an Ontario case, specific performance would be regarded an appropriate remedy.

Note. A side-effect of the enforcement of non-monetary orders is that they fall outside the category of "debt," which traditionally is the rubric under which monetary judgments have been held enforceable. In *PT ATPK Resources TBK (Indonesia) v Diversified Energy & Resource Corp*,[118] the enforcement of a Singapore court order, declaring that the defendant held shares on trust for the plaintiff, was not subject to a limitation period because, for the purpose of the limitations statute, it was not a claim for a debt but a "proceeding to enforce an order of a court."[119]

Jurisdiction of the original court — attornment

Note. An Ohio default judgment in a product liability claim was held enforceable in *Ward v Nackawic Mechanical Ltd*[120] because the defendant had filed a defence and participated in a telephonic pre-trial

---

[117] Authority for the discretion, based on non-monetary orders being viewed as equitable orders, is *Pro Swing Inc v Elta Golf Inc*, 2006 SCC 52, [2006] 2 SCR 612.

[118] *PT ATPK Resources TBK (Indonesia) v Diversified Energy & Resource Corp*, 2013 ONSC 5913.

[119] *Limitations Act*, SO 2002, s 16(1)(b).

[120] *Ward v Nackawic Mechanical Ltd*, 2013 NBQB 296, 408 NBR (2d) 315.

hearing. It was immaterial that it chose to be represented, not by a lawyer, but by one of its executives, or that after the pre-trial hearing it had taken no further part.

Jurisdiction of the originating court — default judgment against non-resident of originating country — real and substantial connection

Amtim Capital Inc v Appliance Recycling Centers of America, 2013 ONSC 4867, 116 OR (3d) 379, aff'd 2014 ONCA 62, 118 OR (3d) 617[121]

Amtim, an Ontario company, conducted its business primarily in Ontario and elsewhere in Canada. It had a dispute with the defendant ARCA, a Minnesota corporation, as to the calculation of payments owing by ARCA under the contract. Mediation and arbitration having failed, Amtim advised ARCA of its intention to begin an action for the amounts in question. ARCA proceeded to commence an action in federal court in Minnesota for a declaration that no amount was owing to Amtim. Two weeks later, Amtim brought its action in Ontario claiming $1.6 million from ARCA. Amtim applied for dismissal or a stay of the US proceeding on the basis that the court lacked jurisdiction or should decline it on *forum non conveniens* grounds, but the US court rejected the application. Amtim thereafter took no further part in the proceeding. A few months later, ARCA obtained a default judgment from the US court, which Amtim did not seek to appeal.

ARCA now sought a dismissal or stay of the Ontario action on the basis that the Minnesota judgment made Amtim's claim *res judicata*.[122] The motion judge held in favour of Amtim, primarily on the ground that ARCA's proceeding against Amtim lacked a real and substantial connection with Minnesota and so the judgment was not binding in Ontario. The Court of Appeal upheld his decision. Even if, contrary to his conclusion, *res judicata* and issue estoppel were made out, this was a proper case for the exercise of the equitable discretion not to apply the doctrines. The case had minimal connections to Minnesota; there was no determination of the issues on the merits in the US court; and the US action had no enforcement effect and

[121] Leave to appeal to SCC refused, 35764 (5 June 2014).

[122] An earlier decision had held that the Ontario action should not be stayed on *forum non conveniens* grounds, while leaving open the question whether, when the merits were considered, the Minnesota judgment was to be considered *res judicata*: *Amtim Capital Inc v Appliance Recycling Centers of America*, 2012 ONCA 664, noted at (2012) 50 Can YB Int'l L 591.

was commenced solely as a defensive measure. The jurisprudence suggested that the American court would be concerned by a race to *res judicata* and, as conceded, that court was not informed of the Ontario proceedings or apprised of any calculation with respect to the damages claimed, when it was asked to grant default declaratory judgment. Ontario courts had refused to recognize negative declaratory relief where the purpose of the proceeding is to bar the natural plaintiff's claim in the jurisdiction with the closest connection to the litigation.[123]

Jurisdiction of the originating court in class action — non-resident members of plaintiff class

Meeking v Cash Store Inc, 2013 MBCA 81, 367 DLR (4th) 684[124]

A class proceeding was brought against Cash Store in Ontario on behalf of a national plaintiff class, including all residents of Canada, other than those in British Columbia and Alberta, who had paid certain broker fees to Cash Store that were argued to be illegal. The class action was settled. Meeking, a resident of Manitoba, subsequently sought to bring an action on the same claim against Cash Store in Manitoba. He said he had not noticed the posters in the Manitoba Cash Store premises he frequented nor read the mail he received from Cash Store about the Ontario settlement. The motion judge allowed Cash Store's motion for recognition and enforcement of the Ontario settlement, thus precluding Meeking's action.[125]

On appeal, the court affirmed the motion judge's decision. There was jurisdiction *simpliciter* in respect of the claims of non-residents of Ontario that did business with Cash Store in their home province. The fact that Cash Store did business in Ontario provided a presumptive connecting factor so far as the Ontario customers were concerned. So far as the residents in other provinces were concerned, based on *Van Breda*,[126] the presumptive connecting factor

---

[123] The Court of Appeal cited *Wolfe v Pickar*, 2011 ONCA 347, 332 DLR (4th) 157, noted (2011) 49 Can YB Int'l L 584.

[124] Leave to appeal to SCC granted, 35608 (27 February 2014).

[125] The motion judge held against recognizing the settlement so far as it concerned certain types of loans, because the notices did not indicate clearly enough that those loans were included in the proceeding.

[126] *Van Breda, supra* note 2.

was the common issues that their claims shared with the Ontario residents and militated in favour of a single class proceeding. That presumptive connecting factor could be rebutted but was not rebutted in this case. Fairness to non-resident plaintiffs is achieved through the notification process and opt-out provisions and the constitutional principle of federalism is respected. A settlement does not bind non-resident plaintiffs if the notice they received of the proceeding was inadequate, but the motion judge here had found that the Cash Store customers had received ample notice of the proceeding.

Note. In *Silver v IMAX Corp.,*[127] a United States class action against the defendant, brought on behalf of all purchasers of the defendant's securities on exchanges in the United States, was held good reason to exclude such purchasers from the plaintiff class in a parallel Canadian class action against the same defendant. The decision was based on two grounds. One was recognition of the settlement in the US class action, which was reached while the Canadian action was still ongoing. The other was that, with respect to purchasers on exchanges in the United States, in light of their being included in the United States proceeding, the Canadian class proceeding was not the "preferable procedure" for determining their rights.

Defences to Recognition or Enforcement

Penal judgment

Note. A British Columbia judge refused to hold that a damage award obtained against the defendant by the Securities and Exchange Commission in proceedings in the United States, for violation of securities laws, was a penal judgment: *United States (Securities and Exchange Commn) v Peever.*[128] The defendants had not shown that the damage award was for the benefit of the United States government. There was evidence that the policy of the Commission was to distribute awards to injured investors, and the award itself specified a mechanism for the Commission to achieve that distribution.

---

[127] *Silver v IMAX Corp*, 2013 ONSC 1667, 36 CPC (7th) 254, leave to appeal to Div. Ct. refused, 2013 ONSC 6751.

[128] *United States (Securities and Exchange Commn.) v Peever*, 2013 BCSC 1090, 17 BLR (5th) 332, aff'd 2014 BCCA 141.

Arbitral Awards

UNCITRAL Model Law

Note. Recognition in Ontario of an arbitral award made in the United States was held to be unimpeded by the fact that the debtor had applied to the Securities and Exchange Commission for a stay of enforcement of the award: *New York Stock Exchange LLC v Orbixa Technologies Inc.*[129]

CHOICE OF LAW (INCLUDING STATUS OF PERSONS) / CONFLITS DE LOIS (Y COMPRIS STATUT PERSONNEL)

Common Law and Federal

Contract

Statutory regulation of contract — territorial application of consumer protection legislation

Jones v Zimmer GmbH, 2013 BCCA 21, 358 DLR (4th) 499

This was a class proceeding by patients who had been implanted in British Columbia hospitals with an artificial hip component (the "Durom Cup") manufactured by the defendants. The claims were based on negligence in the design of the product as well as failures to state material facts in its marketing and distribution. The claims included compensation under the British Columbia *Business Practices and Consumer Protection Act*[130] for alleged deceptive acts and practices. In an appeal from the decision to certify the class proceeding, one of the issues raised was whether the pleaded facts disclosed any breach of the act in British Columbia. The Court of Appeal held the certification judge had rightly let the claim under the act stand. So far as it rested on allegedly deceptive or misleading statements made in a press release published only in the United States, the claim was outside the act. It was a provincial statute and did not apply to deceptive acts and practices that occurred outside the territorial boundaries of British Columbia. However, a deceptive act or practice under the act could include a failure to state a material fact if the effect of the failure was misleading. There was a basis in fact for a statutory common issue on the ground that the defendants

---

[129] *New York Stock Exchange LLC v Orbixa Technologies Inc,* 2013 ONSC 5521, aff'd 2014 ONCA 219.

[130] *Business Practices and Consumer Protection Act,* SBC 2004, c 2, s 4-5.

had failed to state a material fact and that that failure took place in British Columbia.

Note. This decision is of interest as an example of the territorial scope of a consumer protection statute being determined, not on the basis of the law that governs the consumer contract, but on the basis of the place where the consumer was solicited. The matter is one of the construction of the statute in the light, as the court pointed out, of the constitutional rule that a province can only legislate intra-territorially.

Tort

Applicable law — personal injury suffered abroad — parties resident in the forum

Long (Litigation guardian of) v Dundee Resort Development LLC, 2013 ONSC 4238

The plaintiff, then aged fifteen and a member of the Ontario Alpine Ski Team, was seriously injured in a skiing accident in Colorado while training with the team. He sued several individuals and corporations, all of whom were also resident in Ontario, in connection with his injuries. Before he was allowed to travel to Colorado to train with the team, the plaintiff, together with his parents, had to sign certain documents. One was an Athlete's Declaration for Registration with the International Ski Federation. It stipulated that disputes arising out of an event in the Federation's calendar were to be governed by Swiss law and settled by arbitration in Lausanne. Another document, an Alpine Canada Membership Registration form, included a purported release of liability and assumption of risk agreement.

The defendants brought a motion for an order that the law of Colorado applied to the plaintiff's claims. The plaintiff argued that, as this was an international case, the court had a discretion to depart from the *lex loci delicti* rule.[131] The court held that Colorado law should apply to all the tort issues. The authorities were to the effect that the discretion was to be exercised only in exceptional cases. Courts had held against a departure from the law of the place

---

[131] The possible departure from the *lex loci delicti* in international cases (but not intra-Canadian cases) was expressly contemplated by *Tolofson v Jensen,* [1994] 3 SCR 1022.

of the tort even where all the parties to the action were from the forum province and the only connection with the foreign jurisdiction was the place of the accident.[132] There was no basis in the present case for holding that a law other than the *lex loci delicti* should apply.

Personal Legal Capacity

Foreign guardianship order — recognition

Cariello v Perrella, 2013 ONSC 7605

A retired Italian priest, Fr Perrella, who had worked in Canada for many years, came back to Canada from his home in Italy in 2011. He already suffered from declining mental capacity, but soon after he arrived he suffered a stroke that further affected his mental processes. At the instance of his family in Italy, an Italian court appointed an interim guardian because Fr Perrella appeared no longer capable of looking after himself or his financial matters. The interim guardian had travelled to Ontario to try to persuade Fr Perrella to return to Italy but encountered difficulties in doing so. The Italian court issued an order that Fr Perrella be examined by a representative of the Italian Embassy to determine his capacity, but execution of this order was impeded by third parties. Residents of Ontario now applied to be appointed Fr Perrella's guardian.

The Ontario court held that, when the Italian court made its decision, Fr Perrella, although present in Canada, was still domiciled as well as ordinarily resident in Italy. On the evidence, he did not intend to adopt a domicile of choice in Ontario when he travelled to Ontario in 2011. It was also more than likely that when he came to Canada he was already incapable of forming the requisite intention to change his domicile. Personal capacity is a question of status and status is governed by the law of the domicile. It was therefore the Italian court, as the court of the domicile, that must take jurisdiction to determine Fr Perrella's capacity and ancillary matters arising from that determination. The court's order recognized that the interim guardian appointed by the Italian court had the authority and the responsibility in Ontario to make decisions on behalf of Fr Perrella.

---

[132] As the strongest example the court referred to *Castillo v Castillo*, 2005 SCC 83, [2005] 3 SCR 870.

Matrimonial Causes

Marriage — essential validity — capacity to marry polygamously

Azam v Jan, 2013 ABQB 301, 362 DLR (4th) 111

Mr. Jan was born in Pakistan but immigrated to Canada and became a lawyer in Alberta. He married Ms. Naz in Pakistan in 2000 and sponsored her immigration to Canada as his wife. They lived together in Calgary until the present and had three children. In 2007, Jan went through a form of marriage with Ms. Azam. The government of Pakistan issued a marriage certificate, and Jan sponsored Ms. Azam's immigration to Canada, not as his spouse but to obtain a student visa. At the time of this proceeding, Ms. Azam was a doctoral candidate at the University of Calgary. Jan did not tell Ms. Naz about his purported marriage to Ms. Azam. The latter was aware that Jan was already married. Ms. Azam eventually broke off her relationship with Jan and now sought a divorce. Jan argued there was no valid marriage and applied for a nullity decree. An initial dismissal of the divorce petition was set aside by the Court of Appeal on the basis that the parties' marital status had not been properly determined in light of the possibility that the marriage might be polygamous.[133]

In the present proceeding, the Court of Queen's Bench decided there was no valid marriage between Jan and Ms. Azam because Jan lacked the capacity to enter into a polygamous marriage in 2007. As a preliminary point, the court had to decide whether it even had jurisdiction to grant matrimonial relief, such as a nullity decree, if the marriage was or might be polygamous. The court held that the exclusion of polygamous marriages from any form of matrimonial relief, which stemmed from *Hyde v Hyde,*[134] was obsolete. The law should provide remedies to meet the needs of all Canadians including both citizen and permanent resident. Immigrant families should not be excluded from rights accorded to other Canadians when marriages, however concluded, break down.

It was agreed that the marriage between Jan and Ms. Azam was regarded as a valid polygamous marriage in Pakistan. However, the Canadian conflicts rule required the essential validity of a marriage to be judged by the "dual domicile theory" by which each party must have capacity to marry the other in the country in which they were domiciled at the time of the marriage. It was clear from the

---

[133] *Azam v Jan,* 2012 ABCA 197, 533 AR 173, noted at (2012) 50 Can YB Int'l L 617.
[134] *Hyde v Hyde* (1866), LR 1 PD 130 (Eng PDA).

case law that this theory was preferred to the "intended matrimonial home theory" by which a marriage can be valid if it complies with the law of the jurisdiction where the parties intend to live after the marriage. At the time of her marriage to Jan, Ms. Azam was domiciled in Pakistan and had capacity to enter into a polygamous union, but Jan was domiciled in Canada, where polygamous marriages are not possible, and he therefore lacked the legal capacity to marry Ms. Azam. The court dismissed the petition for divorce and granted an order of annulment.

Marriage — civil partnership entered into abroad — whether to be treated as marriage for purpose of divorce

Hincks v Gallardo (2013), 358 DLR (4th) 702, 113 OR (3d) 654 (SCJ)

Hincks, a dual citizen of Canada and the United Kingdom, practised architecture in the United Kingdom. He formed a relationship with Gallardo, who owned a business in Ontario; he was a dual citizen of Canada and Mexico. The parties decided to live together in the United Kingdom. Marriage between same-sex partners was not possible in the United Kingdom, so the parties entered into a civil partnership under United Kingdom legislation that gave same-sex civil partners the same rights and responsibilities as in a civil marriage.[135] Some months later, the parties decided to move to Toronto. Eventually, the relationship broke up, by which time Hincks had a job in Toronto. Hincks commenced a proceeding for divorce and for a division of family property and spousal support. Gallardo took the position the parties were not married. Hincks brought a motion for a declaration that the parties' civil partnership was a marriage within the Canadian *Civil Marriage Act*.[136]

The court granted the declaration. By its statutory requirements in the United Kingdom, the parties' civil partnership was a lawful union of two persons to the exclusion of others, which *prima facie* fell into the definition of civil marriage under the *Civil Marriage Act*. Not to recognize this as a marriage would be contrary to the express values of Canadian society and would be discriminatory. To distinguish, as English law did, between a marriage and a civil partnership was contrary to Canadian public policy. There was no reason why the civil partnership, which was a marriage in everything but name, could not be treated as a marriage in Canada. Moreover, refusing

---

[135] *Civil Partnership Act, 2004* (UK), c 33.
[136] *Civil Marriage Act*, SC 2005, c 33.

to treat the parties' partnership as a marriage would frustrate the choice they made to change their status from single to something functionally equal to marriage.

The potential option that the parties could have married in Ontario was no answer. To require a second marriage ceremony would introduce a distinction in Canada between those who had become civil partners in the UK and those who had been married in the UK, and so would perpetuate unequal treatment that the *Civil Partnership Act* was designed to eliminate. Nor was it an answer that the parties had the option of seeking dissolution of their partnership in England. Had they been a couple of opposite sex they would have had the option of seeking a divorce in either country, so that denial of the right to be divorced in Canada was, once again, discriminatory. The parties should be considered spouses for the purposes both of the *Divorce Act*[137] and of the *Family Law Act*,[138] which deals with matters of property and support.

Divorce — recognition of foreign decree

S(R) v S(K), 2013 BCCA 406, 367 DLR (4th) 749

The wife appealed from a judgment after summary trial[139] that a divorce her husband had obtained in Western Australia was recognized in Canada. The parties had been married and lived for the first four years in Australia and then moved to British Columbia, where they were living when they separated. The husband was still living in British Columbia when he obtained a divorce in Western Australia. The divorce therefore did not meet the statutory recognition test that either party be ordinarily resident in the foreign jurisdiction for one year immediately preceding the commencement of proceedings.[140] However, the summary trial judge held that the husband had a real and substantial connection with Australia, which brought the divorce within the common law grounds for recognition as preserved by the *Divorce Act*.[141]

The Court of Appeal affirmed the decision. The judge had not erred by basing recognition on a real and substantial connection with Australia rather than specifically with the state of Western

---

[137] *Divorce Act*, RSC 1985 (2nd Supp), c 3.

[138] *Family Law Act*, RSO 1990, c F.3.

[139] *Salfinger v Salfinger*, 2012 BCSC 1874, noted at (2012) 50 Can YB Int'l L 618.

[140] *Divorce Act*, RSC 1985 (2nd Supp), c 3, s 22(1).

[141] *Ibid* at s 22(3).

Australia. Divorce was a matter of federal law in Australia. There was no basis upon which a British Columbia court could question the jurisdiction of the court in Western Australia to grant what on its face was an order under a federal statute to a person with a real and substantial connection with Australia. The Court of Appeal also rejected arguments based on forum shopping by the husband and on public policy. The latter was said to be contravened because to recognize the divorce would be to deprive the wife of her ability to claim support in the court in British Columbia. This was held to be incorrect in two respects. One was that there was no evidence that the wife could not have sought support from the court in Australia, or that what the Australian court might award would be less favourable to her. The other was that, although corollary relief under the *Divorce Act* was unavailable if the marriage was dissolved already, the wife could still claim child and spousal support under provincial legislation. She had initiated those claims in British Columbia before the Australian divorce. Moreover, the legislation now in effect includes former spouses in the definition of spouse, without restricting former spouses to those divorced in Canada.[142]

Québec

Obligations

Responsabilité professionnelle

Wightman c Succession Widdrington, 2013 QCCA 1187, [2013] RJQ 1054[143]

Wightman, associé de la firme de comptables agréés Coopers, et d'autres en appellent du jugement de la Cour supérieure qui a accueilli l'action de la Succession de Widdrington et les a condamné solidairement à des dommages de 2 672 960 $. La faillite en 1992 de Castor Holdings Ltd (Castor), société incorporée au Nouveau-Brunswick mais ayant son siège social à Montréal, a engendré une série de poursuites judiciaires en responsabilité professionnelle à l'encontre de Coopers et des associés canadiens de celle-ci. Près de 100 créanciers réclament à Coopers plus d'un milliard de dollars, alléguant que Coopers a fait preuve de négligence dans ses travaux comptables. Le dossier de Widdrington a procédé en tant que dossier type. Widdrington, un résident ontarien, a investi dans

---

142 *Family Law Act*, SBC 2011, c 25, s 3(2).

143 Autorisation d'appeler à la CSC refusée, 35438 (9 janvier 2014).

Castor une somme de 1 130 400 $ en décembre 1989, puis 292 560 $ en octobre 1991, après s'être joint au conseil d'administration de la société en mars 1990.

Une des questions soulevées par le litige était, selon la juge, "Taking into account that Castor is incorporated under the New Brunswick *Corporation Act*, that Coopers performed its work in various worldwide locations under the responsibility of a Montreal engagement partner and always issued the consolidated financial statements and other opinions out of its Montreal offices, that Widdrington resided in Ontario while various other claimants live in different European countries, what is the governing law applicable: New Brunswick or Ontario common law, Quebec civil law or another law?"

La Cour d'appel accueille l'appel en partie. Seulement sa décision sur la question de la loi applicable est notée ici. La proposition principale des appelants veut que le débat soit régi par la loi du Nouveau-Brunswick, puisque Castor y a été incorporée. De façon subsidiaire, les appelants plaident que c'est la loi ontarienne qui s'applique au litige parce que ce serait l'endroit où Widdrington a reçu l'information trompeuse et a subi la perte économique réclamée. La Cour décide que l'indépendance du comptable agissant à titre de vérificateur est consacrée tant en droit professionnel que corporatif, et la règle de la *lex societatis* ne peut donc être invoquée en l'espèce.

C'est la *lex loci delicti* qui s'applique. D'un point de vue étatique, le Québec est la seule province intéressée par le respect des normes de conduite et de comportement attendues des professionnels qui œuvrent sur son territoire. Les liens les plus substantiels du dossier renvoient le tribunal invariablement aux activités professionnelles de Coopers à Montréal pour une cliente montréalaise. Le lien avec l'Ontario est ténu. Il repose sur un seul élément: une perte économique y fut subie. Si on devait retenir le lieu du préjudice pour déterminer la loi applicable, il s'ensuivrait une situation à tout le moins chaotique où les comptables montréalais, pour un travail fait en majeure partie à Montréal, pour le compte d'une société montréalaise, verraient leur responsabilité déterminée en fonction d'autant de lois étrangères qu'il y a de demandeurs dont le domicile est étranger. Puisque le comportement fautif ayant donné lieu aux dommages s'est produit principalement au Québec, la juge de première instance s'est bien dirigée en droit et en fait en appliquant les règles du droit civil pour trancher la question de la responsabilité de Coopers.

Book Reviews / Recensions de livres

Le droit de l'OMC et l'agriculture: analyse critique et prospective du système de régulation des subventions agricoles. Par Hervé Agbodjan Prince. Montréal : Éditions Thémis, 2012. 557 pages.

L'ouvrage d'Hervé Agbodjan Prince traite d'un sujet relativement peu connu des juristes, mais qui revêt une importance considérable dans le droit du commerce multilatéral: les subventions agricoles. L'actualité récente de l'Organisation mondiale du commerce (OMC) le confirme. En effet, lors de la récente réunion ministérielle de Bali en décembre 2013, l'OMC a conclu son premier accord depuis sa création en 1995; la question des subventions agricoles a été l'un des points-clés des négociations. Un groupe de pays en développement, le G33, exigeait un assouplissement des règles relatives aux subventions afin de permettre l'achat de denrées destinées à la constitution de stocks à prix administrés. L'Inde, leader de ce groupe d'États, demandait une règle permanente sur ce point. Les pourparlers ont finalement abouti à l'adoption d'une "clause de paix" par laquelle les membres s'engagent à ne pas porter plainte contre les mesures de subventionnement et à rechercher des solutions pérennes d'ici la prochaine conférence ministérielle de 2017. L'actualité récente de l'OMC témoigne par conséquent de la pertinence et de l'importance du sujet.

Tiré de sa thèse de doctorat, le livre d'Agbodjan Prince, fait 555 pages, dont 406 pages de développement. Il se propose d'analyser le système des subventionnements agricoles à la lumière des règles du commerce multilatéral et de proposer des pistes de réforme "du système de régulation multilatéral." L'objectif affirmé de la recherche est double: d'une part, mesurer l'effectivité du droit de l'OMC relatif aux subventions agricoles et, d'autre part, mesurer l'efficacité du système qui en assure la mise en œuvre.

L'approche se veut novatrice, originale et résolument favorable à l'intégration de l'agriculture dans le droit commun de l'OMC. En effet, l'auteur, fervent défenseur du commerce multilatéral, "milite" tout au long de l'étude pour un abandon de la spécificité agricole qu'il qualifie de "péché originel" du droit du commerce international. C'est sur ce postulat qu'est construite l'analyse critique et prospective du cadre normatif des subventions agricoles.

L'ouvrage commence dans l'introduction par une critique de la spécificité agricole et des tenants de la reconnaissance de cette spécificité selon lesquels le commerce agricole ne devrait pas dépendre exclusivement des lois du marché. S'il reconnaît que l'agriculture présente des spécificités en raison de son caractère vital, il conteste son traitement juridique spécifique au nom de l'efficacité économique, notamment pour les pays en développement. Cette critique de la spécificité agricole est traitée, selon nous, de manière trop rapide pour être pleinement convaincante. Si l'on perçoit clairement l'argument selon lequel cette "spécificité" nuit à la création d'un ordre juridique commercial unique et uniforme pour tous les produits, il est en revanche plus difficile pour le lecteur d'en mesurer les enjeux concrets pour les États et pour les peuples. Une mise en perspective de cette "spécificité" de l'agriculture dans l'ordre commercial avec les droits de l'homme, et particulièrement le droit à l'alimentation, aurait été utile dans cette introduction au même titre que des données économiques et sociologiques (et la littérature sur ces questions est abondante) relatives à l'agriculture et à l'alimentation du monde. On aurait ainsi aimé trouver dans cette introduction riche et longue (cinquante-cinq pages) des informations sur la sécurité alimentaire et des chiffres sur le commerce international des produits agricoles, comme le fait que près d'un milliard d'êtres humains souffrent de la faim et 80 % d'entre eux sont des agriculteurs de pays en développement. Si l'agriculture constitue toujours un point d'achoppement des négociations internationales, sa part dans le commerce mondial demeure faible: seuls 10 à 11 % de produits agricoles font l'objet d'échanges internationaux.

De manière "désincarnée" et détachée des données factuelles, le commerce des produits agricoles est appréhendé dans cette étude à travers le prisme du droit de l'OMC et de la libéralisation des échanges: l'auteur précise dans cette introduction que "la régulation multilatérale initiée et menée par l'OMC ... constitue le cadre de cette étude." L'objet de l'étude est donc tout autant l'étude du droit des subventions agricoles dans le cadre de l'OMC que l'organisation mondiale du commerce elle-même, ce que l'auteur appelle "l'étude du cadre structurel des subventions." L'objet de l'étude est donc particulièrement vaste: il s'étend de la notion de subventions à l'analyse des règles du subventionnement en passant par l'asymétrie des pouvoirs de négociation au sein de l'OMC.

La méthode d'analyse choisie est "l'analyse économique": on comprend à la lecture qu'il s'agit d'apprécier la pertinence du droit positif dans le commerce agricole à la lumière des concepts d'efficacité et d'efficience. Les longs développements de l'introduction sur l'histoire de la pensée économique, de A. Smith à nos jours, ne permettent toutefois pas toujours de savoir avec certitude à quelle école de l'analyse économique se rattache l'auteur. S'agit-il d'apprécier l'effectivité des règles de droit, leur efficacité au regard des objectifs de développement ou au regard de l'objectif de libéralisation des échanges et d'abandon de la spécificité agricole? Les développements organisés en deux parties ne permettent pas toujours aux lecteurs d'en avoir une idée précise.

La première partie intitulée "Du *GATT* à l'OMC: le cadre de régulation des politiques de subventionnement agricole," formée de 2 chapitres, s'attache à retracer l'histoire des politiques et des normes qui régissent les subventions agricoles depuis le *General Agreement on Tariffs and Trade* (*GATT*) de 1947 jusqu'au cycle de Doha.

Le premier chapitre est consacré à une étude détaillée et historique du traitement particulier réservé au secteur agricole. Après avoir montré que le "péché originel", l'exception agricole, naît avec le *GATT* de 1947, l'auteur en analyse les fondements économiques, politiques et sociaux. L'intervention de l'État et les politiques de soutien des pays industrialisés poursuivaient — et poursuivent encore — des objectifs de sécurité alimentaire, de garantie de revenus décents aux agriculteurs et d'accroissement de la compétitivité sur les marchés extérieurs. De nombreuses dérogations ponctuelles ont été accordées par le *GATT* de 1947 aux pays industrialisés; il faut attendre le *Kennedy Round* puis la mise en place du TSD (du traitement spécial et différencié) pour que l'exception agricole soit étendue aux pays en développement. Ce "péché originel" se serait ensuite "enraciné dans les politiques publiques" des États, principalement des États-Unis et des États membres de la Communauté européenne, par l'instauration de la Politique agricole commune (PAC). Le régime institué par le *GATT* de 1947 n'a pas su, nous dit l'auteur, "définir un cadre juridique rigoureux pour le commerce agricole"; le subventionnement agricole est demeuré le parent pauvre des négociations multilatérales jusqu'au cycle de l'Uruguay.

Le second chapitre traite précisément du cycle de l'Uruguay et "de la réintégration de l'agriculture au 'droit commun' de l'OMC à l'émergence du système de régulation du subventionnement agricole." En réalité, il faudrait parler d'intégration plus que de réintégration puisque l'étude montre que jusqu'aux accords de Marrakech, l'agriculture relevait d'un régime spécifique. Les accords de Marrakech marquent une "réintégration" de l'agriculture dans le droit commun du commerce multilatéral: le commerce des produits agricoles est désormais soumis aux principes fondamentaux des accords de 1994, aux accords multilatéraux de l'annexe I-A et aux dispositions de l'*Accord sur l'Agriculture*. Ce sont ces accords qui constituent le nouveau cadre normatif du commerce agricole et du subventionnement agricole. La conclusion de l'*Accord sur l'Agriculture* marque pour l'auteur la fin de l'exception agricole, au moins d'un point de vue formel; le système d'engagements de réduction des mesures de soutien amorce un processus de réforme des règles de subventionnement agricole.

L'analyse du régime juridique applicable au subventionnement agricole particulièrement détaillée, appuyée sur une étude exhaustive des textes et de la jurisprudence, permet de prendre la mesure de la complexité de la notion même de subvention au sens du droit commercial multilatéral. Aux termes de l'article de l'*Accord sur les subventions et les mesures compensatoires*, une subvention se caractérise par la réunion de trois éléments: une contribution financière, un financement public et un avantage conféré au destinataire de la subvention. Cette définition d'une apparente simplicité suscite nombre de contentieux et de débats pour déterminer avec précision quelles sont les subventions interdites et celles qui peuvent donner lieu à l'octroi de droits compensateurs. En matière agricole, le subventionnement est entendu comme toutes formes de soutien à l'agriculture, les mesures de soutien interne de la "boîte orange" et les mesures de soutien à l'exportation. L'*Accord sur l'Agriculture* instaure une distinction entre les subventions à l'exportation proprement dites, les mesures d'effet équivalant aux subventions à l'exportation et les mesures de contournement. Pour l'auteur "cette distinction fragilise le cadre réglementaire des subventions" et ouvre un "espace d'impunité" pour les États qui subventionnent leurs secteurs agricoles. Derrière l'aide alimentaire internationale se dissimulent souvent des subventions à l'exportation. L'encadrement des mesures de soutien internes laisse lui aussi une large — trop large pour l'auteur — marge de manœuvre aux États: les critères des soutiens de la "boîte bleue" et de la "boîte verte" devraient au moins être clarifiés.

On l'aura compris, dans la première partie de l'ouvrage, l'auteur fait une étude exhaustive des règles juridiques qui régissent le commerce agricole et les subventions agricoles depuis 1947 et de leur effectivité. Il en conclut que le droit positif ne permet pas de véritablement faire entrer l'agriculture dans le "droit commun" du commerce multilatéral; plus encore que le subventionnement constitue un obstacle au développement des pays en développement.

La seconde partie de l'ouvrage, "Limites et nouvelles perspectives pour le système de régulation des subventions agricoles," est plus prospective. Le premier chapitre, qui remet en question "[l]'efficacité et l'effectivité du système de régulation des subventions agricoles," s'appuie non seulement sur le droit positif, mais aussi sur la sociologie juridique et politique. Sont ainsi successivement étudiés les mécanismes de négociation et d'adoption des décisions à l'Organisation mondiale du commerce, les mécanismes de règlement des différends et le système de sanction. Sont également envisagés les rapports de force politiques et les asymétries de pouvoir économique entre les membres de l'OMC. Dans ce chapitre, l'auteur identifie trois catégories de causes de l'inefficacité du système de régulation des subventions agricoles. La première de ces causes est la "faiblesse structurelle" de l'OMC, cadre de régulation du commerce multilatéral; plus précisément, ce sont les techniques de négociation et la règle du consensus qui sont considérées comme des obstacles à l'efficacité. La seconde cause identifiée est l'incohérence et la carence normative. À cet égard, l'exemple des règles relatives aux entreprises commerciales d'État est convaincant. Le régime juridique spécial de ces entreprises qui n'est pas articulé avec celui des subventions agricoles permet aux États de contourner les engagements de réduction des soutiens. L'inefficacité de la régulation tiendrait enfin au mode de règlement des différends et à la mise en œuvre des sanctions en cas de non-conformité.

La régulation juridique des subventions agricoles n'est pas seulement appréhendée en termes d'effectivité, mais aussi d'efficacité. Il s'agit donc de s'interroger également sur "la capacité du système à atteindre ses objectifs." L'auteur met en lumière l'inefficacité du système: en matière agricole les objectifs de suppression progressive des soutiens n'ont pas été atteints. Plus encore, les pays en développement sont les premières victimes de cette inefficacité et des distorsions de concurrence induites par le subventionnement direct ou indirect. La démonstration faite, pour convaincante qu'elle soit, aurait été renforcée par l'apport d'informations chiffrées sur les niveaux de subventionnement et leur évolution du commerce agricole international.

Face à ce constat, Agbodjan Prince propose, dans le second chapitre, des éléments de solution visant deux objectifs principaux: "une refonte du cadre structurel et normatif qui viendrait approfondir l'intégration des pays en développement dans le système multilatéral et une réforme du cadre fonctionnel des négociations agricoles." La première proposition consiste à redéfinir et à moderniser la notion de subvention agricole et de là, à reconstruire le régime juridique des soutiens internes. Cette reconstruction reposerait sur une définition élargie de la subvention et l'intégration des mesures d'effets équivalents dans le champ d'application du droit des subventions à l'exportation (article 9.1 de l'*Accord sur l'Agriculture*). Ensuite, afin d'atteindre l'objectif de développement des pays en développement membres de l'OMC, l'auteur envisage une refonte du Traitement spécial et différencié (TSD) dont bénéficient ces pays et l'instauration d'un système obligatoire d'accès préférentiel aux marchés étrangers. Serait ainsi instituée une obligation d'accorder des préférences commerciales fondées sur des critères objectifs comme le PIB par habitant. Enfin, la troisième série de propositions est d'ordre institutionnel, ou pour reprendre les termes de l'auteur, d'ordre "structuralo-institutionnel." Les réformes envisagées visent à pallier l'asymétrie des pouvoirs de négociation entre pays en développement et pays développés. L'auteur appelle à une institutionnalisation de l'implication de la Conférence des Nations-Unies sur le commerce et le développement (CNUCED) dans les négociations multilatérales agricoles au soutien des pays en développement; l'objectif étant ici de créer une "bipolarisation institutionnelle" au sein de l'OMC. L'idée est séduisante, mais ne serait pas sans soulever de difficultés: difficultés politiques liées à la souveraineté des États, d'une part; difficultés juridiques relatives à la substitution d'une organisation internationale à des États souverains, d'autre part.

L'ouvrage d'Agbodjan Prince est riche et ambitieux; ses développements démontrent une solide connaissance du droit international économique et du droit du commerce multilatéral. Qu'il partage ou non la foi de l'auteur dans le libre-échange et son combat contre la spécificité agricole, tout juriste (étudiant, avocat, universitaire ou membre d'une organisation non gouvernementale) qui s'intéresse à la question agricole y trouvera une source importante d'informations et de réflexion. On regrettera toutefois que les questions de la spécificité agricole et des subventions ne soient à aucun moment appréhendées sous l'angle de la sécurité alimentaire, du droit à l'alimentation et de la souveraineté alimentaire; les récentes négociations de Bali nous ont montré combien la sécurité et la souveraineté alimentaire pèsent sur l'adoption d'une nouvelle réglementation du subventionnement agricole.

CATHERINE DEL CONT
Enseignante-chercheure HDR à la Faculté de droit de Nantes
Laboratoire UMR CNRS Droit et Changement social

The Interpretation of International Investment Law: Equality, Discrimination and Minimum Standards of Treatment in Historical Context. By Todd Weiler. Leiden: Martinus Nijhoff, 2013. 526 pages.

Anyone who has followed the development of international investment law and the explosion of investor-state arbitration — the distinctive mechanism that permits a foreign investor to seek damages for a state's breach of its investment treaty obligations — will be aware that investor-state awards have sometimes reached inconsistent conclusions regarding the interpretation of the basic investor protection provisions found in more than 3,000 treaties worldwide. There is disagreement regarding the nature and seriousness of the problem. However, few would deny that inconsistency in investor-state arbitration awards and the resulting uncertainty regarding investment law obligations is a significant concern. Indeed, many would agree that it threatens the legitimacy of investor-state arbitration. In this context, a systematic analysis is sorely needed to describe how the broad standards of investor protection should be interpreted. This new book by well-known claimant counsel, arbitrator, and scholar, Todd Weiler, provides such an analysis.

Weiler employs an inductive, historical approach to debunk what he sees as four fundamental myths regarding the meaning of investor-protection standards in investment treaties. He describes these myths as follows:

1. State obligations to provide "protection and security" and "fair and equitable treatment" (FET) to foreign investors are both part of the customary international law minimum standard

for the treatment of aliens (CILMSTA) and, as such, "neither standard portends a meaning independent from that which is intended under the CILMSTA."

2. "The only way it has ever been possible to demonstrate non-compliance with the CILMSTA has been to satisfy the orthodox test of establishing binding international custom (that is, by tendering sufficient evidence of State practice and *opinio juris* — about the existence of a specific rule of conduct — to rebut the (implicit) assumption that State action cannot be bound absent explicit consent)."

3. "[T]he FET standard is either a facsimile or a limited outgrowth of the customary international law prohibition against denial of justice. As a general rule, denials of justice can only occur through a systemic failure of the administration of justice in the host state."

4. Non-compliance with either a national treatment or a most-favoured nation treatment obligation in an investment treaty "can only be established in cases where it has also been demonstrated that host state officials intended to discriminate on the basis of nationality."

Weiler's essential argument is that these myths have been embraced by arbitrators and commentators but "do not measure up to the scrutiny of historical analysis." While it is likely that not everyone will agree with all of Weiler's conclusions regarding these "myths," there is no doubt that he has marshalled an impressive array of historical evidence in support of his analysis, going back, in some cases, thousands of years for examples of state practice. His work also displays an impressive fluency with arbitral decisions, treaty practice, and secondary commentary on international investment law. In both ways, it represents a significant contribution to the rapidly expanding literature on international investment law.

Following an introductory chapter, Weiler sets out his approach to treaty interpretation in Chapter 2. He rejects seeking the state parties' subjective intention and what he calls an "abstract exercise in plain language construction." Instead, he adopts an inductive approach based on the work of well-known international law scholar Georg Schwarzenberger that seeks to give meaning to investment treaty provisions based on an understanding of their historical development. Without this historical guidance, he argues, interpretation is reduced to a "rudderless excursion in subjective analysis." Weiler argues that to resort to subjective intention is especially pernicious in the context of investor-state arbitration. Where an investor is challenging a state's action as contrary to its obligations, allowing arguments by the state regarding what it meant at the time it signed the treaty would accord a significant and inappropriate advantage to the state in defending against the investor's claim. He also rejects one common prescription for enhancing certainty and consistency in arbitral decision making — greater efforts by arbitral tribunals to follow well-established trends in the interpretation of specific provisions. Of course, this is not surprising, since Weiler views many established trends as wrong-headed.

In Chapter 3, Weiler traces the development of the customary international law standard requiring states to provide "protection and security" to foreign investors. Using his inductive approach, he catalogues state practice with respect to host state protection of foreigners engaged in commercial activities — not limited to investment — beginning with the Bronze Age. He comes to the conclusion that, historically, protection and security represented an obligation for states to honour specific commitments undertaken to foreigners and, more significantly, to "make good faith efforts to provide protection and security to foreigners and their legal interests." His strong conclusion that protection and security was not just an obligation to protect property rights is tempered by his view that this obligation did not require a state to go beyond the protection provided to its own citizens.[1]

Chapter 4 provides an interesting portrayal of how, in Weiler's view, developed countries — with the complicity of leading scholars of international investment law — hijacked the customary protection and security rule and transformed it into a "standard of civilization" that was used to justify European policies of expansion and colonization. He uses two examples to demonstrate that international investment has a Euro-centric character and is fundamentally malleable: European oppression of the Haudenosaunee Confederacy, a First Nation whose territory straddles the border of what are now Canada and the United States, and the Qing Dynasty in China. Weiler argues that both were societies that respected the basic protection and security standard but were exploited as being

---

[1] Some other commentators note that this standard is traditionally limited to the protection of property, though some arbitral awards have adopted a broader interpretation. See Andrew Newcombe and Lluis Paradell, *Law and Practice of International Investment Law: Standards of Protection* (Deventer: Wolters Kluwer, 2009) at 308, 310-13.

uncivilized by European powers. This exposition produces important insights into the nature of international legal relations in the
eighteenth and nineteenth centuries, illuminating key aspects of
the historical context for contemporary international investment
law, including why assertions of a minimum customary standard of
investor protection have been viewed with suspicion by developing
countries.

In the remainder of this chapter, Weiler leads the reader through
developments in the use of protection and security in treaties, especially the friendship, commerce, and navigation treaties negotiated by the United States, describing how protection and security
standards contributed to the development of contemporary human
rights law. Finally, he describes how, beginning in the 1920s, treaty
provisions adopted by developed countries added "full" or "constant" to protection and security or set out additional proscriptions
for arbitrary or discriminatory treatment. He argues that these
additions were part of a deliberate, two-pronged strategy of developed countries to improve investor protection. The first and
more obvious prong was to create treaty provisions that would
guarantee greater protection than was required under the customary international law standard of protection and security. The second
prong was to argue that these words modifying the customary
international law protection and security standard should be understood as integral parts of the customary standard. Weiler argues that
developed countries sought to revise the customary standard in this
way to provide a level of protection in excess of the true historical
customary law standard that he describes in Chapter 3.

In Chapter 5, he plunges into what has become one of the most
complex contemporary issues regarding investor protection: to
what extent FET is part of customary international law. Weiler's
clear answer is that FET was first adopted as a treaty standard. He
argues forcefully that its origin was in treaties establishing mixed
claims commissions, such as the Mexico-US Claims Commission.
These treaties created a state obligation of equitable treatment to
ensure that commissions had a broad, if uncertain, standard to
apply to state behaviour. The breadth of "fair and equitable treatment" encouraged first the United States and then other developed
countries to adopt this language beginning seven decades ago in
various international economic law treaties to express a basic commitment to provide non-discriminatory and equal treatment that
goes beyond customary international law. Part of the subsequent
confusion regarding the extent to which FET was part of customary

law was caused by what Weiler characterizes as an intentional lack of specificity in that regard in the treaty language used. Developing his argument in Chapter 4, he asserts that the United States and other developed countries adopted this approach to support their efforts to characterize FET as incorporated in the minimum standard of treatment under customary law.

Chapter 6 is a scathing critique of the 2001 interpretation of the FET obligation in Article 1105 of the *North American Free Trade Agreement* (*NAFTA*), which was adopted by the Free Trade Commission (FTC), a ministerial level body created under the treaty. The commission said the obligation to provide "treatment in accordance with international law, including fair and equitable treatment and full protection and security" was no more than an obligation to meet the customary international law standard for the treatment of aliens. Weiler describes the statement as an abrupt and "disingenuous" reversal of the US position described in Chapter 5 that attempted to cut back the level of protection in Article 1105 to the level of the historical customary law standard. He cites evidence that, at least as recently as 1996, US officials considered FET to be additive to customary law. He explains the statement as a "panicky" response by Canadian and US government officials to cases being brought by investors against Canada and the United States. The statement has meant that "tribunals have accordingly been left to grope around, as if in the dark, for a means of interpreting FET provisions with any degree of coherence." He proceeds to review the arbitral awards made under *NAFTA* and other treaties following the FTC statement and comes to the somewhat controversial conclusion that most post-2001 awards have interpreted the customary international law standard as requiring what the FET standard demands in any case.[2] In other words, despite the origin of FET as a purely treaty-based standard to supplement the customary law minimum standard and the FTC's interpretation, the enhanced protection provided by FET is being treated as part of the customary standard.

Chapter 7 is devoted to a lengthy exegesis of what FET requires. Weiler considers the role of FET in prohibiting arbitrary and un-

---

[2] Newcombe and Paradell conclude that investment arbitration awards support the view that fair and equitable treatment (FET) remains a separate treaty-based standard (*ibid* at 269). See the similar conclusion reached in Patrick Dumberry, *The Fair and Equitable Treatment Standard: A Guide to NAFTA Case Law on Article 1105* (Deventer: Wolters Kluwer, 2013) at 307.

reasonable conduct as well as in the denial of justice. He also wrestles with the difficult distinction between what FET requires and what constitutes indirect expropriation requiring state compensation under international investment law. He argues that the most illuminating approach to understanding FET is to view it as a requirement for good faith behaviour by states and as a prohibition on abuse of rights. Somewhat surprisingly, apart from a reference in a footnote at the end of the chapter, Weiler does not address what some consider the most important and controversial element of FET: the extent to which it protects the legitimate expectations of investors.[3]

In Chapters 8 and 9, Weiler turns his attention to national treatment and most favoured nation (MFN) treatment. He argues that MFN is the key obligation in the *General Agreement on Tariffs and Trade* (*GATT*), and its main purpose is to ensure that tariff concessions are extended to all *GATT* parties (now World Trade Organization (WTO) members). He characterizes the national treatment obligation as intended only to ensure that states do not undermine their tariff commitments by internal measures that discriminate against foreign goods. In the investment context, by contrast, national treatment obligations play a fundamental role in ensuring no less favourable treatment to investors in connection with all things that governments do, so long as the treaty protection lasts. The goal, he suggests, is to guarantee equality of competitive opportunity. In light of their different purposes, Weiler argues that the well-developed approach to interpreting national treatment and MFN in the trade context should not be applied to investment treaty provisions guaranteeing national treatment and MFN. To support his argument, Weiler provides a very lengthy discussion in Chapter 8 of the negotiations leading up to the adoption of the *GATT*, with its national treatment and MFN treatment obligations in 1947 and the concurrent failure of the parties to agree to set up an International Trade Organization (ITO) that would have involved some weak obligations regarding investment. The United States' suggestion that there should be limited non-discrimination obligations in the ITO Charter did not even make it into the final draft. Instead, the obligations were introduced in bilateral investment treaties. Weiler's interesting historical account explains the distinct origins of these similar non-discrimination obligations in the trade and investment contexts, but it would have been interesting to read more about how these different origin stories demonstrate that the provisions should be interpreted differently.

---

[3] See, for example, *ibid* at 137-70, 315-16.

Weiler's principal goal in Chapter 9 is to provide additional, more specific arguments to explain why the approach to non-discrimination obligations as they exist in international trade law should not be applied to their interpretation in the investment context. His particular concern is to argue that it should not be necessary to show that a state intended to discriminate on the basis of nationality to find a treaty breach in investment law cases. He provides several compelling arguments. In addition to the absence of language indicating that an intention to discriminate is necessary in investment treaty provisions, he suggests that investors should not have the burden of proving state intention because they have more to lose than traders. Consequently, investors should have a lower burden to establish that a state has failed to comply with its obligations.

As with any treatise, one may critique some of Weiler's specific arguments. For example, in his zeal to distinguish national treatment under the *GATT* from the similar obligation under investment law, Weiler presents a less-than-fully developed conception of national treatment in the trade law context. The purpose of national treatment in the *GATT* was never confined to preventing circumvention of MFN, as he suggests. It was also intended to provide equality of competitive opportunities to imported products compared to domestic goods, a rationale that is similar to what Weiler suggests animates national treatment in the investment context. Over time, this other role for national treatment has become more prominent in the trade context.[4] As well, WTO jurisprudence on MFN reveals a much less consistent and pronounced emphasis on finding state intent to discriminate than Weiler's portrayal suggests.[5] Nevertheless, overall, his assertion that trade-based approaches should not be used in interpreting national treatment and MFN obligations in investment treaties is convincing. Investor-state arbitration awards, as Weiler suggests, confirm that arbitration tribunals are following an independent approach.

Some may find a few of his other conclusions harder to accept. His assertion that investor-state tribunal awards demonstrate a consensus in favour of the conclusion that FET forms part of customary law, for example, is difficult to reconcile with arbitral awards to date and, as noted, runs counter to the views of other commentators.

[4] Nicholas DiMascio and Joost Pauwelyn, "Nondiscrimination in Trade and Investment Treaties: Worlds Apart of Two Sides of the Same Coin" (2008) 102 AJIL 48 at 60.
[5] *Ibid* at 62-66.

Overall, however, Weiler's book provides a treasure trove of historical references, especially regarding US treaty practice and its rationale, which will be a very useful resource for subsequent scholars and others interested in investment law. Perhaps, more importantly, his historically supported narrative for the development of basic investor protection obligations provides a potentially fruitful approach that may help to address the significant problem of inconsistent interpretation of these standards by investment tribunals.

J. Anthony VanDuzer
Professor, Common Law Section, University of Ottawa

Law on the Battlefield. Par A.P.V. Rogers. 3ᵉ edition. Manchester, Manchester University Press, 2012. 384 pages.

Le droit international humanitaire (DIH) ne cherche pas à éliminer la guerre, mais plutôt à humaniser les conditions dans lesquelles elle est menée. Issu du droit international public, ce droit

peut être défini comme une branche du droit international qui limite l'usage de la violence dans les conflits armés pour : a) épargner celles et ceux qui ne participent pas — ou plus — directement aux hostilités ; b) la restreindre au niveau nécessaire pour atteindre le but du conflit qui — indépendamment des causes au nom desquelles on se bat — ne peut viser qu'à affaiblir le potentiel militaire de l'ennemi.[1]

Bien que ses règles soient généralement acceptées par les États, comme en fait foi l'ensemble des ratifications des *Conventions de Genève* et de leurs protocoles,[2] il faut, pour qu'elles aient un effet réel, qu'elles soient mises en application sur le terrain par les forces armées nationales. D'ailleurs, bien qu'il s'agisse d'une des branches du droit international les plus codifiées, le DIH n'est toujours pas appliqué dans sa totalité par les militaires, soit parce que la règle n'est pas assez précise, soit parce qu'il y a restriction de temps,

---

[1] Marco Sassòli, Antoine A. Bouvier et Anne Quentin, *Un droit dans la guerre? Cas, documents et supports d'enseignement relatifs à la pratique contemporaine du droit international humanitaire. Volume 1: Présentation du droit humanitaire*, 2ᵉ éd, Genève, Comité international de la Croix-Rouge, 2012, à la p 1.

[2] En effet, les quatre *Conventions de Genève* ont été entérinées chacune par 194 États, tandis que le *Protocole I* l'a été par 177 États, le *Protocole II* par 163 États et

soit parce que la situation est inédite. Tous ces obstacles à l'application efficace du DIH peuvent s'expliquer notamment par l'écart important qui subsiste entre le droit tel que théorisé par les universitaires, et les situations concrètes auxquelles sont confrontés les militaires.

C'est pour répondre à ce problème qu'APV Rogers a écrit *Law on the Battlefield*,[3] dont la première édition a été récompensée par le prix Paul Reuter remis par le Comité international de la Croix-Rouge en 1997, et dont la dernière édition, la troisième, a été publiée en 2012. Si une personne a le profil pour relever ce défi de taille, il s'agit bien d'APV Rogers. D'une part, il a eu une carrière militaire remarquable: il a atteint le rang de Major-général en 1994 et a occupé le poste de directeur des services juridiques de l'armée britannique. D'autre part, il a entrepris une carrière universitaire tout aussi réussie; il a notamment été *Senior Fellow* au *Lauterpacht Center for International Law* de l'Université Cambridge.

Sans introduction ni conclusion, le livre comprend douze chapitres, dont trois sont un ajout à la deuxième édition. Dans son livre, Rogers ne procède pas à une recension systématique des règles du DIH, mais aborde plutôt de manière critique ses principaux énoncés, et ce, à la lumière des problèmes courants vécus par les forces armées lors de la conduite des hostilités. Comme l'indique l'auteur, "l'idée était de prendre une proposition du droit humanitaire, d'examiner ses origines historiques et sa compréhension actuelle, d'examiner les problèmes d'interprétation et d'application, particulièrement en fonction de l'expérience, et de parvenir à une conclusion sur la méthode d'application" [notre traduction].[4]

Les lecteurs sont ainsi amenés à se familiariser avec les principales règles et principes du DIH ainsi qu'avec les différents débats qu'ils suscitent, et ce, dans un langage clair et précis, rendant ainsi le livre accessible à un large public, qu'il s'agisse de commandants militaires

---

finalement le *Protocole III*, le plus récent (2005), par 114 États, dont cinquante-cinq ne sont que signataires. Comité international de la Croix-Rouge, "Les Conventions de Genève de 1949 et leurs Protocoles additionnels," en ligne: icrc. org <http://www.icrc.org/fre/war-and-law/treaties-customary-law/geneva -conventions/index.jsp>.

3 APV Rogers, *Law on the Battlefield*, 3ᵉ éd, Manchester, Manchester University Press, 2012.

4 *Ibid* à la p xx.

sans notions approfondies de droit humanitaire ou d'avocats sans expérience du champ de bataille. Le résultat est un livre de référence actualisé en matière de conduite des hostilités par les forces armées de terre. Le livre ne remet pas en question la dynamique du DIH ni l'adéquation entre ses grands principes et les changements toujours plus rapides sur le terrain. Bien au contraire, l'auteur adopte une vision conservatrice du droit, s'alignant ainsi sur le courant dominant du positivisme juridique.

Le premier chapitre porte sur les principes généraux du DIH. L'auteur y définit l'ensemble des concepts centraux, comme la notion d'attaque, de conflit armé ou encore les principes d'humanité, de nécessité militaire et de proportionnalité, concepts qui seront repris tout au long de l'ouvrage. Il poursuit avec un chapitre sur les forces ennemies (chapitre 2) et un autre sur les blessés, les malades et les naufragés (chapitre 3), définissant les contours de ces catégories ainsi que les protections qui y sont rattachées. Les trois chapitres qui suivent portent respectivement sur la notion d'objectif militaire (chapitre 4), les précautions à prendre lors d'une attaque (chapitre 5) et celles à prendre pour limiter les effets d'une attaque (chapitre 6). L'auteur aborde ensuite des régimes de droit spécialisés, soit celui sur les biens culturels, protégés par la *Convention pour la protection des biens culturels lors de conflit armé* (chapitre 7); sur l'environnement, protégé notamment par la *Convention sur l'interdiction d'utiliser des techniques de modification de l'environnement à des fins militaires ou toutes autres fins hostiles* (chapitre 8); sur l'occupation militaire (chapitre 9); et finalement sur la conduite des hostilités lors de conflits armés internes (chapitre 10). L'auteur conclut sur la responsabilité du commandant (chapitre 11) et sur la mise en œuvre du droit humanitaire (chapitre 12).

L'auteur a choisi de se concentrer sur les règles qui sont pertinentes pour les militaires lors des opérations de l'armée de terre; par conséquent, il n'aborde les règles encadrant les opérations aériennes et navales que de manière marginale. Ce choix impose aussi une limite quant aux règles qu'il aborde. Ainsi, dans la section portant sur l'occupation, l'auteur limite son analyse aux règles directement liées à l'action militaire; "les sujets de nature plus politique, comme jusqu'où la puissance occupante peut légitimement modifier la structure politique et économique du territoire occupé, ne sont pas abordés" [notre traduction].[5]

---

[5] *Ibid* à la p 238.

Ce désir de s'en tenir à des problématiques auxquelles les militaires sont directement confrontés a l'avantage de permettre à l'auteur d'atteindre son objectif, soit de faire le lien entre les règles théoriques et la réalité. La retenue dans le nombre de règles abordées assure un degré élevé de précision pour expliquer les différentes obligations qui y sont liées, ce qui est nécessaire pour assurer leur mise en œuvre efficace, en particulier dans des domaines plus techniques. De cette façon, l'auteur détaille les différents types de protection qui existent pour les biens culturels (la protection de base, la protection spéciale et la protection améliorée), ainsi que les différentes mesures qu'un commandant doit prendre avant de lancer une attaque contre un bâtiment protégé. Le même souci du détail se retrouve dans le chapitre consacré à la protection de l'environnement, dans lequel l'auteur énumère plusieurs types d'armes afin de juger de leur légalité compte tenu des dommages qu'ils causent à l'environnement. Dernier exemple, dans le chapitre consacré aux blessés, aux malades et aux naufragés, l'auteur précise le type d'armes que peut porter le personnel médical ainsi que les motifs qui justifient leur utilisation. Bien que ces règles soient parfois extrêmement techniques, leur compréhension est nécessaire pour en assurer le respect. Loin d'un ouvrage de droit théorique, l'auteur fait constamment le lien entre le droit humanitaire et la réalité sur le terrain, tirant certains exemples de l'actualité récente.

Entre la deuxième et la troisième édition, huit ans se sont écoulés et plusieurs évènements se sont en effet produits sur le plan juridique, autant avec la parution notamment du *Guide interprétatif sur la notion de participation directe aux hostilités en droit international humanitaire*[6] par le Comité international de la Croix-Rouge et le rôle de plus en plus important des avocats militaires, que sur le plan universitaire avec la publication des deux volumes intitulés *Le Droit international humanitaire coutumier*,[7] et le plan militaire, avec les problématiques très actuelles concernant la torture, les détentions de terroristes présumés et les hostilités en Afghanistan et en Irak. Ces nouveaux développements ont été pris en compte par l'auteur lors de la réédition, améliorant ainsi la qualité du volume. Les trois nouveaux chapitres, soit celui sur les malades, les blessés et les

---

6 Nils Melzer, *Guide interprétatif sur la notion de participation directe aux hostilités en droit international humanitaire*, Genève, Comité international de la Croix-Rouge, 2010.

7 Jean-Marie Henckaerts et Louise Doswald-Beck, dir, *Customary International Humanitarian Law*, Cambridge, Cambridge University Press, 2005.

naufragés (chapitre 3), celui sur l'occupation militaire (chapitre 9) et celui sur la mise en œuvre et le respect du droit humanitaire (chapitre 12), sont autant d'exemples de cette volonté de l'auteur d'examiner les problématiques actuelles. Comme le mentionne Michael N. Schmitt dans la préface, les évènements actuels ont démontré la complexité de ces enjeux, que ce soit l'utilisation de transports médicaux à des fins militaires, les différents défis rencontrés lors de l'occupation d'un territoire en Afghanistan, en Irak ou en Palestine, ou encore, les effets dévastateurs des violations importantes du DIH lorsqu'elles sont publicisées.[8]

Le traitement de la question des prisonniers lors de l'occupation d'un territoire illustre très bien cette volonté d'ancrer son livre dans le débat actuel. L'auteur commence par rappeler que de nombreux crimes de guerre et crimes contre l'humanité ont eu lieu dans des centres de détention. Pour illustrer la situation existante, Rogers soulève le cas de Baha Mousa, un civil irakien décédé lors de sa captivité sous autorité anglaise, un évènement qui a donné lieu à une commission d'enquête dont le rapport, publié en 2011, met en lumière les pratiques discutables de l'armée britannique. Il revient aussi sur l'arrêt *Al-Saadoon et Mufdhi c Royaume-Uni*[9] plaidé en 2010 devant la Cour européenne des droits de l'homme et qui portait sur l'application extraterritoriale de la Convention européenne des droits de l'homme. En l'espèce, les requérants ont été arrêtés par les forces britanniques et incarcérés dans un centre de détention administré par les Britanniques. Les autorités britanniques ont finalement décidé de les transférer aux autorités irakiennes. C'est ce transfert qui était contesté devant la Cour européenne.

L'une des raisons qui expliquent le nombre important d'abus commis sur les détenus serait le peu de règles que l'on retrouve sur ce sujet en droit humanitaire. Pour l'auteur, la situation des prisonniers ne peut s'améliorer qu'avec l'adoption de lignes directrices claires, qu'il définit à la toute fin de la partie sur les prisonniers de guerre. Il est évident que cette section, relativement longue par rapport aux autres, est une réponse directe aux évènements récents. L'auteur n'a pas simplement augmenté le nombre de sujets abordés, il a aussi mis à jour les différents débats et exemples auxquels faisait référence la deuxième édition. De ce fait, il renvoie à l'étude publiée en 2010 par la Croix-Rouge, aux derniers jugements du Tribunal pénal international pour l'ex-Yougoslavie, aux

---

[8] APV Rogers, *Law on the Battlefield*, *supra* note 3 à la p xvii.

[9] N° 61498/08, CEDH 2010.

opérations en Irak et en Afghanistan, aux derniers manuels militaires et enfin à des articles savants récents. Cette actualisation du contenu est essentielle pour que l'ouvrage puisse rapprocher le droit et la pratique selon son objectif.

Bien qu'il s'agisse d'un excellent livre de référence, il ne permet pas réellement de se questionner sur les fondements du droit humanitaire ou encore sur son utilité. Au contraire, l'auteur adopte un point de vue conservateur en symbiose avec le positivisme juridique. Ceci est évident lorsqu'il fait l'historique des règles. Il n'y a aucune explication des débats, des positions adoptées, des enjeux ou encore des raisons qui expliquent la règle actuelle, ce qui perpétue le mythe selon lequel le droit est apolitique. Cette omission s'explique peut-être par la brièveté des historiques.

Le point de vue positiviste de l'auteur est aussi illustré par la place importante qu'il accorde aux traités par rapport à la coutume. En effet, la règle coutumière n'est habituellement mentionnée que lorsqu'aucune règle conventionnelle n'existe. Ainsi, lorsque l'auteur parle de la perfidie et des ruses de guerre, il ne fait pas référence à l'étude réalisée par la Croix-Rouge sur le droit humanitaire coutumier, mais seulement au Protocole additionnel 1. Cela pourrait s'expliquer par la volonté de l'auteur de limiter au maximum les incertitudes et les zones grises contenues dans le DIH. D'ailleurs, l'auteur utilise la jurisprudence, non pas comme preuve d'une pratique généralisée, mais comme outil de précision des règles conventionnelles. Par exemple, dans son chapitre sur l'occupation, l'auteur s'appuie sur le jugement de la Cour internationale de Justice pour aborder la question de la colonisation. Il ne s'agit pas d'expliquer les fondements du raisonnement, mais simplement d'illustrer le fait que la colonisation telle que pratiquée par les Israéliens est une violation des *Conventions de Genève*.

L'absence du droit coutumier explique-t-elle l'analyse limitée que l'auteur consacre aux conflits non internationaux? De fait, bien que la majorité des conflits aient aujourd'hui un caractère non international, seul un chapitre est consacré à cette problématique. Peut-être est-ce en raison du fait que c'est un domaine où le droit codifié est presque totalement absent?

L'auteur tente de décrire dans son livre le droit tel qu'il est, de manière neutre et objective, et lorsqu'il se permet une opinion, il prend soin d'utiliser des formules d'atténuation comme "pour l'auteur" ou "l'auteur est d'avis que" pour assurer une séparation claire entre le fait et l'opinion. Cela a donc pour résultat un texte qui se veut neutre et apolitique. L'un des problèmes de cette approche est que certaines difficultés dans la mise en œuvre du droit humanitaire n'ont pas été abordées. Ainsi, les risques liés à la conduite d'une action militaire multilatérale lorsque les obligations internationales des États diffèrent pour chacun n'ont pas été traités. Comme les États ne sont soumis qu'aux obligations contenues dans les traités qu'ils ont ratifiés, en plus des règles coutumières sur lesquelles persiste beaucoup de désaccord, il y a des disparités dans les règles à mettre en œuvre. Il faut donc toujours garder à l'esprit que les règles énumérées dans le livre peuvent ne pas s'appliquer ou encore être plus ou moins sévères selon le pays en cause.

En conclusion, il s'agit d'un ouvrage de référence pour toutes les personnes qui s'intéressent au droit humanitaire et aux problématiques qui y sont liées, même si certaines questions comme celle des réfugiés ou encore des victimes de la guerre n'ont pas été abordées. La structure du livre, quoique peu innovatrice, a permis à l'auteur de classer les principales règles du DIH dans différentes catégories, permettant ainsi aux lecteurs de s'y retrouver facilement. De plus, la clarté et la justesse du langage ainsi que l'actualisation des enjeux permettent une lecture aisée de sujets parfois très techniques. Bien ancré dans son positivisme juridique, l'auteur n'innove pas énormément, livrant un résumé du droit humanitaire conventionnel. Cependant, dans cet ouvrage, l'auteur a réussi son pari de rapprocher la pratique de la guerre aux règles qui l'encadrent. Ce qui est le plus malheureux avec cet ouvrage, c'est qu'il s'agit de la dernière édition, puisque comme l'auteur nous l'apprend dans son avant-propos, il prend officiellement sa retraite du monde universitaire.

CLAUDINE BOUVIER
Doctorante, Faculté de droit, Université d'Ottawa

Cross-Border Torts: Canadian-U.S. Litigation Strategies. By Wyatt Pickett. Markham: LexisNexis, 2013. 350 pages.

With an estimated 90 percent of the Canadian population living within 100 miles (or 160 kilometres) of the US border,[1] it is not surprising that Canadians would sometimes be implicated in lawsuits involving American parties. A shopper from St. Catharines, Ontario, for instance, might cross the border for a weekend shopping trip in Buffalo, New York, and purchase products in New York

---

[1] "By the Numbers," *CBC News* (15 May 2009), online: CBC News <http://www.cbc.ca/news/canada/by-the-numbers-1.801937>.

that ultimately cause injury in Ontario. Or a resident of Seattle, Washington, might get into a car accident with a British Columbia resident while visiting Stanley Park in Vancouver. The possibilities are endless. To date, no author has endeavoured to consolidate and synopsize, in book form, the legal principles that are relevant to a Canadian litigator's decision to sue in Canada or the United States. Accordingly, Pickett's book fills a gap in the relevant literature and could prove to be a handy resource for litigators confronting cross-border litigation issues.

Pickett's book reflects a solid understanding of the conflict of laws principles of Canada and the United States. The book is very well researched and provides extensive discussion of case law in both jurisdictions. The best part of the book is the practical nuggets of wisdom that Pickett often shares with his readers. For instance, Pickett notes early on that litigators should probably not consider bringing suit in the United States, unless the amount likely to be recovered exceeds $100,000.[2] He also instructs Canadian litigators to not "allow defendants in U.S. actions to define 'Canada' as a forum ... Aggregation of interprovincial contacts into one group of 'Canadian' interests rarely works to the Canadian plaintiff's advantage."[3] These types of insights, which are scattered throughout the book, are the real value-added that Pickett brings to his readers.

Pickett states that his primary objective in writing the book is "to raise awareness within the Canadian plaintiff's bar of the potential circumstances in which an action in the United States *may* benefit the client — and when those advantages become significant enough to make litigation there worthwhile."[4] He emphasizes that his intent is for the book to be a "practical 'beginner's guide' to the multitude of legal concepts which may arise in cross-border tort litigation."[5] Much of this book, however, is written in a manner that does not resemble a "practical beginner's guide" and, as such, is sometimes apt to lose its audience.

Pickett's book is divided into four chapters: an overview chapter and three substantive chapters dealing with the issues of personal jurisdiction, choice of law, and *forum non conveniens*. The structure of the book is somewhat non-intuitive, since Pickett interposes the

---

[2] Wyatt Pickett, *Cross-Border Torts: Canadian-U.S. Litigation Strategies* (Markham: LexisNexis, 2013) at 26.

[3] *Ibid* at 220.

[4] *Ibid* at 5 [emphasis in original].

[5] *Ibid*.

choice of law chapter between jurisdiction and *forum non conveniens* — two doctrines that are customarily considered in tandem. In addition, Pickett only briefly describes judgment enforcement as a relevant consideration for a Canadian litigator in deciding where to sue. The analysis of judgment enforcement feels rushed, particularly for a topic that has the potential to be so significant to litigants and to litigation decisions. There are a number of issues that Pickett's book does not cover (or does not cover in any detail): arbitration or jurisdiction clauses; class actions; defamation; parallel proceedings; pleading or proving foreign law; and Internet jurisdiction. It is not clear whether the choice to omit these topics was deliberate or inadvertent.

The first chapter of Pickett's book ("Considering Cross-Border Torts") discusses forum shopping — or, in the author's preferred words, forum selection.[6] Pickett makes his views on forum shopping clearly known, and, accordingly, the chapter takes on more of an "advocacy" flavour than a "primer" flavour. For example, he refers to judicial admonitions of forum shopping as "schizophrenic and one sided"[7] and states that "[m]uch like an accusation of witchcraft in the 17th century, or an inference of Communist sympathies made in the 1950s, the term 'forum shopping' is employed by one's American adversaries in the hopes of inciting a viscerally negative reaction in the relevant tribunal."[8] Pickett, in fact, refers to the phenomenon of "forum shopping" in quotations throughout the entire chapter, presumably to distance himself from the use of what he considers a pejorative term.

As part of his defence of forum shopping, Pickett briefly discusses the parallel system of federal and state courts in the United States. The topic is not delineated by a heading or anything else to indicate the discussion is significant beyond understanding Pickett's position on forum shopping. In discussing the federal and state court system, Pickett mentions diversity jurisdiction, amount in controversy, pendent jurisdiction, and removal — all in one short paragraph. A Canadian litigator who is unfamiliar with the state/federal court divide in the United States would have benefited from a more fulsome discussion of the topic, particularly because Pickett returns to this divide in the *forum non conveniens* chapter.[9] Moreover, Pickett

---

6 Pickett writes: "'Forum shopping' is nothing more than a pejorative way of referring to the process of *forum selection*" (*ibid* at 6).

7 *Ibid* at 14.

8 *Ibid* at 5-6.

fails to discuss why a litigator, as a strategic matter, would prefer to litigate in state court or in federal court. In a book devoted to discussing the topic of where to sue, a Canadian reader might have expected some guidance on the election between federal or state courts in the United States and not just the election between "Canada" and the "United States," broadly speaking. In the final part of the chapter, Pickett does a very good job identifying the circumstances where a Canadian litigator might consider filing suit in the United States. Pickett clearly lays out the differences in substantive and procedural law between the two countries that might make forum shopping worthwhile for a Canadian litigator. This is one of the most useful sections of the book. Ideally, Pickett would have expanded the section to discuss in more detail the circumstances that could impact forum selection.

Chapter 2 of Pickett's book addresses the topic of personal jurisdiction ("'Where Can I Sue?': A Few Brief Words on Personal Jurisdiction and Territorial Competence"). He notes at the outset of the chapter that his coverage of jurisdiction is abridged in comparison to the other topics in his book, reasoning that "[o]f the three key challenges posed in cross-border litigation, jurisdiction should be the least of your worries — and if it is not, you have an uphill battle ahead of you."[10] This is another of Pickett's practical nuggets of wisdom that is likely to resonate with his intended audience.

Pickett divides his analysis of American law into "general jurisdiction" and "specific jurisdiction." Pickett's lead-in to the discussion[11] could be confusing for a Canadian litigator who would not likely

---

9 For instance, Pickett notes that "actions filed by a plaintiff in state court which possess the requisite diversity between litigants and amounts in controversy may be removed to the federal system by motion of a defendant" *(ibid* at 7). Pickett, however, fails to mention the concept of remand, whereby a federal court may send an action back to state court in the event that it does not possess jurisdiction over the case. Similarly, Pickett does not discuss a very important limitation on the ability of a defendant to remove an action: that a defendant sued in the state court of his domicile cannot remove an action to federal court. See 28 USC § 1441(b)(2) (2012): "A civil action otherwise removable solely on the basis of the jurisdiction under section 1332(a) of this title may not be removed if any of the parties in interest properly joined and served as defendants is a citizen of the State in which such action is brought."

10 Pickett, *supra* note 2 at 34.

11 For instance, Pickett references *International Shoe Co v Washington*, 326 US 310 (1945) [*International Shoe*] multiple times in his discussion of general jurisdiction even though the case, on its facts, dealt with specific jurisdiction (that is, minimum

be familiar with these labels, as Canadian courts do not use the general/specific construct for personal jurisdiction. While Pickett's discussion of general jurisdiction is accurate, it fails to discuss the controversial idea of "doing business" jurisdiction.[12] That is, over the past few decades, lower American courts have endorsed the idea that a company is subject to general jurisdiction if it is "doing business" in the forum, in the sense of having continuous and systematic contacts with the forum. Thus, large companies such as Home Depot and Wal-Mart, for instance, were regarded as being subject to general jurisdiction anywhere they were "doing business." Both American and international commentators have questioned the legitimacy of "doing business" jurisdiction.[13] Pickett alludes to this controversy at the end of his discussion of general jurisdiction, observing that the new "at home" language from the recent *Goodyear Dunlop Tires Operations, SA v Brown* case could place a "significant restriction on the scope of general jurisdiction as previously interpreted."[14] However, he fails to make any mention as to how general jurisdiction

---

contacts). As such, an unfamiliar reader might be puzzled as to why Pickett keeps referring to *International Shoe* when discussing general jurisdiction. The answer is that *International Shoe* first erected the bipartite jurisdictional structure even though general jurisdiction was not relevant or applicable on that case's facts. Moreover, the language of general jurisdiction derived largely from *Helicopteros Nacionales de Colombia, SA v Hall*, 466 US 408 (1984) ("continuous and systematic general business contacts") is oddly similar to the language of specific jurisdiction from *International Shoe*. "[T]he activities carried on in behalf of appellant in the State of Washington were neither irregular nor casual. They were systematic and continuous throughout the years in question" (*ibid* at 320). This similarity in phraseology again has the potential to confuse a Canadian reader who is making a foray into these concepts for the first time.

12 Likewise, Pickett does not mention corporate registration as providing a basis for jurisdiction, whether general or specific. Compare, for example, *The Rockefeller University v Ligand Pharmaceuticals*, 581 F Supp (2d) 461 at 467 (SDNY 2008) ("[Defendant's] unrevoked authorization to do business and its designation of a registered agent for service of process amount to consent to personal jurisdiction in New York") with *Leonard v USA Petroleum*, 829 F Supp 882 at 888-89 (SD Tex 1993) ("[b]y registering to do business, a foreign corporation only *potentially subjects* itself to jurisdiction; it does not subject itself to *potential jurisdiction* ... [i]n complying with the Texas registration statute, USA Petroleum consented to personal jurisdiction in Texas only if the jurisdiction were constitutional").

13 See, for example, Mary Twitchell, "Why We Keep Doing Business with Doing Business Jurisdiction" (2001) U Chicago Legal F 171.

14 Pickett, *supra* note 2 at 40. See also *Goodyear Tires Operations, SA v Brown*, 131 S Ct 2846 (2011).

was, in fact, "previously interpreted." In other words, Pickett signals a new direction for the law, without really discussing the initial direction the law had taken.

Pickett's discussion of specific jurisdiction is likewise a little difficult for an unfamiliar reader to understand. For instance, Pickett's entire discussion of specific jurisdiction focuses on "stream of commerce." A reader could easily be left to wonder what stream of commerce has to do with minimum contacts. Pickett never actually explains that stream of commerce is the particularized test or metaphor for minimum contacts in product liability cases. It is unclear why Pickett chose to focus exclusively on stream of commerce case law, to the exclusion of other US Supreme Court case law on minimum contacts, including *Calder v Jones*,[15] *Keeton v Hustler Magazine*,[16] and *Burger King Corp v Rudzewicz*.[17] Such an omission is glaring because it leaves the reader with the distinct impression that "minimum contacts" is somehow synonymous with "stream of commerce."[18] Even within the discussion of the stream of commerce case law, Pickett fails to reference the well-established, two-part jurisdictional test first articulated in *World-Wide Volkswagen Corp v Woodson*: contacts and reasonableness.[19] To the extent that the contacts/reasonableness construct survives *J McIntyre Machinery Ltd v Nicastro*, it is something that a Canadian litigator should know about and be prepared to address in his or her jurisdictional submissions.[20]

---

[15] *Calder v Jones*, 465 US 783 (1984).

[16] *Keeton v Hustler Magazine*, 465 US 770 (1984).

[17] *Burger King Corp v Rudzewicz*, 471 US 462 (1985).

[18] Indeed, much of the book is geared towards the discussion of more territorial torts, such as negligence and products liability actions, with no mention of torts such as defamation or fraud. With defamation, in particular, American (and Canadian) courts have developed very specific jurisdictional principles, which are not discussed, or even alluded to, in Pickett's book.

[19] See *World-Wide Volkswagen Corp v Woodson*, 444 US 286 (1980). See also *Asahi Metal Industry Co v Superior Court*, 480 US 102 (1987).

[20] See *J McIntyre Machinery v Nicastro*, 131 S Ct 2780 at 2798 (2011) [*McIntyre*]. Since the Supreme Court did not expressly refer to the two-pronged test, it was unclear in the aftermath of *McIntyre* whether the test still applied. However, the recent case of *Daimler AG v Bauman*, 134 S Ct 746 (2014) (US), decided after Pickett's book was published, confirms that the two-part test is alive and well: "[t]rue, a multipronged reasonableness check was articulated in *Asahi*, but not as a free-floating test. Instead, the check was to be essayed when *specific* jurisdiction is at issue. First, a court is to determine whether the connection between the forum and the episode-in-suit could justify the exercise of specific jurisdiction.

Pickett then moves on to discussing jurisdictional principles in Canada. Pickett's discussion of the Canadian law on jurisdiction is longer than his discussion of American law (seventeen pages versus fourteen pages). The page allocation is a little perplexing, given that his intended audience would likely be familiar with the jurisdictional principles prevailing in the province where he or she practises. While Pickett's description of Canadian law is accurate, he takes a largely detailed and descriptive approach, rather than drawing all of the cases together to provide some practical pointers for litigators.

In Chapter 3 ('"Where Should I Sue?': Introducing Conflict of Laws"), Pickett addresses choice of law concerns and how they impact forum selection. Pickett starts off the section by offering the reader some practical advice: courts are inclined to apply forum law and "you and your client are always 'swimming upstream' when you urge a court to consider applying foreign law to your fact pattern."[21] He next moves on to some common themes in the choice of law analysis. His four themes (defining the place of the tort, substance/procedure, *renvoi*, and *dépeçage*) do a good job of introducing the core issues that a litigator will face when confronted with choice of law issues. Pickett then succinctly summarizes the various approaches to choice of law in tort that prevail in the United States. This section succeeds in providing a Canadian reader with a flavour for the various choice of law approaches that exist south of the

---

Then, in a second step, the court is to consider several additional factors to assess the reasonableness of entertaining the case." Further, Pickett casts his entire analysis of specific jurisdiction as reflecting a tension between the 'personal subjection' and 'administration of justice' approach to jurisdiction (Pickett, *supra* note 2 at 41). Pickett derives the labels from a 1991 article by Canadian academic Vaughan Black and notes himself that the labels are used in Canada, not the United States. Consequently, it is unclear why Pickett proceeds to analyze the stream of commerce case law (as well as the Canadian cases) with reference to these constructs. It is apparent from the most recent US Supreme Court case on point, *McIntyre*, that the constitutional debate is one between sovereignty/purposeful availment and due process/fairness. See McIntyre, *supra* note 20 at 2798, Ginsburg J dissenting (responding to plurality by noting "the constitutional limits on a state court's adjudicatory authority derive from considerations of due process, not state sovereignty"). Even if the Canadian labels are roughly analogous — which it is not clear that they are — their use in describing the approaches in the United States is unhelpful to understanding the relevant American case law.

21 Pickett, *supra* note 2 at 79.

border, without getting overly bogged down in the nuances of each approach.

The bulk of Chapter 3 is devoted to looking at "Choice of Law in Practice," where Pickett examines the choice of law approach in thirteen American "border" jurisdictions. He acknowledges early on in his book that the border approach is "admittedly ... arbitrary" given that these border states, first, represent only a quarter of the US population and, second, fail to include some of the most populous American jurisdictions as well as jurisdictions that might be tourism destinations for Canadians (such as Florida and Arizona).[22] It is unclear whether Pickett needed to examine any "sample" jurisdictions in order for his book to be an effective primer for his intended audience. Unless a Canadian litigator happens to have a case that can be filed in Montana, Idaho, New Hampshire, or ten other border jurisdictions, more than 40 percent of the book is of no use to him or her.[23] Another problem with this section is that the discussion of choice of law is not uniform from state to state. In other words, Pickett does not have a pre-existing structure whereby he seeks to answer a set of defined questions regarding choice of law such as: Does the state allow for *dépeçage?* Does the state regard statutes of limitations as substantive or procedural? Does the state have a borrowing statute? Instead, Pickett discusses whatever law there is in that particular jurisdiction, making it potentially confusing for a reader who is reasoning by extrapolation. Granted, Pickett's intention is not to have his audience read the entire chapter but, rather, to select only the jurisdictions that are relevant. Nonetheless, the discussion could have benefited from additional consistency and structure.

Certain parts of Pickett's synopsis of the choice of law approaches of the thirteen border states read more like an academic critique than a primer. For instance, Pickett spends six pages outlining and disagreeing with the New York Court of Appeals' decision in *Edwards v Erie Coach Lines Co.*[24] Pickett notes that the "result in *Edwards* is

---

22 *Ibid* at 29-30.

23 Seventy-seven pages are devoted in Chapter 3 to forum-specific choice of law rules. Similarly, sixty-one pages are devoted in Chapter 4 to forum-specific *forum non conveniens* law. Consequently, 138 out of 347 pages (almost 40 percent of the book) are dedicated to forum-specific law.

24 *Edwards v Erie Coach Lines Co,* 17 NY (3d) 306 (NY Ct App 2011) [*Edwards*]. This is particularly strange considering that Pickett spent only three pages discussing US Supreme Court jurisprudence on general jurisdiction.

troubling on a number of levels" and proceeds to deconstruct all the reasons why he believes the decision is flawed.[25] Canadian litigators are not likely to concern themselves with the perceived incongruities or errors in the *Edwards* court's reasoning in assessing whether to sue in New York. This interjection of Pickett's personal opinion into the book is sometimes a distraction to his main aim of providing a practical guide to cross-border litigation.[26]

Pickett then turns to the Canadian choice of law approach. He devotes considerable attention to the historical development of the rule and to synopsizing the leading case, *Tolofson v Jensen*.[27] Much of this fifteen-page discussion is unnecessary given that it is all a lead up to one fairly straightforward point: Canada uses the *lex loci* approach to choice of law. In fact, on multiple occasions in this part of the chapter, Pickett's discussion of Canadian law is protracted, walking the reader through years of case law before getting to the "bottom line" that a litigator is likely looking for.

Chapter 4 ("'Can I Keep My Case Where I Want It?': The Doctrine of *Forum Non Conveniens*") deals with the issue of *forum non conveniens*. At the outset of the chapter, Pickett does a solid job outlining the general approach to *forum non conveniens* in the United States. He is particularly adept at synthesizing and providing an overview of the "public" and "private" interest factors at the heart of the American *forum non conveniens* analysis. As with the choice of law chapter, however, too many pages are devoted to the subtle differences in *forum non conveniens* laws between jurisdictions. Here, Pickett not only examines state *forum non conveniens* law in each of the thirteen border jurisdictions but also federal law that would be applicable if the action were filed in federal court in any of the thirteen states. Thus, he examines twenty-six different bodies of *forum non conveniens* law, plus any other potentially applicable federal law.[28]

---

25 See Pickett, *supra* note 2 at 149-52.

26 See, for example, Pickett's lengthy critique of *Somers v Fournier* (2002), 214 DLR (4th) 611 (Ont CA) and *Wong v Wei*, [1999] 10 WWR 296 (BCSC) (Pickett, *supra* note 2 at 214-15). If Pickett's personal opinion on cases or doctrines were couched in litigation terms (for example: "Here are arguments that a litigator can use to get around [x or y rule]"), then one could understand Pickett venturing into some of these issues. However, Pickett's thoughts on various cases read like an academic critique within a practice guide, making the book potentially less useful for its intended reader.

27 *Tolofson v Jensen*, [1994] 3 SCR 1022.

28 For instance, Pickett examines Maine state law, Maine federal law, and general First Circuit case law that might be relevant in Maine federal court (Pickett, *supra*

This section is a cumbersome read and, for the reasons outlined earlier, Pickett's choice to survey the thirteen border jurisdictions is questionable. Presumably, a litigator who is considering one of those states as a potential forum would conduct his or her own research into both the applicable choice of law precedents as well as the nuances of the *forum non conveniens* doctrine. As such, it is unclear how valuable Pickett's description of the relevant law is, even for those Canadian litigators with an action that could potentially be brought in a border state. It probably would have been more helpful to a Canadian litigator for Pickett to emphasize broad trends and themes, rather than the precise particulars of *forum non conveniens* law in various state and federal courts.

Overall, Pickett's book is a bit of a mixed bag. At times, Pickett does an excellent job of distilling the relevant legal principles and take-away points that a Canadian litigator would need to know in assessing whether to file suit in the United States. At other times, Pickett's book reads more like a treatise — with a historical narrative, overly detailed examination of cases, and sustained academic critiques. The book ebbs and flows between these extremes, sometimes leaving a reader bewildered as to which information is actually important. With that said, Pickett's book is the only one of its kind and, for that reason, is certainly worth a look.

TANYA J. MONESTIER
Associate Professor, Roger Williams University School of Law

Responsibility of International Organizations: Essays in Memory of Sir Ian Brownlie. Dirigé par Maurizio Ragazzi. Leiden-Boston, Martinus Nijhoff Publishers, 2013. 470 pages.

L'ouvrage faisant l'objet de la présente recension est un ouvrage collectif édité par Maurizio Ragazzi et dédié à la mémoire de Sir Ian Brownlie. Il regroupe quelque trente-quatre contributions d'auteurs du monde entier issus du milieu académique, de la Com-

---

note 2 at 278-81, 337-38). As with the forum-specific choice of law analysis, Pickett examines *forum non conveniens* law in each jurisdiction in a non-systematized manner. Many of the cases he discusses involve parties from countries with legal systems that differ significantly from the United States (for example, Turkey, Colombia, and so on). One might question how applicable those precedents are when applied to Canada-US litigation.

mission du droit international, de diverses juridictions, ou occupant des fonctions au sein d'organisations internationales. Si certains d'entre eux ont eu le privilège de rencontrer et de travailler avec Sir Ian Brownlie, tous admettent avoir été influencés par ses écrits. Cette unanimité et la qualité des contributions réunies illustrent en soi l'impact qu'a eu le dédicataire de ce recueil sur l'ensemble du droit international et plus particulièrement, sur la thématique de la responsabilité des organisations internationales.

Le présent ouvrage, qui brosse un paysage aussi riche qu'hétéroclite de la doctrine sur le sujet, est le pendant d'un autre ouvrage collectif édité également par Maurizio Ragazzi, dédié à Oscar Schachter, et portant sur la responsabilité des États. Prenant pour point de départ le projet d'articles de la Commission du droit international sur la responsabilité des organisations internationales, le mélange ici recensé offre au lecteur un panorama de la doctrine en analysant ce qui restera sans doute le projet de la Commission du droit international le plus critiqué sur sa méthodologie.

Maurizio Ragazzi a choisi de scinder l'ouvrage en quatre parties que nous aborderons successivement. Il n'est toutefois pas anodin de noter que cet ordonnancement n'a été réalisé qu'après réception des différentes contributions. Ce choix procède de la volonté assumée par l'éditeur de laisser toute latitude aux auteurs quant à la détermination de leur sujet, sans qu'aucune contrainte, serait-ce thématique ou autre, ne leur soit imposée. Ce parti pris est assurément à double tranchant. Alors qu'il permet d'entrevoir toute la diversité de la doctrine, il est également, à l'occasion, source de certaines redondances. Quoi qu'il en soit, c'est ici la première considération qui l'emporte, et l'on ne peut que se réjouir de voir réunis autant de regards sur la responsabilité des organisations internationales. Pour autant, on ne sera pas surpris que la localisation de certains articles dans la structure déterminée *a posteriori* soit sujette à discussion. Chaque contribution ayant été envisagée de manière autonome, il est en effet normal que certaines d'entre elles se situent à la convergence de deux parties. De nouveau, la critique est mineure et l'on ne peut que saluer l'ordonnancement de l'ouvrage qui contribue largement à son accessibilité.

La première partie a trait au rôle de la Commission du droit international. Le projet d'articles de la Commission balance entre codification et développement progressif, sans doute plus que tout autre projet avant lui ce que la Commission admet d'ailleurs elle-même dans le commentaire général de son projet: "Le fait que plusieurs des présents projets d'article sont fondés sur une pratique limitée déplace le curseur entre codification et développement progressif en direction de ce dernier."

Partant de ce commentaire, fort remarqué, cinq auteurs, trois membres de la Commission du droit international — Sean Murphy, Alain Pellet, et Sir Michael Wood — et deux juges à la Cour internationale de Justice — A.A. Cançado Trindade et Kenneth Keith — évaluent la portée qu'il convient d'accorder au projet d'articles au vu de cet accent inédit sur la dimension de développement progressif du travail de la Commission. On notera dans cette partie l'intéressante contribution de Sean Murphy qui détaille, de manière limpide, les différentes nomenclatures qu'a, jusqu'ici, adoptées la Commission pour présenter ses travaux. Projet d'articles, projet de convention, guide de la pratique, modèle de règles ... La nomenclature est aussi diverse que parfois incompréhensible pour le béotien. On se réjouit donc de trouver ici une contribution qui explique les raisons de cette variété. Pour Sean Murphy, cette nomenclature est un emballage, un moyen de présenter le travail de la Commission et de ménager les attentes vis-à-vis de celui-ci. Reste que, et cette conclusion est partagée par bon nombre de contributeurs de cet ouvrage, la postérité des articles sera fonction de la réception de ceux-ci dans la pratique des États et des organisations internationales, quelles que soient les précautions prises par la Commission pour présenter son travail.

La seconde partie du mélange recensé rassemble des contributions évaluant l'approche de la Commission. Largement commenté, au vu du caractère limité de la pratique, le projet d'articles sur la responsabilité des organisations est ici mis en perspective avec le projet d'article sur la responsabilité des États. Dans une première sous-partie, C.F. Amerasinghe, Dan Sarooshi ainsi que Chusei Yamada formulent un certain nombre de commentaires généraux sur le projet d'articles. La contribution du professeur Sarooshi renvoie à ses travaux sur une typologie des transferts de compétences des États vers les organisations internationales. Pour stimulante qu'elle soit, cette contribution n'en est pas moins frustrante. On aurait en effet souhaité qu'elle puisse dépasser les 5 000 mots impartis afin de mieux illustrer la pratique. On eut ainsi souhaité que l'auteur explicite pourquoi, à son sens, une organisation internationale peut être considérée comme une entité habilitée par un État à exercer des prérogatives de puissance publique, au sens de l'article 5 du projet d'article sur la responsabilité des États. On voit mal, en effet, comment cet article pourrait constituer le fondement de la responsabilité d'un État pour le fait d'une organisation inter-nationale alors que l'article 57 de ce projet d'articles précise sans ambiguïté que le projet d'articles sur la responsabilité des États a été rédigé sans préjudice de toute question relative à la responsa-bilité d'un État pour le comportement d'une organisation interna-tionale. On touche ici à une autre spécificité de l'ouvrage: la brièveté des contributions. Voulue par l'éditeur afin de permettre une vaste gamme de points de vue, cette brièveté est parfois source de frus-trations tant on voudrait que les contributions soient plus étoffées. C'est toutefois la règle du genre, et l'on ne saurait en tenir rigueur ni à l'éditeur ni aux auteurs dont on ira consulter utilement d'autres écrits lorsque le besoin s'en fera sentir.

La seconde partie de l'ouvrage se poursuit avec des contributions de Maurizio Arcari, Vincent-Joël Proulx et Tullio Scovazzi qui exa-minent les liens entre le projet d'articles sur la responsabilité des États et celui sur la responsabilité des organisations. On aura déjà compris que cette thématique est commune à l'ensemble de l'ou-vrage. Elle est ici abordée de manière plus précise par ces auteurs qui s'attardent à voir dans quelle mesure le projet concernant les États a pu servir de point de départ à celui concernant les organi-sations. La troisième sous-partie aborde quant à elle la place accor-dée par la Commission aux règles de l'organisation en tant que *lex specialis* du droit de la responsabilité. Cette sous-partie regroupe des contributions de Kristen Boon, d'Arnoldo Pronto et d'Emmanuel Roucounas. On notera que ce dernier apporte ici une contribution fort documentée et particulièrement stimulante sur la pratique de l'organisation envisagée en tant que règle de l'organisation.

La troisième partie comprend, quant à elle, des contributions exposant le point de vue d'organisations internationales ou d'autres entités au statut plus incertain sur le travail de la Commission. Sont ainsi passés en revue les contextes particuliers des Nations Unies (Daphna Shraga), de l'Union européenne (José Manuel Cortés Martin), de l'OMS (Gian Luca Burgi et Clemens Feinäugle), ainsi que des institutions financières internationales (Laurence Boisson de Chazournes, Ross Leckow et Erik Plith, ainsi que Maurizio Ragazzi). Ces contributions, d'une originalité et d'une rigueur certaine, sont suivies par celle d'un ancien conseiller juridique du Saint-Siège, Robert John Araujo, qui propose ici un article ayant, de manière surprenante, bien peu à voir avec la responsabilité des orga-nisations internationales. Au prétexte d'examiner la notion d'acte *ultra vires,* ce dernier critique un rapport de la Haute-Commissaire des Nations Unies aux droits de l'homme portant sur les "Lois et pratiques discriminatoires et actes de violence dont sont victimes des personnes en raison de leur orientation sexuelle ou de leur identité de genre."[1] Dans cette contribution, l'auteur avance qu'en ne définissant pas la notion d'"identité de genre" en accord avec la "réalité objective de la nature humaine," l'ONU manquerait au respect que doit l'organisation à son mandat. Il n'est nullement question ici de critiquer la position de M. Araujo sur la définition à donner à la notion d'"identité de genre," quand bien même nous ne la partagerions pas. On peine en revanche à voir en quoi cette question envisageant à ce point des règles primaires est pertinente dans un ouvrage traitant de la responsabilité. De surcroît, on reste dubitatif sur le caractère *ultra vires*, que l'auteur ne démontre en rien. En quoi la production d'un rapport concernant l'orientation sexuelle et l'identité de genre excède-t-elle le mandat de l'ONU? Le rédacteur de cette recension ne trouve pas de réponse et la lecture de la contribution de M. Araujo ne l'éclaire pas sur le sujet. Quoi qu'il en soit, si cette contribution détonne, elle est immédiatement suivie par deux articles forts intéressants sur des sujets jusqu'ici encore relativement peu traités: le quartet pour le Moyen-Orient (John Dugard et Annemarieke Vermeer-Künzli) et le récent avis consultatif rendu par la Cour internationale de Justice concernant le jugement N° 2867 du Tribunal administratif de l'Organisation internationale du Travail[2] (Rutsel Silvestre J. Martha).

La dernière partie du recueil contient des contributions portant sur la responsabilité des États membres d'une organisation du fait de cette organisation (Kazuhiro Nakatani, Paolo Palchetti, Pavel Sturma, Sienho Yee), sur la justiciabilité des différends impliquant la responsabilité d'une organisation internationale (Sergio Puig, Hugh Thirlway), sur les contre-mesures visant les organisations internationales (Antonios Tzanakopoulos, Simone Vezzani), sur l'autorisation de l'usage de la force (PS Rao), ainsi que sur les opérations de maintien de la paix (Blanca Montejo, Francesco Salerno).

Ce mélange en l'honneur de Sir Ian Brownlie est voué à rester une référence sur le sujet. Il regroupe en un seul volume un nombre impressionnant d'articles de très grande qualité et constitue assurément une lecture captivante pour toute personne intéressée par la responsabilité des organisations, mais aussi, de manière plus générale, par le droit des organisations internationales. On note ainsi que

---

1 Doc off Conseil des droits de l'homme, 19e sess, Doc NU A/HCR/19/41 (2011).

2 Sur requête contre le Fonds international de développement agricole, avis consultatif, [2012] CIJ rec 10.

sont traités de nombreux sujets emblématiques du droit des organisations internationales: personnalité juridique, actes *ultra vires*, règles de l'organisation, pratique établie de l'organisation, voile institutionnel. Quels que soient ses centres d'intérêt, il est fort probable que le lecteur y trouvera plusieurs articles susceptibles d'attirer son attention. C'est ici un fort bel hommage à Sir Ian Brownlie que signent les auteurs ayant participé à ce mélange: un ouvrage riche, varié et rigoureux.

ARNAUD LOUWETTE
Assistant, Centre de Droit International, Université Libre de Bruxelles

Unimaginable Atrocities: Justice, Politics, and Rights at the War Crimes Tribunals. By William Schabas. Oxford: Oxford University Press, 2012. 240 pages.

International criminal law has been controversial since its inception because of its seemingly inextricable link with politics and the self-interests of states. For instance, the fact that Roman Andreyevich Rudenko, a Soviet lieutenant-general widely accused of war crimes during the Second World War, was a prosecutor at the Nuremburg trial is seen by many as strong evidence not only of victor's justice but also of the immutable force of *realpolitik* in international law. At the same time, the establishment of individual criminal liability under international law has also been praised for transcending political interests because it has allowed the international community to hold some of the worst and most powerful perpetrators to account.

In *Unimaginable Atrocities: Justice, Politics, and Rights at the War Crimes Tribunals,* William Schabas addresses the major controversies that surround modern atrocity trials.[1] Schabas addresses eight specific topics that he identifies as central to the current debates about international criminal law. Each issue is addressed in a separate chapter. The unifying theme for all of the topics and arguments is the close relationship between politics and justice in this area of the law.[2]

The views expressed in this review are those of the author and not necessarily of the Ministry of the Attorney General.

1 William Schabas, *Unimaginable Atrocities: Justice, Politics, and Rights at the War Crimes Tribunals* (Oxford: Oxford University Press, 2012).

2 *Ibid* at 3.

Schabas is ideally suited and qualified for the task. He has published more than twenty books and hundreds of articles on international criminal and human rights law and has taught at universities
in Canada, the United States, Europe, and Africa. Schabas is currently a professor of international law at Middlesex University in
London. He also has appointments at the National University of
Ireland, Galway, the Chinese Academy of Social Sciences, Kellogg
College, Oxford, and at the Université du Québec à Montréal. He
is the editor-in-chief of *Criminal Law Forum* and was awarded the
Order of Canada in 2006.

A great strength of this book is Schabas' approach to providing
a broad overview of the major international criminal law issues.
Indeed, the central goal of the book is to "de-mystify" some of the
legal arguments — to make the issues more accessible to non-lawyers
who wish to better understand the politics and policy underlying
international criminal justice.[3] Schabas' approach accomplishes this
goal. *Unimaginable Atrocities* is more a policy examination than a
legal analysis. The book contains explanations of relevant legal
doctrines, but the object of the discussion is to contextualize the
law in a broader policy debate. Schabas' ability to go beyond legal
doctrine to discuss the foundational theories and political issues
of international criminal law speaks to his broad expertise and
versatility.

The issues and arguments are consistently presented in an accessible, engaging style. Schabas assumes little legal knowledge, succinctly explaining the basic legal concepts that are essential to
understanding his discussion. He does not burden the reader with
dense, legalistic prose. He makes the discussion relevant by drawing
on a great deal of historical context and precedent, particularly
from the Nuremburg trials. He does not, however, shy away from
making reasoned legal arguments and grounding them in sources
of international law. He frequently explains and refers to treaties,
custom, case law, and works of pre-eminent international law
scholars.

For example, the entirety of Chapter 2 addresses the principle of
nullum crimen sine lege. Schabas makes this Latin-cloaked legal principle vibrantly relevant to current political and philosophical debates
by explaining how it relates to the theories of international criminal
law's origins and development. *Nullum crimen sine lege* requires that
no one be subject to criminal sanction, except where the crime and

[3] *Ibid* at 2-3.

associated penalty are prescribed by law. The doctrine also encompasses the principle of non-retroactivity, which holds that no one may be punished for a crime that was not prohibited in law at the time the acts occurred. Schabas explains how the doctrine operates differently, depending on whether one theorizes the law's genesis and evolution as a "big bang" or a "constant state." He describes how these two theories stem from the original debates leading up to the Nuremburg trials and how they relate to whether international criminal law can be applied retroactively. He also demonstrates how such theories are reflected in the statutes and jurisprudence of the various international criminal tribunals. In addition to Chapter 2, Schabas takes time throughout the book to explain basic international legal concepts such as *jus cogens, jus in bello,* and *jus ad bellum,* before he relates them to the broader political debate.[4]

As previously mentioned, although Schabas takes on the "law and policy" theme, he does not overtly state a main thesis. Nevertheless, throughout the book, Schabas defends international criminal law from the criticism that its political dimensions necessarily undermine its legitimacy. He seems to be implicitly urging the reader to accept that international criminal law should incorporate and account for its significant political dimensions, rather than attempt to hide and suppress them. According to Schabas, politics has a proper place in both the substantive and administrative aspects of international criminal law.

For example, Chapter 3 is about victor's justice and selective prosecution. Both the International Criminal Court (ICC) and the International Criminal Tribunal for Yugoslavia have been criticized for ignoring the crimes of people from powerful states, while targeting investigations and indictments against people from less influential states. Schabas takes a thorough, balanced, and interesting approach to addressing this issue. He acknowledges that the critique that international criminal law is an exercise in victor's justice is a significant attack on the legitimacy of international criminal law. He further identifies the selection of cases for prosecution as perhaps the law's most significant challenge.[5] He argues that in the case of the ICC, the *Rome Statute* artificially applies judicial criteria to the necessarily political process of selecting cases for investigation and indictment. He argues that the façade of legal criteria shrouds

---

[4] *Ibid* at 118, 211.

[5] *Ibid* at 4, 73-77.

the selection process in secrecy when, given its inherently political nature, it should be more transparent.

Although Schabas does not claim that the scope of the book is exhaustive, there are controversial topics that call out for more attention. Since the book is meant to address major international criminal law issues, the discussion could have benefited from Schabas' thoughts on two additional key questions: (1) which authorities in international law have the legitimacy to hold individuals accountable for violations of international criminal law and (2) can and does the emerging system of international criminal justice adequately protect the rights of accused people?

According to Schabas, the first generation of international crimes is classified by less serious offences that required international cooperation to enforce. They were merely trans-border offences commonly prohibited in states' domestic law, such as piracy and trafficking. Thus, a violation of these rules was a violation of states' laws, not substantive international law.[6] By contrast, the body of rules forming the second generation of international criminal law is quintessentially international. These crimes are so serious that their commission offends the entire international legal community, rather than merely the laws of individual states.[7] A second-generation violation is an offence under international law, not the law of a given state.

Considering the absence of a single sovereign entity to hold perpetrators accountable for violations of second-generation offences, Schabas' reader is left to wonder which international authorities have the legitimacy to enforce this new cohort of offences on behalf of the international community — perhaps the tribunal that issues the conviction, the Security Council, or the international community as a whole? National criminal justice systems do not struggle with this question. Traditional criminal law requires a sovereign law-making entity before which accused persons are tried and offenders are held to account. In a given state, a violation of criminal law may be viewed as an offence against the public, the monarch, or the state itself. Who and what the state represents varies by jurisdiction. Nevertheless, in the eyes of international law, the creation and enforcement of criminal law is a sovereign act of the state, regardless of who or what the state claims to represent.

This foundational criminal law theory does not translate well into the international legal context. There is no unified law-making

6 *Ibid* at 29-30.

7 *Ibid* at 30-33.

sovereign. All members of the society of states are themselves independent, sovereign lawmakers. Schabas explains that international tribunals can be distinguished from national judicial institutions by determining whether the tribunal could be abolished by the act of a single state.[8] Tribunals created by treaty or Security Council resolution are beyond the authority of any one state. In this way, they are truly international. Thus, when the accused is tried before a truly international tribunal, she or he is not answering to any unified sovereign authority.

Arguably, in light of the absence of a clear sovereign legal authority, international criminal law may not be criminal law at all. At least, it is not criminal law as it has been traditionally understood. Perhaps international criminal law is better defined as an amalgamation of political processes, restrained by legal principles, and designed to reprimand people who commit atrocities. These processes may be meant to deter and punish atrocities, and they may be more reasoned and principled than summary executions or automatic imprisonment, but they do not reflect criminal law as it was understood prior to the Nuremburg precedent.

A discussion about this topic would have fit well into Schabas' theme relating to the interaction between politics and justice, particularly in light of ongoing attacks on the legitimacy of the ICC on the basis of selective prosecution. Are these highly politicized judicial processes a legitimate and fitting approach to criminal justice? Should groups of states creating and enforcing international law be entrusted with prosecuting individuals? Are there better approaches to ending impunity for these acts that offend the international community as a whole? For example, should states take the more conventional approach of agreeing by treaty to enact these crimes in their domestic legislation and to exercise universal jurisdiction to prosecute anyone who commits these offences regardless of where they occurred?

Further, Schabas specifies in the book's title that an important subject of this work is rights at international war crimes tribunals. Chapter 6 discusses victims' right to truth. Chapter 7 discusses amnesties, addressing the balance between the right to peace and victims' right to justice. Chapter 8 discusses the crime of aggression with reference to the right to peace and its relationship to international humanitarian law and human rights law. Surprisingly, however, Schabas does not specifically address one important body

---

[8] *Ibid* at 19.

of rights central to the legitimacy, nature, and function of criminal tribunals: the rights of the accused. Although Schabas discusses the political aspects of prosecutorial selection, he does not discuss the trial process itself. The reader is left wondering whether, with such powerful political forces at play, an internationalized trial can ever be truly fair?

Criticisms about due process and independence have plagued international tribunals since Nuremburg. A whole set of concerns have arisen, including: lengthy trial delays, the gathering of evidence through proxies, lax rules of evidence, perceived and actual problems relating to judicial and institutional independence, and under-funded defence counsel for indigent accused. Schabas suggests that although Nuremburg may not be a shining example of due process, it must be judged by the standards of the period and not by modern expectations.[9] He does not go so far as to say that the people accused of war crimes at Nuremburg were given a fair trial, and he does not further pursue this issue in relation to contemporary prosecutions.

There are a great many mechanisms to dispense international justice. Perhaps most international judicial and quasi-judicial institutions would be best described as dispute resolution mechanisms, designed to resolve legal issues that arise in the course of inter-state relations. For example, even the International Court of Justice may only exercise its jurisdiction with the agreement of the states that would be bound by the decision.[10] The notion that an international judicial mechanism should have independent and coercive authority over any legal entity, whether it is a state or an individual, is a relatively recent and novel development in international law.

Criminal trials are not designed to serve as dispute resolution mechanisms. They are not voluntary and, unlike other international judicial bodies, included among their intended outcomes are severe stigma and deprivation of liberty. Given these serious potential consequences, the design of the trial process is meant, perhaps above all else, to carefully protect the rights of the person liable to criminal sanction and punishment. Although the establishment of a tribunal is necessarily a matter of policy, the trials themselves cannot be political. They are meant to be justice processes insulated

---

9 *Ibid* at 73-74.

10 *Statute of the International Court of Justice, annexed to the Charter of the United Nations,* 26 June 1945, Can TS 1945 No 7, Article 36(1); *Monetary Gold Removed from Rome in 1943 (Italy v France, UK and US),* Judgment of 15 June 1954, [1954] ICJ Rep 19.

from outside political influence. Rules of procedure and evidence are meant to ensure guilt is established beyond a reasonable doubt and that the accused's legal rights are not violated in the prosecutor's pursuit of obtaining a conviction.

The right to a fair trial does not require the intention of fairness — it requires a guarantee of fairness. Given the highly politicized nature of international criminal justice, can international law guarantee the accused a fair trial? Considering Schabas' focus on the intermingling of the legal and political aspects of international criminal justice, a discussion about whether and how international criminal tribunals have been successful at respecting the rights of the accused would have been relevant. Schabas quotes the famous opening statement of American prosecutor Robert Jackson more than once in the book.[11] In his opening, Jackson states that one reason Nuremburg was a major historical event is the Allies's choice to stay the hand of vengeance in favour of a principled approach to justice. The incorporation of legal rights for the accused was meant to eliminate political influence over the justice process. In this way, it is the rights-focused nature of the trial process that made Nuremburg such a major legal innovation. In light of Schabas' expertise in both the legal and political sides of international human rights and criminal law, the reader would benefit from his comments on this topic.

Although these further discussions would have been enlightening, this book is not substantially incomplete. Schabas states from the outset that his intention is to address some of the major policy and legal issues in international criminal justice and to relate them to a broad audience. The work does in the end constitute an accessible, logically organized survey of a number of major issues being debated today. Perhaps the main underlying assumption of this book is that politics and international criminal law need not exist in separate, watertight compartments. By contrast, their relationship is both inevitable and foundational to the proper administration of international criminal law.

NATHAN KRUGER
Crown Counsel, Crown Law Office — Criminal,
Ministry of the Attorney General of Ontario

---

[11] Schabas, *supra* note 1 at 12, 106-7.

The Regulation of International Shipping: International and Comparative Perspectives: Essays in Honor of Edgar Gold. Dirigé par Aldo Chircop et al. Leiden (Pays-Bas), Martinus Nijhoff Publishers, 2012. 586 pages.

Le transport maritime international est un domaine commercial pour lequel le besoin d'être assujetti à des règles de droit international s'est très tôt fait sentir. Le présent ouvrage fait valoir l'importance de ces règles pour le droit maritime dans une perspective de droit comparé.

L'objectif du livre est de rendre hommage à Edgar Gold et de le remercier pour sa contribution dans le domaine du droit maritime international. Edgar Gold est un marin, praticien et professeur de droit maritime, considéré aujourd'hui comme un grand expert dans ce domaine au niveau canadien et mondial. Une liste "limitée" des publications d'Edgar Gold, soit quelque 200, figure dans les pages 568-76 de l'ouvrage. Dans ses différentes sections, la collection réussit largement à couvrir des sujets extrêmement variés qui sont au centre des intérêts d'Edgar Gold et au cœur du transport maritime international comme, par exemple, la protection de l'environnement marin, les politiques maritimes au niveau canadien et international, la sécurité des navires, les marins et l'assurance maritime.

Le livre est publié sous la direction d'Aldo Chircop, professeur à la *Schulich School of Law* de l'Université Dalhousie et directeur du *Marine and Environmental Law Institute*; Norman Letalik, associé chez Borden Ladner Gervais s.r.l. à Toronto; Ted L. McDorman, professeur à la faculté de droit de l'Université Victoria; et Susan J. Rolston, directrice de *Seawinds Consulting Services* et associée au *Marine and Environmental Law Institute* de la *Schulich School of Law.*

L'ouvrage est divisé en cinq sections. Chaque section contient des contributions de différents auteurs qui connaissent ou admirent Edgar Gold. Le nombre de contributions dans les différentes sections s'élève à vingt-sept. Les sections I et II s'intitulent *Law of the Sea and Ocean Governance* et *Governance in the Arctic Ocean* respectivement. Les deux sections s'inscrivent dans le cadre du droit international public et portent sur différents sujets d'actualité, comme la délimitation et la règlementation des zones maritimes, les questions juridiques et autres que pose la navigation dans l'Arctique, la piraterie et la règlementation des détroits. Les sections III, IV et V contiennent la majorité des contributions de l'ouvrage et s'intitulent respectivement *Shipping and International Maritime Law, Seafaring and Maritime Labour Law* et *Canadian Maritime Law.* Leur contenu relève du droit maritime, mais s'inscrit plutôt dans le cadre du droit international privé. Les sujets traités dans cette section sont aussi très variés et incluent le transport maritime, les marins, le *forum shopping*, la compétence judiciaire en matière maritime, la libéralisation de la navigation et les privilèges maritimes. Cette variété de sujets traités permet d'appréhender l'éventail des domaines auxquels s'intéressent les auteurs et Edgar Gold, à qui ce livre est dédié.

La contribution de cette collection au domaine du droit maritime n'est pas négligeable. Comparé à d'autres branches de droit comme le droit commercial international ou le droit pénal international, le droit maritime n'a pas donné lieu à une abondance d'ouvrages. Par conséquent, les publications sur cette matière sont bien reçues. En outre, la qualité du présent ouvrage est attribuable à son contenu. En effet, les différentes contributions font bien ressortir l'importance des règles internationales en matière de transport maritime et la nécessité d'une coopération internationale afin d'établir des règles efficaces et communément admises. Les textes sont par ailleurs pluridisciplinaires: ils portent sur le droit, les sciences politiques, l'administration publique, l'histoire, les études maritimes et l'administration commerciale. L'analyse adoptée comporte souvent une perspective comparée qui enrichit la qualité des chapitres. Par exemple, on y traite de législation dans différents ressorts de common law et de droit civil, et d'autres traditions juridiques. Les auteurs utilisent fréquemment des exemples pratiques, rendant ainsi leur analyse plus intéressante. Leur langage est clair et précis. Ils se livrent généralement à une analyse critique des sujets traités. De fait, l'approche critique et l'analyse comparée exhibée dans les contributions ajoutent de la valeur à la collection.

L'éventail des sources utilisées est aussi remarquable. Pour appuyer leurs textes, les auteurs ont recours à la documentation des institutions nationales, régionales et internationales, aux rapports nationaux et internationaux, à la jurisprudence des différents pays maritimes (de common law et de droit civil), à la doctrine nationale et internationale, ainsi qu'à des cartes géographiques, des tableaux, des statistiques et des représentations graphiques. Dans presque toutes les contributions, on relève des incidents maritimes, des arrêts de principe et des développements d'actualité afin d'illustrer un point précis ou de soutenir un argument.

L'organisation des sections de la collection est conséquente et logique. Les thèmes de chaque contribution sont bien regroupés dans des sections correspondantes. Même s'il n'est pas très courant de traiter, dans un même ouvrage, du droit de la mer (domaine de droit international public, dans les sections I et II) et du droit maritime (domaine de droit international privé, dans les sections III, IV, V), le fait que ces sections représentent des domaines d'intérêt d'Edgar Gold et qu'elles traitent des sujets d'actualité explique entièrement le choix de ceux qui ont dirigé la collection. La section V sur le *Droit maritime canadien* est singulièrement intéressante et originale en ce qu'elle porte principalement sur le Canada, le pays d'origine des directeurs de l'ouvrage et de nombreux auteurs des textes de la collection.

La qualité du présent ouvrage n'est pas surprenante si l'on considère que les auteurs des contributions sont des professeurs, des juges, des avocats, des chercheurs et d'autres professionnels qui se spécialisent depuis des années dans le domaine du transport maritime. Certains ont entretenu des relations professionnelles avec Edgar Gold: ils ont travaillé avec lui dans des bureaux d'avocats, des facultés universitaires ou des agences gouvernementales, ou ils ont été ses étudiants. Comme mentionné, un bon nombre d'entre eux travaillent au Canada. D'autres auteurs proviennent de différents pays maritimes du monde — surtout des pays développés — comme Singapour, l'Australie, la Suède, la Norvège et la Chine. Cela confère à la collection une dimension multinationale et permet au lecteur de connaître les règles applicables dans différents pays, ainsi que les enjeux auxquels font face les professionnels œuvrant dans le domaine du droit maritime international. Les points de vue des auteurs sont souvent convergents, par exemple, concernant la collaboration internationale qu'on devrait promouvoir relativement à la piraterie ou à la pollution marine. Cela est justifié par le caractère international des enjeux présents dans le domaine du transport maritime international.

Comme on peut s'y attendre dans un ouvrage de ce genre, certaines contributions sont nettement plus structurées, mieux écrites et plus riches en contenu, suggestions et analyse critique que d'autres. Nous considérons, par exemple, que les contributions de Mary R. Brooks, "Maritime Cabotage: International Market Issues in the Liberalization of Domestic Shipping," de Tommy Koh, "Straits Used for International Navigation: Some Recent Developments," de Ted L. McDorman, "Canada's Vessel Traffic Management Regime: an Overview in the Context of International Law" et de Brian Flemming, "A Commentary on the Great Arctic Melt and its Potential Impact on Global Shipping Patterns" font partie de cette catégorie de contributions extraordinaires. Cependant, d'autres auteurs pourraient adopter un style de présentation plus intéressant pour le lecteur et mener une analyse plus approfondie des déclarations contenues dans leur conclusion. C'est le cas, par exemple, de la contribution d'Aref Fakhry, "Piracy Across Maritime Law: Is there a Problem of Definition?" et d'Alfred Popp, "The Treaty Making Work of the Legal Committee of the International Maritime Organization." Pour le reste, on a observé des manquements mineurs dans certaines contributions. Il s'agit d'erreurs d'expression ou de rédaction[1] et de mises à jour d'information[2] qui selon nous, devraient être considérées plus attentivement par les auteurs concernés et, pour certains d'entre eux, par la maison d'édition.

Malgré ces critiques mineures, la qualité supérieure de l'ouvrage ne fait aucun doute. Les contributions de ses auteurs sont, en général, riches en information, suggestions et analyse critique. Elles sont bien structurées, très intéressantes à lire et clairement écrites. Les points de vue des auteurs sont convaincants et basés sur une bonne connaissance de la matière et sur une recherche approfondie des sujets traités. C'est un ouvrage que nous recommandons sans réserve. Il peut servir de référence aux professionnels tels les juristes, les professeurs de droit, les avocats et autres praticiens qui œuvrent dans les domaines du droit maritime, du droit de la mer, du droit comparé, du droit international privé et du droit commercial international. De plus, les étudiants qui suivent des cours sur ces matières pourront puiser dans la richesse de son contenu. L'ouvrage mérite, par conséquent, une place dans les bibliothèques de droit de tous les pays du monde.

Marel Katsivela
Professeure adjointe, Programme de common law en français, Faculté de droit, Université d'Ottawa

---

[1] Les mots en italique marquent les termes à considérer dans les exemples suivants. Dans la contribution de L Dolliver M. Nelson, "Reasonable Bond and the Jurisprudence of the International Tribunal for the Law of the Sea: Some Brief Remarks" à la p 74, l'auteur note: "It may be remarked here that the use of the word 'suffisante' in the French text, and the meanings attributed to it by France and Australia, certainly reflects the *open nature texture* of the expression 'reasonable'." *Ibid* à la p 68: "The Tribunal has *to a certain extent* qualified this observation when it went on to add" au lieu de "The Tribunal has, *to a certain extent*, qualified this observation when it went on to add."

[2] Dans la contribution de Proshanto K Mukherjee, "Economic Losses and Environmental Damage in the Law of Ship-Source Pollution" à la p 348, note de bas de page 22, l'auteur mentionne les articles 1053 et 1075 du Code civil du

The Proposed Nordic Saami Convention: National and International Dimensions of Indigenous Property Rights. Edited by Nigel Bankes and Timo Koivurova. Portland, OR: Hart Publishing, 2013. 417 pages.

This collection of fifteen essays, edited by University of Calgary professor Nigel Bankes and University of Lapland professor Timo Koivurova, is the result of a multi-year collaboration financed by the Nordic Council of Ministers. What inspired the research project are the renewed negotiations between Norway, Sweden, and Finland and the Saami Parliaments within each country, which began in 2011 with the aim at arriving at a final version of a *Nordic Saami Convention* by 2015. The essays in the collection provide a theoretical or doctrinal analysis of the contents and possible implications of the convention and propose modifications to the draft to perhaps influence public policy. While the main area of law that is addressed in the volume is the recognition of property interests within the context of the draft convention, the collection will appeal to anyone who is broadly interested in indigenous property rights within settler states.

The book is divided into four sections. The first section looks at the general doctrinal and theoretical framework within which the proposed *Nordic Saami Convention* can be situated. The section begins with a piece by Nigel Bankes who outlines three different conceptual approaches for recognizing — or refusing to recognize — the property interests of indigenous peoples. Jonnette Watson Hamilton considers the implications of the proposed convention in terms of legal pluralism and, more specifically, of normative theories of recognition, reconciliation, and transitional justice. Since legal pluralism implies at least partially autonomous societies, Watson Hamilton finds the convention inconsistent in this regard. Finally, Jeremy Webber closes the section with a chapter entitled "The Public Law Dimension of Indigenous Property Rights," where he argues that the recognition of property rights prior to the assertion of sovereignty necessarily entails recognition of the pre-existing indigenous normative order that governed property rights. Using examples from Western legal orders, Webber illustrates that even

Québec concernant les pertes purement économiques, et cite un article de 1985 de Deana Silverstone à titre d'appui. Les articles 1053 et 1075 du Code civil du Bas-Canada correspondent aux articles 1457 et 1607 du Code civil du Québec qui s'applique dans cette province depuis 1994. Il aurait été préférable de citer ces articles.

in this context the separation of the public and private aspects of property is artificial.

The second section includes three chapters that look at the public international law dimensions of the proposed Nordic Saami accord — in particular, its transnational character and its relevance to human rights law. The fourth chapter by Timo Koivurova takes on the question of the Saami as a transnational indigenous people as well as the implications of their status as a people in international law and their right to self-determination. Koivurova provides an insightful history of the notion of self-determination under international law and arrives at the conclusion that, for indigenous peoples, it is limited to self-determination within existing states. In the fifth chapter, Leena Heinämäki considers the inclusion of a "Right of a People to Control Issues Important to Them" in the draft convention. Her contribution also examines the question of self-determination and arrives at the conclusion that, much like Koivurova insofar as the *Declaration of the Rights of Indigenous Peoples* is concerned, the right as it is expressed in the convention is *sui generis* in international law. She argues, however, that the international law standard related to control of "issues of importance to them," is that of prior informed consent and not simply consultation. Else Grete Broderstad closes the second section with an examination of the difficulty of reaching a cross-border reindeer management agreement between Norway and Sweden and the existence of conflicting legal norms between Saami communities.

The same subject that is in Broderstad's chapter leads into the third section, which further delves into reindeer grazing rights, and Saami land use in general, in each of the three Nordic states. Øyvind Ravna looks at the assessment of land use in section 34 of the draft convention. Like most indigenous peoples, Saami land and water use leaves few visible traces, creating problems for state recognition of their title. Christina Allard considers the question of identifying rights holders in Sweden for the purposes of reindeer herding. While the *Reindeer Herding Act* invests the Saami people collectively with herding rights, Allard suggests that the right may be more properly located in a village or even a group within the village. Juha Joona looks more specifically at right holders under the draft convention and argues that it is not sensitive enough to historical patterns of settlement in Saami areas. In Finland, settlers displaced Forest Lapps, but Mountain Lapps from Norway subsequently migrated into Finland. In Joona's view, using language as a criterion to identify rights holders is problematic, as it favours Mountain

Lapps who have retained the language and tends to exclude Forest Lapps who have suffered language loss. Tanja Joona also focuses on section 4 of the draft convention when asking who the subjects of the draft convention are in fact. On the one hand, the convention insists on the unity of the Saami people and developing a cohesive legal approach, yet the four prescribed ways of identifying a right holder largely depend on the actions of each individual state to be operationalized. Elina Helander-Renvall closes the third section with a closer look at Saami customary law. She remarks that customary norms are dynamic, flexible, and adaptable and, for this reason, may come into conflict with state law or lose these qualities in the process of state recognition.

The fourth and final section provides a comparative law perspective on the recognition of land rights in other jurisdictions, most notably Ecuador, Australia, and Canada. Verónica Potes' contribution looks specifically at the Achuar people — who are also a transnational people that straddle the Ecuador-Peru boundary — in relation to the introduction of the concept of a "pluri-national state" in the 2008 Ecuador Constitution. Despite this development, the Ecuadorian state continues to resist any meaningful implementation of the pluri-national principle by refusing to cede control over land and resources or grant political autonomy to the Achuar. For her part, Sharon Mascher focuses on the *Mabo* decision in Australia and the ensuing adoption of the *Native Title Act 1993*. In Mascher's view, if legislation in Australia has led to a strict statutory interpretation of indigenous title and truncated the broader recognition at common law, it is doubtful the language of the draft convention will lend itself to a similar restrictive view of indigenous title, given the role of the Norwegian legislature and courts. Nigel Bankes then considers the Saami convention in light of modern land claims agreements in Canada. He notably situates the issue within the debate over titling indigenous lands to allow access to capital, and the accompanying concern that this will lead to commodification and even potentially to the loss of a land base. Jennifer Koshan closes the section with lessons from Canada concerning equal rights for indigenous women. Taking a relational view of rights according to which collective and individual rights are congruous, Koshan explores the relevancy of including an equal rights clause for indigenous men and women in the draft convention, as was done in the Canadian Constitution.

In their concluding chapter, Bankes and Koivurova pull together many of the threads that cut across various chapters by providing a general overview, divided into seven themes. These themes render even more evident the similarity of indigenous legal issues in Canada and the issues the convention raises for the Saami. For example, several indigenous nations in Canada — most notably, the Haudenosaunee (Iroquois), the Anishinaabeg (Ojibwa), the Dakota (Sioux), and the Inuit — are in fact transnational peoples who find their nations artificially divided by the Canada-US border and even by Russia and Greenland in the case of the Inuit. Though it is also true that in North America the only bilateral international treaty that deals with indigenous migration is the Jay Treaty of 1794, while the Saami have been the subject of several bilateral international treaties between the Nordic countries since 1751. The convention also has the potential to replicate the same problems encountered with the *Indian Act*. For instance, treaty membership and Métis status remain contentious issues in Canada, in part because of the difficulties in identifying treaty members and individual rights holder. Another common issue is the familiar question of equality between indigenous men and women.

There are at the same time noteworthy differences that seem to benefit the Saami relative to indigenous peoples in Canada. Interestingly, Ravna's chapter points out that Norway's *Reindeer Husbandry Act, 1996* reversed the burden of the proof so that Nordic property owners have to demonstrate that there is no right to herd. In Canada, the courts constantly repeat that there is "no question as to the underlying title of the Crown," a principle founded on the doctrine of discovery, and, as a result, they have shifted the burden to indigenous peoples of proving territorial rights that pre-exist the affirmation of sovereignty. Another difference is that Nordic courts seem more willing to integrate international standards for assessing Saami claims. For example, the international criterion for sovereignty is proof of effective control of the territory and not simply the affirmation of sovereignty. In light of this proof, the Supreme Court of Canada's decision in *R. v Powley* is not the anomaly it appears to be but, in fact, states the appropriate norm for all indigenous peoples' claims.[1]

Overall, the collection delivers what it promises: a consideration of the convention within an international and comparative law perspective. The various contributions provide the reader with a useful and timely reference work on the draft convention as well as insightful analyses of some of its key substantive provisions. The

---

[1] *R v Powley*, [2003] 2 SCR 207, 2003 SCC 43.

volume does not attempt to provide a monolithic interpretation of the draft convention or of its potential effects. This approach is a comprehensible one given the hypothetical nature of questioning a proposed draft version. Furthermore, a diversity of conclusions from one author to another is reflective of a normal, healthy academic debate. For those who teach indigenous legal issues in a Canadian context, it provides a useful comparative tool that relativizes the issue of "race" and provides a broader perspective for considering colonization and indigenous claims in Canada.

DARREN O'TOOLE
Assistant Professor, Faculty of Law, University of Ottawa

Analytical Index / Index analytique

(A) Articles; (NC) Notes and Comments; (Ch) Digest;
(P) Practice; (C) Cases; (BR) Book Reviews

(A) Articles; (NC) Notes et commentaires; (Ch) Chronique;
(P) Pratique; (C) Jurisprudence; (BR) Recensions de livres

Index of Cases /
Index de la jurisprudence

___

683